Introduction to Management Accounting

Introduction

CHARLES T. HORNGREN

Ph.D., C.P.A.
Stanford University

to Management Accounting

(Formerly Accounting for Management Control: An Introduction)

FOURTH EDITION

PRENTICE-HALL, INC., ENGLEWOOD CLIFFS, NEW JERSEY 07632

Library of Congress Cataloging in Publication Data

Horngren, Charles T
  Introduction to management accounting—(formerly
Accounting for management control: an introduction)

    First-3d. ed. published under earlier title.
    Bibliography: p.
    Includes index.
    1. Managerial accounting. 2. Cost accounting.
I. Title.
HF5635.H814 1978   658.1'5   77-14973
ISBN 0-13-487595-8

To
Joan, Scott, Mary, Susie, Cathy

Introduction to Management Accounting, Fourth Edition
(Formerly Accounting for Management Control: An Introduction)

CHARLES T. HORNGREN

© 1978, 1974, 1970, 1965 by Prentice-Hall, Inc., Englewood Cliffs, N.J. 07632

Printed in the United States of America

10 9 8 7 6 5 4 3 2 1

Cover: View of the World Trade Center, New York City
Photo by Four By Five, Inc.

Prentice-Hall International, Inc., *London*
Prentice-Hall of Australia Pty. Limited, *Sydney*
Prentice-Hall of Canada, Ltd., *Toronto*
Prentice-Hall of India Private Limited, *New Delhi*
Prentice-Hall of Japan, Inc., *Tokyo*
Prentice-Hall of Southeast Asia Pte. Ltd., *Singapore*
Whitehall Books Limited, *Wellington, New Zealand*

Contents

Preface xvii

PART ONE
Focus on Decision Making 1

1 Perspective: Scorekeeping, Attention Directing, and Problem Solving 3

THREE BROAD PURPOSES OF AN ACCOUNTING SYSTEM.
THE MANAGEMENT PROCESS AND ACCOUNTING.
Nature of Planning and Controlling.   Management by Exception.
Illustration of the Budget and the Performance Report.
Organizations, Processes, and Systems.
COST-BENEFIT PHILOSOPHY.
TYPES OF INFORMATION SUPPLIED BY ACCOUNTING.

Three Questions.
MANAGEMENT ACCOUNTING AND SERVICE ORGANIZATIONS.
ROLE OF THE ACCOUNTANT IN THE ORGANIZATION.
Line and Staff Authority.   The Controller.
Distinctions between Controller and Treasurer.
MANAGEMENT ACCOUNTING AND FINANCIAL ACCOUNTING.
Freedom of Choice.   Behavioral Impact.
Certified Management Accountant.
SUMMARY.   SUMMARY PROBLEMS FOR YOUR REVIEW.
ASSIGNMENT MATERIAL.
Fundamental Assignment Material.   Additional Assignment Material.

2 Introduction to Cost-Volume Relationships 24

VARIABLE COSTS AND FIXED COSTS.
COMPARISON OF VARIABLE AND FIXED COSTS.
Relevant Range.   Some Simplifying Assumptions.
ILLUSTRATION OF COST-VOLUME-PROFIT ANALYSIS.
1. Break-even Point—Two Analytical Techniques.
2. Graphical Technique.   3. Changes in Fixed Expenses.
4. Changes in Contribution Margin per Unit.
5. Target Net Profit and an Incremental Approach.
6. Multiple Changes in the Key Factors.
USES AND LIMITATIONS OF COST-VOLUME ANALYSIS.
Optimum Combination of Factors.   Limiting Assumptions.
Contribution Margin and Gross Margin.
SUMMARY.   SUMMARY PROBLEM FOR YOUR REVIEW.
APPENDIX 2-A: THE P/V CHART AND SALES-MIX ANALYSIS.
The P/V Chart.   Effects of Sales Mix.
APPENDIX 2-B: IMPACT OF INCOME TAXES.
ASSIGNMENT MATERIAL.
Fundamental Assignment Material.   Additional Assignment Material.
ASSIGNMENT MATERIALS FOR APPENDIXES.

3 Introduction to Manufacturing Costs 54

CLASSIFICATIONS OF COSTS.
Cost Accumulation and Cost Objectives.
Elements of Manufacturing Costs.
**RELATIONSHIPS OF INCOME STATEMENTS AND BALANCE
    SHEETS.**
Product Costs and Period Costs.   Balance Sheet Presentation.
Unit Costs for Product Costing.   Costs and Income Statements.
Common Mistakes.   Relation to Balance Sheet Equation.
Direct and Indirect Costs.
TWO TYPES OF INCOME STATEMENTS.
Detailed Costs of Manufacturing Company.   Functional Approach.

Contribution Approach.
JOB AND PROCESS COSTING.   SUMMARY.
SUMMARY PROBLEM FOR YOUR REVIEW.
APPENDIX 3: CLASSIFICATION OF LABOR COSTS.
ASSIGNMENT MATERIAL.
Fundamental Assignment Material.   Additional Assignment Material.

Relevant Costs
and Special Decisions—Part One 81

THE ACCOUNTANT'S ROLE IN SPECIAL DECISIONS.
Accuracy and Relevance.   Qualitative and Quantitative Factors.
MEANING OF RELEVANCE: THE MAJOR CONCEPTUAL LESSON.
Definition of Relevance.   Examples of Relevance.
Role of Predictions.
THE SPECIAL SALES ORDER.
Illustrative Example.   Correct Analysis.
Variable and Absorption Costing.   Incorrect Analysis.
Spreading Fixed Costs.   Total Costs and Unit Costs.
ROLE OF COSTS IN PRICING.
Factors that Influence Prices.   Target Pricing.
DELETION OR ADDITION OF PRODUCTS OR DEPARTMENTS.
CONTRIBUTION TO PROFIT PER UNIT OF LIMITING FACTOR.
SUMMARY.   SUMMARY PROBLEM FOR YOUR REVIEW.
ASSIGNMENT MATERIAL.
Fundamental Assignment Material.   Additional Assignment Material.

Relevant Costs
and Special Decisions—Part Two 113

MAKE OR BUY.
Make or Buy and Idle Facilities.
Essence of Make or Buy: Utilization of Facilities.
OPPORTUNITY COSTS.
JOINT PRODUCT COSTS AND INCREMENTAL COSTS.
Danger of Allocation.   Incremental or Differential Costs.
IRRELEVANCE OF PAST COSTS.
Obsolete Inventory.   Book Value of Old Equipment.
Examining Alternatives over the Long Run.
MOTIVATION AND CONFLICT OF MODELS.
Influence of Loss.   Distinguishing between Decisions.
Reconciling the Models.
IRRELEVANCE OF FUTURE COSTS THAT WILL NOT DIFFER.
BEWARE OF UNIT COSTS.
DECISION MODELS AND UNCERTAINTY.   SUMMARY.
SUMMARY PROBLEM FOR YOUR REVIEW.
ASSIGNMENT MATERIAL.
Fundamental Assignment Material.   Additional Assignment Material.

PART TWO
Accounting for Planning and Control 145

 6 ## The Master Budget: The Overall Plan 147

CHARACTERISTICS OF BUDGETS.
Definition of Budget.   Advantages of Budgets.
Formalization of Planning.
Expectations as a Framework for Judging Performance.
Coordination and Communication.
HUMAN RELATIONS.   TYPES OF BUDGETS.
Time Span.   Classification of Budgets.
ILLUSTRATION OF PREPARATION OF A MASTER BUDGET.
Description of Problem.   Basic Steps in Preparing Master Budget.
Explanation of Cash Budget.   Budgeted Balance Sheet.
THE DIFFICULTIES OF SALES FORECASTING.
FINANCIAL PLANNING MODELS AND SIMULATION.
SUMMARY.   SUMMARY PROBLEM FOR YOUR REVIEW.
ASSIGNMENT MATERIAL.
Fundamental Assignment Material.   Additional Assignment Material.
SUGGESTED READINGS.

7 ## Flexible Budgets and Standards for Control 171

FLEXIBLE BUDGETS.
Static Budget Comparisons.   Flexible Budget Comparisons.
Isolating the Variances.   Development of Control Systems.
STANDARDS FOR MATERIAL AND LABOR.
Difference between Standards and Budgets.   Role of Past Experience.
Current Attainability: The Most Widely Used Standard.
Price and Efficiency Variances.   A General Approach.
Graphical Approach.   Limitations of Price and Efficiency Variances.
CONTROLLABILITY AND VARIANCES.
Responsibility for Material Variances.
Responsibility for Labor Variances.   Causes of Efficiency Variances.
Trade-offs among Variances.   When to Investigate Variances.
SUMMARY.   SUMMARY PROBLEM FOR YOUR REVIEW.
APPENDIX: MUTUAL PRICE AND EFFICIENCY EFFECTS.
ASSIGNMENT MATERIAL.
Fundamental Assignment Material.   Additional Assignment Material.
SUGGESTED READING.

Variations of Cost Behavior Patterns 205

ENGINEERED, DISCRETIONARY, AND COMMITTED COSTS.
Fixed Costs and Capacity.   Committed Fixed Costs.
Discretionary Fixed Costs.
Engineered and Discretionary Variable Costs.
ENGINEERED VERSUS DISCRETIONARY COSTS.
Work Measurement for Control.   Origins of Work Measurement.
Control-Factor Units.   The Engineered-Cost Approach.
The Discretionary-Fixed-Cost Approach.
Choosing among Control Systems.
DETERMINING HOW COSTS BEHAVE.
Major Assumptions.   Focus on Costs and Benefits.
Criteria for Choosing Functions.   Variety of Cost Functions.
Methods of Linear Approximation.
APPROXIMATING A COST FUNCTION.
Mixed Costs.   Budgeting Mixed Costs.   Data for Illustration.
Analysis of Graphs.   Focus on Relevant Range.
Use of High-Low Method.   Unreliability of High-Low Method.
SUMMARY.   SUMMARY PROBLEMS FOR YOUR REVIEW.
APPENDIX:
METHOD OF LEAST SQUARES.
ASSIGNMENT MATERIAL.
Fundamental Assignment Material.   Additional Assignment Material.

Motivation and Responsibility Accounting 241

GOAL CONGRUENCE AND INCENTIVE.
Cost-Benefit Assessment.   Goal Congruence.
Top-Management Objectives.   Incentive.   Behavioral Focus.
USE OF MULTIPLE GOALS.
Choosing Subgoals.   Interaction of Goals.
ORGANIZATION STRUCTURE AND RESPONSIBILITY.
Responsibility Accounting Approach.   Cost Centers and Profit Centers.
Illustration of Responsibility Accounting.   Format of Feedback Reports.
Responsibility and Incentive.
RESPONSIBILITY ACCOUNTING AND CONTROLLABILITY.
Nature of Controllability.   Management by Objectives.
Who Gets Blamed?   Cooperation versus Competition.
Confusion among Cost Classifications.
Reporting Controllable and Uncontrollable Items.
BEHAVIORAL PROBLEMS WITH CONTROL SYSTEMS.
Obtaining Acceptance.   Budget Padding.   Accurate Scorekeeping.
RESPONSIBILITY BUDGETING IN NONPROFIT ORGANIZATIONS.
Goals, Incentives, and Complexities.
Budgeting as Ongoing Procedure.   Zero-Based Budgeting.

Experience to Date.   Zero-Based Revenue.   Program Budgeting.
SUMMARY.   SUMMARY PROBLEM FOR YOUR REVIEW.
ASSIGNMENT MATERIAL.
Fundamental Assignment Material.   Additional Assignment Material.
SUGGESTED READINGS.

Responsibility Accounting and Cost Allocation 280

COST ALLOCATION IN GENERAL.
Cost Allocation as a Term.   Four Purposes of Allocation.
Cost Allocation Bases.
THE CONTRIBUTION APPROACH TO ALLOCATION.
Contribution Margin.   Subunit and Manager Performance.
Contribution Controllable by Segment Managers.
Contribution by Segments.   Alternative Definitions of Segments.
HOW TO ALLOCATE FOR PLANNING AND CONTROL.
General Guides.   Using the Guides.   Variable Cost Pool.
Fixed Cost Pool.   Fixed Pool and Actual Usage.
Troubles with Using Lump Sums.   Allocating Central Costs.
Using Budgeted Allocation Bases.
THE PRODUCT COSTING PURPOSE.
Relating Costs to Outputs.   Allocation of Service Department Costs.
Applying the Steps.
SUMMARY.   SUMMARY PROBLEM FOR YOUR REVIEW.
ASSIGNMENT MATERIAL.
Fundamental Assignment Material.   Additional Assignment Material.

Profit Centers and Transfer Pricing 314

EVOLUTION OF ACCOUNTING TECHNIQUES.
DECENTRALIZATION.
Costs and Benefits.   Middle Ground.   Meaning of Profit Centers.
TRANSFER PRICING.
Nature of Transfer Pricing.   Transfers at Cost.   Market Price.
Variable Cost.   Dysfunctional Behavior.   Use of Incentives.
THE NEED FOR MANY TRANSFER PRICES.
MEASURES OF PROFITABILITY.
Return on Investment.   ROI or Residual Income?
DISTINCTION BETWEEN MANAGERS AND INVESTMENTS.
THE BUDGET AND THE COST-BENEFIT APPROACH.
DEFINITIONS OF INVESTED CAPITAL AND INCOME.
Many Investment Bases.   Allocation to Divisions.
MEASUREMENT ALTERNATIVES.
Valuation of Assets.   Plant and Equipment: Gross or Net?
CHOOSING DESIRED RATES OF RETURN.
ALTERNATIVES OF TIMING.   WHY PROFIT CENTERS?
SUMMARY.   SUMMARY PROBLEMS FOR YOUR REVIEW.

ASSIGNMENT MATERIAL.
Essential Assignment Material.   Additional Assignment Material.
SUGGESTED READINGS.

PART THREE

Selected Topics for Further Study 349

12 Capital Budgeting 351

FOCUS ON PROGRAMS OR PROJECTS.
DISCOUNTED-CASH-FLOW MODEL.
Major Aspects of DCF.   Net Present Value.
Assumptions of DCF Model.   Internal Rate of Return.
Meaning of Internal Rate.   Depreciation and Discounted Cash Flow.
Review of Decision Rules.   Two Simplifying Assumptions.
Choosing the Minimum Desired Rate.
CAPITAL BUDGETING AND NONPROFIT ORGANIZATIONS.
UNCERTAINTY AND SENSITIVITY ANALYSIS.
No Single Way.   Applying Sensitivity Analysis.
THE NET-PRESENT-VALUE COMPARISON OF TWO PROJECTS.
Incremental versus Total Project Approach.
Analysis of Typical Items under Discounted Cash Flow.
CAPITAL BUDGETING AND INFLATION.
OTHER MODELS FOR ANALYZING LONG-RANGE DECISIONS.
Payback Model.   Accounting Rate-of-Return Model.
WEIGHING DOLLARS DIFFERENTLY.   CONFLICT OF MODELS.
Reconciliation of Conflict.
SUMMARY.   SUMMARY PROBLEM FOR YOUR REVIEW.
APPENDIX 12: CALCULATIONS OF INTERNAL RATES OF RETURN.
Expansion of Existing Gasoline Station.   Investment in an Oil Well.
Purchase of a New Gasoline Station.
ASSIGNMENT MATERIAL.
Fundamental Assignment Material.   Additional Assignment Material.
SUGGESTED READINGS.

13 Impact of Income Taxes on Management Planning 391

INCOME TAXES AND CAPITAL BUDGETING.
General Characteristics.   Effects of Depreciation Deductions.
The Best Depreciation Method.

Comprehensive Illustration: Effects of Income Taxes on Cash Flow.
Income Tax Complications.
MISCELLANEOUS TAX PLANNING MATTERS.
Form of Organization.   Changes in Income Tax Rates.   Lifo or Fifo.
Effect of Lifo on Purchase Decisions.
Contributions of Property Rather Than Cash.   Operating Losses.
Tax-Free Interest.   Capital Gains Alternative.
Other General Considerations.   Desirability of Losses.
SUMMARY.   SUMMARY PROBLEM FOR YOUR REVIEW.
Fundamental Assignment Material.   Additional Assignment Material.

14 Job and Process Systems and Overhead Application 420

CONTROL AND PRODUCT COSTING PURPOSES.
Two Purposes and Two Cost Objectives.
Distinction between Job Costing and Process Costing.
ILLUSTRATION OF JOB-ORDER COSTING.
Cost Application.   Predetermined Overhead Application Rates.
The Year's Events.
PROBLEMS OF OVERHEAD APPLICATION.
Normalized Overhead Rates.
Disposition of Underapplied or Overapplied Overhead.
The Use of Variable and Fixed Application Rates.
Actual versus Normal Costing.
PRODUCT COSTING IN NONPROFIT ORGANIZATIONS.
SUMMARY.   SUMMARY PROBLEM FOR YOUR REVIEW.
**APPENDIX 14A: JOB-COSTING DETAILS: JOURNAL ENTRIES
    AND LEDGERS.**
General Systems Design.   Basic Records.
Relationships among Source Documents, Subsidiary Ledgers, and General
    Ledger.   Disposition of Factory Overhead.
APPENDIX 14B: ILLUSTRATION OF PROCESS COSTING.
ASSIGNMENT MATERIAL.
Essential Assignment Material.   Additional Assignment Material.

15 Overhead Application: Direct and Absorption Costing 454

DIRECT VERSUS ABSORPTION COSTING.
Accounting for Fixed Manufacturing Overhead.   Facts for Illustration.
Direct-Costing Method.   Absorption-Costing Method.
FIXED OVERHEAD AND ABSORPTION COSTS OF PRODUCT.
Variable and Fixed Unit Costs.   Selecting the Denominator Level.
Nature of Denominator Variance.
**RECONCILIATION OF DIRECT COSTING AND ABSORPTION
    COSTING.**
EFFECT OF OTHER VARIANCES.
DISPOSITION OF STANDARD COST VARIANCES.

SUMMARY.   SUMMARY PROBLEMS FOR YOUR REVIEW.
APPENDIX 15: COMPARISONS OF DENOMINATOR VARIANCES
    WITH OTHER VARIANCES.
Denominator Variance Is Unique.   Lost-Contribution Margins.
ASSIGNMENT MATERIAL.
Fundamental Assignment Material.   Additional Assignment Material.

16   Influences of Quantitative Techniques on Management Accounting 486

DECISION THEORY AND UNCERTAINTY.
Formal Decision Models.   Payoff Tables and Decision Tables.
Decisions under Certainty.   Decisions under Risk or Uncertainty.
Expected Value and Standard Deviation.
The Accountant and Uncertainty.
Example of General Approach to Uncertainty.
Obtaining Additional Information.
LINEAR-PROGRAMMING MODELS.
Characteristics.   The Techniques, the Accountant, and the Manager.
Illustration of Product Mix.
INVENTORY PLANNING AND CONTROL MODELS.
Characteristics.   How Much to Order?   Order-Size Formula.
When to Order?   Minimum Inventory: Safety Allowance.
SUMMARY.   SUMMARY PROBLEM FOR YOUR REVIEW.
ASSIGNMENT MATERIAL.
Fundamental Assignment Material.   Additional Assignment Material.
SUGGESTED READINGS.

PART FOUR

Basic Financial Accounting for Managers 521

17   Basic Accounting: Concepts, Techniques, and Conventions 523

THE RUDIMENTS OF ACCOUNTING.
The Accounting Process.   Economic Activity.   Financial Statements.
Relationship of Balance Sheet and Income Statement.
The Analytical Power of the Balance Sheet Equation.
Accrual Basis and Cash Basis.   Formal Adjustments.
The Measurement of Expenses: Assets Expire.   Pause for Reflection.

SUMMARY PROBLEM FOR YOUR REVIEW.
ACCOUNTING FOR WAGES.
ACCOUNTING FOR DEFERRED REVENUE.
DIVIDENDS AND RETAINED INCOME.
PROPRIETORSHIPS AND PARTNERSHIPS.
NONPROFIT ORGANIZATIONS.
GENERALLY ACCEPTED ACCOUNTING PRINCIPLES.
"Principles" Is a Misnomer.   Realization.   Matching.   Stable Dollar.
Additional Conventions.   The Entity.   Going Concern.
Consistency.   Objectivity or Verifiability.   Conservatism.
Disclosure.   Materiality.   Cost-Benefit.
SUMMARY.   SUMMARY PROBLEM FOR YOUR REVIEW.
APPENDIX 17: USING LEDGER ACCOUNTS.
The Account.   General Ledger.   Debits and Credits.
ASSIGNMENT MATERIAL.
Fundamental Assignment Material.   Additional Assignment Material.
ASSIGNMENT MATERIAL FOR APPENDIX.

18 Understanding Corporate Annual Reports—Part One 569

CLASSIFIED BALANCE SHEET.
Current Assets.   Plant Assets.   Intangible Assets.   Liabilities.
Stockholders' Equity.
Meaning of Stockholders' Equity Section: Stock Splits and Stock Dividends.
Reserves and Funds.   Alternate Form of Balance Sheet.
INCOME STATEMENT.
Use of Subtotals.   Operating and Financial Management.
Income, Earnings, Profits.
RECONCILIATION OF RETAINED EARNINGS.
STATEMENT OF CHANGES IN FINANCIAL POSITION.
Concept and Format of Funds Statement.
Example of Funds Statement.   Role of Depreciation.
Effects of Different Patterns of Depreciation.
Depreciation, Income Taxes, and Cash Flow.
Alternative Concepts and Formats.   Cash Flow.
SUMMARY.   SUMMARY PROBLEMS FOR YOUR REVIEW.
ASSIGNMENT MATERIAL.
Fundamental Assignment Material.   Additional Assignment Material.

19 Understanding Corporate Annual Reports—Part Two 606

ACCOUNTING FOR INTERCORPORATE INVESTMENTS.
CONSOLIDATED FINANCIAL STATEMENTS.
The Acquisition.   After Acquisition.   Minority Interests.
Unconsolidated Subsidiaries.

RECAPITULATION OF ACCOUNTING FOR INVESTMENTS.
ACCOUNTING FOR GOODWILL.
Purchased Goodwill.   Nature of Goodwill.
ANALYSIS OF FINANCIAL STATEMENTS.
Do Ratios Provide Answers?   Operating Performance.
Trading on the Equity.   Common Stock Statistics.
Senior Securities and Safety.   Short-Term Credit Analysis.
SUMMARY.   SUMMARY PROBLEM FOR YOUR REVIEW.
ASSIGNMENT MATERIAL.
Fundamental Assignment Material.   Additional Assignment Material.

 Difficulties
in Measuring Net Income 640

INFLATION AND INCOME MEASUREMENT.
Historical Cost and Current Value.   Restated Historical Cost.
Maintaining Invested Capital.   Restated Current Value.
Misinterpretations of Current-Value Accounting.
UNIFORMITY VS. FLEXIBILITY.   INVENTORY METHODS.
Fifo and Lifo.   Lower of Cost or Market.
THE INVESTMENT TAX CREDIT.
DEFERRED FEDERAL INCOME TAXES.   SUMMARY.
SUMMARY PROBLEMS FOR YOUR REVIEW.
APPENDIX 20: DISPUTES ABOUT INCOME MEASUREMENT.
EFFECTS OF CURRENT VALUE.
What Is Income?   Replacement-Cost Basis.
Income Tax Effects of Current Value.
GENERAL PURCHASING-POWER GAINS AND LOSSES.
Monetary Items.   Nonmonetary Items.
ASSIGNMENT MATERIAL.

PART FIVE

Appendixes 683

 Recommended Readings 685

Fundamentals of Compound Interest and the Use of Present-Value Tables 687

NATURE OF INTEREST.
TABLE 1: PRESENT VALUE OF $1.
TABLE 2: PRESENT VALUE OF AN ORDINARY ANNUITY OF $1.

C Glossary 695

Index 704

xvi

Preface

This book is an introduction to internal accounting—most often called *management accounting*. The important topics with which it deals are those that all undergraduates of business should study. The book is written primarily for students who have had one or two terms of basic accounting. It is appropriate for a one-term course in managerial accounting at either the undergraduate or graduate level. It is also appropriate for executive educational programs of varying lengths in which the students have had no formal training in accounting. My twin goals have been to choose relevant subject matter and to present it clearly.

The change in title indicates that this is a major revision. The publisher solicited over 25 reviews of the preceding edition. After pondering the oft-conflicting advice of the reviewers, I decided to concentrate on a theme of "more." This edition should: (1) be more readable than ever; (2) have more emphasis on the fundamentals of management accounting; (3) have more stress on how accounting affects management behavior; (4) give more attention to nonmanufacturing activities and to not-for-profit organizations; and (5) contain **more** product costing for those who desire it. **In short, more than ever, this is a basic book that is aimed at a reader who has a minimal background in accounting, if any.**

This book attempts a balanced, flexible approach. For example, it deals as much with not-for-profit, retail, wholesale, selling, and administrative situations as it does with manufacturing. The fundamental accounting concepts and techniques for planning and control are applicable to all types and functions of organizations, not just to manufacturing. This more general approach makes it easier for the student to relate the book's examples and problems to his particular interests. Moreover, many valuable concepts (for example, master budgets) are more easily grasped if they are not complicated by intricate manufacturing situations.

Stress is on planning and control, not on product costing for purposes of inventory valuation and income determination. This approach, which excludes the troublesome but unimportant complications introduced by changes in inventory levels, simplifies the presentation of planning and control techniques in the classroom. Instead of the simultaneous discussion of costs for control and for product costing found in most texts, this text concentrates on planning and control without dwelling on product costing at all until Chapter 14. At that point, the implications of overhead application for product costing may be considered in perspective and in relation to management policy decisions regarding the "best" inventory valuation method.

Major specific changes in this edition include:

1. There are three new chapters. The first expands the study of relevant cost analysis, a topic that deserves more stress early in the course (see Chapters 4 and 5). The second explores cost allocation (Chapter 10), a subject that affects almost every organization imaginable. The third presents job order costing (Chapter 14), a topic that eases comparisons of the various purposes of a cost accounting system.

2. The four chapters on financial accounting (old Chapters 2–5) have been moved to the end of the book and are now Chapters 17–20. They have been thoroughly revised. The first of these (Chapter 17) provides a digestible introduction to basic financial accounting. It assumes that the reader has not studied accounting previously. The materials on intercorporate investments, consolidations, and goodwill are new and are in the third chapter of the sequence (rather than the second chapter). The fourth chapter has a new presentation on accounting for inflation; advanced coverage is in the appendix. Past users of the book are especially urged to scrutinize these new materials and the new organization.

   The shifting of the financial chapters provides a more self-contained arrangement of topics. That is, the financial accounting topics do not intrude into the presentation of the management accounting topics. When using previous editions, many teachers felt obligated to defend the deferring or elimination of the financial chapters.

3. There are several changes in the content █████████
   accounting chapters, principally to improv█████
   (a) Old Chapter 8 (Cost Behavior and Income██████
       revised and is now Chapter 3 (Introduction to ██
   (b) Old Chapter 12 (Relevant Costs and the Contrib██
       Problem Solving) is now Chapters 4 and 5.
   (c) Old Chapter 11 (Motivation, Responsibility Accounting██
       Allocation) is thoroughly redone and expanded. It is now Cha███
       and 10.
   (d) Old Chapter 16 (Decentralization, Performance Measurement, and
       Transfer Pricing) has also been revamped and is now Chapter 11.
   (e) Chapter 14 and the first part of Chapter 3 have been introduced in
       response to demands for more product costing. They contain a de-
       scription of how costs flow through accounts and relate manufacturing
       costs to balance sheets and income statements.

4. Chapters 9, 10, and 11 now form a sub-part of the book that focuses more
   sharply on the impact of accounting control systems on human behavior.

5. More attention is given to not-for-profit organizations. For example, see
   sections of Chapters 1, 9, 12, 14, and 17. In addition, many chapter
   illustrations use not-for-profit settings. For instance, see Chapters 8, 10,
   and 12.

6. The *Student Guide* (by Dudley W. Curry) that is available as supplementary
   material stresses learning objectives. These clearly define what the student
   is expected to learn from the corresponding textbook chapters. Therefore,
   the student is easily able to determine whether he or she has achieved the
   learning objectives.

Alternative Ways of Using This Book

In my opinion, the first nine chapters provide the foundation of the field of
management accounting. These nine chapters may be amplified by assigning
the subsequent chapters in the given order, or by inserting them after the
earlier chapters as desired. **Such insertion may be achieved without disrupting
the readers' flow of thought.** The most obvious candidates for insertion are
indicated below:

Chapters   1   2   3   4   5   6   7   8   9 ⟶ 10–20
            ↑   ↑   ↑   ↑
           17   14   12   15
           18   13
           19
           20

If they are going to be covered in a course in management accounting,
any or all of the financial accounting chapters (17–20) may be undertaken
anytime. (For example, to provide a change of pace, I have even used such
chapters in the midst of a course.)

fer to assign the chapters in the sequence provided
...ot enslaved by the sequence. Through the years, I
...ment of sequences, depending on the readers' back-

...on Decision Making) provides a bedrock introduction,
...irety. Sometimes I assign Chapter 17 immediately after
...rly if the readers have little or no background in financial
...ver, if there is time in the course for students to get more
...luct costing, I frequently assign Chapter 14 immediately
...Furthermore, there is much logical appeal to studying the
...tal budgeting (Chapters 12 and 13) immediately after the
...evant costs (Chapters 4 and 5). Tradition has prevented my
...chapters there, plus the fact that capital budgeting is often
...d in other courses.

...wo (Accounting for Planning and Control) emphasizes the
attention... recting functions of accounting. I often assign Chapter 15 immediately after Chapter 7 because it stresses the product costing aspects of
standard costs, whereas Chapter 7 focuses on the control aspects.

Part Three (Selected Topics for Further Study) contains chapters on
capital budgeting, product costing, and quantitative techniques. These topics
are important, but the decision to study them will depend on the teachers'
preferences, the other courses in the curriculum, and the students' previous
courses.

Part Four introduces, interprets, and appraises basic financial accounting. These chapters form a unified package that covers all elementary
financial accounting in capsule form with heavy stress on interpretation and
uses and, except in Chapter 17, with little attention given to the accumulation
of the information. In my view, a major objective of basic financial accounting should be to equip the student with enough fundamental concepts and
terminology so that he can reasonably comprehend any industrial corporate
annual report.

Chapters 17–20 may be skipped entirely or may be used in a variety of
ways:

1. In courses or executive programs where the students have *no* accounting
   background but where the main emphasis is on management rather than
   financial accounting.

2. In courses where the chapters may be used as a quick review by students
   who have had some financial accounting previously.

3. In courses where one or two of Chapters 17–20 may be chosen to remedy
   weaknesses or gaps in the background of the students.

Chapters 17–20 need not be used in total, page by page or topic by
topic. The teacher is free to pick and choose those topics (particularly in
Chapter 20) that seem most suitable for his students.

On the other hand, some teachers may want to use these chapters to teach the fundamentals of financial accounting to students with no prior background in accounting. Classroom testing has shown that such teaching can be done successfully, provided that the homework material is chosen carefully.

The front of the solutions manual contains several alternate detailed assignment schedules and ample additional recommendations to teachers regarding how best to use this book.

ACKNOWLEDGMENTS

I have received ideas, assistance, miscellaneous critiques, and assorted assignment material in conversations and by mail from many students and professors. Each has my gratitude, but the list is too long to enumerate here.

Professor Dudley W. Curry (Southern Methodist) has my special thanks for offering many helpful suggestions and **for preparing the quiz and examination material and a student guide that are available as supplementary material.**

The following professors supplied helpful reviews of the previous edition or drafts of this edition: M. Robert Carner, J. F. Cook, William F. Crum, Joseph R. Curran, Patrick R. Delaney, Billy Goetz, S. Michael Groomer, Wilber C. Haseman, W. Morley Lemon, Mohamed E. Moustafa, Ray M. Powell, C. Stevenson Rowley, E. J. Schmidlein, Douglas Sharp, and Robert J. West.

Christiane Jose has my special appreciation for her cheerful and skillful typing and related help. Pamela Adler also helped considerably. The following students ably performed assorted editorial chores: Thomas Dawson, Jules Goins, Sarah Johnson, John Otterlei, and Susan Reynolds Rosenberg.

Sally Lewis has my gratitude for her flawless typing of the solutions manual.

My thanks to the American Institute of Certified Public Accountants (problem material designated as CPA), the National Association of Accountants (NAA), the Society of Management Accountants of Canada (SMA), and the Institute of Management Accounting (CMA) for their generous permission to use some of their problems and to quote from their publications.

And finally, my thanks to Ron Ledwith, Ann Marie McCarthy, Elinor Paige, and Mark A. Binn (designer) at Prentice-Hall.

Comments from users are welcome.

Charles T. Horngren

Charles T. Horngren is the Edmund W. Littlefield Professor of Accounting at Stanford University. A graduate of Marquette University, he received his MBA from Harvard University, and his Ph.D. from the University of Chicago. He is also a recipient of an honorary DBA from Marquette University.

Dr. Horngren was President of the American Accounting Association, 1976–1977, and was Director of Research, 1964–1966. He received the Outstanding Accounting Educator Award in 1973, when the Association initiated an annual series of such awards. Horngren served on the Accounting Principles Board, 1968–1973, and is a member of the American Institute of Certified Public Accountants, the National Association of Accountants, and the Financial Accounting Standards Board Advisory Council. He is the author of two other best selling Prentice-Hall titles—Cost Accounting: A Managerial Emphasis, Fourth Edition, 1977, and CPA Problems and Approaches to Solutions, Fourth Edition, 1974 (with J. A. Leer).

PART ONE

Focus on Decision Making

CHAPTER 1

Perspective: Scorekeeping, Attention Directing, and Problem Solving

Because accounting is so pervasive, an understanding of its usefulness—and its limitations—is desirable for all managers in all types of organizations. Company presidents, production managers, public accountants, hospital administrators, controllers, school administrators, sales managers, and politicians are better equipped to perform their duties when they have a reasonable grasp of accounting data.

The study of management accounting can be especially fruitful, because it helps us see through the eyes of those who are subject to accounting measures of performance and who often depend heavily on accounting data for guidance in decision making. There is no escaping the linkage of accounting and management, so the study of management accounting will help you regardless of whether you become a manager or an accountant, or whether you will work in retailing, manufacturing, health care, public administration, or some other activity.

The objective of this chapter is to gain an overall view of the accountant's role in an organization. We shall see that the accountant must fulfill three jobs simultaneously: scorekeeping, attention directing, and problem solving.

THREE BROAD PURPOSES OF AN ACCOUNTING SYSTEM

The accounting system is the major quantitative information system in almost every organization. An effective accounting system provides information for three broad purposes: **(1) internal reporting to managers, for use in planning and controlling routine operations; (2) internal reporting to managers, for use in strategic planning, that is, the making of special decisions and the formulating of overall policies and long-range plans; and (3) external reporting to stockholders, government, and other outside parties.**

Both management (internal parties) and external parties share an interest in all three important purposes, but the emphases of financial accounting and of management (internal) accounting differ. Financial accounting has been mainly concerned with the third purpose and has traditionally been oriented toward the historical, stewardship aspects of external reporting. The distinguishing feature of management accounting is its emphasis on the planning and control purposes. **Management accounting is concerned with the accumulation, classification, and interpretation of information that assists individual executives to fulfill organizational objectives as revealed explicitly or implicitly by top management.**

THE MANAGEMENT PROCESS AND ACCOUNTING

Nature of Planning and Controlling

The nucleus of the management process is decision making, the purposeful choosing from among a set of alternative courses of action in light of some objective. These decisions range from the routine (making daily production schedules) to the nonroutine (launching a new product line).

Decision making underlies the commonly encountered twofold division of the management process into (1) planning and (2) control. The left-hand side of Exhibit 1-1 clearly demonstrates the planning and control cycle of current operations. **Planning** (the top box) means deciding on objectives and the means for their attainment. It provides the answers to two questions: What is desired? When and how is it to be accomplished? **Controlling** (the two boxes labeled "Action" and "Evaluation" immediately below) means implementation of plans and the use of feedback so that objectives are optimally attained. The feedback loop is the central facet of any concept of control, and timely, systematic measurement is the chief means of providing

EXHIBIT 1-1. Accounting Framework for Planning and Control

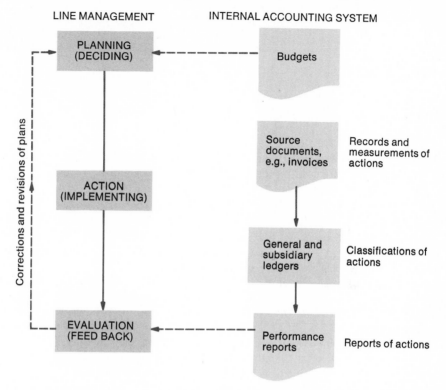

LINE MANAGEMENT INTERNAL ACCOUNTING SYSTEM

useful feedback. Planning and controlling are so intertwined that it seems artificial to draw rigid lines of separation between them; yet at times we will find it useful to concentrate on one or the other phase of the planning-control cycle.

Management by Exception

The right-hand side of Exhibit 1-1 shows that accounting formalizes plans by expressing them in the language of figures as **budgets.** Accounting formalizes control as **performance reports** (the last box), which provide feedback by comparing results with plans and by highlighting **variances** (i.e., deviations from plans).

Exhibit 1-2 shows the form of a simple performance report for a management consulting firm. Such reports spur investigation of exceptions. Operations are then brought into conformity with the plans, or the plans are revised. This is an example of management by exception.

Management by exception means that the executive's attention and effort are concentrated on the significant deviations from expected results

EXHIBIT 1-2

Performance Report

	BUDGETED AMOUNTS	ACTUAL AMOUNTS	DEVIATIONS OR VARIANCES	EXPLANATION
Revenue from fees	xxx	xxx	xx	—
Various expenses	xxx	xxx	xx	—
Net income	xxx	xxx	xx	—

and that the information system highlights the areas most in need of investigation. Management should not ordinarily be concerned with results that conform closely to plans. However, well-conceived plans should incorporate enough discretion or flexibility so that the manager may feel free to pursue any unforeseen opportunities. In other words, **the definition of control does not mean that managers should blindly cling to a preexisting plan when unfolding events indicate the desirability of actions that were not authorized specifically in the original plan.**

Illustration of the Budget and the Performance Report

An assembly department constructs electric fans. The assembly of the parts and the installation of the electric motor are basically hand operations. Each fan is inspected before being transferred to the painting department. In light of the present sales forecast, a production schedule of 4,000 window fans and 6,000 table fans is planned for the coming month. Cost classifications are shown in Exhibit 1-3, the Assembly Department Budget.

EXHIBIT 1-3

ASSEMBLY DEPARTMENT BUDGET FOR THE MONTH ENDING MARCH 31, 19x1

Material (detailed by type: metal stampings, motors, etc.)	$ 38,000
Assembly labor (detailed by job classification, number of workers, etc.)	73,000
Other labor (foremen, inspectors)	12,000
Utilities, maintenance, etc.	7,500
Supplies (small tools, lubricants, etc.)	2,500
Total	$133,000

The operating plan, which is crystallized in the form of a department budget for the coming month, is prepared in conferences attended by the foreman, his supervisor, and an accountant. Each of the costs subject to the foreman's control is scrutinized. Its average amount for the past few months

6

7

*Perspective:
Scorekeeping,
Attention
Directing, and
Problem
Solving*

is often used as a guide, especially if past performance has been reasonably efficient. However, the budget is a **forecast** of costs. Each cost is projected in light of trends, price changes, alterations in product mix, specifications, labor methods, and changes in production volume from month to month. The budget is then formulated, and it becomes the foreman's target for the month.

As actual factory costs are incurred during the month, the accounting department collects them and classifies them by departments. At the end of the month (or perhaps weekly, or even daily, for such key items as materials or assembly labor), the accounting department prepares an Assembly Department Performance Report (Exhibit 1-4). In practice, this report may be very detailed and contain explanations of variances from the budget.

The foreman and his[1] superiors use this report to help appraise performance. **The spotlight is cast on the variances—the deviations from the budget.** It is through management's investigation of these variances that better ways of doing things are discovered. The budget is an aid to planning; the performance report is the tool that aids controlling. The accounting system thus helps to direct managerial attention to the exceptions. Exhibit 1-1 shows that accounting does *not* do the controlling. Controlling consists of actions performed by the managers and their workmen and of the evaluation that follows actions. Accounting assists the managerial control function by providing prompt measurements of actions and by systematically pinpointing trouble spots. This management-by-exception approach frees managers from needless concern with those phases of operations that are adhering to plans.

EXHIBIT 1-4
ASSEMBLY DEPARTMENT PERFORMANCE REPORT FOR THE MONTH ENDING MARCH 31, 19x1

	BUDGET	ACTUAL	VARIANCE
Material (detailed by type: metal stampings, motors, etc.)	$ 38,000	$ 39,000	$1,000 U
Assembly labor (detailed by job classification, number of workers, etc.)	73,000	74,300	1,300 U
Other labor (foremen, inspectors)	12,000	11,200	800 F
Utilities, maintenance, etc.	7,500	7,400	100 F
Supplies (small tools, lubricants, etc.)	2,500	2,600	100 U
Total	$133,000	$134,500	$1,500 U

U = Unfavorable.
F = Favorable.

[1] For conciseness "he" and "his" are usually used in this book rather than "he or she" or "his or hers" or "person." If you prefer, substitute "she" or "hers" where appropriate.

Managers work within organizations, which are groups of individuals who are assumed to have some common objectives or goals. The framework in Exhibit 1-1 focuses on the relation of the internal accounting system to a single manager. If you imagine this framework applying to several or hundreds of managers within an organization, you can see how accounting systems might evolve. That is, the multitude of management decisions being made day after day can be perceived as a **process.** The dictionary defines a process as a series of actions or operations leading to a definite end. Data collection via an accounting **system** facilitates the best collective decision making. The dictionary defines a system as an assemblage of objects united by some form of regular interaction or interdependence. Put another way, the accounting *system* is often the principal formal means of gathering data to *aid* and *coordinate* the *process* of making the best collective operating or routine decisions in light of the overall goals or objectives of an organization.

Ordinarily, the process of a particular organization should be the dominant influence in deciding what system to design. Therefore, the system can be modified to fit whatever seems to be the preferable process. Unfortunately, the systems designer sometimes has the reverse attitude, such as: "We can't do that. It won't fit on our punched card."

COST-BENEFIT PHILOSOPHY

The **cost-benefit philosophy** (or call it a theme or state of mind, if you prefer) is our fundamental approach to choosing among accounting systems and accounting methods. It will dominate this book. Systems and methods are economic goods that are available at various costs. Which system does a manager want to buy? A simple file drawer for amassing receipts and canceled checks? An elaborate budgeting system based on computerized descriptive models of the organization and its subunits? Or something in between?

Of course, the answer depends on the buyer's perceptions of the **expected incremental (additional) benefits in relation to the incremental costs.** For example, a hospital administrator may contemplate the installation of a TECHNICON computerized system for controlling hospital operations. Such a system uses a single document of original entry for automatic accumulation of data for financial records, medical records, costs by departments, nurse staffing requirements, drug administration, billings for patients, revenue generated by physicians, and so forth. This system will lead to more efficiency, less waste, and fewer errors. But the system costs $14 million. Thus, the system is not good or bad by itself. It must meet the tests of the economics of information—its value must exceed its cost.

Steak and butter may be "good buys" for many people at 50¢ per pound, but they may become "bad buys" at $5 per pound. Similarly, a

9

*Perspective:
Scorekeeping,
Attention
Directing, and
Problem
Solving*

particular accounting system may be a wise investment in the eyes of the buyer if it will generate a sufficiently better collective set of decisions to justify its added cost. However, an existing accounting system is only *one* source of information for decision making. In many organizations it may be more economical to gather data by one-shot special efforts than by having a ponderous system gathering data repetitively that are rarely used.

The cost-benefit philosophy provides innate appeal to both the hard-headed manager and the theoretician. Managers have been employing the cost-benefit test for years, even though they may not have expressed it as such. Instead, they may have referred to the philosophy as "having to be practical" despite what theory may say. But the cost-benefit philosophy has an exceedingly rich underlying theory of information economics.[2] It is good theory that can supply the missing rationale for many management practices.

TYPES OF INFORMATION SUPPLIED BY ACCOUNTING

Three Questions

Accounting data can be classified and reclassified in countless ways. A helpful overall classification was proposed in a research study of seven large companies with geographically dispersed operations:

> By observation of the actual decision-making process, specific types of data needs were identified at particular organizational levels—the vice-presidential level, the level of the factory manager, and the level of the factory head [foreman], for example—each involving quite distinct problems of communication for the accounting department.[3]

The research team found that three types of information, each serving a different purpose, often at various management levels, raise and help to answer three basic questions:

1. *Scorecard questions:* Am I doing well or badly?
2. *Attention-directing questions:* Which problems should I look into?
3. *Problem-solving questions:* Of the several ways of doing the job, which is the best?

The scorecard and attention-directing uses of data are closely related. The same data may serve a scorecard function for a foreman and an

---

[2] J. Demski and G. Feltham, *Cost Determination: A Conceptual Approach* (Ames, Iowa: Iowa State University Press, 1976).

[3] H. A. Simon, *Administrative Behavior,* 2nd ed. (New York: The Macmillan Company), p. 20.

attention-directing function for his superior. For example, many accounting systems provide performance reports in which actual results are compared with previously determined budgets or standards. Such a performance report often helps to answer scorecard questions and attention-directing questions simultaneously. Furthermore, the actual results collected serve not only control purposes but also the traditional needs of financial accounting, which is chiefly concerned with the answering of scorecard questions. This collection, classification, and reporting of data is the task that dominates day-to-day accounting.

Problem-solving data may be used in long-range planning and in making special, nonrecurring decisions, such as whether to make or buy parts, replace equipment, add or drop a product, etc. These decisions often require expert advice from specialists such as industrial engineers, budgetary accountants, statisticians, and others.

In sum, the accountant's task of supplying information has three facets:

1. *Scorekeeping.* The accumulation of data. This aspect of accounting enables both internal and external parties to evaluate organizational performance and position.

2. *Attention directing.* The reporting and interpreting of information that helps managers to focus on operating problems, imperfections, inefficiencies, and opportunities. This aspect of accounting helps managers to concern themselves with important aspects of operations promptly enough for effective action either through perceptive planning or through astute day-to-day supervision. Attention directing is commonly associated with current planning and control and with the analysis and investigation of recurring, routine internal-accounting reports.

3. *Problem solving.* This aspect of accounting involves the concise quantification of the relative merits of possible courses of action, often with recommendations as to the best procedure. Problem solving is commonly associated with nonrecurring decisions, situations that require special accounting analyses or reports.

The above distinctions sometimes overlap or merge. Consequently, it is often difficult to pinpoint a particular accounting task as being scorekeeping, attention directing, or problem solving. Nevertheless, attempts to make these distinctions provide insight into the objectives and tasks of both accountants and managers.

MANAGEMENT ACCOUNTING AND SERVICE ORGANIZATIONS

The basic ideas of management accounting were developed in manufacturing organizations. However, they have evolved so that they are applicable to all types of organizations, including **service organizations.** Service organizations

11

*Perspective:
Scorekeeping,
Attention
Directing, and
Problem
Solving*

or industries are defined in various ways. For our purposes, they are organizations that produce a service rather than a tangible good. Examples are public accounting firms, law firms, management consultants, real estate firms, transportation companies, banks, and hotels. Almost all **nonprofit** or **not-for-profit**[4] **organizations** are service industries. Examples are hospitals, schools, and a department of forestry.

The characteristics of service organizations include:

1. *Labor is intensive.* For example, the highest costs in schools and law firms are wages, salaries, and payroll-related costs, not the costs relating to the use of machinery, equipment, and extensive physical facilities.

2. *Output is usually difficult to define.* For example, the output of a university might be defined as the number of degrees granted, but many critics would maintain that the real output is "what is contained in the students' brains." In such a manner the output of schools and hospitals is often idealized; attempts to measure output are often considered immoral.

3. *Major inputs and outputs cannot be stored.* For example, although raw materials and store merchandise may be stored, a hotel's available labor force and rooms are either used or unused as the day expires.

Many activities of nonprofit organizations are little different from business organizations, as the following illustrates:

St. Mary's College aimed at luring working adults back to the campus. Backed by a yearly advertising and marketing budget of $20,000, the adult division is thriving. . . . The new adult programs are helping to carry the school financially. It's very profitable.[5]

In this book, references are made to service industry applications as the various management accounting techniques are discussed. A major generalization is worth mentioning at the outset. Simplicity is the watchword for installation of systems in service industries and nonprofit organizations, especially in the health industry, where highly paid professionals such as physicians barely bother with a written medical record, much less a time card. In fact, simplicity is a fine watchword for the design of any accounting system. Complexity tends to generate data-gathering and data-interpreting costs that often exceed prospective benefits. Simplicity is sometimes referred to as KISS (which means keep it simple, stupid).

---

[4] *Not-for-profit* is more accurately descriptive of these organizations, but it is more awkward than *nonprofit,* which will be used henceforth for brevity. See Chapter 9 for a fuller discussion.

[5] "Colleges Learn to Hard Sell," *Business Week,* February 14, 1977, p. 92.

Line and Staff Authority

The organization chart in Exhibit 1-5 portrays how many manufacturing companies are divided into subunits. In particular, consider the distinction between line and staff authority. Most organizations specify certain activities as their basic mission, such as the production and sale of goods or services. All subunits of the organization that are *directly* responsible for conducting these basic activities are called **line** departments. The others are called **staff** departments, because their principal task is to support or service the line departments. Thus, staff activities are *indirectly* related to the basic activities of the organization. For instance, Exhibit 1-5 shows a series of factory-service departments that perform the staff function of supporting the line functions carried on by the production departments.

The controller fills a staff role, in contrast to the line roles of sales and production executives. The accounting department has responsibility for providing other managers with specialized service, including advice and help in budgeting, analyzing variances, pricing, and the making of special decisions. The accounting department does not exercise direct authority over line departments: its authority to prescribe uniform accounting and reporting methods is delegated to the controller by top-line management. The uniform accounting procedure is authorized by the company president and is installed for him by the controller. When the controller prescribes the line department's role in supplying accounting information, he is not speaking as the controller, a staff person; he is speaking for top-line management.

Theoretically, the controller's decisions regarding the best accounting procedures to be followed by line people are transmitted to the president. In turn, the president communicates these procedures through a manual of instructions, which comes down through the line chain of command to all people affected by the procedures. In practice, however, the daily work of the controller, and his face-to-face relationships with the production manager or foreman, may require him to direct how production records should be kept or how work tickets should be completed. The controller usually holds delegated authority from top-line management over such matters.

Exhibit 1-6 shows how a controller's department may be organized. In particular, note the distinctions between the scorekeeping, attention-directing, and problem-solving roles. Unless some internal accountants are given the latter two roles as their primary responsibilities, the scorekeeping tasks tend to be too dominating and the system less responsive to facilitating management's decision making.

The Controller

The title of controller is applied to various accounting positions, the stature and duties of which vary from company to company. In some firms the

EXHIBIT 1-5. Organization Chart of a Manufacturing Company

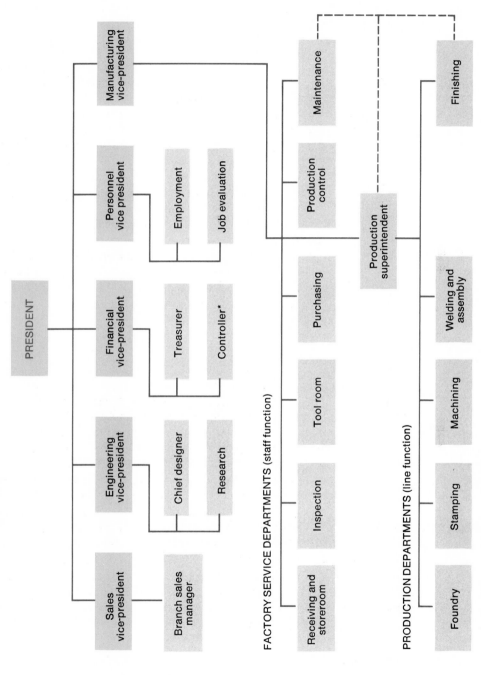

FACTORY SERVICE DEPARTMENTS (staff function)

PRODUCTION DEPARTMENTS (line function)

*For detailed organization of a controller's department, see Exhibit 1-6.

Dotted line represents staff authority.

EXHIBIT 1-6. Organization Chart of a Controller's Department

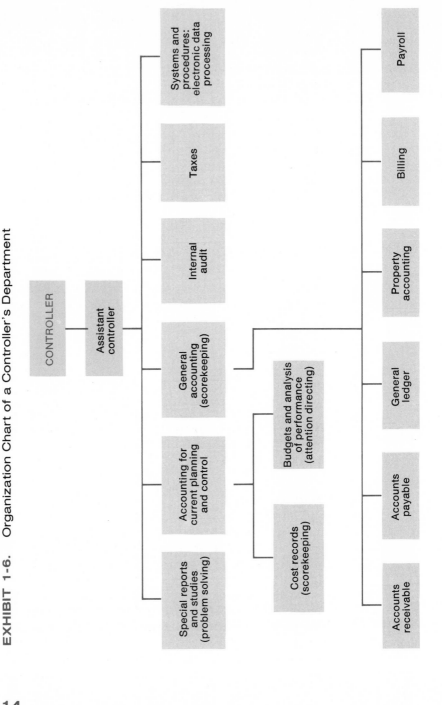

*Perspective:
Scorekeeping,
Attention
Directing, and
Problem
Solving*

controller is little more than a glorified bookkeeper who compiles data, primarily for external reporting purposes. In General Electric he is a key executive who aids managerial planning and control in over 160 company subdivisions. In most firms he has a status somewhere between these two extremes. For example, his opinion on the tax implications of certain management decisions may be carefully weighed, yet his opinion on other aspects of these decisions may not be sought. In this book, **controller** (sometimes called **comptroller**) means the chief management accounting executive. We have already seen that the modern controller does not do any controlling in terms of line authority, except over his own department. Yet the modern concept of controllership maintains that, in a special sense, the controller *does* control: by reporting and interpreting relevant data, the controller exerts a force or influence or projects an attitude that impels management toward logical decisions that are consistent with objectives.

Distinctions between Controller and Treasurer

Many people confuse the offices of controller and treasurer. The Financial Executives Institute, an association of corporate treasurers and controllers, distinguishes their functions as follows:

Controllership	*Treasurership*
1. Planning for control	1. Provision of capital
2. Reporting and interpreting	2. Investor relations
3. Evaluating and consulting	3. Short-term financing
4. Tax administration	4. Banking and custody
5. Government reporting	5. Credits and collections
6. Protection of assets	6. Investments
7. Economic appraisal	7. Insurance

Note how management accounting is the controller's primary *means* of implementing the first three functions of controllership.

We shall not dwell at length on the treasurer's functions. As the seven points indicate, he is concerned mainly with financial, as distinguished from operating, problems. The exact division of various accounting and financial duties obviously varies from company to company.

The controller has been compared to the ship's navigator. The navigator, with the help of his specialized training, assists the captain. Without the navigator, the ship may flounder on reefs or miss its destination entirely, but the captain exerts his right to command. The navigator guides and informs the captain as to how well the ship is being steered. This navigator role is especially evident in points 1 through 3 of the seven functions.

Freedom of Choice

Financial accounting and management accounting would be better labeled as external accounting and internal accounting, respectively. "Financial accounting" emphasizes the preparation of reports of an organization for external users such as banks and the investing public. "Management accounting" emphasizes the preparation of reports of an organization for its internal users such as presidents, deans, and head physicians.

Keep in mind that the same basic accounting system compiles the fundamental data for both financial accounting and management accounting. Furthermore, external forces (for example, income tax authorities and regulatory bodies, such as the United States Securities and Exchange Commission and the California Health Facility Commission) often limit management's choices of accounting methods. Organizations frequently limp along with a system that has been developed in response to the legal requirements imposed by external parties. In short, many existing systems are primarily oriented toward external rather than internal users.

Consider our cost-benefit theme that accounting systems are commodities like steak or butter. As just noted, generally accepted accounting standards or principles affect both internal and external accounting. However, change in internal accounting is not inhibited by generally accepted financial accounting standards. The manager who buys an internal accounting system can have anything his heart desires—as long as he is willing to pay the price. For instance, for its own management purpose, a hospital, a manufacturer, or a university can account for its assets on the basis of *current values,* as measured by estimates of replacement costs. No outside agency can prohibit such accounting.

There are no "generally accepted management accounting principles" that forbid particular measurements. Indeed, the cost-benefit philosophy refrains from stating that any given accounting is bad or good. Instead, the philosophy says that any accounting system or method (no matter how crazy it appears at first glance) is desirable as long as it brings incremental benefits in excess of its incremental costs.

Of course, satisfying internal demands for data (as well as external demands) means that organizations may have to keep more than one set of records. At least in the United States, there is nothing immoral or unethical about having many simultaneous sets of books—but they are expensive. The cost-benefit test says that their perceived increases in benefits must exceed their perceived increases in costs. Ultimately, benefits are measured by whether better decisions are forthcoming in the form of increased net cost savings or profit (or, in the case of many nonprofit institutions, in the form of increased quality or quantity of service rendered for each dollar spent).

Behavioral Impact

Financial accounting is often looked upon as being a cold, objective discipline. But management accounting is not; it is wrapped up in behavioral ramifications. The buyer of an accounting system should be concerned with how it will affect the decisions (behavior) of the affected managers. Earlier we saw how budgets and performance reports may play a key role in helping management. Emphasis on the future is a major feature of management accounting, whereas it is not as prominent in financial accounting. Budgets are the chief devices for compelling and disciplining management planning. Without budgets, planning may not get the front-and-center focus that it usually deserves.

The performance reports that are so widely used to judge decisions, subunits, and managers have enormous influence on the behavior of the affected individuals. Performance reports not only provide feedback to improve future economic decisions; they may also provide desirable or undesirable incentives. The choices of the content, format, timing, and distribution of performance reports are heavily influenced by their probable impact on incentives.

In a nutshell, management accounting can be best understood by using a cost-benefit philosophy coupled with an awareness of the importance of behavioral effects. Even more than financial accounting, management accounting spills over into related disciplines, such as economics, the decision sciences, and the behavioral sciences.

Certified Management Accountant

The distinction between financial accounting and management accounting became institutionalized in 1972, when the National Association of Accountants or NAA (the largest association of internal accountants in the United States) established the Institute of Management Accounting. The Institute administers a program leading to the Certificate in Management Accounting (CMA).[6] The objectives of the program are threefold:

1. To establish management accounting as a recognized profession by identifying the role of the management accountant and the underlying body of knowledge, and by outlining a course of study by which such knowledge can be acquired.
2. To foster higher educational standards in the field of management accounting.
3. To establish an objective measure of an individual's knowledge and competence in the field of management accounting.

[6]Information may be obtained from the Institute, 570 City Center Building, Ann Arbor, Michigan 48104.

The highlight of the program is a qualifying examination covering five parts: (1) economics and business finance, (2) organization and behavior, (3) public reporting, (4) periodic reporting for internal and external purposes, and (5) decision analysis, including modeling and information systems.

SUMMARY

An understanding of the overall purposes of the accounting system provides perspective for the study of the usefulness of accounting to management. The accounting system of the future is likely to be a multiple-purpose system with a highly selective reporting scheme. It will be highly integrated and will serve three main purposes: (1) routine reporting to management, primarily for planning and controlling current operations (scorekeeping and attention directing); (2) special reporting to management, primarily for long-range planning and nonrecurring decisions (problem solving); and (3) routine reporting on financial results, oriented primarily for external parties (scorekeeping). The first two purposes are the distinguishing characteristics of internal accounting for planning and control.

Internal accounting is interwoven with management itself. Accounting is a service function. Internal accounting is not management as ordinarily conceived, but it helps management do a better job.

The chief of internal accounting is usually called the *controller.* His responsibilities usually encompass all phases of accounting, including income taxes and routine reporting to outside parties. But accounting techniques for planning and control are his main tools for helping managers to get things done. Besides being a combination scorekeeper, attention director, and problem solver, he must constantly provide an objective view of operations and avoid seizing or accepting line authority. The human or organizational facets of his work often provide his most challenging and delicate tasks.

This book will stress the cost-benefit philosophy toward buying accounting systems. The choice of a system or method should be based on weighing the value of the system against its cost. This weighing often entails making predictions of how individuals will collectively behave under one system versus another. Therefore, the behavioral impact of alternatives is given ample attention throughout this book.

SUMMARY PROBLEMS FOR YOUR REVIEW

(Try to solve these problems before examining the solutions that follow.)

Problem One

The scorekeeping, attention-directing, and problem-solving duties of the accountant have been described in this chapter and elsewhere in literature. The accountant's usefulness to management is said to be directly influenced by how good an attention director and problem solver he is.

Evaluate this contention by specifically relating the accountant's duties to the duties of operating management.

Problem Two

Using the organization charts in this chapter (Exhibits 1-5 and 1-6), answer the following questions:

1. Do the following have line or staff authority over the machining foreman: maintenance foreman, manufacturing vice-president, production superintendent, purchasing agent, storekeeper, personnel vice-president, president, chief budgetary accountant, chief internal auditor?
2. What is the general role of service departments in an organization? How are they distinguished from operating or producing departments?
3. Does the controller have line or staff authority over the cost accountants? The accounts receivable clerks?
4. What is probably the *major duty* (scorekeeping, attention directing, or problem solving) of the following:

   Payroll clerk   Budgetary accountant
   Accounts receivable clerk   Cost analyst
   Cost record clerk   Head of special reports and studies
   Head of general accounting   Head of accounting
   Head of taxes   for planning and control
   Head of internal auditing   Controller

Solution to Problem One

Operating managers may have to be good scorekeepers, but their major duties are to concentrate on the day-to-day problems that most need attention, to make longer-range plans, and to arrive at special decisions. Accordingly, because the manager is concerned mainly with attention directing and problem solving, he will obtain the most benefit from the alert internal accountant who is a useful attention director and problem solver.

Solution to Problem Two

1. The only executives having line authority over the machining foreman are the president, the manufacturing vice-president, and the production superintendent.
2. A typical company's major purpose is to produce and sell goods or services. Unless a department is directly concerned with producing or selling, it is called a service or staff department. Service departments exist only to help

the production and sales departments with their major tasks: the efficient production and sale of goods or services.

3. The controller has line authority over all members of his own department, all those shown in the controller's organization chart (Exhibit 1-6).

4. The major duty of the first five—through the head of taxes—is typically scorekeeping. Attention directing is probably the major duty of the next three. Problem solving is probably the primary duty of the head of special reports and studies. The head of accounting for planning and control and the controller should be concerned with all three duties: scorekeeping, attention directing, and problem solving. However, there is a perpetual danger that day-to-day pressures will emphasize scorekeeping. Therefore, accountants and managers should constantly see that attention directing and problem solving are also stressed. Otherwise, the major management benefits of an accounting system may be lost.

ASSIGNMENT MATERIAL

The assignment material for each chapter is divided into two groups: *fundamental* and *additional*. The first group consists of carefully designed, relatively straightforward material aimed at conveying the essential concepts and techniques of the particular chapter. These assignments provide a solid introduction to the major concepts of accounting for management control.

The first question in each chapter usually concerns terminology, an extremely important and often troublesome phase of the learning process. A fuzzy understanding of terms hampers the learning of concepts. Many instructors will not require written answers to the question on terminology; in this case, the reader should check his comprehension of new terms by consulting the glossary at the end of the book.

The second group of assignment material in each chapter should not be regarded as inferior to the fundamental group. Many of these problems can be substituted for ones in the fundamental group.

Fundamental Assignment Material

1-1. Terminology. Define the following terms: *scorekeeping; attention directing; problem solving; management by exception; planning; controlling; performance report; budget; variance; line authority; staff authority; controller; comptroller; source document.*

1-2. Role of the accountant in the organization: line and staff functions.

1. Of the following, who have line authority over a cost record clerk: budgetary accountant; head of accounting for current planning and control; head of general accounting; controller; storekeeper; production superintendent; manufacturing vice-president; president; production control chief?

21

*Perspective:
Scorekeeping,
Attention
Directing, and
Problem
Solving*

2. Of the following, who have line authority over an assembler: stamping foreman; assembly foreman; production superintendent; production control chief; storekeeper; manufacturing vice-president; engineering vice-president; president; controller; budgetary accountant; cost record clerk?

1-3. **Scorekeeping, attention directing, and problem solving.** For each of the following, identify the function the accountant is performing—i.e., scorekeeping, attention directing, or problem solving. *Also state* whether the departments mentioned are service or production departments.

1. Processing the weekly payroll for the maintenance department.
2. Explaining the welding foreman's performance report.
3. Analyzing the costs of several different ways to blend raw materials in the foundry.
4. Tallying sales, by branches, for the sales vice-president.
5. Analyzing, for the president, the impact on net income of a contemplated new product.
6. Interpreting why a branch did not meet its sales quota.
7. Interpreting variances on a machining foreman's performance report.
8. Preparing the budget for research and development.
9. Adjusting journal entries for depreciation on the personnel manager's office equipment.
10. Preparing a customer's monthly statement.

Additional Assignment Material

1-4. "The accounting system is intertwined with operating management. Business operations would be a hopeless tangle without the paperwork that is so often regarded with disdain." Do you agree? Explain, giving examples.

1-5. What are the three broad purposes of an accounting system?

1-6. "The emphases of financial accounting and management accounting differ." Explain.

1-7. Distinguish among scorekeeping, attention directing, and problem solving.

1-8. Give examples of special nonrecurring decisions and of long-range planning.

1-9. Briefly describe the probable business information system of the future.

1-10. "Planning is much more vital than control." Do you agree? Explain.

1-11. Distinguish among a source document, a subsidiary ledger, and a general ledger.

1-12. Distinguish among a budget, a performance report, and a variance.

1-13. "Management by exception means abdicating management responsibility for planning and control." Do you agree? Explain.

1-14. "Good accounting provides automatic control of operations." Do you agree? Explain.

1-15. Distinguish between line and staff authority.

1-16. "The controller does control in a special sense." Explain.

1-17. "The importance of accurate source documents cannot be overemphasized." Explain.

1-18. **Organization chart.** Draw an organization chart for a single-factory company with the following personnel. Which represent factory service departments? Producing departments?

Punch press foreman
Vice-president and controller
Storekeeper
Drill press foreman
Production superintendent
Chairman of the board
Engineering vice-president
Manufacturing vice-president
President

Personnel vice-president
Maintenance foreman
Sales vice-president
Production control chief
Production planning chief
Assembly foreman
Purchasing agent
Secretary and treasurer

1-19. **Focus on financial data.** *Business Week* (January 10, 1977, p. 58) reported:

> Rockwell's Anderson, a veteran of the company's automotive operations, recalls that when he sat in on meetings at Rockwell's North American Aircraft Operations in the late 1960s, "there'd be 60 or 70 guys talking technical problems, with never a word on profits." Such inattention to financial management helped Rockwell lose the F-15 fighter to McDonnell Douglas, Pentagon sources say. Anderson brought in profit-oriented executives, and he has now transformed North American's staff meetings to the point that "you seldom hear talk of technical problems any more," he says. "It's all financial."

What is your reaction to Anderson's comments? Are his comments related to management acccounting?

1-20. **Costs and benefits.** Marks & Spencer, a giant retailer in the United Kingdom, has used a cost-benefit approach to the paper bureaucracy. Looked at in isolation, each form seemed reasonable:

23

*Perspective:
Scorekeeping,
Attention
Directing, and
Problem
Solving*

. . . but in terms of the total procedure, the substantial effort required in each department to confirm the accuracy of the information or verify completion of the task seemed to be out of proportion to any value achieved. By challenging the need for detail and highlighting the fact that sensible approximation costs less, the committee succeeded in simplifying many documents and eliminating others.[7]

Describe the rationale that should underlie systems design.

1-21. Nonprofit systems. The following comments were made by a certified public accountant who has had extensive experience in consulting in service industries and nonprofit organizations: "Valid accounting principles are so basic that, once accepted, it seems incredible that there was ever any question. Accounting doesn't advance on theory, only when somebody's money is at stake."

Required | During the 1970s hospitals hired consultants in droves to install cost accounting systems. Why hadn't hospitals used much cost accounting before?

[7] Derek G. Rayner, "A Battle Won in the War on the Paper Bureaucracy," *Harvard Business Review,* Vol. 53, No. 1 (January–February 1975), p. 14.

CHAPTER 2

Introduction to Cost-Volume Relationships

How do the costs and revenues of a hospital change as one more patient is admitted for a four-day stay? How are the costs and revenue of an airline affected when one more passenger is boarded at the last moment, or when one more flight is added to the schedule? How should the budget request by the California Department of Motor Vehicles be affected by the predicted increase in the state's population? These questions have a common theme: What will happen to financial results if a specified level of activity or volume fluctuates? Their answers are not easy to obtain, and managers usually resort to some simplifying assumptions, especially concerning cost behavior (that is, how total costs are affected as volume changes). Nevertheless, implicitly or explicitly, managers must frequently answer these questions in order to reach intelligent decisions.

The managers of profit-seeking organizations usually study the relationships of revenue (sales), expenses (costs), and net income (net profit). This study is commonly called cost-volume-profit analysis. The managers of nonprofit organizations also will benefit from the study of cost-volume-profit relationships, primarily because knowledge of how costs fluctuate in response to changes in volume is valuable regardless of whether profit is an objective. After all, no organization has unlimited resources.

The subject matter of this chapter is straightforward. No knowledge of the accountant's assumptions underlying financial reporting is required. After all, in its most fundamental sense, an income statement is merely a presentation of the financial results from matching sales and related costs.

VARIABLE COSTS AND FIXED COSTS

Variable costs and fixed costs are usually defined in terms of how a total cost changes in relation to fluctuations in the quantity of some selected activity. Activity bases are diverse: They may be the number of orders processed, the number of lines billed in a billing department, the number of admissions to a theater, the number of pounds handled in a warehouse, the hours of labor worked in an assembly department, the number of rides in an amusement park, the seat-miles on an airline, the dollar sales in a grocery store, or some other index of volume.

If Watkins Products pays its door-to-door sales personnel a 40 percent straight commission, then the total cost of sales commissions should be 40 percent of the total sales dollars. If a garden shop buys bags of weed killer at $2 each, then the total cost of weed killer should be $2 times the total number of bags. These are variable costs. **They are uniform *per unit*, but their *total* fluctuates in direct proportion to the total of the related activity or volume.** These relationships are depicted graphically in Exhibit 2-1. The costs of most merchandise, materials, parts, supplies, commissions, and many types of labor are variable.

EXHIBIT 2-1. Variable-Cost Behavior

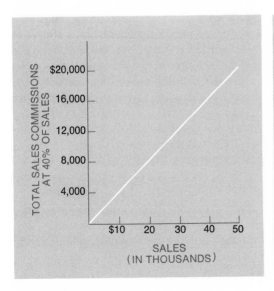

If a manufacturer of picture tubes for color television rents a factory for $100,000 per year, then the unit cost of rent applicable to each tube will depend on the total number of tubes produced. If 100,000 tubes are produced, the unit cost will be $1; if 50,000 tubes are produced, $2. This is an example of a fixed cost, a cost that does not change in *total* but becomes progressively smaller on a *per-unit* basis as volume increases. Real estate taxes, real estate insurance, many executive salaries, and straight-line depreciation charges are fixed costs.

COMPARISON OF VARIABLE AND FIXED COSTS

Note carefully from the foregoing examples that the "variable" or "fixed" characteristic of a cost relates to its *total dollar amount* and not to its per-unit amount. A variable cost (the 40 percent sales commission) is constant per unit, and its *total* dollar amount *changes* proportionally with changes in activity or volume. A fixed cost (the factory rent) varies inversely with activity or volume changes on a per-unit basis but is *constant* in *total* dollar amount.

Relevant Range

A fixed cost is fixed only in relationship to a given period of time—the budget period—and a given, though wide, range of activity called the "relevant range." Fixed costs may change from budget year to budget year solely because of changes in insurance and property tax rates, executive salary levels, or rent levels. But these items are highly unlikely to change within a given year. In addition, the total budgeted fixed costs may be formulated on the basis of an expected activity level (i.e., volume), say, within a relevant planning range of 40,000 to 85,000 units of production per month. However, operations on either side of the range will result in major salary adjustments or in the layoff or hiring of personnel. For example, assume the total monthly fixed cost within the relevant range is $100,000. If operations fall below 40,000 units, changes in personnel and salaries will slash fixed costs to $60,000. If operations rise above 85,000 units, increases in personnel and salaries will raise fixed costs to $115,000.

These assumptions—a given time period and a given range—are shown graphically at the top of Exhibit 2-2. The possibility that operations will be outside the relevant range is usually remote. Therefore, the three-level refinement at the top of Exhibit 2-2 is usually not graphed. A single horizontal line is usually extended through the plotted activity levels, as at the bottom of the exhibit.

EXHIBIT 2-2. Fixed Costs and the Relevant Range

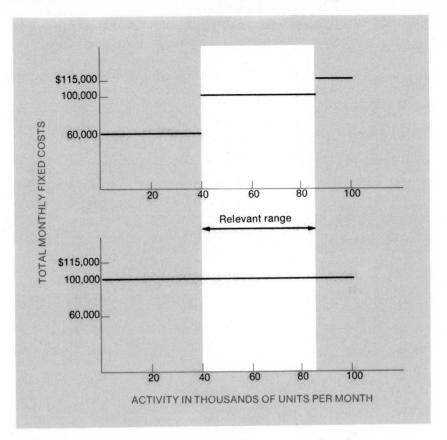

Some Simplifying Assumptions

Nearly every organization has some variable costs and some fixed costs. As you may suspect, it is often difficult to classify a cost as exactly variable or exactly fixed. Many complications arise, including the possibility of costs behaving in some nonlinear way (not behaving as a straight line). For example, as workers learn to process incoming income tax forms, productivity rises. This means that total costs may behave like this:

but not like this:

Moreover, costs may be simultaneously affected by more than one activity base. For example, the costs of shipping labor may be affected by *both* the weight and the number of units handled. We shall investigate various facets of this problem in succeeding chapters; for now, we shall assume that any cost may be classified as either variable or fixed. A given variable cost is associated with *one* measure of volume, and that relationship is linear.

ILLUSTRATION OF COST-VOLUME-PROFIT ANALYSIS

The following situation will be used to demonstrate the techniques and the analytical power of cost-volume-profit analysis. Amy Winston, the manager of food services for the State of California, is trying to decide whether to rent a line of food vending machines for the state's Sacramento buildings. Although the unit prices and acquisition costs differ among individual food items, Winston feels that an average unit selling price of 50¢ and an average unit acquisition cost of 40¢ will suffice for purposes of this analysis. The following revenue and expense relationships are predicted:

	Per Unit	Percent of Sales
Selling price	$.50	100%
Cost of each item	.40	80
Contribution margin	$.10	20%
Monthly fixed expenses:		
Rent	$1,000	
Wages for replenishing and servicing	4,500	
Other fixed expenses	500	
Total fixed expenses per month	$6,000	

The following six sections will explore various aspects of the above data. A new question or requirement will be stated at the start of each section.

1. Break-even Point—Two Analytical Techniques

Express the monthly break-even point in number of units and in dollar sales.

The study of cost-volume-profit relationships is often called break-even analysis. The latter is a misnomer because the break-even point—the point of zero net income—is often only incidental to the planning decision at hand. Still, knowledge of the break-even point provides insights into the possible riskiness of certain courses of action.

There are three basic techniques for computing a break-even point: equation, contribution margin, and graphing. The graphical technique is shown in the solution to Requirement 2.

a. **Equation technique.** This is the most general form of analysis, the one that may be adapted to any conceivable cost-volume-profit situation. You are familiar with a typical income statement. Any income statement can be expressed in equation form, as follows:

$$\text{Sales} - \text{Variable expenses} - \text{Fixed expenses} = \text{Net income} \qquad (1)$$

or

$$\text{Sales} = \text{Variable expenses} + \text{Fixed expenses} + \text{Net income} \qquad (1)$$

Let X = number of units to be sold to break even. Then

$$\$.50X = \$.40X + \$6,000 + 0$$

$$\$.10X = \$6,000 + 0$$

$$X = \frac{\$6,000 + 0}{\$.10}$$

$$X = 60,000 \text{ units}$$

Total sales in the equation is a price-times-quantity relationship. In the above equation, this was expressed as $\$.50X$. Of course, the *dollar* sales answer in this case could be obtained in shortcut fashion by multiplying 60,000 *units* by 50¢, which would yield the break-even dollar sales of $30,000. Another approach is to solve the equation method for total sales *dollars* directly. This method becomes important in those situations where *unit* price and *unit* variable costs are not given. Rather, you must work with variable cost as a *percentage* of each sales *dollar*. Moreover, most companies sell more than one product, and the overall break-even point is often expressed in sales dollars because of the variety of product lines. For example, although radios and television sets cannot be meaningfully added, their sales prices provide an automatic common denominator.

The same equation, this time using the relationship of variable costs and profits as a *percentage* of sales, may be used to obtain the sales in dollars:

Let $\qquad\qquad X$ = sales in dollars needed to break even.

$$X = .80X + \$6,000 + 0$$

$$.20X = \$6,000 + 0$$

$$X = \frac{\$6,000 + 0}{.20}$$

$$X = \$30,000$$

b. Contribution-margin technique. If algebra is not one of your strong points, you may prefer to approach cost-volume-profit relationships in the following common-sense arithmetic manner. Every unit sold generates a contribution margin or marginal income, which is the excess of the sales price over the variable expenses pertaining to the units in question:

Unit sales price	$.50
Unit variable expenses	.40
Unit contribution margin to fixed expenses and net income	$.10

The $.10 unit contribution is divided into total fixed expenses plus a target net income[1] to obtain the number of *units* that must be sold to break even: ($6,000 + 0) ÷ $.10 = 60,000 units.

The computation in terms of *dollar* sales is

Sales price	100%
Variable expenses as a percentage of dollar sales	80
Contribution-margin ratio	20%

Therefore, 20 percent of each sales dollar is the amount available for the recovery of fixed expenses and the making of net income: ($6,000 + 0) ÷ .20 = $30,000 sales needed to break even.

c. Relationship of the two techniques. Reflect on the relationship between the equation technique and the contribution-margin technique. As you can see, the contribution-margin technique is merely a shortcut version of the equation technique. Look at the second-last line in the solutions to Equation (1). They read:

Target Volume

In Units	*In Dollars*
$.10X = \$6,000 + 0$	$.20X = \$6,000 + 0$
$X = \dfrac{\$6,000 + 0}{\$.10}$	$X = \dfrac{\$6,000 + 0}{.20}$

This gives us the shortcut general formulas:

$$\frac{\text{Target volume}}{\text{in units}} = \frac{\text{Fixed expenses + Net income}}{\text{Contribution margin per unit}} \quad (2)$$

$$\frac{\text{Target volume}}{\text{in dollars}} = \frac{\text{Fixed expenses + Net income}}{\text{Contribution-margin ratio}} \quad (3)$$

Which should you use, the equation or the contribution-margin technique?

---

[1]The terms **net income** and **net profit** are used interchangeably. Similarly, variable and fixed **expenses** and variable and fixed **costs** are used interchangeably. In this context, costs refer to the costs expiring during the period in question.

Use either; the choice is a matter of personal preference or convenience within a particular case.

2. Graphical Technique

Graph the cost-volume-profit relationships in Requirement 1.

The break-even point is represented by the intersection of the sales line and the total expenses line in Exhibit 2-3. Exhibit 2-3 was constructed by using a sales line and a total expenses line that combined variable and fixed expenses. The procedure (see Exhibit 2-3) is as follows:

Step 1. Select a convenient sales volume, say 100,000 units, and plot the point for total sales dollars at that volume: 100,000 × 50¢ = $50,000. Draw the revenue (i.e., sales) line from the origin to the $50,000 point.

Step 2. Draw the line showing the $6,000 fixed portion of expenses. It should be a horizontal line intersecting the vertical axis at $6,000.

Step 3. Determine the variable portion of expenses at a convenient level of activity: 100,000 units × 40¢ = $40,000. Add this to the fixed expenses: $40,000 + $6,000 = $46,000. Plot the point for 100,000 units and $46,000. Then draw a line between this point and the $6,000 fixed cost intercept of the

EXHIBIT 2-3. Cost-Volume-Profit Graph

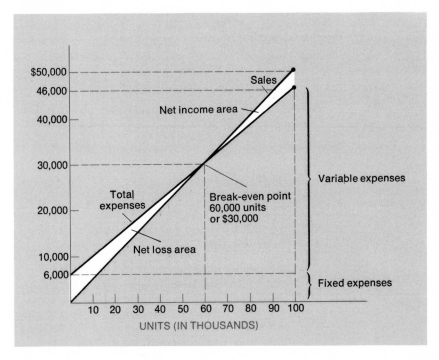

vertical axis. This is the total expenses line. The break-even point is where this line crosses the sales line, 60,000 units or $30,000, namely where total sales revenues exactly equal total costs.

Exhibit 2-3 is the completed break-even graph. The break-even point is only one facet of this cost-volume-profit graph. More generally, the graph shows the profit or loss at *any* rate of activity. Namely, at any given volume, the vertical distance between the sales line and the total expenses line measures the net income or net loss.

The graph portrays only one of a number of methods for picturing cost-volume-profit relationships. The graph often has educational advantages because it shows potential profits over a wide range of volume more easily than numerical exhibits. Whether graphs or other types of exhibits are used depends largely on management's preference.

3. Changes in Fixed Expenses

If the rent were doubled, find the monthly break-even point: (a) in number of units, (b) in dollar sales.

The fixed expenses would increase from $6,000 to $7,000. Then:

$$\text{Target volume in units} = \frac{\text{Fixed expenses + Net income}}{\text{Contribution margin per unit}} = \frac{\$7,000}{\$.10} = \frac{70,000}{\text{units}} \quad (2)$$

$$\text{Target volume in dollars} = \frac{\text{Fixed expenses + Net income}}{\text{Contribution-margin ratio}} = \frac{\$7,000}{.20} = \$35,000 \quad (3)$$

Note that a one-sixth increase in fixed expenses altered the break-even point by one-sixth: from 60,000 to 70,000 units and from $30,000 to $35,000. This relationship always exists, everything else held constant.

4. Changes in Contribution Margin per Unit

Assume that the fixed rent is unchanged. (a) If the owner is paid 1¢ per unit as additional rent, find the monthly break-even point in number of units; in dollar sales. (b) If the selling price falls from 50¢ to 45¢ per unit, and the original variable expenses are unchanged, find the monthly break-even point, in number of units; in dollar sales.

a. The variable expenses would be increased from 40¢ to 41¢, the unit contribution margin would be reduced from 10¢ to 9¢, and the contribution-margin ratio would become only 18 percent (9¢ ÷ 50¢).

The original fixed expenses of $6,000 would be unaffected, but the denominators are changed as compared with the denominators used in the solutions to Requirements 1 and 3. Thus:

$$\text{Break-even point in units} = \frac{\$6,000}{\$.09} = 66,667 \text{ units} \qquad (2)$$

$$\text{Break-even point in dollars} = \frac{\$6,000}{.18} = \$33,333 \qquad (3)$$

b. A change in unit contribution margin can also be caused by a change in selling price. If the selling price fell from 50¢ to 45¢, and the original variable expenses were unchanged, the unit contribution would be reduced from 10¢ to 5¢ (i.e., 45¢ − 40¢) and the break-even point would soar to 120,000 units (6,000 ÷ 5¢). The break-even point in dollars would also change, because the selling price and contribution-margin ratio change: the contribution-margin ratio would be 11.11 percent (5¢ ÷ 45¢). The break-even point, in dollars, would be $54,000 (120,000 units × 45¢), or, using the formula:

$$\text{Break-even point in dollars} = \frac{\$6,000}{.1111} = \$54,000 \qquad (3)$$

5. Target Net Profit and an Incremental Approach

Refer to the original data. If Winston considers $480 per month the minimum acceptable net income, how many units will have to be sold to warrant the renting of the machines? Convert your answer into dollar sales.

$$\text{Target sales volume in units} = \frac{\text{Fixed expenses} + \text{Net income}}{\text{Contribution margin per unit}}$$

$$= \frac{\$6,000 + \$480}{\$.10} = 64,800 \text{ units} \qquad (2)$$

Another way of getting the same answer is to use your knowledge of the break-even point and adopt an incremental approach. If 60,000 units is the break-even point, all fixed expenses would be recovered at that volume. Therefore, every *additional* unit beyond 60,000 would represent a unit contribution to *net profit* of 10¢. If $480 were the target net profit, $480 ÷ 10¢ would show that the target volume must exceed the break-even volume by 4,800 units; it would therefore be 60,000 + 4,800 = 64,800 units.

The answer, in terms of *dollar* sales, can then be computed by multiplying 64,800 units by 50¢, or by using the formula:

$$\text{Target sales volume in dollars} = \frac{\text{Fixed expenses} + \text{Net income}}{\text{Contribution margin ratio}}$$

$$= \frac{\$6,000 + \$480}{.20} = \$32,400 \qquad (3)$$

To solve directly for sales dollars with the alternative incremental approach, the break-even point, in dollar sales of $30,000, becomes the frame of reference. Every sales dollar beyond that point contributes 20¢ to net profit. Divide $480 by 20¢. The dollar sales must therefore exceed the break-even volume by $2,400 to produce a net profit of $480; thus the total dollar sales would be $30,000 + $2,400 = $32,400.

6. Multiple Changes in the Key Factors

Suppose, after the machines have been in place awhile, Winston is considering locking them from 6 P.M. to 6 A.M., which she estimates will save $820 in wages monthly. The cutback from 24-hour service would hurt volume substantially, because many nighttime employees use the machines. However, employees could find food elsewhere, so not too many complaints are expected. Should the machines remain available 24 hours per day? Assume that monthly sales would decline by 10,000 units from current sales of (a) 62,000 units and (b) 90,000 units.

First, whether 62,000 or 90,000 units are being sold is irrelevant to the decision at hand. The analysis of this situation consists of constructing and solving equations for conditions that prevail under either alternative and selecting the volume level that yields the highest net profit. However, the incremental approach is much quicker. What is the essence of this decision? We are asking whether the prospective savings in cost exceed the prospective loss in *total* contribution margin in dollars:

Lost total contribution margin, 10,000 units @ $.10	$1,000
Savings in fixed expenses	820
Prospective decline in net income	$ 180

Regardless of the current volume level, whether it be 62,000 or 90,000 units, if we accept the prediction that sales will decline by 10,000 units as accurate, the closing from 6:00 P.M. to 6:00 A.M. will decrease the profit by $180:

	Decline from 62,000 to 52,000 Units		Decline from 90,000 to 80,000 Units	
Units	62,000	52,000	90,000	80,000
Sales	$31,000	$26,000	$45,000	$40,000
Variable expenses	24,800	20,800	36,000	32,000
Contribution margin	$ 6,200	$ 5,200	$ 9,000	$ 8,000
Fixed expenses	6,000	5,180	6,000	5,180
Net profit	$ 200	$ 20	$ 3,000	$ 2,820
Change in net profit	($180)		($180)	

USES AND LIMITATIONS
OF COST-VOLUME ANALYSIS

Optimum Combination of Factors

The analysis of cost-volume-profit relationships is one of management's paramount responsibilities. The knowledge of patterns of cost behavior offers insights valuable in planning and controlling short- and long-run operations. This is a major theme of this book, so we should regard the current material as introductory. Our purpose in this chapter is to provide perspective, rather than to impart an intimate knowledge of the niceties of cost behavior.

The example of the vending machines demonstrated some valuable applications of cost-volume-profit analysis. One of management's principal duties is to discover the most profitable combination of the variable and fixed cost factors. For example, automated machinery may be purchased, causing more fixed costs but reducing labor cost per unit. On the other hand, it may be wise to reduce fixed costs in order to obtain a more favorable combination. Thus, direct selling by a salaried sales force may be supplanted by the use of manufacturers' agents who are compensated via sales commissions (variable costs).

Generally, companies that spend heavily for advertising are willing to do so because they have high contribution margins (airlines, cigarette, and cosmetic companies). Conversely, companies with low contribution margins usually spend less for advertising and promotion (manufacturers of industrial equipment). The size of the contribution margin influences such outlays. Obviously, a company with a volume of 100,000 units and a contribution margin of 10¢ per unit is not going to risk the same promotional outlay to obtain, say, a 10 percent increase in volume as a company with a contribution margin of 90¢ per unit.

Therefore, when the contribution-margin ratio is low, great increases in volume are necessary before significant increases in net profits can occur. As sales exceed the break-even point, a high contribution-margin ratio increases profits faster than a small contribution-margin ratio.

Limiting Assumptions

The notion of **relevant range,** which was introduced when fixed expenses were discussed, is applicable to the entire break-even graph. Almost all break-even graphs show revenue and cost lines extending back to the vertical axis. This is misleading, because **the relationships depicted in such graphs are valid only within the relevant range that underlies the construction of the graph.** Exhibit 2-4(B), a modification of the conventional break-even graph, partially demonstrates the multitude of assumptions that must be made in constructing the typical break-even graph. Some of these assumptions are:

EXHIBIT 2-4. Conventional and Modified Break-even Graphs

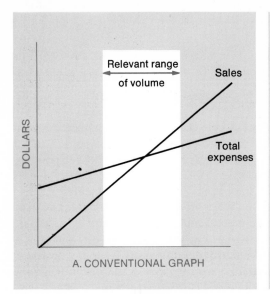

A. CONVENTIONAL GRAPH

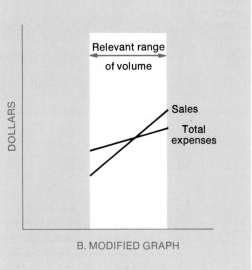

B. MODIFIED GRAPH

1. The behavior of revenues and expenses is accurately portrayed and is linear over the relevant range. The principal difference between the accountant's break-even chart and the economist's are: (a) the accountant's sales line is drawn on the assumption that selling prices do not change with production or sales, and the economist assumes that reduced selling prices are normally associated with increased sales volume; (b) the accountant usually assumes a constant variable expense per unit, and the economist assumes that variable expense per unit does change with production.

2. Expenses may be classified into variable and fixed categories. Total variable expenses vary directly with volume. Total fixed expenses do not change with volume.

3. Efficiency and productivity will be unchanged.

4. Sales mix will be constant. The sales mix is the relative combination of quantities of a variety of company products that compose total sales.

5. The difference in inventory level at the beginning and at the end of a period is insignificant. (The impact of inventory changes on cost-volume-profit analysis is discussed in Chapter 15.)

Contribution Margin and Gross Margin

Recall that contribution margin was defined as the excess of sales over *all* variable expenses. It may be expressed as a *total* absolute amount, a *unit* absolute amount, and a *percentage*. Sometimes a variable expense ratio or variable cost ratio may be encountered; it is defined as the variable expenses

36

divided by sales. Thus, a contribution margin ratio of 20 percent means that the variable cost ratio is 80 percent.

The most confusion about terms seems to be the mix-up between *contribution margin* and **gross margin** (which is also called **gross profit**). *Gross margin* is a widely used concept, particularly in the retailing industry. It is defined as the excess of sales over the *cost of goods sold* (that is, the cost of the merchandise that is acquired and resold). The following comparisons from our chapter illustration show the similarities and differences between the contribution margin and gross margin:

Sales	$.50
Variable costs: Acquisition cost of unit sold	.40
Contribution margin and gross margin are equal	$.10

Thus, the basic data for Requirement 1 resulted in no difference between the measure of contribution margin and gross margin. However, recall that Requirement 4a introduced a variable portion of rent. There would now be a difference:

	4a	1
Sales	$.50	$.50
Acquisition cost of unit sold	$.40	.40
Variable rent	.01	
Total variable expense	.41	
Contribution margin	$.09	
Gross margin		$.10

As the preceding tabulation indicates, and as the next chapter will explain more fully, contribution margin and gross margin are not the same concepts. Contribution margin focuses on sales in relation to *all* variable cost behavior, whereas gross margin focuses on sales in relation to a lone item, the acquisition cost of the *merchandise* that has been sold.

SUMMARY

An understanding of cost behavior patterns and cost-volume-profit relationships can help guide a manager's decisions.

Variable costs (and expenses) and fixed costs (and expenses) have contrasting behavior patterns. Their relationship to sales, volume, and net profit is probably best seen on a cost-volume-profit graph. However, the graph should be used with great care. The portrayal of all profit-influencing factors on such a graph entails many assumptions that may hold over only a relatively narrow range of volume. As a tool, the graph may be compared to a meat-ax rather than to a surgeon's scalpel. Cost-volume-profit analysis, as depicted on a graph, is a framework for analysis, a vehicle for appraising overall performance, and a planning device.

The assumptions that underlie typical cost-volume-profit analysis are static. A change in one assumption (e.g., total fixed cost or the unit price of merchandise) will affect all the cost-volume-profit relationships on a given graph. The static nature of these assumptions should always be remembered by the managers who use this valuable analytical technique.

SUMMARY PROBLEM FOR YOUR REVIEW

Problem

The income statement of Wiley Company is summarized as follows:

Net revenue	$800,000
Less: Expenses, including $400,000 of fixed expenses	880,000
Net loss	$(80,000)

The manager believes that an increase of $200,000 in advertising outlays will increase sales substantially. His plan was approved by the chairman of the board.

Required

1. At what sales volume will the company break even?
2. What sales volume will result in a net profit of $40,000?

Solution

1. Note that all data are expressed in dollars. No unit data are given. Most companies have many products, so the overall break-even analysis deals with dollar sales, not units. The variable expenses are $880,000 − $400,000, or $480,000. The variable expense ratio is $480,000 ÷ $800,000, or .60. Therefore, the contribution-margin ratio is .40.

Let
S = break-even sales, in dollars. Then

$$S = \text{Variable expenses} + \text{Fixed expenses} + \text{Net profit} \qquad (1)$$
$$S = .60S + (\$400,000 + \$200,000) + 0$$
$$.40S = \$600,000 + 0$$

$$S = \frac{\$600,000 + 0}{.40} = \frac{\text{Fixed expenses} + \text{Target net profit}}{\text{Contribution-margin ratio}} \qquad (3)$$

$$S = \$1,500,000$$

2. Required sales $= \dfrac{\text{Fixed expenses} + \text{Target net profit}}{\text{Contribution-margin ratio}}$ (3)

Required sales $= \dfrac{\$600,000 + \$40,000}{.40} = \dfrac{\$640,000}{.40}$

Required sales $= \$1,600,000$

Alternatively, we can use an incremental approach and reason that all dollar sales beyond the $1,500,000 break-even point will result in a 40 percent contribution to net profit. Divide $40,000 by .40. Sales must therefore be $100,000 beyond the $1,500,000 break-even point in order to produce a net profit of $40,000.

APPENDIX 2-A:
THE P/V CHART AND SALES-MIX ANALYSIS

The P/V Chart

Exhibit 2-3 can be recast in another form as a so-called P/V chart (a profit-volume graph). This form is preferred by many managers who are interested mainly in the impact of changes in volume on net income. The first graph in Exhibit 2-5 illustrates the chart, using the data in our example. The chart is constructed as follows:

1. The vertical axis is net income in dollars. The horizontal axis is volume in units (or in sales dollars, in many cases).

EXHIBIT 2-5. P/V Chart

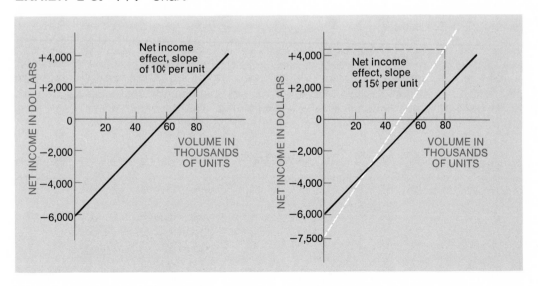

2. At zero volume, the net loss would be approximated by the total fixed costs: $6,000 in this example.

3. A net income line will slope upward from the −$6,000 intercept at the rate of the unit contribution margin of 10¢. The line will intersect the volume axis at the break-even point of 60,000 units. Each unit sold beyond the break-even point will add 10¢ to net income. For example, at a volume of 80,000 units, the net income would be $(80,000 − 60,000) \times 10¢ = \$2,000$.

The P/V chart provides a quick, condensed comparison of how alternatives on pricing, variable costs, or fixed costs may affect net income as volume changes. For example, the second graph in Exhibit 2-5 shows how net income and the break-even point would be affected by an increase in selling price from 50¢ to 55¢ and a $1,500 increase in rent. The unit contribution would become 15¢, and the break-even point would fall from 60,000 to 50,000 units:

$$\text{New break-even point} = \$7,500 \div \$.15$$

$$= 50,000 \text{ units}$$

Note also that the net income will increase at a much faster rate as volume increases. At a volume of 80,000 units, the net income would be $(80,000 − 50,000) \times 15¢ = \$4,500$.

Effects of Sales Mix

The cost-volume-profit analysis in this chapter has focused on a single line of products. In multiproduct firms, sales mix is an important factor in calculating an overall company break-even point. If the proportions of the mix change, the cost-volume-profit relationships also change. When managers choose a sales mix, it can be depicted on a break-even chart or P/V chart by assuming average revenues and costs for a given mix.

For example, suppose that a two-product company has a unit contribution margin of $1 for Product A and $2 for Product B, and that fixed costs are $100,000. The break-even point would be 100,000 units if only A were sold and 50,000 units if only B were sold. Suppose that the planned mix is three units of A for each unit of B. The contribution margin for each "package" of products would be $3 \times \$1$ plus $1 \times \$2$, or $5. The average contribution margin per unit of product would be $5 ÷ 4 units in each package = $1.25[2]. The break-even point, assuming that the mix is main-

---

[2]An alternate computation would use a weighted-average approach:

	Planned Sales	Weights	Unit Contribution Margin	Weighted Average
A	3	$\frac{3}{4}$	$1.00	$ .75
B	1	$\frac{1}{4}$	2.00	.50
	4			$1.25

tained, would be:

$100,000 ÷ $1.25 = 80,000 units (consisting of 60,000 units of A
and 20,000 of B)

These relationships are shown in Exhibit 2-6. The slopes of the solid lines depict the unit contribution margins of each product. The slope of the broken line depicts the average contribution per unit. Suppose that the total planned sales are 160,000 units, consisting of 120,000 units of A and 40,000 of B. Exhibit 2-6 shows that if overall unit sales and mix targets are achieved, net income would be $100,000. However, if the mix changes, net income may be much greater because the proportion of sales of B might be higher than anticipated. The opposite effect would occur if A sold in a higher proportion than expected. **When the sales mix changes, the break-even point and the expected net income at various sales levels are altered.**

EXHIBIT 2-6.   P/V Chart and Sales Mix

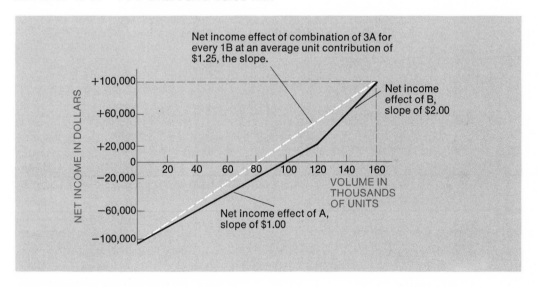

APPENDIX 2-B:
IMPACT OF INCOME TAXES

Private enterprises are subject to income taxes. Reconsider Requirement 5 of the basic illustration in the chapter, where the target income before income taxes was $480. If an income tax were levied at 40 percent, relationships would be:

Income before income tax	$480	100%
Income tax	192	40
Net income	$288	60%

Note that:

$$\text{Income before income taxes} = \frac{\text{Target after-tax net income}}{1 - \text{tax rate}}$$

$$\text{Income before income taxes} = \frac{\$288}{1 - .40} = \frac{\$288}{.60} = \$480$$

Suppose the target net income after taxes were $288. The only change in the general equation approach would be:

$$\text{Target sales} = \text{Variable expenses} + \text{Fixed expenses} + \frac{\text{Target after-tax net income}}{1 - \text{tax rate}}$$

Thus, letting X be the number of units to be sold at 50¢ each with a variable cost of 40¢ each and total fixed costs of $6,000:

$$\$.50X = \$.40X + \$6,000 + \frac{\$288}{1 - .4}$$

$$\$.10X = \$6,000 + \frac{\$288}{.6}$$

$$\$.06X = \$3,600 + \$288 = \$3,888$$

$$X = \$3,888 \div \$.06 = 64,800 \text{ units}$$

Suppose the target net income after taxes were $480. The needed volume would rise to 68,000 units, as follows:

$$\$.50X = \$.40X + \$6,000 + \frac{\$480}{1 - .4}$$

$$\$.10X = \$6,000 + \frac{\$480}{1 - .4}$$

$$\$.06X = \$3,600 + \$480 = \$4,080$$

$$X = \$4,080 \div \$.06 = 68,000 \text{ units}$$

ASSIGNMENT MATERIAL

Fundamental Assignment Material

2-1. **Terminology.** Define: *fixed cost; relevant range; contribution margin; marginal income;* and *variable cost.*

2-2. Cost-volume-profits and vending machines. The Putnam Company operates and services beverage vending machines located in restaurants, gas stations, factories, etc. The machines are rented from the manufacturer. In addition, Putnam must rent the space occupied by its machines. The following expense and revenue relationships pertain to a contemplated expansion program of 20 machines.

Fixed monthly expenses:

Machine rental: 20 machines @ $26.75	$ 535
Space rental: 20 locations @ $14.40	288
Wages to service the additional 20 machines	660
Payroll fringe costs: 10%	66
Other fixed costs	41
Total monthly fixed costs	$1,590

Other data:

	Per Unit	*Per $100 of Sales*
Selling price	$.50	100%
Cost of beverage	.40	80
Contribution margin	$.10	20%

Required

These questions relate to the above data unless otherwise noted. **Consider each question independently.**

1. What is the monthly break-even point in dollar sales? In number of units?

2. If 20,000 units were sold, what would be the company's net income?

3. If the space rental were doubled, what would be the monthly break-even point in dollar sales? In number of units?

4. If, in addition to the fixed rent, the vending machine manufacturer was also paid 1¢ per unit sold, what would be the monthly break-even point in dollar sales? In number of units? Refer to the original data.

5. If, in addition to the fixed rent, the machine manufacturer was paid 1¢ for each unit sold in excess of the break-even point, what would the new net income be if 20,000 units were sold? Refer to the original data.

2-3. The Wexler Trucking Company specializes in long-haul intercity transportation. Pertinent budget data for next year are as follows:

Sales volume	1,000,000 miles[a]
Average selling price (revenue)	25¢ per mile[a]
Fixed expenses	$40,000
Average variable expenses	20¢ per mile[a]

[a] *Mile* is an abbreviation for "intercity-vechicle mile."

Compute the new profit for each of the following changes. (Consider each case independently.)

a. A 10 percent increase in sales volume.

b. A 10 percent decrease in sales volume.

c. A 4 percent increase in selling price.

d. A 4 percent decrease in selling price.

e. A 1¢ per mile increase in variable expenses.

f. A 1¢ per mile decrease in variable expenses.

g. A 10 percent increase in fixed costs.

h. A 10 percent decrease in fixed costs.

i. A decrease in variable expenses of 1¢ per mile and a decrease in selling price of 4¢.

j. A decrease in selling price of 4¢ and an increase in miles of sales volume at 10 percent.

k. A 10 percent increase in fixed costs and 10 percent increase in miles of sales volume.

Additional Assignment Material

2-4. Why is "break-even analysis" a misnomer?

2-5. Distinguish between the equation technique and the unit contribution technique.

2-6. What are the principal differences between the accountant's and the economist's break-even graphs?

2-7. What is the sales mix?

2-8. **Nature of variable and fixed costs.** "As I understand it, costs such as the salary of the vice-president of transportation operations are variable because the more traffic you handle the less your unit cost. In contrast, costs such as fuel are fixed because each ton-mile should entail consumption of the same amount of fuel and hence bear the same unit cost." Do you agree? Explain.

2-9. **Extension of chapter illustration.** Refer to the basic facts in the chapter illustration. Suppose the selling price was changed to 60¢ in response to a rise in unit variable cost from 40¢ to 45¢. The original data are on page 28.

Required

1. Compute the monthly break-even point in number of units and in dollar sales.

2. Refer to the original data. If the rent were halved, what would be the monthly break-even point in number of units and in dollar sales?

2-10. **Hospital costs.** A hospital has overall variable costs of 20 percent of total revenue and fixed costs of $1.2 million per year.

1. What is the break-even point expressed in total revenue?

2. A patient-day is frequently used to measure the volume of a hospital. If there are going to be 10,000 patient-days next year, what average daily charge should be made to patients to break even?

2-11. Fixed costs and relevant range. Maxwell Engineering Consultants has a substantial year-to-year fluctuation in billings. Top management has the following policy regarding the employment of key personnel and staff engineers:

Number of Engineers	Engineers' Salaries	Gross Annual Billings
4	$52,000	$100,000 or less
5	70,000	100,001–$200,000
6	88,000	200,001 or more

For the past four years, gross annual billings have fluctuated between $120,000 and $180,000. You are preparing a budget for the coming year. Expectations are that gross billings will be between $165,000 and $185,000. What amount should be budgeted for engineers' salaries? Graph the relationships on an annual basis using the two approaches illustrated in Exhibit 2-2. Indicate the relevant range on each graph. You need not use graph paper; simply approximate the graphical relationships.

2-12. Estimating cost behavior patterns. The Mideastern Railroad showed the following results (in millions of dollars):

	19x3	19x2
Operating revenues	$218	$196
Operating expenses:		
Transportation	$ 87	$ 84
Maintenance of way and structures	34	32
Maintenance of equipment	37	34
Traffic	7	6
General	12	11
Payroll taxes	9	9
Property taxes	7	7
Equipment and other rentals	13	12
Total operating expenses	$206	$195
Net railway operating income	$ 12	$ 1

Based solely on your analysis of these figures, what is the percentage relationship of *variable* operating expenses to operating revenue? Explain any assumptions that underlie your answer.

2-13. Movie manager. Sam Baker is the manager of Stanford's traditional Sunday Flicks. Each Sunday a film has two showings. The admission price is 50¢. A maximum of 1,650 tickets are sold for each showing. The rental of the auditorium is $100 and labor is $280, including $30 for Baker. Baker must pay the film distributor a guarantee, ranging from $200 to $600 or 50 percent of gross admission receipts, whichever is higher.

Before and during the show, refreshments are sold; these sales average 12 percent of gross admission receipts and yield a contribution margin of 40 percent.

1. On June 3, Baker played "The Graduate." The film grossed $1,400. The guarantee to the distributor was $500 or 50 percent of gross admission receipts. What operating income was produced for the Students Association, which sponsors the showings?

2. Recompute the results if the film grossed $900.

3. The "four-wall" concept is being increasingly adopted by movie producers. This means that the producer pays a fixed rental for the theater for, say, a week's showing of a movie. As a theater owner, how would you evaluate a "four-wall" offer?

2-14. Hotel rentals. The Skillern Hotel has annual fixed costs applicable to its rooms of $1,500,000 for its 400-room hotel, average daily room rents of $30, and average variable costs of $5 for each room rented. It operates 365 days per year.

Required

1. How much net income on rooms will be generated (a) if the hotel is completely full throughout the entire year? and (b) if the hotel is half-full?

2. Compute the break-even point in number of rooms rented. What percentage occupancy for the year is needed to break even?

2-15. Promotion of championship fight. Newspaper accounts of a Joe Frazier-Muhammad Ali boxing match stated that each fighter would receive a flat fee of $2.5 million in cash. The fight would be shown on closed-circuit television. The central promoter would collect 100 percent of the receipts and would return 30 percent to the individual local promoters. He expected to sell 1,100,000 seats at a net average price of $10 each. He also was to receive $250,000 from Madison Square Garden (which had sold out its 19,500 seats, ranging from $150 for ringside down to $20, for a gross revenue of $1.25 million); he would not share the $250,000 with the local promoters.

Required

1. If the central promoter wanted to break even on sales of 1,100,000 tickets for closed-circuit television, how much fixed costs could he bear in addition to the $5 million paid to the boxers?

2. If the central promoter desired an operating income of $500,000, how many seats would have to be sold? Assume that the average price was $10 and the total fixed costs were $8 million.

2-16. Cost-volume-profit analysis and barbering. Sidney's Barber Shop has five barbers. (Sidney is not one of them.) Each barber is paid $6 per hour and works a 40-hour week and a 50-week year. Depreciation on store fixtures is $500 annually and depreciation on equipment is $1,000 annually. Rent is $500 per month. Since the shop is located near a large Midwestern university and the clientele is almost exclusively students, the only service performed is the giving of haircuts, the unit price of which is $5.

1. Contribution margin per haircut.

2. Annual break-even point, in number of haircuts.

3. What will be operating income if 20,000 haircuts are sold?

4. Suppose the landlord decides to revise the monthly rent to $100 + 10 percent of revenue per haircut. What is the new contribution margin per haircut? What is the annual break-even point (in number of haircuts)?

5. Ignore Requirements 3 and 4, and assume that the barbers cease to be paid by the hour but receive a 50 percent commission for each haircut. What is the new contribution margin per haircut? The annual break-even point (in number of haircuts)?

6. Refer to Requirement 5. What would be the operating income if 20,000 haircuts are sold? Compare your answer with the answer in Requirement 3.

7. Refer to Requirement 5. What would be the operating income if the barbers received an 80 percent commission for each haircut and 20,000 haircuts are sold?

8. Refer to Requirement 5. If 20,000 haircuts are sold, at what rate of commission would Sidney earn the same operating income as he earned in Requirement 3?

2-17. **Hospital cost-volume-profit relationships.** Dr. Brown and Dr. Black, the two radiologists of the San Susi Hospital, have submitted the following costs for operating the Department of Radiology:

Radiologists' salaries	30% of gross receipts
Technicians' and clerical salaries	$70,000
Supplies (fixed)	80,000
Depreciation	60,000

This year the department processed 65,000 films with three 200-milliampere X-ray machines. (Their original cost was $200,000 each, their original life expectancy, ten years.) For these processed films the average charge was $6. The 65,000 films represent maximum volume possible with the present equipment.

Drs. Brown and Black have submitted a request for two new 300-milliampere X-ray machines. (Their cost will be $250,000 each, their life expectancy ten years.) They will increase the capacity of the department by 35,000 films per year. Because of their special attachments (i.e., fluoroscopes) it will be possible to take more intricate films, for which a higher charge will be made. The average charge to the patient for each of these additional 35,000 films is estimated at $10. In order to operate the new machines, one highly trained technician must be hired at an annual salary of $15,000. The added capacity will increase the cost of supplies by $20,000.

1. Determine the break-even point in films for the three 200-milliampere X-ray machines. How much do they contribute to the hospital's overall profits?

2. Determine the break-even point if the two new 300-milliampere X-ray machines are added to the department, assuming a sales mix based on

maximum capacity. How much will be contributed to the hospital's overall profit, assuming they are operated at maximum volume?

2-18. Church enterprise. A California law permits a game of chance called BINGO, when it is offered by specified not-for-profit institutions, including churches. Reverend John O'Toole, the pastor of a new parish in suburban Los Angeles, is investigating the desirability of conducting weekly BINGO nights. The parish has no hall, but a local hotel would be willing to commit its hall for a lump-sum rental of $300 per night. The rent would include cleaning, setting up and taking down tables and chairs, and so on.

1. BINGO cards would be provided by a local printer in return for free advertising thereon. Door prizes would be donated by local merchants. The services of clerks, callers, security force, and others would be donated by volunteers. Admission would be $2.50 per person, entitling the player to one card; extra cards would be $1.50 each. Father O'Toole also learns that many persons buy extra cards, so there would be an average of four cards played per person. What is the maximum in total cash prizes that the church may award and still break even if 100 persons attend each weekly session?

2. Suppose the total cash prizes are $400. What will be the church's operating income if 50 persons attend? If 100 persons attend? If 150 persons attend? Briefly explain effects of the cost behavior on income.

3. After operating for ten months, Father O'Toole is thinking of negotiating a different rental arrangement but keeping the prize money unchanged. Suppose the rent is $200 weekly plus $1 per person. Compute the operating income for attendance of 50, 100, and 150 persons, respectively. Explain why the results differ from those in Requirement 2.

2-19. Effects of changes in costs. (CMA.) All-Day Candy Company is a wholesale distributor of candy. The company services grocery, convenience, and drug stores in a large metropolitan area.

Small but steady growth in sales has been achieved by the All-Day Candy Company over the past few years while candy prices have been increasing. The company is formulating its plans for the coming fiscal year. Presented below are the data used to project the current year's after-tax net income of $110,400.

Average selling price per box	$4.00
Average variable costs per box:	
Cost of candy	$2.00
Selling expenses	.40
Total	$2.40
Annual fixed costs	
Selling	$160,000
Administrative	280,000
Total	$440,000
Expected annual sales volume	
(390,000 boxes)	$1,560,000
Tax rate	40%

Manufacturers of candy have announced that they will increase prices of their products an average of 15 percent in the coming year, owing to increases in raw material (sugar, cocoa, peanuts, etc.) and labor costs. All-Day Candy Company expects that all other costs will remain at the same rates or levels as the current year.

Required

1. What is All-Day Candy Company's break-even point in boxes of candy for the current year?

2. What selling price per box must All-Day Candy Company charge to cover the 15 percent increase in the cost of candy and still maintain the current contribution-margin ratio? (Also see Problem 2-28.)

2-20. Traveling expenses. (A. Roberts.) Harold Nuget is a traveling inspector for the Environmental Protection Agency. He uses his own car and the agency reimburses him at 10¢ per mile. Harold claims he needs 12¢ per mile just to break even.

George Barr, the district manager, decides to look into the matter. He is able to compile the following information about Harold's expenses:

Oil change every 3,000 miles	$ 6.00
Maintenance (other than oil) every 6,000 miles	78.00
Yearly insurance	400.00
Auto cost $6,800 with an average cash trade-in value of $2,900; has a useful life of three years.	
Gasoline is approximately 80¢ per gallon and Harold averages 20 miles per gallon.	

When Harold is on the road, he averages 120 miles a day. The manager knows that Harold does not work Saturdays or Sundays, has ten working days vacation, six holidays, and spends approximately fifteen working days in the office.

Required

1. How many miles a year would the inspector have to travel to break even at the current rate of reimbursement?

2. What would be an equitable mileage rate?

2-21. Promotion of entertainment. George Doherty, a theatrical promoter, is trying to decide whether to engage The Bugs, a very popular singing group, for a one-night appearance at the local arena, which has a salable capacity of 5,000 seats. He has gathered the following data:

Rental, including ushering and cleanup service	$ 4,000
Advertising	3,000
Ticket service and ticket printing	1,000
Miscellaneous expenses	2,000
Entertainers' fee	10,000
Total	$20,000

Sales and entertainment taxes are 10 percent of the price (excluding the tax) on each ticket, and ticket prices include this tax. That is, if the price of the ticket is $5 (excluding taxes), the total price is $5.50. Therefore, the tax is one-eleventh of the total price of the ticket.

All prices include the sales and entertainment taxes.

1. What average price for each ticket is needed for Doherty to break even, assuming that the arena can be filled to capacity?
2. Suppose Doherty thinks that he can maximize his return by pricing as follows: 1,000 seats @ $10; 1,000 @ $8; 1,000 @ $6; and 2,000 @ $4. If the house were sold out, how much net income would be produced for Doherty at such prices?
3. Suppose that The Bugs appeal mainly to young people who are unlikely to pay high prices. Suppose further that 300 seats are sold @ $10; 700 @ $8; 900 @ $6; and 2,000 @ $4.
   a. How much net income would Doherty make?
   b. What is the average price of the sold tickets? How does it compare with your answer in Requirement 1? In your own words, explain the difference.
4. a. The Bugs' agent phoned Doherty and offered an alternate arrangement for compensation: $5,000 plus $1 per ticket sold regardless of the ticket price. How would this arrangement affect your answers to Requirements 1, 2, and 3a? Show your computations.
   b. If you were Doherty, which arrangement would you prefer? Why?
   c. Would your answer to part b change if the compensation were based on $1.20 per ticket rather than $1? Why?

2-22. **Hospital costs.** (Heavily adapted from CPA.) The Columbus Hospital operates several special departments. Each department pays space and bed charges on a fixed yearly basis, and services such as meals, laundry, etc. are charged as used. During 19x5 the Pediatrics Department billed each patient an average of $65 per day, had a capacity of 60 beds, and collected a gross revenue of $1,138,800.

Expenses charged by the hospital to the Pediatrics Department for 19x5 are detailed below.

	Basis of Allocation	
	Patient-Days	Bed Capacity
Meals	$ 42,952	
Janitorial		$ 12,800
Laundry	28,000	
Laboratory	94,800	
Maintenance	5,200	7,140
General administrative services		131,760
Rent		275,320
Pharmacy	73,800	
Other	18,048	25,980
	$262,800	$453,000

A separate contract is negotiated each year regarding nursing staff. Each nurse receives an annual salary of $15,000 from the hospital, and at the end of the year each department is charged according to the following schedule.

Annual Patient-Days	Nurses Supplied (*assumed*)
10,000-14,000	20
Over 14,000	25

You have been asked to assist the head of the Pediatrics Clinic in determining the 19x6 operating budget and renegotiating the nursing contract for 19x6. The cost system for space and services will be unchanged in 19x6.

Required

1. Considering only the space and service fees charged by the hospital (before nursing fees), how many patient-days will be required in 19x6 for the Pediatrics Department to break even?

2. Now *including* the nursing charges, how many patient-days will be required for the Pediatrics Department to break even in 19x6?

3. The head of the Pediatrics Department is considering offering the nursing center a flat nursing rate of $22.50 per patient-day, rather than the two-level system employed in 19x5. What will be the break-even point (in patient-days) under this plan (including the proposed nursing fee)?

ASSIGNMENT MATERIALS FOR APPENDIXES

2-23. **P/V chart.** Consider the example in Appendix 2-A. Suppose the rent were cut from $1,000 to $504, the cost per item raised from 40¢ to 47¢, and the selling price raised to 55¢. (The original data are on page 28.)

Required

1. Compute the new break-even point in units.

2. Draw a new P/V chart similar to the second one in Exhibit 2-5.

3. Compute and plot the new net income at a volume of 80,000 units.

2-24. **P/V chart and sales mix.** The Grimm Company has three products—X, Y, and Z—having contribution margins of $2, $3, and $6, respectively. The president is planning to sell 200,000 units in the forthcoming period, consisting of 80,000 X, 100,000 Y, and 20,000 Z. The company's fixed costs for the period are $406,000.

Required

1. What is the company's break-even point in units, assuming that the given sales mix is maintained?

2. Prepare a P/V chart for a volume of 200,000 units. Have a broken line represent the average contribution margin per unit and have solid lines represent the net income effects of each product by showing their unit contributions as the slopes of each line. What is the total contribution margin at a volume of 200,000 units? Net income?

3. What would net income become if 80,000 units of X, 80,000 of Y, and 40,000 units of Z were sold? What would be the new break-even point if these relationships persisted in the next period?

2-25. Product mix and break-even analysis. The Frozen Entree Company specializes in preparing two delicious food items that are frozen and shipped to many of the finer restaurants in the New York area. As a diner orders the item, the restaurant heats and serves it. The budget data for 19x4 are:

	Product	
	Veal Oscar	Chicken Kiev
Selling price	$5	$4
Variable expenses	2	2
Contribution margin	$3	$2
Number of units expected to be sold	20,000	30,000

Fixed expenses have been assigned, $33,000 to veal and $16,000 to chicken.

Required

1. Compute the break-even point in units for each product.

2. Suppose that the entrees were made in the same facilities, delivered on the same trucks, and so on. Suppose that a local chicken processor began a competitive operation on the chicken item, cutting the price so severely that Frozen Entree instantly dropped the chicken item for all of 19x4. Suppose also that the company's fixed costs were unaffected.

   a. What would be the break-even point for the company as a whole, assuming no chicken were produced?

   b. Suppose instead that only chicken and no veal were produced. What would be the break-even point for the company as a whole?

3. Draw a break-even graph for the company as a whole, using an average selling price and an average variable expense per unit. What is the break-even point under this aggregate approach? What is the break-even point if you add together the individual break-even points that you computed in Requirement 1? Why is the aggregate break-even point different from the sum of the individual break-even points?

2-26. Patient mix. [Adapted from J. Suver and B. Neumann, "Patient Mix and Break-even Analysis," *Management Accounting,* Vol. LVIII, No. 7 (January 1977), pp. 38–40.] A hospital has the following cost structure and patient mix: fixed costs, $1,000,000; daily revenue rate, $120; variable costs, $40 per patient-day.

Type of Patient		Reimbursement Basis Per Patient-Day	
Self-pay	20%	Revenue rate	$120
Private insurance	25	Revenue rate	120
Medicare	30	Specified costs or revenue rate, whichever is lower	110
Medicaid	25	Specified costs only	100

Required

1. What level of total revenue must be achieved to break even?

2. How many patient-days must be achieved to break even? If the mix is

unchanged, how many patient-days for each type of patient are necessary to break even?

3. The application of cost-volume-profit analysis in a hospital will depend on many objectives of top management. For instance, the hospital may be committed to take all types of patients as a matter of its community responsibilities. Suppose that the hospital is able to eliminate the Medicare and Medicaid patients; how many patient-days are required to break even?

2-27. **Income taxes.** Review the illustration in Appendix 2-B. Suppose the income tax rate were 30 percent instead of 40 percent.

How many units would have to be sold to achieve a target net income of (1) $288 and (2) $480? Show your computations.

2-28. **Income taxes.** (CMA.) Refer to Problem 2-19. What volume of sales in dollars must the All-Day Candy Company achieve in the coming year to maintain the same net income after taxes as projected for the current year if the selling price of candy remains at $4 per box and the cost of candy increases 15 percent?

2-29. **Income taxes.** The Quick Snack Company has a chain of local restaurants with the following income pattern:

Average sales check for each customer		$3.00
Costs of food	$1.10	
Other variable costs	.30	1.40
Contribution margin		$1.60

Fixed costs are $200,000 per year. The income tax rate is 35 percent.

What total revenue must be achieved to obtain a desired net income after taxes of $100,000?

2-30. **Income taxes on hotels.** The Young Hotel has annual fixed costs applicable to rooms of $1,500,000 for its 300-room hotel, average daily room rates of $40, and average variable costs of $6 for each room rented. It operates 365 days per year. The hotel is subject to an income tax rate of 30 percent.

1. How many rooms must the hotel rent to earn a net income after taxes of $1,000,000? Of $500,000?

2. Compute the break-even point in number of rooms rented. What percentage occupancy for the year is needed to break even?

CHAPTER 3

Introduction to Manufacturing Costs

Some form of cost accounting is applicable to manufacturing companies, retail stores, insurance companies, medical centers, and nearly all types of organizations. Throughout this book we shall consider both nonmanufacturing and manufacturing organizations, but we shall start with the manufacturing company because it is the most general case—embracing production, marketing, and general administration functions. You can then apply this overall framework to any organization.

In this chapter we shall examine some commonly encountered manufacturing costs and how they appear on financial statements. After studying the chapter, you should be acquainted with many new cost terms and with the two different approaches to preparing an income statement: the functional approach and the contribution approach.

CLASSIFICATIONS OF COSTS
Cost Accumulation and Cost Objectives

A cost may be defined as a sacrifice or giving up of resources for a particular purpose. Costs are frequently measured by the monetary units (for example, dollars or francs) that must be paid for goods and services. Costs are initially recorded in elementary form and then grouped in different ways to facilitate various decisions such as evaluating managers and subunits of the organization, expanding or deleting products or territories, replacing equipment, and so on.

To help make decisions, managers want the *cost of something*. This something is called a **cost objective,** which may be defined as *any activity for which a separate measurement of costs is desired.* Examples of cost objectives include departments, products, territories, miles driven, bricks laid, patients seen, tax bills sent, checks processed, student hours taught, and library books shelved.

The cost accounting system typically (1) accumulates costs by some "natural" classification such as materials or labor and (2) then allocates (traces) these costs to cost objectives. Exhibit 3-1 illustrates how a company might use materials in two main departments for manufacturing several different products. Note that the cost of, say, the metal used may be accumulated initially by keeping a tabulation of the amounts withdrawn from the raw-material storage center by each department. The same tabulation may be reclassified to provide an allocation of metal usage to the machining department and to the finishing department. In turn, the metal used by each department is allocated to the products worked on in that department.

EXHIBIT 3-1.   Cost Accumulation and Allocation

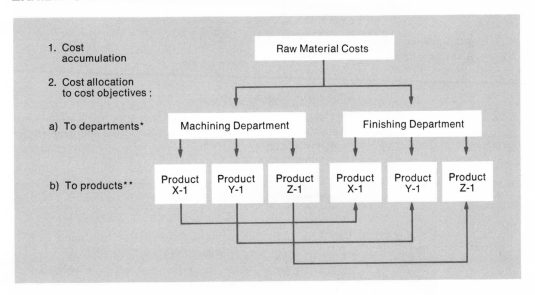

*Purpose: to evaluate performance of manufacturing departments.
**Purpose: to obtain costs of various products for valuing inventory, determining income, and judging product profitability.

Elements of Manufacturing Costs

The same general approach of cost accumulation and cost allocation that was just illustrated for raw materials is also applicable to other manufacturing costs. Manufacturing is the transformation of materials into other goods through the use of labor and factory facilities. There are three major elements in the cost of a manufactured product: (1) direct materials, (2) direct labor, and (3) factory overhead.

1. **Direct materials.** All materials that are physically identified as a part of the finished goods and that may be traced to the finished goods in an economically feasible way. Examples are grey iron castings, lumber, aluminum sheets, and subassemblies. Direct materials often do *not* include minor items such as nails or glue. Why? Because the costs of tracing insignificant items do not seem worth the possible benefits of having more precise product costs. Such items are usually called *supplies* or *indirect materials* and are classified as a part of the factory overhead described below.

2. **Direct labor.** All labor that is physically traceable to the finished goods in an economically feasible way. Examples are the labor of machine operators and of assemblers. Much labor, such as that of janitors, fork-lift truck operators, plant guards, and storeroom clerks, is considered to be **indirect labor** because of the impossibility or economic infeasibility of tracing such activity to specific products via physical observation. Indirect labor is classified as a part of factory overhead.

3. **Factory overhead.** All costs other than direct material or direct labor that are associated with the manufacturing process. Other terms used to describe this category are: **factory burden, manufacturing overhead, manufacturing expenses,** and **indirect manufacturing costs.** The latter term is a clearer descriptor than factory overhead, but factory overhead will be used most frequently in this book because it is briefer. Two major subclassifications of factory overhead are:

   a. **Variable factory overhead.** Examples are power, supplies, and most indirect labor. Whether the cost of a specific category of indirect labor is variable or fixed depends on its behavior in a given company. In this book, unless we specify otherwise, indirect labor will be considered a variable rather than a fixed cost.

   b. **Fixed factory overhead.** Examples are supervisory salaries, property taxes, rent, insurance, and depreciation.

Two of the three major elements are sometimes combined in cost terminology as follows. **Prime cost** consists of (1) + (2), direct materials plus direct labor. **Conversion cost** consists of (2) + (3), direct labor plus factory overhead.

56

RELATIONSHIPS OF INCOME STATEMENTS AND BALANCE SHEETS

This section assumes a basic familiarity with income statements and balance sheets, as covered by any beginning course in financial accounting or by Chapter 17. However, the reader can easily understand most of the terms explained here without having such familiarity.

Product Costs and Period Costs

Accountants frequently refer to *product costs* and *period costs.* **Product costs** generally are identified with goods produced or purchased for resale. Product costs are initially identified as part of the inventory on hand; in turn, these product costs (inventory costs) become expenses (in the form of **cost of goods sold**) only when the inventory is sold. In contrast, **period costs** are costs that are being deducted as expenses during the current period without having been previously classified as product costs.

The distinctions between product costs and period costs are best understood by example. Examine the top half of Exhibit 3-2. A merchandising company (retailer or wholesaler) acquires goods for resale without changing their basic form. The *only* product cost is the purchase cost of the merchandise. Unsold goods are held as merchandise inventory cost and shown as an asset on a balance sheet. As the goods are sold, their costs become expense in the form of "cost of goods sold."

A merchandising company also has a variety of selling and administrative expenses, which are the major examples of period costs. They are referred to as period costs because they are deducted from revenue as expenses without ever having been regarded as a part of inventory.

In manufacturing accounting, as the bottom half of Exhibit 3-2 illustrates, direct materials are transformed into salable form with the help of direct labor and factory overhead. All these costs are product costs because they are allocated to inventory until the goods are sold. As in merchandising accounting, the selling and administrative expenses are not regarded as product costs.

Balance Sheet Presentation

As Exhibit 3-2 shows, balance sheets of manufacturers and merchandisers differ with respect to inventories. The merchandise inventory account is supplanted in a manufacturing concern by three inventory classes. The purpose of these various classifications is to trace all product costs through the production process to the time of sale. The classes are: **direct-material inventory, work-in-process inventory** (cost of uncompleted goods still on the

EXHIBIT 3-2. Relationships of Product Costs and Period Costs

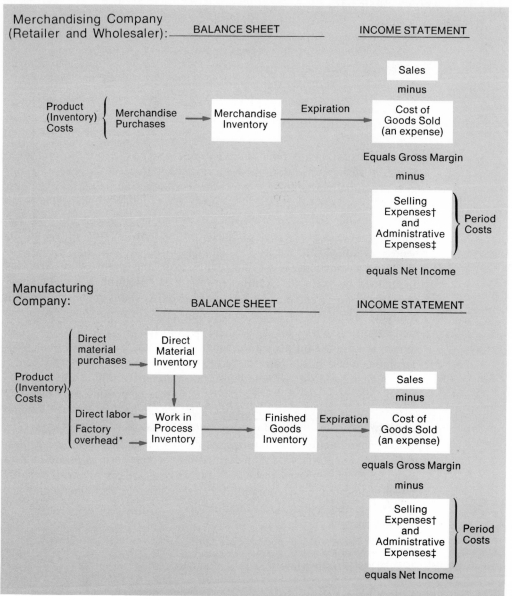

†Examples: insurance on salesmen's cars, depreciation on salesmen's cars, salesmen's salaries.

‡Examples: insurance on corporate headquarters building, depreciation on office equipment, clerical salaries.

*Examples: indirect labor, factory supplies, insurance and depreciation on plant.

Note particularly that where insurance and depreciation relate to the manufacturing function, they are inventoriable; but where they relate to selling and administration, they are not inventoriable.

production line containing appropriate amounts of the three major manufacturing costs: direct material, direct labor, and factory overhead), and **finished goods** (fully completed goods). The only essential difference between the structure of the balance sheet of a manufacturer and that of the balance sheet of a retailer would appear in their respective current-asset sections (numbers are assumed):

CURRENT-ASSET SECTIONS OF BALANCE SHEETS

Manufacturer			*Merchandiser*	
Cash		$ 4,000	Cash	$ 4,000
Receivables		25,000	Receivables	25,000
Finished goods	$32,000			
Work in process	22,000			
Direct material	23,000		Merchandise	
Total inventories		77,000	inventories	77,000
Other current assets		1,000	Other current assets	1,000
Total current assets		$107,000	Total current assets	$107,000

Unit Costs for Product Costing

Most often, product costing is accomplished by heavy use of unit costs. Assume the following:

Total cost of goods manufactured (10,000,000 units)	$40,000,000
Total units manufactured	10,000,000
Unit cost of product for inventory purposes ($40,000,000 ÷ 10,000,000)	$4

The unit cost facilitates the accounting for inventory valuation and income measurement. If some of the 10,000,000 units manufactured are still unsold at the end of the period, a part of the $40,000,000 cost of goods manufactured will be "held back" as a cost of the ending inventory of finished goods (and shown as an asset on a balance sheet). The remainder will be allocated to "cost of goods sold" for the current period (that is, shown as an expense on the income statement).

Costs and Income Statements

In the income statements, the detailed reporting of selling and administrative expenses is typically the same for manufacturing and merchandising organizations, but the cost of goods sold is different:

Retailer or Wholesaler	*Manufacturer*
Merchandise cost of goods sold, usually composed of the purchase cost of items, including freight in, that are acquired and then resold.	Manufacturing cost of goods produced and then sold, usually composed of the three major elements of cost: direct materials, direct labor, and factory overhead

Consider the additional assumed details as they are presented in the model income statement of Exhibit 3-3. The $40,000,000 cost of goods manufactured is subdivided into the major components of direct materials, direct labor, and factory overhead.

EXHIBIT 3-3 *See & Compare to Pg 65*

Model Income Statement, Manufacturing Company

Sales (8,000,000 units @ $10)			$80,000,000
Cost of goods manufactured and sold:			
Beginning finished goods inventory		-0-	
Cost of goods manufactured:			
Direct materials used	$20,000,000		
Direct labor	12,000,000		
Factory overhead:			
Variable factory overhead	2,000,000		
Fixed factory overhead	6,000,000	40,000,000	
Cost of goods available for sale		$40,000,000	
Ending finished goods inventory, 2,000,000			
units @ $4		8,000,000	
Cost of goods sold (an expense)			32,000,000
Gross margin or gross profit			$48,000,000
Less other expenses:			
Selling costs (an expense)		$30,000,000	
General and administrative costs (an expense)		8,000,000	38,000,000
Operating income			
(also net income in this example)			$10,000,000

The terms "costs" and "expenses" are often used loosely by accountants and managers. "Expenses" denote all costs being deducted from (matched against) revenue in a given period. On the other hand, "costs" is a much more generic term; for example, "cost" is used to describe an asset (the cost of inventory) and an expense (the cost of goods sold). Thus, manufacturing costs are funneled into an income statement as an expense (in the form of cost of goods sold) via the multistep inventory procedure, as indicated earlier in Exhibit 3-2. In contrast, selling and general administrative costs are commonly deemed expenses immediately as they are incurred.

Common Mistakes

Before proceeding, please take a moment to review some key distinctions made in Exhibits 3-2 and 3-3. Otherwise, these new terms and classifications become blurred.

Distinguish sharply between the merchandising accounting and the manufacturing accounting for such costs as insurance, depreciation, and wages. In merchandising accounting, all such items are period costs (expenses of the current period). In manufacturing accounting, many of such items are related to production activities and thus, as factory overhead, are product costs (become expenses as the inventory is sold).

In both merchandising accounting and manufacturing, selling and general administrative costs are period costs. Thus, the inventory cost of a manufactured product *excludes* sales salaries, sales commissions, advertising, legal, public relations, and the president's salary. *Manufacturing* overhead is traditionally regarded as a part of finished-goods inventory cost, whereas *selling* expenses and *general administrative* expenses are not.[1]

Relation to Balance Sheet Equation

Exhibit 3-4 relates the theory of product costing to the analysis of the balance sheet equation. For simplicity, all acquisitions and dispositions of resources are assumed to be for cash. The same dollar amounts are used in Exhibits 3-3 and 3-4, except that Exhibit 3-4 introduces the idea of an inventory of materials. That is, $30 million of direct materials were acquired, $20 million were used, and $10 million were left in inventory at the end of the period.

Trace the effects of each summary transaction, step by step, in Exhibit 3-4. As the bottom of Exhibit 3-4 indicates, the ending balance sheet accounts would be:

Cash	$ 92,000,000	Capital stock	$100,000,000
Direct-materials inventory	10,000,000	Retained income	10,000,000[a]
Work-in-process inventory	—		
Finished-goods inventory	8,000,000		
Total assets	$110,000,000	Total equities	$110,000,000

[a] Retained income arose because of profitable operations, which produced income of $10,000,000. For the detailed income statement, see Exhibit 3-3.

[1] Some accountants maintain that product costs become period costs as the goods are sold. In their minds, there is no difference between the terms "period costs" and "expenses," because both represent all costs that are being deducted from revenue during the current period. However, the distinction in this book consists of two steps: (1) Is the cost a product cost or a period cost? and (2) When do the product costs and the period costs become expenses? The product costs become expenses as the goods are sold, whereas the period costs become expenses as incurred.

62

EXHIBIT 3-4

Analysis of Balance Sheet Equation for Manufacturing Costs
(In millions of dollars)

TRANSACTIONS	ASSETS				= LIABILITIES +	EQUITIES — STOCKHOLDERS' EQUITY	
	CASH +	DIRECT-MATERIALS INVENTORY +	WORK-IN-PROCESS INVENTORY +	FINISHED-GOODS INVENTORY	= LIABILITIES +	CAPITAL STOCK +	RETAINED INCOME
Beginning balances	100				=	100	
1. Purchase of direct materials	−30	+30			=		
2. Direct materials used		−20	+20		=		
3. Acquire direct labor	−12		+12		=		
4. Acquire factory overhead	−8		+8		=		
5. Complete the goods			−40	+40	=		
6a. Revenue	+80				=		+80 (Revenue)
6b. Cost of goods sold				−32	=		−32 (Expense)
7. Selling costs	−30				=		−30 (Expense)
8. General and administrative costs	−8				=		−8 (Expense)
Ending balances	92 +	10 +	0 +	8	=	100 +	10

Direct and Indirect Costs

Admittedly, the area of manufacturing costs contains a thicket of new terms. One of your main tasks in studying this chapter is to understand these terms. For example, a distinction was made earlier in this chapter between costs that are "direct" and "indirect" with respect to a *particular* cost objective—the manufactured product. In other settings, the direct-indirect distinction may pertain to a different cost objective, for example, a department. Thus, the wages of a janitor who works solely in the assembly department may be regarded as a direct cost of the department but as an indirect cost of the products worked on within that department. However, unless otherwise stated, throughout this book the direct-indirect distinction will pertain only to the *product* as the cost objective.

TWO TYPES OF INCOME STATEMENTS

Detailed Costs of Manufacturing Company

A fresh example may clarify many of the cost terms and distinctions explored thus far. Assume that the Samson Company for 19x2 has direct-material costs of $7 million and direct-labor costs of $4 million. Assume also that the company incurred the indirect manufacturing costs (factory overhead) illustrated in Exhibit 3-5 and the selling and administrative expenses illustrated in Exhibit 3-6. Total sales were $20 million.

EXHIBIT 3-5
SAMSON COMPANY
Schedules of Indirect Manufacturing Costs (which are product costs)
For the Year Ending December 31, 19x2
(In thousands of dollars)

Schedule 1: Variable Costs		
Supplies (lubricants, expendable tools, coolants, sandpaper)	$ 150	
Indirect labor (janitors, fork-lift operators)	700	
Repairs	100	
Power	50	$1,000
Schedule 2: Fixed Costs		
Foremen's salaries	$ 200	
Employee training	90	
Factory picnic and holiday party	10	
Supervisory salaries, except foremen's salaries	700	
Depreciation, plant and equipment	1,800	
Property taxes	150	
Insurance	50	3,000
Total indirect manufacturing costs		$4,000

EXHIBIT 3-6

SAMSON COMPANY

Schedules of Selling and Administrative Expenses (which are period costs)
For the Year Ending December 31, 19x2
(In thousands of dollars)

Schedule 3: Selling Expenses			
Variable:			
Sales commissions		$ 700	
Shipping expenses for products sold		300	$1,000
Fixed:			
Advertising		$ 700	
Sales salaries		1,000	
Other		300	2,000
Total selling expenses			$3,000
Schedule 4: Administrative Expenses			
Variable:			
Some clerical wages		$ 80	
Computer time rented		20	$ 100
Fixed:			
Office salaries		$ 100	
Other salaries		200	
Depreciation on office facilities		100	
Public-accounting fees		40	
Legal fees		100	
Other		360	900
Total administrative expenses			$1,000

Finally, assume that the units produced are equal to the units sold. That is, there is no change in inventory levels. In this way we avoid some complications that are unnecessary and unimportant at this stage.[2]

Note that Exhibits 3-5 and 3-6 contain subdivisions of costs between variable and fixed classifications. Many companies do not make such subdivisions. Furthermore, when such subdivisions are made, sometimes arbitrary decisions are necessary as to whether a given cost is variable or fixed, or partially variable (for example, some repairs) and partially fixed (for example, other repairs). Nevertheless, to aid decision making, an increasing number of companies are attempting to report the extent to which their costs are approximately variable or fixed.

Functional Approach

Exhibit 3-7 presents the income statement in the form used by most companies. The theory followed is called the **functional approach** or **absorption costing** or **traditional costing** or **full costing**. It is the theory also illustrated in

---

[2]These complexities are discussed in Chapters 14 and 15. (If preferred, Chapters 14 and 15 may be studied immediately after Chapters 3 and 7, respectively, without loss of continuity.)

Exhibit 3-3, whereby all indirect manufacturing costs (both variable plus fixed factory overhead) are considered as inventoriable or product costs that become an expense in the form of manufacturing cost of goods sold as sales occur.

Take a moment to compare Exhibits 3-3 and 3-7. Note that gross profit or gross margin is the difference between sales and the *manufacturing* cost of goods sold. Note too that the *primary classifications* of costs on the income statement are by three major management *functions:* manufacturing, selling, and administrative.

Contribution Approach

Exhibit 3-8 presents the income statement in the "contribution" form used by an increasing number of companies for internal (management accounting) purposes. Even though a standard format is used for external purposes, a

EXHIBIT 3-7

SAMSON COMPANY
FUNCTIONAL INCOME STATEMENT
FOR THE YEAR ENDING
DECEMBER 31, 19x2
(IN THOUSANDS OF DOLLARS)

Sales		$20,000
Less **manufacturing** costs		
of goods sold:		
Direct material	$7,000	
Direct labor	4,000	
Indirect **manufactur-**		
ing costs (Sched-		
ules 1 plus 2)	4,000	15,000
Gross profit or gross		
margin		$ 5,000
Selling expenses		
(Schedule 3)	$3,000	
Administrative expenses		
(Schedule 4)	1,000	
Total **selling** and		
administrative ex-		
penses		4,000
Operating income		$ 1,000

EXHIBIT 3-8

SAMSON COMPANY
CONTRIBUTION INCOME STATEMENT
FOR THE YEAR ENDING
DECEMBER 31, 19x2
(IN THOUSANDS OF DOLLARS)

Sales		$20,000
Less **variable** expenses:		
Direct material	$ 7,000	
Direct labor	4,000	
Variable indirect		
manufacturing		
(Schedule 1)	1,000	
Total **variable** manu-		
facturing cost		
of goods sold	$12,000	
Variable selling		
expenses (Sched-		
ule 3)	1,000	
Variable administra-		
tive expenses		
(Schedule 4)	100	
Total **variable** expenses		13,100
Contribution margin		$ 6,900
Less **fixed** expenses:		
Manufacturing		
(Schedule 2)	$ 3,000	
Selling (Schedule 3)	2,000	
Administrative		
(Schedule 4)	900	5,900
Operating income		$ 1,000

Note: Schedules 1 and 2 are in Exhibit 3-5. Schedules 3 and 4 are in Exhibit 3-6.

company can and often does adopt a different format for internal purposes if the expected benefits of making decisions exceed the extra costs of using different reporting systems simultaneously.

The theory followed in Exhibit 3-8 has been called the **contribution approach, variable costing, direct costing,** or **marginal costing.** For decision purposes, the most important difference between the contribution approach and the functional approach is the emphasis of the former on the distinction between variable and fixed costs. The *primary classifications* of costs are by variable and fixed *cost behavior patterns,* not by *business functions.*

The contribution income statement provides a contribution margin, which is computed after deducting *all* variable costs, *including* variable selling and administrative costs. This approach facilitates the computation of the impact on net income of changes in sales, and it dovetails neatly with the cost-volume-profit analysis illustrated in the preceding chapter.

The contribution approach stresses the lump-sum amount of fixed costs to be recouped before net income emerges. This highlighting of total fixed costs helps to attract management attention to fixed-cost behavior and control when both short-run and long-run plans are being made. Keep in mind that advocates of this contribution approach **do not maintain that fixed costs are unimportant or irrelevant;** but they do stress that the distinctions between behaviors of variable and fixed costs are crucial for certain decisions.

The implications of the *functional approach* and *the contribution approach* for decision making are discussed in the next chapter, using Exhibits 3-7 and 3-8.

JOB AND PROCESS COSTING

The first section of this chapter contains a general diagram of how raw-material costs are accumulated and allocated to departments and products. Direct labor and factory overhead are allocated to products in a similar fashion. The detailed procedures for allocating costs to products vary considerably from industry to industry and company to company. Two contrasting forms of product costing are **job-order costing** and **process costing.** Their principal difference centers around the type of products that are the cost objectives. Job-order costing is found in industries such as printing, construction, and furniture manufacturing, where each unit or batch (job) of product tends to be unique and easily identifiable. Process costing is found where there is mass production of identical units through a sequence of several processes such as mixing, cooking, and so on. Examples include flour, glass, and paint. To see the major difference between job-order costing and process costing, visualize the detail that might support the work-in-process inventory, as diagrammed in Exhibit 3-9.

Job-order accounting is used in many service industries, too, such as in

EXHIBIT 3-9. Comparison of Job-Order and Process Costing

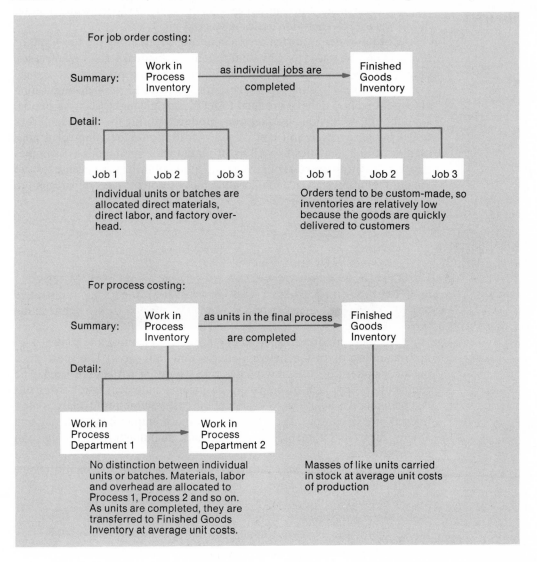

For job order costing:

Summary: Work in Process Inventory → as individual jobs are completed → Finished Goods Inventory

Detail:

Job 1   Job 2   Job 3

Individual units or batches are allocated direct materials, direct labor, and factory overhead.

Job 1   Job 2   Job 3

Orders tend to be custom-made, so inventories are relatively low because the goods are quickly delivered to customers

For process costing:

Summary: Work in Process Inventory → as units in the final process are completed → Finished Goods Inventory

Detail:

Work in Process Department 1 → Work in Process Department 2

No distinction between individual units or batches. Materials, labor and overhead are allocated to Process 1, Process 2 and so on. As units are completed, they are transferred to Finished Goods Inventory at average unit costs.

Masses of like units carried in stock at average unit costs of production

repairing, consulting, legal, and accounting services. Each customer order is a different job with a special account or order number. Sometimes only costs are traced directly to the job, sometimes only revenue is traced, and sometimes both. For example, automobile repair shops typically have a repair order for each car worked on, with space for allocating materials and labor. The customer may see a copy containing only the retail prices of the materials, parts, and labor billed to his or her order. If the repair manager wants cost data, he may also have a system designed so that the "actual" parts and labor costs of each order are traced to a duplicate copy of the job order. That is why you often see auto mechanics "punching in" and "punching out" on "work tickets" as each new order is worked on.

The job-order approach occurs in not-for-profit industries too. Costs or revenues may be traced to individual patients, individual social welfare cases, individual doctoral seminars, and individual research projects.

The process costing approach is less concerned with distinguishing among individual units of product. Instead, accumulated costs for a period, say a month, are divided by quantities produced during that period in order to get broad, average unit costs. Process costing may be adopted in non-manufacturing activities as well as in manufacturing activities. Examples include allocating the costs of giving state automobile driver's license tests to the number of tests given and allocating the costs of an X-ray department to the number of X-rays processed.

SUMMARY

Direct material, direct labor, and factory overhead are traditionally regarded as product costs (inventoriable costs). In contrast, selling and administrative costs are accounted for as period costs and are deducted from revenue in the period incurred.

The most important aspect of intelligent cost planning and control is an understanding of cost behavior patterns and influences. The most basic behavior pattern of costs may be described as either variable or fixed. The contribution approach to preparing an income statement emphasizes this distinction and is a natural extension of the cost-volume-profit analysis used in decisions. In contrast, the functional approach emphasizes the distinction among three major management functions: manufacturing, selling, and administration.

Many new terms were introduced in this chapter. You should review them to make sure you know their exact meanings.

Readers who now desire a more detailed treatment of product costing (particularly job-order costing) may jump to the study of Chapter 14 without losing continuity. In turn, Chapter 15 may be studied immediately after Chapter 7 if desired.

SUMMARY PROBLEM FOR YOUR REVIEW

Problem

1. Review the illustrations in Exhibits 3-5 through 3-8. Suppose that all variable costs fluctuate in direct proportion to units produced and sold, and that all fixed costs are unaffected over a wide range of production and sales.

What would operating income have been if sales (at normal selling prices) had been $20,900,000 instead of $20,000,000? Which statement, the functional income statement or the contribution income statement, did you use as a framework for your answer? Why?

2. Suppose that employee training was regarded as a variable rather than a fixed cost at a rate of $90,000 ÷ 1,000,000 units, or 9¢ per unit. How would your answer in part 1 change?

Solution

1. Operating income would increase from $1,000,000 to $1,310,500, computed as follows:

Increase in revenue	$ 900,000
Increase in total contribution margin	
Contribution-margin ratio in contribution income statement is $6,900,000 ÷ $20,000,000 = .345	
Ratio times revenue increase is .345 × $900,000	$ 310,500
Increase in fixed expenses	-0-
Operating income before increase	1,000,000
New operating income	$1,310,500

The above analysis is readily calculated by using data from the contribution income statement. In contrast, the traditional functional costing income statement must be analyzed and divided into variable and fixed categories before the effect on operating income can be estimated.

2. The contribution-margin ratio would become lower because the variable costs would be higher by 9¢ per unit: $6,810,000 ÷ $20,000,000 = .3405.

Ratio times revenue increase is .3405 × $900,000	$ 306,450
Increase in fixed expenses	-0-
Operating income before increase	1,000,000
New operating income	$1,306,450

APPENDIX 3: CLASSIFICATION OF LABOR COSTS

The terminology for labor costs is usually the most confusing. Each organization seems to develop its own interpretation of various labor-cost classifications. We shall begin by considering some commonly encountered labor-cost terminology.

For our purposes, we shall categorize the terminology as follows:

Direct labor (already defined)
Indirect labor:
  Fork-lift truck operators (internal handling of materials)
  Janitors

Plant guards
Rework labor (time spent by direct laborers redoing defective work)
Overtime premium paid to *all* factory workers
Idle time
Payroll fringe costs

All factory labor costs, other than those for direct labor, are usually classified as **indirect labor costs,** a major component of indirect manufacturing costs. The term *indirect labor* is usually divided into many subsidiary classifications. The wages of fork-lift truck operators are generally not commingled with janitors' salaries, for example, although both are regarded as indirect labor.

Costs are classified in a detailed fashion primarily in an attempt to associate a specific cost with its specific cause, or reason for incurrence. Two classes of indirect labor need special mention: overtime premium and idle time.

Overtime premium paid to all factory workers is usually considered a part of overhead. If a lathe operator earns $8 per hour for straight time, and time and one-half for overtime, his premium is $4 per overtime hour. If he works 44 hours, including four overtime hours, in one week, his gross earnings are classified as follows:

Direct labor: 44 hours × $8	$352
Overtime premium (factory overhead): 4 hours × $4	16
Total earnings	$368

Why is overtime premium considered an indirect cost rather than direct? After all, it can usually be traced to specific batches of work. It is usually not considered a direct charge because the scheduling of production jobs is generally random. For example, assume that Jobs No. 1 through 5 are scheduled for a specific workday of ten hours, including two overtime hours. Each job requires two hours. Should the job scheduled during hours 9 and 10 be assigned the overtime premium? For example, suppose that you brought your automobile to a shop for repair by 8 A.M. Through random scheduling, your auto was repaired during hours 9 and 10 as Job No. 5. When you came to get your car, you learned that all the overtime premium had been added to your bill. You probably would not be overjoyed.

Thus, in most companies, the overtime premium is not allocated to any specific job. Instead, it is prorated to all jobs. The latter approach does not penalize a particular batch of work solely because it happened to be worked on during the overtime hours. Instead, the overtime premium is considered to be attributable to the heavy overall volume of work and its cost is thus regarded as indirect manufacturing costs (factory overhead).

Another subsidiary classification of indirect-labor costs is **idle time.** This cost typically represents wages paid for unproductive time caused by machine breakdowns, material shortages, sloppy production scheduling, and the like. For example, if the same lathe operator's machine broke down for three hours during the week, his earnings would be classified as follows:

Direct labor: 41 hours × $8	$328
Overtime premium (factory overhead): 4 hours × $4	16
Idle time (factory overhead): 3 hours × $8	24
Total earnings	$368

The classification of factory payroll fringe costs (e.g., employer contributions to social security, life insurance, health insurance, pensions, and miscellaneous other employee benefits) differs from company to company. In most companies these are classified as indirect manufacturing costs. In some companies, however, the fringe benefits related to direct labor are charged as an additional direct-labor cost. For instance, a direct laborer, such as a lathe operator whose gross wages are computed on the basis of $8 an hour, may enjoy payroll fringe benefits totaling, say, 75¢ per hour. Most companies tend to classify the $8 as direct-labor cost and the 75¢ as factory overhead. Other companies classify the entire $8.75 as direct-labor cost. The latter approach is preferable, because most of these costs are also a fundamental part of acquiring labor services.

ASSIGNMENT MATERIAL

Fundamental Assignment Material

3-1. **Terminology.** Define: *direct material; direct labor; idle time; overtime premium; indirect labor; indirect manufacturing costs; factory overhead; factory burden; manufacturing overhead; manufacturing expenses;* and *contribution approach.*

3-2. **Straightforward income statements.** (An alternate problem is 3-26.) The Millbrae Company had the following manufacturing data for the year 19x6 (in thousands of dollars):

Beginning inventories	$None
Direct material purchased	400
› Direct material used	360
ı Direct labor	370
Supplies	20
Utilities—variable portion	40
Utilities—fixed portion	12
Indirect labor—variable portion	90
Indirect labor—fixed portion	40
Depreciation	100
Property taxes	20
Supervisory salaries	60

Selling expenses were $300,000 (including $50,000 that were variable) and general administrative expenses were $150,000 (including $30,000 that were variable). Sales were $1,800,000.

Direct labor and supplies are regarded as variable costs.

1. Prepare two income statements, one using the contribution approach and one the functional approach.

2. Suppose that all variable costs fluctuate directly in proportion to sales, and that fixed costs are unaffected over a very wide range of sales. What would operating income have been if sales had been $2,000,000 instead of $1,800,000? Which income statement did you use to help obtain your answer? Why?

3-3. **Meaning of technical terms.** Refer to the functional income statement of your solution to the preceding problem. Give the amounts of the following: (1) prime costs, (2) conversion costs, (3) factory burden, (4) manufacturing expenses, and (5) ending inventory of direct materials.

Additional Assignment Material

3-4. Distinguish between the two prime costs.

3-5. "Glue or nails become an integral part of the finished product, so they would be direct material." Do you agree? Explain.

3-6. What is the advantage of the contribution approach as compared to the traditional approach?

3-7. Distinguish between manufacturing and merchandising.

3-8. "Departments are not cost objects or objects of costing." Do you agree? Explain.

3-9. "Manufacturing cost of goods sold is a special category of expense." Do you agree? Explain.

3-10. "Unexpired costs are always inventory costs." Do you agree? Explain.

3-11. "Miscellaneous supplies are always indirect costs." Do you agree? Explain.

3-12. **Variable or fixed indirect costs.** Many indirect manufacturing costs do not fall easily into the categories of variable and fixed costs. Nevertheless, for the following costs, indicate whether each is more likely to have a variable (use V) or fixed (use F) behavior pattern over a wide range of volume:

1. Supplies	4. Taxes on real estate
2. Depreciation	5. Fuel
3. Patent amortization	6. Purchased power

7. Overtime premium
8. Wages, building employees
9. Hauling within plant
10. Taxes on plant equipment
11. Supervision
12. Small tools
13. Insurance, property
14. Royalties
15. Cost accounting department costs
16. Salaries, production executives
17. Research and development
18. Receiving costs
19. Rework operations
20. Indirect labor

3-13. **Relating costs to cost objectives.** A company uses a job-order cost system. Prepare headings for two columns: (1) assembly department costs and (2) products assembled. Fill in the two columns for each of the costs below. If a specific cost is direct to the department but indirect to the product, place D in column (1) and I in column (2). The costs are: materials used, supplies used, assembly labor, material-handling labor (transporting materials between and within departments), depreciation—building, assembly foreman's salary, and the building and grounds supervisor's salary.

3-14. **Variable costs and fixed costs; manufacturing and other costs.** For each of the numbered items, choose the appropriate classification for a job-order manufacturing company (e.g., custom furniture, job printing). If in doubt about whether the cost behavior is basically variable or fixed, decide on the basis of whether the total cost will fluctuate substantially over a wide range of volume. Most items have two answers from among the following possibilities with respect to the cost of a particular job:

a. Variable cost
b. Fixed cost
c. General and administrative cost
d. Selling cost
e. Manufacturing costs, direct
f. Manufacturing costs, indirect
g. Other (specify)

Sample answers:

Direct material	a,e
President's salary	b,c
Bond interest expense	b,g (financial expense)

Items for your consideration:

1. Sandpaper
2. Supervisory salaries, production control
3. Supervisory salaries, assembly department
4. Supervisory salaries, factory storeroom
5. Company picnic costs
6. Overtime premium, punch press
7. Idle time, assembly
8. Freight out
9. Property taxes
10. Factory power for machines
11. Salesmen's commissions
12. Salesmen's salaries
13. Welding supplies
14. Fire loss
15. Paint for finished products
16. Heat and air conditioning, factory
17. Material-handling labor, punch press
18. Straight-line depreciation, salesmen's automobiles

3-15. Meaning of technical terms. Refer to Exhibit 3-3. Give the amounts of the following with respect to the cost of goods available for sale: (1) prime costs, (2) conversion costs, (3) factory burden, and (4) manufacturing expenses.

3-16. Product and period costs. Refer to Exhibit 3-3. Suppose that $30 million of direct material had been purchased.

Required

Using Exhibit 3-2 as a guide, sketch how the costs in Exhibit 3-3 are related to balance sheets and income statements. In other words, prepare an exhibit like 3-2, inserting the numbers from Exhibit 3-3 to the extent you can.

3-17. Presence of ending work in process. Refer to Exhibits 3-3 and 3-4. Suppose that there were an ending work in process of $5 million. All other facts are unchanged, except that the cost of the completed goods would be $35 million instead of $40 million.

Required

1. Recast the income statement of Exhibit 3-3.

2. What lines and ending balances would change in Exhibit 3-4 and by how much?

3-18. Balance sheet equation. Review Exhibit 3-4. Assume that the G Company had a beginning balance of $800 thousand cash. The following transactions occurred in 19x2 (in thousands):

1. Purchase of direct materials for cash	$350
2. Direct materials used	300
3. Acquire direct labor for cash	160
4. Acquire factory overhead for cash	200
5. Complete all goods that were started	?
6a. Revenue (all sales are for cash)	600
6b. Cost of goods sold (half of the goods completed were sold)	?
7. Selling costs for cash	100
8. General and administrative costs for cash	40

Required

Prepare an analysis similar to Exhibit 3-4. What are the ending balances of cash, direct materials, finished goods, capital stock, and retained income?

3-19. Cost accumulation and allocation. Examine Exhibit 3-1. Suppose a company incurred the following costs:

Direct material	$60,000
Direct labor	30,000
Manufacturing overhead	39,000

Eighty percent of the material was introduced in the machining department, but only 30 percent of the direct labor was incurred there. Manufacturing overhead was allocated to products in proportion to the direct labor in each department.

In the machining department, one-half the direct material was used on Product

X-1 and one-fourth on each of Y-1 and Z-1. Direct labor was split equally among the three products. The manufacturing overhead incurred and allocated to products amounted to $18,000. (*machine dept.*)

In the finishing department, the direct-material cost was split equally among the three products. Direct labor was used as follows: 40 percent for X-1; 40 percent, Y-1; and 20 percent, Z-1.

1. Compute the total costs incurred by the machining department and added by the finishing department.

2. Compute the total costs of each product that would be shown as finished-goods inventory if all the products were transferred to finished stock upon completion.

3-20. Contribution analysis. (CMA, adapted. This problem also reviews Chapter 2, including its appendix on income tax effects.) R. A. Ro and Company, maker of quality handmade pipes, has experienced a steady growth in sales for the past five years. However, increased competition has led Mr. Ro, the president, to believe that an aggressive advertising campaign will be necessary next year to maintain the company's present growth.

To prepare for next year's advertising campaign, the company's accountant has prepared and presented Mr. Ro with the following data for the current year, 19x2:

Cost Schedule

Variable costs per pipe:	
Direct labor	$ 8.00
Direct material	3.25
Variable overhead	2.50
Total variable costs	$13.75
Fixed costs	
Manufacturing	$ 25,000
Selling	40,000
Administrative	70,000
Total fixed costs	$135,000

Selling price per pipe: $25
Expected sales, 19x2 (20,000 units): $500,000
Tax rate: 40%

Mr. Ro has set the sales target for 19x3 at a level of $550,000 (or 22,000 pipes).

1. What is the projected after-tax net income for 19x2?

2. What is the break-even point in units for 19x2?

3. Mr. Ro believes an additional selling expense of $11,250 for advertising in 19x3, with all other costs remaining constant, will be necessary to attain the sales target. What will be the after-tax net income for 19x3 if the additional $11,250 is spent?

4. What will be the break-even point in dollar sales for 19x3 if the additional $11,250 is spent on advertising?

5. If the additional $11,250 is spent on advertising in 19x3, what is the required sales level in dollar sales to equal 19x2's after-tax net income?

6. At a sales level of 22,000 units, what maximum amount can be spent on advertising if an after-tax net income of $60,000 is desired?

3-21. **Overtime premium.** Please read the chapter appendix. An automobile dealer has a service department. You have brought your car for repair at 8 A.M. When you come to get your car at 6 P.M., you notice that your bill contains a charge under "labor" for "overtime premium." When you inquire about the reason for the charge, you are told, "We worked on your car from 5 P.M. to 5:45 P.M. Our union contract calls for wages to be paid at time-and-a-half after eight hours. Therefore, our ordinary labor charge of $25 per hour was billed to you at $37.50."

1. Should the overtime premium be allocated only to cars worked on during overtime hours? Explain.

2. Would your preceding answer differ if the dealer arranged to service your car at 8 P.M. as a special convenience to you? Explain.

3-22. **Payroll fringe costs.** Please read the chapter appendix. Direct labor is often accounted for at the gross wage rate, and the related "fringe costs" such as employer payroll taxes and employer contributions to health-care plans are accounted for as part of overhead. Therefore, the $9 gross pay per hour being paid to George Montrose, a direct laborer, might cause related fringe costs of $3 per hour.

1. Suppose Montrose works 40 hours during a particular week as an auditor for a public accounting firm, 30 hours for Client A and 10 for Client B. What would be the cost of direct labor? Of general overhead?

2. The firm allocates costs to each client. What would be the cost of "direct labor" on the Client A job? The Client B job?

3. How would you allocate general overhead to the Client A job? The Client B job?

4. Suppose Montrose works a total of 50 hours (30 for A and 20 for B), 10 of which are paid on the basis of time-and-one-half. What would be the cost of direct labor? Of general overhead?

5. Given the facts in part 4, what would be the cost of "direct labor" on the Client A job? The Client B job?

3-23. **Distinctions between contribution and functional approaches.** The Dischinger Company provides you with the following miscellaneous data regarding operations in 19x2:

Sales	$100,000
Direct material used	40,000
Direct labor	15,000
Fixed manufacturing overhead	20,000
Fixed selling and administrative expenses	10,000
Gross profit	20,000
Net loss	5,000

There are no beginning or ending inventories.

Required   Compute the following:

1. Variable selling and administrative expenses.
2. Contribution margin in dollars.
3. Variable manufacturing overhead.
4. Break-even point in sales dollars.
5. Manufacturing cost of goods sold.

3-24. Distinctions between contribution and functional approaches. The Dietz Corporation provides you with the following miscellaneous data regarding operations for 19x4:

Break-even point (in sales dollars)	$ 66,667
Direct material used	22,000
Gross profit	25,000
Contribution margin	30,000
Direct labor	30,000
Sales	100,000
Variable manufacturing overhead	5,000

There are no beginning or ending inventories.

Required   Compute the following:

1. Fixed manufacturing overhead.
2. Variable selling and administrative expenses.
3. Fixed selling and administrative expenses.

3-25. Newspaper cost behavior. (CMA.) The *Metropolitan News*, a daily newspaper, services a community of 100,000. The paper has a circulation of 40,000, with 32,000 copies delivered directly to subscribers. The rate schedule for the paper is:

	Daily	*Sunday*
Single issue price	$0.15	$0.30
Weekly subscription	$1.00	
(includes daily and Sunday)		

The paper has experienced profitable operations, as can be seen from the Income Statement for the Year Ended September 30, 19x4 (in thousands):

Revenue:		
Newspaper sales	$2,200	
Advertising sales	1,800	$4,000
Costs and expenses:		
Personnel costs:		
Commissions:		
Carriers	$ 292	

Sales	73	
Advertising	48	
Salaries:		
Administration	250	
Advertising	100	
Equipment operators	500	
Newsroom	400	
Employee benefits	195	$1,858
Newsprint		834
Other supplies		417
Repairs		25
Depreciation		180
Property taxes		120
Building rental		80
Automobile leases		10
Other		90
Total costs and expenses		$3,614
Income before income taxes		$ 386
Income taxes		154
Net income		$ 232

The Sunday edition usually has twice as many pages as the daily editions. Analysis of direct edition variable costs for 19x3–x4 is shown in the schedule below.

	Cost per Issue	
	Daily	*Sunday*
Paper	$0.050	$0.100
Other supplies	0.025	0.050
Carrier and sales commissions	0.025	0.025
	$0.100	$0.175

Several changes in operations are scheduled for the next year, in addition to the need to recognize increasing costs.

1. The building lease expired on September 30, 19x4 and has been renewed with a change in the rental fee provisions from a straight fee to a fixed fee of $60,000 plus 1 percent of newspaper sales.

2. The advertising department will eliminate the payment of a 4 percent advertising commission on contracts sold by its employees. An average of two-thirds of the advertising has been sold on a contract basis in the past. The salaries of the four who solicited advertising will be raised from $7,500 each to $14,000 each.

3. Automobiles will no longer be leased. Employees whose jobs require automobiles will use their own and be reimbursed at 15¢ per mile. The leased cars were driven 80,000 miles in 19x3–x4, and it is estimated that the employees will drive some 84,000 miles next year on company business.

4. Cost increases estimated for next year:
   a. Newsprint 1¢ per daily issue and 2¢ for the Sunday paper.

b. Salaries:
   (1) Equipment operators, 8 percent.
   (2) Other employees, 6 percent.
   c. Employee benefits (from 15 percent of personnel costs excluding carrier
      and sales commissions to 20 percent), 5 percent.
5. Circulation increases of 5 percent in newsstand and home delivery are
   anticipated.
6. Advertising revenue is estimated at $1,890,000 with $1,260,000 from employee solicited contracts.

Required

1. Prepare a projected income statement for the *Metropolitan News* for the
   19x4–x5 fiscal year, using a format that shows the total variable costs and
   total fixed costs for the newspaper (round calculations to the nearest
   thousand dollars).

2. The management of *Metropolitan News* is contemplating one additional
   proposal for the 19x4–x5 fiscal year—raising the rates for its newspaper to
   the following amounts:

	Daily	Sunday
Single issue price	$0.20	$0.40
Weekly subscription (includes daily and Sunday)	$1.25	

It is estimated that the newspaper's circulation will decline to 90 percent of the
currently anticipated 19x4–x5 level for both newsstand and home delivery sales if
this change is initiated. Calculate the effect on the projected 19x4–x5 income if this
proposed rate change is implemented.

3-26. Contribution and functional income statements. (An alternate problem
is 3-2.) The following information is taken from the records of the Kingsville
Company for the year ending December 31, 19x2. There were no beginning or
ending inventories.

Sales	$10,000,000	Long-term rent, factory	$ 100,000
Sales commissions	500,000	Factory superintendent's	
Advertising	200,000	salary	30,000
Shipping expenses	300,000	Foremen's salaries	100,000
Administrative executive		Direct material used	4,000,000
salaries	100,000	Direct labor	2,000,000
Administrative clerical		Cutting bits used	60,000
salaries (variable)	400,000	Factory methods research	40,000
Fire insurance on		Abrasives for machining	100,000
factory equipment	2,000	Indirect labor	800,000
Property taxes on		Depreciation on	
factory equipment	10,000	equipment	300,000

Required

1. Prepare a contribution income statement and a functional income statement. If you are in doubt about any cost behavior pattern, decide on the
   basis of whether the total cost in question will fluctuate substantially over a

wide range of volume. Prepare a separate supporting schedule of indirect manufacturing costs subdivided between variable and fixed costs.

2. Suppose that all variable costs fluctuate directly in proportion to sales, and that fixed costs are unaffected over a very wide range of sales. What would operating income have been if sales had been $10,500,000 instead of $10,000,000? Which income statement did you use to help get your answer? Why?

CHAPTER 4

Relevant Costs and Special Decisions— Part One

Managers' special decisions (often called *problem solving,* as described in Chapter 1) pervade a variety of areas and spans of time. By definition, special decisions occur with less regularity than the typical daily or weekly operating decisions of a hotel, hospital, or manufacturer. The pricing of an unusual sales order is an example of a special decision. Other examples are adding programs, services, or products; selecting equipment; selling products at a certain stage of manufacturing or processing them further; and repairing municipal automobiles internally or buying the repair service from outside suppliers. Unique factors bear on all these special decisions. However, there is a general approach that will help the executive make wise decisions in *any* problem-solving situation. The term "relevant" has been overworked in recent years; nevertheless the general approach herein will be labeled as the **relevant-cost approach.** Coupled with the contribution approach, the ability to distinguish relevant from irrelevant items is the key to making special decisions.

Throughout this and the next chapter, in order to concentrate on a few major points, we shall ignore the time value of money (which is discussed in Chapter 12) and income taxes (which are discussed in Chapter 13).

THE ACCOUNTANT'S ROLE IN
SPECIAL DECISIONS

Accuracy and Relevance

Accountants have an important role in the problem-solving process, not as the decision makers but as collectors and reporters of relevant data. Their reports must provide valid data—numbers that measure the quantities pertinent to the decision at hand. Many managers want the accountant to offer recommendations about the proper decision, even though the final choice always rests with the operating executive.

The distinction between precision and relevance should be kept in mind. Ideally, the data should be **precise** (accurate) and **relevant** (pertinent). However, as we shall see, figures can be precise but irrelevant, or imprecise but relevant. For example, the president's salary may be $100,000 per year, to the penny, but may have no bearing on the question of whether to make or buy a certain part needed in production. As has often been said, it is better to be roughly right than precisely wrong.

Qualitative and Quantitative Factors

The aspects of each alternative may be divided into two broad categories, **qualitative** and **quantitative.** Qualitative factors are those whose measurement in dollars and cents is difficult and imprecise; yet a qualitative factor may easily be given more weight than a measurable saving in cost. For example, the opposition of a militant union to new labor-saving machinery may cause an executive to defer or even reject completely the contemplated installation. Or, the chance to manufacture a component oneself for less than the supplier's selling price may be rejected because acceptance might lead to the company's long-run dependency on the supplier for other subassemblies. Quantitative factors are those that may more easily be reduced to dollars and cents—for example, projected costs of alternative materials, of direct labor, and of overhead. The accountant, statistician, and mathematician try to express as many decision factors as feasible in quantitative terms. This approach reduces the number of qualitative factors to be judged.

MEANING OF RELEVANCE:
THE MAJOR CONCEPTUAL LESSON

Problem solving is essentially decision making—choosing among several courses of action. The available courses of action are the result of an often time-consuming formal or informal search and screening process, perhaps

82

carried on by a company team that includes engineers, accountants, and operating executives.

The accountant's role in problem solving is primarily that of a technical expert on cost analysis. His responsibility is to be certain that the manager is guided by relevant data, information that will lead him to the best decision.

Definition of Relevance

Consider the final stages of the decision-making process. Two (or more) courses of action are aligned, and a comparison is made. The decision is based on the difference in the effect of the two on future performance. **The key question is: What difference does it make? The relevant information is the** *expected future data* **that will** *differ* **among alternatives.**

The ideas in the previous paragraph deserve elaboration because they have such wide application. Historical, or past, data have no direct bearing on the decision. Historical data may be helpful in the formulation of *predictions,* but past figures, in themselves, are irrelevant simply because they are not the expected future data that managers must use in intelligent decision making. Decisions affect the future. Nothing can alter what has already happened; all past costs are down the drain as far as current or future decisions are concerned.

Of the expected future data, **only those that will differ among alternatives are relevant.** Any item is irrelevant if it will remain the same regardless of the alternative selected. For instance, if the department manager's salary will be the same regardless of the products stocked, his salary is irrelevant to the selection of products.[1]

Examples of Relevance

The following examples will help us summarize the sharp distinctions needed for proper cost analysis for special decisions.

You habitually buy gasoline from either of two nearby gasoline stations. Yesterday you noticed that one station is selling gasoline at 90¢ per gallon; the other, at 88¢. Your automobile needs gasoline, and, in making your choice of stations, you *assume* that these prices are unchanged. The relevant costs are 90¢ and 88¢, the expected future costs that will differ between the alternatives. You use your past experience (i.e., what you observed yesterday) for predicting today's price. Note that the relevant cost is not what you paid in the past, or what you observed yesterday, but what you *expect to pay* when you drive in to get gasoline. This cost meets our two

---

[1]The time value of money is ignored here; it is discussed in Chapter 12. Strictly interpreted, differences in future data are affected by both magnitude and timing. Therefore, expected future data with the same magnitude but different timing can be relevant.

criteria: (a) it is the expected future cost, and (b) it differs between the alternatives.

You may also plan to have your car lubricated. The recent price at each station was $6.50, and this is what you anticipate paying. This expected future cost is irrelevant, because it will be the same under either alternative. It does not meet our second criterion.

Exhibit 4-1 sketches the decision process and uses the following decision as an illustration. A manufacturer is thinking of using aluminum instead of copper in a line of desk lamps. The cost of direct material will decrease from 30¢ to 20¢. The elaborate mechanism in Exhibit 4-1 seems unnecessary for this decision. After all, the analysis in a nutshell is:

	Aluminum	Copper	Difference
Direct material	$.20	$.30	$.10

The cost of copper used for this comparison undoubtedly came from historical-cost records, but note that the relevant costs in the above analysis are both expected future costs.

The direct-labor cost will continue to be 70¢ per unit regardless of the material used. It is irrelevant because our second criterion—an element of difference between the alternatives—is not met. Therefore, we can safely exclude direct labor from our cost comparisons. Of course, many companies would not bother to exclude direct labor. In such a case, the following comparison would be made:

	Aluminum	Copper	Difference
Direct material	$.20	$.30	$.10
Direct labor	.70	.70	—

There is no harm in including irrelevant items in a formal analysis, provided that they are included properly. However, clarity is usually enhanced by confining the reports to the relevant items only.

Role of Predictions

Reflect on Exhibit 4-1. It provides a helpful overview. Box 1(a) represents historical accounting data that are usually supplied by the accounting system, whereas box 1(b) represents other data, such as price indices or industry statistics, that are usually gathered from outside the accounting system. Regardless of their source, the historical data in step 2 help the formulation of *predictions*. Although historical data are often used as a guide to predicting, they are irrelevant per se to the decision itself.

In turn, in step 3 these predictions become inputs to the *decision model,* the method for making the choice. In this case our decision model has a simple form: compare the predicted unit costs and select the alternative bearing the lesser cost.

EXHIBIT 4-1. Decision Process and Role of Information

The decision is whether to use aluminum instead of copper.
The objective is to minimize costs.

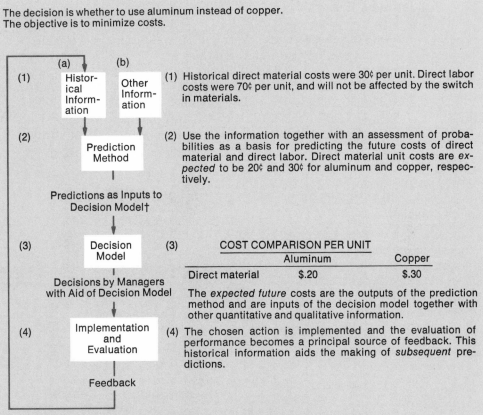

(1) Historical direct material costs were 30¢ per unit. Direct labor costs were 70¢ per unit, and will not be affected by the switch in materials.

(2) Use the information together with an assessment of probabilities as a basis for predicting the future costs of direct material and direct labor. Direct material unit costs are *expected* to be 20¢ and 30¢ for aluminum and copper, respectively.

(3)

COST COMPARISON PER UNIT		
	Aluminum	Copper
Direct material	$.20	$.30

The *expected future* costs are the outputs of the prediction method and are inputs of the decision model together with other quantitative and qualitative information.

(4) The chosen action is implemented and the evaluation of performance becomes a principal source of feedback. This historical information aids the making of *subsequent* predictions.

*Note that historical data may be relevant for prediction methods.
†Historical data are never relevant *per se* for decision models. Only those expected future data that are different are really relevant. For instance, in this example, direct material makes a difference and direct labor does not. Therefore, under our *definition* here, direct labor is irrelevant.

Exhibit 4-1 will be referred to frequently. It displays the major conceptual lesson in this chapter. This and the next chapter will show how the notion of relevant costs combined with the contribution approach may be applied to various particular decisions. **Note that the analytical approach is consistent, regardless of the particular decision encountered.** The contribution approach to cost analysis, which was introduced in the preceding chapter, facilitates analysis for a variety of decisions. In this chapter we shall examine the following decisions: (1) special sales orders, (2) pricing policies, (3) deleting or adding product lines or departments, and (4) using available capacity.

Illustrative Example

Consider the special sales order decision by selecting data from Exhibits 3-7 and 3-8. We are deliberately returning to these exhibits to underscore their general importance. The main data are summarized again in Exhibit 4-2.

The differences in the emphasis and format of the two income statements in Exhibit 4-2 may be unimportant as long as the accompanying cost analysis leads to the same set of decisions. But these two approaches sometimes lead to different unit costs that must be interpreted warily.

EXHIBIT 4-2

FUNCTIONAL AND CONTRIBUTION FORMS OF THE INCOME STATEMENT

Samson Company
Income Statement
For the Year Ended December 31, 19x2
(In thousands of dollars

FUNCTIONAL FORM		CONTRIBUTION FORM		
Sales	$20,000	Sales		$20,000
Less manufacturing cost of		Less variable expenses:		
goods sold	15,000	Manufacturing	$12,000	
Gross profit or gross margin	$ 5,000	Selling and adminis-		
Less selling and administrative		trative	1,100	13,100
expenses	4,000	Contribution margin		$ 6,900
Operating income	$ 1,000	Less fixed expenses:		
		Manufacturing	$3,000	
		Selling and adminis-		
		trative	2,900	5,900
		Operating income		$ 1,000

In our illustration, suppose that 1,000,000 units of product, such as some automobile replacement part, were made and sold. Under the functional costing approach, the unit manufacturing cost of the product would be $15,000,000 ÷ 1,000,000, or $15 per unit. Suppose a mail order house near year-end offered Samson $13 per unit for a 100,000-unit special order that would not affect regular business in any way, would not raise any antitrust issues concerning price discrimination, would not affect total fixed costs, would not entail any additional variable selling and administrative expenses, and would use some otherwise idle manufacturing capacity. Should Samson accept the order? Perhaps the question should be stated more sharply: What is the difference in the short-run financial results between not accepting and accepting? Again, the key question is: What difference does it make?

Correct Analysis

The correct analysis employs the contribution approach and concentrates on the final overall results. As Exhibit 4-3 shows, only the variable manufacturing costs are affected by the particular order, at a rate of $12 per unit. All other variable costs and all fixed costs are unaffected and may therefore be safely ignored in making this special-order pricing decision. Note how the necessary cost analysis is facilitated by the contribution approach's distinction between variable- and fixed-cost behavior patterns. The total short-run income will increase by $100,000 if the order is accepted—despite the fact that the unit selling price of $13 is less than the functional manufacturing cost of $15 computed below:

Total manufacturing costs from Exhibit 4-2	$15,000,000
Divided by units produced	1,000,000
Unit cost	$15

Variable and Absorption Costing

When accountants compare the contribution and functional approaches for product costing (inventory valuation) purposes, they frequently call them the variable-costing and absorption-costing approaches, respectively. Thus, if 1,000,000 units were produced, the unit manufacturing product cost for inventory purposes would be $12 under variable costing and $15 under absorption costing.

EXHIBIT 4-3
COMPARATIVE PREDICTED INCOME STATEMENTS
CONTRIBUTION APPROACH

For the Year Ended December 31, 19x2
(In thousands of dollars)

	WITHOUT SPECIAL ORDER, 1,000,000 UNITS	WITH SPECIAL ORDER, 1,100,000 UNITS	SPECIAL-ORDER DIFFERENCE, 100,000 UNITS TOTAL	SPECIAL-ORDER DIFFERENCE, 100,000 UNITS PER UNIT
Sales	$20,000	$21,300	$1,300	$13
Less variable expenses:				
Manufacturing	$12,000	$13,200	$1,200	$12
Selling and administrative	1,100	1,100	—	—
Total variable expenses	$13,100	$14,300	$1,200	$12
Contribution margin	$ 6,900	$ 7,000	$ 100	$ 1
Less fixed expenses:				
Manufacturing	$ 3,000	$ 3,000	—	—
Selling and administrative	2,900	2,900	—	—
Total fixed expenses	$ 5,900	$ 5,900	—	—
Operating income	$ 1,000	$ 1,100	$ 100	$ 1

Variable costing differs from absorption costing in one major respect: *fixed* indirect manufacturing costs are regarded as expenses immediately and *not* as costs of the manufactured product. The implications of this theory for product costing and income measurement are explored more fully in Chapter 15, but for our immediate purposes they are unimportant.

The variable-costing and absorption-costing terms are introduced here because in practice all kinds of terms are sometimes used to denote particular costs. Be sure to get their exact meaning in a specific decision situation. For example, the terms "full cost" or "fully distributed cost" or "fully allocated cost" sometimes are used as synonyms for absorption cost. However, in other situations "full cost" per unit means "absorption cost *plus* an allocation of selling and administrative costs." For example, using Exhibit 4-2:

	Per Unit
Absorption cost, $15,000,000 ÷ 1,000,000 units	$15
Selling and administrative expenses, $4,000,000 ÷ 1,000,000 units	4
Full cost	$19

For external reporting purposes, American companies must use the $15 amount for inventory valuation. The $4 period cost must, of course, be excluded from inventory. However, you can readily see that for internal decision purposes, managers are free to allocate costs to products in any way that seems helpful. For instance, for setting long-run target prices for products, managers may desire "full-cost" computations.

Incorrect Analysis

Faulty cost analysis sometimes occurs because of misinterpretation of unit fixed costs. Some managers may erroneously use the $15 unit absorption cost to make the following prediction for the year (in thousands of dollars):

	Without Special Order	*With Special Order*	*Special-Order Difference*
Sales	20,000	21,300	1,300
Less manufacturing cost of goods sold @ $15	15,000	16,500	1,500
Gross profit	5,000	4,800	(200)
Other costs	4,000	4,000	—
Operating income	1,000	800	(200)

The $1,500,000 increase in costs is computed by multiplying $15 times 100,000 units. Of course, the fallacy in this approach is the regarding of a fixed cost (fixed manufacturing cost) as though it behaved in a variable manner. Avoid the assumption that unit costs may be used indiscriminately as a basis for predicting how total costs will behave. Instead, follow what was called Robert McNamara's First Law of Analysis when he was U.S. Secretary of Defense: "Always start by looking at the grand total. Whatever problem you are studying, back off and look at it in the large." In this context, that law means, "Beware of unit costs. When in doubt, convert all costs into totals to get the big picture."

Spreading Fixed Costs

As we just saw, the unit cost-total cost distinction can become particularly troublesome when analyzing fixed-cost behavior. Assume the same facts concerning the special order as before, except that the order was for 250,000 units at a selling price of $11.50. Some managers have been known to argue for acceptance of such an order as follows: Of course, we will lose 50¢ each on the variable manufacturing costs, but we will gain 60¢ per unit by spreading our fixed manufacturing costs over 1,250,000 units instead of 1,000,000 units. Consequently, we should take the offer because it represents an advantage of 10¢ per unit:

Old fixed manufacturing cost per unit, $3,000,000 ÷ $1,000,000	$3.00
New fixed manufacturing cost per unit, $3,000,000 ÷ 1,250,000	2.40
"Saving" in fixed manufacturing costs per unit	$ .60
Loss on variable manufacturing costs per unit, $11.50 − $12.00	.50
Net saving per unit in manufacturing costs	$ .10

Again, the analytical pitfalls of unit-cost analysis can be avoided by using the contribution approach and concentrating on totals (in thousands of dollars):

	Without Special Order	With Special Order	Special-Order Difference
Sales	20,000	22,875	2,875[a]
Variable manufacturing costs	12,000	15,000	3,000[b]
Other variable costs	1,100	1,100	—
Total variable costs	13,100	16,100	3,000
Contribution margin	6,900	6,775	(125)[c]

[a] 250,000 × $11.50 selling price of special order.
[b] 250,000 × $12.00 variable manufacturing cost per unit of special order.
[c] 250,000 × $.50 negative contribution margin per unit of special order.

Short-run income will fall by $125,000 (that is, 250,000 units × $.50) if the special order is accepted. No matter how the fixed manufacturing costs are "unitized" and "spread" over the units produced, their total of $3,000,000 will be *unchanged* by the special order (in thousands of dollars):

	Without Special Order	With Special Order	Special-Order Difference
Contribution margin (as above)	6,900	6,775	(125)
Fixed costs:			
As originally allocated at a per-unit rate of $3.00	3,000		
As newly allocated at a per-unit rate of $2.40		3,000	—
Contribution to other fixed costs and operating income	3,900	3,775	(125)

Total Costs and Unit Costs

The term "absorption costing" arises from the procedure of taking a cost that behaves as a fixed cost in total (the fixed manufacturing cost of $3,000,000) and then allocating the cost *as though it was variable.* The fixed costs are thus said to be "absorbed" by "attaching" themselves to units of product as those units are manufactured. By the end of the year, if predictions were *flawless,* the total fixed costs absorbed by the product would indeed exactly equal the total actual fixed costs.

Of course, predictions are rarely flawless, so the cost analysis can become more complicated. Such complexities of the role of fixed overhead in product costing are explored in detail in Chapter 15, so do not be concerned here with anything beyond the major lesson: no matter how fixed costs are spread for *unit* product costing purposes, the *total* fixed costs will be unchanged. This is true even though fixed costs *per unit* have fallen from $3 to $2.40. **The moral is: beware of unit costs when analyzing fixed costs. Think in terms of totals instead.**

To recapitulate, a common error is to regard all unit costs indiscriminately, as if all costs were variable costs. Changes in volume will affect *total* variable costs but not *total* fixed costs. The danger then is to predict total costs assuming that all unit costs are variable. The correct relationships are:

Behavior as Volume Fluctuates

	Variable Cost	Fixed Cost
Cost per unit	No change	Change
Total cost	Change	No change

ROLE OF COSTS IN PRICING

Factors that Influence Prices

Many businessmen say that they use cost-plus pricing—that is, they compute an average unit cost and add a "reasonable" markup that will generate an adequate return on investment. This entails circular reasoning because price, which influences sales volume, is based upon full cost, which in turn is partly determined by the underlying volume of sales. Also, the plus in cost-plus is rarely an unalterable markup. Its magnitude depends on the behavior of competitors and customers. Three major factors influence pricing decisions: customers, competitors, and costs.

Customers always have an alternative source of supply, can substitute one material for another, and may make a part rather than buy it if the vendor's prices are too high.

Competitors will usually react to price changes made by their rivals. Tinkering with prices is usually most heavily influenced by the price setter's expectations of competitors' reactions.

The maximum price that may be charged is the one that does not drive the customer away. The minimum price is zero; companies may give out free samples to gain entry into a market. A more practical guide is that, in the short run, the *minimum* price to be quoted, *subject to consideration of long-run effects,* should be the costs that may be avoided by not landing the order—often all variable costs.

Target Pricing

When a company has little influence over price, it usually sells at the market price and tries, by controlling costs, to achieve profitable operations. When a company can set its own prices, its procedures are often a combination of shrewd guessing and mysterious folklore. Often the first step is to accumulate costs and add a markup. This is the target price. Subsequent adjustments may be made "in light of market conditions."

Earlier in this chapter the relationship between "absorption cost" and "full cost" was discussed. Sometimes these terms are used interchangeably, but more often absorption cost refers to all manufacturing costs while full cost refers to all manufacturing costs plus an allocation of selling and administrative costs too. Target prices might be based on a host of different markups based on a host of different definitions of cost. Thus, there are many ways to arrive at the same target price. They simply reflect different arrangements of the components of the same income statement.

However, when it is used intelligently, the contribution approach has distinct advantages over the traditional full-costing (absorption-costing) approach, which fails to highlight different cost behavior patterns.

First, the contribution approach offers more detailed information than the traditional full-costing approach because variable- and fixed-cost behavior patterns are explicitly delineated. Because the contribution approach is sensitive to cost-volume-profit relationships, it is a better, easier basis for developing pricing formulas.

Second, a normal or target-pricing formula can be as easily developed by the contribution approach as by traditional full-costing approaches. Consider the facts in Exhibit 4-2. Note that under traditional approaches the target markup percentage may be expressed as a percentage of absorption cost—that is, the total manufacturing cost—or as a percentage of some total cost in the fullest sense, whereby all selling and administrative costs are also unitized.

For a volume of 1,000,000 units, assume that the target selling price is $20 per unit. Therefore, the target percentage (sometimes called a *markup* or *markon* percentage) that would obtain a selling price of $20 would be:

As a percentage of manufacturing cost,

$$\frac{\$20,000 - \$15,000}{\$15,000} = 33.33\%$$

As a percentage of manufacturing, selling, and administrative cost,

$$\frac{\$20,000 - (\$15,000 + \$4,000)}{(\$15,000 + \$4,000)} = 5.26\%$$

As a percentage of variable manufacturing cost,

$$\frac{\$20,000 - \$12,000}{\$12,000} = 66.67\%$$

As a percentage of variable manufacturing, selling, and administrative cost,

$$\frac{\$20,000 - \$13,100}{\$13,100} = 52.67\%$$

The percentages above are only a few of the possible variations in formula approaches to pricing. Under *either* the absorption (full) costing or the contribution approach, the pricing decision maker will have a formula that will lead him toward the *same* target price. **If he is unable to obtain such a price consistently, the company will not achieve its $1,000,000 operating-income objective or its desired operating-income percentage of sales.**

Third, the contribution approach offers insight into the short-run versus long-run effects of cutting prices on special orders. For example, assume the same cost behavior patterns as in Exhibit 4-3. The 100,000-unit order added $100,000 to operating income at a selling price of $13, which was $7 below the target selling price of $20 and $2 below the absorption cost of $15. The implication there, given all the stated assumptions, was in favor of accepting the order. No general answer can be given, but the relevant information was more easily generated by the contribution approach. Recall the possible analyses:

	Contribution Approach	Traditional Absorption (full) Costing Approach
Sales, 100,000 units @ $13	$1,300,000	$ 1,300,000
Variable manufacturing costs @ $12	1,200,000	
Absorption manufacturing costs @ $15		1,500,000
Apparent change in income	$ 100,000	$ − 200,000

Should the offer be accepted? Compare the two approaches. Under the traditional approach, the decision maker has no direct knowledge of cost-volume-profit relationships. He makes his decision by hunch. On the surface the offer is definitely unattractive, because the price of $13 is $2 below factory absorption costs.

Under the contribution approach, the decision maker sees a short-run advantage of $100,000 from accepting the offer. Fixed costs will be unaffected by whatever decision is made and net income will increase by $100,000. Still, there often are long-run effects to consider. Will acceptance of the offer undermine the long-run price structure? In other words, is the short-run advantage of $100,000 more than offset by high probable long-run financial disadvantages? The decision maker may think so and may reject the offer. But—and this is important—by doing so he is, in effect, saying that he is willing to forego $100,000 now in order to protect his long-run market advantages. Generally, he can assess problems of this sort by asking whether the probability of long-run benefits is worth an "investment" equal to the foregone contribution margin ($100,000 in this case). Under traditional approaches, he must ordinarily conduct a special study to find the immediate effects; under the contribution approach, he has a system that will routinely provide such information.

Our general theme of focusing on relevant costs also extends into the area of pricing. To say that the contribution approach or absorption (full-cost) approach provides the best guide to pricing decisions is a dangerous oversimplification of one of the most perplexing problems in business. Lack of understanding and judgment can lead to unprofitable pricing regardless of the kind of cost data available or cost accounting system used.

Frequently, managers are reluctant to employ a contribution approach because of fears that variable costs will be substituted indiscriminately for full costs and will therefore lead to suicidal price cutting. This should *not* occur if the data are used wisely. However, if the top managers perceive a pronounced danger of underpricing when variable-cost data are revealed, they may justifiably prefer a full-cost approach for guiding pricing decisions.

A complete discussion of pricing is beyond the scope of this book.[2] However, a contribution approach should clarify the major classes of information that bear on the pricing decision.

DELETION OR ADDITION OF PRODUCTS OR DEPARTMENTS

Consider a discount department store that has three major departments: groceries, general merchandise, and drugs. Management is considering dropping groceries, which have consistently shown a net loss. The present annual net income is reported as follows (in thousands of dollars):

| | | Departments | | |
	Total	Groceries	General Merchandise	Drugs
Sales	$1,900	$1,000	$800	$100
Variable cost of goods sold and expenses	1,420	800	560	60
Contribution margin	$ 480 (25%)	$ 200 (20%)	$240 (30%)	$ 40 (40%)
Fixed expenses (salaries, depreciation, insurance, property taxes, etc.)				
Avoidable[a]	$ 265	$ 150	$100	$ 15
Unavoidable[b]	180	60	100	20
Total fixed expenses	$ 445	$ 210	$200	$ 35
Net income	$ 35	$ (10)	$ 40	$ 5

[a] Includes department salaries and other costs that could be avoided by not operating the specific department.
[b] Unavoidable costs include many common costs, which are defined as those costs of facilities and services that are shared by user departments. Examples are store depreciation, heating, air conditioning, and general management expenses.

Sometimes the terms *avoidable* and *unavoidable* costs are used in conjunction with special decision making. Avoidable costs are those costs that will not continue if an ongoing operation is changed or deleted; in contrast, unavoidable costs are those costs that will continue.

Assume first that the only alternatives to be considered are to drop or continue the grocery department. Assume further that the total assets invested would not be affected by the decision. The vacated space would be idle, and the unavoidable costs would not be changed. Which alternative would you recommend? An analysis follows (in thousands of dollars):

[2] For example, many laws prohibit price discrimination—that is, quoting different selling prices for identical goods or services. Obviously, there are also many other complications, which are explored in books on economics and marketing.

| | Store as a Whole | | |
| | A | B | A − B |
Income Statements	Keep Groceries	Drop Groceries	Difference
Sales	$1,900	$900	$1,000
Variable expenses	1,420	620	800
Contribution margin	$ 480	$280	$ 200
Avoidable fixed expenses	265	115	150
Profit contribution to common space			
and other unavoidable costs	$ 215	$165	$ 50
Common space and other			
unavoidable costs	180	180	—
Net income	$ 35	$(15)	$ 50

The preceding analysis shows that matters would be worse, rather than better, if groceries were dropped and the vacated facilities left idle. In short, as the income statement shows, groceries bring in a contribution margin of $200,000, which is $50,000 more than the $150,000 fixed expenses that would be saved by closing the grocery department.

Assume now that the space made available by the dropping of groceries would be used by an expanded general merchandise department. The space would be occupied by merchandise that would increase sales by $500,000, generate a 30 percent contribution-margin percentage, and have avoidable fixed costs of $70,000. The operating picture would then be improved by an increase in net income of $30,000—from $35,000 to $65,000:

| | | General | |
| | Total | Merchandise | Drugs |
	(in thousands of dollars)		
Sales	$1,400	$800 + $500	$100
Variable expenses	970	560 + 350	60
Contribution margin	$ 430	$240 + $150	$ 40
Avoidable fixed expenses	185	100 + 70	15
Contribution to common space and			
other unavoidable costs	$ 245	$140 + $ 80	$ 25
Common space and other unavoidable costs[a]	180		
Net income	$ 65		

[a] Former grocery fixed costs, which were allocations of common costs that will continue regardless of how the space is occupied.

As the following summary analysis demonstrates, the objective is to obtain, *from a given amount of space or capacity,* the maximum contribution to the payment of those costs that remain unaffected by the nature of the product sold:

Profit Contribution of Given Space

	Groceries	Expansion of General Merchandise	Difference
		(*in thousands of dollars*)	
Sales	$1,000	$500	$500 U
Variable expenses	800	350	450 F
Contribution margin	$ 200	$150	$ 50 U
Avoidable fixed expense	150	70	80 F
Contribution to common space and other unavoidable costs	$ 50	$ 80	$ 30 F

F = Favorable difference resulting from replacing groceries with general merchandise.
U = Unfavorable difference.

In this case, the general merchandise will not achieve the dollar sales volume that groceries will, but the higher markups and the lower wage costs (mostly because of the diminished need for stocking and checkout clerks) will bring more favorable net results.

CONTRIBUTION TO PROFIT PER UNIT OF LIMITING FACTOR

When a multiple-product plant is being operated at capacity, decisions as to which orders to accept must often be made. The contribution approach is also applicable here, because the product to be pushed or the order to be accepted is the one that makes the biggest *total* profit contribution per unit of the limiting factor.

The contribution approach must be used wisely, however. Sometimes, a major pitfall is the erroneous tendency to favor those products with the biggest contribution-margin ratios per sales dollar.

Assume that a company has two products:

	Product	
Per Unit	A	B
Selling price	$20	$30
Variable costs	16	21
Contribution margin	$ 4	$ 9
Contribution-margin ratio	20%	30%

Which product is more profitable? Product B apparently is more profitable than A: however, one important fact has been purposely withheld—the time that it takes to produce each product. If 10,000 hours of capacity are available, and three units of A can be produced per hour in contrast to one unit of B, your choice would be A, because it contributes the most profit per hour, the **limiting, critical,** or **scarce factor** in this example:

	A	B
1. Units per hour	3	1
2. Contribution margin per unit	$4	$9
Contribution margin per hour (1) × (2)	$12	$9
Total contribution for 10,000 hours	$120,000	$90,000

The limiting, critical, or scarce factor is the item that restricts or constrains the production or sale of a given product. **Thus the criterion for maximizing profits, for a given capacity, is to obtain the greatest possible contribution to profit per unit of the limiting or critical factor.** The limiting factor in the above example may be machine-hours or labor-hours. In the discount store example it was square feet of floor space. It may be cubic feet of display space. In such cases, a ratio such as the conventional gross-profit percentage (gross profit ÷ selling price) is an insufficient clue to profitability because profits also depend on the stock turnover (number of times the average inventory is sold per year).

The success of the suburban discount department stores illustrates the concept of the contribution to profit per unit of limiting factor. These stores have been satisfied with subnormal markups because they have been able to increase turnover and thus increase the contribution to profit per unit of space, as Exhibit 4-4 illustrates, using hypothetical numbers.

EXHIBIT 4-4

	REGULAR DEPARTMENT STORE	DISCOUNT DEPARTMENT STORE
Retail price	$4.00	$3.50
Cost of merchandise	3.00	3.00
Contribution to profit per unit	$1.00 (25%)	$ .50 (14+%)
Units sold per year	10,000	22,000
Total contribution to profit, assuming the same space allotment in both stores	$10,000	$11,000

SUMMARY

The accountant's role in problem solving is primarily that of a technical expert on cost analysis. His responsibility is to be certain that the manager uses *relevant data* in guiding his decisions. Accountants and managers must have a penetrating understanding of relevant costs.

To be relevant to a particular decision, a cost must meet two criteria:

(1) it must be an expected *future* cost; and (2) it must be an element of *difference* as among the alternatives. All *past* (*historical* or *sunk*) costs are in themselves irrelevant to any *decision* about the future, although they often provide the best available basis for the *prediction* of expected future data.

The combination of the relevant costing and contribution approaches is a fundamental framework, based on economic analysis, that may be applied to a vast range of problems. The following are among the more important generalizations regarding various decisions:

1. Wherever feasible, think in terms of total costs rather than unit costs. Too often, unit costs are regarded as an adequate basis for predicting changes in total costs. This assumption is satisfactory when analyzing variable costs, but it is frequently misleading when analyzing fixed costs.

2. The contribution approach to pricing special sales orders offers helpful information because the foregone contribution can be quantified as the investment currently being made to protect long-run benefits.

3. The key to obtaining the maximum profit from a given capacity is to obtain the greatest possible contribution to profit per unit of the limiting or scarce factor.

SUMMARY PROBLEM FOR YOUR REVIEW

Problem

Return to the basic illustration in Exhibit 4-3. Suppose a special order like that described in conjunction with Exhibit 4-3 had the following terms: selling price would be $13.50 instead of $13, but a manufacturer's agent who had acquired the potential order would have to be paid a flat fee of $40,000 if the order was accepted. What would be the new operating income if the order was accepted?

Solution

The easiest way to solve this part is to work from the $100,000 increase in income already shown in the final column of Exhibit 4-3:

Operating income based on $13 price	$100,000
Increase in selling price per unit is $13.50	
minus $13, or $.50. Increase in revenue,	
$.50 × 100,000 units	50,000
Increase in fixed expenses, special fee	(40,000)
New operating income	$110,000

ASSIGNMENT MATERIAL

Fundamental Assignment Material

4-1. Terminology. Define: *decision model, limiting factor.*

4-2. Cost analysis and pricing. The budget for the Bright Printing Company for 19x2 follows:

Sales		$1,000,000
Direct material	$180,000	
Direct labor	320,000	
Overhead	400,000	900,000
Net income		$ 100,000

The company typically uses a so-called cost-plus pricing system. Direct material and direct labor are computed, overhead is added at a rate of 125 percent of direct labor, and one-ninth of the total cost is added to obtain the selling price.

Mr. Bright has placed a $10,000 bid on a particularly large order with a cost of $1,800 direct material and $3,200 direct labor. The customer informs him that he can have the business for $8,900, take it or leave it. If Mr. Bright accepts the order, total sales for 19x2 will be $1,008,900.

Mr. Bright refuses the order, saying: "I sell on a cost-plus basis. It is bad policy to accept orders at below cost. I would lose $100 on the job."

The company's annual fixed overhead is $160,000.

Required

1. What would net income have been with the order? Without the order? Show your computations.

2. Give a short description of a contribution approach to pricing that Bright might follow. Include a stipulation of the pricing formula that Bright should routinely use if he hopes to obtain a target net income of $100,000.

4-3. Unit costs and choice of most profitable product. The Frange Corporation sells two molding powders, known as A and B. A detail of the unit income and costs follows:

	Product	
	A	B
Selling price	$12	$20
Direct material	$ 2	$ 4
Direct labor	2	1
Variable factory overhead[a]	2	4
Fixed factory overhead[a]	2	4
Total cost of goods sold	$ 8	$13
Gross profit per unit	$ 4	$ 7

[a] On a machine-hour basis.

99

As far as can be determined, the sales outlook is such that the plant could operate at full capacity on either or both products. Both A and B are processed through the same cost centers. Selling costs are completely fixed and may be ignored.

Which product should be produced? If more than one should be produced, indicate the proportions of each. Explain your answer briefly.

Additional Assignment Material

4-4. "The distinction between precision and relevancy should be kept in mind." Explain.

4-5. Distinguish between the quantitative and qualitative aspects of decisions.

4-6. "Any future cost is relevant." Do you agree? Explain.

4-7. Why are historical or past data irrelevant to special decisions?

4-8. Give four examples of limiting or scarce factors.

4-9. "A ratio such as the conventional gross-profit percentage is an insufficient clue to profitability." Do you agree? Explain.

4-10. What three major factors influence pricing decisions?

4-11. Why are customers one of the three factors influencing prices?

4-12. "I don't believe in assigning only variable costs to a job for guiding pricing. This results in suicidal underpricing." Do you agree? Why?

4-13. Unit costs and total costs. You are a college professor who belongs to a faculty club. Annual dues are $120. You use the club solely for lunches, which cost $3 each. You have not used the club much in recent years and are wondering whether to continue your membership.

Required

1. You are confronted with a variable-cost plus a fixed-cost behavior pattern. Plot each on a graph, where the vertical axis is total cost and the horizontal axis is volume in number of lunches. Also plot a third graph that combines the previous two graphs.

2. What is the cost per lunch if you pay for your own lunch once a year? Twelve times a year? Two hundred times a year?

3. Suppose the average price of lunches elsewhere is $4. (a) How many lunches must you have at the faculty club so that the total costs of the lunches would be the same regardless of where you ate for that number of lunches? (b) Suppose you ate 250 lunches a year at the faculty club. How much would you save in relation to the total costs of eating elsewhere?

4-14. Dropping a product line. Assume that a company has three product lines, all produced in one factory. Management is considering dropping Product C, which has consistently shown a net loss. The predicted income statements follow:

| | Product | | | |
	A	B	C	Total
Sales	$500,000	$400,000	$100,000	$1,000,000
Variable expenses	295,000	280,000	75,000	650,000
Contribution margin	$205,000 (41%)	$120,000 (30%)	$ 25,000 (25%)	$ 350,000 (35%)
Fixed expenses (salaries, depreciation, property taxes, insurance)	165,000	90,000	45,000ᵃ	300,000
Operating income	$ 40,000	$ 30,000	$(20,000)	$ 50,000

ᵃ Includes product-line supervisor's salary of $20,000.

1. Assume that the only available alternatives are to drop Product C or to continue with Product C. Assume further that the total assets invested will not be affected by the decision, but the product supervisor will be discharged. Should C be dropped? Explain.

2. Another important alternative besides the two discussed above is the possibility of dropping Product C, keeping the supervisor, and using the vacant facilities to produce, say, Product A to satisfy its expanding demand. If this happened, and if sales of Product A were expanded by $100,000, by how much would company income be affected? Explain.

4-15. Demand analysis. (SMA, adapted.) The Aurora Manufacturing Limited produces and sells one product. During 19x4 the company manufactured and sold 50,000 units at $25 each. Existing production capacity is 60,000 units a year.

In formulating the 19x5 budget management is faced with a number of decisions concerning product pricing and output. The following information is available:

1. A market survey shows that the sales volume is very much dependent on the selling price. For each $1 drop in selling price, sales volume would increase by 10,000 units.

2. The company's expected cost structure for 19x5 is as follows:

   a. Fixed cost (regardless of production or sales activities), $360,000.

   b. Variable costs per unit (including production, selling and administrative expenses), $16.

3. To increase annual capacity from the present 60,000 to 90,000 units, additional investment for plant, building, equipment, etc. of $200,000 would be necessary. The estimated average life of the additional investment would be 10 years, so the fixed costs would increase by an average of $20,000 per year. (Expansion of less than 30,000 additional units of capacity would cost only slightly less than $200,000.)

Indicate, with reasons, what the level of production and the selling price should be for the coming year. Also indicate whether the company should approve the plant expansion. Show your calculations. Ignore income tax considerations and the time value of money.

4-16. Pricing strategy. The Dreker Company has the following cost behavior pattern for the unique ashtrays that it manufactures and sells:

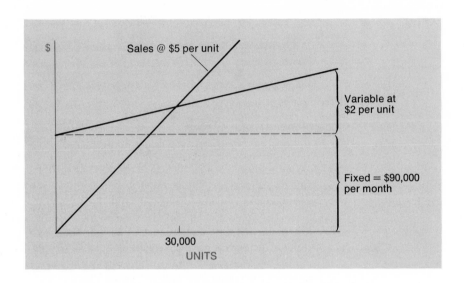

1. What is the break-even point in units?
2. If sales were at 40,000 units, would you then be inclined to cut the selling price? Why?
3. If sales were at 20,000 units, would you then be inclined to cut the selling price? Why?

4-17. Variable costs and prices. A supplier to a large appliance manufacturer has the following conversation with the manufacturer's purchasing manager:

SUPPLIER: You did not predict the heavy demands. To keep up with your unforeseen demands over the coming quarter, we will have to work six days per week instead of five. Therefore, I want a price increase in the amount of the overtime premium that I must pay.

MANUFACTURER: You have already recouped your fixed costs, so you are enjoying a hefty contribution margin on the sixth day. So quit complaining!

Should the supplier get an increase in price? Explain.

4-18. Accepting a low bid. The Vittetaw Company, a maker of a variety of metal and plastic products, is in the midst of a business downturn and is saddled with many idle facilities. The National Hospital Supply Company has approached Vittetaw to produce 300,000 nonslide serving trays. National will pay $1.20 each.

Vittetaw predicts that its variable costs will be $1.30 each. However, its fixed costs, which had been averaging $1 per unit on a variety of other products, will now be spread over twice as much volume. The president commented, "Sure, we'll lose 10¢ each on the variable costs, but we'll gain 50¢ per unit by spreading our fixed costs. Therefore, we should take the offer, because it represents an advantage of 40¢ per unit."

Required

Do you agree with the president? Why? Suppose the regular business had a current volume of 300,000 units, sales of $600,000, variable costs of $390,000, and fixed costs of $300,000.

4-19. Various costing techniques for pricing. Budgeted income statement items for the Doyle Company include: sales, $1,200,000; total factory cost of goods sold, $900,000; total selling and administrative expenses, $200,000; operating income, $100,000; direct material, $350,000; direct labor, $200,000; fixed factory overhead, $300,000; and variable selling and administrative expenses, $100,000.

Operations were exactly in accordance with the budget. Target selling prices were achieved on every order.

Required

1. Prepare two income statements for the year, one with a functional format and a second with a contribution format. Show alternate percentage breakdowns of major items.

2. For an item with total variable costs of $583 (including variable selling and administrative costs) and total factory costs of $750, what markup percentage would be used on a price-quotation sheet that would yield the same target price under (a) the contribution approach and (b) the functional approach? Under (a), the percentage would be based on some version of variable costs; under (b), percentage would be on some version of full costs.

3. During the year, the president personally rejected an offer of $8,500 for some items whose total factory cost of goods was $9,000. The president said, "We never take orders for less than cost." What was the effect of his decision on net income for the year? Did he make a wise decision? Explain.

4-20. Pricing by auto dealers. Many automobile dealers have an operating pattern similar to Lance Motors, a dealer in Ohio. Each month, Lance initially aims at a unit volume quota that approximates a break-even point. Until the break-even point is reached, Lance has a policy of relatively lofty pricing, whereby the "minimum deal" must contain a sufficiently high markup to assure a contribution to profit of no less than $250. After the break-even point is attained, Lance tends to quote lower prices for the remainder of the month.

Required

What is your opinion of this policy? As a prospective customer, how would you react to this policy?

4-21. Dispute about defense contract. During the late 1960s and early 1970s, fury arose in Washington, D.C., about the scenario involved in developing weapons. The frequently encountered situation was begun by the contractor's signing a fixed-price contract with the Defense Department. Later, the contractor encountered cost problems and managed to renegotiate the contract at a higher price. The Pentagon's budget soared, and congressmen demanded a tougher posture.

In 1969, Grumman Corporation agreed to build as many as 313 F-14 Tomcat fighter-bombers at a price of $16.8 million each. The Navy ordered various production lots, and 86 planes were in various stages of completion at the end of 1972. However, when the Navy placed an order for 48 more planes in late 1972, Grumman announced that it would not deliver the planes at that price. The company claimed that it was losing $1 million each on the 86 planes already in production. Furthermore, building 48 more planes at contract prices would cause the company to lose another $105 million and threaten its survival. The company's sales during the first nine months of 1972 were $45 million; its net income was $1.4 million.

The company chairman claimed that the rising costs were not the company's fault. He blamed unexpectedly fast inflation and the phasing out of other government work (including the lunar module for Apollo), not the "bad management" and "inefficiencies" that critics had attributed to another troubled defense contractor, Lockheed.

Required

1. Elaborate on the reasoning of the company chairman. What has the phasing out of other government work got to do with the F-14 contract? Be specific.

2. If you were Senator Proxmire, a habitual critic of defense contracting, what would be your major argument against renegotiation?

4-22. **Evening college operations; revenue potential and unit costs.** (R. C. John.) The budget officer of a large university informed the dean of the Adult Education College that his college was supposed to produce a revenue of $25,000 in excess of expenses. The dean's anticipated revenues are $165,000, from 1,650 enrollments. His total predicted costs are $140,000, including $39,600 of general programmed costs and committed costs. The dean classified his costs as follows:

a. *Direct event or course costs.* All costs that will be incurred if the specific event or course in question is held and that will be avoided if the course is not held. Examples: instructor's salary, specific promotional costs, rental of visual aid equipment.

b. *General programmed costs.* All costs that are fixed, in total, for a given period, in light of a general forecast of overall enrollment or scope of activity. Examples are part-time clerical salaries, printings and mailings of general promotional literature, general space leasing, advertising, and supplies.

c. *Committed costs.* All costs that entail long-range obligations or responsibilities. Decisions about these costs usually involve a longer planning horizon than a single budget period. These costs are also fixed, in total, for a budget period. Examples are full-time administrative and clerical salaries.

Precious Stones, a new course, had been scheduled in response to some requests. The dean had hired a geology professor who was very distinguished in lapidary science. His salary for the course would be $1,700. Required audiovisual equipment would be rented for $100. The class was budgeted for an enrollment of 25 and was assigned to a room that would comfortably accommodate 60. Tuition for the course was $100. In addition, the college furnished a stone kit that was to be bought in the exact quantity needed, from a local supplier, at a special price of $10 per kit.

The dean had learned a little about cost-volume-profit relationships. His enthusiasm for this course diminished after he computed the following break-even point:

Let X = number of enrollments. Then

Tuition revenue = Direct event costs
$$+ \text{(General programmed costs} + \text{Committed costs)}$$

$$\$100X = \$1,700 + \$100 + \$10X + (25/1,650 \times \$39,600)$$
$$\$90X = \$1,800 + \$600$$
$$\$90X = \$2,400$$
$$X = 26.67$$

He was unenthused about adding a course that would bring in a net of $2,250 (25 × $90) and cost $2,400.

1. Should the dean hold the class? Why or why not? Be specific. Show computations and assumptions that underlie your decision.

2. Show an alternate way of computing a break-even point.

3. What is probably the limiting, restricting, or scarce factor that is most crucial in most evening college operations? What is probably the key to the maximum financial performance of a particular course, assuming that the course will definitely be offered?

4-23. **Dropping or adding products.** (CPA, adapted.) The officers of Bradshaw Company are reviewing the profitability of the company's four products and the potential effect of several proposals for varying the product mix. An excerpt from the income statement and other data follow:

	Totals	Product P	Product Q	Product R	Product S
Sales	$62,600	$10,000	$18,000	$12,600	$22,000
Cost of goods sold	44,274	4,750	7,056	13,968	18,500
Gross profit	18,326	5,250	10,944	(1,368)	3,500
Operating expenses	12,012	1,990	2,976	2,826	4,220
Income before income taxes	$ 6,314	$ 3,260	$ 7,968	$(4,194)	$ (720)
Units sold		1,000	1,200	1,800	2,000
Sales price per unit		$ 10.00	$ 15.00	$ 7.00	$11.00
Variable cost of goods sold per unit		$ 2.50	$ 3.00	$ 6.50	$ 6.00
Variable operating expenses per unit		$ 1.17	$ 1.25	$ 1.00	$ 1.20

Each of the following proposals is to be considered independently of the others. Consider only the product changes stated in each proposal; the activity of other products remains stable. Ignore income taxes.

1. If Product R is discontinued, the effect on income will be
   a. a $900 increase.   c. a $12,600 decrease.   e. None of the above.
   b. a $4,194 increase.   d. a $1,368 increase.

2. If Product R is discontinued and a consequent loss of customers causes a decrease of 200 units in sales of Q, the total effect on income will be
   a. a $15,600 decrease.   c. a $2,044 increase.   e. None of the above.
   b. a $2,866 increase.   d. a $1,250 decrease.

3. If the sales price of Product R is increased to $8 with a decrease in the number of units sold to 1,500, the effect on income will be
   a. a $2,199 decrease.   c. a $750 increase.   e. None of the above.
   b. a $600 decrease.   d. a $2,199 increase.

4. The plant in which R is produced can be utilized to produce a new product, T. The total variable costs and expenses per unit of T are $8.05, and 1,600 units can be sold at $9.50 each. If T is introduced and R is discontinued, the total effect on income will be
   a. a $2,600 increase.   c. a $3,220 increase.   e. None of the above.
   b. a $2,320 increase.   d. a $1,420 increase.

5. Part of the plant in which P is produced can easily be adapted to the production of S, but changes in quantities may make changes in sales prices advisable. If production of P is reduced to 500 units (to be sold at $12 each) and production of S is increased to 2,500 units (to be sold at $10.50 each), the total effect on income will be
   a. a $1,765 decrease.   c. a $2,060 decrease.   e. None of the above.
   b. a $250 increase.   d. a $1,515 decrease.

6. Production of P can be doubled by adding a second shift, but higher wages must be paid, increasing variable cost of goods sold to $3.50 for each of the additional units. If the 1,000 additional units of P can be sold at $10 each, the total effect on income will be
   a. a $10,000 increase.   c. a $6,500 increase.   e. None of the above.
   b. a $5,330 increase.   d. a $2,260 increase.

Note: Ignore fixed costs. Be careful when you compute differences—it is easy to get algebraic signs confused. Note how the contribution approach facilitates getting the solution.

4-24. Utilization of passenger jets. In 19x2, Continental Air Lines, Inc., filled 50 percent of the available seats on its Boeing 707 jet flights, a record about 15 percent below the national average.

Continental could have eliminated about 4 percent of its runs and raised its average load considerably. But the improved load factor would have reduced profits. Give reasons for or against this elimination. What factors should influence an airline's scheduling policies?

When you answer this question, suppose that Continental had a basic package of 3,000 flights per month that had an average of 100 seats available per flight. Also suppose that 52 percent of the seats were filled at an average ticket price of $50 per flight. Variable costs are about 70 percent of revenue.

Continental also had a marginal package of 120 flights per month that had an average of 100 seats available per flight. Suppose that only 20 percent of the seats were filled at an average ticket price of $40 per flight. Variable costs are about 50 percent of this revenue. Prepare a tabulation of the basic package, marginal package, and total package, showing percentage of seats filled, revenue, variable expenses, and contribution margin.

4-25. Airline costs. An executive of Trans World Airlines (TWA) stated: "Under the Civil Aeronautics Board load factor standard, any shortfall below 55 percent is treated as presumptive managerial guilt of overscheduling. Thus, if the industry expects 116 billion *passenger miles* of traffic (a *passenger mile* is one person moved one mile), all we have to do is limit *seat miles* to 211 billion (a *seat mile* is one seat moved one mile) .... For us the smallest meaningful unit in capacity planning is not the seat mile, but the schedule. And each schedule generates a large, inflexible, indivisible batch of seat miles .... We cannot slice 5 percent off the airplane."

TWA analyzed its New York-Phoenix schedule for the year ended October 1977. This round trip produced revenues of $4.9 million. Fully allocated costs were $5.2 million, consisting of (a) $3.5 million "out-of-pocket costs" specifically created by this schedule (examples are fuel, crew pay, landing fees, and passenger handling costs), and (b) $1.7 million of allocated fixed costs (examples are the rental of the terminal at Kennedy Airport, the depreciation on the central overhaul base in Kansas City).

Required | Should TWA give up its New York-Phoenix round-trip schedule? Explain.

4-26. Profit planning in a developing country. The subsidiary of a multinational drug company was the largest firm in a developing nation's pharmaceutical industry (comprising some 30 manufacturers) with sales in the vicinity of $20 million. The manufacturing operation consisted primarily of processing and packing imported bulk materials into finished products. The 98 finished products were made from some 50 different kinds of raw (bulk) materials, almost all of which were imported. The firm had its own well-trained "detail" sales force and distribution network.

The subsidiary had grown rapidly after commencing operations in the mid-1950s and became the largest company in terms of sales in 1966 after overtaking its British rival. Although sales had grown phenomenally, the profit performance of the subsidiary had been relatively poor as measured by profits as a percentage of sales. The first president of the company had stressed sales and volume and had provided the sales force with all the financial benefits and assistance possible. His successor, in an effort to improve profitability, had concentrated on reducing costs.

The country in which the subsidiary was located was typical of many developing nations in that it suffered from severe foreign-exchange problems. Some 80 percent of the foreign exchange available was devoted to the import of food and defense equipment, the remainder being made available for all other imports, including drugs. The amount of foreign exchange available was rationed by industry and by company on a six-month basis. Firms then received permits of X of foreign exchange, which they could use to import materials (not available in the country) in any quantities and in any combination. The permitted amount for each company could vary by significant amounts, but planning beyond a six-month period was almost impossible.

The foreign-exchange limitation made the market for drugs in the country a seller's market. The government kept a close watch on prices, and the pharmaceutical industry was extremely sensitive to arousing public hostility due to pricing, as had been the case in some other developing countries. The task, therefore, was to find a straightforward technique—which did not require sophisticated quantitative skills—that could be used as a guide to maximizing profits.

There are practically no constraints in manufacturing, and a wide range in production quantities of the 98 different products is possible. For the purpose of this problem assume that any product can be dropped if necessary.

Required
The following information was chosen at random. Rank the products in order of desired production and sales effort. Explain your ranking:

	Per Unit of Product		
	A	*B*	*C*
Selling price (in dollar equivalents)	$10.50	$12.00	$8.00
Cost of imported materials	2.00	1.00	1.00
Variable costs of production and selling[a]	2.50	5.00	2.00

[a] Excluding imported materials.

4-27. Utilization of capacity. (CMA, adapted.) Anchor Company manufactures several different styles of jewelry cases. Management estimates that during the third quarter of 19x6 the company will be operating at 80 percent of normal capacity. Because the company desires a higher utilization of plant capacity, it will consider a special order.

Anchor has received special-order inquiries from two companies. The first is from JCP Inc., which would like to market a jewelry case similar to one of Anchor's cases. The JCP jewelry case would be marketed under JCP's own label. JCP Inc. has offered Anchor $5.75 per jewelry case for 20,000 cases to be shipped by October 1, 1976. The cost data for the Anchor jewelry case, which would be similar to the specifications of the JCP special order, are as follows:

Regular selling price per unit	$9.00
Costs per unit:	
Raw materials	$2.50
Direct labor .5 hr @ $6	3.00
Overhead .25 machine-hr @ $4	1.00
Total costs	$6.50

According to the specifications provided by JCP Inc., the special-order case requires less expensive raw materials, which will cost only $2.25 per case. Management has estimated that the remaining costs, labor time, and machine time will be the same as the Anchor jewelry case.

The second special order was submitted by the Krage Co. for 7,500 jewelry cases at $7.50 per case. These cases would be marketed under the Krage label and would have to be shipped by October 1, 19x6. The Krage jewelry case is different from any jewelry case in the Anchor line; its estimated per-unit costs are as follows:

Raw materials	$3.25
Direct labor .5 hr @ $6	3.00
Overhead .5 machine-hr @ $4	2.00
Total costs	$8.25

In addition, Anchor will incur $1,500 in additional set-up costs and will have to purchase a $2,500 special device to manufacture these cases; this device will be discarded once the special order is completed.

The Anchor manufacturing capabilities are limited to the total machine-hours available. The plant capacity under normal operations is 90,000 machine-hours per year or 7,500 machine-hours per month. The budgeted *fixed* overhead for 19x6 amounts to $216,000. All manufacturing overhead costs are applied to production on the basis of machine-hours at $4 per hour.

Anchor will have the entire third quarter to work on the special orders. Management does not expect any repeat sales to be generated from either special order. Company practice precludes Anchor from subcontracting any portion of an order when special orders are not expected to generate repeat sales.

Required

Should Anchor Company accept either special order? Justify your answer and show your calculations. *Hint:* Distinguish between variable and fixed overhead.

4-28. Using available facilities. The Krambo Company manufactures electronic subcomponents that can be sold at the end of Process A or can be processed further in Process B and sold as special parts for a variety of intricate electronic equipment. The entire output of Process A can be sold at a market price of $2 per unit. The output of Process B has been generating a sales price of $5.50 for three years, but the price has recently fallen to $5.10 on assorted orders.

Helen Tobin, the vice-president of marketing, has analyzed the markets and the costs. She thinks that the B output should be dropped whenever its price falls below $4.50 per unit. The total available capacity of A and B is interchangeable, so all facilities should currently be devoted to producing B. She has cited the following data:

Output of A

Selling price, after deducting relevant selling costs		$2.00
Direct materials	$1.00	
Direct labor	.20	
Manufacturing overhead	.60	
Cost per unit		1.80
Operating profit		$ .20

Output of B

Selling price, after deducting relevant selling costs		$5.10
Transferred-in variable cost from A	$1.20	
Additional direct materials	1.50	
Direct labor	.40	
Manufacturing overhead	1.20	
Cost per unit		4.30
Operating profit		$ .80

Direct-materials and direct-labor costs are variable. The total overhead is fixed; it is allocated to units produced by predicting the total overhead for the coming year and dividing this total by the total hours of capacity available.

The total hours of capacity available are 600,000. It takes one hour to make 60 units of A and two hours of additional processing to make 60 units of B.

Required

1. If the price of B for the coming year is going to be $5.10, should A be dropped and all facilities devoted to the production of B? Show computations.

2. Prepare a report for the vice-president of marketing to show the lowest possible price for B that would be acceptable.

3. Suppose that 50 percent of the manufacturing overhead were variable. Repeat Requirements 1 and 2. Do your answers change? If so, how?

4-29. **Review of Chapters 2, 3, 4.** The Smart Co. has the following cost behavior patterns:

Production range in units	0–5,000	5,001–10,000	10,001–15,000	15,001–20,000
Nonvariable costs	$150,000	$220,000	$250,000	$270,000

Maximum production capacity is 20,000 units per year. Variable costs per unit are $30 at all production levels.

Required

Each situation described below is to be considered independently.

1. Production and sales are expected to be 11,000 units for the year. The sales price is $50 per unit. How many additional units need to be sold, in an unrelated market, at $40 per unit to show a total overall net income of $8,000 for the year?

2. The company has orders for 23,000 units at $50. If it desired to make a minimum overall net income of $148,000 on these 23,000 units, what unit purchase price would it be willing to pay a subcontractor for 3,000 units? Assume that the subcontractor would act as Smart's agent, deliver the units to customers directly, and bear all related costs of manufacture, delivery, etc. The customers, however, would pay Smart directly as goods were delivered.

3. Production is currently expected to be 7,000 units for the year at a selling price of $50. By how much may advertising or special promotion costs be increased to bring production up to 14,500 units and still earn a total net income of 4 percent of dollar sales?

4. Net income is currently $125,000. Nonvariable costs are $250,000. However, competitive pressures are mounting. A 5 percent decrease in price will not affect sales volume but will decrease net income by $37,500. What is the present volume, in units? Refer to the original data.

4-30. **Review of Chapters 2, 3, 4.** The Hansen Company is a processor of a Bacardi-mix concentrate. Sales are made principally to liquor distributors throughout the country.

The company's income statements for the past year and the coming year are being analyzed by top management.

HANSEN COMPANY
Income Statements

	For the year 19x1 Just ended		For the year 19x2 Tentative Budget	
Sales 1,500,000 gallons in 19x1		$900,000		$1,000,000
Cost of goods sold:				
Direct material	$450,000		$495,000	
Direct labor	90,000		99,000	
Factory overhead:				
Variable	18,000		19,800	
Fixed	50,000	608,000	50,000	663,800
Gross margin		$292,000		$ 336,200
Selling expenses:				
Variable:				
Sales commissions (based on dollar sales)	$ 45,000		$ 50,000	
Shipping and other	90,000		99,000	
Fixed:				
Salaries, advertising, etc.	110,000		138,000	
Administrative expenses:				
Variable	12,000		13,200	
Fixed	40,000	297,000	40,000	340,200
Net income		$ – 5,000		$ – 4,000

Required

Consider each requirement independently.

Unless otherwise stated, assume that all unit costs of inputs such as material and labor are unchanged. Also, assume that efficiency is unchanged— that is, the labor and quantity of material consumed per unit of output are unchanged. Unless otherwise stated, assume that there are no changes in fixed costs.

1. The president has just returned from a management conference at a local university, where he heard an accounting professor criticize conventional income statements. The professor had asserted that knowledge of cost behavior patterns was of key importance in determining managerial strategies. The president now feels that the income statement should be recast to harmonize with cost-volume-profit analysis—that is, the statement should have three major sections: sales, variable costs, and fixed costs. Using the 19x1 data, prepare such a statement, showing the contribution margin as well as net income.

2. Comment on the changes in each item in the income statement. What are the most likely causes for each increase? For example, have selling prices been changed for 19x2? How do sales commissions fluctuate in relation to units sold or in relation to dollar sales?

3. The president is unimpressed with the 19x2 budget: "We need to take a fresh look in order to begin moving toward profitable operations. Let's tear up the 19x2 budget, concentrate on 19x1 results, and prepare a new comparative 19x2 budget under each of the following assumptions:
   a. A 5 percent average price cut will increase unit sales by 20 percent.
   b. A 5 percent average price increase will decrease unit sales by 10 percent.
   c. A sales commission rate of 10 percent and a $3\frac{1}{3}$ percent price increase will boost unit sales by 10 percent."
   Prepare the budgets for 19x2, using a contribution-margin format and three columns. Assume that there are no changes in fixed costs.

4. The advertising manager maintains that the advertising budget should be increased by $100,000 and that prices should be increased by 10 percent. Resulting unit sales will soar by 25 percent. What would be the expected operating income under such circumstances?

5. A nearby distillery has offered to buy 300,000 gallons in 19x2, if the unit price is low enough. The Hansen Company would not have to incur sales commissions or shipping costs on this special order, and regular business would be undisturbed. Assuming that 19x2's regular operations will be exactly like 19x1's, what unit price should be quoted in order for the Hansen Company to earn an operating income of $5,000 in 19x2?

6. The company chemist wants to add a special ingredient, an exotic flavoring that will add 2¢ per gallon to the Bacardi-mix costs. He also wants to replace the ordinary grenadine now used, which costs 3¢ per gallon of mix, with a more exquisite type costing 4¢ per gallon. Assuming no other changes in cost behavior, how many units must be sold to earn an operating income of $5,000 in 19x2?

CHAPTER 5

Relevant Costs and Special Decisions— Part Two

The key question in relevant cost analysis was introduced and explained in the preceding chapter: What difference does it make? This chapter extends the application of such analysis. The contribution approach is illustrated for make-or-buy decisions and sell-or-process-further decisions. Particular attention is given to the relationships between past and future data, using the decision to replace equipment as an illustration.

MAKE OR BUY

Make or Buy and Idle Facilities

Manufacturers are often confronted with the question of whether to make or buy a product. For example, should we manufacture our own parts and subassemblies or buy them from vendors? The qualitative factors may be of paramount importance. Sometimes the manufacture of parts requires special know-how, unusually skilled labor, rare materials, and the like. The desire to control the quality of parts is often the determining factor in the decision to make them. Then, too, companies hesitate to destroy mutually advantageous long-run relationships by erratic order giving, which results from making parts during slack times and buying them during prosperous times. They may have difficulty in obtaining any parts during boom times, when there are shortages of material and workers and no shortage of sales orders.

What are the quantitative factors relevant to the decision of whether to make or buy? The answer, again, depends on the context. A key factor is whether there are idle facilities. Many companies make parts only when their facilities cannot be used to better advantage.

Assume that the following costs are reported:

B COMPANY
Cost of Making Part No. 900

	Total Cost for 20,000 Units	Cost Per Unit
Direct material	$20,000	$ 1
Direct labor	80,000	4
Variable factory overhead	40,000	2
Fixed factory overhead	80,000	4
Total costs	$220,000	$11

Another manufacturer offers to sell B Company the same part for $10. Should B Company make or buy the part?

Although the $11 unit cost shown above seemingly indicates that the company should buy, the answer is rarely obvious. The key question is the difference in expected future costs as between the alternatives. If the $4 fixed overhead assigned to each unit represents those costs (e.g., depreciation, property taxes, insurance, reapportioned executive salaries) that will continue regardless of the decision, the entire $4 becomes irrelevant.

Again, it is risky to say categorically that only the variable costs are relevant. Perhaps $1 of the fixed costs will be saved if the parts are bought instead of made. For instance, suppose $20,000 is the salary of a supervisor who will be released or transferred to another productive assignment. In other words, fixed costs that may be avoided in the future are relevant.

For the moment, let us assume that the capacity now used to make parts will become idle if the parts are purchased. The relevant computations follow:

	Per Unit		Totals	
	Make	Buy	Make	Buy
Direct material	$1		$ 20,000	
Direct labor	4		80,000	
Variable factory overhead	2		40,000	
Fixed factory overhead that can be avoided by not making (supervisor's salary)	1		20,000	
Total relevant costs	$8	$10	$160,000	$200,000
Difference in favor of making		$2		$40,000

Essence of Make or Buy: Utilization of Facilities

The choice in our example is not really whether to make or buy; it is how best to utilize available facilities. Although the data above indicate that making the part is the better choice, the figures are not conclusive—primarily because we have no idea of what can be done with the manufacturing facilities if the component is bought. Only if the released facilities are to remain idle are the figures above valid.

If the released facilities can be used advantageously in some other manufacturing activity (to produce a contribution to profits of, say, $55,000) or can be rented out (say, for $35,000), these alternatives also may merit consideration. The two courses of action have become four (figures are in thousands):

	Make	Buy and Leave Facilities Idle	Buy and Rent	Buy and Use Facilities for Other Products
Rent revenue	$ —	$ —	$ 35	$ —
Contribution from other products	—	—	—	55
Obtaining of parts	(160)	(200)	(200)	(200)
Net relevant costs	$(160)	$(200)	$(165)	$(145)

The analysis indicates that buying the parts and using the vacated facilities for the production of other products is the alternative that should yield best results in this case.

In sum, the make-or-buy decision should focus on relevant costs in a particular decision context. In all cases, companies should relate make-or-buy decisions to the long-run policies for the use of capacity:

> One company stated that it solicits subcontract work for *other* manufacturers during periods when sales of its own products do not fully utilize the plant, but that such work cannot be carried on regularly without expansion of its plant. The profit margin on subcontracts is not sufficiently large to cover these additional costs and hence work is accepted only when other business is lacking. The same company sometimes meets a period of high volume by *purchasing* parts or having them made by subcontractors. While the cost of such parts is usually higher than the cost to make them in the company's own plant, the additional cost is less than it would be if they were made on equipment which could be used only part of the time.[1]

[1] *The Analysis of Cost-Volume-Profit Relationships,* National Association of Accountants, Research Series No. 17, p. 552.

OPPORTUNITY COSTS

An opportunity cost is the *maximum* available contribution foregone by using limited resources for a particular purpose. It represents a forsaken alternative, so the "cost" differs from the usual kind in the sense that it is not the *outlay cost* that accountants and managers typically encounter and discuss. An outlay cost entails a cash disbursement sooner or later; that is, the outlay-cost idea provides the basis for the typical historical-cost valuations of assets.

Consider a hospital administrator who is trying to decide how to use some space vacated by the pediatrics clinic. He has tabulated three choices in a straightforward way. The numbers favor laboratory testing, which will generate a contribution to income that is $30,000 greater than that of the eye clinic:

	(1) Expand Laboratory Testing	(2) Expand Eye Clinic	(3) Rent to Gift Shop Manager[a]
Expected future revenue	$70,000	$50,000	$4,000
Expected future costs	30,000	40,000	—
Contribution to income	$40,000	$10,000	$4,000

[a] The gift shop is run by an independent retailer who pays the hospital a yearly rental. She wants to expand her present space.

In fact the manager may have a dozen possible uses for that space. Instead of listing all of them, he may pick the *best* (the rental) from among the ten alternatives that he does not want to consider in any detail and incorporate the foregone contribution as a cost of his final two alternatives. Therefore, the foregoing data could also be tabulated as follows, using the notion of opportunity cost:

	(1) Expand Laboratory Testing		(2) Expand Eye Clinic	
Expected future revenue		$70,000		$50,000
Expected future costs:				
Outlay costs	$30,000		$40,000	
Opportunity cost—				
rent foregone	4,000	34,000	4,000	44,000
Contribution to income		$36,000		$ 6,000

The numbers have been analyzed correctly under both tabulations. They show a $30,000 difference in favor of the laboratory and thus answer the key query: What difference does it make? A comparison of the two tabulations shows how the concept of opportunity cost is a practical means of narrowing the number of alternatives under consideration.

Sometimes an individual may want to focus on only two alternatives from the start. For instance, Joan Bickerton, a Certified Public Accountant, may be employed by a large accounting firm at a salary of $35,000 per year. She may want to begin her own independent practice. Her analysis of alternatives follows:

	Independent Practice	Employee
Revenue	$90,000	$35,000
Costs	43,000	—
Net income	$47,000	$35,000

Like many individuals, Bickerton may prefer to tabulate the numerical effects as follows:

		Independent Practice
Revenue		$90,000
Costs:		
Outlay costs	$43,000	
Opportunity cost—		
foregone salary	35,000	78,000
Net income		$12,000

The correct key difference, $12,000, will be generated by either tabulation. Some accountants and managers regard the opportunity-cost format of the second tabulation as being more confusing than the straightforward presentation of the first tabulation. Choose either approach. *The choice is a matter of taste.* Obviously, if the choice is framed as in the second tabulation (entering practice versus not entering), the failure to recognize an opportunity cost will misstate the difference between alternatives.

Note that opportunity costs are seldom incorporated in formal accounting systems, particularly for external reporting. Such costs represent incomes foregone by rejecting alternatives; therefore, opportunity costs do not involve cash receipts or outlays. Accountants usually confine their recording to those events that ultimately involve exchanges of assets. Accountants confine their history to alternatives selected rather than those rejected, primarily because of the impracticality or impossibility of accumulating meaningful data on what might have been.

JOINT PRODUCT COSTS
AND INCREMENTAL COSTS

Danger of Allocation

Joint product cost is the term most often used to describe the costs of manufactured goods that are produced by a single process and that are not identifiable as different individual products until after a certain stage of production known as the split-off point. Examples include chemicals, lumber, petroleum products, flour milling, copper mining, meat packing, leather tanning, soap making, and gas manufacturing. A meat-packing company cannot kill a sirloin steak; it has to slaughter a steer, which supplies various cuts of dressed meat, hides, and trimmings.

Joint product costs are the costs of a single process, or a series of processes, that simultaneously produces two or more products of significant sales value. There are many elaborate schemes for assigning these joint costs to the various products. Most are based on the relative sales value of the products. But managers need not be overly concerned with how various joint products are costed for inventory purposes.

No technique for allocating joint product costs is applicable to decisions of whether a product should be sold at the split-off point or processed further. When a product results from a joint process, the decision to process further is not influenced either by the size of the joint costs or the portion of the joint costs that is assigned to the particular product. Joint costs are irrelevant to these decisions.

Suppose that a company produces two chemical products, X and Y, as a result of a particular joint process. Both products are sold to the petroleum industry to be used as ingredients of gasoline. Data are given in Exhibit 5-1.

The 500,000 liters of Y can be processed further and sold to the plastics industry as Product YA, an ingredient for plastic sheeting, at an additional cost of 8¢ per liter for manufacturing and distribution. The net sales price of YA would be 16¢ per liter.

EXHIBIT 5-1

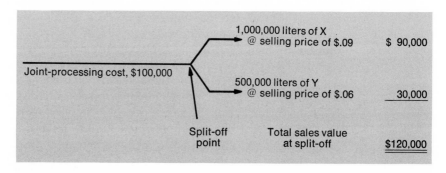

1,000,000 liters of X @ selling price of $.09		$ 90,000
Joint-processing cost, $100,000		
500,000 liters of Y @ selling price of $.06		30,000
Split-off point	Total sales value at split-off	$120,000

EXHIBIT 5-2

	SELL AT SPLIT-OFF AS Y	PROCESS FURTHER AS YA	DIFFERENCE
Revenue	$30,000	$80,000	$50,000
Separable costs beyond split-off, @ $.08	—	40,000	40,000
Income effects	$30,000	$40,000	$10,000

Product X will be sold at the split-off point, but management is undecided about Product Y. Should Y be sold or should it be processed into YA? The joint costs must be incurred to reach the split-off point, so they do not differ among alternatives and are completely irrelevant to the question of whether to sell or process further.[2] The only approach that will yield valid results is to concentrate on the separable costs and revenue *beyond* split-off, as shown in Exhibit 5-2.

Separable cost is defined as any cost that is directly identifiable with a particular cost objective such as a department or process; that is, the cost is exclusively related to the process and not common to two or more processes. A **common cost** was defined in the preceding chapter as a cost of facilities and services that are shared by user departments.

Briefly, it is profitable to extend processing or to incur additional distribution costs on a joint product if the difference in revenue exceeds the difference in expenses (including the cost of capital, which will be discussed in Chapter 12).

For decisions regarding whether to sell or process further, the most straightforward analysis is as shown in Exhibit 5-2. Alternatively, an opportunity-cost format would be:

		Process Further
Revenue		$80,000
Outlay cost: separable cost beyond split-off, @ $.08	$40,000	
Opportunity cost: net realizable value of Y at split-off	30,000	70,000
Income effects		$10,000

[2] For such decisions, joint cost allocations should be ignored. They are useful for inventory costing purposes *only*. Not only are they irrelevant, they may be downright misleading. Two conventional ways are widely used: physical weights such as liters and net realizable value. Costing per liters would show allocated joint cost of $.06667 per liter ($100,000 ÷ 1,500,000 liters). This would erroneously indicate that Product Y is a loss product. Costing by net realizable value (relative sales value) would show a profit for both products at split-off. Product X would bear $75,000 of the joint cost ($90,000/$120,000 × $100,000), and Product Y, $25,000 (which is $30,000/$120,000 × $100,000). Clearly, the indicated profitability of the individual products depends on the method used for allocating a joint cost that is unallocable by its nature: Product X cannot be obtained without obtaining Product Y, and vice versa.

This format merely is a different way of recognizing another alternative (sell Y at split-off) when considering the decision to process further individually. When they are properly analyzed, decision alternatives may be compared by either excluding the idea of opportunity costs altogether, as Exhibit 5-2 shows, or by encompassing opportunity costs, as is shown here. The key difference, $10,000, is generated either way.

Incremental or Differential Costs

Two important points deserve mentioning here. First, the allocation of joint costs would not affect the decision, as Exhibit 5-3 demonstrates. The joint costs are not allocated in the exhibit, but no matter how they might be allocated, the total income effects would be unchanged.

EXHIBIT 5-3
Firm as a Whole

	ALTERNATIVE ONE			ALTERNATIVE TWO			INCREMENTAL OR DIFFERENTIAL
	X	Y	TOTAL	X	YA	TOTAL	
Revenue	$90,000	$30,000	$120,000	$90,000	$80,000	$170,000	$50,000
Joint costs			$100,000		—	$100,000	—
Separable costs			—		40,000	40,000	40,000
Total costs			$100,000			$140,000	$40,000
Income effects			$ 20,000			$ 30,000	$10,000

Second, the title of the last column in Exhibit 5-3 contains terms that are frequently encountered in cost analysis for special decisions. **Incremental costs** (sometimes called **differential costs**) are, in any given situation, the difference between the total costs of each alternative. In this situation, the *incremental revenue* is $50,000, the *incremental cost* is $40,000, and the *incremental income* is $10,000. Each is the difference between the corresponding items under the alternatives being considered. In an analysis that showed only the differences, called an **incremental analysis,** only column 3 would be shown. In a **total analysis** all three sets of columns are shown. The choice of an incremental or a total analysis is a matter of individual preference.

IRRELEVANCE OF PAST COSTS

As defined early in Chapter 4, a relevant cost is (a) an expected future cost that will (b) differ among alternatives. The contribution aspect of relevant-cost analysis has shown that those expected future costs that will not differ are irrelevant to choosing among alternatives. Now we return to the idea that all past costs are also irrelevant to such decisions.

Obsolete Inventory

A company has 100 obsolete missile parts that are carried in inventory at a manufacturing cost of $100,000. The parts can be: (1) remachined for $30,000, and then sold for $50,000; or (2) scrapped for $5,000. Which should be done?

This is an unfortunate situation; yet the $100,000 cost is irrelevant to the decision to remachine or scrap. The only relevant factors are the expected future revenue and costs:

	Remachine	Scrap	Difference
Expected future revenue	$ 50,000	$ 5,000	$45,000
Expected future costs	30,000	—	30,000
Relevant excess of revenue over costs	$ 20,000	$ 5,000	$15,000
Accumulated historical inventory costs[a]	100,000	100,000	—
Net overall loss on project	$(80,000)	$(95,000)	$15,000

[a] Irrelevant because it is not an element of difference as between the alternatives.

We could completely ignore the historical cost and still arrive at the $15,000 difference, the key figure in the analysis.

Book Value of Old Equipment

For now, we shall not consider all aspects of equipment-replacement decisions, but we shall turn to one that is widely misunderstood—the role of the book value of the old equipment. **Book value** is defined here as the original (historical) acquisition cost of a fixed asset less its accumulated depreciation. Suppose that an old machine has four years of useful life remaining, originally cost $10,000, has accumulated depreciation of $6,000, and thus has a book value of $4,000. It can be sold for $2,500 cash now, but it will have no disposal value at the end of the four years. A new machine, which (to simplify the analysis) will also have a useful life of four years, is available for $6,000. The new machine will reduce cash operating costs (maintenance, power, repairs, coolants, and the like) from $5,000 to $3,000 annually, but it will have no disposal value at the end of four years. Prepare a comparative analysis of the two alternatives.

Before making such an analysis, we consider some important concepts. The most widely misunderstood facet of replacement analysis is the role of the book value of the old equipment in the decision. The book value, in this context, is sometimes called a **sunk cost,** which is really just another term for historical or past cost. All historical costs are always irrelevant to choosing among alternative courses of action. Therefore the book value of the old equipment is always irrelevant to replacement decisions. At one time or another, we all like to think that we can soothe our wounded pride arising from having made a bad purchase decision by using the item instead of replacing it. The fallacy here is in erroneously thinking that a current or future action can influence the long-run impact of a past outlay. All past costs are down the drain. *Nothing* can change what has already happened.

We can apply our definition of decision relevance to four commonly encountered items:

1. *Book value of old equipment.* Irrelevant, because it is a past (historical) cost. Therefore, depreciation on old equipment is irrelevant.

2. *Disposal value of old equipment.* Relevant (ordinarily), because it is an expected future inflow that usually differs among alternatives.

3. *Gain or loss on disposal.* This is the algebraic difference between 1 and 2. It is therefore a meaningless combination of book value, which is always irrelevant, and disposal value, which is usually relevant. The combination form, *loss* (or *gain*) *on disposal,* blurs the distinction between the irrelevant book value and the relevant disposal value. Consequently, it is best to think of each separately.[3]

4. *Cost of new equipment.* Relevant, because it is an expected future outflow that will differ among alternatives. Therefore, depreciation on new equipment is relevant.

Exhibit 5-4 should clarify the above assertions. It deserves close study. Book value of old equipment is irrelevant regardless of the decision-making technique used. The "difference" columns in Exhibit 5-4 show that the $4,000 book value of the old equipment is not an element of difference between alternatives and could be completely ignored without changing the $1,125 difference in average annual net income. No matter what the *timing* of the charge against revenue, the *amount* charged is still $4,000, regardless of any available alternative. In either event, the undepreciated cost will be written off with the same ultimate effect on profit.[4] The $4,000 creeps into the income

[3] For simplicity, we ignore income tax considerations and the effects of the interest value of money in this chapter. But book value is irrelevant even if income taxes are considered, because the relevant item is then the tax cash flow, not the book value. Using the approach in Exhibit 4-1, the book value is essential information for the *prediction method* (step 2), but the expected future income tax cash outflows are the relevant information for the *decision model* (step 3). The prediction method would be: Disposal value, $2,500 − Book value, $4,000 = Loss on disposal, $1,500. If the income tax rate is 50 percent, the income tax cash saving would be $750. This $750 would be the expected future cash flow that is relevant input to the decision model. For elaboration, see Chapter 13.

[4] We are deliberately ignoring income tax factors for the time being. If income taxes are considered, the *timing* of the writing off of fixed-asset costs may influence income tax payments. In this example, there will be a small real difference: the present value of $40,000 as a tax deduction now versus the present value of a $10,000 tax deduction each year for four years. But this difference in *future* income tax flows is the *relevant* item—not the book value of the old fixed asset per se. See Chapter 13.

4000 is irrelevant

	FOUR YEARS TOGETHER			ANNUALIZED (DIVIDED BY 4)		
	KEEP	REPLACE	DIFFERENCE	KEEP	REPLACE	DIFFERENCE
Cash operating costs	$20,000	$12,000	$8,000	$5,000	$3,000	$2,000
Old equipment (book value):						
Periodic write-off as depreciation	4,000	—	—	1,000	—	—
or						
Lump-sum write-off		4,000ᵃ	—	—	1,000	—
Disposal value	—	−2,500ᵃ	2,500	—	−625	625
New machine, written off periodically as						
depreciation	—	6,000	−6,000	—	1,500	−1,500
Total costs	$24,000	$19,500	$4,500	$6,000	$4,875	$1,125

ᵃ In a formal income statement, these two items would be combined as "loss on disposal" of $1,500.

statement either as a $4,000 offset against the $2,500 proceeds to obtain the $1,500 *loss on disposal* in one year, or as $1,000 depreciation in each of four years. But how it appears is irrelevant to the replacement decision. In contrast, the $1,500 annual depreciation on the new equipment *is* relevant because the total $6,000 depreciation is a future cost that may be avoided by not replacing.

The advantage of replacement is $4,500 for the four years together; the average annual advantage is $1,125.

Examining Alternatives Over the Long Run

The foregoing is the first example that has looked beyond one year. A useful technique is to view the alternatives over their entire lives and then to compute annual average results. In this way, peculiar nonrecurring items (such as loss on disposal) will not obstruct the long-run view that must necessarily be taken in almost all special managerial decisions.

Exhibit 5-5 concentrates on relevant items only. Note that the same answer (the $4,500 net difference) will be produced even though the book value is completely omitted from the calculations. The only relevant items are the cash operating costs, the disposal value of the old equipment, and the depreciation on the new equipment. To demonstrate that the amount of the book value will not affect the answer, suppose the book value of the old equipment is $500,000 rather than $4,000. Your final answer will not be changed. The cumulative advantage of replacement will still be $4,500. (If you are in doubt, rework this example, using $500,000 as the book value.)

123

EXHIBIT 5-5

Cost Comparison—Replacement of Equipment,
Relevant Items Only

	FOUR YEARS TOGETHER			ANNUALIZED (DIVIDED BY 4)		
	KEEP	REPLACE	DIFFERENCE	KEEP	REPLACE	DIFFERENCE
Cash operating costs	$20,000	$12,000	$8,000	$5,000	$3,000	$2,000
Disposal value of old equipment	—	−2,500	2,500	—	−625	625
Depreciation—new equipment	—	6,000	−6,000	—	1,500	−1,500
Total relevant costs	$20,000	$15,500	$4,500	$5,000	$3,875	$1,125

MOTIVATION AND CONFLICT OF MODELS

Influence of Loss

Reconsider Exhibit 4-1 in conjunction with our illustration of equipment replacement. If the decision model says that the comparison should be on the total change in costs over the four years, as was assumed in our analysis, the choice would be to replace. Would the manager use that decision model? The answer might depend on how his or her performance was being evaluated. Conflict arises when managers are told to use one model for decision making, and their performance is then evaluated via a performance evaluation model that is inconsistent with the decision model. In this instance, if the manager's performance were to be evaluated by the typical accrual accounting model, a loss of $1,500 on the disposal of the old equipment would appear for the first year under the "replace" choice, but not under the "keep" choice.

Note the motivational factors here. A manager may be reluctant to replace simply because the large loss on disposal would severely harm his reported profit performance in the first year. Many managers and accountants would not replace the old machine because it would entail recognizing the $1,500 "loss on disposal," whereas retention would allow spreading the $4,000 book value over four years in the form of "depreciation expense" (a more appealing term than "loss on disposal"). This demonstrates how overemphasis on short-run income may conflict with the objective of maximizing income over the long run, especially if managers are transferred periodically to different responsibilities.

Distinguishing between Decisions

Review Exhibit 4-1. Step 4, the evaluation of performance, is the means of gathering feedback on one decision (Decision A) that often sharpens the

124

predictions of a second decision (Decision B). Feedback on Decision A helps Decision B, feedback on B helps Decision C, and so forth. Thus, the feedback provided by the evaluation of performance is a major way of improving decisions. However, the financial impact of Decision B should not be mingled with the financial impact of Decision A. The analysis of relevant data should not mix the evaluation of Decision A with the steps of Decision B. For example, Decision B should not be forced to bear any "loss" already suffered by Decision A.

The equipment illustration demonstrates that the blunders of a Decision A should not become inputs to the decision model for a Decision B. In this example, having the loss from Decision A (the old decision to buy the existing equipment) affect the measurement of year one's performance for Decision B (replacing) would be faulty thinking. That is, Decisions A and B should be analyzed separately. The analytical difficulties are imposing, because the performance evaluation model (which is based on the typical accrual accounting model) does not ordinarily distinguish various special decisions. Instead, these decisions become mixed together, sometimes in ways that may lead to the wrong choice when Decision B is made.

How are Decisions A and B related? In equipment-replacement decisions, the feedback regarding Decision A may easily affect the predictions concerning Decision B. For instance, if existing equipment was supposed to last ten years, and it only lasted six, how credible is the new prediction that the proposed equipment will last, say, four years? Thus, the evaluation of the performance of past decisions provides vital feedback that should improve later decisions.

Reconciling the Models

The conflict between decision models and performance evaluation models just described is a pervasive problem in practice. Unfortunately, there are no easy solutions. In theory, the synchronization of these models seems obvious. Merely design a performance evaluation model that harmonizes exactly with the decision model. In our equipment example, this would mean predicting year-by-year income effects over the planning horizon of four years, noting that the first year would be poor, and following up accordingly.

The trouble is that systems rarely accommodate each decision in this fashion, one at a time. Consequently, the results of a single decision are encompassed along with many other decisions in an overall performance report. In such cases, the manager may predict the first-year effects and be inhibited from taking the longer view that may be preferable in the eyes of top management.

This one-year-at-a-time approach is especially prevalent in many not-for-profit organizations, where budgets are approved on a year-to-year basis and the use of feedback is not well developed. Occasionally, managers will be tempted to underestimate costs in order to obtain initial approval and then come back year after year for supplementary amounts that were not provided for in the original budget request. Moreover, through the years many colleges and universities have accepted donations for new facilities such as buildings and research equipment without providing sufficiently for lifelong maintenance and repairs. There is a danger that the value of such resources will be exceeded by the costs of operating them.

IRRELEVANCE OF FUTURE COSTS THAT WILL NOT DIFFER

The past costs in the preceding two examples were not an element of difference among the alternatives. As noted, the $100,000 inventory and the $4,000 book value were included under both alternatives and were irrelevant because they were the same for each alternative under consideration.

There are also expected *future* costs that may be irrelevant because they will be the same under all feasible alternatives. These, too, may be safely ignored for a particular decision. The salaries of many members of top management are illustrations of expected future costs that will not be affected by the decision at hand.

Other examples include many fixed costs that will be unaffected by such considerations as whether Machine A or Machine B is selected, or whether a special order is accepted. However, it is not merely a case of saying that fixed costs are irrelevant and variable costs are relevant. Variable costs can be irrelevant. For instance, sales commissions might be paid on an order regardless of whether the order is filled from Plant A or Plant B. Variable costs are irrelevant whenever they do not differ among the alternatives at hand. Our preceding example showed that fixed costs (cost of new equipment) can be relevant. Fixed costs are relevant whenever they differ under the alternatives at hand.

BEWARE OF UNIT COSTS

The pricing illustration in the preceding chapter showed that unit costs should be analyzed with care in decision making. There are two major ways to go wrong: (a) the inclusion of irrelevant costs, such as the $3 allocation of unavoidable fixed costs in the make-or-buy example that would result in a unit cost of $11 instead of the relevant unit cost of $8; and (b) comparisons of unit costs not computed on the same volume basis, as the following example demonstrates. Generally, it is advisable to use total costs rather than unit costs. Then, if desired, the totals may be unitized. Machinery salesmen, for example, often brag about the low unit costs of using the new machines.

Sometimes they neglect to point out that the unit costs are based on outputs far in excess of the volume of activity of their prospective customer.

Assume that a new $100,000 machine with a five-year life can produce 100,000 units a year at a variable cost of $1 per unit, as opposed to a variable cost per unit of $1.50 with an old machine. Is the new machine a worthwhile acquisition?

It is attractive at first glance. If the customer produces 100,000 units, unit-cost comparisons are valid, provided that new depreciation is also considered. Assume that the disposal value of the old equipment is zero. Because depreciation is an allocation of historical cost, the depreciation on the old machine is irrelevant. In contrast, the depreciation on the new machine is relevant, because the new machine entails a future cost that can be avoided by not acquiring it:

	Old Machine	New Machine
Units	100,000	100,000
Variable costs	$150,000	$100,000
Straight-line depreciation	—	20,000
Total relevant costs	$150,000	$120,000
Unit relevant costs	$ 1.50	$ 1.20

However, if the customer's expected volume is only 30,000 units a year, the unit costs change:

	Old Machine	New Machine
Units	30,000	30,000
Variable costs	$45,000	$30,000
Straight-line depreciation	—	20,000
Total relevant costs	$45,000	$50,000
Unit relevant costs	$ 1.50	$1.6667

DECISION MODELS AND UNCERTAINTY

The decision models illustrated in this and the preceding chapter employed accrual accounting models, whereby the effects on net income under various alternatives were compared and the alternative with the best income effect was chosen. Other decision models are discussed in later chapters. (For example, Chapters 12 and 13 cover discounted-cash-flow models for equipment-replacement decisions. Many readers may prefer to jump directly to Chapters 12 and 13 immediately after completing their study of this chapter. This can be done without breaking continuity.)

It is vitally important to recognize that throughout this and other chapters, dollar amounts of future sales and operating costs are assumed to be known with certainty in order to highlight and to simplify various important points. In practice, the forecasting of these key figures is generally the most difficult aspect of decision analysis. For elaboration, see Chapter 16, which explores the implications of uncertainty in decision contexts.

SUMMARY

Relevant-cost analysis, which makes heavy use of the contribution approach, concentrates on expected future data that will differ among alternatives. As Exhibit 4-1 shows, clear distinctions should be made between past data, which may be helpful in formulating predictions, and the predicted data that are the inputs to decision models.

Highlights of this approach are (1) each cost used must be an expected *future* cost, and (2) it must be an element of *difference* among the alternatives. All *past* (*historical* or *sunk*) costs are in themselves irrelevant to any decision about the future, although they often provide the best available basis for the prediction of expected future data.

The combination of the relevant-costing and contribution approaches is a fundamental framework, based on economic analysis, that may be applied to a vast range of problems. The following are among the more important generalizations regarding various decisions:

1. Make-or-buy decisions are, fundamentally, examples of obtaining the most profitable utilization of given facilities.
2. Sometimes the notion of an opportunity cost is helpful in cost analysis. An opportunity cost is the maximum sacrifice in rejecting an alternative; it is the maximum earning that might have been obtained if the productive good, service, or capacity had been applied to some alternative use. The opportunity-cost approach does not affect the important final differences between the courses of action, but the format of the analysis differs.
3. Joint product costs are irrelevant in decisions about whether to sell at split-off or process further.
4. Incremental costs or differential costs are the differences in the total costs under each alternative.
5. The book value of old equipment is always irrelevant in replacement decisions. This cost is often called a *sunk cost*. Disposal value, however, is generally relevant.
6. Generally, it is advisable to use total costs, rather than unit costs, in cost analysis.
7. Managers are often motivated to reject desirable economic decisions because of a conflict between the measures used in the decision model and the performance evaluation model.

SUMMARY PROBLEM FOR YOUR REVIEW

Problem

Exhibit 5-6 contains data for the Block Company for the year just ended. The company makes parts that are used in the final assembly of its finished product.

EXHIBIT 5-6

	A + B COMPANY AS A WHOLE	A FINISHED PRODUCT[a]	B PARTS
Sales: 100,000 units, @ $100	$10,000,000		
Variable costs:			
Direct material	$ 4,900,000	$4,400,000	$ 500,000
Direct labor	700,000	400,000	300,000
Variable factory overhead	300,000	100,000	200,000
Other variable costs	100,000	100,000	—
Sales commissions, @ 10%			
of sales	1,000,000	1,000,000	—
Total variable costs	$ 7,000,000	$6,000,000	$1,000,000
Contribution margin	$ 3,000,000		
Separable fixed costs	$ 2,300,000	$1,900,000	$ 400,000
Common fixed costs	400,000	320,000	80,000
Total fixed costs	$ 2,700,000	$2,220,000	$ 480,000
Operating income	$ 300,000		

[a]Not including the cost of parts (column B).

Required

1. During the year, a prospective customer in an unrelated market offered $82,000 for 1,000 finished units. The latter would be in addition to the 100,000 units sold. The regular sales commission rate would have been paid. The president rejected the order because "it was below our costs of $97 per unit." What would operating income have been if the order had been accepted?

2. A supplier offered to manufacture the year's supply of 100,000 parts for $13.50 each. What would be the effect on operating income if the Block Company purchased rather than made the parts? Assume that $350,000 of the separable fixed costs assigned to parts would have been avoided if the parts were purchased.

3. The company could have purchased the parts for $13.50 each and used the vacated space for the manufacture of a deluxe version of their major product. Assume that 20,000 deluxe units could have been made (and sold in addition to the 100,000 regular units) at a unit variable cost of $70, exclusive of parts and exclusive of the 10 percent sales commission. The sales price would have been $110. All of the fixed costs pertaining to the parts would have continued, because these costs related primarily to the

129

manufacturing facilities utilized. What would operating income have been if Block had bought the necessary parts and made and sold the deluxe units?

Solution

1. Costs of filling special order:

Direct material	$49,000
Direct labor	7,000
Variable factory overhead	3,000
Other variable costs	1,000
Sales commission, @ 10% of $82,000	8,200
Total variable costs	$68,200
Selling price	82,000
Contribution margin	$13,800

Net income would have been $300,000 + $13,800, or $313,800, if the order had been accepted. In a sense, the decision to reject the offer implies that the Block Company is willing to invest $13,800 in immediate gains foregone (an opportunity cost) in order to preserve the long-run selling-price structure.

2. Assuming that $350,000 of the fixed costs could have been avoided by not making the parts and that the other fixed costs would have been continued, the alternatives can be summarized as follows:

	Make	Buy
Purchase cost		$1,350,000
Variable costs	$1,000,000	
Avoidable fixed costs	350,000	
Total relevant costs	$1,350,000	$1,350,000

If the facilities used for parts were to become idle, the Block Company would be indifferent as to whether to make or buy. Operating income would be unaffected.

3.
Sales would increase by 20,000 units, @ $110		$2,200,000
Variable costs exclusive of parts would increase by 20,000 units, @ $70	$1,400,000	
Plus the sales commission, 10% of $2,200,000	220,000	1,620,000
Contribution margin on 20,000 units		$ 580,000
Parts: 120,000 rather than 100,000 would be needed		
Buy 120,000, @ $13.50	$1,620,000	
Make 100,000, @ $10 (only the variable costs are relevant)	1,000,000	
Excess cost of outside purchase		620,000
Fixed costs, unchanged		—
Disadvantage of making deluxe units		$ (40,000)

Operating income would decline to $260,000 ($300,000 − $40,000, the disadvantage of selling the deluxe units). The deluxe units bring in a contribution margin of $580,000, but the additional costs of buying rather than making parts is $620,000, leading to a net disadvantage of $40,000.

ASSIGNMENT MATERIAL

Fundamental Assignment Material

5-1. Terminology. Define: *sunk cost; historical cost; joint product costs; incremental cost; differential cost; and opportunity cost.*

5-2. Role of old equipment in replacement. On January 2, 19x1, the Buxton Company installed a brand-new $81,000 special molding machine for producing a new product. The product and the machine have an expected life of three years. The machine's expected disposal value at the end of three years is zero.

On January 3, 19x1, Jim Swain, a star salesman for a machine tool manufacturer, tells Mr. Buxton: "I wish I had known earlier of your purchase plans. I can supply you with a technically superior machine for $100,000. The old machine can be sold for $16,000. I guarantee that our machine will save $35,000 per year in cash operating costs, although it too will have no disposal value at the end of three years."

Mr. Buxton examines some technical data. Although he had confidence in Swain's claims, Buxton contends: "I'm locked in now. My alternatives are clear: (a) disposal will result in a loss; (b) keeping and using the 'old' equipment avoids such a loss. I have brains enough to avoid a loss when my other alternative is recognizing a loss. We've got to use that equipment till we get our money out of it."

The annual operating costs of the old machine are expected to be $60,000, exclusive of depreciation. Sales, all in cash, will be $900,000 per year. Other annual cash expenses will be $800,000 regardless of this decision. Assume that the equipment in question is the company's only fixed asset. Note that the facts in this problem are probed more deeply in Problems 12-25 and 13-24.

Required

Ignore income taxes and the time value of money.

1. Prepare statements of cash receipts and disbursements as they would appear in each of the next three years under both alternatives. What is the total net difference in cash flow for the three years?

2. Prepare income statements as they would appear in each of the next three years under both alternatives. Assume straight-line depreciation. What is the total difference in net income for the three years?

3. Assume that the cost of the "old" equipment was $1,000,000 rather than $81,000. Would the net difference computed in Requirements 1 and 2 change? Explain.

4. As Jim Swain, reply to Buxton's contentions.

5. What are the irrelevant items in each of your presentations for Requirement 1 and 2? Why are they irrelevant?

5-3. Decision and performance models. Refer to the preceding problem.

1. Suppose the "decision model" favored by top management consisted of a comparison of a three-year accumulation of wealth under each alternative. Which alternative would you choose? Why?

2. Suppose the "performance evaluation model" emphasized the net income of a subunit (such as a division) each year rather than considering each project, one by one. Which alternative would you choose? Why?

3. Suppose the same quantitative data existed, but the "enterprise" was a post office of the United States Postal Service. Would your answers to the first two parts change? Why?

Additional Assignment Material

5-4. Which of the following items are relevant in replacement decisions? Explain.
   a. Book value of old equipment.
   b. Disposal value of old equipment.
   c. Cost of new equipment.

5-5. "No technique applicable to the problem of joint product costing should be used for management decisions regarding whether a product should be sold at the split-off point or processed further." Explain. Do you agree?

5-6. "Incremental cost is the addition to costs from the manufacture of one unit." Do you agree? Explain.

5-7. "I had a chance to rent my summer cottage for two weeks for $150. But I chose to have it idle. I didn't want strangers living in my summer house." What term in this chapter describes the $150? Why?

5-8. There are two major reasons why unit costs should be analyzed with care in decision making. What are they?

5-9. "Accountants do not formally record opportunity costs in the accounting records." Why?

5-10. Distinguish between an opportunity cost and an outlay cost.

5-11. Distinguish between an incremental cost and a differential cost.

5-12. "Past costs are indeed relevant in most instances, because they provide the point of departure for the entire decision process." Do you agree? Why?

5-13. Relevant investment. Tom Thorp had obtained a new truck with a list price, including options, of $10,000. The dealer had given him a "generous trade-in allowance" of $3,000 on his old truck that had a wholesale price of $2,000. Sales tax was $600.

The annual cash operating costs of the old truck were $3,000. The new truck was expected to reduce these costs by one-third.

Required Compute the original investment in the new truck. Explain your reasoning.

5-14. Weak division. (S. Goodman.) The Goodman Company paid $5 million in cash four years ago to acquire a company manufacturing magnetic tape drives. This company has been operated as a division of Goodman and has lost $500,000 each year since its acquisition.

The outlook for this division is: (a) it should break even this year and the next; and (b) two years from now, when a new product is fully developed, it should return a net profit of $500,000 per year for the foreseeable future.

Recently, the Apex Corporation offered to purchase the division from Goodman for $3 million. The president of Goodman commented, "I've got an investment of $7 million to recoup ($5 million plus losses of $500,000 for each of four years). I have finally got this situation turned around, so I oppose selling the division now."

Prepare a response to the president's remarks. Indicate how to make this decision. Be as specific as possible.

5-15. Opportunity cost. Francine Abrams, M.D., is a psychiatrist who is in heavy demand. Even though she has raised her fees considerably during the past five years, Dr. Abrams still cannot accommodate all the patients who wish to see her.

Abrams has conducted six hours of appointments a day, six days a week, for 48 weeks a year. Her fee averages $130 per hour.

Her variable costs are negligible and may be ignored for decision purposes. Ignore income taxes.

Required

1. Abrams is weary of working a six-day week. She is considering taking every other Saturday off. What would be her annual income (a) if she worked every Saturday and (b) if she worked every other Saturday?

2. What would be her opportunity cost for the year of not working every other Saturday?

3. Assume that Dr. Abrams has definitely decided to take every other Saturday off. She loves to repair her sports car by doing the work herself. If she works on her car during half a Saturday when she otherwise would not see patients, what is her opportunity cost?

5-16. Hospital opportunity cost. The University Hospital has some extra space that has been idle for some time because of the declining birth rates in the area. Alice Zaloff, the chief administrator, has been considering several alternatives:

a. Use the space for a new diagnostic laboratory for conducting tests that have been sent to outside laboratories until now.

b. Rent the space to an outside contractor who wants to expand the gift shop space already being leased from the hospital.

c. Do nothing because other demands for space are bound to arise later.

The outside laboratory tests in question amount to 3,000 per year at an average cost to the hospital of $60 each. The administrator predicts that the same tests could

133

be conducted internally for $110,000 per year, including the cost of technicians and depreciation on new equipment, which would have a useful life of three years with zero residual value.

The gift shop operator has offered a three-year agreement that would provide the hospital with $60,000 in yearly rent.

Required

Prepare a tabulation of the total relevant costs of the decision alternatives, omitting the concept of opportunity costs in one tabulation and using it in the second tabulation. As the administrator, which tabulation would you prefer to get if you could only receive one?

5-17. Hotel rooms and opportunity costs. The Remson Corporation owns many hotels throughout the world. Its Los Angeles hotel, located in the center of the city, is anticipating hard times because of the opening of several new competing hotels.

Gala Tours has offered Remson a contract for the coming year that provides for a minimum fee of $400,000 in return for a guarantee of having 100 rooms available for Gala's tourists on 200 specified nights, including all the peak nights of the hotel season. For example, Gala would have 100 rooms available during the New Year season, when football fans fill all available rooms in the downtown area at an average expected rate of $60 per room for the 100 rooms in question.

Required

Suppose the Gala offer is accepted. What is the opportunity cost of the 100 rooms to Remson on December 31? On January 28, when only 30 rooms would be expected to be rented at an average rate of $40? If the year-round rate per room averaged $50, what percentage of occupancy of the 100 rooms in question would have to be rented for the 200 days to make Remson indifferent about accepting the Gala offer?

5-18. Opportunity cost. (CMA, adapted.) George Jackson operates a small machine shop. He manufactures one standard product available from many other similar businesses and he also manufactures products to customer order. His accountant prepared the annual income statement shown below:

	Custom Sales	Standard Sales	Total
Sales	$50,000	$25,000	$75,000
Material	$10,000	$ 8,000	$18,000
Labor	20,000	9,000	29,000
Depreciation	6,300	3,600	9,900
Power	700	400	1,100
Rent	6,000	1,000	7,000
Heat and light	600	100	700
Other	400	900	1,300
Total expenses	$44,000	$23,000	$67,000
Net income	$ 6,000	$ 2,000	$ 8,000

The depreciation charges are for machines used in the respective product lines. The power charge is apportioned on the estimate of power consumed. The rent is for the building space, which has been leased for ten years at $7,000 per year. The rent and heat and light are apportioned to the product lines based on amount of floor space occupied. All other costs are current expenses identified with the product line causing them.

A valued custom-parts customer has asked Mr. Jackson if he would manufacture 5,000 special units for him. Mr. Jackson is working at capacity and would have to give up some other business in order to take this business. He can't cancel custom orders already agreed to, but he could reduce the output of his standard product about one-half for one year while producing the specially requested custom part. The customer is willing to pay $7 for each part. The material cost will be about $2 per unit and the labor $3.60 per unit. Mr. Jackson will have to spend $2,000 for a special device, which will be discarded when the job is done.

Required

1. Calculate and present the following costs related to the 5,000-unit custom order:
   a. The incremental cost of the order.
   b. The full cost of the order.
   c. The opportunity cost of taking the order.
2. Should Mr. Jackson take the order? Explain your answer.

5-19. Conceptual approach. A large automobile-parts plant was constructed four years ago in an Ohio city served by two railroads. The PC Railroad purchased forty specialized 60-foot freight cars as a direct result of the additional traffic generated by the new plant. The investment was based on an estimated useful life of twenty years.

Now the competing railroad has offered to service the plant with new 86-foot freight cars, which would enable more efficient shipping operations at the plant. The automobile company has threatened to switch carriers unless PC Railroad buys ten new 86-foot freight cars.

The PC marketing management wants to buy the new cars, but PC operating management says: "The new investment is undesirable. It really consists of the new outlay plus the loss on the old freight cars. The old cars must be written down to a low salvage value if they cannot be used as originally intended."

Required

Evaluate the comments. What is the correct conceptual approach to the quantitative analysis in this decision?

5-20. Meaning of allocation of joint costs.

1. Examine the illustration on joint costs that appears in this chapter. Suppose the joint costs were allocated on the basis of liters. Prepare an income statement by product line on the assumption that Product Y was (a) sold at split-off, or (b) processed further.
2. Repeat Requirement 1, assuming that the joint costs were allocated on the basis of net realizable values (relative sales values) at split-off.
3. Which set of income statements is more meaningful, those in Requirement 1 or in 2? Why?

5-21. Joint products: sell or process further. The Burns Company produced three joint products at a joint cost of $100,000. These products were processed further and sold as follows:

Product	Sales	Additional Processing Costs
A	$245,000	$200,000
B	330,000	300,000
C	175,000	100,000

The company has had an opportunity to sell at split-off directly to other processors. If that alternative had been selected, sales would have been: A, $56,000; B, $28,000; and C, $56,000.

The company expects to operate at the same level of production and sales in the forthcoming year.

Required

Consider all the available information, and assume that all costs incurred after split-off are variable.

1. Could the company increase net income by altering its processing decisions? If so, what would be the expected overall net income?

2. Which products should be processed further and which should be sold at split-off?

5-22. Joint costs and decisions. A petrochemical company has a batch process whereby 1,000 gallons of a raw material are transformed into 100 pounds of X-1 and 400 pounds of X-2. Although the joint costs of their production are $900, both products are worthless at their split-off point. Additional separable costs of $250 are necessary to give X-1 a sales value of $750 as Product A. Similarly, additional separable costs of $100 are necessary to give X-2 a sales value of $750.

Required

You are in charge of the batch process and the marketing of both products. (Show your computations for each answer.)

1. a. Assuming that you believe in assigning joint costs on a physical basis, allocate the total profit of $250 per batch to Products A and B.
   b. Would you stop processing one of the products? Why?

2. a. Assuming that you believe in assigning joint costs on a net-realizable-value (relative-sales-value) basis, allocate the total profit of $250 per batch to Products A and B. If there is no market for X-1 and X-2 at their split-off point, a net realizable value is usually imputed by taking the ultimate sales values at the point of sale and working backward to obtain approximated "synthetic" relative sales values at the split-off point. These synthetic values are then used as weights for allocating the joint costs to the products.
   b. You have internal product-profitability reports in which joint costs are assigned on a net-realizable-value basis. Your chief engineer says that, after seeing these reports, he has developed a method of obtaining more of Product B and correspondingly less of Product A from each batch,

without changing the per-pound cost factors. Would you approve this new method? Why? What would the overall net profit be if 50 more pounds of B were produced and 50 less pounds of A?

5-23. Joint products. (CPA.) From a particular joint process, Watkins Company produces three products, X, Y, and Z. Each product may be sold at the point of split-off or processed further. Additional processing requires no special facilities, and production costs of further processing are entirely variable and traceable to the products involved. In 19x3, all three products were processed beyond split-off. Joint production costs for the year were $60,000. Sales values and costs needed to evaluate Watkins' 19x3 production policy follow:

			Additional Costs and Sales Values if Processed Further	
		Net Realizable		
	Units	Values (sales values)	Sales	Added
Product	Produced	at Split-Off	Values	Costs
X	6,000	$25,000	$42,000	$9,000
Y	4,000	41,000	45,000	7,000
Z	2,000	24,000	32,000	8,000

Joint costs are allocated to the products in proportion to the relative physical volume of output.

1. For units of Z, the unit production cost most relevant to a sell-or-process-further decision is
   a. $5.
   b. $12.
   c. $4.
   d. $9.

2. To maximize profits, Watkins should subject the following products to additional processing:
   a. X only.
   b. X, Y, and Z.
   c. Y and Z only.
   d. Z only.

5-24. Joint costs. Two products, A and B, had been allocated $30,000 of joint costs each, using the net-realizable-value method. Their ultimate sales values were $70,000 and $90,000, respectively. The separable costs for A were $20,000. What were the separable costs for B?

5-25. Sell equipment. (H. Schaefer.) Dearborn Company is phasing out a production process during the next 12 months. The process uses a piece of special-purpose equipment that has a remaining book value of $10,000 and is depreciated at the rate of $4,000 per year. The equipment operator earns $10,000 (straight time) per year and the equipment consumes $1,000 of power annually. The production supervisor earns $18,000 annually and spends about 10 percent of his time supervising this process. Building depreciation allocated to the process amounts to $1,500 per year.

During the phase-out period the equipment operator will work about 20 percent more time at overtime rates (time-and-one-half) performing some manual tasks. This causes the supervisor to consider the possibility of performing the process manually—100 percent, without the equipment. The equipment can be sold today for $7,000. If the process is done manually, the existing operator will not have to work overtime, but a second man will have to be hired at $9,000 per year. The equipment can be sold at the end of the phase-out period for $4,000.

Required

Should the process be performed with the equipment or 100 percent manually (without the equipment)? Support your answer with quantitative analysis. Do *not* consider the effect of taxes or the time value of money.

5-26. Analysis of four alternatives. (CPA.) Marshall Manufacturing, Inc., has produced two products, Z and P, at its Richmond plant for several years. On March 31, 19x3, P was dropped from the product line. Marshall manufactures and sells 50,000 units of Z annually, and this is not expected to change. Unit material and direct-labor costs are $12 and $7, respectively.

The Richmond plant is in a leased building; the lease expires June 30, 19x7. Annual rent is $75,000. The lease provides Marshall the right of sublet; all non-removable leasehold improvements revert to the lessor. At the end of the lease, Marshall intends to close the plant and scrap all equipment.

P has been produced on two assembly lines, which occupy 25 percent of the plant. The assembly lines will have a book value of $135,000 and a remaining useful life of seven years as of June 30, 19x3. This is the only portion of the plant available for alternative uses.

Marshall uses one unit of D to produce one unit of Z. D is purchased under a contract requiring a minimum annual purchase of 5,000 units. The contract expires June 30, 19x7. A list of D unit costs follows:

Annual Purchases (units)	Unit Cost
5,000– 7,499	$2.00
7,500– 19,999	1.95
20,000– 34,999	1.80
35,000– 99,999	1.65
100,000–250,000	1.35

Alternatives are available for using the space previously used to manufacture P. Some may be used in combination. All can be implemented by June 30, 19x3. Should no action be taken, the plant is expected to operate profitably, and manufacturing overhead is not expected to differ materially from past years when P was manufactured. Following are the alternatives:

1. Sell the two P assembly lines for $70,000. The purchaser will buy only if he can acquire the equipment from both lines. The purchaser will pay all removal and transportation costs.

2. Sublet the floor space for an annual rental of $12,100. The lease will require that the equipment be removed (cost nominal) and leasehold improvements costing $38,000 be installed. Indirect costs are expected to increase $3,500 annually as a result of the sublease.

3. Convert one or both P assembly lines to produce D at a cost of $45,500 for each line. The converted lines will have a remaining useful life of ten years. Each modified line can produce any number of units of D up to a maximum of 37,000 units at a unit direct-material and direct-labor cost of 10¢ and 25¢, respectively. Annual manufacturing overhead is expected to increase from $550,000 to $562,000 if one line is converted and to $566,000 if both lines are converted.

Prepare a schedule to analyze the best utilization of the following alternatives for the four years ended June 30, 19x7. Ignore income taxes and the time value of money.

1. Continue to purchase D; sell equipment; rent space.
2. Continue to purchase D; sell equipment.
3. Produce D on two assembly lines; purchase D as needed.
4. Produce D on one assembly line; purchase D as needed.

Set up your workpaper allowing one column for the evaluation of each alternative. The columns should be numbered 1, 2, 3, and 4.

5-27. **Make or buy.** (CMA, adapted.) The Vernom Corporation, which produces and sells to wholesalers a highly successful line of summer lotions and insect repellents, has decided to diversify in order to stabilize sales throughout the year. A natural area for the company to consider is the production of winter lotions and creams to prevent dry and chapped skin.

After considerable research, a winter products line has been developed. However, because of the conservative nature of the company management, Vernom's president has decided to introduce only one of the new products for this coming winter. If the product is a success, further expansion in future years will be initiated.

The product selected (called Chap-Off) is a lip balm that will be sold in a lipstick-type tube. The product will be sold to wholesalers in boxes of 24 tubes for $8 per box. Because of available capacity, no additional fixed charges will be incurred to produce the product. However, a $100,000 fixed charge will be absorbed by the product to allocate a fair share of the company's present fixed costs to the new product.

Using the estimated sales and production of 100,000 boxes of Chap-Off as the expected volume, the accounting department has developed the following costs per box:

Direct labor	$2.00
Direct material	3.00
Total overhead	1.50
Total	$6.50

Vernom has approached a cosmetics manufacturer to discuss the possibility of purchasing the tubes for Chap-Off. The purchase price of the empty tubes from the

Required

cosmetics manufacturer would be 90¢ per 24 tubes. If the Vernom Corporation accepts the purchase proposal, it is predicted that direct-labor and variable-overhead costs would be reduced by 10 percent and direct-material costs would be reduced by 20 percent.

1. Should the Vernom Corporation make or buy the tubes? Show calculations to support your answer.

2. What would be the maximum purchase price acceptable to the Vernom Corporation for the tubes? Support your answer with an appropriate explanation.

3. Instead of sales of 100,000 boxes, revised estimates show sales volume at 125,000 boxes. At this new volume, additional equipment, at an annual rental of $10,000, must be acquired to manufacture the tubes. However, this incremental cost would be the only additional fixed cost required even if sales increased to 300,000 boxes. (The 300,000 level is the goal for the third year of production.) Under these circumstances, should the Vernom Corporation make or buy the tubes? Show calculations to support your answer.

4. The company has the option of making and buying at the same time. What would be your answer to Requirement 3 if this alternative were considered? Show calculations to support your answer.

5. What nonquantifiable factors should the Vernom Corporation consider in determining whether they should make or buy the lipstick-type tubes?

5-28. Make or buy. The Fram Company's old equipment for making subassemblies is worn out. The company is considering two courses of action: (a) completely replacing the old equipment with new equipment, or (b) buying subassemblies from a reliable outside supplier, who has quoted a unit price of $1 on a seven-year contract for a minimum of 50,000 units per year.

Production was 60,000 units in each of the past two years. Future needs for the next seven years are not expected to fluctuate beyond 50,000 to 70,000 units per year. Cost records for the past two years reveal the following unit costs of manufacturing the subassembly:

Direct material	$ .25
Direct labor	.40
Variable overhead	.10
Fixed overhead (including $.10 depreciation and $.10 for supervision and other direct departmental fixed overhead)	.25
	$1.00

The new equipment will cost $188,000 cash, will last seven years, and will have a disposal value of $20,000. The current disposal value of the old equipment is $10,000.

The salesman for the new equipment has summarized his position as follows: The increase in machine speeds will reduce direct labor and variable overhead by 35¢ per unit. Consider last year's experience of one of your major competitors with identical equipment. They produced 100,000 units under operating conditions very comparable to yours and showed the following unit costs:

Direct material	$.25
Direct labor	.10
Variable overhead	.05
Fixed overhead, including $.24 depreciation	.40
	$.80

Required

For purposes of this case, assume that any idle facilities cannot be put to alternative use. Also assume that 5¢ of the old Fram unit cost is allocated fixed overhead that will be unaffected by the decision.

1. The president asks you to compare the alternatives on a total-annual-cost basis and on a per-unit basis for annual needs of 60,000 units. Which alternative seems more attractive?

2. Would your answer to Requirement 1 change if the needs were 50,000 units? 70,000 units? At what volume level would Fram be indifferent between make and buy? Show your computations.

3. What factors, other than the above, should the accountant bring to the attention of management to assist them in making their decision? Include the considerations that might be applied to the outside supplier.

For additional analyses, see Problems 12-32 and 13-26.

5-29. Relevant-cost analysis. The following are the unit costs of making and selling a single product at a normal level of 5,000 units per month and a current unit selling price of $75:

Manufacturing costs:	
Direct material	$20
Direct labor	12
Variable overhead	8
Fixed overhead	
(total for the year, $300,000)	5
Selling and administrative expenses:	
Variable	15
Fixed (total for the year, $540,000)	9

Required

Consider each requirement separately. Label all computations, and present your solutions in a form that will be comprehensible to the company president.

1. This product is usually sold at a rate of 60,000 units per year. It is predicted that a rise in price to $80 will decrease volume by 5 percent. How much may advertising be increased under this plan without having annual net profit fall below the current level?

2. The company has received a proposal from an outside supplier to make and ship this item directly to the company's customers, as sales orders are forwarded. Variable selling and administrative costs would fall 40 percent. If the supplier's proposal is accepted, the company will use its own plant to produce a new product. The new product would be sold through manufac-

turers' agents at a 10 percent commission based on a selling price of $20 each. The cost characteristics of this product, based on predicted yearly normal volume, are as follows:

	Per Unit
Direct material	$ 3
Direct labor	6
Variable overhead	4
Fixed overhead	3
Manufacturing costs	$16
Selling and administrative expenses:	
Variable	10% of selling price
Fixed	$ 1

What is the maximum price per unit that the company can afford to pay to the supplier for subcontracting the entire old product? Assume the following:

a. Total fixed factory overhead and total fixed selling expenses will not change if the new product line is added.
b. The supplier's proposal will not be considered unless the present annual net income can be maintained.
c. Selling price of the old product will remain unchanged.

5-30. Relevant costs of auto ownership. Joan Robbins, a dairy inspector for the State of Wisconsin, used her private automobile for work purposes and was reimbursed by the state at a rate of 22¢ per mile. Robbins was unhappy about the rate, so she was particularly interested in a publication of the Federal Highway Administration, "The Cost of Owning and Operating an Automobile."

The publication contained a "worksheet for first-year auto costs":

1. Amount paid for your car	$........
2. First-year mileage	$........
3. First-year depreciation	$........
4. Insurance	$........
5. License, other fees or taxes	$........
6. Interest on auto loan	$........
7. Maintenance, repairs, tires	$........
8. Fuel and oil	$........
9. Parking, garaging, tolls	$........
10. Total of Lines 3 through 9	$........
11. Line 10 divided by Line 2	$........
Line 11 is your first-year per-mile cost.	

Robbins paid $9,000 for her new car. She expected to drive it 20,000 miles per year. The highway administration worksheet calls for depreciation at 33 percent of original cost for the first year, 25 percent the second year, and 20 percent the third year.

Insurance is $400. License and other fees amount to $200. Interest on her $6,000 auto loan is $720 for the first year, $480 for the second year, and $240 for the third year. The highway booklet said that the following charges might be expected for maintenance for every 10,000 miles: $120 for the first year, $240 for the second year, and $480 for the third year. Parking and tolls would cost an average of 1¢ per mile, and fuel and oil 6¢ per mile.

Required

1. Compute the total first-year cost of automobile ownership. Compute the cost per mile if the following miles were driven: 10,000, 20,000, and 30,000.

2. Is the reimbursement rate of 22¢ a "fair" rate?

3. Joan and a friend use her car for a 400-mile journey. They agree in advance "to split the costs of using the car, fifty-fifty." How much should Joan's friend pay?

4. What if Joan had paid cash for her car rather than borrowed $6,000? Would the costs change? By how much? Explain.

5. Suppose Joan were thinking of buying a second car exactly like the first and on the same financial terms, but she would confine the second car to personal use of 5,000 miles per year. The total mileage of the two cars taken together would still be 20,000 miles. What would be the first-year cost of operating a second car? The average unit cost? What costs are relevant? Why?

6. Robbins has owned the car one year. She has switched to a local job that does not require a car. What costs are relevant to the question of selling the car and using other means of transportation?

Accounting for Planning and Control

CHAPTER 6

The Master Budget: The Overall Plan

Management—and many investors and bank loan officers—have become increasingly aware of the merits of formal business plans. This chapter provides a condensed view of the overall business plan for the forthcoming year (or less)—the **master budget.** The major technical work of the budgetary accountant involves expected future data rather than historical data. There is also a major philosophical difference: The advocates of budgeting maintain that the process of preparing the budget forces executives to become better administrators. Budgeting puts planning where it belongs—in the forefront of the manager's mind.

This chapter provides a bird's-eye view of planning for the organization as a whole. We will see that planning requires all the functions of a business to blend together. We will see the importance of an accurate sales forecast. Most of all, we should begin to appreciate why budgeting is helpful. Budgeting is primarily attention directing, because it helps managers to focus on operating or financial problems early enough for effective planning or action.

This book stresses how accounting helps the **operating** performance of management (how effectively assets are acquired and utilized). But the financing function (how funds for investment in assets are obtained) is also important. That is why this chapter examines cash budgets as well as operating budgets. Successful organizations are usually characterized by both superior operating management *and* superior financial management. Business failures are frequently traceable to management's shirking of the financial aspects of its responsibilities.

CHARACTERISTICS OF BUDGETS

Definition of Budget

A budget is a formal quantitative expression of management plans. The master budget summarizes the goals of all subunits of an organization—sales, production, distribution, and finance. It quantifies targets for sales, production, net income, and cash position, and for any other objective that management specifies. The master budget usually consists of a statement of expected future income, a balance sheet, a statement of cash receipts and disbursements, and supporting schedules. These statements are the culmination of a series of planning decisions arising from a detailed, rigorous look at the organization's future.

Advantages of Budgets

Many skeptics who have never used budgets are quick to state, "I suppose budgeting is okay for the other fellow's business, but *my* business is different. There are too many uncertainties and complications to make budgeting worthwhile for me." But the same managers, when prodded for details, usually reveal that they are planning incessantly, but in an informal way. Perhaps the best way to combat such a short-sighted attitude is to name others in the same industry who are zealous about budgeting and who, inevitably, are among the industry's leaders. An organization that adopts formal budgeting usually becomes rapidly convinced of its helpfulness and would not consider regressing to its old-fashioned, nonbudgeting days. The benefits of budgeting almost always clearly outweigh the cost and the effort.

Some kind of budget program is bound to be useful to any organization, regardless of its size or its uncertainties. The major benefits are:

1. Budgeting, by formalizing their responsibilities for planning, compels managers to think ahead.
2. Budgeting provides definite expectations that are the best framework for judging subsequent performance.
3. Budgeting aids managers in coordinating their efforts, so that the objectives of the organization as a whole harmonize with the objectives of its parts.

Formalization of Planning

The principal advantage of budgeting is probably that it forces managers to think ahead—to anticipate and prepare for changing conditions. The budgeting process makes planning an explicit management responsibility. Too often, managers operate from day to day, extinguishing one business brush fire after another. They simply have no time for any tough-minded thinking beyond the next day's problems. Planning takes a back seat or is actually obliterated by workaday pressures.

The trouble with the day-to-day approach to managing an organization is that objectives are never crystallized. Without goals, company operations lack direction, problems are not foreseen, and results are hard to interpret. Advocates of budgeting correctly maintain that most business emergencies can be avoided by careful planning.

Expectations as a Framework for Judging Performance

As a basis for judging actual results, budgeted goals and performance are generally regarded as being more appropriate than past performance. The news that a company had sales of $10 million this year, as compared with $8 million the previous year, may or may not indicate that the company has been effective and has achieved maximum success. Perhaps sales should have been $11 million this year. **The major drawback of using historical data for judging performance is that inefficiencies may be concealed in the past performance.** Moreover, the usefulness of comparisons with the past is also limited by intervening changes in economic conditions, technology, competitive maneuvers, personnel, etc.

Another benefit of budgeting is that key personnel are informed of what is expected of them. Nobody likes to drift along, not knowing what his boss expects or hopes to achieve.

Coordination and Communication

Coordination is the meshing and balancing of an organization's resources so that its overall objectives are attained—so that the goals of the individual manager harmonize with goals of the organization as a whole. The budget is the means for communicating overall objectives and for blending the objectives of all departments.

Coordination requires, for example, that purchasing officers integrate their plans with production requirements, and that production officers use the sales budget to help them anticipate and plan for the manpower and plant facilities they will require. **The budgetary process obliges executives to visualize the relationship of their department to other departments, and to the company as a whole.**

A budget is not a cure-all for existing organizational ills. It will not

149

solve the problems created by a bumbling management or a faulty information system. The budget is a device whose value depends on its being administered astutely in conjunction with an information system that is attuned to a coordinated organization.

HUMAN RELATIONS

Middle management's attitude toward budgets will be heavily influenced by the attitude of top management. The chief executives must offer wholehearted support if a budgetary program is to achieve maximum benefits.

The ability to adhere to a budget is often an important factor in judging a manager's performance, and naturally, budgets are usually not the most popular feature of a manager's business life. Budgets pinpoint a manager's performance and direct his superior's attention to trouble spots. Few individuals are ecstatic about any techniques used by the boss to check their performance. Budgets are therefore sometimes regarded by middle management as embodiments of nickel-nursing, restrictive, negative top-management attitudes.

These misconceptions can be overcome by persuasive education and salesmanship. The budget should not be an unpleasant instrument for harassing the employee. Properly used, it will be a positive aid in setting standards of performance, in motivating toward goals, in metering results, and in directing attention to the areas that need investigation. *The budget is inanimate;* however, its administration is a delicate task, because everyone it affects must understand and accept the notion that the budget is primarily designed to help, not hinder.

The supreme importance of the human relations aspects of budgeting cannot be overemphasized. Too often, top management and its accountants are overly concerned with the mechanics of budgets, whereas the effectiveness of any budgeting system depends directly on whether the managers it affects understand it and accept it. Ideally, managers should be cooperative and cost-conscious. This subject is explored more fully in Chapter 9.

TYPES OF BUDGETS

Time Span

The planning horizon for budgeting may vary from a year or less to many years, depending on budget objectives and on the uncertainties involved. Long-range budgets, called **capital budgets,** are often prepared for particular projects such as equipment purchases, locations of plant, and additions of product lines. **Master budgets,** which consolidate an organization's overall plans for a shorter span of time, are usually prepared on an annual basis. The annual budget may be subdivided on a month-to-month basis, or perhaps on a monthly basis for the first quarter and on a quarterly basis for the three remaining quarters.

Continuous budgets are increasingly used. **These are master budgets which perpetually add a month in the future as the month just ended is dropped.** Continuous budgets are desirable because they compel managers to think specifically about the forthcoming twelve months and thus maintain a stable planning horizon.

Classification of Budgets

The terms used to describe assorted budget schedules vary from company to company. Sometimes budgets are called **pro-forma** statements because they are forecasted financial statements.

Budgets, accompanied by subsidiary schedules, may be classified as follows:

1. Master budget
   a. Operating budget
      (1) Sales budget
      (2) Production budget (for manufacturing companies)
         (a) Materials used and material purchases
         (b) Direct labor
         (c) Indirect manufacturing overhead
         (d) Changes in inventory levels
      (3) Cost-of-goods-sold budget (for merchandising and manufacturing companies)
      (4) Selling-expense budget
      (5) Administrative-expense budget
   b. Financial budget
      (1) Cash budget: cash receipts and disbursements
      (2) Budgeted balance sheet
      (3) Budgeted statement of sources and applications of funds (net working capital) or budgeted statement of changes in financial position

2. Special budget reports
   a. Performance reports (comparisons of results with plans)
   b. Capital budgets (long-range expectations for specific projects)

ILLUSTRATION OF PREPARATION OF A MASTER BUDGET

Description of Problem

Try to prepare the budget schedules required for the solution of this illustrative problem. Use the basic steps described after the problem. **Do not rush.** This is a comprehensive illustration that will require some step-by-step thinking and some reflection before a full understanding can be achieved. Although this illustration may seem largely mechanical, remember that the master-budgeting process generates key decisions regarding pricing, product lines, capital expenditures, research and development, personnel assignments, and so forth. **Therefore, the first draft of a budget leads to decisions that prompt subsequent drafts before a final budget is chosen.** Suppose that R Company is a retailer of a wide variety of household items. The company rents a number of retail stores and also has a local door-to-door sales force.

The R Company's newly hired accountant has persuaded management to prepare a budget to aid financial and operating decisions. Because this is the company's first attempt at formal budgeting, the planning horizon is only four months, April through July. In the past, sales have increased during the spring season. Collections lag behind and cash is needed for purchases, wages, and other operating outlays. In the past, the company has met this cash squeeze with the help of six-month loans from banks.

Exhibit 6-1 is the closing balance sheet for the fiscal year just ended. Sales in March were $40,000. Monthly sales are forecasted as follows:

April	$50,000	June	$60,000	August	$40,000
May	$80,000	July	$50,000		

EXHIBIT 6-1
R COMPANY

Balance Sheet
March 31, 19x1

ASSETS		
Current assets:		
Cash	$10,000	
Accounts receivable,		
net (.4 × March sales of $40,000)	16,000	
Merchandise inventory,		
$20,000 + .8 (.7 × April sales of $50,000)	48,000	
Unexpired insurance	1,800	$ 75,800
Plant assets:		
Equipment, fixtures, and other	$37,000	
Accumulated depreciation	12,800	24,200
Total assets		$100,000

EQUITIES		
Current liabilities:		
Accounts payable		
(.5 × March purchases of $33,600)	$16,800	
Accrued wages and commissions payable		
($1,250 + $3,000)	4,250	$ 21,050
Owners' equity		78,950
Total equities		$100,000

Sales consist of 60 percent cash and 40 percent credit. All credit accounts are collected in the month following the sales. The accounts receivable on March 31 represent credit sales made in March (40 percent of $40,000). Uncollectible accounts are negligible and are to be ignored.

At the end of any month, the R Company wishes to maintain a basic inventory of $20,000 plus 80 percent of the cost of goods to be sold in the following month. The cost of merchandise sold averages 70 percent of sales. Therefore, the inventory, on March 31, is $20,000 + .8 (.7 × April sales of $50,000) = $20,000 + $28,000 = $48,000. The purchase terms available to the R Company are net, 30 days. Fifty percent of a given month's purchases is paid during that month and 50 percent during the following month.

Wages and commissions are paid semimonthly, half a month after they are earned. They are divided into two portions: monthly fixed wages of $2,500 and commissions, equal to 15 percent of sales, which are uniform throughout each month. Therefore, the March 31 balance of Accrued Wages and Commissions Payable consists of (.5 × $2,500) + .5 (.15 × $40,000) = $1,250 + $3,000 = $4,250. This $4,250 will be paid on April 15. A used delivery truck will be purchased for $3,000 cash in April.

Other monthly expenses are:

Miscellaneous expenses	5% of sales, paid as incurred
Rent	$2,000, paid as incurred
Insurance	$200 expiration per month
Depreciation, including truck	$500

The company desires to maintain a minimum cash balance of $10,000 at the end of each month. Money can be borrowed or repaid in multiples of $1,000, at an interest rate of 6 percent per annum. Management does not want to borrow any more cash than necessary and wants to repay as promptly as possible. Interest is computed and paid *when the principal is repaid.* Assume that borrowing takes place at the beginning, and repayment at the end, of the months in question.

Required

Special note: By now it must be obvious that a basic knowledge of financial accounting (see Chapter 17) is necessary to cope with this illustrative problem.

1. Using the data given, prepare the following detailed schedules:
   a. Sales forecast.
   b. Cash collection from customers.
   c. Purchases.
   d. Disbursements for purchases.
   e. Wages and commissions.
   f. Disbursements for wages and commissions.
2. Using the data given and the schedules you have compiled, prepare the following major statements:

Required

a. Budgeted income statement for four months ending July 31, 19x1.
b. Budgeted statement of cash receipts and disbursements by months, including details of borrowings, repayments, and interest.
c. Budgeted balance sheet as of July 31, 19x1.

Solution Schedules a–f

	March	April	May	June	July	April–July Total
Schedule a: Sales Forecast						
Credit sales, 40%	$16,000	$20,000	$ 32,000	$24,000	$20,000	
Cash sales, 60%	24,000	30,000	48,000	36,000	30,000	
Total sales, 100%	$40,000	$50,000	$ 80,000	$60,000	$50,000	$240,000
Schedule b: Cash Collections						
Cash sales this month		$30,000	$ 48,000	$36,000	$30,000	
100% of last month's credit sales		16,000	20,000	32,000	24,000	
Total collections		$46,000	$ 68,000	$68,000	$54,000	
Schedule c: Purchases						
Ending inventory	$48,000	$64,800	$ 53,600	$48,000	$42,400	
Cost of goods sold	28,000^a	35,000	56,000	42,000	35,000	$168,000
Total needed	$76,000	$99,800	$109,600	$90,000	$77,400	
Beginning inventory	42,400^b	48,000	64,800	53,600	48,000	
Purchases	$33,600	$51,800	$ 44,800	$36,400	$29,400	

^{a} .7 × March sales of $40,000 = $28,000.
^{b} $20,000 + .8(.7 × March sales of $40,000) = $20,000 + $22,400 = $42,400.

	March	April	May	June	July	April–July Total
Schedule d: Disbursements for Purchases						
50% of last month's purchases		$16,800	$ 25,900	$22,400	$18,200	
50% of this month's purchases		25,900	22,400	18,200	14,700	
Disbursements for merchandise		$42,700	$ 48,300	$40,600	$32,900	
Schedule e: Wages and Commissions						
Wages, all fixed	$ 2,500	$ 2,500	$ 2,500	$ 2,500	$ 2,500	
Commissions (15% of current month's sales)	6,000	7,500	12,000	9,000	7,500	
Total	$ 8,500	$10,000	$ 14,500	$11,500	$10,000	$ 46,000
Schedule f: Disbursements for Wages and Commissions						
50% of last month's expenses		$ 4,250	$ 5,000	$ 7,250	$ 5,750	
50% of this month's expenses		5,000	7,250	5,750	5,000	
Total		$ 9,250	$ 12,250	$13,000	$10,750	

For consistency with the numbering scheme used in this book, label your responses to Requirement 2 as Exhibits 6-2, 6-3, and 6-4, respectively. Note that Schedules *a*, *c*, and *e* will be needed to prepare Exhibit 6-2, and Schedules *b*, *d*, and *f* will be needed to prepare Exhibit 6-3.

Basic Steps in Preparing Master Budget

The basic steps in preparing budgeted financial statements follow. Use the steps to prepare your own schedules. Then examine the schedules in the Solution.

Step 1. The sales forecast (Schedule *a*) is the starting point for budgeting, because inventory levels, purchases, and operating expenses are generally geared to the rate of sales activity. Trace the final column in Schedule *a* to Exhibit 6-2. In nonprofit organizations, forecasts of revenue or some level of services are also the focal point for budgeting. Examples are patient revenues expected by hospitals and donations to be received by churches. If no revenues are generated, as in the instances of municipal fire protection, a desired level of service is predetermined.

Step 2. After sales are budgeted, the purchases budget (Schedule *c*) may be prepared. The total merchandise needed will be the sum of the desired ending inventory plus the amount needed to fulfill budgeted sales demand. The total need will be partially met by the beginning inventory; the remainder must come from planned purchases. Therefore, these purchases are computed as follows: **Purchases = Desired ending inventory + Cost of goods sold − Beginning inventory.** Trace the final column of Schedule *c* to Exhibit 6-2.

EXHIBIT 6-2
R COMPANY
Budgeted Income Statement
For the Four Months Ending July 31, 19x1

	DATA		SOURCE OF DATA
Sales		$240,000	Schedule *a*
Cost of goods sold		168,000	Schedule *c*
Gross margin		$ 72,000	
Operating expenses:			
Wages and commissions	$46,000		Schedule *e*
Rent	8,000		*
Miscellaneous expenses	12,000		5% of sales
Insurance	800		*
Depreciation	2,000	68,800	*
Income from operations		$ 3,200	
Interest expense		220	Exhibit 6-3
Net income		$ 2,980	

*Monthly amounts are given in the statement of the problem.

Step 3. The budgeting of operating expenses is dependent on various factors. Many operating expenses are directly influenced by month-to-month fluctuations in sales volume. Examples are sales commissions and delivery expenses. Other expenses are not directly influenced (e.g., rent, insurance, depreciation, certain types of payroll). In this solution, Schedule *e* should be prepared for wages and commissions. Trace the final column of Schedule *e* to Exhibit 6-2. The other operating expenses are entered in the budgeted income statement, as shown in Exhibit 6-2.

Step 4. Steps 1 through 3 will provide enough information for a budgeted statement of income from operations (Exhibit 6-2).

Step 5. Predict the month-to-month effects on the cash position of the level of operations summarized in Exhibit 6-2. The preparation of the cash budget (Exhibit 6-3) is explained below.

Explanation of Cash Budget

The cash budget (budgeted statement of cash receipts and disbursements, Exhibit 6-3) has the following major sections:

w. The beginning cash balance plus cash receipts yield the total cash available for needs, before financing. Cash receipts depend on collections from customers' accounts receivable and cash sales (Schedule *b*) and on other operating sources such as miscellaneous rental income. Trace Schedule *b* to Exhibit 6-3. **Studies of the collectibility of accounts receivable are a prerequisite to accurate forecasting.** Key factors include collection experience and average time lag between sales and collections.

x. Cash disbursements:
  (1) Purchases depend on the credit terms extended by suppliers and the bill-paying habits of the buyer (Schedule *d*, which should be traced to Exhibit 6-3).
  (2) Payroll depends on wage, salary, or commission terms and on payroll dates (Schedule *f*, which should be traced to Exhibit 6-3).
  (3) Other costs and expenses depend on timing and credit terms. **Note that depreciation does not entail a cash outlay.**
  (4) Other disbursements include outlays for fixed assets, long-term investments, installment payments on purchases, and the like. In this problem, the only "other disbursement" is $3,000 for the truck.

y. Financing requirements depend on how the total cash available *w* (in Exhibit 6-3) compares with the total cash needed. Needs include the disbursements *x* plus the ending cash balance *z* desired. The financing plans will depend on the relationship of cash available to cash sought. If there is an excess, loans may be repaid or temporary investments made. The pertinent outlays for interest expenses are usually contained in this section of the cash budget. Trace the calculated interest expense to Exhibit 6-2, which will then be complete (ignoring income taxes).

z. The ending cash balance is $w + y - x$. Financing *y* may have a positive (borrowing) or a negative (repayment) effect on the cash balance. **The illustrative cash budget shows the pattern of short-term, self-liquidating**

EXHIBIT 6-3

R COMPANY

Budgeted Statement of Cash Receipts and Disbursements
For the Four Months Ending July 31, 19x1

	APRIL	MAY	JUNE	JULY
Cash balance, beginning	$10,000	$10,550	$10,990	$10,240
Cash receipts:				
Collections from customers (Schedule b)	46,000	68,000	68,000	54,000
w.ᵃ Total cash available for needs, before financing	56,000	78,550	78,990	64,240
Cash disbursements:				
Merchandise (Schedule d)	42,700	48,300	40,600	32,900
Wages and commissions (Schedule f)	9,250	12,250	13,000	10,750
Miscellaneous expenses, 5% of sales	2,500	4,000	3,000	2,500
Rent	2,000	2,000	2,000	2,000
Truck purchase	3,000	—	—	—
x. Total disbursements	59,450	66,550	58,600	48,150
Minimum cash balance desired	10,000	10,000	10,000	10,000
Total cash needed	69,450	76,550	68,600	58,150
Excess (deficiency) of total cash available over total cash needed before current financing	(13,450)	2,000	10,390	6,090
Financing:				
Borrowings (at beginning)	14,000ᵇ	—		
Repayments (at end)	—	(1,000)	(10,000)	(3,000)
Interest (at 6% per annum)	—	(10)	(150)	(60)
y. Total effects of financing	14,000	(1,010)ᶜ	(10,150)	(3,060)
z. Cash balance, ending (w + y − x)	$10,550	$10,990	$10,240	$13,030

Note: Expired insurance and depreciation do not entail cash outlays.
ᵃ Letters are keyed to the explanation in the text.
ᵇ Borrowings and repayments of principal are made in multiples of $1,000, at an interest rate of 6 percent per annum.
ᶜ $2,000 is not repaid here because the repayment, plus interest of $20, would result in an ending cash balance of $9,980, which—strictly interpreted—is insufficient.

financing. Seasonal peaks often result in heavy drains on cash, for merchandise purchases and operating expenses, before the sales are made and cash collected from customers. The resulting loan is self-liquidating—that is, the borrowed money is used to acquire merchandise for sale, and the proceeds from the sale are used to repay the loan. This "working-capital cycle" moves from cash to inventory to receivables and back to cash.

Cash budgets help management to avoid having unnecessary idle cash, on the one hand, and unnecessary nerve-racking cash deficiencies, on the other. An astutely mapped financing program keeps cash balances in reasonable relation to needs.

Budgeted Balance Sheet

The final step is the preparation of the budgeted balance sheet (Exhibit 6-4). Each item is projected in accordance with the business plan as expressed in

157

EXHIBIT 6-4
R COMPANY
Budgeted Balance Sheet
July 31, 19x1

ASSETS		
Current assets:		
Cash (Exhibit 6-3)	$13,030	
Accounts receivable (.40 × July sales of $50,000) (Schedule a)	20,000	
Merchandise inventory (Schedule c)	42,400	
Unexpired insurance ($1,800 old balance − $800 expired)	1,000	$ 76,430
Plant:		
Equipment, fixtures, and other ($37,000 + truck, $3,000)	$40,000	
Accumulated depreciation ($12,800 + $2,000 depreciation)	14,800	25,200
Total assets		$101,630

EQUITIES		
Current liabilities:		
Accounts payable (.5 × July purchases of $29,400) (Schedule d)	$14,700	
Accrued wages and commissions payable (.5 × $10,000) (Schedule e)	5,000	$ 19,700
Owners' equity ($78,950 + $2,980 net income)		81,930
Total equities		$101,630

Note: Beginning balances were used as a start for the computations of unexpired insurance, plant, and owners' equity.

the previous schedules. Specifically, the beginning balances at March 31 would be increased or decreased in light of the expected cash receipts and disbursements in Exhibit 6-3 and in light of the effects of noncash items appearing on the income statement in Exhibit 6-2. For example, unexpired insurance of $1,800 (the balance on March 31) minus the $800 expiring over four months would affect the balance sheet, even though it is a noncash item.

When the complete master budget is formulated, management can consider all the major financial statements as a basis for changing the course of events. For example, the initial formulation may prompt management to try new sales strategies to generate more demand. Or management may explore the effects of various ways of adjusting the timing of receipts and disbursements. In any event, the first draft of the master budget is rarely the final draft. In this way, the budgeting process becomes an integral part of the management process itself in the sense that *planning* and *budgeting* are indistinguishable.

THE DIFFICULTIES OF SALES FORECASTING

As you have seen in the foregoing illustration the sales forecast is the foundation of the entire master budget. The accuracy of estimated production

158

schedules and of cost to be incurred depends on the detail and accuracy, in dollars and in units, of the forecasted sales.

The sales forecast is usually prepared under the direction of the top sales executive. All of the following factors are important: (1) past patterns of sales; (2) the estimates made by the sales force; (3) general economic and competitive conditions; (4) specific interrelationships of sales and economic indicators, such as gross national product or industrial production indexes; (5) changes in prices; (6) market research studies; and (7) advertising and sales promotion plans.

Sales forecasting usually combines various techniques. Opinions of the sales staff are sought. Statistical methods are often used. Correlations between sales and economic indicators help make sales forecasts more reliable. In most cases, the quantitative analysis provided by economists and members of the market research staff provide valuable help but not outright answers. The opinions of line management heavily influence the final setting of sales forecasts.

Pricing policies can have pronounced effects on sales. Management's assessment of price elasticities (the effect of price changes on the physical volume sold) will influence the sales forecast. A company may not offer the same unit price to all customers (because of differences in costs of serving different markets). In such cases, a detailed analysis of both units to be sold as well as dollar sales is needed for each price category before a final sales forecast can be aggregated.

Sales forecasting is still somewhat mystical, but its procedures are becoming more formal and are being viewed more seriously because of the intensity of competitive pressures. Although this book does not encompass a detailed discussion of the preparation of the sales budget, the importance of an accurate sales forecast cannot be overstressed.

In recent years, the formal use of statistical probabilities has been applied to the problem of sales forecasting. (See Chapter 16 for an elaboration.) Moreover, financial planning models and simulation have enabled managers to get a quantitative grasp on the ramifications of various sales strategies.[1]

FINANCIAL PLANNING MODELS AND SIMULATION

In most cases, the master budget is the best practical approximation to a formal model of the total organization: its objectives, its inputs, and its outputs. If the master budget serves as a "total decision model" for top

---

[1]For a survey of forecasting techniques, see S. Wheelwright and D. Clarke, "Corporate Forecasting: Promise and Reality," *Harvard Business Review* (November–December 1976), p. 40.

management, then decisions about strategies for the forthcoming period may be formulated and altered during the budgetary process. Traditionally, this has been a step-by-step process whereby tentative plans are gradually revised as executives exchange views on various aspects of expected activities.

In the future, much of the interaction and interdependence of the decisions will probably be formalized in mathematical simulation models—"total models" that are sometimes called **financial-planning models.**[2] These models are mathematical statements of the relationships in the organization among all the operating and financial activities, and of other major internal and external factors that may affect decisions.

Financial models include all the ingredients for preparing a master budget. However, they can also be used for long-range planning decisions. For example, if managers want to predict the impact of adding a new product line, they can obtain budgeted financial statements for many future years. For instance, at Dow Chemical Company, 140 separate cost inputs, constantly revised, are fed into the model. Such factors as major raw-material costs and prices by country and region are monitored weekly. Multiple contingency plans rather than a single master plan are used more widely than before.[3]

Many models are constructed and working. They are used for budgeting, for revising budgets with little incremental effort, and for comparing a variety of decision alternatives as they affect the entire firm. The models speed the budgetary process because the sensitivity of income and cash flows to various decisions can be tested promptly via a simulation. Management can react quickly to events and to revisions in predictions of various aspects of operations. Moreover, mathematical probabilities can be incorporated in these models, so that uncertainty can be dealt with explicitly rather than informally.

SUMMARY

The master budget expresses management's overall operating and financing plan. It outlines company objectives and steps for achieving them. The budgetary process compels managers to think ahead and to prepare for changing conditions. Budgets are aids in setting standards of performance, motivating personnel toward goals, measuring results, and directing attention to the areas that most need investigation.

The human factors in budgeting are more important than the mechanics. Top management must support a budgetary program wholeheartedly. The job of educating personnel and selling them on the budget is everlasting, but essential, if those who are affected by the budget are to

---

[2]Vincent R. LoCascio, "Financial Planning Models," *Financial Executive,* Vol. XL, No. 3.

[3]"Piercing Future Fog in the Executive Suite," *Business Week* (April 28, 1975), p. 46.

understand it and accept it. The master budget should be a powerful aid to the most crucial decisions of top management. Often, it falls far short of that role because its potential is misunderstood. Instead of being regarded as a management tool, in many cases the budget is unfortunately looked upon as a necessary evil.

The cornerstone of the budget is the sales forecast. All current operating and financial planning is generally tied to the expected volume of sales.

SUMMARY PROBLEM FOR YOUR REVIEW

Problem

Before attempting to solve the homework problems, review the R Company illustration in this chapter.

ASSIGNMENT MATERIAL

Fundamental Assignment Material

6-1. Terminology. Define *master budget; continuous budget; pro-forma statements;* and *cash budget.*

6-2. Master budget. (Alternate to 6-24 and 6-25.) A retailing subsidiary of a widely diversified company has a strong belief in using highly decentralized management. You are the new manager of one of its small "Apex" stores (Store No. 82). You know much about how to buy, how to display, how to sell, and how to reduce shoplifting. However, you know little about accounting and finance.

Top management is convinced that training for higher management should include the active participation of store managers in the budgeting process. You have been asked to prepare a complete master budget for your store for April, May, and June. You are responsible for its actual full preparation. All accounting is done centrally, so you have no expert help on the premises. In addition, tomorrow the branch manager and the assistant controller will be here to examine your work; at that time they will assist you in formulating the final budget document. The idea is to have you prepare the budget a few times so that you gain more confidence about accounting matters. You want to make a favorable impression on your superiors, so you gather the following data as of March 31, 19x1:

Cash	$ 11,000	*Recent and Projected Sales:*	
Inventory	300,000		
Accounts receivable	261,000	February	$200,000
Net furniture and fixtures	150,000	March	250,000
Total assets	$722,000	April	500,000
Accounts payable	$340,000	May	300,000
Owner's equity	382,000	June	300,000
Total equities	$722,000	July	200,000

[handwritten margin note: END INV = NEXT MONTHS COST OF GOODS SOLD]

Credit sales are 90 percent of total sales. Credit accounts are collected 80 percent in the month following the sale and 20 percent in the next following month. Assume that bad debts are negligible and may be ignored. The Accounts Receivable on March 31 are the result of the credit sales for February and March: $(.20 \times .90 \times \$200,000 = \$36,000) + (1.00 \times .90 \times \$250,000 = \$225,000) = \$261,000$. The average gross profit on sales is 40 percent.

The policy is to acquire enough inventory each month to equal the following month's projected sales. All purchases are paid for in the month following purchase.

Salaries, wages, and commissions average 20 percent of sales; all other expenses, excluding depreciation, 4 percent of sales. Fixed expenses for rent, property taxes, and miscellaneous payroll and other items are $40,000 monthly. Assume that these expenses require cash disbursements each month. Depreciation is $2,000 monthly.

In April, $40,000 is going to be disbursed for fixtures acquired in March. The March 31 balance of Accounts Payable includes this amount.

Assume that a minimum cash balance of $10,000 is to be maintained. Also assume that all borrowings are effective at the beginning of the month and all repayments are made at the end of the month of repayment. Interest is paid only at the time of repaying principal. Interest rate is 8 percent per annum; round out interest computations to the nearest ten dollars. All loans and repayments of principal must be made in multiples of a thousand dollars.

Required

1. Prepare a budgeted income statement for the coming quarter, a budgeted statement of monthly cash receipts and disbursements (for the next three months), and a budgeted balance sheet for June 30, 19x1. All operations are evaluated on a before-income-tax basis. Also, because income taxes are disbursed from corporate headquarters, they may be ignored here.

2. Explain why there is a need for a bank loan and what operating sources supply cash for repaying the bank loan.

Additional Assignment Material

6-3. What are the major benefits of budgeting?

6-4. Why is budgeted performance better than past performance, as a basis for judging actual results?

6-5. What is coordination?

6-6. "Education and salesmanship are key features of budgeting." Explain.

6-7. "Capital budgets are plans for managing long-term debt and common stock." Do you agree? Explain.

6-8. "*Pro-forma* statements are those statements prepared in conjunction with continuous budgets." Do you agree? Explain.

6-9. What is the difference between an operating budget and a financial budget?

6-10. Why is the sales forecast the starting point for budgeting?

6-11. What is a self-liquidating loan?

6-12. What is the principal objective of a cash budget?

6-13. What factors influence the sales forecast?

6-14. "There are too many uncertainties and complications to make budgeting worthwhile in my business." Do you agree? Explain.

6-15. What is the major technical difference between historical and budgeted financial statements?

6-16. **Cash budget.** Kay Sharon is the manager of an extremely successful gift shop, Gifts for Charities, that is operated for the benefit of local charities. From the data below, she wants a cash budget showing expected cash receipts and disbursements for the month of April, and the cash balance expected as of April 30, 19x1:

Bank note due April 10, $100,000 plus $5,000 interest.
Depreciation for April, $3,000.
Two-year insurance policy due April 14 for renewal: $3,000, to be paid in cash.
Planned cash balance, March 31, 19x1: $100,000.
Merchandise purchases for April: $700,000, 40 percent paid in month of purchase, 60 percent paid in next month.
Customer receivables as of March 31: $100,000 from February sales, $600,000 from March sales.
Payrolls due in April, $120,000.
Other expenses for April, payable in April: $60,000.
Accrued taxes for April, payable in June: $9,000.
Sales for April: $1,400,000, half collected in month of sale, 40 percent in next month, 10 percent in third month.
Accounts payable, March 31, 19x1: $600,000.

Required | Prepare the cash budget.

6-17. **Miscellaneous computations.** (H. Schaefer.) These questions relate to the preparation of budgets for *the year 19x6*. Each question is independent of the others.

a. Sales are predicted to be 30,000 units per month for the first six months and 40,000 units per month for the last six months. The January 1 balance in Accounts Receivable is $50,000. The accounts receivable are predicted to experience a one-month turnover cycle. The predicted sales price is $2. All sales are on a credit basis. Compute: (1) predicted sales revenue, (2) predicted December 31 balance in Accounts Receivable, (3) predicted cash collections from accounts receivable.

b. The January 1 balance in Prepaid Rent is $400. Rent is paid on the last day of the month prior to the month for which it applies; e.g., the April rent is paid on March 31. The present rent contract is for $400 per month, and the last payment is scheduled for May 31. A new contract is expected to be signed for $500 per month, the first payment being on June 30. The new contract is expected to be in effect for 12 months. Compute: (1) predicted rent expense, (2) predicted December 31 balance in Prepaid Rent, (3) predicted cash payments for rent.

6-18. Multiple choice. (CPA.) The Zel Co., a wholesaler, budgeted the following sales for the indicated months:

	June 19x1	July 19x1	August 19x1
Sales on account	$1,500,000	$1,600,000	$1,700,000
Cash sales	200,000	210,000	220,000
Total sales	$1,700,000	$1,810,000	$1,920,000

All merchandise is marked up to sell at its invoice cost plus 25 percent. Merchandise inventories at the beginning of each month are at 30 percent of that month's projected cost of goods sold.

1. The cost of goods sold for the month of June 19x1 is anticipated to be
   a. $1,530,000.   c. $1,275,000.   e. None of the above.
   b. $1,402,500.   d. $1,190,000.

2. Merchandise purchases for July 19x1 are anticipated to be
   a. $1,605,500.   c. $1,448,000.   e. None of the above.
   b. $1,474,400.   d. $1,382,250.

6-19. Multiple choice. (CPA, adapted.) Choose the best answer for each item. Give supporting computations.

The Dilly Company marks up all merchandise at 25 percent of gross purchase price. All purchases are made on account with terms of 1/10, net/60. Purchase discounts, which are recorded as miscellaneous income, are always taken. Normally, 60 percent of each month's purchases are paid for in the month of purchase, while the other 40 percent are paid during the first ten days of the first month after purchase. Inventories of merchandise at the end of each month are kept at 30 percent of the next month's projected cost of goods sold.

Terms for sales on account are 2/10, net/30. Cash sales are not subject to discount. Fifty percent of each month's sales on account are collected during the month of sale, 45 percent are collected in the succeeding month, and the remainder are usually uncollectible. Seventy percent of the collections in the month of sale are subject to discount, while 10 percent of the collections in the succeeding month are subject to discount.

Projected sales data for selected months follow:

	Sales on Account—Gross	Cash Sales
December	$1,900,000	$400,000
January	1,500,000	250,000
February	1,700,000	350,000
March	1,600,000	300,000

1. Projected gross purchases for January are
   a. $1,400,000.   c. $1,472,000.   e. None of the above.
   b. $1,470,000.   d. $1,248,000.

2. Projected inventory at the end of December is
   a. $420,000.   c. $552,000.   e. None of the above.
   b. $441,600.   d. $393,750.

3. Projected payments to suppliers during February are
   a. $1,551,200.   c. $1,528,560.   e. None of the above.
   b. $1,535,688.   d. $1,509,552.

4. Projected sales discounts to be taken by customers making remittances during February are
   a. $5,250.   c. $30,500.   e. None of the above.
   b. $15,925.   d. $11,900.

5. Projected total collections from customers during February are
   a. $1,875,000.   c. $1,511,750.   e. None of the above.
   b. $1,861,750.   d. $1,188,100.

Hints: 1/10, net/60 means that 1 percent of the gross purchase price may be deducted as a purchase discount if payment is made within 10 days. In any event, the invoice is payable within 60 days. Similar reasoning applies to sales terms. This problem requires painstaking attention to detail.

6-20. **Importance of sales forecast.** A retail department of a local chain of department stores sells a plain and a fancy pound box of hard candy. The candy is purchased in bulk from a local candy manufacturer, and two types of pound containers are purchased from a local container manufacturer. The store clerks use a back room for packaging the candy, as the need arises. Purchasing and selling prices have been stable, and no price changes are anticipated.

It is near the end of October. Orders must be placed today for delivery by November 1. These orders are to provide sufficient stock to last through the Christmas season.

Federal Reserve statistics for the local area show retail department store sales to be 2 percent over last year, for the period January 1–September 30. The store's top management anticipates an increase of 1 percent in dollar sales of ordinary items and of 10 percent in dollar sales of luxury items this year, as compared with last year. Other data are:

| | Last Year | | This Year | |
| | | | Inventory Oct. 31 | Target Inventory Dec. 31 |
	November	December		
Selling price per pound, $1.50 fancy and $1.00 plain				
Pounds sold:				
Plain	4,000	7,000		
Fancy	4,000	12,000		
Pounds			1,000	600

Number of containers:		
Plain	200	100
Fancy	500	100

Purchase costs:
Candy, per pound $.40
Container, plain $.05
Container, fancy $.20

Required

Prepare the following:

1. Budgeted sales of plain candy, in pounds and in total dollars, for November and December.
2. Budgeted sales of fancy candy, in pounds and in total dollars, for November and December.
3. Pounds and total cost of needed candy purchases.
4. Number and total cost of needed plain containers.
5. Number and total cost of needed fancy containers.

6-21. Sales forecasting. In each of the diagrams A through E on page 167, the dollar value of a sales order is contrasted with the quantity of product or service sold. Assume a single product in each case.

Required

1. What pricing policy is reflected by these order patterns (assuming that all customers are rational)?
2. Why are these patterns relevant to a sales forecast?

6.22. Comprehensive budgeting for a college. (CPA, adapted.) DeMars College has asked your assistance in developing its budget for the coming 19x1–x2 academic year. You are supplied with the following data for the current year:

a.

	Lower Division (Freshman– Sophomore)	Upper Division (Junior– Senior)
Average number of students per class	25	20
Average salary of faculty member	$10,000	$10,000
Average number of credit hours carried each year per student	33	30
Enrollment including scholarship students	2,500	1,700
Average faculty teaching load in credit hours per year (10 classes of 3 credit hours)	30	30

For 19x1–x2, lower division enrollment is expected to increase by 10 percent, while the upper division's enrollment is expected to remain stable. Faculty salaries will be increased by a standard 5 percent, and additional merit increases to be awarded to individual faculty members will be $90,750 for the lower division and $85,000 for the upper division.

b. The current budget is $210,000 for operation and maintenance of plant and equipment; this includes $90,000 for salaries and wages. Experience of the

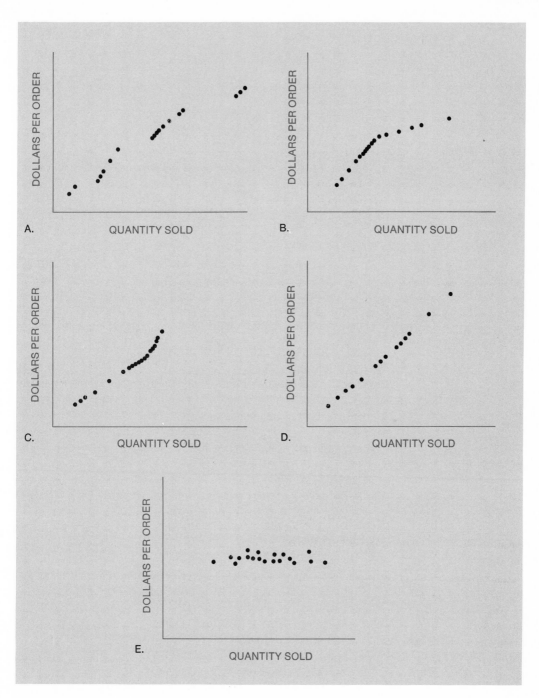

past three months suggests that the current budget is realistic, but that expected increases for 19x1–x2 are 5 percent in salaries and wages and $9,000 in other expenditures for operation and maintenance of plant and equipment.

c. The budget for the remaining expenditures for 19x1–x2 is as follows:

Administrative and general	$240,000
Library	160,000
Health and recreation	75,000
Athletics	120,000
Insurance and retirement	265,000
Interest	48,000
Capital outlay	300,000

d. The college expects to award 25 tuition-free scholarships to lower division students and 15 to upper division students. Tuition is $22 per credit hour; no other fees are charged.

e. Budgeted revenues for 19x1–x2 are as follows:

Endowment income	$114,000
Net income from auxiliary services	235,000
Athletics	180,000

The college's remaining source of revenue is an annual support campaign held during the spring.

Required

1. Prepare a schedule computing for 19x1–x2 by division (a) the expected enrollment, (b) the total credit hours to be carried, and (c) the number of faculty members needed.

2. Prepare a schedule computing the budget for faculty salaries by division for 19x1–x2.

3. Prepare a schedule computing the tuition revenue budget by division for 19x1–x2.

4. Assuming that the faculty salaries budget computed in Requirement 2 was $2,400,000 and that the tuition revenue budget computed in Requirement 3 was $3,000,000, prepare a schedule computing the amount that must be raised during the annual support campaign in order to cover the 19x1–x2 expenditures budget.

6-23. Cash budget. Prepare a statement of estimated cash receipts and disbursements for October 19x2, for the Rourk Company, which sells one product. On October 1, 19x2, part of the trial balance showed:

Cash	$ 6,000	
Accounts receivable	19,500	
Allowance for bad debts		$2,400
Merchandise inventory	12,000	
Accounts payable, merchandise		9,000

The company's purchases are payable within ten days. Assume that one-third of the purchases of any month are due and paid for in the following month.

The unit invoice cost of the merchandise purchased is $10. At the end of each month it is desired to have an inventory equal in units to 50 percent of the following month's sales in units.

Sales terms include a 1 percent discount if payment is made by the end of the calendar month. Past experience indicates that 60 percent of the billings will be collected during the month of the sale, 30 percent in the following calendar month, 6 percent in the next following calendar month. Four percent will be uncollectible. The company's fiscal year begins August 1.

Unit selling price	$ 15
August actual sales	15,000
September actual sales	45,000
October estimated sales	36,000
November estimated sales	27,000
Total sales expected in the fiscal year	450,000

Exclusive of bad debts, total budgeted selling and general administrative expenses for the fiscal year are estimated at $68,500, of which $21,000 is fixed expense (inclusive of a $9,000 annual depreciation charge). These fixed expenses are incurred uniformly throughout the year. The balance of the selling and general administrative expenses vary with sales. Expenses are paid as incurred.

6-24. **Prepare master budget.** (Alternate to 6-2 and 6-25.) The Loebl Company wants a master budget for the next three months, beginning January 1, 19x2. It desires an ending minimum cash balance of $4,000 each month. Sales are forecasted at average selling price of $4 per unit. Inventories are supposed to equal 125 percent of the next month's sales in units, except for the end of March. The March 31 inventory in units should be 75 percent of the next month's sales. Merchandise costs are $2 per unit. Purchases during any given month are paid in full during the following month. All sales are on credit, payable within thirty days, but experience has shown that 40 percent of current sales are collected in the current month, 40 percent in the next month, and 20 percent in the month thereafter. Bad debts are negligible.

Monthly operating expenses are as follows:

Wages and salaries	$12,000
Insurance expired	100
Depreciation	200
Miscellaneous	2,000
Rent	100 + 10% of sales

Cash dividends of $1,000 are to be paid quarterly, beginning January 15, and are declared on the fifteenth of the previous month. All operating expenses are paid as incurred, except insurance, depreciation, and rent. Rent of $100 is paid at the beginning of each month, and the additional 10 percent of sales is paid quarterly on the tenth of the month following the quarter. The next settlement is due January 10.

The company plans to buy some new fixtures, for $2,000 cash, in March.

Money can be borrowed and repaid in multiples of $500, at an interest rate of 6 percent per annum. Management wants to minimize borrowing and repay rapidly. Interest is computed and paid when the principal is repaid. Assume that borrowing takes place at the beginning, and repayments at the end, of the months in question. Money is never borrowed at the beginning and repaid at the end of the *same* month. Compute interest to the nearest dollar.

Assets as of December 31:		Liabilities as of December 31:	
Cash	$ 4,000	Accounts payable	
Accounts receivable	16,000	(merchandise)	$28,750
Inventory	31,250	Dividends payable	1,000
Unexpired insurance	1,200	Rent payable	7,000
Fixed assets, net	10,000		$36,750
	$62,450		

Recent and forecasted sales:

October	$30,000	December	$20,000	February	$60,000	April	$36,000
November	20,000	January	50,000	March	30,000		

Required

1. Prepare a master budget, including a budgeted income statement, balance sheet, statement of cash receipts and disbursements, and supporting schedules.

2. Explain why there is a need for a bank loan and what operating sources provide the cash for the repayment of the bank loan.

6-25. Deviations from master budget. (Alternate to 6-2 and 6-24.) Review the major illustration in the chapter. It is the end of July. Operations have been exactly in accordance with the budget, except that July sales were $40,000 instead of $50,000. Purchases for July were not affected by the drop in sales, but commissions, cash, accounts receivable, and notes payable were among the accounts affected.

Prepare a summary analysis of the effects. That is, how would Schedules *a*, *b*, *e*, and *f* be affected, as well as Exhibits 6-2, 6-3, and 6-4? Include a list of all new balances in Exhibit 6-4.

SUGGESTED READINGS

WELSCH, G., *Budgeting: Profit Planning and Control,* 4th ed. (Englewood Cliffs, N.J.: Prentice-Hall, Inc., 1976).

The following references pertain especially to the difficult problem of sales forecasting:

BUTLER W., R. KAVESH, and R. PLATT (ed.), *Methods and Techniques of Business Forecasting* (Englewood Cliffs, N.J.: Prentice-Hall, Inc., 1974).

GREEN, PAUL E., and DONALD S. TULL, *Research for Marketing Decisions,* 2nd ed. (Englewood Cliffs, N.J.: Prentice-Hall, Inc., 1970). Chapter 16 covers sales forecasting.

CHAPTER 7

Flexible Budgets and Standards for Control

The essence of control is feedback—the comparison of actual performance with planned performance. Flexible budgets and standard costs are major attention-directing techniques for planning and for providing feedback regarding individual costs. Throughout this chapter, to stress some basic ideas, we shall continue to assume that all costs are either variable or fixed; in the next chapter we shall consider various cost behavior patterns in more detail.

FLEXIBLE BUDGETS

Static Budget Comparisons

As Chapter 6 shows, budgets may be developed on a companywide basis to cover all activities, from sales to direct materials to sweeping compounds, and from spending on a new plant to expected drains on petty cash. A budget may be expressed on an accrual basis or on a cash-flow basis; it may be highly condensed or exceedingly detailed. All the budgets discussed in

Chapter 6 are *static* (inflexible). To illustrate: A typical master planning budget is a plan tailored to a single target volume level of, say, 100,000 units. All results would be compared with the original plan, regardless of changes in ensuing conditions—even though, for example, volume turned out to be 90,000 units instead of the original 100,000.

Consider a simplified illustration. Suppose that the Dominion Company, a one-department firm, manufactured and sold a special kind of carry-on flight luggage that required several hand operations. The product had some variations, but it was essentially viewed as a single product bearing one selling price.

The master budget for the forthcoming month included the condensed income statement shown in Exhibit 7-1, column 2. The actual results are in

EXHIBIT 7-1
DOMINION COMPANY
Performance Report Using Static Budget
For the Month Ending June 30, 19x1

	ACTUAL	MASTER (STATIC) BUDGET	VARIANCE
Units	7,000	9,000	2,000
Sales	$168,000	$216,000	$48,000 *U*
Variable costs:			
Direct material	$ 21,350	$ 27,000	$ 5,650 *F*
Direct labor	61,500	72,000	10,500 *F*
Labor to transport materials internally and provide general support	11,100	14,400	3,300 *F*
Idle time	3,550	3,600	50 *F*
Cleanup time	2,500	2,700	200 *F*
Other indirect labor	800	900	100 *F*
Miscellaneous supplies	4,700	5,400	700 *F*
Variable manufacturing costs	$105,500	$126,000	$20,500 *F*
Shipping expenses (selling)	5,000	5,400	400 *F*
Duplication, telephone, etc. (administrative)	2,000	1,800	200 *U*
Total variable costs	$112,500	$133,200	$20,700 *F*
Contribution margin	$ 55,500	$ 82,800	$27,300 *U*
Fixed costs:			
Factory supervision	$ 14,700	$ 14,400	$ 300 *U*
Rent of factory	5,000	5,000	—
Depreciation of factory equipment	15,000	15,000	—
Other fixed factory costs	2,600	2,600	—
Fixed manufacturing costs	$ 37,300	$ 37,000	$ 300 *U*
Fixed selling and administrative costs	33,000	33,000	—
Total fixed costs	$ 70,300	$ 70,000	$ 300 *U*
Operating income (loss)	$(14,800)	$ 12,800	$27,600 *U*

F = Favorable cost variances occur when actual costs are less than budgeted costs.
U = Unfavorable cost variances occur when actual costs are greater than budgeted costs.

column 1. The master budget called for the production and sales of 9,000 units, but only 7,000 units were actually produced and sold. There were no beginning or ending inventories.

The master budget was based on detailed expectations for the given month, including a careful forecast of sales. The performance report in Exhibit 7-1 compares the actual results with the master budget. **Performance report** is a general term that usually means a comparison of actual results with some budget. In particular, note that the volume of activity, as measured by sales, was substantially below the budget. The budget in Exhibit 7-1 is an example of a *static* budget.

Exhibit 7-1 is difficult to analyze. Clearly, sales are below expectations, but the favorable variances regarding the variable costs are deceptive. Considering the lower-than-projected level of activity, was cost control really satisfactory? The comparison of actual results with a static budget does not give much help in answering that question.

Flexible Budget Comparisons

As president of the Dominion Company, you probably would want a performance report that better pinpoints some major variances between the master budget and the actual results. To get a better basis for analysis, a flexible budget is introduced. The **flexible budget** (also called **variable budget**) is based on knowledge of cost behavior patterns. **It is essentially a set of budgets that may be tailored to any level of activity.** Ideally, the flexible budget is compiled after obtaining a detailed analysis of how each cost is affected by changes in activity. Exhibit 7-2 shows how a flexible budget might appear.

The costs in Exhibit 7-2 may be graphed as in Exhibit 7-3. As these exhibits show, a mathematical function or formula can summarize the cost behavior as $70,000 per month plus $14.80 per unit. Although we have assumed that the graph is valid for the range of 7,000 to 9,000 units, costs are unlikely to behave in accordance with such a pat formula beyond either side of this range. Inasmuch as the activity was 7,000 units, the pertinent flexible budget is in the 7,000-unit column of Exhibit 7-2.

Flexible budgets have the following distinguishing features: (a) they are prepared for a range of activity instead of a single level; (b) they supply a dynamic basis for comparison because they are automatically geared to changes in volume.

The flexible-budget approach says, "Give me any activity level you choose, and I'll provide a budget tailored to that particular volume." Flexible budgets may be useful either before or after the period in question. They may be helpful when managers are trying to choose among various ranges of activity for planning purposes. They also may be helpful at the end of the period when managers are trying to analyze actual results.

EXHIBIT 7-2
DOMINION COMPANY

Flexible Budget
For the Month Ending June 30, 19x1

	BUDGET FORMULA PER UNIT	VARIOUS LEVELS OF ACTIVITY		
Units	—	7,000	8,000	9,000
Sales	$24.00	$168,000	$192,000	$216,000
Variable costs:				
Direct material	$ 3.00	$ 21,000	$ 24,000	$ 27,000
Direct labor	8.00	56,000	64,000	72,000
Labor to transport materials internally and provide general support	1.60	11,200	12,800	14,400
Idle time	.40	2,800	3,200	3,600
Cleanup time	.30	2,100	2,400	2,700
Other indirect labor	.10	700	800	900
Miscellaneous supplies	.60	4,200	4,800	5,400
Variable manufacturing costs	$14.00	$ 98,000	$112,000	$126,000
Shipping expenses (selling)	.60	4,200	4,800	5,400
Duplication, telephone, etc.	.20	1,400	1,600	1,800
Total variable costs	$14.80	$103,600	$118,400	$133,200
Contribution margin	$ 9.20	$ 64,400	$ 73,600	$ 82,800
Fixed costs:				
Factory supervision		$ 14,400	$ 14,400	$ 14,400
Rent of factory		5,000	5,000	5,000
Depreciation of factory equipment		15,000	15,000	15,000
Other fixed factory costs		2,600	2,600	2,600
Fixed manufacturing costs		$ 37,000	$ 37,000	$ 37,000
Fixed selling and administrative costs		33,000	33,000	33,000
Total fixed costs[a]		$ 70,000	$ 70,000	$ 70,000
Operating income (loss)		$ (5,600)	$ 3,600	$ 12,800

[a] Note that the budget formula for fixed costs is $70,000 per month. Therefore, the budget formula for total costs is $14.80 per unit plus $70,000 per month. The graph in Exhibit 7-3 portrays these relationships.

Isolating the Variances

Pause a moment to reflect on the analytical problem. The company had an original plan, and the president may seek an explanation of why the plan was not achieved; in other words, a manager may desire a more penetrating analysis of the variances in Exhibit 7-1. The analysis may become quite detailed. However, as a start, consider how the variances may be divided into two major categories:

174

EXHIBIT 7-3
DOMINION COMPANY
Graph of Flexible Budget of Costs

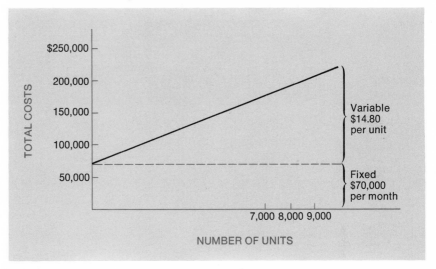

1. Variances from a revenue target (sometimes called a volume target or, in the case of a production manager, a scheduled production target).[1] In this book, this variance will be called a *marketing variance,* although its label will vary from company to company. It emphasizes the idea that the marketing function usually has the primary responsibility for reaching the sales level called for in the master budget.

2. Variances arising from changes in unit prices (or unit costs) and from inefficient utilization of inputs, here called *price* and *efficiency* variances.

The trouble with the static budget, as Exhibit 7-1 shows, is its failure to distinguish between these two facets of a manager's performance. However, Exhibit 7-4 gives a condensed view of how these variances can be isolated by using a flexible budget as an explanatory bridge between the master (static) budget and the actual results.

---

[1]Sometimes this is generically called an *effectiveness* variance, as distinguished from all other measures, which are loosely called *efficiency* variances. Effectiveness is the accomplishment of a predetermined objective. Efficiency is an optimum relationship between input and output. Given any level of output, did the manager control his inputs as he should have? Performance may be both effective and efficient, but either condition can occur without the other. For example, a company may set 200,000 units as a production objective. Subsequently, because of material shortages, only 150,000 units may be produced with 100 percent efficiency—performance would be ineffective but efficient. In contrast, 200,000 units may be produced on schedule but with a considerable waste of labor and materials—performance would be effective but inefficient.

EXHIBIT 7-4
DOMINION COMPANY

Summary of Performance
For the Month Ending June 30, 19x1

	(1) ACTUAL RESULTS AT ACTUAL PRICES^a	(2) (1) − (3) VARIANCES BECAUSE OF PRICE CHANGES AND INEFFICIENCY^b	(3) FLEXIBLE BUDGET FOR ACTUAL OUTPUT ACHIEVED^c	(4) (3) − (5) MARKETING VARIANCES	(5) MASTER (STATIC) BUDGET^a
Physical units	7,000	—	7,000	2,000	9,000
Sales	$168,000	$ —	$168,000	$48,000	$216,000
Variable costs	112,500	8,900 U	103,600	29,600	133,200
Contribution margin	$ 55,500	$8,900 U	$ 64,400	$18,400	$ 82,800
Fixed costs	70,300	300 U	70,000	—	70,000
Operating income	$(14,800)	$9,200 U	$ (5,600)	$18,400 U	$ 12,800

U = Unfavorable.
^{a} = Figures are from Exhibit 7-1.
^{b} = Figures are shown in more detail in Exhibit 7-5.
^{c} = Figures are from the 7,000-unit column in Exhibit 7-2.

Column 4 in Exhibit 7-4 focuses on the marketing variance. It shows that the underachievement of sales by 2,000 units and $48,000 resulted in an $18,400 decrease in attained contribution margin and hence an $18,400 decrease in operating income. Note that unit prices are held constant in this part of the analysis—that is, the net marketing variance is computed by using the budgeted contribution margin per unit:

Net marketing variance = Budgeted unit contribution margin × Difference between the master budgeted sales in units and the actual sales in units

$$= \$9.20 \times (9,000 - 7,000) = \$18,400,$$ unfavorable

Without the flexible budget in column 3, this marketing variance cannot be isolated.

Column 2 focuses on the variances arising from price changes and inefficient uses of inputs. The focus is on the difference between actual costs and flexible budgeted costs at the 7,000-unit level of activity. Again, without the flexible budget in column 3, these variances cannot be separated from the effects of changes in sales volume.

If the president wants to pursue his analysis of cost control beyond the summary in Exhibit 7-4, he may be helped by the cost performance report in Exhibit 7-5. Even if the president were not interested in probing further, some lower-level managers might be so inclined. Exhibit 7-5 gives a line-by-line sizeup, showing how most of the costs that had favorable variances

176

EXHIBIT 7-5
DOMINION COMPANY

Cost Control Performance Report
For the Month Ending June 30, 19x1

	ACTUAL COSTS INCURRED	FLEXIBLE BUDGET[a]	VARIANCES BECAUSE OF PRICE CHANGES AND INEFFICIENCY[b]	EXPLANATION
Units	7,000	7,000	—	
Variable costs:				
Direct material	$ 21,350	$ 21,000	$ 350 U	Lower prices but higher usage
Direct labor	61,500	56,000	5,500 U	Higher wage rates and higher usage
Labor to transport materials internally and provide general support	11,100	11,200	100 F	
Idle time	3,550	2,800	750 U	Excessive machine breakdowns
Cleanup time	2,500	2,100	400 U	Needs more investigation
Other indirect labor	800	700	100 U	
Miscellaneous supplies	4,700	4,200	500 U	Higher prices and higher usage
Variable manufacturing costs	$105,500	$ 98,000	$7,500 U	
Shipping expenses (selling)	5,000	4,200	800 U	Use of air freight
Duplication, telephone, etc.	2,000	1,400	600 U	Needs more investigation
Total variable costs	$112,500	$103,600	$8,900 U	
Fixed costs:				
Factory supervision	$ 14,700	$ 14,400	$ 300 U	Unanticipated raise
Rent of factory	5,000	5,000	—	
Depreciation of factory equipment	15,000	15,000	—	
Other fixed factory costs	2,600	2,600	—	
Fixed manufacturing costs	$ 37,300	$ 37,000	$ 300 U	
Fixed selling and administrative costs	33,000	33,000	—	
Total fixed costs	$ 70,300	$ 70,000	$ 300 U	
Total variable and fixed costs	$182,800	$173,600	$9,200 U	

F = Favorable.   U = Unfavorable.
[a] From 7,000-unit column in Exhibit 7-2.
[b] This represents a line-by-line breakdown of the variances in column 2 of Exhibit 7-4.

when a static budget was used as a basis for comparison have, in reality, unfavorable variances. These "price and efficiency variances" may be analyzed in even more depth by being subdivided further, at least for the more important material and labor costs, as shown later in the section, "Standards for Material and Labor."

Development of Control Systems

In most organizations, systems for accumulating and analyzing data evolve gradually. For example, when small businesses are founded, planning and control decisions are based at first almost wholly on the manager's *physical observations* of operations. It does not take long for him to realize that keeping some *historical records* would be a net benefit. That is, the additional bookkeeping costs are clearly outweighed by the greater likelihood of a series of better decisions regarding extensions of trade credit to customers, negotiating with suppliers and bankers, and so on. Furthermore, comparing the current period's sales, costs, or income with the preceding period's helps in the evaluation of performance and the preparation of new plans.

Physical observation and historical records, however, are often not enough. Managers desire to reduce emergency decision making by doing more careful planning, and the *master (static) budget* is helpful in this regard. Furthermore, the master budget provides a better benchmark for evaluating performance. That is, managers want to know more than how they have done currently in relation to last period's performance; they also want to know how they have done *currently* in relation to their *current* targeted performance.

This chapter has shown that some managers are willing to pay for more help in the form of *flexible budgets,* which are key aids in mapping an explanatory trail from the master budget to the actual results.

Thus, the evolution of control systems is often from physical observation, to historical records, to master (static) budgets, to flexible budgets (and standard costs, which are described in the next section). Note that one control tool does not *replace* another; instead, each control tool is *added* to the others. The systems become more costly, but somehow they are perceived by the managers who buy them as leading to net benefits in the form of a better set of collective operating decisions.

This concludes the presentation of an overall view of flexible budgets and standards. Subsequent sections probe the subject more deeply.

STANDARDS FOR MATERIAL AND LABOR

Standard costs are the building blocks of a budgeting and feedback system. They are carefully predetermined costs—targets that should be achieved.

Difference between Standards and Budgets

What is the difference between a standard amount and a budget amount? If standards are currently attainable, as they are assumed to be in this book, there is no conceptual difference. The term standard cost, as it is most widely used, is a unit concept; for example, the standard cost of direct material shown in Exhibit 7-2 is $3 per unit. The term **budgeted cost,** as it is most widely used, is a total concept; that is, the budgeted cost of material is $21,000 if 7,000 units are to be produced at a standard cost of $3 per unit. It may be helpful to think of a standard as a budget for the production of a single unit. In many companies, the terms **budgeted performance** and **standard performance** are used interchangeably.

In practice, direct material and direct labor are often said to be controlled with the help of *standard costs,* whereas all other costs are usually said to be controlled with the help of **departmental overhead budgets.** This distinction probably arose because of different timing and control techniques for various costs. Direct material and direct labor are generally relatively costly, and are easily identifiable for control purposes. Therefore, techniques for planning and controlling these costs are relatively refined. Overhead costs are combinations of many individual items, none of which justifies an elaborate control system. In consequence, use of direct material may be closely watched on an hourly basis; direct labor, on a daily basis; and factory overhead, on a weekly or monthly basis.

All this leads to the following straightforward approach (using assumed figures), which we will pursue throughout the remainder of this book. The *standard* is a *unit* idea; the *budget* is a *total* idea. Using the data in Exhibit 7-2:

	STANDARDS		
	---	---	---
	(1) STANDARD INPUTS ALLOWED FOR EACH UNIT OF OUTPUT ACHIEVED	(2) STANDARD PRICE PER UNIT OF INPUT	BUDGET FOR 7,000 UNITS OF OUTPUT*
Direct material	5 pounds	$ .60	$21,000
Direct labor	2 hours	4.00	56,000
Other costs (detailed)	Various	Various	96,600

* Col. (1) × (2) × 7,000

Role of Past Experience

The study of past behavior patterns is typically a fundamental step in formulating a standard or a budgeted cost. Although the study of past cost behavior is a useful starting point, a budgeted cost should not be merely an extension of past experience. Inefficiencies may be reflected in prior costs. Changes in technology, equipment, and methods also limit the usefulness of comparisons with the past. Also, performance should be judged in relation to some currently attainable goal, one that may be reached by skilled, diligent, superior effort. **Concern with the past is justified only insofar as it helps**

prediction. Management wishes to plan what costs *should be,* not what costs *have been.*

Current Attainability:
The Most Widely Used Standard

What standard of expected performance should be used? Should it be so severe that it is rarely, if ever, attained? Should it be attainable 50 percent of the time? Eighty percent? Twenty percent? Individuals who have worked a lifetime in setting standards for performance cannot agree, so there are no universal answers to these questions.

Two types of standards deserve mention here, perfection standards and currently attainable standards. **Perfection standards** (often also called **ideal standards**) are expressions of the absolute minimum costs possible under the best conceivable conditions, using existing specifications and equipment. No provision is made for shrinkage, spoilage, machine breakdowns, and the like. Those who favor this approach maintain that the resulting unfavorable variances will constantly remind managers of the perpetual need for improvement in all phases of operations. These standards are not widely used, however, because they have an adverse effect on employee motivation. Employees tend to ignore unreasonable goals.

Currently attainable standards are those that can be achieved by *very efficient* operations. Expectations are set high enough so that employees regard their fulfillment as possible, though perhaps not probable. Allowances are made for normal shrinkage, waste, and machine breakdowns. Variances tend to be unfavorable, but managers accept the standards as being reasonable goals.

The major reasons for using currently attainable standards are:

1. The resulting standard costs serve multiple purposes. For example, the same cost may be used for cash budgeting, inventory valuation, and budgeting departmental performance. In contrast, perfection standards cannot be used per se for cash budgeting, because financial planning will be thrown off.[2]

2. They have a desirable motivational impact on employees. The standard represents reasonable future performance, not fanciful ideal goals or antiquated goals geared to past performance.

[2] If standards are not currently attainable because they are perfection or outdated, the amount budgeted for financial (cash) planning purposes has to differ from the standard. Otherwise, projected income and cash disbursements will be forecasted incorrectly. In such cases, ideal or outdated standards may be used for compiling performance reports, but "expected variances" are stipulated in the master budget for financial planning. For example, if unusually strict labor standards are used, the standard cost per finished unit may be $8 despite the fact that top management anticipates an unfavorable performance variance of 40¢ per unit. In the master budget, the total labor costs would be $8.40 per unit: $8 plus an expected variance of 40¢.

180

Price and Efficiency Variances

The assessment of performance is facilitated by separating the items that are subject to the manager's direct influence from those that are not. The general approach is to separate *price* factors from *efficiency* factors. Price factors are less subject to immediate control than are efficiency factors, principally because of external forces, such as general economic conditions and unforeseeable price changes. Even when price factors are regarded as outside of company control, it is still desirable to isolate them to obtain a sharper focus on the efficient usage of the goods or services in question.

To see how the analysis of variances can be pursued more fully, reconsider the direct material and direct labor in Exhibit 7-5. The variances there can be subdivided into two major types: *price* and *efficiency*.[3]

To demonstrate this general approach for direct material and direct labor, we continue our illustration and assume that the following actually occurred:

Direct material: 36,810 pounds of inputs used at an actual unit price of 58¢ for a total actual cost of $21,350.

Direct labor: 15,000 hours of inputs were used at an actual hourly price (rate) of $4.10, for a total actual cost of $61,500.

The budget variance for materials may be analyzed as follows:

Price variance	= Actual inputs used × Difference between the actual unit price and the standard unit price
	= 36,810 pounds × ($.58 − $.60)
	= $736 *F*
Efficiency variance	= Standard unit price × Difference between the actual inputs used and the standard inputs allowed for the outputs achieved
	= $60 × [36,810 − (7,000 units of finished product × 5 pounds of materials per unit)]
	= $.60 × (36,810 − 35,000)
	= $.60 × 1,810 = $1,086 *U*
Flexible budget variance explained	= Price variance + Efficiency variance
	= $736 *F* + $1,086 *U* = $350 *U*

"Efficiency" is a relative measure that is often expressed as the ratio of inputs to outputs. That is, the concept of efficiency requires our knowing both

[3]Price and efficiency will be used throughout this book to describe these two classes of variances. In practice, the price variance is often called a *rate* variance when it is used in conjunction with labor. Similarly, the efficiency variance is often called a *usage* or *quantity* variance when it is used in conjunction with materials.

inputs and *outputs* and their interrelationship. "Perfect" efficiency would be some approximation of an optimal relationship between inputs and outputs.

Variance analysis does *not* provide any answers. But it raises questions, provides clues, and directs attention. For instance, one possible explanation, among many, for this set of variances is that a manager might have made a trade-off and lost—that is, he might have purchased, at a favorable price, some materials that were slightly substandard, resulting in excessive waste as indicated by the unfavorable efficiency variance.

The analysis for direct labor is similar:

Price variance	$= 15{,}000 \text{ hours} \times (\$4.10 - \$4.00)$
	$= 15{,}000 \times \$.10 = \$1{,}500 \ U$
Efficiency variance	$= \$4.00 \times [15{,}000 - (7{,}000 \text{ product}$
	$\text{units} \times 2 \text{ allowed hours of labor}$
	$\text{per unit})]$
	$= \$4.00 \times 1{,}000 = \$4{,}000 \ U$
Flexible budget variance explained	$= \$1{,}500 \ U + \$4{,}000 \ U = \$5{,}500 \ U$

Evidently, direct labor warrants further investigation, because it is easily the largest variance of all.

A General Approach

Exhibit 7-6 presents the foregoing analysis in a format that deserves close study. The general approach is at the top of the exhibit; the specific applications then follow. **Even though the exhibit may seem unnecessarily complex at first, its repeated use will solidify your understanding of variance analysis.** Of course, the other budget variances in Exhibit 7-5 could be further analyzed in the same manner in which direct material and direct labor are analyzed in Exhibit 7-6. The pursuit of such a detailed investigation depends on the manager's perceptions as to whether the extra benefits will exceed the extra cost of such detective work.

Graphical Approach

A graphical approach sometimes clarifies the relationships. For example, the direct-labor analysis in the middle of Exhibit 7-6 is also portrayed in Exhibit 7-7. The cost function is linear, sloping upward at a standard rate (price) of $4 per hour.

Note that volume is expressed in hours instead of in physical units of product. This is a common practice. Most departments have a variety of products; when the variety of units is added together, the result is frequently a nonsensical sum. Therefore, all units of output are expressed in terms of the standard inputs of hours allowed for their production. Hours thus become

EXHIBIT 7-6

General Approach to Analysis of Variable Cost Variances

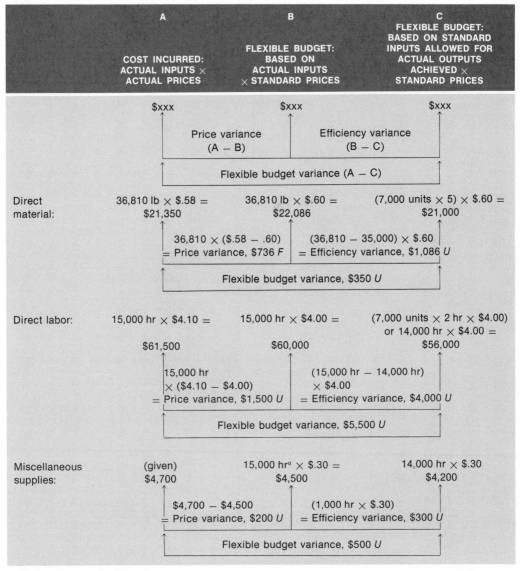

	A	B	C
	COST INCURRED: ACTUAL INPUTS × ACTUAL PRICES	**FLEXIBLE BUDGET: BASED ON ACTUAL INPUTS × STANDARD PRICES**	**FLEXIBLE BUDGET: BASED ON STANDARD INPUTS ALLOWED FOR ACTUAL OUTPUTS ACHIEVED × STANDARD PRICES**

$xxx → $xxx → $xxx

Price variance (A − B)   Efficiency variance (B − C)

Flexible budget variance (A − C)

Direct material:

36,810 lb × $.58 = $21,350

36,810 lb × $.60 = $22,086

(7,000 units × 5) × $.60 = $21,000

36,810 × ($.58 − .60) = Price variance, $736 *F*

(36,810 − 35,000) × $.60 = Efficiency variance, $1,086 *U*

Flexible budget variance, $350 *U*

Direct labor:

15,000 hr × $4.10 = $61,500

15,000 hr × $4.00 = $60,000

(7,000 units × 2 hr × $4.00) or 14,000 hr × $4.00 = $56,000

15,000 hr × ($4.10 − $4.00) = Price variance, $1,500 *U*

(15,000 hr − 14,000 hr) × $4.00 = Efficiency variance, $4,000 *U*

Flexible budget variance, $5,500 *U*

Miscellaneous supplies:

(given) $4,700

15,000 hr[a] × $.30 = $4,500

14,000 hr × $.30 $4,200

$4,700 − $4,500 = Price variance, $200 *U*

(1,000 hr × $.30) = Efficiency variance, $300 *U*

Flexible budget variance, $500 *U*

U = Unfavorable.   *F* = Favorable.
[a] For comments, see the section, "Limitations of Price and Efficiency Variances," in text.

the common denominator for measuring total volume. Production, instead of being expressed as, say, 12,000 chairs and 3,000 tables, is frequently expressed as 14,000 *standard hours allowed* (or *standard hours worked,* or *standard hours earned,* or most accurately as *standard hours of input allowed for outputs achieved*).

EXHIBIT 7-7. Graphical Analysis of Direct Labor

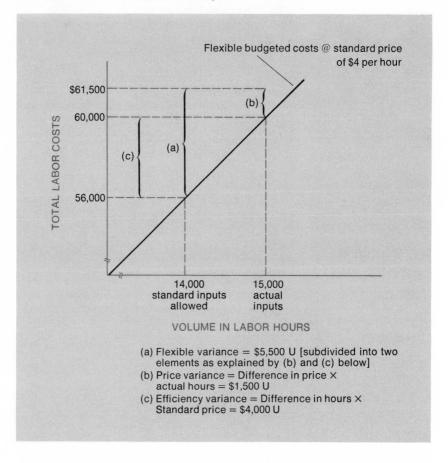

(a) Flexible variance = $5,500 U [subdivided into two elements as explained by (b) and (c) below]
(b) Price variance = Difference in price ×
    actual hours = $1,500 U
(c) Efficiency variance = Difference in hours ×
    Standard price = $4,000 U

Another key idea illustrated in Exhibits 7-6 and 7-7 is the versatility of the flexible budget. A flexible budget is geared to volume, and Exhibit 7-7 shows that volume can be measured in terms of *actual inputs* alone, *actual outputs achieved* alone, or both. Both measures are shown in the graph; they are necessary to obtain separate identification of price and efficiency variances.

When used in this book, unless stated otherwise, the term *flexible budget variance* will mean the difference between columns A and C in Exhibit 7-6, the difference between actual costs and the flexible budget based on the standard inputs allowed for actual outputs achieved.

Please reread the preceding four paragraphs before going on. They contain key ideas and terms that warrant scrutiny.

Limitations of Price and Efficiency Variances

The division of variances into two neat categories of "price" and "efficiency" is a good first step. However, it is a crude split, and its limitations should be kept in mind. In particular, the individual overhead items may be hard to subdivide in this way. For instance, the flexible budget for supplies is budgeted in Exhibit 7-5 at $4,200, based on a formula of 60¢ per unit.

In practice, a simple but fragile assumption underlies the usual efficiency-variance computation for variable-overhead items: Variable-overhead costs fluctuate in direct proportion to direct-labor hours. Therefore, the efficiency variance for a variable-overhead item such as supplies is a measure of the extra overhead (or savings) incurred *solely* because the actual *direct-labor hours* used differed from the standard hours allowed:

$$\begin{aligned}
\text{Overhead efficiency variance} &= \text{Standard overhead rate per hour} \times \\
&\quad \text{(Actual direct-labor hours of inputs} \\
&\quad - \text{Standard direct-labor hours allowed)} \\
&= \$.30 \times (15,000 - 14,000) \\
&= \$300 \text{ unfavorable}
\end{aligned}$$

Because direct labor was inefficiently used by 1,000 hours under this approach, we would expect the related usage of supplies to be proportionately excessive wholly because of labor inefficiency. However, whether in fact this direct relationship exists depends on specific circumstances.

To recapitulate, let us investigate why there was a $500 unfavorable supplies variance in Exhibit 7-5. The analysis in Exhibit 7-6 implies:

Actual costs		$4,700
Efficiency variance—The amount that would be expected to be incurred *because of the inefficient use of direct labor,* 1,000 hr × $.30 =	$300	
Price variance—The amount unexplained by the efficiency variance. It could arise from unit price changes for various supplies—but it could also arise simply from the general waste and sloppy use of these supplies. In short, this, too, could be partially or completely traceable to *more inefficiency,* even though it is labeled as a price variance. (Incidentally, for this reason, many practitioners call this type of overhead variance a *spending* variance rather than a price variance.)	200	
Budget variance		500
Budgeted amount in flexible budget		$4,200

Above all, the limitations of these analyses of variances should be underscored. The *only* way to discover why overhead performance did not

185

agree with a budget is to investigate possible causes, line item by line item. However, the price-efficiency distinctions provide a handy springboard for a more rigorous analysis.

CONTROLLABILITY AND VARIANCES

Responsibility for Material Variances

In most companies, the *acquisition* of materials or merchandise entails different control decisions than their *use*. The purchasing executive of a manufacturing company worries about getting raw materials at favorable prices, whereas the production executive concentrates on using them efficiently. The merchandise manager of a large grocery company will be responsible for skillful buying of foodstuffs, but the store manager will be responsible for their sale and for minimizing losses from shrinkage, shoplifting, and the like. Thus the responsibility for price variances usually rests with the purchasing officer, and the responsibility for efficiency variances usually rests with the production manager or sales manager.

Price variances are often regarded as measures of forecasting ability rather than of failure to buy at specified prices. Some control over the price variance is obtainable by getting many quotations, buying in economical lots, taking advantage of cash discounts, and selecting the most economical means of delivery. Price variances may lead to decisions to change suppliers or freight carriers.

However, failure to meet price standards may result from a sudden rush of sales orders or from unanticipated changes in production schedules, which in turn may require the purchasing officer to buy at uneconomical prices or to request delivery by air freight. In such cases, the responsibility may rest with the sales manager or the head of production scheduling, rather than with the purchasing officer.

Responsibility for Labor Variances

In most companies, because of union contracts or other predictable factors, labor prices can be foreseen with much greater accuracy than can prices of materials. Therefore, labor price variances tend to be relatively insignificant.

Labor, unlike material and supplies, cannot ordinarily be stored for later use. The acquisition and use of labor occur simultaneously. For these reasons, labor rate variances are usually charged to the same manager who is responsible for labor usage.

Labor price variances may be traceable to faulty predictions of the labor rates. However, the more likely causes include: (1) the use of a single average standard labor price for a given operation that is, in fact, performed by individuals earning slightly different rates because of seniority; (2) the assignment of a worker earning, perhaps, $6 per hour to a given operation that should be appointed to a less skilled worker earning, say, $4 per hour; and (3) the payment of hourly rates, instead of prescribed piece rates, because of low productivity.

Causes of Efficiency Variances

The general approach to analyzing efficiency variances is probably best exemplified by the control of direct materials in standard cost systems. The budget of the production department manager is usually based on a **standard formula** or a **Standard Bill of Materials**. This is a specification of the physical quantities allowed for producing a specified number of acceptable finished units. These quantities are then compared to the quantities actually used.

What does the manager do with the variances? He seeks explanations for their existence. Common causes of efficiency variances include: improper handling, inferior quality of material, poor workmanship, changes in methods, new workmen, slow machines, broken cutting tools, and faulty blueprints.

Trade-offs among Variances

Variance analysis can be useful for focusing on how various aspects of operations are meeting expectations. **However, a standard cost system should not be a straightjacket that prevents the manager from aiming at the overall organization objectives.** Too often, each unfavorable variance is regarded as, ipso facto, bad; and each favorable variance is regarded as, ipso facto, good.

Managers sometimes deliberately acquire off-standard material at unusually low prices. They hope that the favorable price variances will exceed any resulting unfavorable efficiency variances caused by heavy spoilage or unusual labor-hours. Thus, if the manager guesses correctly, the decision was favorable despite the unfavorable label pinned on the efficiency variances. **Because there are so many interdependencies among activities, an "unfavorable" or a "favorable" label should not lead the manager to jump to conclusions. By themselves, such labels merely raise questions and provide clues. They are attention directors, not answer givers.** The chapter appendix discusses these interdependencies in more depth.

When to Investigate Variances

When should variances be investigated? Frequently the answer is based on subjective judgments, hunches, guesses, and rules of thumb. The most troublesome aspect of feedback is deciding when a variance is significant enough to warrant management's attention. For some items, a small devia-tion may prompt follow-up. For other items, a minimum dollar amount or 5, 10, or 25 percent deviations from budget may be necessary before investiga-tions commence. Of course, a 4 percent variance in a $1 million material cost may deserve more attention than a 20 percent variance in a $10,000 repair cost. Therefore, rules such as "Investigate all variances exceeding $5,000, or 25 percent of standard cost, whichever is lower" are common.

Variance analysis is subject to the same cost-benefit test as other phases of an information system. The trouble with the foregoing rules of thumb is that they are too frequently based on subjective assessments, guesses, or hunches. The field of statistics offers tools to help reduce these subjective features. These tools help answer the cost-benefit question, and they help separate variances caused by random events from variances that are con-trollable.

Accounting systems have traditionally implied that a standard is a single acceptable measure. Practically, the accountant (and everybody else) realizes that the standard is a *band* or *range* of possible acceptable outcomes. Consequently, he expects variances to fluctuate randomly within some normal limits. A random variance, by definition, calls for no corrective action to an existing process. In short, random variances are attributable to chance rather than to management's implementation decisions.

SUMMARY

Management is best aided by carefully prepared standards and budgets representing what *should* be accomplished. These standards should be based on material specifications and on work measurement rather than on past performance, because the latter too often conceals past inefficiencies.

Currently attainable standards are the most widely used because they usually have the most desirable motivational impact and because they may be used for a variety of accounting purposes, including financial planning, as well as for monitoring departmental performance.

When standards are currently attainable, there is no logical difference between standards and budgets. A standard is a *unit* concept, whereas a budget is a *total* concept. In a sense, the standard is the budget for one unit.

Flexible budgets are geared to changing levels of activity rather than to a single static level. They may be tailored to a particular level of sales or production volume—*before* or *after* the fact. They tell how much cost *should be* or *should have been* incurred for any level *of output,* which is usually expressed either in product units of output or in standard direct labor hours allowed for that output.

The evaluation of performance is aided by a feedback comparison of actual results with budgeted expectations, as summarized in Exhibit 7-4. The flexible budget idea helps managers to get an explanation of why the master budget was not achieved. Variances are often divided into marketing, price, and efficiency variances. In practice, the efficiency factors are more important because they are subject to more direct management influence than are prices of materials or labor.

There is a similarity in approach to the control of all costs that are regarded as variable. The *price* variance is the *difference in price multiplied by actual quantity.* The *efficiency* variance is the *difference in quantity multiplied by standard price.*

Variances raise questions; they do not provide answers. The analysis and follow-up of variances are the keys to successful management control. Variances provide clues, jog memories, and open pertinent avenues for management investigation. If managers do not do anything with the variances, then either the reporting system needs overhauling or the managers need to be educated and convinced of the benefits that can be derived from a careful analysis of the variances.

Variance analysis is subject to the same cost-benefit test as other phases of an information system. The decision on whether to investigate a variance depends on expected net benefits.

Chapter 15, which may be studied now if desired, probes the analysis of variances in more depth, particularly with respect to fixed overhead and inventories.

SUMMARY PROBLEM FOR YOUR REVIEW

Problem

The following questions are based on the data contained in the illustration used in the chapter:

1. Suppose that actual production and sales were 8,500 units instead of 7,000 units. (a) Compute the marketing variance. Is the performance of the marketing function the sole explanation for this variance? Why? (b) Using a flexible budget, compute the budgeted contribution margin, the budgeted operating income, budgeted direct material, and budgeted direct labor.
2. Suppose the following were the actual results for the production of 8,500 units:

   Direct material: 46,000 pounds of inputs were used at an actual unit price of 55¢, for a total actual cost of $25,300.
   Direct labor: 16,500 hours of inputs were used at an actual hourly price (rate) of $4.20, for a total actual cost of $69,300.

   Compute the flexible budget variance and the price and efficiency variances for direct material and direct labor. Present your answers in the form shown in Exhibit 7-6.
3. Suppose that the company is organized so that the purchasing manager bears primary responsibility for the acquisition prices of materials, and the production manager bears the primary responsibility for efficiency but no

responsibility for unit prices. Assume the same facts as in Requirement 2, except that the purchasing manager acquired 60,000 pounds of materials. This means that there is an ending inventory of 14,000 pounds. Would your variance analysis of materials in Requirement 2 change? Why? Show computations to support your answer.

Solution

1. (a) Marketing variance = Budgeted unit contribution margin
   × Difference between the master-budgeted sales in units and the actual sales in units

   $$= \$9.20 \times (9,000 - 8,500) = \$4,600 \ U$$

   This variance is labeled as a marketing variance because it quantifies the impact on net income of the deviation from an original sales target—while holding price and efficiency factors constant. Of course, the failure to reach target sales may be traceable to a number of causes beyond the control of the marketing force, including strikes, material shortages, and storms.
   (b) The budget formulas in Exhibit 7-2 are the basis for the following answers:

   Budgeted contribution margin = $9.20 × 8,500 = $78,200
   Budgeted operating income   = $78,200 − $70,000 fixed costs = $8,200
   Budgeted direct material   = $3.00 × 8,500 = $25,500
   Budgeted direct labor   = $8.00 × 8,500 = $68,000

2.

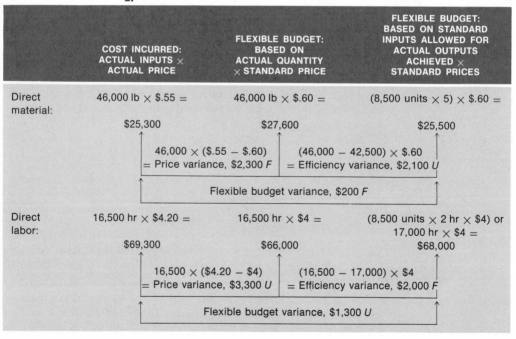

	COST INCURRED: ACTUAL INPUTS × ACTUAL PRICE	FLEXIBLE BUDGET: BASED ON ACTUAL QUANTITY × STANDARD PRICE	FLEXIBLE BUDGET: BASED ON STANDARD INPUTS ALLOWED FOR ACTUAL OUTPUTS ACHIEVED × STANDARD PRICES
Direct material:	46,000 lb × $.55 =	46,000 lb × $.60 =	(8,500 units × 5) × $.60 =
	$25,300	$27,600	$25,500

46,000 × ($.55 − $.60)
= Price variance, $2,300 F   (46,000 − 42,500) × $.60
= Efficiency variance, $2,100 U

Flexible budget variance, $200 F

Direct labor:	16,500 hr × $4.20 =	16,500 hr × $4 =	(8,500 units × 2 hr × $4) or 17,000 hr × $4 =
	$69,300	$66,000	$68,000

16,500 × ($4.20 − $4)
= Price variance, $3,300 U   (16,500 − 17,000) × $4
= Efficiency variance, $2,000 F

Flexible budget variance, $1,300 U

3. Whether the variance analysis in Requirement 2 would change depends on how the information system is designed. In many organizations, price variances for materials are isolated at the most logical control point—time of purchase rather than time of use. In turn, the production or operating departments that later use the materials are always charged at some predetermined so-called budget or standard unit price, never at actual unit prices. Under this procedure the price-variance analysis would be conducted in the purchasing department and the efficiency-variance analysis in the production department. This represents a slight modification of the approach in Requirement 2 as follows:

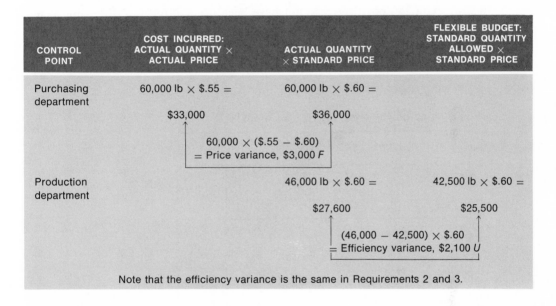

CONTROL POINT	COST INCURRED: ACTUAL QUANTITY × ACTUAL PRICE	ACTUAL QUANTITY × STANDARD PRICE	FLEXIBLE BUDGET: STANDARD QUANTITY ALLOWED × STANDARD PRICE
Purchasing department	60,000 lb × $.55 = $33,000	60,000 lb × $.60 = $36,000	
		60,000 × ($.55 − $.60) = Price variance, $3,000 F	
Production department		46,000 lb × $.60 = $27,600	42,500 lb × $.60 = $25,500
		(46,000 − 42,500) × $.60 = Efficiency variance, $2,100 U	

Note that the efficiency variance is the same in Requirements 2 and 3.

APPENDIX:
MUTUAL PRICE AND EFFICIENCY EFFECTS

The usual breakdown of variances into price and efficiency is not theoretically perfect because there may be a small mutual price-efficiency effect. A production foreman and a purchasing agent might argue over the following situation. The direct material is 1,000 pounds @ $1, and is intended to produce 1,000 good finished units. The performance report shows the use of 1,150 pounds @ $1.20 to produce 1,000 good finished units.

The ordinary analysis of variances would appear as follows:

Actual quantity × Actual price or 1,150 × $1.20 = $1,380

Price variance = Difference in price ×
   Actual pounds = ($1.20 − $1) × 1,150 = $230 U

Efficiency variance = Difference in quantity ×
   Standard price = (1,150 − 1,000) × $1 =   <u>150 U</u>

Total variance explained   <u>380 *U*</u>

Standard quantity of inputs allowed for units

     produced × Standard price = 1,000 × $1 =   <u>$1,000</u>

      The small area in the upper right-hand corner of the graphic analysis (Exhibit 7-8) may be the area of controversy. The purchasing officer might readily accept responsibility for the price variance on the 1,000 pounds in the standard allowance, but he might claim that the extra $30 buried in his $230 total variance is more properly attributable to the production foreman. After all, if the foreman had produced in accordance with the standard, the extra 150 pounds would not have been needed. But this distinction is not often made, simply because it usually involves a small sum. However, we

EXHIBIT 7-8.   Graphic Analysis of Variances

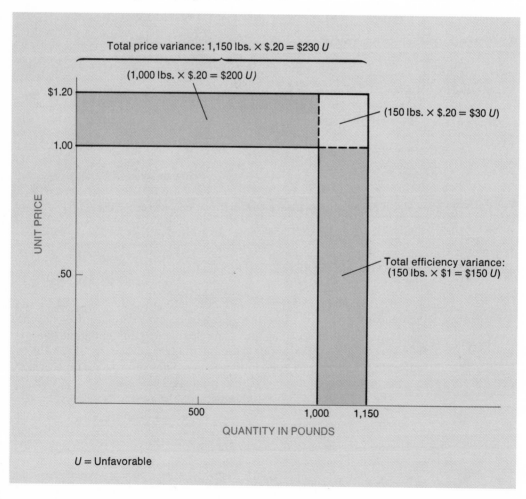

should be aware that the conventional variance analysis, which includes the joint price-efficiency variance ($30, in this case) as a part of an overall price variance, has logical deficiencies.

In practice, the efficiency variance is considered much more important than the price variance because the manager can exert more direct influence over the efficiency variance. Consequently, the performance report on efficiency should minimize the possibility of the production manager's criticisms of any accounting or measurement methods. Joint price-efficiency variance is less likely to cause arguments if it is buried in the total price variance than if it is buried in the efficiency variance.

ASSIGNMENT MATERIAL

Fundamental Assignment Material

7-1. Terminology: Define: *currently attainable standards; standard cost; price variance; rate variance; quantity variance; usage variance; flexible budget; variable budget; static budget; spending variance;* and *efficiency variance.*

7-2.[4] Flexible and static budgets. Azure Transportation Company executives have had trouble interpreting operating performance for a number of years. The company has used a budget based on detailed expectations for the forthcoming quarter. For example, the condensed performance report for a recent quarter for a midwestern branch was (in dollars):

	Budget	*Actual*	*Variance*
Net revenue	10,000,000	9,500,000	500,000 *U*
Fuel	200,000	196,000	4,000 *F*
Repairs and maintenance	100,000	98,000	2,000 *F*
Supplies and miscellaneous	1,000,000	985,000	15,000 *F*
Variable payroll	6,700,000	6,500,000	200,000 *F*
Total variable costs[a]	8,000,000	7,779,000	221,000 *F*
Supervision	200,000	200,000	—
Rent	200,000	200,000	—
Depreciation	600,000	600,000	—
Other fixed costs	200,000	200,000	—
Total fixed costs	1,200,000	1,200,000	—
Total costs charged against revenue	9,200,000	8,979,000	221,000 *F*
Operating income	800,000	521,000	279,000 *U*

U = Unfavorable.   *F* = Favorable.

[a] For purposes of this analysis, assume that all these costs are totally variable. In practice, many are mixed and have to be subdivided into variable and fixed components before a meaningful analysis can be made. Also assume that the prices and mix of services remain unchanged.

[4]Problems 7-23 or 7-36 may be used instead of 7-2.

Although the branch manager was upset about not obtaining enough revenue, he was happy that his control performance was favorable; otherwise his net operating income would be even worse.

His immediate superior, the Vice-President for Operations, was totally unhappy and remarked: "I can see some merit in comparing actual performance with budgeted performance because we can see whether actual revenue coincided with our best guess for budget purposes. But I can't see how this performance report helps me evaluate the cost control performance of the department head."

Required

1. Prepare a columnar flexible budget for expected costs at $9, $10, and $11 million levels of revenue. Include both variable and fixed costs in your budget.

2. Express Requirement 1 in formula form.

3. Prepare a condensed summary similar to Exhibit 7-4 that might better trace the effects on operating income of the deviations of actual results from the original plans.

Additional Assignment Material

7-3. "A standard is a band or range of acceptable outcomes." Explain.

7-4. What are standard costs? Why is their use preferable to comparisons of actual data with past data?

7-5. "Direct material and direct labor may be included in a flexible budget." Do you agree? Explain.

7-6. Why should a budgeted cost not be merely an extension of past experience?

7-7. Distinguish between perfection and currently attainable standards.

7-8. What is the difference between a standard amount and a budget amount?

7-9. What are expected variances?

7-10. "Price variances should be computed even if prices are regarded as outside of company control." Do you agree? Explain.

7-11. "Failure to meet price standards is the responsibility of the purchasing officer." Do you agree? Explain.

7-12. Why do labor price variances tend to be insignificant?

7-13. What are the key questions in the analysis and follow-up of variances?

7-14. What are some common causes of quantity variances?

7-15. Why is the joint price-quantity variance buried in the price variance rather than in the quantity variance?

7-16. What two basic questions must be asked in approaching the control of all costs?

7-17. Why do the techniques for controlling overhead differ from those for controlling direct material and direct labor?

7-18. "The flex in the flexible budget relates solely to variable costs." Do you agree? Explain.

7-19. How does the overhead price variance differ from the labor price variance?

7-20. Why are standard hours superior to actual hours as an index of activity?

7-21. Federal Park Service. The Federal Park Service prepared the following budget for one of its national parks for 19x4:

Revenue from fees	$4,000,000
Variable costs (miscellaneous)	400,000
Contribution margin	$3,600,000
Fixed costs (miscellaneous)	3,600,000
Operating income	$ 0

The fees were based on an average of 50,000 vehicle-admission days (vehicles multiplied by number of days in parks) per week for the twenty-week season, multiplied by average entry and other fees of $4 per vehicle-admission day.

The season was booming for the first four weeks. However, there was a wave of thievery and violence during the fifth week. Grizzly bears killed four campers during the sixth week and two during the seventh week. As a result, the number of visitors to the park dropped sharply during the remainder of the season.

Total revenue fell by $1,000,000. Moreover, extra rangers and police had to be hired at a cost of $200,000. The latter was regarded as a fixed cost.

Required

Prepare a columnar summary of performance, showing the original budget, marketing variance, and actual results.

7-22. Explanation of variance in income. The Olson Company makes a variety of products that result in standard contribution margins averaging 30 percent of dollar sales and average unit selling prices of $8. Average productivity is three units per standard direct-labor hour. The master budget for 19x1 had predicted sales of 500,000 units, but only 460,000 units were produced and sold. As many as 156,000 actual direct-labor hours were used to produce the 460,000 units.

Fixed manufacturing costs were $700,000 and fixed nonmanufacturing costs were $300,000. There were no beginning or ending inventories.

The president was upset because the budgeted net income of $200,000 was not attained, particularly since the only budget variances were variable-cost efficiency variances amounting to merely $6,000, unfavorable.

1. What is the net income for the year?
2. Explain fully why the target net income was not achieved. Use a presentation similar to Exhibit 7-4.

7-23. University flexible budgeting. (CMA.) The University of Boyne offers an extensive continuing education program in many cities throughout the state. For the convenience of its faculty and administrative staff and also to save costs, the university operates a motor pool. The motor pool operated with 20 vehicles until February this year, when an additional automobile was acquired. The motor pool furnishes gasoline, oil, and other supplies for the cars and hires one mechanic who does routine maintenance and minor repairs. Major repairs are done at a nearby commercial garage. A supervisor manages the operations.

Each year the supervisor prepares an operating budget, informing university management of the funds needed to operate the pool. Depreciation on the automobiles is recorded in the budget in order to determine the costs per mile.

The schedule below presents the annual budget approved by the university. The actual costs for March are compared to one-twelfth of the annual budget. The annual budget was constructed upon the following assumptions:

a. 20 automobiles in the pool.
b. 30,000 miles per year per automobile.
c. 15 miles per gallon per automobile.
d. $.60 per gallon of gas.
e. $.006 per mile for oil, minor repairs, parts, and supplies.
f. $135 per automobile in outside repairs.

The supervisor is unhappy with the monthly report comparing budget and actual costs for March; he claims it presents his performance unfairly. His previous employer used flexible budgeting to compare actual costs to budgeted amounts.

UNIVERSITY MOTOR POOL

Budget Report
For March 19x6

	ANNUAL BUDGET	ONE-MONTH BUDGET	MARCH ACTUAL	OVER[a] UNDER
Gasoline	$24,000	$2,000	$2,800	$800[a]
Oil, minor repairs, parts, and supplies	3,600	300	380	80[a]
Outside repairs	2,700	225	50	175
Insurance	6,000	500	525	25[a]
Salaries and benefits	30,000	2,500	2,500	—
Depreciation	26,400	2,200	2,310	110[a]
	$92,700	$7,725	$8,565	$840[a]
Total miles	600,000	50,000	63,000	
Cost per mile	$.1545	$.1545	$.1359	
Number of automobiles	20	20	21	

1. Employing flexible budgeting techniques, prepare a report that shows budgeted amounts, actual costs, and monthly variation for March.
2. Explain briefly the basis of your budget figure for outside repairs.

7-24. Comparing budgeted and actual performance. The Reliance Company recently constructed a factory that can manufacture 100,000 units of a product per year. The forecasted demand averaged 84,000 units per year over a planning horizon of fifteen years. The bigger plant was built because management decided that this was the most economical way to prepare for growth and seasonality in demand.

The sales forecast used in a master budget for 19x1 was 90,000 units. Average productivity is one-half unit per direct-labor hour, but it took 164,000 labor-hours to produce the 78,000 units that were sold.

The average unit selling price was $32. There were no beginning or ending inventories. The standard direct-labor rate was $6 per hour. Standard direct material was $8 per unit and standard variable overhead was $2 per hour. Variable nonmanufacturing costs were $1 per unit. Fixed manufacturing costs were $400,000 and fixed nonmanufacturing costs were $200,000.

All prices, rates, and fixed costs were incurred as foreseen in the master budget, except that the advertising budget allowance was underspent by $40,000 and actual material prices on the last 10,000 units produced were $9 per unit.

1. Present a schedule of the marketing variance, material price variance, efficiency variances, and advertising variances. Show your computations.
2. Prepare two sets of reports: (a) a summary of performance similar to Exhibit 7-4 and (b) a cost-control performance report similar to Exhibit 7-5.
3. Suppose there were no variable- or fixed-cost variances whatsoever. Compute the budgeted net income if the master-budgeted level were at the average long-run demand of 84,000 units. What is the break-even point? What alternatives should management explore to increase profitability?

7-25. Reconstructing financial statements. On New Year's Eve, December 31, 19x1, a fire partially destroyed the records of the Valentino Manufacturing Company. You are asked to prepare a summary of performance similar to Exhibit 7-4 for the year 19x1 based on scattered data.

Production and sales were 52,000 units. The unfavorable marketing variance, based on the unit contribution margin, was $40,000. The average selling price was $20 per unit. Total actual operating income was $17,000. The standard contribution margin per unit was $5. Budgeted and actual fixed costs were the same. Efficiency variances were $43,000, unfavorable.

7-26. Efficiency variances. Assume that 10,000 units of a particular item were produced. Suppose that the standard direct-material allowance is two pounds per unit, at a cost per pound of $2. Actually, 21,000 pounds of materials (input) were used to produce the 10,000 units (output).

Similarly, assume that it is supposed to take four direct-labor hours to produce one unit, and that the standard hourly labor cost is $3. But 41,000 hours (input) were used to produce the 10,000 units.

Compute the efficiency variances for direct material and direct labor.

7-27. Straightforward variance analysis. The Dixon Company uses a standard cost system. The month's data regarding its single product follow:

Variable overhead rate, $.90 per hour
Standard direct-labor cost, $4 per hour
Standard material cost, $1 per pound
Standard pounds of material in a finished unit, 3
Standard direct-labor hours per finished unit, 5
Material purchased and used, 6,700 lb
Direct-labor costs incurred, 11,000 hours, $41,800
Variable overhead costs incurred, $9,500
Finished units produced, 2,000
Actual material cost, $.90 per pound

Prepare schedules of all variances, using the format of Exhibit 7-6.

7-28. Hospital costs. A hospital cafeteria used a flexible budget. The expectation for January volume was 20,000 meals. Hourly paid extra dishwashers were budgeted at $4,000, computed on the basis of an average wage rate of $4 per hour. The following data were compiled for January, when 20,000 meals were actually served and the dishwashers actually worked 1,200 hours:

	Actual	Budget	Variance
Dietary department:			
Wages—dishwashers	$4,560	$4,000	$560 U

U = Unfavorable.

1. Compute the price and efficiency variances. What might be some possible reasons for the variances?
2. Suppose 24,000 meals had been served. Compute the price and efficiency variances.

7-29. Similarity of direct-labor and variable-overhead variances. The Acme Company has had great difficulty controlling costs during the past three years. Last month, a standard cost and flexible budget system was installed. A condensation of results for a department follows:

	Expected Behavior per Standard Direct-Labor Hour	Total Budget Variance
Lubricants	$ .30	$200 F
Other supplies	.20	150 U
Rework	.40	300 U
Other indirect labor	.50	300 U
Total variable overhead	$1.40	$550 U

F = Favorable.   U = Unfavorable.

198

The department had initially planned to manufacture 6,000 units in 4,000 standard direct-labor hours allowed. However, material shortage and a heat wave resulted in the production of 5,400 units in 3,900 actual direct-labor hours. The standard wage rate is $3.50 per hour, which was 20¢ higher than the actual average hourly rate.

Required

1. Prepare a detailed performance report with two major sections: direct labor and variable overhead.

2. Prepare a summary analysis of price and efficiency variances for direct labor and for variable overhead, using the format of Exhibit 7-6.

3. Explain the similarities and differences between the direct-labor and variable-overhead variances. What are some of the likely causes of the overhead variances?

7-30. **Variance analysis.** The Kaplan Company uses standard costs and a flexible budget. The purchasing agent is responsible for material price variances, and the production manager is responsible for all other variances. Operating data for the past week are summarized as follows:

Finished units produced: 5,000.
Direct material: Purchases, 10,000 lb @ $1.50. Standard price, $1.60 per lb.
Used, 5,400 lb. Standard allowed per unit produced, 1 lb.
Direct labor: Actual costs, 8,000 hours @ $3.05, or $24,400. Standard allowed per good unit produced, $1\frac{1}{2}$ hours. Standard price per direct-labor hour, $3.
Variable manufacturing overhead: Actual costs, $8,800. Budget formula is $1 per standard direct-labor hour.

Required

1. a. Material purchase-price variance.
   b. Material efficiency variance.
   c. Direct-labor price variance.
   d. Direct-labor efficiency variance.
   e. Variable manufacturing-overhead price variance.
   f. Variable manufacturing-overhead efficiency variance.

   (*Hint:* For a format, see Requirement 3 of the solution to the Summary Problem for Your Review.)

2. a. What is the budget allowance for direct labor?
   b. Would it be any different if production were 6,000 good units?

7-31. **Labor variances.** The City of New York has a sign shop where street signs of all kinds are manufactured and repaired. The manager of the shop uses standards to judge performance. However, because a clerk mistakenly discarded some labor records, the manager has only partial data for October. He knows that the total direct-labor variance was $880, favorable, and that the standard labor price was $6 per hour. Moreover, a recent pay raise produced an unfavorable labor price variance for October of $320. The actual hours of input were 1,600.

1. Find the actual labor price per hour.

2. Determine the standard hours allowed for the output achieved.

7-32. **Variable-overhead variances.** You have been asked to prepare an analysis of the overhead costs in the billing department of a hospital. As an initial step, you prepare a summary of some events that bear on overhead for the most recent period. The variable-overhead budget variance was $4,000, unfavorable. The standard variable-overhead price per billing was 5¢. Ten bills per hour is regarded as standard productivity per clerk. The total overhead incurred was $168,500, of which $110,000 was fixed. There were no variances for fixed overhead. The variable-overhead price variance was $2,000, favorable.

Find the following:

1. Variable-overhead efficiency variance.

2. Actual hours of input.

3. Standard hours allowed for output achieved.

7-33. **Analyzing direct labor.** (CMA.) The Felton Company manufactures a complete line of radios. Because a large number of models have plastic cases, the company has its own molding department for producing the cases. The month of April was devoted to the production of the plastic case for one of the portable radios—Model SX76.

The Molding Department has two operations—molding and trimming. There is no interaction of labor in these two operations. The standard labor cost for producing ten plastic cases for Model SX76 is as follows:

Molders	.50 hr @ $6 =	$3
Trimmers	.25 hr @ $4 =	1
		$4

During April, 70,000 plastic cases were produced in the Molding Department. However, 10 percent (7,000) had to be discarded as defective at final inspection. The Purchasing Department had changed to a new plastic supplier to take advantage of a lower price for comparable plastic. The new plastic turned out to be of a lower quality and resulted in the rejection of completed cases.

Direct-labor hours of input and direct-labor costs charged to the Molding Department are shown below.

Actual Direct-Labor Costs in the Molding Department

Molders	3,800 hr @ $6.25 =	$23,750
Trimmers	1,600 hr @ $4.15 =	6,640
		$30,390

As a result of poor scheduling by the Production Scheduling Department, the foreman of the Molding Department had to shift molders to the trimming operation for 200 hours during April. The company paid the molding workers their regular hourly rate even though they were performing a lower-rated task. No significant loss of efficiency was caused by the shift. In addition, the foreman of the department indicated that 75 hours and 35 hours of idle time occurred in the molding and trimming operations, respectively, as a result of unexpected machinery repairs required during the month.

Required

1. The monthly report, which compares actual costs with standard cost of output for the month of April, shows the following labor variance for the Molding Department:

Actual labor costs for April	$30,390
Standard labor cost of output	
(63,000 × $4/10)	25,200
Unfavorable labor variance	$ 5,190

This variance is significantly higher than normal, and management would like an explanation. Prepare a detailed analysis of the unfavorable labor variance for the Molding Department that shows the variance resulting from (1) labor rates; (2) labor substitution, (3) material substitution, (4) operating efficiency, and (5) idle time.

2. The foreman of the Molding Department is concerned with the large variances charged to his department. He feels that the variances due to labor substitution and change in raw materials should not be charged to his department. Does the foreman have a valid argument? Briefly justify your position.

7-34. **Combined or joint price-quantity variance and incentives.** Read the chapter appendix. The Melbourne Company had an incentive system that rewarded managers each Christmas for cost savings on materials. The manager of purchasing received 10 percent of any favorable price variance accumulated for the fiscal year ending November 30. Similarly, the production manager received 10 percent of the favorable efficiency (quantity) variances. In addition, each manager received 10 percent of the favorable net material variances. Note, however, that all variances were included in the computations—that is, an unfavorable variance in one month would offset a favorable variance in another month.

In the opinion of the company president, this system had worked reasonably well in past years. Of course, because of the sensitivity of the incentive system, the standards were carefully specified and adjusted each quarter. Only minimal inventories were kept at any time. Bonuses had varied from zero to 20 percent of the managers' base salaries. The purchasing manager's base salary for a recent fiscal year ending November 30 was $24,000; the production manager's was $30,000.

The operating results on Material A for a recent month were:

Purchase-price variance	$ 72,000 U
Efficiency variance	36,000 U
Net material variance	$108,000 U

Two pounds of Material A was the standard quantity allowed for every unit of a particular finished product, a chemical used in petroleum refining. One hundred thousand units of the chemical had been manufactured. The average price actually paid for Material A was 30¢ per pound in excess of the standard price.

1. What number of pounds of Material A was purchased?
2. Find the standard price per pound of Material A.
3. What is the total standard cost allowed for material components of the finished product?
4. As the purchasing manager, what is your opinion of the bonus system? Would your answer be the same if the actual raw-material price paid had been 70¢ per pound? Explain fully.
5. As the production manager, what is your opinion of the bonus system? Why?
6. Why is part of the bonus dependent on the net material variance?
7. Assume that some bonus system tied to variance analysis is maintained. What changes would you recommend?

7-35. **Comprehensive variance analysis.** (CMA, adapted.) The Carberg Corporation manufactures and sells a single product. The cost system used by the company is a standard cost system. The standard variable cost per unit of product is shown below:

Material—1 pound plastic @ $2	$ 2.00
Direct labor, 1.6 hours @ $4	6.40
Variable overhead cost	3.00
	$11.40

The variable-overhead cost per unit was calculated from the following annual overhead cost budget for a 60,000-unit volume. Variable overhead cost:

Indirect labor, 30,000 hours @ $4	$120,000
Supplies—Oil 60,000 gallons @ $.50	30,000
Allocated variable service department costs	30,000
Total variable-overhead cost	$180,000

The charges to the manufacturing department for November, when 5,000 units were produced, are given below:

Material—5,300 pounds @ $2	$10,600
Direct labor, 8,200 hours @ $4.10	33,620
Indirect labor, 2,400 hours @ $4.10	9,840
Supplies—Oil 6,000 gallons @ $0.55	3,300
Allocated variable service department costs	3,200
Total variable costs	$60,560

The purchasing department normally buys approximately the same quantity as is used in production during a month. In November, 5,200 pounds were purchased at a price of $2.10 per pound.

1. Calculate the following variances from standard costs for the data given:
   a. material purchase price
   b. material efficiency
   c. direct-labor price
   d. direct-labor efficiency
   e. overhead budget

2. The company has divided its responsibilities so that the purchasing department is responsible for the price at which material and supplies are purchased, and the manufacturing department is responsible for the quantities of material used. Does this division of responsibilities solve the conflict between price and efficiency variances? Explain your answer.

3. Prepare a report that details the overhead budget variance. The report, which will be given to the manufacturing department manager, should display only the part of the variance that is the responsibility of the manager and should highlight the information in ways that would be useful to him in evaluating departmental performance and when considering corrective action.

7-36. **Review of major points in chapter.** The following questions are based on the data contained in the illustration used in the chapter:

1. Suppose that actual production and sales were 8,000 units instead of 7,000 units. (a) Compute the marketing variance. Is the performance of the marketing function the sole explanation for this variance? Why? (b) Using a flexible budget, compute the budgeted contribution margin, the budgeted operating income, budgeted direct material, and budgeted direct labor.

2. Suppose the following were the actual results for the production of 8,000 units:

   Direct material: 42,000 pounds were used at an actual unit price of 56¢, for a total actual cost of $23,520.

   Direct labor: 16,500 hours were used at an actual hourly rate of $4.10, for a total actual cost of $67,650.

   Compute the flexible-budget variance and the price and efficiency variances for direct materials and direct labor. Present your answers in the form shown in Exhibit 7-6.

3. Suppose the company is organized so that the purchasing manager bears primary responsibility for the acquisition prices of materials, and the production manager bears the primary responsibility for efficiency but no responsibility for unit prices. Assume the same facts as in Requirement 2, except that the purchasing manager acquired 60,000 pounds of materials. This means that there is an ending inventory of 18,000 pounds. Would your variance analysis of materials in Requirement 2 change? Why? Show your computations.

7-37. **Review problem on standards and flexible budgets; answers provided.** The Morrow Company makes a variety of leather goods. It uses standard costs and a flexible budget to aid planning and control. Budgeted variable overhead at a 60,000-direct-labor-hour level is $36,000.

During April the company had an unfavorable variable-overhead efficiency variance of $1,200. Material purchases were $322,500. Actual direct-labor costs incurred were $187,600. The direct-labor efficiency variance was $6,000, unfavorable. The actual average wage price was 20¢ lower than the average standard wage price.

The company uses a variable-overhead rate of 20 percent of standard direct-labor *cost* for flexible budgeting purposes. Actual variable overhead for the month was $41,000.

Required

Compute the following amounts; then use *U* or *F* to indicate whether requested variances are favorable or unfavorable.

1. Standard direct-labor cost per hour.

2. Actual direct-labor hours worked.

3. Total direct-labor price variance.

4. Total flexible budget for direct-labor costs.

5. Total direct-labor variance.

6. Variable-overhead price variance in total.

Answers to Problem 7-37

1. $3. The variable-overhead price is $.60, obtained by dividing $36,000 by 60,000 hours. Therefore, the direct-labor price must be $.60 ÷ .20 = $3.

2. 67,000 hours. Actual costs, $187,600 ÷ ($3 − $.20) = 67,000 hours.

3. $13,400 *F*. 67,000 actual hours × $.20 = $13,400.

4. $195,000. Efficiency variance was $6,000, unfavorable. Therefore, excess hours must have been $6,000 ÷ $3 = 2,000. Consequently, standard hours allowed must be 67,000 − 2,000 = 65,000. Flexible budget = 65,000 × $3 = $195,000.

5. $7,400 *F*. $195,000 − $187,600 = $7,400 *F*; or $13,400 *F* − $6,000 *U* = $7,400 *F*.

6. $800 *U*. Flexible budget = 65,000 × $.60 = $39,000. Total variance = $41,000 − $39,000 = $2,000 *U*. Price variance = $2,000 − $1,200 efficiency variance = $800 *U*.

SUGGESTED READING

BEYER, R., and D. TRAWICKI, *Profitability Accounting for Planning and Control*, 2nd ed. (New York: The Ronald Press Company, 1972). Especially strong in the area of flexible budgeting.

CHAPTER 8

Variations of Cost Behavior Patterns

When we refer to "cost behavior patterns," we generally mean the relationship of total costs to changes in the volume of activity. Until this chapter, we have concentrated on two basic linear-cost behavior patterns: variable and fixed. Now we shall examine some variations of these patterns that have proven helpful for planning and control. Then we shall explore the problem of how to determine cost behavior patterns so that useful predictions and evaluations may be made.

ENGINEERED, DISCRETIONARY, AND COMMITTED COSTS

During the 1960s, a classification of costs evolved as follows:

Fixed Costs:	*Variable Costs:*
Committed	Engineered
Discretionary	Discretionary[a]

[a] Only a few variable costs belong in the discretionary classification, as explained below.

We shall describe these types of costs, beginning with fixed committed costs.

Fixed Costs and Capacity

Fixed costs, also called capacity costs, measure the capacity for manufacturing, sales, administration, and research. They reflect the capability for sustaining a planned volume of activity.

The size of fixed costs is influenced by long-run marketing conditions, technology, and the methods and strategies of management. Examples of the methods and strategies of management include sales salaries versus sales commissions and one-shift versus two-shift operations. Fixed costs are often the result of a trade-off decision whereby lower variable costs are attained in exchange for higher fixed costs. For example, automatic equipment may be acquired by banks, post offices, or hospitals to reduce labor costs.

Generally, a heavier proportion of fixed to variable costs lessens management's ability to respond to short-run changes in economic conditions and opportunities. Still, unwillingness to incur fixed costs reveals an aversion to risk that may exclude a company from profitable ventures. For instance, the launching of new products often requires very large fixed costs for research, advertising, equipment, and working capital.

Committed Fixed Costs

For planning and control, fixed costs may be usefully subdivided into committed and discretionary categories. Committed fixed costs consist largely of those fixed costs that arise from the possession of plant, of equipment, and of a basic organization. Examples are depreciation, property taxes, rent, insurance, and the salaries of key personnel. These costs are affected primarily by long-run sales forecasts that, in turn, indicate the long-run capacity needs.

The behavior of committed fixed costs may best be viewed by assuming a zero volume of activity in an enterprise that fully expects to resume normal activity (for example, during a strike or a shortage of materials that forces a complete shutdown of activity). The committed fixed costs are all those organization and plant costs that continue to be incurred and that cannot be reduced without injuring the organization's competence to meet long-range goals. Committed fixed costs are the least responsive of the fixed costs, because they tend to be less affected by month-to-month and year-to-year decisions.

In planning, the focus is on the impact of these costs over a number of years. Such planning usually requires tailoring the capacity to future demand for the organization's products in the most economical manner. For example, should the store size be 50,000 square feet, or 80,000, or 100,000? Should the gasoline station have one, or two, or more stalls for servicing automobiles? Such decisions usually involve selecting the point of optimal trade-off between present and future operating costs. That is, constructing excess

206

capacity now may save costs in the long run, because construction costs per square foot may be much higher later. On the other hand, if the forecast demand never develops, the organization may own facilities that are idle.

These decisions regarding capital expenditures are generally shown in an annual budget called the **capital budget** or **capital-spending budget.** As you recall, the *master budget* is based primarily on the annual sales forecast, the cornerstone of budgeting. Similarly, all capital-spending decisions are ultimately based on long-range sales forecasts. Capital budgeting is discussed in Chapter 12.

Once buildings are constructed and equipment is installed, little can be done in day-to-day operations to affect the *total level* of committed costs. From a control standpoint, the objective is usually to increase current utilization of facilities, because this will ordinarily increase net income.

There is another aspect to the control problem, however. A follow-up, or audit, is needed to find out how well the ensuing utilization harmonizes with the decision that authorized the facilities in the first place. The latter approach helps management to evaluate the wisdom of its past long-range decisions and, in turn, should improve the quality of future decisions.

Discretionary Fixed Costs

Discretionary fixed costs (sometimes called **managed** or **programmed costs**) are fixed costs (a) that arise from periodic (usually yearly) appropriation decisions that directly reflect top-management policies regarding the maximum permissible amounts to be incurred, and (b) that do not have a demonstrable optimum relationship between inputs (as measured by the costs) and outputs (as measured by sales, services, or production). Discretionary costs may have no particular relation to volume of activity. Examples vary among organizations and include child day-care services, staging an opera, research and development, advertising, sales promotion, charitable donations, management consulting services, and many employee-training programs. Conceivably, such costs could be reduced almost entirely for a given year in dire times, whereas the committed costs would be much more difficult to reduce.

Discretionary fixed costs are decided upon by management at the start of the budget period. Goals are selected, the means for their attainment are chosen, the maximum expense to be incurred is specified, and the total amount to be spent is appropriated. For example, a state government may appropriate $5 million for an advertising campaign to encourage tourism. In the give-and-take process of preparing the master budget, the discretionary costs are the most likely to be revised.

Discretionary fixed costs represent an assortment of manufacturing, selling, administrative, and research items. For example, a large portion of discretionary fixed costs may consist of salaries for salesmen, accountants, clerks, and engineers, and often appear in the income statement lumped under the heading "General Selling and Administrative Expense." As in the case of committed costs, the resources acquired should be carefully planned and fully utilized if net income is to be maximized. Unlike committed costs, discretionary costs can be influenced more easily from period to period. It is also harder to measure the utilization of resources acquired via discretionary costs, principally because the results of services such as creative personnel, advertising, research, and training programs are much more difficult to isolate and quantify than the results of utilizing plant and equipment to make products.

The behavior of some discretionary fixed costs is easy to delineate. Advertising, research, donations, and training programs, for example, are usually formulated with certain objectives in mind. The execution of such projects is measured by comparing total expenditures with the appropriation. Because the tendency is to spend the entire appropriation, the resulting dollar variances are generally trivial. But planning is far more important than this kind of day-to-day control. The perfect execution of an advertising program—in the sense that the full amount authorized was spent in specified media at predetermined times—will be fruitless if the advertisements are unimaginative and lifeless and if they reach the wrong audience.

The most noteworthy aspect of discretionary fixed costs is that, unlike most other costs, they are not subject to ordinary engineering input-output analysis. For example, an optimum relationship between inputs and outputs can be specified for direct materials because it takes three pounds or five gallons or two square feet to make a finished product. In contrast, we are usually unsure of the "correct" amount of advertising, research, management training, donations, management consulting costs, police protection, and programs for health care, education, or consumer protection.

An agency within the U.S. Department of Health, Education and Welfare (HEW) can quantify the inputs (for example, the amount spent on planning, research, and evaluation and on writing regulations), but the outputs and the relation between inputs and outputs are harder to quantify. Systems can be designed to insure that the research and the regulations are concerned with the subjects deemed most important by the decision makers, but there is no convincing way of knowing how much is enough in any absolute sense.

Engineered and Discretionary Variable Costs

An engineered cost is any cost that has an explicit, specified physical relationship with a selected measure of activity. Most variable costs fit this classification. An "engineered" variable cost exists when an optimum relationship between inputs and outputs has been carefully determined by work-measurement techniques, which are described below. In fact, efficiency has been defined as just such an optimum relationship. For example, an automobile may have exact specifications: one battery, one radiator, two fan belts, and so forth. Direct material and direct labor are prime examples of engineered costs.

Many managers and accountants tend to use "variable cost" and "engineered cost" interchangeably, as if they were synonymous. Usually, this error is harmless. However, as noted at the start of the chapter, although most variable costs are engineered, some fit a discretionary classification; depending on management policy, other costs may go up and down with sales (or production) merely because management has predetermined that the organization can afford to spend a certain percentage of the sales dollar for items such as research, donations, and advertising. These costs would have a graphical pattern of variability, but not for the same reasons as direct materials or direct labor. An increase in such costs may be due to management's authorization to spend "because we can afford it" rather than to an engineered cause-and-effect relationship between such costs and sales.

ENGINEERED VERSUS DISCRETIONARY COSTS

Work Measurement for Control

Work measurement is the careful analysis of a task, its size, the methods used in its performance, and its efficiency. Its objective is to determine the work load in an operation and the number of employees necessary to perform that work efficiently.

The work-measurement approach is based on a fundamental premise: Permanent improvement in any performance is impossible unless the work is measured. The premise is a natural accompaniment for the definition of *efficiency,* which is an optimal relationship between inputs and outputs. Therefore, to know whether efficiency exists, we must have some quantification of both inputs and outputs.

Origins of Work Measurement

Work-measurement techniques were initially developed for planning and control of manufacturing rather than of nonmanufacturing activities. This occurred because inputs and outputs in the manufacturing areas are easier to identify and measure. The measurement of direct material consumed and finished units produced is straightforward. It is much more difficult to obtain a measurement for relating the inputs of advertising and sales promotion activity to the outputs of sales or contribution margins.

As the input-output relationships become less defined, management tends to abandon any formal work-measurement techniques and, instead, relies almost wholly on the individual and his supervisor for successful control. Consequently, physical observation is paramount and formal cost control is approached from a discretionary-cost rather than from an engineered-cost (work-measurement) viewpoint, especially in many areas of nonmanufacturing. However, despite the difficulties of implementation, work measurement is getting more attention from nonmanufacturing organizations as they seek to improve their efficiency.

In recent years, work measurement has been extended into nonprofit organizations as well as into the selling and administrative clerical areas of profit-seeking organizations. In fact, federal government agencies are heavy users of work measurement in such diverse areas as the auditing of income tax returns, the processing of social security checks, and the sorting of mail.

Control-Factor Units

The specific techniques used to measure the work include time and motion study, observation of a random sample of the work (work sampling), and the estimation, by a work-measurement analyst and a line supervisor, of the amount of time required for the work (time analysis).

The work load is often expressed in *control-factor units,* which are used in formulating the budget. For example, the control-factor units in a payroll department might include operations performed on time cards, on notices of change in the labor rate, on notices of employee promotion, on new employment and termination reports, and on routine weekly and monthly reports. All of these would be weighed. The estimated work load would then be used for determining the required labor force and budgetary allowance.

Examples of other operations and appropriate control-factor units include:

Operation	Unit of Measure (control-factor unit)
Billing	Lines per hour
Warehouse labor	Pounds or cases handled per day
Packing	Pieces packed per hour
Posting accounts receivable	Postings per hour
Mailing	Pieces mailed per hour

The Engineered-Cost Approach

There is much disagreement about how clerical costs should be controlled. Advocates of work measurement favor a more rigorous approach, which essentially regards these costs as engineered. In practice, a discretionary-fixed-cost approach is more often found.

Assume that ten payroll clerks are employed by a government agency, and that each clerk's operating efficiency *should be* the processing of the payroll records of 500 employees per month. This might be called the *perfection standard* for the work. In the month of June, the payroll records of 4,700 individuals were processed by these ten clerks. Each clerk earns $600 per month.

The engineered-cost approach to this situation is to base the budget formula on the unit cost of the individual pay record processed: $600 ÷ 500 records, or $1.20. Therefore, the budget allowance for payroll-clerk labor would be $1.20 × 4,700, or $5,640. Assume that the ten employees worked throughout the month. The following performance report would be prepared:

	Actual Cost	Flexible Budget: Total Standard Inputs Allowed for Good Units Produced	Budget Variance
Payroll-clerk labor	$6,000	$5,640	$360 U
	(10 × $600)	(4,700 × $1.20)	

Essentially, two decisions must be made in this operation. The first is a policy decision: How many clerks do we need? How flexible should we be? How divisible is the task? Should we use part-time help? Should we hire and fire as the volume of work fluctuates? The implication of these questions is that once the hiring decision is made, the total costs incurred can be predicted easily—$6,000 in our example.

The second decision concentrates on day-to-day control, on how efficiently the given resources are being utilized. The work-measurement approach is an explicit and formal attempt to measure the utilization of resources by:

1. Assuming a proportionately variable budget and the complete divisibility of the work load into small units.

2. Generating a budget variance that assumes a comparison of actual costs with the perfection standard—the cost that would be incurred if payroll-clerk labor could be turned on and off like a faucet. In this case, the variance of $360 informs management that there was overstaffing. The workload capability was 5,000 pay records, not the 4,700 actually processed. The extra cost of $360 resulted from operating in a way that does not attain the lowest possible cost. The $360 might also be considered as the amount that management is currently investing to provide stability in the work force.

Critics of work measurement will often assert that such a formal approach is not worth its cost because strong labor unions and other forces prevent managers from fine-tuning the size of the work force. Defenders of work measurement will respond that managers must know the costs of various labor policies. For instance, if the cost of overstaffing becomes exorbitant, the pertinent provisions in a labor contract may become key bargaining issues when the contract is about to be renewed.

The Discretionary-Fixed-Cost Approach

Work-measurement techniques are not used in the vast majority of organizations. Consequently, the tendency is to rely on the experience of the department head and his superior for judging the size of the work force needed to carry out the department's functions. There is a genuine reluctance to overhire because there is a corresponding slowness in discharging or laying off people when volume slackens. As a result, temporary peak loads are often met by hiring temporary workers or by having the regular employees work overtime.

In most cases, the relevant range of activity during the budget period can be predicted with assurance, and the work force needed for the marketing and administrative functions can be readily determined. If management refuses, consciously or unconsciously, to control costs in rigid accordance with short-run fluctuations in activity, these costs become discretionary—that is, their total amount is relatively fixed and unresponsive to short-run variations in volume.

The practical effects of the discretionary-fixed-cost approach are that the budgeted costs and the actual costs tend to be very close, so that resulting budget variances are small. Follow-ups to see that the available resources are being fully and efficiently utilized are regarded as the managers' responsibility, a duty that can be carried through by face-to-face control and by records of physical quantities (for example, pounds handled per day in a warehouse, pieces mailed per hour in a mailing room) that do not have to be formally integrated into the accounting records in dollar terms.

Hence, there is a conflict between common practice and the objective of work measurement, which is to treat most costs as engineered and to therefore subject them to short-range management control. **The moral is that management's attitudes and its planning and controlling decisions often determine whether a cost is discretionary fixed or engineered variable. A change in policy can transform a budgeted fixed cost into a budgeted variable cost, and vice versa.**

In sum, the two approaches may be compared as in Exhibit 8-1. The graphs there provide an overview of how differing philosophies of budgeting and control may be adopted for a cost that has *the same underlying behavior pattern.*

EXHIBIT 8-1

	BUDGET AS AN ENGINEERED COST	BUDGET AS A DISCRETIONARY COST
Actual cost incurred	$6,000	$6,000
Budget allowance	5,640[a]	6,000
Variance	360 *U*	0

[a] Rate = $6,000 ÷ 5,000 records or $1.20 per record; total = 4,700 records @ $1.20 = $5,640.

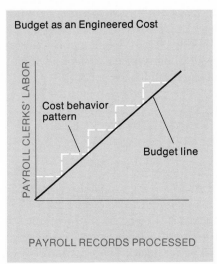

Budget as an Engineered Cost

PAYROLL CLERKS' LABOR

Cost behavior pattern

Budget line

PAYROLL RECORDS PROCESSED

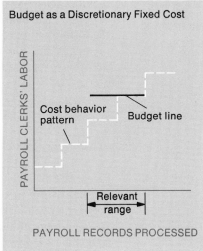

Budget as a Discretionary Fixed Cost

PAYROLL CLERKS' LABOR

Cost behavior pattern

Budget line

Relevant range

PAYROLL RECORDS PROCESSED

Choosing among Control Systems

As we have just seen, costs may be divided for planning and control purposes as follows:

Type of Cost	Major Control Techniques	Time Span and Feedback
Engineered	Flexible budgets and standards	Short
Discretionary	Physical observation and budget negotiation	Longer
Committed	Capital budgeting[1]	Longest

From time to time, you will undoubtedly find these distinctions among engineered, discretionary, and committed costs to be useful. However, these are subjective decisions, so expect some ambiguity as to whether a given cost is, say, committed or discretionary. For example, the salaries of supervisory or other highly prized personnel that would be kept on the payroll at zero activity levels are often regarded as committed costs; but some organizations may classify them as discretionary costs. Arguments about whether such types of costs are committed or discretionary are a waste of time—these matters must be settled on a case-by-case basis. In a given organization, quick agreement regarding an appropriate classification is usually possible.

The section on work measurement illustrates the overall theme of this book regarding control systems. Two alternative systems have been *described*, but note that one is not *advocated* here as being superior to the other. Such judgments can be safely made only in the specific circumstances facing a given organization.

Although a particular *system* has not been advocated here, a *method for choosing* among the systems is favored. Essentially, it is the cost-benefit

[1] Discussed in Chapters 12 and 13.

method. That is, the manager or systems designer should assess (1) the expected benefits from, say, a proposed clerical work-measurement system in the form of a better collective set of operating behavior or decisions against (2) the expected costs of a more formal system, including behavioral costs and the costs of educating employees.

DETERMINING HOW COSTS BEHAVE

Major Assumptions

Before costs can be classified and appropriately controlled, managers must be familiar with how the costs in question behave. As we know, costs often do not fit snugly into strictly variable and strictly fixed categories. Instead, there are a variety of *cost behavior patterns,* more technically described as *cost functions.* A cost function is a relationship between two or more variables. The dependent variable is frequently denoted as y (for example, some measure of total cost of repairs); the independent variable, as x (for example, some measure of activity or volume of inputs or outputs). The problem facing the accountant or manager is frequently called *cost estimation* or *cost approximation,* which is the attempt to specify some underlying relation between x and y over a stipulated *relevant range* of x that may be of interest. That is, given any quantification of the independent variable x (e.g., total miles driven), how much will the dependent variable y be (e.g., total repair costs)?

In practice, such cost approximations are typically based on two major simplifying and often heroic assumptions:

1. The cost function is linear over the relevant range. This straight-line approximation is often regarded as sufficiently precise for most decision uses.

2. The "true" cost behavior can be sufficiently explained by one independent variable (miles driven) instead of more than one (miles driven, weather, weight carried, model year of the vehicle, and so forth).

Focus on Costs and Benefits

As this book has stressed, whether these simplifying assumptions are justified is a cost-benefit question to be answered on a situation-by-situation basis. The manager tends to rely on exceedingly rough approximations until he realizes that buying finer cost estimation models may lead to net collective benefits from more desirable operating decisions.

To summarize, given assumptions of linearity and of one independent variable, each item of cost has some underlying "true" behavior pattern, whose expected value, $E(y)$, has the form:

$$E(y) = A + Bx$$

where *A* and *B* are the true (but unknown) parameters. (A *parameter* is a constant, such as *A*, or a coefficient, such as *B*, in a model or system of equations.)

Working with historical data, the cost analyst usually develops a formula approximation of the underlying relationship:

$$y' = a + bx$$

where *y'* is the calculated value as distinguished from the observed value *y*, and *a* and *b* are the approximations of the true *A* and *B*.

Criteria for Choosing Functions

The critical tasks in choosing among possible cost functions are to approximate the appropriate slope coefficient (defined as the amount of increase in *y* for each unit increase in *x*) and the constant or intercept (defined as the value of *y* when *x* is zero). The cost function is determined on the basis of some plausible theory that supports the relationships between the dependent and the independent variable—not on the basis of sample observations alone. There are many variables that move together and are therefore referred to as being highly *correlated.* But no conclusions about causes and effects are warranted. For instance, studies have shown a high positive correlation between teachers' salaries and liquor consumption. There are also many teacher members of Alcoholics Anonymous, but no cause-and-effect relationships have been demonstrated.

The following criteria should help in obtaining accurate approximations of cost functions:

1. *Economic plausibility.* The relationship must be credible. Physical observation, when it is possible, probably provides the best evidence of a relationship. The engineered-cost approach described earlier is an example of heavy reliance on observed technical relationships between inputs and outputs.

2. *Goodness of fit.* The cost analyst uses tests of closeness of fit for personal reassurance about the choice of a plausible cost function. Such tests, which are briefly described later, may be limited to scatter diagrams or may entail full-fledged formal statistical regression analysis.[2]

Note especially that both of these criteria are used together in choosing a cost function; each is a check on the other. Knowledge of both cost

---

[2] In the latter case, so-called *specification analysis* is also conducted to be sure that certain assumptions are satisfied. Then the sample values *a* and *b* are the best available estimates of the population values *A* and *B*. For an expanded discussion, see C. Horngren, *Cost Accounting: A Managerial Emphasis* (4th ed., Englewood Cliffs, N.J.: Prentice-Hall, Inc., 1977), Chap. 25.

accounting and operations is helpful. For example, repairs are often made when output is low because the machines can be taken out of service at these times. Therefore, if repair costs were recorded as each repair was made, scatter diagrams and regression analysis would show repair costs declining as output increased, whereas engineers know that the *timing* of the repair is often discretionary—the true cause-and-effect relationship is a tendency for many repair costs to increase (perhaps in steplike fashion) as activity increases. Consequently, these costs should be analyzed separately; otherwise, the true extent of variability of costs with output will be masked.[3]

Note too how criteria 1 and 2 interrelate. For example, a clerical overhead cost may show a high correlation with the number of records processed and an even higher correlation with the number of factory machine-hours worked. Our knowledge of operations confirms the first relationship; in contrast, there is a less convincing theoretical basis for the second.

Variety of Cost Functions

To illustrate the major types of cost functions, we now examine the corresponding graphic solutions to the basic formula: $y' = a + bx$.

A **proportionately variable cost** is the classical variable cost that we introduced in Chapter 2. Its total fluctuates in direct proportion to changes in x:

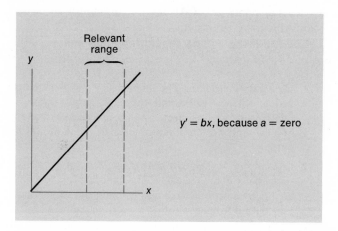

A *fixed cost* does not fluctuate in total as x changes within the relevant range:

[3]George J. Benston, "Multiple Regression Analysis of Cost Behavior," *Accounting Reveiw,* Vol. XLI, No. 4, p. 663.

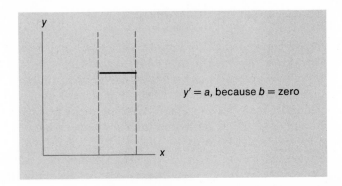

$y' = a$, because b = zero

A mixed or semivariable cost is a combination of variable and fixed elements. That is, its total fluctuates as x changes within the relevant range, but not in direct proportion. Instead, its behavior accords with the basic formula:

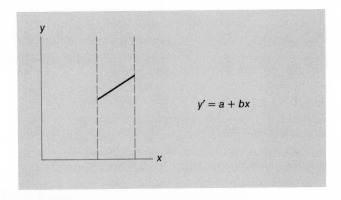

$y' = a + bx$

A step-function cost is nonlinear because of the breaks in its behavior pattern:

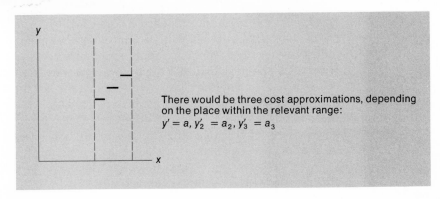

There would be three cost approximations, depending on the place within the relevant range:
$y' = a, y_2' = a_2, y_3' = a_3$

Methods of Linear Approximation

There are many methods of approximating cost functions, including (a) *industrial engineering method,* (b) *account analysis,* (c) *high-low points,* (d) *visual fit,* (e) *simple regression, and* (f) *multiple regression.* These methods are not mutually exclusive; frequently, two or more are used to prevent major blunders. In many organizations, each of these five methods is used in succession over the years as the need for more accurate approximations becomes evident.

The **industrial engineering method,** sometimes called the **analytic method,** searches for the most efficient means of obtaining wanted output. It entails a systematic review of materials, supplies, labor, support services, and facilities. Time and motion studies are sometimes used. Any input-output relationship that is physically observable is an obvious candidate for the engineering method. For example, in the manufacturing of bicycles, one handlebar and two wheels are needed per bicycle. But the engineering method is of little help when relationships are infeasible or impossible to observe on an individual cost basis. Examples are relationships between various overhead costs and output. Then other methods come to the fore.

In **account analysis,** the analyst proceeds through the accounts, one by one, and classifies each into one of two categories, variable or fixed. In so doing, he may use his past experience intuitively and nothing else. More likely, he will at least study how total costs behave over a few periods before making judgments.

An examination of the accounts is obviously a necessary first step, no matter whether cost functions are approximated by means of simple inspection of the accounts or by multiple regression. Familiarity with the data is needed to avoid the analytical pitfalls that abound in regression analysis.

A major disadvantage of the account classification method is its inherent subjectivity. The **high-low** method is slightly less subjective because at least it employs a series of samples and relies on two of their results, the highest cost and the lowest cost. It will be illustrated in a subsequent section.

The **visual-fit, simple-regression,** and **multiple-regression** methods have a distinct advantage because all sample points are used in determining the cost function. A visual fit is applied by drawing a straight line through the cost points on a scatter diagram, which consists of a plotting on a graph of individual dots that represent various experienced costs at various activity levels. The line in Exhibit 8-2 could have been fitted visually.

There are no objective tests to assure that the line fitted visually is the most accurate representation of the underlying data. Consequently, regression analysis is a more systematic approach.[4] Under certain assumptions, it has measures of probable error. Regression analysis refers to the measurement of the average amount of change in one variable (e.g., shipping cost)

---

[4]For elaboration, see Horngren, *Cost Accounting,* Chap. 25.

EXHIBIT 8-2. Mixed Cost

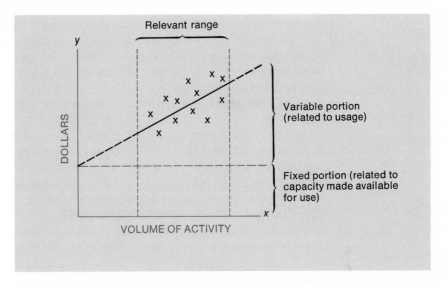

that is associated with unit increases in the amounts of one or more other variables. When only two variables are studied (e.g., shipping costs in relation to units shipped), the analysis is called **simple regression**; when more than two variables are studied (e.g., shipping costs in relation to units shipped and to the weight of those units shipped), it is called **multiple regression.**[5]

APPROXIMATING A COST FUNCTION

Mixed Costs

We have previously discussed the nature of the proportionately variable cost, the fixed cost, and the step-function cost, so this section will concentrate on the *mixed cost* (often called *semivariable cost*). Exhibit 8-2 gives a closer look at a mixed cost. The fixed portion is usually the result of *providing* capacity, whereas the variable portion is the result of *using* the capacity, given its availability. For example, a copy-making machine often has a fixed monthly rental plus a variable cost based on the copies produced. Other examples include costs of rented trucks, power, telephone, repairs and maintenance, clerks, accountants, and janitors.

Ideally, there should be no accounts for mixed costs. All such costs should be subdivided into two accounts, one for the variable portion and one for the fixed portion. In practice, these distinctions are rarely made in the

[5] For elaboration, see Benston, "Multiple Regression Analysis of Cost Behavior," 657–72.

recording process, because of the difficulty of analyzing day-to-day cost data into variable and fixed sections. Costs such as power, indirect labor, repairs, and maintenance are generally accounted for in total. It is typically very difficult to decide, as such costs are incurred, whether a particular invoice or work ticket represents a variable or fixed item. Moreover, even if it were possible to make such distinctions, the advantages might not be worth the additional clerical effort and costs. Whenever cost classifications are too refined, the perpetual problem of getting accurate source documents is intensified.

In sum, mixed costs are merely a blend of two unlike cost behavior patterns; they do not entail new conceptual approaches. Anybody who obtains a working knowledge of the planning and controlling of variable and fixed costs, separately, can adapt to a mixed-cost situation when necessary.

In practice, where a report is divided into two main cost classifications, variable and fixed, mixed costs tend to be included in the variable category even though they may not have purely variable behavior. At first glance, such arbitrary classification may seem undesirable and misleading. However, within a particular organization, the users of the reports usually have an intimate knowledge of the fundamental characteristics of the cost in question. Therefore, they can temper their interpretation accordingly.

Budgeting Mixed Costs

How should mixed costs be budgeted? Sometimes it is relatively easy to separate the cost into its fixed and variable elements. For example, the rental for a leased computer or photographic reproduction machine may be subdivided:

Clerical reproduction costs—variable @ 3¢ per copy	xxxx
Clerical reproduction costs—fixed @ $200 per month	xxxx

Alternatively, a flexible budget may be prepared that contains a single line item:

Totals at Various Volumes

Clerical reproduction costs ($200 per month plus 3¢ per copy)	xxxx	xxxx	xxxx

Other mixed costs are harder to analyze: For example, how do repairs and maintenance, indirect factory labor, clerical labor, and miscellaneous overhead relate to decisions concerning changes in general volume of work in the form of more sales, more inquiries, more telephone calls, more letters, and so forth? The relationships are often hazy and difficult to pinpoint in any systematic way. Still, the decision maker wants to know how these costs are affected by volume so that he can weigh his operating alternatives more intelligently.

Data for Illustration

The City of Northvale operates several municipal golf courses that require varying maintenance attention, depending on the season of the year. The assistant city manager has begun to collect data on the cost of repairing the various types of power equipment used (for example, golf carts and power lawn mowers). She is concerned because repairs have been billed individually by an outside firm as each piece of equipment fails to perform. She is considering various alternatives, including buying a service contract for a flat fee or creating her own equipment repair department.

To date she has compiled the following data:

	Groundskeeper Labor-Hours (x)	Repair Expense (y)
August	2,200	$2,300
September	2,300	2,500
October	1,900	2,000
November	1,200	2,000
December	1,200	2,000
January	900	1,500
February	700	1,400
March	1,100	1,400
April	1,400	1,600

She realizes that much more data should be gathered before jumping to conclusions about how costs behave. She also wishes that more detailed classifications were available (for example, by acreage in specific golf courses, by types and age of equipment, and perhaps by number of rounds played at each course). But she has decided to use the above data as a start.

Analysis of Graphs

The first graph in Exhibit 8-3 is a scatter diagram of the preceding data. The analyst should scrutinize the data to see whether a strong relationship exists between the costs of repair and groundskeeper labor-hours. Also, the analyst uses the scatter diagram as a key to deciding whether the relationship can be followed sufficiently closely by a *linear* approximation—that is, a straight line fitted through the dots.

The second graph in Exhibit 8-3 shows the straight line that has been fitted by the *statistical method of least squares,* which is described in more detail in the appendix to this chapter. The formula for the straight line is:

$$y' = a + bx$$

$$y' = \$983 + \$.609x$$

That is, repair costs fluctuate *over the relevant range of 700 to 2,300 hours* at a rate of $983 per month plus $.609 per labor-hour.

221

EXHIBIT 8-3

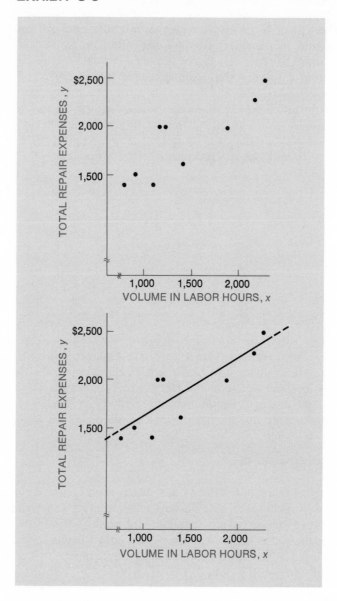

Focus on Relevant Range

The line in Exhibit 8-3 is extended backward from the relevant range to intersect the *y*-axis at $983. The extension is deliberately shown as a dashed line to emphasize the focus on the relevant range. The manager is concerned with how costs behave *within the relevant range,* not with how they behave at zero volume. Therefore, the $983 intercept must be kept in perspective. It is often called a fixed cost, but it is really a fixed or constant component of the formula that provides the best available linear approximation of how a mixed cost behaves within the relevant range. The manager is ordinarily not concerned about cost behavior at extremely low or high volumes.

Use of High-Low Method

The high-low method uses two observations rather than all the observations for constructing the line. A high representative point (rather than an "outlier" that seems nonrepresentative) and a low representative point are chosen. The resultant line is extended back to intersect the vertical axis. The intercept becomes the "fixed" portion and the slope becomes the "variable" portion of the formula for the mixed cost.

The same results can be achieved via algebra:

	Labor-Hours (x)	Repair Expense (y)
High (h)	2,300	$2,500
Low (l)	700	1,400
Difference	1,600	$1,100

$$\text{Variable rate} = \frac{y_h - y_l}{x_h - x_l} = \frac{\$1,100}{1,600} = \$.6875 \text{ per labor-hour}$$

Fixed overhead component = Total mixed cost less
variable component

$$\text{At } x_h = \$2,500 - \$.6875(2,300)$$
$$= \$2,500 - \$1,581 = \$919$$

or

$$\text{At } x_l = \$1,400 - \$.6875(700)$$
$$= \$1,400 - \$481 = \$919$$

Therefore,

Mixed-cost formula = $919 per month plus $.6875 per labor-hour

Compare this high-low formula with the least-squares formula, which was $983 per month plus $.609 per labor-hour. At a 1,000-hour level of volume, cost predictions would be:

High-low formula:	$919 + \$.6875(1,000) = \$1,606.50$
Least-squares formula:	$983 + \$.609(1,000) = \$1,592.00$

In this illustration, the differences seem too small to have any influence on decisions. However, the high-low method is statistically inefficient. For example, if 40 data points were available, the high-low would use only 2 and disregard the other 38. Because of the danger of relying on extreme points, which may not be representative of normal situations, the high-low method is not recommended.

EXHIBIT 8-4

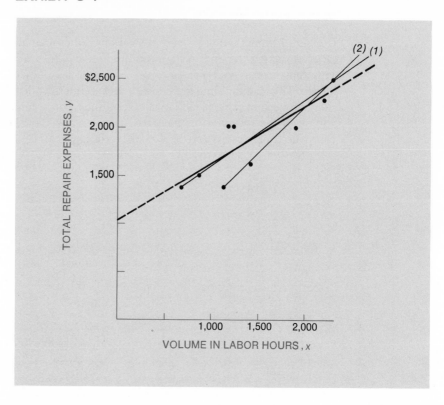

Unreliability of High-Low Method

The graph in Exhibit 8-4 shows the unreliability of the high-low method. The graph is merely the second one of Exhibit 8-3, which showed a least-squares line fitted to the data, plus two high-low lines, marked as (1) and (2). High-low line (1) is the one we just computed algebraically. High-low line (2) is based on the choice of the alternative low point in the data:

	Labor-Hours (x)	Repair Expenses (y)
High (h)	2,300	$2,500
Low (l)	1,100	1,400
Difference	1,200	$1,100

$$\text{Variable rate} = \frac{y_h - y_l}{x_h - x_l} = \frac{\$1,100}{1,200} = \$.9167 \text{ per labor-hour}$$

Fixed overhead component = Total mixed cost less
variable component

$$\text{At } x_h = \$2,500 - \$.9167(2,300)$$
$$= \$2,500 - \$2,108 = \$392$$

or

$$\text{At } x_l = \$1,400 - \$.9167(1,100)$$
$$= \$1,400 - \$1,008 = \$392$$

Therefore,

$$\text{Mixed-cost formula} = \$392 \text{ per month plus } \$.9167$$
$$\text{per labor-hour}$$

Thus, we have two strikingly different mixed-cost formulas provided by the same high-low method. The watchword is beware. Use all, or nearly all, the data points, not just two, as a basis for cost estimation.

SUMMARY

Managers who know cost behavior patterns are better equipped to make intelligent planning and control decisions. The division of costs into engineered, discretionary, and committed categories highlights the major factors that influence cost incurrence. Management policies often determine whether a cost will be planned and controlled as an engineered cost or as a discretionary cost.

Predictions of how costs will behave in response to various actions usually have an important bearing on a wide number of decisions. The cost function used to make these predictions is usually a simplification of underlying relationships. Whether this simplification is justified depends on how sensitive the manager's decisions are to the errors that the simplifications may generate. In some cases, additional accuracy may not make any difference; in other cases, it may be significant. The choice of a cost function is a decision concerning the cost and value of information.

SUMMARY PROBLEMS FOR YOUR REVIEW

Problem One

The Alic Company has many small accounts receivable. Work measurement of billing labor has shown that a billing clerk can process 2,000 customers' accounts per month. The company employs thirty billing clerks at an annual salary of $9,600 each. The outlook for next year is for a decline in the number of customers, from 59,900 to 56,300 per month.

1. Assume that management has decided to continue to employ the thirty clerks despite the expected drop in billings. Show two approaches, the engineered-cost approach and the discretionary-fixed-cost approach, to the budgeting of billing labor. Show how the *performance report* for the year would appear under each approach.

2. Some managers favor using tight budgets as motivating devices for controlling operations. In these cases, the managers really expect an unfavorable variance and must allow, in financial planning, for such a variance so that adequate cash will be available as needed. What would be the budgeted variance, also sometimes called expected variance, in this instance?

3. Assume that the workers are reasonably efficient. (a) Interpret the budget variances under the engineered-cost approach and the discretionary-fixed-cost approach. (b) What should management do to exert better control over clerical costs?

Problem Two

The Delite Company has its own power plant. All costs related to the production of power have been charged to a single account, Power. We know that the total cost for power was $24,000 in one month and $28,000 in another month. Total machine hours in those months were 120,000 and 160,000, respectively. Express the cost behavior pattern of the Power account in formula form.

Solution to Problem One

1. Engineered-cost approach:

Standard unit rate = $9,600 ÷ 2,000 = $4.80 per customer per year
or = $.40 per customer per month

	Actual Cost	Flexible Budget: Total Standard Quantity Allowed for Good Units Produced × Standard Unit Rate	Budget Variance
Billing-clerk labor	(30 × $9,600) $288,000	(56,300 × $.40 × 12 months) $270,240	$17,760 U

Discretionary-fixed-cost approach:

	Actual Cost	Budget	Budget Variance
Billing-clerk labor	$288,000	$288,000	—

2. The budgeted variance would be $17,760, unfavorable. The master budget for financial planning must provide for labor costs of $288,000; therefore, if the engineered-cost approach were being used for control, the master budget might specify:

226

Billing-clerk labor:

Control-budget allowance	$270,240
Expected control-budget variance	17,760
Total budget allowance for financial planning	$288,000

3. As the chapter explains, management decisions and policies are often of determining importance in categorizing a cost as fixed or variable. If management refuses, as in this case, to control costs rigidly in accordance with short-run fluctuations in activity, these costs are discretionary. The $17,760 variance represents the price that management, consciously or unconsciously, is willing to pay currently in order to maintain a stable work force geared to management's ideas of "normal needs."

Management should be given an approximation of such an extra cost. There is no single "right way" to keep management informed on such matters. Two approaches were demonstrated in the previous parts of this problem. The important point is that clerical workloads and capability must be measured before effective control may be exerted. Such measures may be formal or informal. The latter is often achieved through a supervisor's regular observation, so that he knows how efficiently work is being performed.

Solution to Problem Two

$$\text{Variable rate} = \frac{\text{Change in mixed cost}}{\text{Change in volume}} = \frac{\$28,000 - \$24,000}{160,000 - 120,000}$$

$$= \frac{\$4,000}{40,000} = \$.10 \text{ per machine-hour}$$

Fixed component = Total mixed cost less variable component

At 160,000-hour level = $28,000 − $.10(160,000) = $12,000

Or, at 120,000-hour level = $24,000 − $.10(120,000) = $12,000

Cost formula = $12,000 per month + $.10 per machine-hour

APPENDIX

Method of Least Squares

The method of least squares is the most accurate device for formulating the *past behavior* of a mixed cost.

The line itself is not plotted visually, however; it is located by means of two simultaneous linear equations:

$$\Sigma xy = a\Sigma x + b\Sigma x^2 \tag{1}$$

$$\Sigma y = na + b\Sigma x \tag{2}$$

where a is the fixed component, b is the variable cost rate, x is the activity measure, y is the mixed cost, n is the number of observations, and Σ means summation.

For example, assume that nine monthly observations of repair costs are to be used as a basis for developing a budget formula. A scatter diagram indicates a mixed-cost behavior in the form $y = a + bx$. Computation of the budget formula by the method of least squares is shown in Exhibit 8-5. Substitute the values from Exhibit 8-5 into Equations (1) and (2):

EXHIBIT 8-5

Least-Squares Computation of Budget Formula for Mixed Cost

MONTH	LABOR-HOURS x	TOTAL MIXED COST y	xy	x^2
August	2,200	$ 2,300	$ 5,060,000	4,840,000
September	2,300	2,500	5,750,000	5,290,000
October	1,900	2,000	3,800,000	3,610,000
November	1,200	2,000	2,400,000	1,440,000
December	1,200	2,000	2,400,000	1,440,000
January	900	1,500	1,350,000	810,000
February	700	1,400	980,000	490,000
March	1,100	1,400	1,540,000	1,210,000
April	1,400	1,600	2,240,000	1,960,000
	12,900	$16,700	$25,520,000	21,090,000

SOURCE: Adapted from "Separating and Using Costs As Fixed and Variable," N.A.A. Bulletin, *Accounting Practice Report No. 10* (New York, June 1960), p. 13. For a more thorough explanation, see any basic text in statistics or Horngren, *Cost Accounting*, Chap. 25.

$$\$25{,}520{,}000 = 12{,}900a + 21{,}090{,}000b \quad (1)$$

$$\$16{,}700 = 9a + 12{,}900b \quad (2)$$

Repeat Equation (1): $\qquad \$25{,}520{,}000 = 12{,}900a + 21{,}090{,}000b$

Multiply Equation (2) by 1,433.3333
(which is $12{,}900 \div 9$): $\qquad \underline{\$23{,}936{,}667 = 12{,}900a + 18{,}490{,}000b}$

Subtract: $\qquad \$1{,}583{,}333 = 2{,}600{,}000b$

$$b = \$.6089742$$

Substitute $.6089742 for b in

Equation (2):

$$\$16,700 = 9a + 12,900(\$.6089742)$$

$$\$16,700 = 9a + \$7,855.7671$$

$$9a = \$8,844.233$$

$$a = \$982.69255$$

Therefore, the formula for the total repair expenses is $983 per month plus $.609 per labor-hour.

A scatter diagram also should be prepared to see whether the derived line seems to fit the existing cost data to a satisfactory degree. If not, then factors other than volume or activity have also significantly affected total cost behavior. In such instances, multiple regression techniques may have to be used.

ASSIGNMENT MATERIAL

Fundamental Assignment Material

8-1. **Terminology:** Define: *committed costs; discretionary costs; managed costs; appropriation;* and *parameter.*

8-2. **Clerical work measurement.** The Northeastern Transportation Company has many small customers. Billing labor used to be controlled by careful physical observation, but a year ago a formal system of work measurement was added to aid control.

A management consultant developed work standards that allowed 150 bills per day per billing clerk. The company employs ten clerks at a salary of $300 per five-day week.

To avoid confusion regarding comparisons from month to month, interim performance focuses on reporting periods of four weeks each. A recent four-week period showed that 27,000 bills had been processed by the ten clerks.

1. How would a performance report show the budget variance for the four-week period under (a) a discretionary-cost approach and (b) an engineered-cost approach?

2. What factors might influence management regarding the size of the clerical force for the billing operation?

3. Sometimes top management uses one budget for cash planning purposes and a second budget for cost control purposes. If an engineered-cost approach is used, top management might have an "expected variance" embedded in the cash planning budget. What would be the "expected" or "budgeted" variance in this case?

8-3. Classification of cost behavior. Identify the following as (a) proportionately variable costs, (b) committed fixed costs, (c) discretionary fixed costs, (d) mixed costs, (e) step costs. More than one letter can be used in an answer. If in doubt, write a short explanation of why doubt exists.

1. Straight-line depreciation on a building.
2. Fork-lift truck operators' wages. One operator is needed for every 5,000 tons of steel sold monthly by a steel warehouse.
3. Property taxes on plant and equipment.
4. Advertising costs.
5. Research costs.
6. Total rental costs of salesmen's automobiles. Charge is a flat $60 per month plus 15¢ per mile.
7. Salesmen's total compensation, including salaries and commissions.
8. Total repairs and maintenance.
9. Foremen's salaries. A new foreman is added for every ten workers employed.
10. Management consulting costs.
11. Public accounting fees.
12. Management training costs.

8-4. Division of mixed costs into variable and fixed components. The president and the controller of the Warner Transformer Company have agreed that refinement of the company cost classifications will aid planning and control decisions. They have asked you to approximate the formula for variable-and fixed-cost behavior of repairs and maintenance from the following sparse data:

Monthly Activity in Direct-Labor Hours	Monthly Repair and Maintenance Costs Incurred
3,000	$1,700
5,000	2,300

Additional Assignment Material

8-5. Why are fixed costs also called capacity costs?

8-6. How do committed costs differ from discretionary costs?

8-7. How do the methods and philosophies of management affect cost behavior?

8-8. "Ideally, there should be no accounts for mixed costs." Explain.

8-9. Describe how mixed costs are budgeted.

8-10. "Variable costs are those that should fluctuate directly in proportion to sales." Do you agree? Explain.

8-11. How does the basic behavior of the cost of raw materials differ from that of clerical services?

8-12. "For practical budgeting purposes, costs do not have to be proportionately variable in order to be regarded as variable." Explain.

8-13. "The objective in controlling step costs is to attain activity at the highest volume for any given step." Explain.

8-14. What is the primary determinant of the level of committed costs?

8-15. What is the primary determinant of the level of discretionary costs?

8-16. "Planning is far more important than day-to-day control of discretionary costs." Do you agree? Explain.

8-17. Distinguish between order getting and order filling.

8-18. When are planning and control techniques most effective?

8-19. What is the central purpose of analyzing order-getting costs?

8-20. What is the best single gauge of a salesman's effectiveness?

8-21. What is work measurement?

8-22. Why are committed costs the stickiest of the fixed costs?

8-23. "An unfavorable variance for discretionary costs would measure the failure to spend the entire appropriation." Do you agree? Explain.

8-24. Attitudes toward work measurement. At a management conference, a proponent of work measurement stated, "Before you can control, you must measure." Another executive complained, "Why bother to measure when workrules and guaranteed employment provisions in labor union contracts prevent discharging workers, using part-time employment, and using overtime!"

Required | Evaluate these comments. Summarize your personal attitudes toward the use of work measurement.

8-25. Government work measurement. The auditor general of the State of California conducted a study of the Department of Motor Vehicles. The auditor's report said that the department's work standards, which were set in 1939, allow ten minutes for typing and processing a driver's license application. But a 1977 study of 40 of its 147 field offices showed that it takes only six minutes. The report said: "The continued use of the ten-minute standard results in the overstaffing of 158 positions at an unnecessary annual cost of $1.9 million."

Name four governmental activities that are likely candidates for using work measurement as a means for control.

8-26. Work measurement in a hospital. The billing procedures in a hospital require ponderous detail. A large hospital introduced a work-measurement program and established a standard rate of four bills per hour. Extensive studies had concluded that the typical bill contains 40 lines. Each billing clerk received an hourly labor rate of $8 and worked five days per week, eight hours per day.

1. The billing supervisor has asked you to prepare a performance report for billing labor for a recent eight-week period when ten clerks were employed and 10,000 bills were processed. Show the actual cost, flexible budget, and the variance.

2. The hospital administrator has followed the work-measurement application with intense interest. A consultant had suggested that all variances should be expressed in terms of "equivalent persons" in addition to dollar amounts. The administrator has asked you to compute the variance in terms of "equivalent persons."

3. The administrator told the supervisor: "As you know, the trustees, the government agencies, and the patients are really criticizing us for soaring hospitalization costs. This work-measurement system leads me to think we are overstaffed with billing labor. As a start, we ought to reduce the work force by the number of equivalent persons shown by the variance analysis."

   The supervisor was upset. She then took a careful random sample of 500 of the bills that were processed. Her count showed a total of 25,000 lines in the sample. As the supervisor, prepare a reply to the administrator.

8-27. Identifying cost behavior patterns. At a seminar, a cost accountant spoke on the classification of different kinds of cost behavior.

Mr. Falk, a hospital administrator who heard the lecture, identified several hospital costs and classified them. After his classification, Falk presented you with the following list of costs and asked you to classify their behavior as one of the following: variable; step; mixed; discretionary fixed; or committed fixed:

1. Straight-line depreciation of operating room equipment.
2. Costs incurred by Dr. Raun in cancer research.
3. Costs of services of ABC Hospital Consultant Firm.
4. Repairs made on hospital furniture.
5. Nursing supervisors' salaries (a supervisor is added for each 45 nursing personnel).
6. Leasing costs of X-ray equipment ($9,500 a year plus $.05 per film).
7. Training costs of an administrative resident.
8. Blue Cross insurance for all full-time employees.

8-28. Separation of hospital X-ray mixed costs into variable and fixed components. A staff meeting has been called at the Hugh G. Dephicit Memorial Hospital by the new administrator, Buck Saver. Mr. Saver has examined the income statement and is particularly interested in the X-ray department. The chief radiologist, Dr. I. C.

Throoyou, has demanded an increase in prices to cover the increased repair costs because of the opening of an outpatient clinic. He claims it is costing more per X-ray for this expense.

Mr. Saver asks the controller, Mr. Adam Upp, to approximate the fundamental variable- and fixed-cost behavior of repairs and maintenance for the X-ray department and to prepare a graphic report he can present to Dr. Throoyou. Data for the relevant range follow:

	X-rays per Month	Monthly Repair and Maintenance Cost Incurred
Low volume	6,000	$3,400
High volume	10,000	5,400

Required

As the controller, prepare the requested information.

8-29. University budgeting. Saratoga Business College, a private institution, is preparing a budgeted income statement for the coming academic year ending August 31, 19x4. Tuition revenue for the past two years ending August 31 were 19x3, $500,000; and 19x2, $550,000. Total expenses in 19x3 were $510,000 and in 19x2 were $530,000. No tuition rate changes occurred in 19x2 or 19x3, nor are any expected to occur in 19x4. Tuition revenue is expected to be $520,000 for the year ending August 31, 19x4. What net income should be budgeted for next year, assuming that the implied cost behavior patterns remain unchanged?

8-30. Least squares. Assume that total operating overhead of a trucking company is a function of the gross ton-miles of work to be performed. The past records show (in thousands):

Gross ton miles	800	1,200	400	1,600
Total operating costs	$350	$350	$150	$550

Required

1. Draw a scatter diagram.

2. Use simple regression to fit a line to the data. What is the equation of the line? Plot the line. This example is used only to illustrate the least-squares method. When the number of observations is small, as in this example, additional analysis should be performed to determine whether the results are reliable.

8-31. Method of least squares and sales forecasts. (SMA, adapted.) The Progressive Company, Ltd., has recorded the following sales since its inception in 19m2:

19m2	$ 10,000	19m8	$125,000
19m3	20,000	19m9	150,000
19m4	30,000	19n0	180,000
19m5	45,000	19n1	220,000
19m6	70,000	19n2	270,000
19m7	90,000		

1. Calculate 19n3 sales, using the least-squares method.

2. If the directors have determined from an outside consultant that the cyclical factor in 19n4 will cause sales to be 10 percent above the forecast trend, what will they amount to?

8-32. **Least-squares analysis.** Suppose that a manufacturer is troubled by fluctuations in labor productivity and wants to compute how direct-labor costs are related to the various sizes of batches of output. The workers in question set up their own jobs on complex machinery. The following data show the results of a random sample of ten batches of a given kind:

Batch Size x	Direct-Labor Costs y
15	$180
12	140
20	230
17	190
12	160
25	300
22	270
9	110
18	240
30	320

1. Prepare a scatter diagram.

2. Using least-squares analysis, compute the equation of the line relating labor costs and size of batch.

3. Predict the labor costs for a lot size of 20.

4. Using a high-low method, repeat Requirements 2 and 3. Should the manager use the high-low method or the least-squares method? Explain.

8-33. **Nonlinear costs.** The U.S. Government Printing Office has used a flexible budget for the overhead of one of its press departments. At a level of 15,000 direct-labor hours, its total overhead is budgeted at $80,000; at a level of 23,000 hours, at $96,000.

In March, the department took 21,000 hours of input for work that should have taken 19,000 standard allowed hours. Actual overhead costs incurred were $98,000.

1. Compute the flexible budget variance for March. Subdivide the variance into a price variance and an efficiency variance.

2. Special cost studies were conducted later in the year that developed the following approximation for relating overhead to direct-labor hours (DL):

$$\text{Total overhead} = \$53,000 + \$1DL + \$100 \sqrt{DL}$$

If this cost function had been used in March as the flexible-budget formula (instead of the linear budget used previously), what would have been the flexible-budget variance for March? The price variance? The efficiency variance? Round your square roots to the nearest hour.

8-34. Nonlinear behavior. The following graph contains a linear function, which is the linear approximation of the nonlinear "true" cost function also shown.

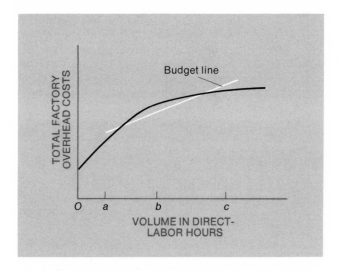

1. Will the flexible budget be higher or lower than what the budgeted "true" costs would be at *Oa, Ob,* and *Oc?*
2. Would you prefer to use the "true" cost curve for budgeting and for decision purposes? Why?

8-35. Two independent variables in hospital. The underlying cost behavior pattern of overhead in Santa Clara Hospital is linear but affected by two independent variables: number of patients and the number of days each patient stays. The latter, called *patient-days,* is computed by multiplying the number of patients times the days each stayed. The number of patients influences costs because the first day of the stay tends to require more overhead costs than subsequent days. In sum, the actual cost behavior pattern is:

$$\text{Total overhead} = a + bx_1 + cx_2$$

where a = intercept, b = rate per patient-day, and c = rate per patient.

For simplicity, the flexible budget for overall overhead behavior is based on patient-days:

$$\text{Total overhead} = a + bx_1$$

At the end of a period, the hospital administrator was disturbed that the overhead variance was highly unfavorable. He commented, "A large part of that

235

variance is attributable to Medicare and similar reimbursement plans. Some people place aged parents in the hospital for a couple of days and go away for a short holiday."

Required | Given these facts and the underlying cost behavior, was the flexible budget variance overstated or understated? Suppose the more costly and more accurate flexible-budget formula had been developed. Would the variance be higher or lower than the variance produced by the simpler formula? Why?

8-36. **Various cost behavior patterns.** In practice, there is often a tendency to simplify approximations of cost behavior patterns, even though the "true" underlying behavior is not simple. Choose from among the accompanying graphs A through H the one that matches the numbered items. Indicate by letter which graph best fits each of the situations described.

The vertical axes of the graphs represent total dollars of factory costs incurred and the horizontal axes represent total production. The graphs may be used more than once.

1. Natural gas bill consisting of a fixed component, plus a constant variable cost per thousand cubic feet after a specified number of cubic feet are used.
2. Availability of quantity discounts, where the cost per unit falls as each price break is reached.
3. Price rise of an increasingly scarce raw material as the volume used increases.
4. Cost of sheet steel for a manufacturer of refrigerators.
5. Guaranteed annual wage plan, whereby workers get paid for 40 hours of work per week at zero or low levels of production that require working only a few hours weekly.

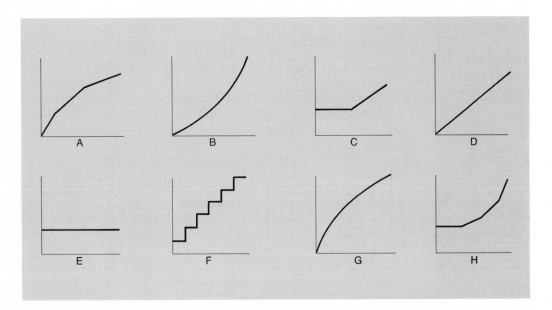

6. Cost of machining labor that tends to decrease per unit as workers gain experience.
7. Depreciation on a straight-line basis.
8. Water bill under drought conditions, which entails a flat fee for the first 100,000 gallons and then an increasing unit cost for every additional batch of 10,000 gallons used.
9. Salaries of assistant foremen, where one assistant foreman is added for every ten assembly workers added.

8-37. **Nonlinear behavior and banking.** Managers are often troubled by not really knowing how overhead is affected by their operating decisions. As a result, they are uncomfortable when they use the simple "linear approximations" that are commonly encountered. Suppose a bank is contemplating the introduction of a new "one-price" banking service, whereby a flat monthly fee will provide a combination of "free" checking, safety deposit, and other services.

Suppose the underlying (but unidentified) overhead cost behavior would be:

Volume Level in Number of Accounts	Total Overhead Costs per Year
1,000	$34,000
2,000	40,000
3,000	45,000
4,000	49,000
5,000	64,000
6,000	85,000

Required

1. A committee is trying to predict what costs are relevant. After much heated discussion predictions were made for two "representative" volumes: 2,000 accounts and 5,000 accounts. A flexible budget was to be constructed based on a "high-low" analysis of these two volumes. Compute the formula for the flexible-budget line.

2. What predictions would be produced by the flexible budget developed in Requirement 1 for each of the tabulated levels of activity? Use a table to compare these predictions with the "true" cost behavior, showing the difference between the "true" cost behavior and the linear approximation.

3. Plot the two sets of predictions on a graph.

4. Assume that the new service has been introduced. The manager in charge is convinced that a special television campaign can increase volume from the current level of 2,000 accounts to a level of 4,000 accounts. These additional accounts would bring an additional contribution to income of $64,000 before considering the predicted increase in total overhead cost and before considering the cost of $50,000 for the television campaign. If the manager were guided by the linear flexible-budget formula, would he launch the campaign? Show computations. If he did launch the campaign, by how much would income change if 2,000 more accounts were achieved?

5. As an operating manager responsible for budgetary control of overhead, would you regard the linear budget allowances for 4,000 and 6,000 accounts as too tight or too loose? Why?

6. A top executive of the bank commented, "I think we should have a more accurate budgetary system." Do you agree? Explain.

8-38. Controlling nursing costs. (P. Fry.) Royal Hospital is located in an older established community on the west coast. A nonprofit hospital, it has had a close and peaceful relationship with area residents. Although the days have long passed when meals were served on real china and silver to staff and patients alike, the sense of tradition remains strong.

Most of the patients, physicians, and employees have lived and worked in the community the majority of their lives. A large proportion of employees have worked at the hospital over 15 years; those in administrative positions over 25 years. A handsome annual bonus goes to those with over five years of employment at Royal. Only under extraordinary circumstances has anyone been fired. Turnover is due to resignations (mostly among the younger employees) or retirement at age 65.

In 19x5 Royal Hospital was faced with a problem of increased costs and decreasing revenues. Cost increases over the years had been passed directly on to patients in the form of increased charges. Seldom had there been a vociferous complaint; the quality and amenities at Royal were clearly superior.

Demand for care had remained strong. Royal operated at 90 percent of its 320-patient capacity. This meant that during an average day, 288 patients were treated there.

As more of the costs were assumed by third-party payors (e.g., Blue Cross, Medicare), the hospital was forced to cut back on the "extras" that had long characterized Royal. Patient fee increases were now being severely limited, but skyrocketing material and labor costs made cost containment a difficult task.

One of the biggest areas of increased costs has been labor, which makes up 70 percent of the annual budget. The largest division is nursing, under the firm hand of Ms. Willa Conrad, Director of Nursing.

Under considerable pressure from Frank Krauss (Hospital Administrator) to control costs, Ms. Conrad has identified two areas with potential for cost reduction: (1) turnover costs—next year's level is expected to be 45 nurses (the annual level over the past few decades has been 30 nurses each year); (2) staffiing costs (i.e., nursing division wages and salaries). Some of the nurses work part-time; however, the turnover cost per person is $600 regardless of their work status.

Unfortunately, these two areas are related. As the hospital has aged, so have the community residents. This has been reflected in a dramatic rise in the number of elderly and chronically ill patients. Compared with younger patients with the same illness, these patients require much more nursing time.

Although nurses always seem to complain about being overworked, Ms. Conrad is convinced this is the major cause of the increased turnover. To reduce turnover, she feels compelled to increase staffing. However, she suspects that the increased costs of more nurses would offset the savings realized by reducing turnover.

"If only the costs could be reduced in some other ways," she thinks, as she reviews her present staffing methods and costs.

Staffing Method. Although each nurse is hired for one of the 12 nursing units, she may be assigned to work anywhere in the hospital. Every day the supervisor for each shift calculates the number of patients in each unit and the total number of nurses on duty; the nurses are then assigned to units according to the staffing formula described on p. 239.

The formula is based strictly on the number of nurses; it ignores the type of nurse assigned (could be RN, LVN, or nurse aide). The supervisor uses her judgment to ensure that the mix of skills among the nurses is appropriate to the level of care required by the patients in each unit. This is generally accepted as a safe and equitable method.

A veteran head nurse has observed, "No matter what combination of nurses the supervisor assigns to my unit today, you can bet that half the time I'll get RN's, 45 percent of the time nurse aides, and 5 percent of the time LVN's."

Staffing Formula. The universal method for determining the number of nurses to be assigned to a unit is in terms of nursing hours per patient per day. At Royal Hospital the formula (strictly adhered to) is 5.1 nursing hours per patient per day. This means that in any 24-hour period, each unit is allocated 5.1 nursing hours for each patient in that unit. Thus a unit with 16 patients would be allocated 81.6 nursing hours (16 patients times 5.1 nursing hours/patient/day). This is equivalent to 10.2 nurses, who would be assigned over the three shifts (e.g., 5 nurses on day shift, 3 on evening shift, 2 on night shift). The head nurse of each unit is ignored in these calculations.

Wages and salaries are as follows:

Nurse Aide	$4.20/hour	Head Nurse	$15,000/year
LVN	5.20/hour	Supervisor	19,000/year
RN	6.20/hour	Coordinator	21,000/year

As Ms. Conrad glances up, she noticed the organizational chart on her wall (Figure 1). She is reminded of another pressing problem that seems unrelated to her cost-reduction campaign—the five coordinators.

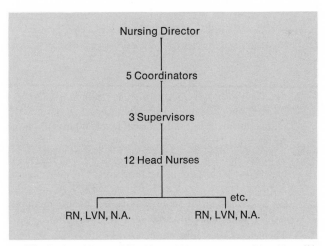

RN = Registered Nurse   LVN = Licensed Vocational Nurse   N.A. = Nurse Aide

These trustworthy and respected individuals have been promoted through the ranks to their current level. Only one is under the age of 60. Although everyone seems to enjoy their presence, Ms. Conrad is painfully aware of the hospitalwide joke about how these women are always scurrying to meetings that have been called by, and attended by, only themselves.

This adds to considerable dysfunctional behavior by the head nurses. In theory, they are to report problems to the shift supervisor, who then requests assistance from the coordinators. In actuality, the head nurses try resolving most problems by themselves. Usually they do not communicate the problem or their actions to anyone. Difficulties arise when the head nurse has neither the responsibility nor authority to resolve the issue; too often the problem is ignored or only temporarily resolved.

Ms. Conrad has been considering changing the formal structure of her division to reflect more accurately the informal changes that have been evolving (Figure 2). Her major purpose is to strengthen communication channels by having the head nurses report directly to herself while formally placing additional responsibility and authority in their hands. It is generally agreed that this increased autonomy might contribute to more permanent solutions to recurring problems as well as increase morale (which in turn might help stabilize turnover). She realizes the potential benefits of such a change cannot be measured.

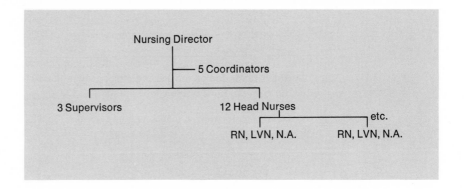

Required

1. Ms. Conrad has decided to increase staffing by changing the formula from 5.1 to 5.3 nursing hours per patient per day. Assume this will immediately reduce turnover to the historical level. What will be the change in annual costs?

2. Suppose she could change the mix of nurses to reflect the proportions that exist in the labor pool of the local area. The pool consists of 35 percent RN, 55 percent nurse aides, and 10 percent LVN. Assume this change is made at the beginning of the same year as the changes mentioned in question one. Now what will be the change in annual costs?

3. The ages of the coordinators are as follows: 62, 60, 64, 59, 62. Assume that each coordinator retires at the end of the year in which she turns 65. If the vacancies created by the retirements are not filled, what will be the cost savings in each of the next five years (coordinator salaries only)?

4. What should Ms. Conrad do about the staffing level, the mix of nurses, and the coordinators?

CHAPTER 9

Motivation and Responsibility Accounting

This chapter takes an overview of the problem of management control and the design of control systems. It emphasizes behavioral factors and introduces responsibility accounting.

GOAL CONGRUENCE AND INCENTIVE

Cost-Benefit Assessment

How should managers and accountants judge a given management accounting system? We need some criteria, some benchmarks to gauge the quality of a planning and control system. Too often, criteria concentrate on physical or data-processing aspects, emphasizing the detection of fraud and compliance with various legal requirements. However, such criteria are incomplete because they overlook the central purpose of a management control system—to improve the decisions within an organization. That is, the selection of a control system should be governed by a cost-benefit assessment.

241

The chooser should weigh the relative collective costs and benefits, given the particular circumstances of the specific organization that is considering one control system versus others. The trade-offs of costs and benefits form the dominant criterion for systems design and appraisal.

Goal Congruence

As a part of the cost-benefit assessment, two major problems should be explicitly faced when a system is chosen: obtaining *goal congruence* and strengthening *incentive*. **Goal congruence** exists when individuals and groups aim at the goals desired by top management. *Incentive* is discussed later.

Goal congruence is achieved as managers, when working in their own perceived best interests, make decisions that harmonize with the overall objectives of top management. The challenge is to specify goals (or behaviors) to induce (or at least not discourage) decisions that will blend with top-management goals.

For example, four main functions of business—sales, production, purchasing, and finance—generate four views of inventories that are often in conflict. The sales manager has a natural desire to have plenty of everything on hand so that no customer is ever turned away or forced to wait because of lack of stock. The production manager likes to concentrate on continuous, single-product runs so as to spread such costs as set-ups, changeover, spoilage, and training over longer runs of product. The purchasing officer often prefers to buy in large quantities to take advantage of quantity discounts and lower freight costs. Sometimes he would like to outguess changing market prices and to postpone or accelerate purchases accordingly. Thus, if the natural tendencies of these three executives were unchecked, inventories would become quite large. However, the financial manager wants to pry loose as much inventory capital from inventory investment as is feasible so that it may be channeled into other profitable opportunities. Because of these conflicting functional objectives, any inventory-control system must be carefully drawn if it is to benefit the business as a whole. Accounting information is essential in the formulation of a goal-congruent system.

Top-Management Objectives

To evaluate the accounting system for planning and control, the manager and the systems designer must **begin by determining top management's stated (or implied) objectives.** For example, top management may *state* that the objective of the organization is the maximization of long-run earnings. Nevertheless, management may *act* so that the objective is perceived by subordinates to be to "maximize reported earnings for next year regardless of other consequences." To minimize confusion, top management's words and actions must coincide.

242

The resulting system should be judged in relation to how well any *given* objective is achieved. For example, top managers may specify that earnings for the following year should be $50 million. They may use the accounting system to communicate and enforce this objective. Near the end of the year, if the earnings prospects are gloomy, top managers may exert immense pressure to reach the budgeted target. To reach the earnings objective, subordinates may be inclined to reduce current expenses by postponing outlays for maintenance, sales promotion, or research, even though such decisions could cripple future earning power.

We may deplore these decisions, but our criticism should be aimed at top management's choice of objectives rather than at the system. Given the objective, the accounting system performed admirably as the helpmate of top management. The system should be judged in light of the objectives, whatever they may be. In this example, goal congruence was actually achieved; the trouble was that the goals may not have been appropriate.

Incentive

Incentive is a matter of degree; it is maximized when individuals and groups *strive* (run rather than walk) toward their goals. Goal congruence can exist with little incentive, and vice versa. For example, students can enroll for a university course because their goal is to learn about, say, managing a government agency. The dean of the school, the professors, and the students may share the same goal. But goal congruence is not enough. Educators also introduce incentives in the form of a grading system.

Grading is a formal tool of *performance evaluation,* as are accounting performance reports in various organizations. Performance evaluation is a widely used means of improving incentives because most individuals tend to perform better when they expect such feedback.

During the course some students may be irresistibly tempted to skip class sessions and play tennis instead. This would be an example of having plenty of incentive aimed at a different and less important goal. Similarly, managers may eagerly pursue sales in the aggregate without paying sufficient attention to the specified and more important goal of profits, which may be affected differently by different products.

The problem of incentives arises in a variety of organization contexts. For example, should bonuses be given? Should standards and budgets be relatively tight or loose? Should performance be judged on the basis of sales, gross profit, contribution to fixed costs, net income, return on investment, or on some other basis? Should central corporate costs be fully allocated to divisions and departments? There are no clear-cut answers to these questions. A method that works well in one organization may flop in the next. Nevertheless, the answers must be framed in terms of the predicted incentive impact of the various alternatives.

Behavioral Focus

Motivation has been defined as the need to achieve some *selected goal* (the goal-congruence problem) together with the *resulting drive* (the incentive problem) that influences action toward that goal. So the systems designer's problems of goal congruence and incentive may be wrapped together as the problem of motivation—a problem that often is fruitfully divided into its congruence and incentive aspects. Hereafter in this book, the terms "motivational" or "motivation" will refer to both the goal-congruence effects and the incentive effects.

Obtaining goal congruence and incentive is essentially a behavioral problem. The incessant focus is on the motivational impact of a particular accounting system or method versus another system or method. It may seem strange to view accounting systems in terms of their behavioral effects, but the task of the accountant is more complex, more ill-structured, and more affected by the human aspects than many people believe at first glance. A simple awareness of the importance of goal congruence and the incentive impact of systems is at least a first step toward getting a perspective on the design of accounting systems and the selection of accounting techniques.

USE OF MULTIPLE GOALS

Choosing Subgoals

The starting point for judging a system is the specification of a top-management goal (or set of goals). Some managements will delineate a single goal, such as the maximization of profit over the long run. Such a lofty overall goal is too vague for most subordinates. Consequently, many organizations specify multiple goals and accompany them with some form of measurement for evaluating performance.[1]

Top management's subgoals are frequently called by other names, such as *key-result areas, critical success factors, key variables,* or *critical variables.* Some critics maintain that they should not be called goals at all; instead they should be labeled as key *means* of obtaining a single, dominant overall goal such as long-run profitability.

---

[1]Some organizations express goals in unique ways. For example, consider the Gavilan Bank of Gilroy, California, Report to Shareholders, 1976: "Greed is our vital force. It is the major influence in our program of expansion . . . . As Samuel Butler said, 'Money is always on the brain so long as there is a brain in reasonable order.'"

244

Interaction of Goals

To illustrate the use of multiple goals, consider the General Electric Company, which has stated that organizational performance will be measured in the following eight areas:

1. Profitability
2. Market position
3. Productivity
4. Product leadership
5. Personnel development
6. Employee attitudes
7. Public responsibility
8. Balance between short-range and long-range goals

Note that the first goal, profitability, usually is measured in terms of a single year's results. The thrust of the other goals is to offset the inclination of managers to maximize short-run profits to the detriment of long-run profits.

Overstress on any single goal, whether it be short-run profits or some other goal, usually does not promote long-run profitability. Instead, coordination of goals is blocked; one goal may be achieved while others are neglected:

Example. An executive of a major corporation described the following situation. Central headquarters ordered all plants to reduce their inventories of supplies from a ninety-day to a sixty-day level. Subsequently, the internal audit staff discovered two interesting developments. Two of the plant managers really rode hard on the inventory amounts and achieved the requested reduction. In the first plant, the employees threw the factory supplies out the back door. In the second plant, their consciences hurt. They did not throw the supplies out. Instead, they hid the items throughout the plant.

Example. The Moscow Cable Company decided to reduce copper wastage, and actually slashed it by 60 percent in a given year. The value of the scrap recovered was only $40,000 instead of the $100,000 originally budgeted. However, when top management in the central government perceived this to be an undesirable shortfall of value, the plant was fined $45,000 for not meeting its scrap budget.

Example. "Though the company lost the sale, the manager of Nippon Fisher Co., of Tokyo, was delighted recently when one of his salesmen refused a customer's request for a discount. The discount would have made the sale unprofitable for the manufacturers of valves . . . 'A year ago the most important thing in the salesmen's minds was getting an order. Some mysterious person someplace was supposed to worry about the profits.'"[2]

[2] "The Profit in Breaking Japanese Traditions," *Business Week,* February 14, 1977, p. 51.

Responsibility Accounting Approach

Another principal way of promoting goal congruence and incentive is to tailor the accounting system to the organization in order to strengthen motivation. The design of an *organizational structure* and a *control system* should be interdependent. Practically, however, the organizational structure is often regarded as a given when systems are modified or constructed. To work optimally, top managers subdivide activities and stipulate a hierarchy of managers who oversee some predetermined sphere of activities and who have some latitude to make decisions in that sphere. Some type of responsibility accounting usually accompanies this delegation of decision making. **Responsibility accounting** is a system of accounting that recognizes various responsibility centers throughout the organization and that reflects the plans and actions of each of these centers by assigning particular revenues and costs to the one having the pertinent responsibility. It is also called **profitability accounting** and **activity accounting.**

The motivational impact of the responsibility accounting approach is described in the following:

> The sales department requests a rush production. The plant scheduler argues that it will disrupt his production and cost a substantial though not clearly determined amount of money. The answer coming from sales is: "Do you want to take the responsibility of losing the *X* Company as a customer?" Of course the production scheduler does not want to take such a responsibility, and he gives up, but not before a heavy exchange of arguments and the accumulation of a substantial backlog of ill feeling. Analysis of the payroll in the assembly department, determining the costs involved in getting out rush orders, eliminated the cause for argument. Henceforth, any rush order was accepted with a smile by the production scheduler, who made sure that the extra cost would be duly recorded and charged to the sales department—"no questions asked." As a result, the tension created by rush orders disappeared completely; and, somehow, the number of rush orders requested by the sales department was progressively reduced to an insignificant level.[3]

Ideally, particular revenues and costs are recorded and automatically traced to the one individual in the organization who shoulders primary responsibility for the item. He is in the best position to evaluate and to influence a situation—to exert control. In practice, however, the diffusion of control throughout the organization complicates the task of collecting relevant data by responsibility centers. The organizational networks, the com-

---

[3]Raymond Villers, "Control and Freedom in a Decentralized Company," *Harvard Business Review,* Vol. XXXII, No. 2, p. 95.

munication patterns, and the decision-making processes are complex—far too complex to yield either pat answers or an ideal management accounting system.

Cost Centers and Profit Centers

Areas of responsibility take many forms, including:

1. **Cost centers**—formal reporting of costs only.
2. **Profit centers**—formal reporting of revenues and expenses.
3. **Investment centers**—formal reporting of revenues, expenses, and related investment.

A **cost center** is the smallest segment of activity or area of responsibility for which costs are accumulated. Typically, cost centers are departments, but in some instances a department may contain several cost centers. For example, although an assembly department may be supervised by one foreman, it may contain several assembly lines. Sometimes each assembly line is regarded as a separate cost center with its own assistant foreman.

A **profit center** is a segment of a business, often called a division, that is responsible for both revenue and expenses.[4] An **investment center** goes a step further; its success is measured not only by its income but also by relating that income to its invested capital. In practice, the term *investment center* is not widely used. **Instead,** *profit center* **is used indiscriminately to describe segments that are always assigned responsibility for revenue and expenses but may or may not be assigned responsibility for the related invested capital.**

Illustration of Responsibility Accounting

The simplified organization chart in Exhibit 9-1 will be the basis for our illustration of how responsibility accounting is used in the motel industry. The manager at the motel level has freedom to make many operating decisions, including some repairs and building improvements.

Exhibit 9-2 provides an overall view of responsibility reporting. Start with the lowest level and work toward the top. See how the reports are integrated through three levels of responsibility. All the variances may be subdivided for further analysis, either in these reports or in more detailed reports.

Trace the $38,000 total from the Los Banos manager's report to the Western vice-president's report. The vice-president's report merely summa-

---

[4]In some settings, particularly in nonprofit organizations, the term *revenue center* is used instead of *profit center* because profit (as ordinarily conceived) is not the primary mission of the subunit. For example, an army motor pool might be called a revenue center if it charged users for its vehicles instead of not charging.

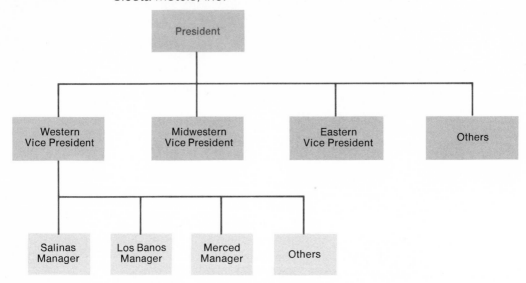

EXHIBIT 9-1. Simplified Organization Chart
Siesta Motels, Inc.

rizes the final results of the motels under his jurisdiction. He may also want copies of the detailed statements for each motel manager responsible to him.

Also trace the $297,000 total from the Western vice-president's report to the president's report. The president's report includes data for her own corporate office plus a summarization of the entire company's operating income performance.

Format of Feedback Reports

This set of illustrative reports shows only the budgeted amount and the variance, which is defined as the difference between the budgeted and the actual amounts. This places the focus on the variances and illustrates **management by exception,** which means that the executive's attention is concentrated on the important deviations from budgeted items. In this way, managers do not waste time on those parts of the reports that reflect smoothly running phases of operations.

Of course, this illustration represents only one possible means of presenting a report of performance. Another common reporting method shows three sets of dollar figures instead of two sets. Moreover, the variances could also be expressed in terms of percentages of budgeted amounts. For example, revenue in Los Banos could appear as follows:

248

EXHIBIT 9-2
SIESTA MOTELS, INC.

Responsibility Accounting at Various Levels
(in thousands of dollars)

| | PRESIDENT'S MONTHLY RESPONSIBILITY REPORT | | | |
| | BUDGET | | VARIANCE: FAVORABLE (UNFAVORABLE) | |
	THIS MONTH	YEAR TO DATE	THIS MONTH	YEAR TO DATE
President's office	(90)	(300)	(9)	(30)
Western vice-president	→297	850	8	50
Midwestern vice-president	400	1,300	20	(100)
Eastern vice-president	350	1,050	30	130
Others	300	1,000	50	100
Operating income	1,257	3,900	99	150

| | WESTERN VICE-PRESIDENT'S MONTHLY RESPONSIBILITY REPORT | | | |
| | BUDGET | | VARIANCE: FAVORABLE (UNFAVORABLE) | |
	THIS MONTH	YEAR TO DATE	THIS MONTH	YEAR TO DATE
Vice-president's office	(20)	(40)	(2)	4
Salinas	29	(20)	(1)	(5)
Los Banos	→38	133	3	16
Merced	30	90	2	10
Others	220	687	(10)	25
Operating income	297	850	8	50

| | LOS BANOS MANAGER'S MONTHLY RESPONSIBILITY REPORT | | | |
| | BUDGET | | VARIANCE: FAVORABLE (UNFAVORABLE) | |
	THIS MONTH	YEAR TO DATE	THIS MONTH	YEAR TO DATE
Revenue	80	250	5	15
Housekeeping and supplies	12	30	1	4
Heat, light, power	3	10	(1)	(2)
Advertising and promotion	2	7	—	(2)
Repairs and maintenance	4	10	(2)	(1)
General	11	30	—	2
Depreciation	10	30	—	—
Total expenses	42	117	(2)	1
Operating income	38	133	3	16

249

	Budget		Actual Results		Variance: Favorable (Unfavorable)		Variance: Percent of Budgeted Amount	
	This Month	Year to Date	This Month	Year to Date	This Month	Year to Date	This Month	Year to Date
Revenue	$80	$250	$85	$265	$5	$15	6.3%	6.0%

The full performance report would contain a similar line-by-line analysis of all items.

Other data are often included in performance evaluation reports. For example, the motel industry characteristically includes the percentage of occupancy of rooms and the average rate per room. Restaurants will show number of meals served and the average selling price per meal.

The exact format adopted in a particular organization depends heavily on user preferences. For instance, some companies focus on the budgeted income statement for the year. As each month unfolds, the managers receive the original plan *for the year* compared against the revised plan *for the year*. The revised plan provides management with the best available prediction of how the year's results will eventually turn out.

Even though formats and intent of responsibility reports may be geared to satisfy the preferences of the managers in a particular organization, the following fundamentals are typically followed:

1. Show total costs, unit costs, and physical amounts of inputs and outputs. Most managers prefer simple reports. Consequently, some of these data may be omitted or condensed; when in doubt, more data rather than less data are furnished.

2. Keep the terminology, time spans, and various internal reports consistent. In this way, budgeted figures can be easily compared with actual results and with budgets and actual results of previous and future periods.

Responsibility and Incentive

Responsibility accounting has innate attraction for most top managers because it facilitates the delegation of decision making. That is, each middle manager is given command of a subunit together with some authority. In return, responsibility accounting supplies the basic means of evaluating each manager's performance. Consequently, in addition to keeping top management informed, a responsibility accounting system helps give individual managers incentive via performance reports.

To try to focus on the manager's performance as an individual administrator, responsibility reporting often excludes or segregates items that are not subject to the manager's control. For example, a foreman's performance report may be confined to usage of direct material, direct labor, and supplies, and exclude depreciation, rent, and property taxes. In a prison or hospital, or in many hotels, the costs on a laundry department performance report might be confined to soap and labor; depreciation on the building and equipment would be excluded.

RESPONSIBILITY ACCOUNTING AND CONTROLLABILITY

Nature of Controllability

Earlier we said that incentive is a matter of degree. Controllability also is a matter of degree. For example, a **controllable cost** has been defined as any cost that is subject to the influence of a given *manager* of a given *responsibility center* for a given *time span*. Responsibility accounting concentrates on human responsibility and focuses on the work of specific managers in relation to a well-defined area of supervision, the responsibility center. Moreover, a specific item may not be influenced for a week, but may be influenced for a month or for a year.

To illustrate, consider the costs of nursing services in a hospital. The extent of the controllability of these costs depends on the availability of short-term or part-time help, the top-management policies regarding intensity of care, the lead time necessary for planning the number of nurses in relation to patient loads, and so on. Some nursing managers may have considerable control over such costs, whereas others may have little control. These factors must be taken into account when judging performance.

Lord Keynes once remarked, "In the long run, we are all dead." In the long run, all costs are controllable by somebody in the organization. But performance reports are prepared for the short run, usually for one year or less. Therefore, an item such as "depreciation on the hospital building" hardly qualifies as a controllable cost on anybody's performance report— perhaps including the president's report. Managers come and go, and they inherit the effects of their predecessors' decisions. The inevitability and long-run effects of costs such as depreciation, property taxes, long-term lease rentals, and the like justifiably spur elaborate studies before the undertaking of such heavy commitments.

Management by Objectives

Management by objectives (MBO) **is a term that describes the joint formulation by a manager and his superior of a set of goals and of plans for achieving the goals for a forthcoming period.**[5] The plans often take the form of a

[5]G. Odiorne, *Management Decisions by Objectives* (Englewood Cliffs, N.J.: Prentice-Hall, Inc., 1970), and R. Brady, "MBO Goes to Work in the Public Sector," *Harvard Business Review,* Vol. 51, No. 2 (March–April 1973), pp. 65–74.

responsibility accounting budget (together with supplementary goals such as levels of management training, safety, and so on that may not be incorporated in the accounting budget). The manager's performance is then evaluated in relation to these agreed-upon budgeted objectives.

Regardless of whether it is so labeled, a management-by-objectives approach lessens the complaints about lack of controllability because of its stress on *budgeted results*. That is, a budget is negotiated between a *particular* manager and his or her superior for a *particular* time period and a *particular* set of expected outside and inside influences. In this way, a manager may more readily accept an assignment to a less successful subunit. This is preferable to a system that emphasizes absolute profitability for its own sake. Unless focus is placed on currently attainable results, able managers will be reluctant to accept responsibility for subunits that are in economic trouble.

Thus, skillful budgeting and intelligent performance evaluation will go a long way toward overcoming the common lament: "I'm being held responsible for costs beyond my control."

Who Gets Blamed?

Responsibility accounting, budgets, variances, and the entire library of accounting techniques are basically neutral devices. However, they are frequently misused as negative weapons, as being a means of placing blame or finding fault. Viewed positively, they are a means of assisting managers so that future improvements in decisions are more easily attained. Moreover, they facilitate the delegation of decision making to lower levels, and autonomy is almost always treasured by managers.

The "blame-placing" attitude reveals a misunderstanding of the rationale of responsibility accounting, which basically asks, "Which individual in the organization is in the best position to explain why a specific outcome occurred? Let's trace costs down to that level so that the feedback coming from performance evaluation is as well-informed as feasible."

In many circumstances, the degree of the manager's control or influence over the outcome may be minimal—but responsibility accounting still is favored. For example, the price of gold to a jewelry manufacturer may be beyond the influence of anybody within the organization. Still, somebody usually is in the best position to explain the *price* of gold, and another is in the best position to explain the *quantity* of gold consumed. The latter individual typically has a budget based on a standard (budgeted) unit price of gold rather than on its actual unit price.

In sum, responsibility accounting presses accountability down to the person who has the greatest potential day-to-day influence over the revenue or cost in question. He must bear the responsibility, and so must his superiors. His fundamental reporting responsibility is to explain the outcome regardless of the degree of his personal influence over the result.

Although terms such as "controllable costs," "controllable profit," and "contribution controllable by the division manager" are widely used, they are deceiving. Note that the "controllable costs" of a foreman of a machining department can be much more highly influenced by him than the "controllable costs" of a sales department can be influenced by a sales manager. **Arguments over degrees of controllability are often a waste of time; they betray a fruitless preoccupation with fixing blame.**

The overall idea of controllability is easily subject to criticism because virtually every revenue and cost is affected by more than one factor. For example, energy *prices* are influenced by forces outside the typical organization, and energy *quantities* are influenced by more than one manager within an organization. Similarly, a purchasing manager may have some influence over unit prices but little influence over usage of materials such as lumber. In some cases, the purchasing manager may influence usage too; after all, he may acquire below-standard lumber that could adversely affect usage through increased rates of spoilage and waste.

A fragile balance must be struck between careful delineation of responsibility on the one hand, and a too-rigid separation of responsibility on the other. Buck passing is a pervasive tendency that is supposedly minimized when responsibility is fixed unequivocally.

> *Example.* A large utility used to hire college graduates and rotate them among all departments in the company during a two-year training program. Their salaries were not assigned to the departments, and individual managers took little interest in the trainees. But now the trainee is assigned to a definite department that fits his primary interest, where he is given direct responsibility as soon as possible. Both the trainees and the managers are much more satisfied with the new responsibility arrangement.

But often the motivational impact boomerangs; too much falls between the chairs. Managers often wear blinders and concentrate more than ever on their individual worlds. Family cooperation is replaced by intracompany competition.

> *Example.* Two departments performed successive operations in a line-production process making automobile frames. The frames were transferred from the first to the second department via an overhead conveyor system. Because of machine breakdowns in his department, the Department 2 manager requested the Department 1 manager to slow down production. He refused, and the frames had to be removed from the conveyor and stacked to await further processing. A bitter squabble ensued regarding which departments should bear the extra labor cost of stacking the frames.

When two or more departments or divisions are heavily interdependent, serious consideration should be given to not pushing the responsibility subunit down too low in the organization.

Confusion among Cost Classifications

Sometimes controllable costs are regarded as indistinguishable from direct costs or variable costs. They may be the same amounts by coincidence, but the concepts differ. **Direct costs are those obviously related to any chosen cost objective (for example, departments or products). Controllable costs are related to an individual manager.** Variable costs are related to fluctuations in a chosen activity base. Some examples of how these costs may be classified are shown in Exhibit 9-3. As the footnotes to the exhibit explain, whether a cost is deemed controllable is affected by who is the department manager in question, his authority over the incurrence of the cost, and the time period in question.

Reporting Controllable and Uncontrollable Items

In a given situation, therefore, some costs may be regarded as controllable with various degrees of influence and others as uncontrollable. Most advocates of responsibility accounting favor excluding the uncontrollable items from a performance report. For example, the report for a shop foreman's department would contain only his controllable costs. Such items as property taxes and rent would not appear on his report; from his standpoint, these are uncontrollable costs.

The countervailing view is that uncontrollable items that are indirectly caused by the existence of the foreman's department should be included in his report. In this way, managers become aware of the whole organization and its costs. The behavioral implication is that some managers in the organization influence almost every cost; by also assigning that cost to some other executives in the organization, these executives will be more inclined to influence the manager who has primary control over the cost.

> *Example.* A president of a large corporation insists that central basic research costs be fully allocated to all divisions despite objections about uncontrollability. His goal is to force division managers' interests toward such research activity. The basic question is whether the accounting system is the best vehicle for reaching such an objective. Indiscriminate cost allocations may undermine the confidence of the managers in the entire accounting system.

But there is also a pitfall here. There can be overdependence on an accounting system as being the prime means of motivation and the final word on the appraisal of performance. Although the system may play a necessary

EXHIBIT 9-3
Classification of Costs

	DIRECT OR INDIRECT		VARIABLE OR FIXED	CONTROLLABLE OR UNCONTROLLABLE		
	TO DEPARTMENT	TO PRODUCT	TO DEPARTMENT	LOWEST DEPARTMENT MANAGER	PRODUCTION MANAGER	SALES MANAGER
1. Raw materials in machining department	Direct	Direct	Variable	Controllable	Controllable	Uncontrollable
2. Power in machining department	Direct	Indirect	Variable	Controllable	Controllable	Uncontrollable
3. Rent on factory building:						
Effect on machining department	Indirect	Indirect	Fixed[a]	Uncontrollable	Controllable	Uncontrollable
Effect on factory buildings and grounds department	Direct	—[b]	Fixed	Uncontrollable[c]	Uncontrollable[c]	Uncontrollable
4. Janitorial service by outside contractor:						
Effect on machining department	Indirect	Indirect	Fixed[a]	Uncontrollable	Controllable	Uncontrollable
Effect on factory building and grounds department	Direct	—[b]	Fixed	Controllable[c]	Controllable	Uncontrollable
5. Supplies in assembly department:						
Effect on machining department	—	—	—	Uncontrollable	Controllable	Uncontrollable
Effect on assembly department	Direct	Indirect	Variable	Controllable	Controllable	Uncontrollable
6. Sales commissions:						
Effect on sales department	Direct	—[d]	Variable	Controllable	Uncontrollable	Controllable
Effect on machining department	—	—	—	Uncontrollable	Uncontrollable	Controllable

[a] Whether the cost is fixed or variable *to the department* will depend on the organization's methods of allocating costs identified as "fixed for the organization as a whole" among the various departments.

[b] Products do not flow through this department.

[c] Controllability is also affected by the time period in question and the level of authority. If the manager of the buildings and grounds department negotiates a long-term contract (longer than one year), the item is regarded as uncontrollable. If the contract is for one year or less, the item is regarded as controllable.

[d] Sales commissions may be linked to departments and products for management control and pricing purposes, but they are not a part of the product cost for inventory valuation purposes.

role in coordination and motivation, its many limitations deserve recognition, too, particularly in matters of cost allocations. A common complaint of managers, often marked by tones of discouragement, is that they are being unfairly charged with uncontrollable costs. **In any event, if management insists that both controllable and uncontrollable costs appear on the same report, these costs should not be mingled indiscriminately.** Instead, they should be separately identified so they may be evaluated differently.

BEHAVIORAL PROBLEMS WITH CONTROL SYSTEMS

Obtaining Acceptance

Top management is faced with trying to get managers to *accept* top management's goals as their own personal goals and their own group goals. The accounting control system is the major formal means of solving problems of goal congruence and incentive in most organizations. But it requires enthusiastic support from senior management if it is to be taken seriously by subordinates. **Top-management support is so important that it almost deserves the same prominence as goal congruence and incentive as key factors in judging systems.**

Personal goals and group goals are affected by many influences beyond the formal control system, including religion, family, profession, and education. Therefore, top management should not expect too much from the accounting control system in some situations. For instance, physicians and research scientists tend not to regard the formal control system as important, unless top management is unusually persuasive. To illustrate, professionals are often unenthusiastic about keeping accurate records, if any. Some top managers are highly successful in explaining the importance of accurate record keeping to all types of employees, whereas other top managers fail.

Many behavioral researchers acclaim participation as a large help in minimizing problems of congruence and incentive. For instance, participation entails the joint setting of budgetary goals by the managers at all levels of the organization, often from the bottom up. In contrast, nonparticipation is exemplified by the authoritarian imposition of budgets from the top down. Participation is not a cure-all for budgetary-system ills. The question in a specific organization is whether acceptance of goals is achieved. Sometimes congruence and desired incentive are obtained via democratic processes and sometimes via dictatorial processes.[6]

---

[6]E. Lawler and J. Rhode, *Information and Control in Organizations* (Pacific Palisades, Calif.: Goodyear Publishing Co., Inc., 1976), and A. Hopwood, *Accounting and Human Behavior* (Englewood Cliffs, N.J.: Prentice-Hall, Inc., 1976), discuss in depth the issues of accounting in relation to authoritative and participative management.

Budget Padding

Almost all managers want as much autonomy as they can get; they do not want to be rigidly constrained in their decision making. They want to keep their options open with respect to running their subunits and demonstrating impressive performance. Consequently, managers might be expected to "protect themselves" when they prepare budgets and when they spend. **When their behavior conflicts with top-management desires, it is often described as** *dysfunctional,* **an oft-used term for describing behavior that is counterproductive because it is not goal-congruent.**

Some examples of dysfunctional behavior include:

1. In all organizations, particularly nonprofit ones, managers spend all available money so as to exhaust any budgetary appropriation (that is, authority to spend up to a specified maximum). This sometimes involves foolish disbursements, especially near the end of a fiscal year. This attitude persists from year to year. Spending is justified as follows: "We'd better spend the money now or forego the benefits forever."

2. Managers are reluctant to reduce costs for fear that their future budget allowances will be reduced. In short, stellar performance now may bring temporary praise and tightened expectations.

3. Managers play games at budget-setting time. They deliberately pad their requests. In turn, top management cuts the budgets because they know padding exists. Padding is sometimes called *slack*; it is the difference between the budgeted costs requested and the costs necessary to get the work accomplished.[7]

How does top management encourage cost reduction and discourage padding? One way is to give rewards such as bonuses or pay raises for changes in methods that will produce cost savings. Another way is to allow the manager to "keep" the prospective savings. For example, the budget for the next year or two would remain at, say $400,000, even though the introduction of a new operating method could warrant its being reduced to $370,000.

Some organizations have convinced managers that a budget reduction is a sign of achievement, so the managers regard cost reduction as a major goal; they see that

". . . a budget reduction, *per se,* should not be viewed as a punishment and that there is top management emphasis on recognizing and rewarding cost reduction. A manager is rewarded by a combination of promotion, salary, and the respect of peers, superiors, and subordinates. If top management stresses

[7]M. Schiff and A. Lewin, "Where Traditional Budgeting Fails," *Financial Executive,* Vol. XXXVI, No. 5, 51–62; and "The Impact of People on Budgets," *The Accounting Review,* Vol. XLV, No. 2 (April 1970), 259–69.

the importance of cost reduction and rewards, there need not be a negative reaction to reducing the budget." [8]

Some accountants and managers regard all padding as undesirable. In their eyes, the perfect budget would contain zero padding. But the cost-benefit test should be applied to budget padding (slack). There may be an optimum amount of padding in every budget. This permits managers to preserve their dignity, their sense of freedom, and their flexibility in coping with unforeseen conditions.

Accurate Scorekeeping

The control system rests on a foundation of accurate records such as time sheets, output measures, and requisitions. They are used for legal purposes, for income tax purposes, for external reporting purposes, for dealing with customers, creditors, employees, and so forth. Above all, accurate records provide a basis for planning and control. Control systems produce two kinds of faulty data: (1) about what can be done (budget) and (2) about what has been done (performance evaluation).[9]

Managers are sometimes tempted to falsify records in order to improve their personal showing on performance reports. For example, a manager commented, "I accidently discovered that the plant manager hoarded some parts that were produced in excess of quota in good months to protect himself against bad months." Such behavior distorts production records in both good and bad months and is misleading for planning purposes.

Obtaining accuracy is a problem of motivation. Managers and subordinates must be convinced that maintaining accuracy is an important feature of an employee's responsibilities. Two major means of motivation are (1) designing records that are not overly difficult to maintain accurately (an uncomplicated time sheet) and (2) top-management emphasis on the matter.

Senior managers can set good examples by openly seeking key records of reports. For example, many partners in public accounting firms express day-to-day concern over how their staffs have allocated their time to various auditing steps. This is done not only for current control, but to ensure that correct data are being compiled as a basis for planning next year's or similar auditing engagements.

[8] R. Anthony and R. Herzlinger, *Management Control in Nonprofit Organizations* (Homewood, Ill.: Richard D. Irwin, Inc., 1975), p. 289.

[9] Lawler and Rhode, *Information and Control,* Chap. 7.

RESPONSIBILITY BUDGETING
IN NONPROFIT ORGANIZATIONS

Goals, Incentives, and Complexities

Most nonprofit organizations have more difficulty in identifying objectives or goals than do profit-seeking organizations. There is no profit, no "bottom line" that so often serves as a powerful incentive in private industry. Furthermore, monetary incentives are generally less effective in nonprofit organizations. For example, many managers seek positions in nonprofit organizations primarily for nonmonetary rewards.

Control systems in nonprofit organizations will never be as highly developed as in profit-seeking organizations for several reasons, including:

1. Organizational goals or objectives are less clear. Moreover, they are often multiple, requiring trade-offs.
2. Professionals (for example, teachers, attorneys, physicians, scientists, economists) tend to dominate nonprofit organizations. They are usually less receptive to the installation or improvement of formal control systems.[10]
3. Measurements are more difficult:
   a. There is no profit measure.
   b. There are heavy amounts of discretionary fixed costs.
   c. The relationships of inputs to outputs are hard to specify and measure. Attempts to relate inputs to outputs via work measurement are often resisted.

Additional difficulties arise because of the lesser role of the marketplace, the greater role of politics, and the vague sense of responsibility because "ownership" of nonprofit organizations is often ill-defined.

Budgeting was originally developed in the public sector as a way of providing accountability. However, the management uses of budgets have been unimpressive. Too often, the budget is regarded as a means of obtaining money, not as a means of planning and control. Thus, the process of budgeting in the public sector is often a matter of playing bargaining games with higher authorities to get the largest possible authorization of discretionary fixed costs.

Budgeting as Ongoing Procedure

Because managers of all organizations are unsure about what amount for a discretionary cost is "correct" or "right" or "optimum," they frequently rely

[10] Anthony and Herzlinger, *Nonprofit Organizations*, pp. 34–58, discuss differences between nonprofit and other organizations. Also see R. Anthony and J. Dearden, *Management Control Systems* (3rd ed., Homewood Ill.: Richard D. Irwin, Inc., 1976), Chap. 15.

on industry or company tradition or custom for deciding on a budgeted amount. For example, a lump sum of 2 percent of last year's sales may be appropriated for the forthcoming year's research budget.

By definition, discretionary costs are not subject to scientific input-output analysis. Nevertheless, managers have attempted to pinpoint relative priorities. For instance, some organizations ask their managers to specify the activities that would be cut back or added if the budgetary allowance were increased or decreased, respectively. This ploy requires the manager to conduct more than the superficial analysis that often accompanies the budgetary ritual.

Zero-Based Budgeting

From time to time, catchy words and phrases arise to describe new budgeting techniques or variations of old ones. An example is *zero-based budgeting,* which arose as a response to the problems of controlling discretionary costs and which refers to the practice of having a manager justify his department's activities from the ground up as though they were being initiated for the first time. Traditionally, proposed budgets have been justified on an incremental basis. That is, managers have tended to prepare new budgets in terms of changes from last year's budget and results. **In contrast, zero-based budgeting gets back to the bedrock questions such as why does this activity or department exist and what are or should be its goals or objectives.**

Zero-based budgeting has been receiving increased attention in non-profit organizations:

> "Zero-based budgeting is especially adaptable to discretionary cost areas in which service and support are the primary outputs. It is this characteristic that has attracted the interest of governmental officials, as most expenditures of government can be classified as discretionary in nature." [11]

Experience to Date

Zero-based budgeting has been adopted by at least twelve state governments. The general idea is for low-level managers to construct alternative budgets for each activity. These alternatives are combined into so-called decision packages.

One alternative says what would occur if the activity were simply

[11] See G. Minmier and R. Hermanson, "A Look at Zero Base Budgeting—The Georgia Experience," *Atlanta Economic Review,* Vol. 26, No. 4 (July–August 1976), p. 6. The practice originally arose in Texas Instruments Company. For elaboration of procedures and descriptions, see Peter A. Phyrr, "Zero-Base Budgeting," *Harvard Business Review* (November–December 1970), pp. 111–21.

eliminated. Another alternative explains how the agency would adapt to a budget cut. Other alternatives indicate what will be achieved with the existing budget and with extra money if supplied.

Charles Travis, the Texas governor's budget chief, has commented on the advantages of zero-based budgeting: "The system itself doesn't save money. What it does is provide better information for the decision makers." [12] The Georgia study[13] cited the same advantage plus two others: (1) more careful planning before the budget itself is prepared and (2) increased involvement of lower-level personnel in the state's budgetary process.

The biggest disadvantage is the cost of zero-based budget preparation in terms of time and effort. For example, a proposed study of one portion of the Federal Elementary and Secondary Education Act will last seven years and cost $7 million during the first year alone. Thus, in some organizations the costs may exceed any expected benefits.

Is complete zero-based budgeting on an annual basis a feasible way to plan? Many critics think that such a traumatic, costly analysis is desirable every five or six years, but not every year. Accordingly, some states (including Colorado and Florida) have passed "sunset laws" that provide a termination date for each state regulatory agency. As the date approaches, a performance review is conducted to determine whether the agency's life should be extended.

Zero-Based Revenue

Many experienced administrators in nonprofit organizations believe that managers should be concerned about revenue as well as costs. As a dean commented, "Responsibility for expenses only, and not for revenue and expenses, leads to different behavior."

Herbert Stein, former chairman of the Council of Economic Advisers, is skeptical of zero-based budgeting:

> There is a missing link in the zero-based budgeting idea, and that is failure to apply it to the revenue side of the budget . . . . First, it means that the test which existing programs must pass in order to be continued is less rigorous than it would otherwise be. A program does not have to meet the test of being worth the expenditure of some of the money that is automatically flowing into the Treasury. Second, it means that if existing programs fail to pass the test, new programs will be adopted because the money is there.[14]

---

[12]"Zero-Based Budgeting," *U.S. News & World Report,* September 20, 1976, p. 80.

[13]Minmier and Hermanson, "The Georgia Experience," p. 11.

[14]Herbert Stein, "How About Zero-Based Revenue?" *Wall Street Journal,* January 3, 1977, p. 6.

Program budgeting is an outgrowth of a concept known as Planning, Programming, and Budgeting (PPB), which was experimented with extensively in the U.S. federal government during the 1960s. The Secretary of Defense and other high officers used PPB to analyze military activities in strategic terms. Programs (such as defending the continental United States or obtaining a first-strike capability) were framed to enable the comparison of alternatives based on explicit criteria and assumptions and incorporating expected costs and benefits. A highlight of the approach was the focus on explicit, long-range program decisions, in contrast to the previous procedure of annually deciding how much of the overall appropriation should be allocated to the Army, Navy, and Air Force.

PPB was implemented successfully in the Defense Department because (1) outputs were definable and measurable (e.g., the probabilities of U.S. weapons' penetrating enemy defenses); (2) top-management support for PPB was heavy and visible; and (3) competent PPB staff was available to top management.

PPB is more a state of mind than a system. It has become widely used, particularly at state and local governmental levels, where it is often called program budgeting rather than PPB.[15] Its central characteristics were described by a former Director of the Budget:

> As the *first* step, PPB calls for a careful specification and analysis of basic program objectives . . . . What are they really trying to accomplish? The objective of our intercity highway program, for example, is *not* to build highways. Highways are useful only as they serve a higher objective, namely transporting people and goods. . . .
>
> The *second* step is to analyze the output of a given program in terms of the objectives . . . .
>
> The *third* step is to measure the *total costs* of the program, not just for one year, but over at least several years ahead . . . not on the basis of the first year costs alone . . . .
>
> The *fourth* and crucial step is to analyze alternatives . . . . It is competition among alternatives which is crucial . . . .
>
> The *fifth* step is establishing PPB as an integral part of the budgetary decisions. The programming concept is the crucial link that relates planning to budgeting, converting planning from paper exercise to an important part of the decision process.[16]

[15] For fuller descriptions, see Anthony and Herzlinger, *Nonprofit Organizations*, Chaps. 8 and 9.

[16] Charles Schultze, U.S. Congress, Senate Committee on Government Operations, *Planning-Programming-Budgeting*. Hearings, 90th Congress, 1st session (Washington, D.C.: Government Printing Office). For a description of designing and installing a PPB system, see Robert J. Mowitz, *The Design and Implementation of Pennsylvania's Planning, Program and Budgeting System* (University Park: Pennsylvania State University, 1970).

The success of the management-control system can be affected both by its technical perfection and by nontechnical factors that influence management behavior. Accounting records, budgets, standards, and reports are inanimate objects. By themselves, they are neither good nor bad. Whether they help or hinder strictly depends on how skillfully they are used by managers.

The trade-offs of the benefits and cost of information form the basic criterion for systems design and appraisal. Motivation is the dominant consideration in pinpointing the value or benefits of a management-control system. Above all, the system should promote goal congruence and incentives by explicitly identifying top-management objectives and then encouraging managers to act in harmony with these objectives. Among the questions that seem particularly important are:

1. Does the system specify goals and subgoals that encourage behavior that blends with top-management goals?
2. Are the goals as specified by top management accepted by managers as their personal goals?
3. Is the accounting system tailored to the organizational structure to strengthen motivation?
4. Does the system properly guide managers in the acquisition and utilization of resources by providing accurate, timely, relevant data?

Subquestions deserving consideration would cover such commonly encountered difficulties as the overemphasis on a subgoal; the overemphasis on short-run performance; failure to pinpoint responsibility; cooperation versus competition; the lack of distinction between controllable and uncontrollable costs; limitations of records as motivation devices; inaccurate source documents; and faulty cost analysis.

SUMMARY PROBLEM FOR YOUR REVIEW

Problem

The Lindhe Co. has a responsibility accounting system. Uncontrollable costs, such as insurance, property taxes, depreciation, and supervisory salaries, are excluded from the periodic performance reports. A summary of the performance of Departments A and B follows:

	Department A		Department B	
	Actual	*Budget*	*Actual*	*Budget*
Direct material	$ 70,000	$ 69,000	$150,000	$155,600
Direct labor	30,000	28,000	70,000	68,000
Supplies	2,000	2,600	3,200	4,000
Idle time	1,100	1,000	5,100	1,500
Rework	3,000	1,400	2,000	2,100
Overtime premium	800	—	2,000	—
Other indirect labor	4,000	4,200	6,700	6,800
	$110,900	$106,200	$239,000	$238,000

During the period reported, one of the important machines in Department A developed a misalignment that was not detected until the machine had been used for a considerable time. The product has an assembly-line production pattern, moving from Department A to Department B.

Required | Explain the possible causes of the variations noted above in light of the information given here. Comment on the controllability of the cost elements.

Solution

Neither department shows significant deviations from budget *totals*. However, the detailed items reveal clues for investigation. A major point here is that summary analysis often buries significant, but offsetting, variances.

The high rework costs in Department A are probably due to the faulty machine. The idle time in Department B was probably spent waiting for goods reworked in Department A. The overtime premiums in both departments may have resulted from efforts to adhere to scheduled production requirements. For example, in Department A the rework cost was $1,600 in excess of budget; the overtime premium was $800 (50 percent of $1,600). Therefore, the idle time and the overtime premium in Department B may not have been controllable by the head of that department. And this raises the possibility that these costs might more properly be charged to Department A.

The notable savings in supplies in both departments are difficult to explain with the sketchy information we have. One possible explanation is an honest-to-goodness bearing down on the cost of supplies. Other possible explanations are faulty budget figures, errors in record keeping, or deliberate holding back of new orders for supplies in an effort to keep costs within the overall budget.

The direct-material and direct-labor performances are difficult to evaluate because no distinctions are available between prices or labor rates, on the one hand, and usage, on the other. We have no assurance that the direct-material and direct-labor figures shown are computed either at standard or at actual unit rates. The department heads probably have control over usage but not over prices or rates.

ASSIGNMENT MATERIAL

Fundamental Assignment Material

9-1. Terminology. Define *responsibility accounting, goal congruence, cost centers, profit centers, investment centers, controllable cost,* and *zero-based budgeting.*

9-2. Responsibility of purchasing agent. Acme Manufacturing Company has received an order for 500 special parts, which will require modifications of stock part No. 1739. There is a penalty clause on the order—$1,500 a day for every day delivery is late. It will cost the company $7 less per unit to purchase and process raw materials for the special part than to rework standard part No. 1739.

Mr. Smith, the purchasing agent, is responsible for securing the raw material in time to meet the scheduled delivery date. Mr. Smith places the order and receives an acceptable delivery date from his supplier. He checks up several times and does everything in his power to insure prompt delivery of the raw material.

On the delivery date specified by the supplier, Mr. Smith is notified that the raw material was damaged in packaging and will be delivered four days late. As a result, the special order will also be four days late. Consequently, a $6,000 penalty must be paid by Acme Company.

What department should bear the $6,000 penalty? Why?

Additional Assignment Material

9-3. "There are corporate objectives other than profit." Name four.

9-4. What is the most important question in judging the effectiveness of a measure of performance?

9-5. What eight areas has General Electric Company used to avoid overemphasis of one performance measure?

9-6. Give three examples of how managers may improve short-run performance to the detriment of long-run results.

9-7. Illustrate how a measurement system may engender faulty cost analysis.

9-8. What three guides are basic to the accountant's work in current planning and control?

9-9. What are the most glaring sources of error in source documents?

9-10. Why is attention directing such an important accounting function?

9-11. "Collecting relevant data by responsibility centers is difficult." Why?

9-12. "Variable costs are controllable and fixed costs are uncontrollable." Do you agree? Explain.

9-13. "Managers may trade off variable for fixed costs." Give three examples.

9-14. What two major factors influence controllability?

9-15. Describe three guides to deciding how costs should be charged to a responsibility center.

9-16. "Material costs are controllable by a production department foreman." Do you agree? Explain.

9-17. **Responsibility accounting.** (CMA, adapted.) The Fillep Company operates a standard cost system. The variances for each department are calculated and reported to the department manager. It is expected that the manager will use the information to improve his operations and recognize that it is used by his superiors when they are evaluating his performance.

John Smith was recently appointed manager of the assembly department of the company. He has complained that the system as designed is disadvantageous to his department. Included among the variances charged to the departments is one for rejected units. The inspection occurs at the end of the assembly department. The inspectors attempt to identify the cause of the rejection so that the department where the error occurred can be charged with it. But not all errors can be easily identified with a department. The nonidentified units are totalled and apportioned to the departments according to the number of identified errors. The variance for rejected units in each department is a combination of the errors caused by the department plus a portion of the unidentified causes of rejects.

Required

1. Is John Smith's complaint valid? Explain the reason(s) for your answer.
2. What would you recommend the company do to solve its problem with John Smith and his complaint?

9-18. **Management by objectives.** (CMA.) John Press is the chief executive officer of Manfield Company. Press has a financial management background and is known throughout the organization as a "no-nonsense" executive. When Press became chief executive officer, he emphasized cost reduction and savings and introduced a comprehensive cost control and budget system. The company goals and budget plans were established by Press and given to his subordinates for implementation. Some of the company's key executives were dismissed or demoted for failing to meet projected budget plans. Under the leadership of John Press, Manfield has once again become financially stable and profitable after several years of poor performance.

Recently, Press has become concerned with the human side of the organization and has become interested in the management technique referred to as "management by objectives" (MBO). If there are enough positive benefits of MBO, he plans to implement the system throughout the company. However, he realizes that he does not fully understand MBO because he does not understand how it differs from the current system of establishing firm objectives and budget plans.

1. Briefly explain what "management by objectives" entails and identify its advantages and disadvantages.

2. Does the management style of John Press incorporate the human value premises and goals of MBO? Explain your answer.

9-19. Cost classifications. Construct a chart with the following headings:

		Controllable Cost		
Product Cost	Variable Cost	By Sales Vice-President	By Assembly Supervisor	By Production Vice-President

Salesmen's commissions
Direct material
Machining department—
 direct labor
Finishing department—
 supplies
Sales vice-president's
 salary
Straight-line deprecia-
 tion—equipment in
 assembly department
Management consulting
 fee for improving
 labor methods in
 assembly department

For each account, answer "yes" or "no" as to whether the cost is a product cost, a variable cost, and a cost controllable by the three officers indicated. Thus, you will have five answers, entered horizontally, for each account.

9-20. Source documents. (CMA.) The Majina Plant of Reed Manufacturing Co. produces automotive components and accessories. Don Kline recently has been assigned to the accounting department at the Majina Plant. Kline spent a great deal of time reviewing the plant's operations, operating procedures, and reporting practices in order to become familiar with the plant's activities.

During this review period, Kline discovered an inconsistency in the reporting of production and finished-goods inventory to corporate headquarters. The normal rejection rate on components manufactured at the Majina Plant was 5 percent. The production reports indicate that Majina's experience during periods of normal production activity was much better than this rate. Yet when reporting to corporate headquarters, Majina reported spoiled units at above 5 percent rather than the lesser quantity of actual units spoiled.

Further analysis disclosed that the units representing the difference between the actual and reported defective rates were stockpiled in the plant warehouse for future disposition. The plant would release these units whenever they were needed. These "extra" units especially proved convenient when the plant was asked to operate at a higher-than-normal production rate or when there was an unexpected order to be filled. Under such circumstances extra demands were placed on Majina manufacturing facilities. This usually resulted in a larger-than-normal defective rate. The "stockpiled" units could then be released to offset the large spoilage rate.

By the end of the year Majina's inventory and production records were in agreement with the actual activities. Don Kline was concerned about the reporting discrepancies that occurred throughout the year.

Identify the problem, discuss the issues, and recommend the action to be taken by Don Kline.

9-21. Public and private enterprise. A news story described how the New York City police department had turned over some of its duties to a private company, City Towing Service, Inc. Because of the salaries paid to police department personnel, it cost the department $65 to tow away a single car. The new system pays the private company $30 for every car with a traffic ticket that it tows from midtown Manhattan.

Required

1. How do you think the $65 figure may have been computed?
2. Do you think the drivers for the private company will behave any differently than the drivers for the police department? Explain.

9-22. Sales incentives. (CMA, adapted.) The Parsons Co. compensates its field sales force on a commission and year-end bonus basis. The commission is 20 percent of standard gross margin (planned selling price less standard cost of goods sold on a full absorption basis) contingent upon collection of the account. Customer's credit is approved by the company's credit department. Price concessions are granted on occasion by the top sales management, but sales commissions are not reduced by the discount. A year-end bonus of 15 percent of commissions earned is paid to salesmen who equal or exceed their annual sales target. The annual sales target is usually established by applying approximately a 5 percent increase to the prior year's sales.

Required

1. What features of this compensation plan would seem to be effective in motivating the salesmen to accomplish company goals of higher profits and return on investment? Explain why.
2. What features of this compensation plan would seem to be countereffective in motivating the salesmen to accomplish the company goals of higher profits and return on investment? Explain why.

9-23. Performance evaluation. Consider the following excerpt from a company employee newsletter. It announces the creation of a Perpetual Trophy that will be awarded to the branch with the most outstanding performance during a fiscal year:

The Trophy will be several feet high and will be designed to be moved from branch to branch each year. Additionally, a small replica of the trophy will be awarded to the manager of the winning branch.

The Trophy will be awarded to the branch with the best combination of sales percentage increase and net operating percentage increase. The actual calculation will be to take the sales percentage increase, plus the net operating profit percentage increase and divide those two numbers by two, giving equal weight to both sales and profit growth. Only independent branches achieving a minimum 15 percent sales increase will be eligible.

What is your personal evaluation of the way outstanding performance is measured?

9-24. Goal congruence. (CMA, adapted.) NEI, Inc., is a medium-sized manufacturer of precision measurement instruments, which have international recognition for engineering design and quality. Tom Nash, the firm's president and founder, is concerned primarily with product reputation and with a satisfactory return.

A small technical sales force works with NEI's major customers. The salesmen are paid a salary plus commission. A limited number of manufacturers' representatives supplement the sales force and are compensated by a straight commission.

The production area is organized into profit centers, output being valued at standard cost plus 25 percent. Most of the production employees are skilled tradesmen, and many of them have been with the firm since its earliest years of operation. The production employees participate in a year-end profit-sharing bonus, which is allocated on the basis of each profit center's profitability.

Tom Nash believes each production manager should have complete responsibility and control over his profit center. Therefore, they have substantial control over accepting, scheduling, and running jobs. Preference is routinely given to the most profitable jobs over the less profitable ones. Most orders are not completed by the promised delivery date, and usually expediting measures have to be taken.

Jim Case, the chief financial officer of NEI, Inc., wants the production scheduling system changed because the present system has caused several financial problems for the company. For example, the raw-materials and work-in-process inventories are too large. Customers express their irritation over late deliveries by slow payment of their accounts. As a result of the large inventories and slow collection of accounts, the company has a severe cash-flow problem. These factors have adversely affected Case's ability to arrange short-term financing through a local bank.

Case has informed Tom Nash of the difficulties in arranging a short-term loan. Again, as many times in the past, he pointed out that a major contributor to the company's financial problems is the production scheduling system. Nash replied that Case's job was to obtain the necessary financing and not to second-guess experienced production men.

Jim Case has become quite frustrated in his position as chief financial officer of NEI, Inc. He has interviewed for a similar position with several firms. However, he has experienced difficulty in changing firms because NEI has a reputation for its poor financial position.

1. Discuss how the goals of the production managers and Jim Case conflict.
2. Discuss how the goals of Jim Case and Tom Nash conflict.
3. Do NEI's present management policies cause suboptimum behavior? Justify your answer.

9-25. Multiple goals and profitability.[17] The following are multiple goals of the General Electric Company:

---

[17]Adapted from a problem originally appearing in R. H. Hassler and Neil E. Harlan, *Cases in Controllership* (Englewood Cliffs, N.J.: Prentice-Hall, Inc.).

1. Profitability
2. Market position
3. Productivity
4. Product leadership
5. Personnel development
6. Employee attitudes
7. Public responsibility
8. Balance between short-range and long-range goals

General Electric is a Goliath corporation with sales of about $18 billion and assets of $14 billion in 1978. It had approximately 170 responsibility centers called "departments," but that is a deceiving term. In most other companies, these departments would be called divisions. For example, some GE departments have sales of over $300 million.

Each department manager's performance is evaluated annually in relation to the specified multiple goals. A special measurements group was set up in 1952 to devise ways of quantifying accomplishments in each of the areas. In this way, the evaluation of performance would become more objective as the various measures were developed and improved.

Required

1. How would you measure performance in each of these areas? Be specific.
2. Can the other goals be encompassed as ingredients of a formal measure of profitability? In other words, can profitability *per se* be defined to include the other goals?

9-26. Commission plan for new-car salesmen. As an automobile dealer, you are faced with the problem of formulating a new-car salesmen's commissions plan. You have listed the following alternatives:

a. Commissions based on a flat percentage of dollar sales.
b. Commissions based on varying percentages of dollar sales. The higher the sales price of a deal, the higher the commission rate. Also, commissions will differ, depending on various accessories sold.
c. Commissions based on net profit after allocation of a fair share of all operating expenses.

Required

Evaluate these alternatives. Are there other methods that deserve consideration.

9-27. Responsibility for a stable employment policy. The Fast-Weld Metal Fabricating Company has been manufacturing machine tools for a number of years and has an industrywide reputation for doing high-quality work. The company has been faced with irregularity of output over the years. It has been company policy to lay off welders as soon as there was insufficient work to keep them busy, and to rehire them when demand warranted. The company, however, now has poor labor relations and finds it very difficult to hire good welders because of its layoff policy. Consequently, the quality of the work has been continually declining.

The plant manager has proposed that the welders, who earn $6 per hour, be retained during slow periods to do menial plant maintenance work that is normally performed by men earning $3.85 per hour in the plant maintenance department. You, as controller, must decide the most meaningful accounting procedure to handle the wages of the welders doing plant maintenance work. What department or departments should be charged with this work, and at what rate? Discuss the implications of your plan.

9-28. Salesmen's compensation plan. You are sales manager of a manufacturing firm whose sales are subject to month-to-month variations, depending upon the individual salesman's efforts. A new salary-plus-bonus plan has been in effect for four months and you are reviewing a sales performance report. The plan provides for a base salary of $400 per month, a $500 bonus each month if the salesman's monthly quota is met, and an additional commission of 5 percent on all sales over the monthly quota.

		Salesman A	Salesman B	Salesman C
January	Quota	$30,000	$10,000	$50,000
	Actual	10,000	10,000	60,000
February	Quota	$10,300	$10,300	$61,800
	Actual	20,000	10,300	40,000
March	Quota	$20,600	$10,600	$41,200
	Actual	35,000	5,000	60,000
April	Quota	$36,050	$ 5,150	$61,800
	Actual	15,000	5,200	37,000

Evaluate the compensation plan. Be specific. What changes would you recommend?

9-29. Sales responsibility reports. (CMA, adapted.) Mill Company prepares monthly and annual "Salesman Performance Reports" for each of the territorial salesmen. Copies of the annual report for two salesmen—John Fowler and James Barnes—are reproduced in Exhibit 9-4. Mill Company has classified the twelve territories into three types, according to characteristics such as travel required, customer demographics, and product prices. A territory budget is formulated for each of the three classifications to be used for comparison purposes. Fowler and Barnes are assigned to territories that are similar and have the same territorial classification and the same budget.

The purpose of the Salesman Performance Report is to compare the salesman's performance with the planned activity and show the salesman's contribution toward company profits. All costs and expenses that can be identified with the salesman's effort to generate and produce sales are included on the report. Sales administration and promotion costs (including salaries) are charged to the salesmen according to the number of regular and special handling orders the salesmen write. Special-handling orders require approximately twice as much administrative effort as regular orders; consequently, the charge for special-handling orders is double the charge for regular orders ($16 versus $8). The 19x4 rate was determined by dividing the amount budgeted for sales administration salaries and sales administration and promotion costs ($160,000) by the estimated total orders (regular, 18,000; special-handling, 1,000) weighted by the amount of administrative effort. Special-handling orders comprise approximately 5 percent of the total orders handled.

EXHIBIT 9-4

Salesman Performance Reports
For the Fiscal Year Ended December 31, 19x4

	TERRITORY BUDGET FOR EACH			ACTUAL RESULTS: FOWLER			ACTUAL RESULTS: BARNES		
	PLASTIC	METAL	TOTAL	PLASTIC	METAL	TOTAL	PLASTIC	METAL	TOTAL
Sales in units	24,000	16,000	40,000	24,000	17,000	41,000	20,000	20,000	40,000
Sales in dollars	$144,000	$160,000	$304,000	$144,000	$161,500	$305,500	$120,000	$190,000	$310,000
Cost of sales at standard	72,000	120,000	192,000	72,000	127,500	199,500	60,000	150,000	210,000
Gross profit at standard	$ 72,000	$ 40,000	$112,000	$ 72,000	$ 34,000	$106,000	$ 60,000	$ 40,000	$100,000
Operating expenses:									
Salary			$ 4,000			$ 4,000			$ 4,000
Commissions			9,120			9,165			9,300
Employee benefits			1,968			1,975			1,995
Sales administration and promotion:[a]									
Regular orders			11,400			10,000			11,600
Special-handling orders			1,200			800			2,400
Travel and entertainment			6,250			6,000			7,500
Shipping and packing			12,000			12,300			12,000
Total operating expenses			$ 45,938			$ 44,240			$ 48,795
Salesman profit contribution			$ 66,062			$ 61,760			$ 51,205
Other data:									
Salesman miles traveled						32,000			28,000
Salesman calls						1,200			1,000
Number of regular orders						1,250			1,450
Number of special-handling orders						50			150
Average size of order						$235			$194

[a] Sales administration and promotion costs plus sales administration salaries are charged to the salesmen at the rate of $8 per regular order and $16 per special-handling order.

1. Evaluate, from the company's point of view, the performance of the two salesmen whose reports are presented. Use the appropriate numerical data to support your answer.

2. What changes, if any, would you make in the Salesman Performance Report presently employed by Mill Company to make it more useful for evaluating salesmen? Explain your answer.

9-30. Federal budget and slack. Formulation of the budget of the President of the United States is a give-and-take process that starts eight months before the budget is presented and 14–18 months before it goes into effect. This lengthy process means that budgetary decisions must be made far in advance of actual conditions. Hence, the predictions provide a generous amount of "slack" or "padding."

In addition to the problem of a long time span, there is the problem of back-and-forth negotiating among many layers of decision makers in the government agencies and between the agency or department and the Office of Management and Budget (OMB), which is the President's voice of authority. An agency will face this problem internally from May to September. The agency and OMB will negotiate from September until January. Congress and the agency will proceed from February until June or September. The line manager who initiates the request will hardly ever participate beyond the first or second stage.

The OMB tries to exert some control over slack by allocating spendable funds to an agency from quarter to quarter rather than in one lump sum.

One agency in HEW had failed to spend about $5 million of its $70 million program administration account for two consecutive years. The agency budget officer feared that the OMB would cut the budget. The unspent $5 million was caused by a failure to hire enough employees, so the budget officer instructed the personnel office to hire as many temporary employees as possible, without waiting for line office requests.

Because the budget officer knew that OMB could easily discover that these employees were temporary, she also authorized about 40 percent of the $5 million to be spent for hiring consultants to the personnel office to improve the classification, recruitment, and hiring of regular employees. To thwart OMB's investigation, she embargoed the monthly personnel reports and substituted a new "personnel projection report" that predicted what expenditures would be under the new accelerated hiring trends. She submitted a budget request for $17 million for increased personnel based on the premise that all current positions were full.

What are the probable motivational effects of the federal budget process? How would you cope with slack or padding in the federal budget?

9-31. Nonprofit performance. (CMA.) In late 19x1 Mr. Sootsman, the official in charge of the State Department of Automobile Regulation, established a system of performance measurement for the department's branch offices. He was convinced that management by objectives could help the department reach its objective of better citizen service at a lower cost. The first step was to define the activities of the branch offices, to assign point values to the services performed, and to establish performance targets. Point values, rather than revenue targets, were employed because the department was a regulatory agency, not a revenue-producing agency.

Further, the specific revenue for a service did not adequately reflect the differences in effort required. The analysis was compiled at the state office, and the results were distributed to the branch offices.

The system has been in operation since 19x2. The performance targets for the branches have been revised each year by the state office. The revisions were designed to encourage better performance by increasing the target or reducing resources to achieve targets. The revisions incorporated noncontrollable events, such as population shifts, new branches, and changes in procedures.

The Barry County branch is typical of many branch offices. A summary displaying the budgeted and actual performance for three years is presented in Exhibit 9-5.

Mr. Sootsman has been disappointed in the performance of branch offices because they have not met performance targets or budgets. He is especially concerned because the points earned from citizens' comments are declining.

Required

1. Does the method of performance measurement properly capture the objectives of this operation? Justify your answer.
2. The Barry County branch office came close to its target for 19x4. Does this constitute improved performance compared to 19x3? Justify your answer.

9-32. Human-resource accounting. The Barry Corporation is a producer of leisure footwear in Columbus, Ohio. The company has been a pioneer in so-called "human-resource accounting," an outgrowth of research conducted by Rensis Likert, a social psychologist, and others.

For many years, Likert has stressed that accounting systems encourage the misuse of human resources because of undue emphasis on short-run profits. According to Likert, the attempts to maximize immediate earnings have induced managers to exert too much pressure for productivity and to have uneconomical layoffs and discharges. Why? Because increases in employee turnover and later additional spending for hiring and training more than offset the immediate savings. Likert advocates incorporating human-resource accounting as part of the formal accounting system.

Many variations of human-resource accounting are possible. The Barry Corporation has taken a minimum step by recording as assets the outlays for recruiting and training managers. These investments in human assets are then amortized over the expected useful lives of the employees.

Data from the human-resource system have not yet been incorporated in the company's audited financial statements. Nevertheless, as seen in Exhibit 9-6, the company's annual reports contain a *supplementary* balance sheet and income statement that shows the human-resource effects.

Required

1. Were new investments in human assets during 19x7 undertaken more rapidly than they were written off? Explain, using the figures given in Exhibit 9-6.
2. Do you favor implementing human-resource accounting for internal-reporting purposes? Why do you think Likert prefers human-resource accounting to the use of less formal measures, such as employee-attitude surveys, absenteeism, employee-turnover rates, and so on? Be specific.

EXHIBIT 9-5

Barry County Branch Performance Report

	19x2 BUDGET	19x2 ACTUAL	19x3 BUDGET	19x3 ACTUAL	19x4 BUDGET	19x4 ACTUAL
Population served	38,000		38,500		38,700	
Number of employees						
Administrative	1	1	1	1	1	1
Professional	1	1	1	1	1	1
Clerical	3	3	2	3	1½	3
Budgeted Performance Points*						
1. Services	19,500		16,000		15,500	
2. Citizen comments	500		600		700	
	20,000		16,600		16,200	
Actual Performance Points*						
1. Services	14,500		14,600		15,600	
2. Citizen comments	200		900		200	
	14,700		15,500		15,800	
Detail of Actual Performance*						
1. New drivers licenses						
a. Examination and road tests (3 pts.)	3,000		3,150		3,030	
b. Road tests repeat—failed prior test (2 pts.)	600		750		1,650	
2. Renew drivers licenses (1 pt.)	3,000		3,120		3,060	
3. Issue license plates (.5 pts.)	4,200		4,150		4,100	
4. Issue titles						
a. Dealer transactions (.5 pts.)	2,000		1,900		2,100	
b. Individual transaction (1 pt.)	1,700		1,530		1,660	
	14,500		14,600		15,600	
5. Citizen comments						
a. Favorable (+.5 pts.)	300		1,100		800	
b. Unfavorable (−.5 pts.)	100		200		600	
	200		900		200	

*The budget performance points for services are calculated using 3 points per available hour. The administrative employee devotes half his time to administration and half to regular services. The calculations for the services point budget are as follows:

19x2 4½ people × 8 hours × 240 days × 3 pts. × 75% productive time = 19,440 rounded to 19,500
19x3 3½ people × 8 hours × 240 days × 3 pts. × 80% productive time = 16,128 rounded to 16,000
19x4 3 people × 8 hours × 240 days × 3 pts. × 90% productive time = 15,552 rounded to 15,500

The comments targets are based upon rough estimates by department officials. The actual point totals for the branch are calculated by multiplying the weights shown in the report in parentheses by the number of such services performed or comments received.

9-33. Responsibility accounting and decisions. Easthall Company, a manufacturer of a variety of small appliances, has an Engineering Consulting Department (ECD). The department's major task has been to help the production departments improve their operating methods and processes.

For several years, the consulting services have been charged to the production departments based on a signed agreement between the managers involved. The agreement specifies the scope of the project, the predicted savings, and the number of consulting hours required. The charge to the production department is based on the

EXHIBIT 9-6
R. G. BARRY CORPORATION AND SUBSIDIARIES PRO FORMA
(Conventional and Human-Resource Accounting)
Balance Sheet

ASSETS	19x7 CONVENTIONAL AND HUMAN RESOURCE	19x7 CONVENTIONAL ONLY
Total current assets	$16,408	$16,408
Net property, plant and equipment	3,371	3,371
Excess of purchase price over net assets acquired	1,288	1,288
Deferred financing costs	183	183
Net investments in human resources	**1,779**	—
Other assets	232	232
	$23,264*	$21,484*

LIABILITIES AND STOCKHOLDERS' EQUITY		
Total current liabilities	3,218	3,218
Long-term debt, excluding current installments	7,285	7,285
Deferred compensation	116	116
Deferred federal income tax based upon full tax deduction for human-resource costs	**889**	—
Stockholders' equity:		
Capital stock	1,818	1,818
Additional capital in excess of par value	5,047	5,047
Retained earnings:		
Financial	3,998	3,998
Human resources	**889**	—
	$23,264	$21,484

Statement of Income

Net sales	$39,162	$39,162
Cost of sales	25,667	25,667
Gross profit	13,494	13,494
Selling, general and administrative expenses	10,190	10,190
Operating income	3,303	3,303
Interest expense	549	549
Income before federal income taxes	2,754	2,754
Net increase in human-resource investment	**218**	—
Adjusted income before federal income taxes	2,973	2,754
Federal income taxes	1,414	1,305
Net income	$ 1,558	$ 1,449

* 000's deleted, so totals may appear slightly inaccurate.

costs to the engineering department of the services rendered. For example, senior engineer hours cost more per hour than junior engineer hours. An overhead cost is included. The agreement is really a "fixed-price" contract. That is, the production manager knows his total cost of the project in advance. A recent survey revealed that production managers have a high level of confidence in the engineers.

The ECD department manager oversees the work of about forty engineers and ten draftsmen. He reports to the engineering manager, who reports to the vice-president of manufacturing. The ECD manager has the freedom to increase or decrease the number of engineers under his supervision. The ECD manager's performance is based on many factors, including the annual incremental savings to the company in excess of the costs of operating the ECD department.

The production departments are profit centers. Their goods are transferred to subsequent departments, such as a sales department or sales division, at standard cost plus markups that vary from 10 to 40 percent.

Top management is seriously considering a "no-charge" plan. That is, engineering services would be rendered to the production departments at absolutely no cost. Proponents of the new plan maintain that it would motivate the production managers to take keener advantage of engineering talent. In all other respects, the new system would be unchanged from the present system.

Required

1. Compare the present and proposed plans. What are their strong and weak points? In particular, will the ECD manager tend to hire the "optimal" amount of enginering talent?

2. What plan do you favor? Why?

9-34. **College cost allocation.** (CMA.) College Publications (CP) was established in 19x5 by the president of Boyd College to advance the quality and effectiveness of the college's graphic communications. CP provides professional editing, designing, and planning services to all academic and administrative units requesting help in the publication of catalogs, brochures, booklets, posters and other forms of printed material. CP is under the vice-president for public affairs, employs 20 professional staff, and has an annual operating budget of $500,000.

To encourage the use of CP's services, the cost of operating CP have not been allocated or charged to units requesting services. Instead, these operating costs are included in central administration overhead. However, to maintain as much uniformity as possible in the content and design of the college's publications, all items submitted to CP for publication are reviewed and approved by CP. Thus, CP can reject or require the complete revision of a unit's publication. The number of copies for each publication is determined jointly by CP and the unit requesting service.

During the last two years Boyd College has experienced considerable financial pressure. Inflation has increased operating costs, a downturn in the stock market has reduced endowment income, and various governmental agencies have cut back on research support. During the spring of 19x5 the president of the college established a number of task forces to review various aspects of the college's operations. These task forces collectively concluded that there was a need to emphasize and promote fiscal responsibility among administrative and academic units. Consequently, the task force on publications recommended the use of a charge-back system in which user units pay for services they requested from CP.

In the fall of 19x5 the president issued a memorandum requiring the use of a charge-back system for the services of CP. The memorandum stated that the purpose of the new system was "to put control and responsibility for publication expenditures where the benefits were received and to make academic and administrative units more aware of the publication costs they were incurring." The memorandum suggested that the costs of operating CP be charged back to user units on the basis of actual hours used in servicing their publication needs.

The academic and administrative units that purchased publication services through CP were generally pleased with the president's memorandum, even though they had some reservations about how the charge-back rate would be calculated. They had not been happy about having to obtain CP's approval in purchasing publication services. Their major complaint had been that CP imposed excessively high standards that resulted in overly expensive publications.

The director of CP was very upset about the president's memorandum. He believed that the charge-back system was a political maneuver by the president to get the task force pressures off his back. He believed that the task force had paid too much attention to publication costs and that the new system would reduce the effectiveness of CP to the college as a whole. He also was upset that the president took unilateral action in establishing the new system. He believed that it was a big jump from the memorandum to the installation of the new system and he was concerned about whether the new system would achieve the desired results.

Required

1. What are the likely motivational and operational effects of the new system on:
   a. Academic and administrative units requesting and using the services of CP?
   b. College Publications?
   c. Boyd College?
2. Evaluate the president's methods for instituting an organization change with respect to College Publications.

9-35. **Controls of tax accountants.** Smith & Smith is a public accounting firm with offices in several cities throughout the country. Much of its business is tax work. The partners (management) have profit as a principal goal, which in terms of their tax work equals:

$$
\begin{array}{l}
\text{Billable time (accountants' and staff's billing rates} \\
\qquad \text{times the time spent on client work)} \\
\underline{- \text{ Accounts' direct-labor cost}} \\
= \text{Margin} \\
\underline{- \text{ Allocated overhead (includes all nonbillable time)}} \\
= \text{"Profit"}
\end{array}
$$

In order to keep this profit as high as possible, accountants must spend as little time as possible per client while properly completing the job (thus keeping the bills down and therefore keeping the clients happy and hopefully insuring return business) and keeping as fully billable as possible. It is also necessary for the staff to keep current in tax law and other accounting and intracompany matters.

To trace the time spent on each client's work and the total time that staff members spent on various activities, the staff is required to fill out certain reports: (a) *Monthly time sheets* show all time spent on the job each day by category—billable (by client), training time, unassigned time, vacation, holiday, miscellaneous indirect (office chores, etc.), excused time. Staff members are told that this report is used to cross-check the billings to clients. They know that generally the client is billed for the amounts of time actually spent on his account by the accounting staff, clerical, and partners. They also know that the information on the time sheets is used to generate several statistics that are reviewed by the partners. (b) *Weekly productivity reports* show total daily time in the categories of "billable," "unassigned," and "other" for each staff member. Using this time information, each staff member must also calculate his ratio of billable to total time, which is made part of the report. Staff members are told that this report is used by the partners to evaluate work load and to help allocate the future work. In several instances, though, accountants have been asked by a partner to "explain" periods of time in which their billable ratio was "low." No standard had ever been made known to the staff, but it appeared that those staff members being questioned had generally fallen below the 80 percent level. This was the only feedback to the staff regarding the productivity reports.

The staff is evaluated semiannually in what are known as "critical review sessions." At this session each staff accountant meets with the partner with whom he does the most work, and the partner tells him how he is progressing. The review is generally subjective. Once a year the members of the staff are given raises as determined by a board of the partners.

Tax projects are assigned to the staff accountants by the partners. It is known to the staff accountants that some of them work faster (are more efficient) and thus are assigned more work than the others by the partners. It is hard to quantify the difference in working speed, because different tax projects have various complexities.

Required

1. Evaluate the staff reports in light of the true goals of the management. What effect do they have? If they do not have the desired effect, what changes could be made to achieve better results?

2. As a client, what would you think of your billing resulting from such a system?

SUGGESTED READINGS

Anthony, R., and R. Herzlinger, *Management Control in Nonprofit Organizations* (Homewood, Ill.: Richard D. Irwin, Inc., 1975).

Caplan, Edwin H., *Management Accounting and Behavioral Science* (Reading, Mass.: Addison-Wesley Publishing Co., Inc., 1971).

Hopwood, A., *Accounting and Human Behavior* (Englewood Cliffs, N.J.: Prentice-Hall, Inc., 1976).

Lawler, E., and J. Rhode, *Information and Control in Organizations* (Pacific Palisades, CA.: Goodyear Publishing Co., Inc., 1976).

Likert, Rensis, *The Human Organization, Its Management and Value* (New York: McGraw-Hill Book Company, 1967).

Livingstone, J. L., ed., *Managerial Accounting: The Behavioral Foundations* (Columbus, O.: Grid, Inc., 1975).

Schiff, M., and Y. Lewin, eds., *Behavioral Aspects of Accounting* (Englewood Cliffs, N.J.: Prentice-Hall, Inc., 1974).

CHAPTER 10

Responsibility Accounting and Cost Allocation

The term "cost allocation" is used here as a generic label for all tracing of various costs to cost objectives such as departments or products. Like air and water, problems of cost allocation are everywhere. University presidents, city managers, hospital administrators, and corporate executives inevitably face these difficult problems. This chapter describes some general approaches to the solutions, but there are no easy answers.

COST ALLOCATION IN GENERAL

Cost Allocation as a Term

The literature is not consistent in the use of terms in this area, so be sure to pinpoint the meaning of terms in specific situations. You may encounter terms such as *allocate, reallocate, trace, assign, distribute, redistribute, load, apportion,* and *reapportion* being used interchangeably to describe the same cost accounting practice. The terms *apply* or *absorb* tend to have the narrower meaning of costs traced to *products* rather than to *departments*.

Four Purposes of Allocation

What logic should be used for allocating costs from one segment to other segments of an organization? This question bothers many internal users and suppliers of services in all organizations, including nonprofit organizations. The answer should begin with a determination of the principal purpose or purposes of the cost allocation.

Costs are allocated for four major purposes:

1. *To predict the economic effects of planning and control decisions.* Examples are the addition of a new course in a university, the addition of a new flight or an additional passenger on an airline, and the addition of a new specialty in a medical clinic. Some costs are obviously associated with particular decisions. Other costs are admittedly associated, but the nature of the association is hard to establish in any convincing way.

2. *To obtain desired motivation.* Cost allocations sometimes are made to promote goal congruence and incentives. Examples are decisions to allocate or not to allocate a given cost, depending on top management's predictions regarding collective management behavior. Consequently, in some organizations there is no cost allocation for legal or internal auditing services or internal management consulting services because top management wants to encourage their use. In other organizations, there is a cost allocation for such items to spur managers to take an interest in a particular activity or to compare the costs and benefits of the use of specified services. Examples are allocations of research costs and of "carrying" costs, such as an artificial or "imputed" interest cost on the subunit's investment in receivables or inventories.

3. *To compute income and asset valuations.* Costs are allocated to products and projects to measure their inventory costs and their profit contributions.

4. *To obtain a mutually agreeable price.* The best examples are in regulated industries and in government contracts based on a negotiated price that provides for costs plus some profit based on costs.[1] These contracts are used when ordinary market prices do not seem applicable. In these instances, cost allocations become substitutes for the usual working of the market-place. That is, cost allocations are a way of arriving at a "fair" price—even if cause-and-effect logic may be hard to find.

Ideally, all four purposes would be served simultaneously by a single cost allocation. The allocation of raw-material usage to departments, products,

---

[1]"A Whole New Way to Figure AT&T's Rates," *Business Week,* February 14, 1977, pp. 86–89, reports that American Telephone and Telegraph Co. will have a future rate structure tied more closely to the "fully distributed cost" of providing various services: "In the past, it has figured rates on new services according to a complex formula that relied heavily on the incremental costs that such a service was deemed to impose an overall operations. The FCC and Bell's competitors argued that this basis was unfair, since Bell's monopoly business—ordinary telephone service—bore most of the company's costs and thus subsidized the newer services (p. 88)." Regarding government contracts, see the statements on cost allocation being issued by the Cost Accounting Standards Board, 441 G Street N.W., Washington, D.C. 20548.

managers and contracts might reach this ideal occasionally. But thousands of managers and accountants will testify that for most costs the ideal is rarely achieved. Instead, cost allocations are often a major source of discontent and confusion to the affected parties. When all four purposes are unattainable simultaneously, the manager and the accountant should start attacking a cost allocation problem by trying to identify which of the purposes should dominate in the particular situation at hand.

Cost Allocation Bases

As Chapter 3 pointed out, cost allocation is fundamentally a problem of linking (1) some cost or groups of costs with (2) one or more cost objectives (examples are products, departments, and divisions). In short, cost allocation tries to identify (1) with (2) via some cost function. Cost allocation bases are the means of establishing these links or cost functions, preferably using some cause-and-effect logic.

Major costs, such as newsprint for a newspaper and direct professional labor for a law firm, may be allocated to departments, jobs, and projects on an item-by-item basis, using cost allocation bases such as tonnage consumed or direct-labor hours used. Other costs, taken one at a time, are not important enough to justify being allocated individually. These costs are *pooled* (that is, grouped together in some plausible way) and then allocated as pools. An example would be a university's allocating the operating costs of a library to its colleges on the basis of the number of students and faculty in each college. Other examples of typical cost allocation bases are shown in Exhibit 10-1.

EXHIBIT 10-1

Typical Bases for Allocation of Service-Department
Costs to Production Departments

SERVICE DEPARTMENT	BASE FOR ALLOCATION OF COSTS
Building Grounds	Square footage or cubic footage
Cafeteria	Number of workers
Cost Accounting	Labor-hours
Engineering	Analysis of services rendered each department*; labor-hours
Maintenance	Direct charges on basis of materials used plus hours worked for each department
Material Handling	Units carried; tonnage; hours of service rendered
Medical	Number of employees; labor-hours; number of cases
Personnel or Employment	Number of workers; rate of labor turnover; number of workers hired; analysis of time spent for each department*
Production Planning and Control	Machine-hours; labor-hours; analysis of services rendered
Power	Metered usage; capacity of equipment; machine-hours; formula weighting capacity and machine-hours
Receiving, Shipping, and Stores	Pounds handled; requisitions; receiving slips; issues
Tool Room	Requisitions

* Sometimes detailed analyses or surveys are made of services rendered over two, six, or twelve months; the results of the "sample" are used as a basis for allocation until conditions warrant another sample survey.

EXHIBIT 10-2.   Organization Chart of Retail Grocery Company

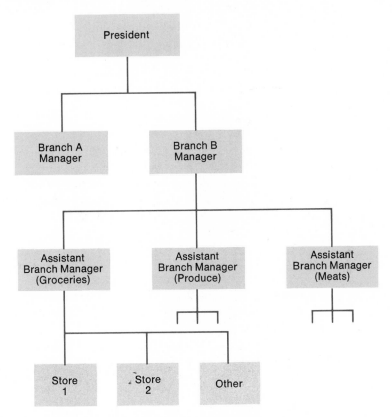

THE CONTRIBUTION APPROACH TO ALLOCATION

Many organizations combine the contribution approach and responsibility accounting; they report by cost behavior pattern as well as by degrees of controllability. To do so, they must contend with problems of cost allocation. Consider an illustration of a retail grocery company. It might have the basic organizational design shown in Exhibit 10-2.

Exhibit 10-3 displays the contribution approach to reporting and cost allocation. Study this important exhibit carefully. It provides perspective on how a reporting system can be designed to stress cost behavior patterns, controllability, manager performance, and subunit performance simultaneously.

Contribution Margin

As demonstrated in previous chapters, the contribution margin, which is revenues minus all variable expenses [line (a) in Exhibit 10-3], is especially helpful for predicting the impact on income of short-run changes in volume.

EXHIBIT 10-3

The Contribution Approach:
Model Income Statement, by Segments*
(In thousands of dollars)

	RETAIL FOOD COMPANY AS A WHOLE	COMPANY BREAKDOWN INTO TWO DIVISIONS		NOT ALLOCATED†	POSSIBLE BREAKDOWN OF BRANCH B ONLY			NOT ALLOCATED†	POSSIBLE BREAKDOWN OF BRANCH B, MEATS ONLY	
		BRANCH A	BRANCH B		GROCERIES	PRODUCE	MEATS		STORE 1	STORE 2
Net sales	$4,000	$1,500	$2,500	—	$1,300	$300	$900	—	$600	$300
Variable costs:										
Cost of merchandise sold	$3,000	$1,100	$1,900	—	$1,000	$230	$670	—	$450	$220
Variable operating expenses	260	100	160	—	100	10	50	—	35	15
Total variable costs	$3,260	$1,200	$2,060	—	$1,100	$240	$720	—	$485	$235
(a) Contribution margin	$ 740	$ 300	$ 440	—	$ 200	$ 60	$180	—	$115	$ 65
Less: Fixed costs controllable by segment managers‡	260	100	160	$ 20	40	10	90	$ 30	35	25
(b) Contribution controllable by segment managers	$ 480	$ 200	$ 280	$(20)	$ 160	$ 50	$ 90	$(30)	$ 80	$ 40
Less: Fixed costs controllable by others§	200	90	110	20	40	10	40	10	22	8
(c) Contribution by segments	$ 280	$ 110	$ 170	$(40)	$ 120	$ 40	$ 50	$(40)	$ 58	$ 32
Less: Unallocated costs**	100									
(d) Income before income taxes	$ 180									

* Three different types of segments are illustrated here: branches, product lines, and stores. As you read across, note that the focus becomes narrower: from Branch A and B, to Branch B only, to Meats in Branch B only.

† Only those costs clearly identifiable to a product line should be allocated.

‡ Examples are certain advertising, sales promotion, salesmen's salaries, management consulting, training and supervision costs.

§ Examples are depreciation, property taxes, insurance, and perhaps the segment manager's salary.

** These costs are not clearly or practically allocable to any segment except by some highly questionable allocation base.

Incidentally, in this case, if management prefers, a gross margin or gross profit (revenue minus the cost of the merchandise sold) could be inserted just after cost of merchandise sold. This is a good example of how gross margin and contribution margin differ. The principal example of variable operating expenses are the wages and payroll-related costs for most store personnel.

Any expected changes in income may be quickly calculated by multiplying increases in dollar sales by the contribution-margin ratio. Suppose the contribution-margin ratio for meats is 20 percent. Then a $1,000 increase in sales of meats should produce a $200 increase in income (.20 × $1,000 = $200).

Subunit and Manager Performance

When they analyze performance, many proponents of responsibility accounting distinguish sharply between the *subunit* (department, division, store, motel) as an economic investment and the *manager* as a professional decision maker. Managers frequently have little influence over many factors that affect economic performance. For instance, the manager of a motel may be relatively helpless if an energy crisis reduces automobile traffic or if unseasonable weather ruins the ski season.

Similarly, the manager of a retail store may have influence over some local advertising but not other advertising, some fixed salaries but not other salaries, and so forth. Moreover, the meat manager at both the branch and store levels for the retail grocery company may have zero influence over store depreciation and the president's salary.

Contribution Controllable by Segment Managers

The controllable contribution [item (b) in Exhibit 10-3] and the segment contribution [item (c) in Exhibit 10-3] are attempts to underscore the distinction between subunit (segment) performance and manager performance.

The term "segment managers" is used in the exhibit to represent a general description of the manager of any subunit of any organization. Examples are nursing supervisors, shipping room foremen, police captains, and fire station chiefs.

Note that fixed costs controllable by the segment manager are deducted from the contribution margin to obtain the contribution controllable by segment managers. These are usually discretionary fixed costs. Examples of these discretionary costs are some local advertising but not all advertising and some fixed salaries but not the manager's own salary.

In many organizations, managers have some latitude to trade off some variable costs for fixed costs. To save variable material and labor costs, managers might make heavier outlays for machinery, labor-saving devices, quality control inspectors, maintenance, management consulting fees, employee training programs, and so on. Moreover, decisions on advertising, research, and sales promotion have effects on sales volumes and hence on contribution margins. That is why the contribution margin is not a satisfactory measure of manager performance. However, the controllable contribution attempts to capture the results of these trade-offs.

The distinctions in Exhibit 10-3 among what items belong in what cost classification are inevitably not clear-cut. For example, determining controllability is always a problem when service department costs are allocated to other departments. Should the store manager bear a part of the branch headquarters costs? If so, how much and on what basis? How much, if any, store depreciation or lease rentals should be deducted in computing the controllable contribution? There are no pat answers to these questions. They are worked out somehow from organization to organization. Again, for management control purposes there are no constraints of external accounting principles[2] on designing acceptable management accounting systems. The answers depend fundamentally on what reporting system will bring the most net benefits in terms of motivation and collective decisions.

Consider the fixed costs that are deducted between items (a) and (b) in Exhibit 10-3. The "not allocated" columns show amounts of $20,000 and $30,000, respectively. This approach recognizes that perhaps some clusters of costs should not be allocated below specified levels in the organization's hierarchy. For instance, the $20,000 may include secretarial salaries of the Branch B general manager that may not be allocated; similarly, the $30,000 in that same line may include costs of meat advertisements that may not be allocated to individual stores.

Contribution by Segments

The contribution by segments, line (c) in Exhibit 10-3, is an attempt to approximate the economic *performance of the subunit,* as distinguished from the *performance of its manager.* The "fixed costs controllable by others" typically include committed costs (such as depreciation and property taxes) and discretionary costs (such as the subunit manager's salary). These costs are examples of items that are minimally influenced by the segment manager within a reporting period of a year or less.

Exhibit 10-3 shows an "unallocated costs" line immediately before line (d). They might include central corporate costs such as the costs of the president's office and many costs of the legal and accounting activities. When a persuasive "cause-and-effect" or "benefits-received" justification for allocating such costs cannot be found, many organizations favor not allocating them to segments.

---

[2] FASB Statement No. 14, *Financial Reporting for Segments of a Business Enterprise,* requires that companies' external financial statements include information about operations in different industries, foreign operations and export sales, and major customers. Disclosure of profit contribution (revenue less only those operating expenses that are directly traceable to a segment) is encouraged but not required.

Managers and accountants with a passion for symmetry may insist on allocation of all costs to all segments. To do so often entails the use of some unconvincing bases for allocation, such as the relative revenues or relative cost of goods sold of the subunits.

However, symmetry is not a basic principle of management accounting, nor is it a basic principle of organizational design. That is, some subunits at the same level of the corporate hierarchy may be cost centers, some may be profit centers, and some investment centers. For instance, some service centers (such as computer centers or printing centers) may be profit centers, selling their services at internal transfer prices that may approximate external market prices for similar services. Other service centers may take the form of cost centers. Examples are buildings and grounds departments, power departments, repair departments, and internal auditing departments.

The contribution approach highlights the relative objectivity of various measures of performance evaluation. The contribution margin tends to be the most objective. As you read downward, the allocations become more difficult, and the resulting measures of contributions or income become more subject to dispute. In contrast, the traditional functional approach to income statements rarely hesitates to use full-cost allocations. Therefore, it tends to offer less-sharp distinctions between variable and fixed costs and between controllable and uncontrollable costs.

Alternative Definitions of Segments

Segments in Exhibit 10-3 were defined by branch and then by product line. Segments may be defined in any manner that seems informative—by divisions, by territories, by products, by product groups, and by functions such as manufacturing, selling, and administration. Thus, school district statements can be broken down by schools, by subject matter, by grade levels, and so on.

Exhibit 10-3 could be recast for our retail grocery company to show the relationships by stores and then by product lines within stores:

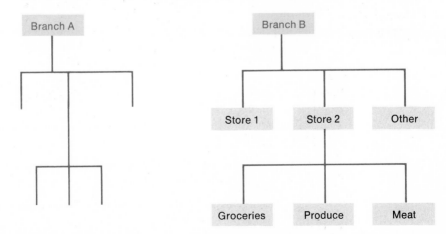

General Guides

What causes costs to occur? The *causes* of costs are the very same activities that are usually chosen to be cost objectives. Examples are products produced, letters typed, and patients seen. The *effects* of these activities are various costs. **Therefore, the manager and the accountant should search for some cost allocation base that establishes a convincing relationship between the cause and the effect and that permits reliable predictions of how costs will be affected by decisions regarding the activities.**

The preferred guides for allocating service department costs are:

1. Use responsibility accounting and flexible budgets for each service (staff) department, just as they are used for each production or operating (line) department. When feasible, maintain distinctions between variable-cost pools and fixed-cost pools.

2. Allocate variable- and fixed-cost pools separately. This is sometimes called the dual method of allocation. Note that one service department (such as a computer department) can contain a variable-cost pool and a fixed-cost pool. That is, costs may be pooled within and among departments if desired.

3. Establish part or all of the details regarding cost allocation in advance of rendering the service rather than after the fact.

Using the Guides

To illustrate these guides, consider a simplified example of a computer department of a university that serves two major users, the School of Earth Sciences and the School of Engineering. The computer mainframe was acquired on a five-year lease that is not cancellable unless prohibitive cost penalties are paid.

How should costs be allocated to the user departments? Suppose there are two major purposes for the allocation: (1) predicting economic effects of the use of the computer and (2) motivating toward optimal usage. Apply the guides enumerated earlier:

1. Analyze the costs of the computer department in detail. Divide the costs into two pools, one for variable costs and one for fixed costs. Suppose the flexible-budget formula for the forthcoming fiscal year is $100,000 monthly fixed costs plus $200 variable costs per hour of computer time used.

2. Allocate the variable-cost pool and the fixed-cost pool separately.

3. Establish the details regarding the cost allocation in advance.

Guides (2) and (3) will be considered together in the following sections on variable cost pools and fixed cost pools.

Variable Cost Pool

Ideally, the variable cost pool should be allocated as follows:

(budgeted unit rate) × (actual quantities of service units used)

The cause-and-effect relationship is clear: the heavier the usage, the higher the total costs. In this example, the rate used would be the budgeted rate of $200 per hour.

The use of *budgeted* cost rates rather than *actual* cost rates for allocating variable costs of service departments protects the using departments from intervening price fluctuations and also often protects them from inefficiencies.

The most desirable procedure for allocating variable cost pools is to know the complete cost of various services in advance. For example, the cost of a repair job would be predetermined based on budgeted cost rates multiplied by the budgeted or standard hours of input allowed for accomplishing specified repairs. User department managers sometimes complain more vigorously about the poor management of a service department than about the choice of a cost allocation base (such as direct labor dollars or number of employees). Such complaints are less likely if the service department managers have budget responsibility and the user departments are protected from short-run price fluctuations and inefficiencies.

Fixed Cost Pool

Ideally, the fixed cost pool should be allocated as follows:

(budgeted fraction of capacity available for use)
                                            × (total budgeted fixed costs)

Before exploring the implications of this approach, consider our example. Suppose that the deans had originally predicted the following long-run average monthly usage: earth sciences, 210 hours, and engineering, 490 hours, a total of 700 hours. The fixed cost pool would be allocated as follows:

	Earth Sciences	Engineering
Fixed costs per month:		
210/700 or 30% of $100,000	$30,000	
490/700 or 70% of $100,000		$70,000

This predetermined lump-sum approach is based on the long-run capacity *available* to the user, regardless of actual usage from month to month. The reasoning is that the level of fixed costs is affected by long-range planning regarding the overall level of service and the *relative* expected usage.

A major strength of the use of capacity *available* rather than capacity *used* for allocating *budgeted* fixed costs is that short-run allocations to user departments are not affected by the *actual* usage of *other* user departments. Such a budgeted lump-sum approach is more likely to have the desired motivational effects with respect to the ordering of service in both the short-run and the long-run.

Fixed Pool and Actual Usage

In practice, the use of capacity available as a base for allocating fixed cost pools is often not followed. Instead, actual usage is the base employed. Suppose the computer department allocated the total actual costs after the fact, a weakness followed by many service departments. At the end of the month, total *actual* costs would be allocated in proportion to the *actual* hours used by the consuming departments. Compare the costs borne by the two schools:

If 600 hours are used:

Total costs incurred, $100,000 + 600 ($200) = $220,000

Earth Sciences: 200/600 × $220,000 =	$ 73,333
Engineering: 400/600 × $220,000 =	146,667
Total cost allocated	$220,000

What happens if Earth Sciences uses only 100 hours during the following month, while Engineering still uses 400 hours?

If 500 hours are used:

Total costs incurred, $100,000 + 500 ($200) = $200,000

Earth Sciences: 100/500 × $200,000 =	$ 40,000
Engineering: 400/500 × $200,000 =	160,000
Total cost allocated	$200,000

Engineering has done nothing differently, but it must bear higher costs of $13,333, an increase of 9 percent. Its short-run costs are dependent on what *other* consumers have used, not on its own actions. This phenomenon is caused by a faulty allocation method for the *fixed* portion of total costs, a method whereby the allocations are highly sensitive to fluctuations in the actual volumes used by the various consuming departments. This weakness is avoided by the dual approach that provides for a predetermined lump-sum allocation of fixed costs.

To consider further the use of *budgeted* rates for allocating *variable* costs, return to our data for 600 hours. Suppose that inefficiencies in the computer department caused the variable costs to be $140,000 instead of the 600 hours × $200, or $120,000 budgeted. A common weakness of cost allocation is to allocate the costs of inefficiencies to the consumer departments. To remedy this weakness, many cost allocation schemes would allocate only the $120,000 to the consuming departments and would let the $20,000 remain as an unallocated unfavorable budget variance of the computer department. This is responsibility accounting in action, and it reduces the resentment of user managers. The allocation of costs of inefficiency seems unjustified because the "consuming departments" have to bear another department's cost of waste.

Most consumers prefer to know the total price in advance. They become nervous when an automobile mechanic or a contractor undertakes a job without specifying prices. As a minimum, they like to know the hourly rates that they must bear.

Cost allocation systems should provide an incentive to the service department manager to control operating costs. Therefore, predetermined unit prices (at least) should be used. Where feasible, predetermined total prices should be used for various kinds of work based on flexible budgets and standards.

To illustrate, when we have our automobiles repaired, we are routinely given firm total prices for various types of services. Furthermore, in the short run these prices are not affected by the volume of work handled on a particular day. Imagine your feelings if you came to an automobile service department to get your car and were told: "Our daily fixed overhead is $1,000. Yours was the only car in our shop today,[3] so we are charging you the full $1,000. If we had 100 cars processed today, your charge would have been only $10."

Troubles with Using Lump Sums

If fixed costs are allocated on the basis of long-range plans, there is a natural tendency on the part of consumers to underestimate their planned usage and thus obtain a smaller fraction of the cost allocation. Top management can counteract these tendencies by monitoring predictions and by following up and utilizing feedback to keep future predictions more honest.

In some organizations there are even definite rewards in the form of salary increases for managers who are skillful as accurate predictors. More-

[3] Similarly, consider a news reporter's comment on medical costs: "When they thought I had a heart attack, I was glad to know they were giving me the Rolls Royce treatment. For 30 hours of observation in a coronary ward the bill topped $700. The cost was higher than needed because I was the only one in it."

over, some cost allocation methods provide for penalties for underpredictions. For example, if a manager predicts usage of 210 hours and then demands 300 hours, either he doesn't get the hours or he pays a dear price for every hour beyond 210.

Allocating Central Costs

Many central costs, such as the president's salary and related expenses, public relations, legal, income tax planning, companywide advertising, and basic research, are difficult to allocate in any feasible, convincing way. Therefore, many companies do not allocate them at all. Other companies use allocation bases such as the revenue of each division, the cost of goods sold of each division, or the total costs of each division (before allocation of the central costs).

The desperate search for such allocation bases is a manifestation of a widespread, deep-seated belief that all costs must somehow be fully allocated to all parts of the organization. The flimsy assumptions that might underlie such allocations are widely recognized, but most managers accept them as a fact of a manager's life—as long as all managers seem to be treated alike and thus "fairly."

The use of the above bases may provide a rough indication of cause-and-effect relationships. Basically, however, they represent a "soak-the-rich" or "ability-to-bear" philosophy of cost allocation. For example, the costs of companywide advertising, such as the goodwill sponsorship of a program on a noncommercial television station, might be allocated to all products and divisions on the basis of the dollar sales in each. But such costs precede sales. They are discretionary costs that are determined by management policies, not by sales results.

Using Budgeted Allocation Bases

Again, if these costs are to be allocated, the use of *budgeted* sales or some other *budgeted* allocation base is preferred to the use of *actual* sales. At least this method means that the short-run costs of a given consuming department will not be affected by the fortunes of other consuming departments.

For example, suppose central advertising were allocated on the basis of potential sales in two territories:

| | Territory | | | |
	A	B	Total	Percent
Budgeted sales	$500	$500	$1,000	100%
Central advertising allocated		50	50	100	10%

Consider the possible differences in allocations when actual sales become known:

	Territories	
	A	B
Actual sales	$300	$600
Central advertising:		
1. Allocated on basis of budgeted sales	$50	$50
or		
2. Allocated on basis of actual sales	$33	$67

Compare allocation 1 with 2. Allocation 1 is preferable. It indicates a low ratio of sales to advertising in Territory A. It directs attention to where it is deserved. In contrast, allocation 2 soaks Territory B with more advertising cost because of the *achieved* results and relieves Territory A because it had lesser success. This is another example of the analytical confusion that can arise when cost allocations to one consuming department are dependent on the activity of other consuming departments.

THE PRODUCT COSTING PURPOSE

Relating Costs to Outputs

Until this point, we have concentrated on cost allocation to divisions, departments, and similar segments of an entity. Cost allocation is often carried one step further—to the outputs of these departments, however defined. Examples are *products* such as automobiles, furniture, and newspapers. Other examples are personal *services,* such as hospitalization and education.

Costs are allocated to products for inventory valuation purposes and for decision purposes such as pricing, adding products, promoting products, and so forth. Cost allocation is also performed for cost reimbursement purposes. For example, many public and private health programs reimburse hospitals for the "costs" of rendering services to patients.

The general approach to allocating costs to final products or services is:

1. Prepare budgets for all departments, including the *operating* (*line*) or *production* or *revenue-producing* departments that work directly on the final product or service and the *service* (*staff* or *support*) departments that help the operating departments.

2. Choose the most logical cost allocation bases that seem economically feasible.

3. Allocate the costs of the service departments to the operating departments. The operating departments now have been allocated all the costs: their direct department costs and the service department costs.

4. Allocate (apply) the total costs accumulated in item 3 to the products or services that are the outputs of the operating departments.

Allocation of
Service Department Costs

The foregoing steps can be illustrated in a hospital setting. The output of a hospital is not as easy to define as the output of a factory. The objective is the improved health of patients, but that is hard to quantify. Consequently, the output of revenue-producing departments might be the following:

Department	Measures of Output*
Radiology	X-ray films processed
Laboratory	Tests administered
Daily patient services†	Patient days of care (that is, the number of patients multiplied by the number of days of each patient's stay)

*These become the product cost objectives, the various revenue-producing activities of a hospital.
† There would be many of these departments, such as obstetrics, pediatrics, orthopedics, and so forth. Moreover, there may be both in-patient and out-patient care.

As you undoubtedly suspect, the allocation of hospital costs to cost objectives is marked by trade-offs between costs and the possible benefits to be derived from more elaborate cost allocations. Because hospitals are often reimbursed by government agencies based on allocated costs, hospital administrators have become increasingly interested in how the costs of various departments might be allocated to the measures of revenue-producing output.

Applying the Steps

To keep the data manageable, suppose there are only three service departments in addition to the revenue-producing departments just mentioned: Administrative and Fiscal Services, Plant Operations and Maintenance, and Laundry.

1. *Prepare departmental budgets.* All six departments would prepare responsibility-center budgets for operating their own areas as efficiently and effectively as possible. These budgets would be confined to their "direct departmental costs" that are the primary responsibility of the particular department manager. Examples of such costs are salaries and supplies.

2. *Choose allocation bases.* Common allocation bases for various hospital service departments are shown in Exhibit 10-4. Exhibit 10-5 shows the allocation bases and relationships of our sample hospital.

   Administrative and Fiscal Services will be allocated on the basis of the relative costs of other departments and will be allocated first. Because it would be nonsense to allocate its own costs to itself, its costs are not included in the allocation base.

294

EXHIBIT 10-4

Hospital Cost Allocation Bases*

Purchasing—Costs of supplies used by each center; "other" direct expenses

Nursing service, administrative office—Hours of nursing service supervised; estimated supervision time

Pharmacy—Amount of requisitions priced at retail; number of requisitions; special studies

Medical records—Estimated time spent on records; number of patient-days; number of admissions

Admitting—Number of admissions

Plant operations and maintenance—Square feet of area occupied; work orders

Laundry and linens—Pounds of soiled laundry processed; pounds weighted by degree of care (nurses' uniforms would be double- or triple-weighted to allow for starching or pressing)

Administrative and Fiscal Services—Accumulated costs in each department before these costs are allocated; number of personnel. This is a general cost center that should be subdivided into several cost centers and be allocated on different bases.

*For a thorough discussion, see *Cost Finding and Rate Setting for Hospitals* (Chicago: American Hospital Association).

Plant Operations and Maintenance will be allocated second on the basis of square feet occupied, and none will be allocated back to Administrative and Fiscal Services. Therefore, no square footage is presented for these two departments in this exhibit.

Laundry will be allocated third; none will be allocated back to the first two departments, *even though the first two departments may have used laundry services.* Sometimes special studies of relative usage of services are made to establish what percentage should go to various consuming departments. For example, the hospital administrator's salary might be allocated separately in proportion to the time she spends on each department. This allocation might be unchanged for a year or two. Similarly, laundry might be weighed periodically on a sampling basis and the results used as a predetermined means of allocation for a year regardless of interim usage.

EXHIBIT 10-5

Cost Allocation Bases by Department

	SERVICE DEPARTMENTS			REVENUE DEPARTMENTS		
	ADMINIS-TRATIVE FISCAL SERVICES	PLANT OPERATIONS AND MAINTENANCE	LAUNDRY	RADIOLOGY	LABORATORY	DAILY PATIENT SERVICES
Direct departmental costs	$ —	$800,000	$200,000	$1,000,000	$400,000	$1,600,000
Percentage	—	20%	5%	25%	10%	40%
Square feet occupied	—	—	5,000	12,000	3,000	80,000
Percentage		5%	12%	3%	80%	
Pounds	—	—	—	80,000	20,000	300,000
Percentage				20%	5%	75%

3. *Allocate service department costs.* There are two popular ways to allocate:

Method One, Direct Method. As the name implies, this method ignores other service departments when any given service department's costs are allocated to the revenue-producing (operating) departments. For example, as Exhibit 10-6 shows, the service rendered by Plant operations and Maintenance to laundry is not considered. The direct method is popular. Its outstanding virtue is simplicity.

Method Two, Step-down Method. Hospitals are increasingly being required to use this method, which has been used by many manufacturing companies for years. As Exhibit 10-6 shows, the step-down method recognizes that service departments render their benefits to other service departments as well as to revenue-producing departments. A sequence of allocations is chosen, usually by starting with the service department that renders the greatest service (as measured by costs) to the greatest number of other departments. The last service department in the sequence is the one that renders the least service to the least number of other departments. There-fore, once a department's costs are allocated to other departments, no subsequent service department costs are allocated back to it.

4. *Allocate (apply)* the total costs to products. The final step is sometimes called *cost application,* whereby total departmental costs are applied to a reve-nue-producing product. Our illustration in Exhibit 10-6 is a hospital, but the same fundamental approach is used for manufactured products, for re-search projects in universities, and for client cases in social welfare depart-ments.

Compare Methods One and Two in Exhibit 10-6. In many instances, the final product costs may not differ enough to warrant investing in a cost allocation method that is any fancier than the direct method.[4] But some-times even small differences may be significant to a government agency or anybody paying for a large volume of services based on costs. For example, in Exhibit 10-6 the "cost" of an "average" laboratory test is either $11.37 or $10.90. This may be significant for the fiscal committee of the hospital's board of trustees, who must decide on hospital prices. Thus, cost allocation often is a technique that helps answer the vital question, "Who should pay for what, and how much?"

SUMMARY

Cost are allocated for four major purposes: (1) prediction of economic effects of decisions, (2) motivation, (3) income and asset measurement, and (4) pricing.

The contribution approach to the income statement and to the prob-lems of cost allocation is accounting's most effective method for helping

---

[4]The most defensible theoretical accuracy is generated by the *reciprocal method,* which is rarely used in practice because of its complexity. Simultaneous equations and linear algebra are used to solve for the impact of mutually interacting services, such as between Administrative and Fiscal Services and Plant Operations. See C. Horngren, *Cost Accounting: A Managerial Emphasis* (4th ed., Englewood Cliffs, N.J.: Prentice-Hall, Inc., 1977), Chap. 16.

EXHIBIT 10-6

Allocation of Service Department Costs:
Two Methods

ALLOCATION BASE—FROM EXHIBIT 10-5	ADMINISTRATIVE AND FISCAL SERVICES (ACCUMULATED COSTS)	PLANT OPERATIONS AND MAINTENANCE (SQ. FOOTAGE)	LAUNDRY (LB)	RADIOLOGY	LABORATORY	DAILY PATIENT SERVICES
Method One, Direct Method						
Direct departmental costs before allocation	$1,000,000	$800,000	$200,000	$1,000,000	$400,000	$1,600,000
Administrative and fiscal services	(1,000,000)	—	—	333,333[a]	133,333	533,334
Plant operations and maintenance		(800,000)		101,052[b]	25,263	673,685
Laundry			(200,000)	40,000[c]	10,000	150,000
Total budgeted costs				$1,474,385	$568,596	$2,957,019
Product output in films, tests, and patient-days, respectively				60,000	50,000	30,000
Cost per unit of output				$ 24.573	$ 11.372	$ 98.567
Method Two, Step-down Method						
Direct departmental costs before allocation	$1,000,000	$800,000	$200,000	$1,000,000	$400,000	$1,600,000
Administrative and fiscal services	(1,000,000)	200,000[d]	50,000	250,000	100,000	400,000
Plant operations and maintenance		(1,000,000)	50,000[e]	120,000	30,000	800,000
Laundry			(300,000)	60,000[f]	15,000	225,000
Total budgeted costs				$1,430,000	$545,000	$3,025,000
Product output in films, tests, and patient-days, respectively				60,000	50,000	30,000
Cost per unit of output				$ 23.833	$ 10.900	$ 100.833

Notes: The percentages below are from Exhibit 10-5:

[a] 25 + 10 + 40 = 75%. 25/75 × 1,000,000 = 333,333; 10/75 × 1,000,000 = 133,333; etc.

[b] 12 + 3 + 80 = 95%. 12/95 × 800,000 = 101,052; 3/95 × 800,000 = 25,263; etc.

[c] 20 + 5 + 75 = 100%. 20/100 × 200,000 = 20,000; 5/100 × 200,000 = 10,000; etc.

[d] 20 + 5 + 25 + 10 + 40 = 100%. 20/100 × 1,000,000 = 200,000; 5/100 × 1,000,000 = 50,000; etc.

[e] 5 + 12 + 3 + 80 = 100%. 5/100 × 1,000,000 = 50,000; 12/100 × 1,000,000 = 120,000; etc.

[f] 20 + 5 + 75 = 100%. 20/100 × 300,000 = 60,000; 5/100 × 300,000 = 15,000; etc.

management to evaluate performance and make decisions. Allocations are made with thoughtful regard for the purpose of the information being compiled. Various subdivisions of net income are drawn for different purposes. The contribution approach distinguishes sharply between various degrees of objectivity in cost allocations.

Where feasible, fixed costs of service departments should be reallocated by using predetermined monthly lump sums for providing a basic capacity to serve. Variable costs should be reallocated by using a predetermined standard unit rate for the services actually utilized.

The complexity of a cost-allocation method should be influenced by how the results of the alternative allocation methods affect decisions. Full-cost allocations are widespread, apparently because accountants and managers feel that these methods generally induce better decisions than partial-cost allocations.

SUMMARY PROBLEM FOR YOUR REVIEW

Problem

Review the section, "How to Allocate for Planning and Control," and the example of the use of the computer by the university. Recall that the flexible-budget formula was $100,000 monthly plus $200 per hour of computer time used. Based on long-run predicted usage, the fixed costs were allocated on a lump-sum basis, 30 percent ot Earth Sciences and 70 percent to Engineering.

1. Show the total allocation if Earth Sciences used 210 hours and Engineering used 420 hours in a given month. Assume that the actual costs coincided exactly with the flexible-budgeted amount.

2. Assume the same facts as in Part 1, except that the fixed costs were allocated on the basis of actual hours of usage. Show the total allocation of costs to each school. As the Dean of Earth Sciences, would you prefer this method or the method in part 1? Explain.

Solution

1.

	Earth Sciences	Engineering
Fixed costs per month:		
210/700, or 30% of $100,000	$30,000	
490/700, or 70% of $100,000		$ 70,000
Variable costs @ $200 per hour:		
210 hours	42,000	
420 hours		84,000
Total costs	$72,000	$154,000

2.

	Earth Sciences	Engineering
Fixed costs per month:		
210/630 × $100,000	$33,333	
420/630 × $100,000		$ 66,667
Variable costs, as before	42,000	84,000
Total costs	$75,333	$150,667

The Dean of Earth Sciences probably would be unhappy. His school has operated exactly in accordance with the long-range plan. Nevertheless, Earth Sciences is bearing an extra $3,333 of fixed costs because of what *another* consumer is using. He would prefer the method in part 1 because it insulates Earth Sciences from short-run fluctuations in costs caused by the actions of other users.

ASSIGNMENT MATERIAL

Fundamental Assignment Material

10-1. Terminology. Define: *segment, allocation, step-down method, cost application.*

10-2. Hospital equipment. A regional health-planning agency must approve the acquisition of specified medical equipment before the hospitals in the region can qualify for cost-based reimbursement related to that equipment. That is, hospitals cannot bill government agencies for the later use of the equipment unless the agencies originally authorized the acquisition.

Two hospitals in the region proposed the acquisition and sharing of some expensive X-ray equipment to be used for unusual cases. The depreciation and related fixed costs of operating the equipment were predicted at $10,000 per month. The variable costs were predicted at $20 per patient procedure.

The planning agency asked each hospital to predict how much each hospital would use the equipment over its expected useful life of five years. Hospital A predicted an average usage of 60 procedures per month; B, of 40 procedures. The agency regarded this information as critical to the size and degree of sophistication that would be justified. That is, if the number of procedures exceeded a certain quantity per month, a different configuration of space, equipment, and personnel would be acquired that would mean higher fixed costs per month.

Required

1. Suppose fixed costs are allocated on the basis of the hospitals' predicted average utilization per month. Variable costs are allocated on the basis of $20 per procedure, the budgeted variable-cost rate for the current fiscal year. In October, A had 40 procedures and B had 40 procedures. Compute the total costs allocated to A and to B.

2. Suppose the manager of the equipment had various operating inefficiencies so that the total October costs were $12,400. Would you change your answers in part 1? Why?

299

3. A traditional method of cost allocation does not use the method in part 1. Instead, an allocation rate depends on the actual costs and actual volume encountered. The actual costs are totaled for the month and divided by the actual number of procedures conducted during the month. Suppose the actual costs agreed exactly with the flexible budget for a total of 80 actual procedures. Compute the total costs allocated to A and to B. Compare the results with those in part 1. What is the major weakness in this traditional method? What are some of its possible behavioral effects?

4. Describe any undesirable behavioral effects of the method described in part 1. How would you counteract any tendencies toward deliberate false predictions of long-run usage?

10-3. Allocating central costs. The Western Railroad allocates all central corporate overhead costs to its divisions. Some costs, such as specified internal auditing and legal costs, are identified on the basis of time spent. However, other costs are harder to allocate, so the revenue achieved by each division is used as an allocation base. Examples of such costs were executive salaries, travel, secretarial, utilities, rent, depreciation, donations, corporate planning, and general marketing costs.

Allocations on the basis of revenue for 19x4 were (in millions):

Divisions	Revenue	Allocated Costs
Shasta	$ 60	$ 3
Southern	120	6
Valley	120	6
Total	$300	$15

In 19x5, Shasta's revenue remained unchanged. However, Valley's revenue soared to $140 million because of unusually bountiful crops. The latter are troublesome to forecast because unpredictable weather has a pronounced influence on volume. Southern had expected a sharp rise in revenue, but severe competitive conditions resulted in a decline to $100 million. The total cost allocated on the basis of revenue was again $15 million, despite rises in other costs. The president was pleased that central costs did not rise for the year.

1. Compute the allocations of costs to each division for 19x5.

2. How would each division manager probably feel about the cost allocation in 19x5 as compared with 19x4? What are the weaknesses of using revenue as a basis for cost allocation?

3. Suppose that the budget revenues for 19x5 were $60, $120, and $140, respectively, and that the budgeted revenues were used as a cost allocation base. Compute the allocations of costs to each division for 19x5. Do you prefer this method to the one used in part 1? Why?

4. Many accountants and managers oppose allocating any central costs. Why?

Additional Assignment Material

10-4. Give examples of segments, as described in this chapter.

10-5. Distinguish between a separable cost and a common cost.

10-6. "The contribution margin is the best measure of short-run performance." Do you agree? Why?

10-7. What is the most controversial aspect of the contribution approach to cost allocation?

10-8. Give two guides to cost allocation.

10-9. "A commonly misused basis for allocation is dollar sales." Explain.

10-10. How should national advertising costs be allocated to territories?

10-11. Give five terms that are sometimes used as substitutes for the term *allocate.*

10-12. How do the terms *apply* or *absorb* differ from *allocate?*

10-13. What is *dual allocation?*

10-14. "Always try to distinguish between the performance of a subunit and its manager." Why?

10-15. "Symmetry in reporting is not a basic principle of management accounting." Explain.

10-16. Give four examples of segments.

10-17. "Common costs should never be allocated." Do you agree? Explain.

10-18. **College cost allocation.** Refer to Problem 4-22. If you have not already solved the problem, please do so now. In addition, solve the requirements below.

Required

1. Sketch how the dean's operating statement would appear under the contribution approach.
2. The "discretionary and committed costs" were allocated on a predicted-enrollment basis. Some deans favor allocating on a course basis instead. If you were required to allocate such costs, which basis would you prefer? Explain.

10-19. **Hospital depreciation allocation.** Many hospital accounting systems are designed so that depreciation on buildings and fixed equipment is collected in a separate cost pool and then allocated to departments, usually on the basis of square feet of space occupied. In contrast, depreciation of major movable equipment is allocated directly to the departments that use such equipment.

Is square feet a logical allocation base? Explain.

10-20. **Allocating public housing costs.** A newly appointed Commissioner of the State Public Housing Agency faced a serious economic problem. On his first appearance before the state legislature, he would have to request a 40 percent increase ($2.5 million) in the annual operating subsidy.

Before 1970, the subsidy was confined to capital outlays; all operating outlays were to be covered by rental fees. But the plight of the poor led to a state law that provided separate operating subsidies for the elderly and family housing programs. This new law changed the role of the State Public Housing Agency from being a dispenser of funds to a regulator of funds and of local management policies.

The operating subsidies grew each year because of:

a. Insufficient revenues generated by the 25 percent income ceiling on rents.
b. Skyrocketing energy costs.
c. Excessive maintenance and repairs.
d. Inability of local management to stay within budgeted standards.

In dealing with the legislature, the Commissioner thought he would get more sympathy regarding the subsidy-for-the-elderly program. Public support for such programs was solid.

The Commissioner also learned that over 50 percent of the local housing budgets was represented by costs common to both the family and the elderly programs. Such costs were prorated by the number of bedrooms in each housing program. For example, consider the Middleboro program:

	Housing Units	Bedrooms	Total Bedrooms	Percentage Allocation
Elderly	300	1	300	35%
Family	50	1	50	
	100	2	200	
	100	3	300 550	65%
Total	550		850	100%

Required

What is the probable rationale for the present cost allocation base in Middleboro? As Commissioner, what cost allocation base would you favor? Why?

10-21. Cost of passenger traffic. Southern Pacific Railroad (SP) has a commuter operation that services passengers along a route between San Jose and San Francisco. Problems of cost allocation were highlighted in a 1978 news story about SP's application to the Public Utilities Commission (PUC) for a rate increase. The PUC staff claimed that the "avoidable annual cost" of running the operation was $700,000, in contrast to SP officials claim of a loss of $9,000,000. PUC's estimate was based on what SP would be able to save if it shut down the commuter operation.

The SP loss estimate was based on a "full-allocation-of-costs" method, which allocates a share of common maintenance and overhead costs to the passenger service.

If the PUC accepted its own estimate, a 25 percent fare increase would have been justified, whereas SP sought a 96 percent fare increase.

The PUC stressed that commuter costs represent less than one percent of the system wide costs of SP, and that 57 percent of the commuter costs are derived from some type of allocation method—sharing the costs of other operations.

SP's representative stated that "avoidable cost" is not an appropriate way to allocate costs. He said that "it is not fair to include just so-called above-the-rail costs" because there are other real costs associated with commuter service. Examples are maintaining smoother connections and making more frequent track inspections.

Required

1. As Public Utilities Commissioner, what approach toward cost allocation would you favor for making decisions regarding fares? Explain.

2. How would fluctuations in freight traffic affect commuter costs under the SP method?

10-22. Responsibility accounting, profit centers, and the contribution approach. Consider the following data for the year's operations of an automobile dealer:

Sales of vehicles	$2,000,000
Sales of parts and service	500,000
Cost of vehicle sales	1,600,000
Parts and service materials	150,000
Parts and service labor	200,000
Parts and service overhead	50,000
General dealership overhead	100,000
Advertising of vehicles	100,000
Sales commissions, vehicles	40,000
Sales salaries, vehicles	50,000

The president of the dealership has long regarded the markup on material and labor for the parts and service activity as the amount that is supposed to cover all parts and service overhead plus all general overhead of the dealership. In other words, the parts and service department is viewed as a cost-recovery operation, and the sales of vehicles as the income-producing activity.

Required

1. Prepare a departmentalized operating statement that harmonizes with the views of the president.

2. Prepare an alternative operating statement that would reflect a different view of the dealership operations. Assume that $10,000 and $50,000 of the $100,000 general overhead can be allocated with confidence to the parts and service department and to sales of vehicles, respectively. The remaining $40,000 cannot be allocated except in some highly arbitrary manner.

3. Comment on the relative merits of Requirements 1 and 2.

10-23. Divisional contribution, performance, and segment margins. The president of the Midwestern Railroad wants to obtain an overview of his operations, particularly with respect to comparing freight and passenger business. He has heard about some new "contribution" approaches to cost allocations that emphasize cost behavior patterns and so-called *contribution margins, contributions controllable by segment managers,* and *contributions by segments.* Pertinent data for the year ended December 31, 19x2, follow:

Total revenue was $100 million, of which $90 million was freight traffic and $10 million was passenger traffic. Half of the latter was generated by Division 1; 40 percent by Division 2; and 10 percent by Division 3.

303

Total variable costs were $56,000,000, of which $44 million was freight traffic. Of the $12 million allocable to passenger traffic, $4.4, $3.7, and $3.9 million could be allocated to Divisions 1, 2, and 3, respectively.

Total separable discretionary fixed costs were $10,000,000, of which $9,500,000 applied to freight traffic. Of the remainder, $100,000 could not be allocated to specific divisions, although it was clearly traceable to passenger traffic in general. Divisions 1, 2, and 3 should be allocated $300,000, $70,000, and $30,000, respectively.

Total separable committed costs, which were not regarded as being controllable by segment managers, were $30,000,000, of which 90 percent was allocable to freight traffic. Of the 10 percent traceable to passenger traffic, Divisions 1, 2, and 3 should be allocated $1,800,000, $420,000, and $180,000, respectively; the balance was unallocable to a specific division.

The common fixed costs not clearly allocable to any part of the company amounted to $1,000,000.

Required

1. The president asks you to prepare statements, dividing the data for the company as a whole between the freight and passenger traffic and then subdividing the passenger traffic into three divisions.

2. Some competing railroads actively promote a series of one-day sight-seeing tours on summer weekends. Most often, these tours are timed so that the cars with the tourists are hitched on with regularly scheduled passenger trains. What costs are relevant for making decisions to run such tours? Other railroads, facing the same general cost picture, refuse to conduct such sightseeing tours. Why?

3. For purposes of this analysis, even though the numbers may be unrealistic, suppose that Division 2's figures represented a specific run for a train instead of a division. Suppose further that the railroad has petitioned government authorities for permission to drop Division 2. What would be the effect on overall company net income for 19x3, assuming that the figures are accurate and that 19x3 operations are in all other respects a duplication of 19x2 operations?

10-24. Contribution analysis. (CMA, adapted.) The Justa Corporation produces three products, A, B, and C, which are sold in a local market and in a regional market. At the end of the first quarter of the current year, the following income statement has been prepared:

	Total	Local	Regional
Sales	$1,300,000	$1,000,000	$300,000
Cost of goods sold	1,010,000	775,000	235,000
Gross margin	$ 290,000	$ 225,000	$ 65,000
Selling expenses	$ 105,000	$ 60,000	$ 45,000
Administrative expenses	52,000	40,000	12,000
Total S&A expenses	$ 157,000	$ 100,000	$ 57,000
Net income	$ 133,000	$ 125,000	$ 8,000

Management has expressed special concern with the regional market because of the extremely poor return on sales. This market was entered a year ago because of excess capacity. It was originally believed that the return on sales would improve with time, but after a year no noticeable improvement can be seen from the results as reported in the above quarterly statement.

In attempting to decide whether to eliminate the regional market, the following information has been gathered:

| | *Products* | | |
	A	*B*	*C*
Sales	$500,000	$400,000	$400,000
Variable manufacturing			
expenses as a percentage of sales	60%	70%	60%
Variable selling expenses			
as a percentage of sales	3%	2%	2%

Sales by Markets

Product	*Local*	*Regional*
A	$400,000	$100,000
B	300,000	100,000
C	300,000	100,000

All administrative expenses and fixed manufacturing expenses are common to the three products and the two markets and are fixed for the period. Remaining selling expenses are fixed for the period and separable by market. All fixed expenses are based upon a prorated yearly amount.

Required

1. Prepare the quarterly income statement showing contribution margins by markets.

2. Assuming there are no alternative uses for the Justa Corporation's present capacity, would you recommend dropping the regional market? Why or why not?

3. Prepare the quarterly income statement showing contribution margins by products.

4. It is believed that a new product can be ready for sale next year if the Justa Corporation decides to go ahead with continued research. The new product can be produced by simply converting equipment presently used in producing Product C. This conversion will increase fixed costs by $10,000 per quarter. What must be the minimum contribution margin per quarter of the new product to make the changeover financially feasible?

10-25. Hospital cost allocation. The laboratory of a hospital has developed the following relative value weightings based on the amount of time necessary to complete specific types of tests:

	Weighting	Number of Tests Performed
Sugar, quantitative	1.0	1,375
Bleeding time	0.8	2,340
White cell count	0.6	4,675
Chlorides	1.9	584
Sedimentation rate	0.7	3,280
Tissues, surgical, frozen section	10.0	603

The total costs of these tests were $139,392. You are to allocate the costs to the tests as a basis for reimbursements from health-care agencies. Compute the cost rate per test.

10-26. Hospital allocation base. Myra Keller, the administrator of Mount Sinai Hospital, has become interested in obtaining more accurate cost allocations on the basis of cause and effect. The $80,000 of laundry costs had been allocated on the basis of 400,000 pounds processed for all departments, or 20¢ per pound.

Keller is concerned that government health-care officials will require weighted statistics to be used for cost allocation. She asks you, "Please develop a revised base for allocating laundry costs. It should be better than our present base, but not be overly complex either."

You study the situation and find that the laundry processed a large volume of uniforms for student nurses and physicians, and for dietary, housekeeping, and other personnel. In particular, the coats or jackets worn by personnel in the radiology department took unusual care.

A special study of laundry for radiology revealed that 5,000 of the 10,000 pounds were jackets and coats that were five times as expensive to process as regular laundry items. A number of reasons explained the difference, but it was principally because of unusual handwork.

Ignore the special requirements of the departments other than radiology. Revise the cost allocation base and compute the new cost allocation rate. Compute the total cost charged to radiology using pounds and using the new base.

10-27. Step-down allocation. A factory has three service departments:

	Budgeted Department Costs
Cafeteria, revenue $100,000 less expenses of $220,000	$ 120,000
Engineering	2,400,000
General factory administration	970,000

Cost allocation bases are budgeted as follows:

Production Departments	Employees	Engineering Hours Worked for Production Departments	Total Labor- Hours
Machining	100	40,000	250,000
Assembly	450	15,000	600,000
Finishing and painting	50	5,000	120,000

1. All service department costs are allocated directly to the production departments without allocation to other service departments. Show how much of the budgeted costs of each service department are allocated to each production department. To plan your work, examine Requirement 2 before undertaking Requirement 1.

2. The company has decided to use the step-down method of cost allocation. General factory administration would be allocated first, then cafeteria, then engineering. Cafeteria employees had 30,000 labor-hours per year. There were 50 engineering employees with 100,000 total labor-hours. Recompute the results in Requirement 1, using the step-down method. Show your computations. Compare the results in Requirements 1 and 2. Which method of allocation do you favor? Why?

10-28. **Step-down allocation.** The X Company has prepared departmental overhead budgets for normal activity levels before reapportionments, as follows:

Building and grounds	$ 10,000
Personnel	1,000
General factory administration*	26,090
Cafeteria—operating loss	1,640
Storeroom	2,670
Machining	34,700
Assembly	48,900
	$125,000

* To be reapportioned before cafeteria.

Management has decided that the most sensible product costs are achieved by using departmental overhead rates. These rates are developed after appropriate service department costs are reapportioned to production departments.

Bases for reapportionment are to be selected from the following:

Department	Direct-Labor Hours	Number of Employees	Square feet of Floor Space Occupied	Total Labor-Hours	Number of Requisitions
Building and grounds	—	—	—	—	
Personnel*	—	2,000	—		
General factory administration	35	7,000	—		
Cafeteria— operating loss	10	4,000	1,000		
Storeroom	5	7,000	1,000		
Machining	5,000	50	30,000	8,000	2,000
Assembly	15,000	100	50,000	17,000	1,000
	20,000	200	100,000	27,000	3,000

* Basis used is number of employees.

1. Allocate service department costs by the step-down method. Develop overhead rates per direct-labor hour for machining and assembly.

2. Same as in 1, using the direct method.

3. What would be the blanket plantwide factory-overhead application rate, assuming that direct-labor hours are used as a cost allocation base?

4. Using the following information about two jobs, prepare three different total-overhead costs for each job, using rates developed in 1, 2, and 3 above.

	Direct-Labor Hours	
	Machining	Assembly
Job 88	18	2
Job 89	3	17

10-29. Reallocation of costs. Trans Company has two operating departments (A and B) and one service department. The actual monthly costs of the service department are reallocated on the basis of the net ton-miles operated. The budgeted-cost behavior pattern of the service department is $200,000 monthly plus 50¢ per 1,000 ton-miles operated in Departments A and B.

1. In May, Trans Company handled 300,000,000 ton-miles of traffic, half in each operating department. The actual costs of the service department were precisely as budgeted. How much cost would be reallocated to each department?

2. Suppose that in Requirement 1 Department B handled only 90,000,000 ton-miles instead of 150,000,000. Department A handled 150,000,000 ton-miles. Also suppose that the actual costs of the service department were precisely as budgeted for this lower level of activity. How much cost would be reallocated to each department?

3. Suppose that in Requirement 1 the actual costs of the service department were $420,000 because of various inefficiencies and unfavorable but controllable rate or price changes in various items. How much cost would be reallocated to each department? Does such reallocation seem justified? If, not, what improvement in the reallocation procedure would you suggest?

4. Suppose that various investment outlays for space and equipment in the service department were made to provide a basic maximum capacity to serve other departments under the assumption that Department A would operate at a maximum monthly level of 160,000,000 ton-miles and Department B at a level of 200,000,000 ton-miles. In Requirement 2, suppose fixed costs are reallocated via a predetermined monthly lump sum for providing a basic maximum capacity to serve; variable costs are reallocated via a predetermined standard rate per 1,000 ton-miles. How much cost would be reallocated to each department? What are the advantages of this method over other methods?

10-30. Allocating Computer Costs. (CMA.) Bonn Company recently reorganized its computer and data-processing activities. The small installations located within the accounting departments at its plants and subsidiaries have been replaced with a single data-processing department at corporate headquarters responsible for the operations of a newly acquired large-scale computer system. The new department has been in operation for two years and has been regularly producing reliable and timely data for the past twelve months.

Because the department has focused its activities on converting applications to the new system and producing reports for the plant and subsidiary managements, little attention has been devoted to the costs of the department. Now that the department's activities are operating relatively smoothly, company management has requested that the departmental manager recommend a cost accumulation system to facilitate cost control and the development of suitable rates to charge users for service.

For the past two years, the departmental costs have been recorded in one account. The costs have then been allocated to user departments on the basis of computer time used. The schedule below reports the costs and charging rate for 19x5.

Data-Processing Department
Costs for the Year Ended December 31, 19x5

(1) Salaries and benefits	$ 622,600
(2) Supplies	40,000
(3) Equipment maintenance contract	15,000
(4) Insurance	25,000
(5) Heat and air conditioning	36,000
(6) Electricity	50,000
(7) Equipment and furniture depreciation	285,400
(8) Building improvements depreciation	10,000
(9) Building occupancy and security	39,300
(10) Corporate administrative charges	52,700
Total costs	$1,176,000

Computer-hours for user processing*		2,750
Hourly rate ($1,176,000 ÷ 2,750)	$	428

*Use of available computer-hours:

Testing and debugging programs	250
Set-up of jobs	500
Processing jobs	2,750
Down-time for maintenance	750
Idle time	742
	4,992

The department manager recommends that the department costs be accumulated by five activity centers within the department: Systems Analysis, Programming, Data Preparation, Computer Operations (processing), and Administration. He then suggests that the costs of the Administration activity should be allocated to the other four activity centers before a separate rate for charging users is developed for each of the first four activities.

The manager made the following observations regarding the charges to the several subsidiary accounts within the department after reviewing the details of the accounts:

1. Salaries and benefits—records the salary and benefit costs of all employees in the department.
2. Supplies—records punch-card costs, paper costs for printers, and a small amount for miscellaneous other costs.

3. Equipment maintenance contracts—records charges for maintenance contracts; all equipment is covered by maintenance contracts.

4. Insurance—records cost of insurance covering the equipment and the furniture.

5. Heat and air conditioning—records a charge from the corporate heating and air-conditioning department estimated to be the incremental costs to meet the special needs of the computer department.

6. Electricity—records the charge for electricity based upon a separate meter within the department.

7. Equipment and furniture depreciation—records the depreciation charges for all owned equipment and furniture within the department.

8. Building improvements—records the amortization charges for the building changes required to provide proper environmental control and electrical service for the computer equipment.

9. Building occupancy and security—records the computer department's share of the depreciation, maintenance, heat and security costs of the building; these costs are allocated to the department on the basis of square feet occupied.

10. Corporate administrative charges—records the computer department's share of the corporate administrative costs. They are allocated to the department on the basis of number of employees in the department.

Required

1. For each of the ten cost items, state whether or not it should be distributed (allocated) to the five activity centers, and for each cost item that should be distributed, recommend the basis upon which it should be distributed. Justify your conclusion in each case.

2. Assume the costs of the Computer Operations (processing) activity will be charged to the user departments on the basis of computer-hours. Using the analysis of computer utilization shown as a footnote to the department cost schedule presented in the problem, determine the total number of hours that should be employed to determine the charging rate for Computer Operations (processing). Justify your answer.

10-31. Allocating fixed overhead. You have recently been hired as an assistant to the Vice-President of Planning and Analysis, Mr. Jackson, of the Thornhill Towing Company. Thornhill Towing owns and operates a large fleet of harbor and ocean-going tugboats. Founded in Galveston in 1923, the company now has ongoing operations in the Gulf of Mexico and the Caribbean, the North Sea, the Far East and the Pacific Northwest.

During your second week on the job you have lunch with Jackson and the Executive Vice-President of Finance, Alex Thomson. Thomson mentions that at an upcoming staff meeting the internal accounting group is going to make a presentation highlighting the top ten most profitable operations from the previous month.

Later that day Jackson calls you into his office. He has an internal operating statement of one of the profit centers in his hand. He says, "I feel fairly comfortable with these reports down through 'revenue after variable operating expenses,' but past that I'm just not too sure. We have had this system for about a year, and I know some of our operating managers have been complaining about how fixed vessel costs are allocated. If we are going to start giving corporate recognition to the top ten profit centers, I think we need to be on firmer ground about the allocated fixed vessel costs. Please investigate how we are allocating fixed vessel costs."

You begin to piece together how the current system works. Usually several boats will be stationed at one location, which is the operating base for several functions such as assisting and docking ships, towing inland oil barges, and offshore contract towing. Each of the functions has an operating manager who is responsible for his function as a profit center. The boats stationed at a location are likely to work in any of the functions based at the location for which they are suited. The annual dollar amount of fixed cost is accumulated for each boat and divided into twelve increments to correspond with the monthly accounting periods. This monthly fixed cost is then allocated to each function in which the boat worked during the month as a percentage of the total revenue-producing hours that the boat worked during the month.

1. Suppose the tug Sam Houston had $3,000 in fixed costs each month. Prepare a tabulation for January, February, and March showing the vessel fixed costs per revenue-hour and the allocated fixed costs to functions A and B if revenue-hours were as follows:

	A	*B*
January	300	300
February	200	300
March	400	300

2. Comment on the tabulation in Requirement 1. What is causing the puzzling results?

3. What cost allocation system would you recommend? For this requirement, assume that the annual revenue-hours for A is 3,600 and for B is 3,600.

10-32. Review of Chapters 1–10. (H. Schaefer.) As you are about to depart on a business trip, your accountant hands you the following information about your Singapore division:

a. Master budget for the fiscal year just ended on October 31, 19x1:

Sales	$700,000
Manufacturing cost of goods sold	560,000
Manufacturing margin	$140,000
Selling and administrative expenses	100,000
Operating income	$ 40,000

b. Budgeted sales production mix:

Product A	40,000 units
Product B	60,000 units

c. Standard variable manufacturing cost per unit:

Product A

Direct material	10 pieces @ $0.25	$2.50
Direct labor	1 hour @ $3.00	3.00
Variable overhead	1 hour @ $2.00	2.00
		$7.50

Product B

Direct material	5 pounds@ $0.10	$0.50
Direct labor	.3 hours @ $2.50	0.75
Variable overhead	.3 hours @ $2.50	0.75
		$2.00

d. All budgeted selling and administrative expenses are common, fixed expenses; 60 percent are discretionary expenses.

e. Actual income statement for the fiscal year ended October 31, 19x1:

Sales	$700,000
Manufacturing cost of goods sold	571,400
Manufacturing margin	$128,600
Selling and administrative expenses	97,000
Operating income	$ 31,600

f. Actual sales and production mix:

Product A	42,000 units
Product B	56,000 units

g. Budgeted and actual sales prices:

Product A	$10
Product B	5

h. Schedule of the actual *variable* manufacturing cost of goods sold by product; actual quantities in parentheses:

Product A:	Material	$106,800	(427,200 pieces)
	Labor	123,900	(42,000 hours)
	Overhead	86,100	(42,000 hours)
Product B:	Material	33,600	(280,000 pounds)
	Labor	42,500	(17,000 hours)
	Overhead	42,500	(17,000 hours)
		$435,400	

i. Products A and B are manufactured in separate facilities. Of the *budgeted* fixed manufacturing cost, $120,000 is separable as follows: $40,000 to product A and $80,000 to product B. Ten percent of these separable costs are discretionary. All other budgeted fixed manufacturing expenses, separable and common, are committed.

The purpose of your business trip is a board of directors meeting. During the meeting it is quite likely that some of the information from your accountant will be discussed. In anticipation you set out to prepare answers to possible questions. (There are no beginning or ending inventories.)

1. Determine the firm's *budgeted* break-even point, overall contribution-margin ratio, and contribution margins per unit by product.
2. Considering products A and B as *segments* of the firm, find the *budgeted* "contribution by segments" for each.
3. It is decided to allocate the *budgeted* selling and administrative expenses to the segments (in part 2 above) as follows: committed costs on the basis of budgeted unit sales mix and discretionary costs on the basis of actual unit sales mix. What are the final expense allocations? Briefly appraise the allocation method.
4. How would you respond to a proposal to base commissions to salesmen on the sales (revenue) value of orders received? Assume all salesmen have the opportunity to sell both products.
5. Determine the firm's *actual* "contribution margin" and "contribution controllable by segment managers" for the fiscal year ended October 31, 19x1. Assume *no* variances in committed fixed costs.
6. Determine the "marketing variance" for each product for the fiscal year ended October 31, 19x1.
7. Determine and identify all variances in *variable* manufacturing costs by product for the fiscal year ended October 31, 19x1.

CHAPTER 11

Profit Centers and Transfer Pricing

The ideas of responsibility accounting, which were explored in the two preceding chapters, are applicable to all types of organizations and organizational subunits. In this chapter, these ideas are examined in relation to profit centers and to two widely used aids in measuring performance: (1) transfer prices and (2) rate of return on investment (hereafter often called ROI).

EVOLUTION OF ACCOUNTING TECHNIQUES

Reconsider the ideas introduced in Chapter 7 in the section, Development of Control Systems. As organizations grow, managers cope with their responsibilities by delegating their decision-making powers to subordinates and by coordinating activities through informal and formal control systems, most notably the accounting system. The initial stages of organizations are usually marked by heavy reliance on personal observation and light reliance on formal accounting techniques. But the founders soon learn that accounting techniques can improve decisions. The evolution occurs as follows:

1. *Physical observation.* The manager relies on his eyes and ears to obtain his objectives.

2. *Historical records.* The manager quickly finds that records help operations. Moreover, assorted records must be kept to satisfy legal requirements such as income tax laws. The cost-benefit tests of system design are easily met; without such records, the manager faces lawsuits, fines, or worse.

3. *Static budgets.* The manager finds that historical records are often insufficient because they do not draw attention to the right questions. For example, he may be depressed if he discovers that his hospital's actual revenue in 1978 was only $50 million instead of the $55 million of the previous year. But he may be even more depressed if the budgeted 1978 revenue was $62 million. The key question, then, is not how did we do in comparison to last year but **how did we do in comparison to our targets for the current year.**

4. *Flexible budgets and standards.* Many organizations introduce these techniques to obtain a sharper focus on explaining the separate impact on operations of price, efficiency, and volume factors.

5. *Profit centers.* Organizations use these techniques to evaluate the performance of subunits that are assigned responsibility for revenue as well as costs and to provide better motivation.

Reflect on this evolution. Steps 1 and 3 through 5 are usually taken voluntarily rather than being imposed by outside forces. Thus, the cost-benefit tests induce managers to invest in more sophisticated accounting systems as their organizations become harder to control. Furthermore, these new features are *additions* to the old features instead of *replacements* for them.

The conceptual overview here is that systems are typically changed on an incremental basis when top management predicts that the benefits from better collective decisions (improved goal congruence and incentive) will exceed the additional costs.

DECENTRALIZATION

Costs and Benefits

Decentralization is the delegation of the freedom to make decisions. The lower in the organization that this freedom exists, the greater the decentralization. Decentralization is a matter of degree along a continuum:

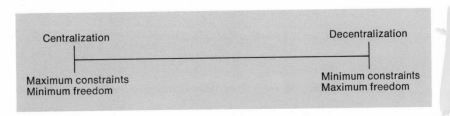

The benefits of decentralization include: (1) the lower-level managers have the best knowledge concerning local conditions and therefore are able to make better decisions than their superiors; (2) managers acquire the ability to make decisions and other management skills that assist their movement upward in the organization; and (3) managers enjoy higher status from being independent and thus are better motivated.

The costs of decentralization include: (1) managers may make dysfunctional decisions (a) by focusing on and acting to improve their own subunit's performance at the expense of the organization, or (b) by not being aware of all relevant facts; (2) managers tend to duplicate central services that might be less expensive when centralized (accounting, advertising, and personnel are examples); and (3) costs of accumulating and processing information frequently rise. The latter is exemplified by responsibility accounting reports that represent a necessary counterbalance to the extension of freedom to make decisions. It is also exemplified by the time that subunit managers often spend with one another in negotiating prices for goods or services that are transferred internally.

Decentralization is more popular in profit-seeking organizations (where outputs and inputs can be measured) than in nonprofit organizations:

> . . . considerable latitude can safely be given to the operating manager . . . . If poor decisions are made, these are soon revealed through the signal of inadequate profits. Without such a signal, such latitude is dangerous . . . . The budgeting process is extremely important in a nonprofit organization. When resource allocation decisions cannot safely be decentralized, the budget is an essential device for communicating how operating managers are expected to act.[1]

Middle Ground

Philosophies of decentralization differ considerably. Cost-benefit considerations usually result in some management decisions being highly decentralized and vice versa. To illustrate, much of the controller's problem-solving and attention-directing functions may be found at the lower levels, whereas income tax planning and mass scorekeeping such as payroll may be highly centralized.

Decentralization tends to be most successful when the subunits are relatively independent of one another—that is, the decisions of one manager will not affect the fortunes of another manager. If subunits do much internal buying or selling, much buying from the same outside suppliers, or much selling to the same outside markets, they are candidates for heavier centralization.

The preceding two chapters stressed cost-benefit tests, goal congruence,

[1]R. Anthony and R. Herzlinger, *Management Control in Nonprofit Organizations* (Homewood, Ill.: Richard D. Irwin, Inc., 1975), p. 77.

and incentive as three major problems that must be considered when designing a control system. **A fourth problem, autonomy, must be added if management has pondered the pros and cons and has decided in favor of heavy decentralization.** The control system should be designed to respect autonomy to the extent specified by top management. In other words, when top managers openly commit themselves to decentralization, they must refrain from interfering in local decisions (except in rare instances).

Meaning of Profit Centers

Do not confuse *profit centers* (accountability for revenue and expenses) with *decentralization* (freedom to make decisions). They are entirely separate concepts, although profit centers clearly are accounting techniques that aim to facilitate decentralization. **However, one can exist without the other.** Some profit-center managers possess vast freedom to make decisions concerning labor contracts, supplier choices, equipment purchases, personnel decisions, and so on. In contrast, other profit-center managers may have to obtain top-management permission for almost all the decisions just mentioned. **Indeed, some cost centers may be more heavily decentralized than profit centers if the cost-center managers have more freedom to make decisions.**

TRANSFER PRICING

Nature of Transfer Pricing

Transfer prices are associated with goods or services that are exchanged among the subunits of an organization. Most often, the term is associated with materials, parts, or finished goods. **In a most fundamental sense, all cost allocation is a form of transfer pricing,** although how to charge the costs of a personnel department to the subunits of a hospital, for example, is referred to as a cost allocation problem, not a transfer pricing problem.

Why do transfer-pricing systems exist? The principal reason is to communicate data that help solve the problems of cost-benefit trade-offs, goal congruence, incentive, and autonomy. Transfer-pricing systems are judged as all facets of control systems should be judged—by determining whether top-management objectives are being obtained as efficiently and effectively as feasible.

Organizations solve their problems by using market prices for some transfers, standard costs for other transfers, negotiated prices for other transfers, and so forth. Therefore, do not expect to obtain a lone, universally applicable answer in the area of transfer pricing. It is a subject of continuous concern to top management. Whenever there is a lull in a conversation with a manager, try asking, "Do you have any transfer-pricing problems?" The response is usually, "Let me tell you about the peculiar transfer-pricing difficulties in my organization."

Transfers at Cost

When the "transfer price" is some version of cost, such transfer pricing is indistinguishable from the "cost allocation" of interdepartmental services that was discussed in the preceding chapter. Therefore, if you want to study the options and pitfalls of "transfer pricing at cost," merely substitute those words for "cost allocation" as you review the section, "How to Allocate for Planning and Control," in the preceding chapter.

As an example of a pitfall, transferring at *actual* cost is generally not recommended because it fails to provide the buying subunit with a reliable basis for planning. More important, it fails to provide the supplying division with the incentive to control its costs. Inefficiencies are merely passed along to the buying division. Thus, the general recommendation of using budgeted or standard costs instead of actual costs applies to all forms of cost allocation, whether the allocation is called transfer pricing, cost reallocation, or by some other name.

Market Price

When an organization has profit centers, market price should be the prime candidate for setting transfer prices. In this way, the buyers and sellers systematically keep abreast of their internal and external opportunities, and problems of goal congruence, incentive, and autonomy are minimized.

Frequently, internal transfers are made at market-price-minus. That is, the supplier division may avoid some shipping or marketing costs by transferring goods to another division instead of marketing them to outside customers. These savings are often deducted when the transfer price is agreed upon.

Sometimes market prices fail to be used because they are nonexistent, inapplicable, or impossible to determine. For example, no intermediate markets may exist for specialized parts, or markets may be too thin or scattered to permit the determination of a credible price. In these instances, versions of "cost-plus-a-profit" are used that are supposed to provide a "fair" or "equitable" substitute for regular market prices.

Variable Cost

Although market prices have innate appeal in a profit-center context, they are not cure-all answers to transfer-pricing problems. To illustrate, consider the analysis in Exhibit 11-1. Division A produces a part that may be sold

318

EXHIBIT 11-1

Analysis of Market Prices

DIVISION A		DIVISION B			
Market price of finished part to outsiders	$15	Sales price of finished product			$17
Variable costs per unit	6	Variable costs:			
Contribution margin	$ 9	Division A		$6	
		Division B			
Total contribution for 10,000 units	$90,000	Processing	$4		
		Selling	4	8	14
		Contribution margin			$ 3
		Total contribution for 10,000 units			$30,000

either to outside customers or to Division B, which incorporates the part in a finished product that is then sold to outside customers. The selling prices and "variable" costs per unit are shown in the exhibit. Whether the part should be manufactured by Division A and transferred to Division B depends on the existence of idle capacity in Division A (insufficient demand from outside customers).

As Exhibit 11-1 shows, if there were no idle capacity in Division A, the optimum action would be for A to sell outside at $15, because Division B would incur $8 of variable costs but add only $2 to the selling price of the product ($17 − $15). Using market price would provide the correct congruence and incentive for such a decision, because, if the part were transferred, Division B's cost would rise to $15 + $8 = $23, which would be $6 higher than B's prospective revenue of $17 per unit. So B would choose not to buy from A at the $15 market price.

As Exhibit 11-1 also shows, if there were idle capacity in Division A, the optimum action would be to produce the part and transfer it to Division B. If there were no production and transfer, Division B and the company as a whole would forego a total contribution of $30,000. In this situation, variable cost[2] would be the better basis for transfer pricing and would lead to the optimum decision for the firm as a whole.

Dysfunctional Behavior

Reconsider the situation depicted in Exhibit 11-1. If there were idle capacity in Division A, the optimum transfer price would be the $6 variable cost.

---

[2]"Variable" is used here (but with misgivings) because the term is so widely used in the literature and in practice. "Variable" should be interpreted broadly here as including all pertinent "outlay" costs (those additional costs that will be incurred by the production of the units in question.) For example, if a special lump-sum outlay such as a set-up cost were engendered by the order for 10,000 units, it would be added to the "variable" costs in Exhibit 11-1 for purposes of this analysis.

Nevertheless, in a decentralized company the Division A manager, working in his own best interests, may argue that the transfer price should be based on the $15 market price rather than $6. If his subunit is a profit center, his incentive is to obtain as high a price as possible above the $6 variable cost, because such a price maximizes the contribution to the subunit profit. (Of course, the latter statement assumes that the number of units transferred will be unaffected by the transfer price—an assumption that is often shaky.)

So the solutions to the problems of goal congruence and incentive may conflict. From the companywide viewpoint, the desired transfers may not occur because each subunit manager, pursuing his own best interest, could decide against a transfer. These conflicts sometimes are overcome by having a superior manager impose a "fair" transfer price and insist that a transfer be made. But the managers of subunits within an organization that has an announced policy of decentralization often regard such orders as undermining their autonomy. So the imposition of a price may solve the congruence and incentive problem but intensify the autonomy problem. Transfer pricing thus becomes a delicate balancing act in systems design.

The general difficulties are exemplified by the following:

> Levels of the subunits tried to make their results look good at each other's expense. One widespread result: Inflated transfer payments among the Gulf subunits as each one vied to boost its own bottom line. A top manager commented, "Gulf doesn't ring the cash register until we've made an outside sale." [3]

Use of Incentives

What should top management of a decentralized organization do if it sees dysfunctional decisions being made at the subunit level? As usual, the answer is, "It depends." If top management steps in and forces transfers, it undermines autonomy. This may have to be done occasionally, but if top management imposes its will too often, the organization is in substance being recentralized. Of course, if the decision were indeed not to give autonomy, the organization could be redesigned by combining the two subunits.

Top managers who are proponents of decentralization will be more reluctant to impose their desires. Instead, they will make sure that both A and B managers understand all the facts, are good company citizens, and will make sacrifices for the company as a whole. If they think a dysfunctional decision is going to be made anyway, some top managers swallow hard and accept the subunit manager's judgments.

Keep in mind that a decentralized set-up is usually initiated primarily because top managers think that the subunit managers have more informa-

---

[3] "Gulf Oil Goes Back to What it Knows Best," *Business Week*, January 31, 1977, p. 80.

tion at the local level that permits these subordinates to make better collective decisions about all sorts of options. Therefore, second-guessing the local managers really means that the top manager is saying, "I know more than you do about the condition of the local markets."

Being a good corporate citizen may be one way to appeal to subunit managers to make goal-congruent decisions, but building in some formal incentives typically is far more persuasive. As a result, some companies would try various incentives in reaction to our illustration in Exhibit 11-1. For example, the contribution to the company as a whole, $30,000 in the idle-capacity case, would be split between A and B, perhaps equally, perhaps in proportion to the variable costs of each, or perhaps via negotiation.[4]

THE NEED FOR MANY TRANSFER PRICES

Previous sections have pointed out that there is seldom a single transfer price that will meet the three criteria for inducing the desired decisions. The "correct" transfer price depends on the economic and legal circumstances and the decision at hand. We may want one transfer price for congruence and a second for incentive. Furthermore, the optimal price for either may differ from that employed for tax reporting or for other external needs.

Income taxes, property taxes, and tariffs often influence the setting of transfer prices so that the firm as a whole will benefit, even though the performance of a subunit may suffer. To minimize tariffs and domestic income taxes, a company may want to set an unusually low selling price for a domestic division that ships goods to foreign subsidiaries in countries where the prevailing tax rates are lower. To maximize tax deductions for percentage depletion allowances, which are based on revenue, a petroleum company may want to transfer crude oil to other subunits at as high a price as legally possible.

Transfer pricing is also influenced in some situations because of state fair-trade laws and national antitrust acts. Because of the differences in national tax structures around the world or because of the differences in the incomes of various divisions and subsidiaries, the firm may wish to shift profits and "dump" goods, if legally possible. These considerations are additional illustrations of the limits of decentralization where heavy interdependencies exist and of why the same company may use different transfer prices for different purposes.

---

[4]Other examples include using the dual allocation described in Chapter 10—that is, transfer at standard variable cost. In addition, a predetermined lump-sum charge is made for fixed costs, based on a long-run commitment of the buyer to support the supplier. In this way the buyer's month-to-month decisions are not influenced by the supplier's fixed costs.

MEASURES OF PROFITABILITY

Return on Investment

A favorite objective of top management is to maximize profitability. The trouble is that profitability does not mean the same thing to all people. Is it net income? Income before taxes? Net income percentage based on revenue? Is it an absolute amount? A percentage?

Too often, managers stress net income or income percentages without tying the measure into the investment associated with the generating of the income. A better test of profitability is the rate of return on investment (ROI). That is, given the same risks, for any given amount of resources required, the investor wants the maximum income. To say that Project A has an income of $200,000 and Project B has an income of $150,000 is an insufficient statement about profitability. The required investment in A may be $500,000, and the required investment in B may be only $150,000. Based on rate of return, all other things being equal, A's return would be much less than B's.

The ROI measure is a useful common denominator. It can be compared with rates inside and outside the organization and with opportunities in other projects and industries. It is affected by two major ingredients:

$$\frac{\text{Rate of return}}{\text{on invested capital}} = \frac{\text{Income}}{\text{Invested capital}}$$

$$= \frac{\text{Income}}{\text{Revenue}} \times \frac{\text{Revenue}}{\text{Invested capital}}$$

$$= \text{Income percentage of revenue} \times \text{Capital turnover}$$

The terms of this equation are deliberately vague at this point because various versions of income, revenue, and invested capital are possible. Ponder the components of the equation. The rate of return is the result of the combination of two items, income percentage of revenue and capital turnover. An improvement in either without changing the other will improve the rate of return on invested capital.

Consider an example of these relationships:

	Rate of return on invested capital	=	Income Revenue	×	Revenue Invested capital
Present outlook	20%	=	$\frac{16}{100}$	×	$\frac{100}{80}$
Alternatives:					
1. Increase income percentage by reducing expenses	25%	=	$\frac{20}{100}$	×	$\frac{100}{80}$
2. Increase turnover by decreasing investment in inventories	25%	=	$\frac{16}{100}$	×	$\frac{100}{64}$

322

Alternative 1 is a popular way to improve performance. An alert management tries to decrease expenses without reducing sales in proportion or to boost sales without increasing related expenses in proportion.

Alternative 2 is less popular, but it may be a quicker way to improve performance. Increasing this turnover of invested capital means generating higher revenue for each dollar invested in such assets as cash, receivables, or inventories. There is an optimal level of investment in these assets. Having too much is wasteful, but having too little may hurt credit standing and the ability to compete for sales.

ROI or Residual Income?

Most managers agree that the rate of return on investment is the ultimate test of profitability. Intelligently used, ROI can help guide decision making. However, some companies favor emphasizing an *absolute amount* of income rather than a *rate* of return. This approach is called *residual income* (RI). For example, residual income may be defined as follows:

	Figures Assumed
Divisional net income after taxes	$900,000
Minus imputed interest on average invested capital	800,000
Equals residual income	$100,000

Suppose that the average invested capital in the division for the year was $10 million. The corporate headquarters assesses an "imputed" interest charge of 8 percent ($.08 \times \$10,000,000 = \$800,000$). The word "imputed" in this context means that the charge is made regardless of whether the corporation as a whole has actually incurred an interest cost in the ordinary sense of a cash disbursement. The rate represents the minimum acceptable rate for investments in that division.

Why do some companies (such as General Electric) prefer RI to ROI? The ROI approach shows:

Divisional net income after taxes	$900,000
Average invested capital	10,000,000
Return on investment	9%

Residual income is favored for reasons of goal congruence and incentive. Under ROI, the basic message is, "Go forth and maximize your rate of return, a percentage." Thus, managers of highly profitable divisions may be reluctant to invest in projects at, say, 8 percent if their division is currently earning, say, 18 percent, because their average ROI would be reduced.

From the viewpoint of the company as a whole, top management may want this division manager to accept any projects that earn 8 percent or more. Under RI, the manager would be inclined to invest in projects earning more than 8 percent even if his division were currently earning 18 percent. The basic message is, "Go forth and maximize residual income, an absolute amount."

DISTINCTION BETWEEN MANAGERS AND INVESTMENTS

As Chapter 10 explained (see Exhibit 10-3), a distinction should be made between the performance of the division manager and the performance of the division as an investment by the corporation. The manager should be evaluated on the basis of his controllable performance (in many cases some controllable contribution in relation to controllable investment). For other decisions, "such as new investment or a withdrawal of funds from the division, the important thing is the success or failure of the divisional venture, not of the men who run it."[5]

This distinction helps clarify some vexing difficulties. For example, top management may want to use an investment base to gauge the economic performance of a retail store, but the *manager* may be best judged by focusing on income and forgetting about any investment allocations. If investment is assigned to the manager, the aim should be to assign controllable investment only. Controllability[6] depends on what *decisions* managers can make regarding the size of the investment base. In a highly decentralized company, for instance, the manager can influence the size of all his assets and can exercise judgment regarding the appropriate amount of short-term credit and perhaps some long-term credit.

THE BUDGET AND THE COST-BENEFIT APPROACH

Many of the troublesome motivational effects of performance evaluation systems can be minimized by the astute use of budgets. The desirability of tailoring a budget to particular managers cannot be overemphasized. For example, either an ROI or an RI system can promote goal congruence and incentive if top management gets everybody to focus on what is currently attainable in the forthcoming budget period. Typically, divisional managers do not have complete freedom to make major investment decisions without checking with senior management.

In sum, our cost-benefit approach provides no universal answers with

---

[5]David Solomons, *Divisional Performance: Measurement and Control* (Homewood, Ill.: Richard D. Irwin, Inc., 1968), p. 84. Solomons also discusses residual income.

[6]See Chapter 9 for an expanded discussion of controllability.

respect to such controversial issues as historical values versus current values or return on investment versus residual income. Instead, each organization must judge for itself whether an alternate control system or accounting technique will improve collective decision making. The latter is the central criterion.

Too often, the literature engages in pro-and-con discussion about which alternative is more perfect or truer than another in some logical sense. The cost-benefit approach is not concerned with "truth" or "perfection" by itself. Instead, it asks, "Do you think your perceived 'truer' or 'more logical' system is worth its added cost? Or will our existing imperfect system provide about the same set of decisions if it is skillfully administered?"

DEFINITIONS OF INVESTED CAPITAL AND INCOME

Many Investment Bases

Consider the following balance sheet classifications:

Current assets	$ 400,000	Current liabilities	$ 200,000
Property, plant and equipment	800,000	Long-term liabilities	400,000
Construction in progress	100,000	Stockholders' equity	700,000
Total assets	$1,300,000	Total equities	$1,300,000

Possible definitions of invested capital include:

1. *Total assets.* All assets are included, $1,300,000.

2. *Total assets employed.* All assets except agreed-upon exclusions of vacant land or construction in progress, $1,300,000 − $100,000 = $1,200,000.

3. *Total assets less current liabilities.* All assets except that portion supplied by short-term creditors, $1,300,000 − $200,000 = $1,100,000. This is sometimes expressed as *long-term invested capital;* note that it can also be computed by adding the long-term liabilities and the stockholders' equity, $400,000 + $700,000 = $1,100,000.

4. *Stockholders' equity.* Focuses on the investment of the owners of the business, $700,000.

All of the above are computed as averages for the period under review. These averages may be based simply on the beginning and ending balances or on more complicated averages that weigh changes in investments through the months.

For measuring the performance of division managers, any of the three asset bases is recommended rather than stockholders' equity. If the division manager's mission is to utilize all assets as best he can without regard to their financing, then base 1 is best. If top management directs him to carry extra assets that are not currently productive, then base 2 is best. If he has direct control over obtaining short-term credit and bank loans, then base 3 is best.[7] In practice, base 1 is used most often, although base 3 is not far behind.

A few companies allocate long-term debt to their divisions and thus have an approximation of the stockholders' equity in each division. However, this practice has doubtful merit. Division managers typically have little responsibility for the long-term *financial* management of their divisions, as distinguished from *operating* management. You might compare how the investment base of a division manager of Company A might differ radically from the investment base of a comparable division manager of Company B, if A bore heavy long-term debt and B were debt-free.

Allocation to Divisions

Various definitions of income for the segments of an organization were discussed in the preceding chapter, so they will not be repeated here. Just as cost allocations affect income, asset allocations affect the invested capital of particular divisions. The aim is to allocate in a manner that will be goal-congruent, will provide incentive, and will recognize autonomy insofar as possible. Incidentally, as long as the managers feel that they are being treated uniformly, they tend to be more tolerant about the imperfections of the allocation.

A frequent criterion for asset allocation is avoidability. That is, the amount allocable to any given segment for the purpose of evaluating the division's performance is the amount that the corporation as a whole could avoid by not having that segment. Commonly used bases for allocation, when assets are not directly identifiable with a specific division, include:

Asset Class	*Possible Allocation Base*
Corporate cash	Budgeted cash needs, as discussed below
Receivables	Sales weighted by payment terms
Inventories	Budgeted sales or usage
Plant and equipment	Usage of services in terms of long-run forecasts of demand or area occupied

The allocation of central corporate assets often parallels the allocation of central corporate costs. Where the allocation of an asset would indeed be arbitrary, many managers feel that it is better not to allocate.

[7]John J. Mauriel and Robert N. Anthony, "Misevaluation of Investment Center Performance," *Harvard Business Review* (March–April 1966), pp. 98–105, summarize the practices of 2,658 companies. Forty-one percent deducted current external payables in arriving at the investment base.

Should cash be included under controllable investment if the balances are strictly controlled by corporate headquarters? Arguments can be made for both sides, but the manager is usually regarded as being responsible for the volume of business generated by the division. In turn, this volume is likely to have a direct effect on the overall cash needs of the corporation.

Central control of cash is usually undertaken to reduce the holdings from what would be used if each division had a separate account. Fluctuations in cash needs of each division will be somewhat offsetting, and back-up borrowing power is increased. These factors make allocation of cash to the subunits difficult.

The allocation of cash on the basis of sales dollars seldom gets at the economic rationale of cash holdings. As Chapter 6 explains, cash needs are influenced by a host of factors, including payment terms of customers and creditors.

If the criterion of avoidability is used, the cash assignments should be done in recognition of offsetting "portfolio" effects. For example, Division A might have a cash deficiency of $1 million in February, but Division B might have an offsetting cash excess of $1 million. Taken together for the year, Divisions A, B, C, D, and others might require a combined investment in cash of, say, $16 million if each were independent entities but only $8 million if cash were controlled centrally. Hence, if Division C would ordinarily require a $4 million investment in cash as a separate entity, it would be allocated an investment of only $2 million as a subunit of a company where cash was controlled centrally.

MEASUREMENT ALTERNATIVES

Valuation of Assets

There is a widespread tendency to have one asset measure serve many masters. Should the assets contained in the investment base be valued at net book value (original cost less accumulated depreciation), some version of current value, or some other way? Until the mid-1970s the answer was overwhelmingly uniform. Most companies throughout the world have used net book value. A survey of 2,658 American companies showed that 73 percent used net book value and 18 percent used gross book value (*undepreciated* original cost). Only 3 percent used some measure that departs from historical cost, such as appraisal value or insurance value.[8]

Historical cost has been widely criticized for many years as providing a faulty basis for decision making and performance evaluation. As Chapters 4 and 5 point out, historical costs are irrelevant per se for making economic decisions. Despite these criticisms, and despite the increasing external re-

[8] Mauriel and Anthony, "Misevaluation," p. 100.

quirements for using current values such as replacement costs for asset valuation,[9] managers have been slow to depart from historical cost.

Why is historical cost so widely used? Some critics would say that sheer ignorance is the explanation. But a more persuasive answer comes from cost-benefit analysis. Accounting systems are costly. Historical records must be kept for many legal purposes; therefore, they are already in place. No additional money must be spent to obtain an evaluation of performance based on the historical-cost system. Furthermore, many managements believe that such a system provides the desired goal congruence and incentive. That is, a more sophisticated system will not radically improve the collective operating decisions that are desired. In short, the historical cost system is good enough for the *routine* evaluation of performance. In nonroutine instances, such as replacing equipment or deleting a product line, managers will conduct special studies to gather any current valuations that seem relevant.

The impending required introduction in external reporting of "current values" in the United Kingdom and Australia and the required disclosures of "replacement costs" in American external reporting will probably also cause their wider use internally. Thus, such current-value information will have to be gathered in a routine manner to satisfy external requirements. When current values are already available, the incremental costs (including the costs of educating users, which are high) of using such values for internal performance measurement purposes are much less imposing than when current values must be installed from scratch.

Plant and Equipment: Gross or Net?

Although net book value is extensively used, gross book value was used by 18 percent of the companies surveyed.[10] The proponents of gross book value maintain that it facilitates comparisons between years and between plants or divisions.

Consider an example of a $600,000 piece of equipment with a three-year life and no residual value:

	Operating Income before		Operating	Net Book	Rate of	Average Investment Gross Book	Rate of
Year	Depreciation	Depreciation	Income	Value	Return	Value	Return
1	$260,000	$200,000	$60,000	$500,000	12%	$600,000	10%
2	260,000	200,000	60,000	300,000	20%	600,000	10%
3	260,000	200,000	60,000	100,000	60%	600,000	10%

[9] See Chapter 20 for a discussion of the use of current values and general price-level indexes as a basis of asset valuation and income measurement.

[10] Mauriel and Anthony, "Misevaluation," p. 101.

The rate of return on net book value goes up as the equipment ages; note that it could increase even if operating income gradually declined through the years. In contrast, the rate of return on gross book value is unchanged if operating income does not change; moreover, the rate would decrease if operating income gradually declined through the years.

The advocates of using net book value maintain:

1. It is less confusing because it is consistent with the assets shown on the conventional balance sheet and with the net income computations.

2. The major criticism of net book value is not peculiar to its use for ROI purposes. It is really a criticism of using historical cost as a basis for evaluation.

This author is not enchanted with the gross book value method because of its inherent inconsistency. To show depreciation on an income statement and not deduct it on the balance sheet seems like an awkward means of remedying some peculiarities of historical cost accounting. Instead, if net book value is yielding unsatisfactory measures of performance, serious consideration should be given to revising the straight-line patterns of depreciation[11] or to using current values.

CHOOSING DESIRED RATES OF RETURN

Whatever their merits, neither the ROI nor the residual-income method can be used without considering the cost of capital. Critical questions include (a) what minimum rates to specify; (b) when and by how much minimum rates should be altered; and (c) whether the same minimum rates should be used in each segment of the organization. If a uniform rate is used and many divisions are currently earning different rates, the use of a very low rate will surely drive ROI down toward such a rate. Moreover, frequent changes in the rate may be demoralizing as well as nonoptimal. For example, it might lead to acceptance of an 11 percent prospective return when the minimum rate is 11 percent, and rejection of a 15 percent prospective rate when the minimum rate is 16 percent.

Modern financial theory supports the use of different rates for different divisions. Portfolio theory provides the analytical framework for the investment decision under uncertainty. The firm would be viewed as a collection of different classes of assets whose income streams bear different risks. The minimum desired rates of return are functions of risk. Various divisions face

[11] David Solomons, *Divisional Performance,* p. 135. He discusses these issues at length on pp. 134–42.

different risks. Therefore, a different minimum desired rate should be used for each division, based on the relative investment risks of each.[12]

The use of different required rates for different divisions is apparently not widespread. The most extensive survey of practice in this area indicated an overwhelming tendency to use the same required rate for all divisions and for all classes of assets.[13] The use of uniform rates is probably attributable to the attitude that managers must be treated fairly (or uniformly unfairly). In this context, fairness means that the same required rate should apply to all divisions. Moreover, even the use of different rates for different classes of assets (that is, one rate for investments in current assets and another rate for plant assets) may be perceived as unfair if divisions have different compositions of such assets.

The foregoing was a description of a central problem in guiding decisions and evaluating performance. Unfortunately, there is no pat solution. Researchers in economics and finance continue to quarrel about these issues. For our purposes, we explore the design of accounting systems given minimum required rates of return, however determined.

ALTERNATIVES OF TIMING

Accounting textbooks, including this one, do not discuss at length the problem of timing. However, timing is an important factor to consider when an information system is designed. For instance, the costs of gathering and processing information and the need for frequent feedback for controlling current operations may lead to using historical-cost measures rather than replacement costs. The need for replacement costs, realizable values, and economic values tends to be less frequent, so the systems are not designed for providing such information routinely.

Admittedly, this point was made earlier in the chapter. Nevertheless, it is repeated here because it is a likely explanation of why actual practice seems to differ so markedly from what theory may prefer. The essence of the matter is that management seems unwilling to pay for more elegant information because its extra costs exceed its prospective benefits.

WHY PROFIT CENTERS?

The literature contains many criticisms of profit centers on the grounds that managers are given profit responsibility without commensurate authority.

---

[12] James Van Horne, *Financial Management and Policy,* 4th ed. (Englewood Cliffs, N.J.: Prentice-Hall, Inc., 1977), Chap. 8, gives a detailed discussion of the finance issues summarized here.

[13] Mauriel and Anthony, in "Misevaluation," report that only 7 percent of the 258 respondents to this question used different rates.

Therefore, the criticism continues, the profit center is "artificial" because the manager is not free to make a sufficient number of the decisions that affect his profit.

Such criticisms confuse profit centers and decentralization; early in this chapter, we stressed that one can exist without the other. The fundamental question in deciding between using a cost center or a profit center for a given subunit is not whether heavy decentralization exists. Instead, the fundamental question is, **"Will a profit center better solve the problems of goal congruence and incentive than a cost center? In other words, do I predict that a profit center will induce the managers to make a better collective set of decisions from the viewpoint of the organization as a whole?"**

All control systems are imperfect. Judgments about their merits should concentrate on which alternative system will bring the actions top management seeks. For example, a plant may be a "natural" cost center because the plant manager has no influence over decisions concerning the marketing of its products. Still, some companies impose profit responsibility on the plant manager by either creating some transfer price above cost or by including the marketing costs on his income statement. Why? Because it has changed the plant manager's behavior. How? Instead of being concerned solely with running an efficient cost center, he now "naturally" considers quality control more carefully and reacts to customers' special requests more sympathetically. The profit center obtained the desired plant-manager behavior that the cost center failed to achieve.

From the viewpoint of top management, plant managers often have more influence on sales than is apparent at first glance. This is an example of how systems may evolve from cost centers to profit centers and an example of the first-line importance of predicting behavioral effects when an accounting control system is designed.

SUMMARY

As organizations grow, decentralization of some management functions becomes desirable. Decentralization immediately raises problems of obtaining decisions that are coordinated with the objectives of the organization as a whole. Ideally, planning and control systems should provide information that (a) aims managers toward decisions that are goal-congruent, (b) provides feedback (evaluation of performance) that improves incentive and future decisions, and (c) preserves autonomy. Note that the common thread of these problems is motivation.

Transfer-pricing systems are often used as a means of communicating data among subunits. There is rarely a single transfer price that will serve all requirements. Instead, there may be one transfer price for making a particular production decision, another for evaluating performance, and another for minimizing tariffs or income taxes. The choice of transfer-pricing systems must contend with problems of cost-benefit trade-offs, goal congruence, incentives, and autonomy.

Many techniques, such as ROI or residual income, fall far short of the ideal goals stipulated above. Nevertheless, in practice their conceptual shortcomings may be unimportant; often they are the best techniques available for obtaining the perceived top-management goals.

Despite the theoretical attractiveness of various nonhistorical accounting methods, most managements have apparently decided that a historical-cost system is good enough for the *routine* evaluation of managers. Evidently, this crude approach provides the desired motivational effects and gives clues as to whether to invest or disinvest in a particular division. The investment decision is evidently not routine enough to justify gathering information regarding replacement costs or realizable values except as special decisions arise.

Profit centers are usually associated with heavily decentralized organizations, whereas cost centers are usually associated with heavily centralized organizations. However, profit centers and decentralization are separate ideas; one can exist without the other.

SUMMARY PROBLEMS FOR YOUR REVIEW

Problem One

Examine Exhibit 11-1. In addition to the data there, suppose that Division A has fixed manufacturing costs of $400,000 and expected annual production of 100,000 units. The "full absorption cost" per unit was computed as follows:

Variable costs per unit	$ 6
Fixed costs, $400,000 ÷ 100,000 units	4
Full absorption cost per unit	$10

Required

Assume that Division A has idle capacity. Division B is considering whether to buy 10,000 units to be processed further and sold for $17. The additional costs shown in Exhibit 11-1 for Division B would prevail. If transfers were based on absorption cost, would the B manager buy? Why? Would the company as a whole benefit if the B manager decided to buy? Why?

Problem Two

A division has assets of $200,000 and operating income of $60,000.

1. What is the division's ROI?

2. If interest is imputed at 14 percent, what is the residual income?

3. What effects on management behavior can be expected if ROI is used to gauge performance?

4. What effects on management behavior can be expected if residual income is used to gauge performance?

Solution to Problem One

B would not buy. Absorption costing occasionally may lead to dysfunctional decisions. The absorption-costing transfer price of $10 would make the acquisition of parts unattractive to B:

Division B:

Sales price of final product			$ 17
Deduct costs:			
Transfer price per unit paid to A (absorption cost)		$10	
Additional costs (from Exhibit 11-1):			
Processing	$4		
Selling	4	8	
Total costs to B			18
Contribution to profit of B			$ –1
Contribution to company as a whole (from Exhibit 11-1)			$ 3

As Exhibit 11-1 shows, the company as a whole would benefit by $30,000 ($10,000 units × $3) if the units were transferred.

The major lesson here is that, when idle capacity exists in the supplier division, transfer prices based on absorption costs may induce the wrong decisions. Working in his own best interests, the B manager has no incentive to buy from A.

Solution to Problem Two

1. $60,000 ÷ $200,000 = 30%

2. $60,000 – .14($200,000) = $60,000 – $28,000 = $32,000

3. If ROI is used, the manager is prone to reject projects that do not earn an ROI of at least 30 percent. From the viewpoint of the organization as a whole, this may be undesirable because its best investment opportunities may lie in that division at a rate of, say, 22 percent. If a division is enjoying a high ROI, it is less likely to expand if it is judged via ROI than if it is judged via residual income.

4. If residual income is used, the manager is inclined to accept all projects whose expected ROI exceeds the minimum desired rate. His division is more likely to expand, because his goal is to maximize a dollar amount rather than a rate.

ASSIGNMENT MATERIAL

Essential Assignment Material

11-1. **Terminology.** Define: *decentralization, profit center, transfer price,* and *capital turnover.*

11-2. Rate of return and transfer pricing. You are given the following data regarding budgeted operations of a company division:

Average available assets:		
Receivables	$100,000	
Inventories	300,000	
Plant and equipment, net	200,000	
Total	$600,000	
Fixed overhead	$200,000	
Variable costs		$1 per unit
Desired rate of return on average available assets	25%	
Expected volume	100,000 units	

Required

1. a. What average unit sales price is needed to obtain the desired rate of return on average available assets?
   b. What would be the expected capital turnover?
   c. What would be the net income percentage on dollar sales?

2. a. If the selling price is as computed above, what rate of return will be earned on available assets if sales volume is 120,000 units?
   b. If sales volume is 80,000 units?

3. Assume that 30,000 units are to be sold to another division of the same company and that only 70,000 units can be sold to outside customers. The other division manager has balked at a tentative selling price of $4. He has offered $2.25, claiming that he can manufacture the units himself for that price. The manager of the selling division has examined his own data. He has decided that he could eliminate $40,000 of inventories, $60,000 of plant and equipment, and $20,000 of fixed overhead if he did *not* sell to the other division and sold only 70,000 units to outside customers. Should he sell for $2.25? Show computations to support your answer.

11-3. Transfer-pricing dispute. A transportation-equipment manufacturer, Chalmers Corporation, is heavily decentralized. Each division head has full authority on all decisions regarding sales to internal or external customers. Division P has always acquired a certain equipment component from Division S. However, when informed that Division S was increasing its unit price to $220, Division P's management decided to purchase the component from outside suppliers at a price of $200.

Division S had recently acquired some specialized equipment that was used primarily to make this component. The manager cited the resulting high depreciation charges as the justification for the price boost. He asked the president of the company to instruct Division P to buy from S at the $220 price. He supplied the following:

P's annual purchases of component	2,000 units
S's variable costs per unit	$190
S's fixed costs per unit	$ 20

Required

1. Suppose that there are no alternative uses of the S facilities. Will the company as a whole benefit if P buys from the outside suppliers for $200 per unit? Show computations to support your answer.

2. Suppose that internal facilities of S would not otherwise be idle. The equipment and other facilities would be assigned to other production operations that would otherwise require an additional annual outlay of $29,000. Should P purchase from outsiders at $200 per unit?

3. Suppose that there are no alternative uses for S's internal facilities and that the selling price of outsiders drops $15. Should P purchase from outsiders?

4. As the president, how would you respond to the request of the manager of S? Would your response differ, depending on the specific situations described in Requirements 1 through 3 above? Why?

Additional Assignment Material

11-4. "The essence of decentralization is the use of profit centers." Do you agree? Explain.

11-5. Distinguish between a profit center and a cost center.

11-6. What is the major benefit of the ROI technique for measuring performance?

11-7. "There is an optimum level of investment in any asset." Explain.

11-8. "Just as there may be different costs for different purposes, there may be different rates of return for different purposes." Explain.

11-9. Why are cost-based transfer prices in common use?

11-10. Why are transfer-pricing systems needed?

11-11. Why are interest expense and income taxes ordinarily excluded in computing incomes that are related to asset bases?

11-12. **Simple calculations.** You are given the following data:

Sales	$100,000,000
Invested capital	$20,000,000
Return on investment	10%

1. Turnover of capital.
2. Net income.
3. Net income as a percentage of sales.

11-13. **Comparison of asset and equity bases.** Company A has assets of $1,000,000 and a long-term, 6 percent debt of $500,000. Company B has assets of $1,000,000 and no long-term debt. The annual operating income (before interest) of both companies is $200,000.

Compute the rate of return on:

1. Assets available.
2. Stockholders' equity.

Evaluate the relative merits of each base for appraising operating management.

11-14. Using gross or net book value of fixed assets. Assume that a particular plant acquires $400,000 of fixed assets with a useful life of four years and no residual value. Straight-line depreciation will be used. The plant manager is judged on income in relation to these fixed assets. Annual net income, after deducting depreciation, is $40,000.

Assume that sales, and all expenses except depreciation, are on a cash basis. Dividends equal net income. Thus, cash in the amount of the depreciation charge will accumulate each year. The plant manager's performance is judged in relation to fixed assets because all current assets, including cash, are considered under central-company control.

1. Prepare a comparative tabulation of the plant's rate of return and the company's overall rate of return based on:
   a. Gross (i.e., original cost) assets.
   b. Net book value of assets. Assume (unrealistically) that any cash accumulated remains idle.
2. Evaluate the relative merits of gross assets and net book value of assets as investment bases.

11-15. Margins and turnover. Return on investment is often expressed as the product of two components—capital turnover and margin on sales. You are considering investing in one of three companies, all in the same industry, and are given the following information.

| | *Company* | | |
	X	*Y*	*Z*
Sales	$5,000,000	$ 2,500,000	$50,000,000
Income	500,000	250,000	250,000
Capital	2,000,000	20,000,000	20,000,000

1. Why would you desire the breakdown of return on investment into margin on sales and turnover on capital?
2. Compute the margin on sales, turnover on capital, and return on investment for the three companies, and comment on the relative performance of the companies as thoroughly as the data permit.

11-16. ROI or residual income. d'Anconia Copper is a large integrated conglomerate with shipping, metals, and mining operations throughout the world. The general manager of the ferrous metals division has been directed to submit his proposed capital budget for 19x1 for inclusion in the company-wide budget.

336

The division manager has for consideration the following projects, all of which require an outlay of capital. All projects have equal risk.

Project	Investment Required	Return
1	$6,000,000	$1,380,000
2	2,400,000	768,000
3	1,750,000	245,000
4	1,200,000	216,000
5	800,000	160,000
6	350,000	98,000

The division manager must decide which of the projects to take. The company has a cost of capital of 15 percent. An amount of $15,000,000 is available to the division for investment purposes.

Required

1. What will be the total investment, total return, return on capital invested, and residual income of the rational division manager if:
   a. The company has a rule that all projects promising at least 20 percent or more should be taken.
   b. The division manager is evaluated on his ability to maximize his return on capital invested (assume that this is a new division with no invested capital).
   c. The division manager is expected to maximize residual income as computed by using the 15 percent cost of capital.

2. Which of the three approaches will induce the most effective investment policy for the company as a whole?

11-17. Different ways of evaluating divisional performance. As the president of Excell Enterprises Company, you have been given the following measures of the performance of three divisions (in thousands of dollars):

	Net Assets		
	(1)	(2)	(3)
Division	Net Book Value	Net Replacement Value	Net Income
A	10,000	10,000	1,800
B	20,000	32,000	3,200
C	30,000	37,500	4,500

Required

1. Compute for each division the rate of return and the residual income based on net book value and on net replacement value. For purposes of computing residual income, use 10 percent as the minimum desired rate of return.

2. Rank the performance of each division under each of the four different measures computed in Requirement 1.

3. What do these measures tell you about the performance of the division? Of the division manager? Which measure do you prefer? Why?

11-18. Use of Ratios. (CMA.) A common measure of a management's performance is "return on net worth." This is a particularly important measure from the shareholder's point of view. This ratio can be expressed as the product of three other ratios, as shown below:

$$\underset{\text{net worth}}{\text{Return on}} = \frac{\text{Net income}}{\text{Net worth}} = \overset{\text{I}}{\frac{\text{Net income}}{\text{Sales}}} \times \overset{\text{II}}{\frac{\text{Sales}}{\text{Assets}}} \times \overset{\text{III}}{\frac{\text{Assets}}{\text{Net worth}}}$$

Required

1. Discuss the "return on net worth" as a management goal and as a measurement of management performance.

2. What management activities are measured by each of the ratios I, II, III?

3. Would separation of the "return on net worth" into the three ratios and use of these ratios for planning targets and performance measures result in goal congruence (or improvement toward goal congruence) among the responsible managers? Explain your answer.

11-19. ROI for measuring performance. (CMA.) The Texon Co. is organized into autonomous divisions along regional market lines. Each division manager is responsible for sales, cost of operations, acquisition and financing of divisional assets, and working-capital management.

The vice-president of general operations for the company will retire in September 19x5. A review of the performance, attitudes, and skills of several management employees has been undertaken. Interviews with qualified outside candidates also have been held. The selection committee has narrowed the choice to the managers of Divisions A and F.

Both candidates were appointed division managers in late 19x1. The manager of Division A had been the assistant manager of that division for the prior five years. The manager of Division F had served as assistant division manager of Division B before being appointed to his present post. He took over Division F, a division newly formed in 19x0, when its first manager left to join a competitor. The financial results of their performance in the past three years are reported in Exhibit 11-2.

EXHIBIT 11-2

	DIVISION A			DIVISION F		
	19x2	19x3	19x4	19x2	19x3	19x4
Estimated industry sales			(000 omitted)			
—market area	$10,000	$12,000	$13,000	$5,000	$6,000	$6,500
Division sales	$ 1,000	$ 1,100	$ 1,210	$ 450	$ 600	$ 750
Variable costs	$ 300	$ 320	$ 345	$ 135	$ 175	$ 210
Discretionary costs	400	405	420	170	200	230
Committed costs	275	325	350	140	200	250
Total costs	$ 975	$ 1,050	$ 1,115	$ 445	$ 575	$ 690
Net income	$ 25	$ 50	$ 95	$ 5	$ 25	$ 60
Assets employed	$ 330	$ 340	$ 360	$ 170	$ 240	$ 300
Liabilities	103	105	115	47	100	130
Net investment	227	235	245	123	140	170
Return on investment	11%	21%	39%	4%	18%	35%

1. Texon Co. measures the performance of the divisions and the division managers on the basis of their return on investment (ROI). Is this an appropriate measurement for the division managers? Explain.

2. Many believe that a single measure, such as ROI, is inadequate to fully evaluate performance. What additional measure(s) could be used for performance evaluation? Give reasons for each measure listed.

3. On the basis of the information given, which manager would you recommend for vice-president of general operations? Present reasons to support your answer.

11-20. Setting multiple objectives. Solve Problem 9-25, which could logically have been placed here.

11-21. Human-resources accounting. Solve Problem 9-32, which could logically have been placed here.

11-22. Judging a control technique. Solve Problem 9-33, which could logically have been placed here.

11-23. Judging a control technique. Solve Problem 9-34, which could logically have been placed here.

11-24. Role of economic value and replacement value. "To me, economic value is the only justifiable basis for measuring plant assets for purposes of evaluating performance. By economic value, I mean the present value of expected future services. Still, we do not even do this upon acquisition of new assets—that is, we may compute a positive net present value, using discounted cash flow; but we record the asset at no more than its cost. In this way, the excess present value is not shown in the initial balance sheet. Moreover, the use of replacement costs in subsequent years is also unlikely to result in showing economic values; the replacement cost will probably be less than the economic value at any given instant of an asset's life.

"Market values are totally unappealing to me because they represent a second-best alternative value—that is, they ordinarily represent the maximum amount obtainable from an alternative that has been rejected. Obviously, if the market value exceeds the economic value of the assets in use, they should be sold. However, in most instances, the opposite is true; market values of individual assets are far below their economic value in use.

"The obtaining and recording of total present values of individual assets based on discounted-cash-flow techniques is an infeasible alternative. I, therefore, conclude that replacement cost (less accumulated depreciation) of similar assets producing similar services is the best practical approximation of the economic value of the assets in use. Of course, it will facilitate the evaluation of the division's performance more easily than the division manager's performance."

Critically evaluate the above comments. Please do not wander; concentrate on the issues described by the quotation.

11-25. Transfer-pricing concession. (CMA, adapted.) The Ajax Division of Gunnco Corporation, operating at capacity, has been asked by the Defco Division of

Gunnco to supply it with Electrical Fitting No. 1726. Ajax sells this part to its regular customers for $7.50 each. Defco, which is operating at 50 percent capacity, is willing to pay $5 each for the fitting. Defco will put the fitting into a brake unit that it is manufacturing on essentially a cost-plus basis for a commercial airplane manufacturer.

Ajax has a variable cost of producing fitting No. 1726 of $4.25. The cost of the brake unit as being built by Defco is as follows:

Purchased parts—outside vendors	$22.50
Ajax fitting No. 1726	5.00
Other variable costs	14.00
Fixed overhead and administration	8.00
	$49.50

Defco believes the price concession is necessary to get the job.

The company uses return on investment and dollar profits in the measurement of division and division-manager performance.

Required

1. Consider that you are the division controller of Ajax. Would you recommend that Ajax supply fitting No. 1726 to Defco? Why or why not? (Ignore any income tax issues.)

2. Would it be to the short-run economic advantage of the Gunnco Corporation for the Ajax Division to supply the Defco Division with fitting No. 1726 at $5 each? (Ignore any income tax issues.) Explain your answer.

3. Discuss the organizational and manager-behavior difficulties, if any, inherent in this situation. As the Gunnco controller, what would you advise the Gunnco Corporation president do in this situation?

11-26. Profit centers and transfer pricing in an automobile dealership. A large automobile dealership is installing a responsibility accounting system and three profit centers: parts and service; new vehicles; and used vehicles. Each department manager has been told to run his shop as if he were in business for himself. However, there are interdepartmental dealings. For example:

a. The parts and service department prepares new cars for final delivery and repairs used cars prior to resale.

b. The used-car department's major source of inventory has been cars traded in in part payment for new cars.

The owner of the dealership has asked you to draft a company policy statement on transfer pricing, together with specific rules to be applied to the examples cited. He has told you that clarity is of paramount importance because your statement will be relied upon for settling transfer-pricing disputes.

11-27. Transfer pricing. The Never Die Division of Durable Motors Company produces 12-volt batteries for automobiles. It has been the sole supplier of batteries to the Automotive Division, and charges $10 per unit, the current market price for very large wholesale lots. The battery division also sells to outside retail outlets, at

$12.50 per unit. Normally, outside sales amount to 25 percent of a total sales volume of 2,000,000 batteries per year. Typical combined annual data for the division follow:

Sales	$21,250,000
Variable costs, @ $8 per battery	$16,000,000
Fixed costs	2,000,000
Total costs	$18,000,000
Gross margin	$ 3,250,000

The Sure Life Battery Company, an entirely separate entity, has offered the Automotive Division comparable batteries at a firm price of $9 per unit. The Never Die Division claims that it can't possibly match this price because it could not earn any margin at $9.

Required

1. Assume you are the manager of the Automotive Division. Comment on the Never Die Division's claim. Assume that normal outside volume cannot be increased.

2. The Never Die Division feels that it can increase outside sales by 1,500,000 batteries per year by increasing fixed costs by $2,000,000 and variable costs by $1 per unit, while reducing the selling price to $12. Assume that maximum capacity is 2,000,000 batteries per year. Should the division reject intracompany business and concentrate on outside sales?

11-28. Variable cost as a transfer price. A product's variable cost is $2 and its market value is $3 at a transfer point from Division S to Division P. Division P's variable cost of processing the product further is $2.25, and the selling price of the final product is $4.75.

Required

1. Prepare a tabulation of the contribution margin per unit for Division P performance and overall performance under the two alternatives of (a) processing further and (b) selling to outsiders at the transfer point.

2. As Division P manager, which alternative would you choose? Explain.

11-29. Transfer pricing. Refer to Problem 11-3, Requirement 1 only. Suppose that Division S could modify the component at an additional variable cost of $10 per unit and sell the 2,000 units to other customers for $225. Then would the entire company benefit if P purchased the 2,000 components from outsiders at $200 per unit?

11-30. Transfer pricing. (CMA.) The Lorax Electric Company manufactures a large variety of systems and individual components for the electronics industry. The firm is organized into several divisions, division managers being given the authority to make virtually all operating decisions. Management control over divisional operations is maintained by a system of divisional profit and return on investment measures, which are reviewed regularly by top management. The top management of Lorax have been quite pleased with the effectiveness of the system they have been using and believe that it is responsible for the company's improved profitability over the last few years.

The Devices Division manufactures solid-state devices and is operating at capacity. The Systems Division has asked the Devices Division to supply a large quantity of integrated circuit IC378. The Devices Division currently is selling this component to its regular customers at $40 per hundred.

The Systems Division, which is operating at about 60 percent capacity, wants this particular component for a digital clock system. It has an opportunity to supply large quantities of these digital clock systems to Centonic Electric, a major producer of clock radios and other popular electronic home entertainment equipment. This is the first opportunity any of the Lorax divisions have had to do business with Centonic Electric. Centonic Electric has offered to pay $7.50 per clock system.

The Systems Division prepared an analysis of the probable costs to produce the clock systems. The amount that could be paid to the Devices Division for the integrated circuits was determined by working backward from the selling price. The cost estimates employed by the division reflected the highest per-unit cost the Systems Division could incur for each cost component and still leave a sufficient margin so that the division's income statement could show reasonable improvement. The cost estimates are summarized below.

Proposed selling price		$7.50
Costs excluding required integrated		
circuits (IC378)		
Components purchased from		
outside suppliers	$2.75	
Circuit-board etching—labor		
and variable overhead	.40	
Assembly, testing, packaging—		
labor and variable overhead	1.35	
Fixed-overhead allocations	1.50	
Profit margin	.50	6.50
Amount that can be paid for		
integrated circuits IC378		
(5 @ $20 per hundred)		$1.00

As a result of this analysis, the Systems Division offered the Devices Division a price of $20 per hundred for the integrated circuit. This bid was refused by the manager of the Devices Division, who felt the Systems Division should at least meet the price of $40 per hundred that regular customers pay. When the Systems Division found that it could not obtain a comparable integrated circuit from outside vendors, the situation was brought to an arbitration committee that had been set up to review such problems.

The arbitration committee prepared an analysis showing that 15¢ would cover variable costs of producing the integrated circuit, 28¢ would cover the full cost including fixed overhead, and 35¢ would provide a gross margin equal to the average gross margin on all of the products sold by the Devices Division. The manager of the Systems Division reacted by stating, "They could sell us that integrated circuit for 20¢ and still earn a positive contribution toward profit. In fact, they should be required to sell at their variable cost—15¢—and not be allowed to take advantage of us."

Lou Belcher, manager of Devices, countered: "It doesn't make sense to sell to the Systems Division at $20 per hundred when we can get $40 per hundred outside on all we can produce. In fact, Systems could pay us up to almost $60 per hundred and they would still have a positive contribution to profit."

The recommendation of the committee, to set the price at 35¢ per unit ($35 per hundred), so that Devices could earn a "fair" gross margin, was rejected by both division managers. Consequently, the problem was brought to the attention of the vice-president of operations and his staff.

Required

1. What would be the immediate economic effect on the Lorax Company as a whole if the Devices Division were required to supply IC378 to the Systems Division at 35¢ per unit—the price recommended by the arbitration committee. Explain your answer.

2. Discuss the advisability of intervention by top management as a solution to transfer-pricing disputes between division managers such as the one experienced by Lorax Electric Company.

3. Suppose that Lorax adopted a policy of requiring that the price to be paid in all internal transfers by the buying division would be equal to the variable costs per unit of the selling division for that product and that the supplying division would be required to sell if the buying division decided to buy the item. Discuss the consequences of adopting such a policy as a way of avoiding the need for the arbitration committee or for intervention by the vice-president.

11-31. Transfer pricing. (CMA, adapted.) A. R. Oma, Inc., manufactures a line of men's perfumes and after-shaving lotions. The manufacturing process is basically a series of mixing operations with the addition of certain aromatic and coloring ingredients; the finished product is packaged in a company-produced glass bottle and packed in cases containing six bottles.

A. R. Oma feels that the sale of its product is heavily influenced by the appearance and appeal of the bottle and has, therefore, devoted considerable managerial effort to the development of certain unique bottle production processes, in which management takes considerable pride.

The two areas (i.e., perfume production and bottle manufacture) have evolved over the years in an almost independent manner; in fact, a rivalry has developed between management personnel as to "which division is the more important" to A. R. Oma. This attitude is probably intensified because the bottle manufacturing plant was purchased intact ten years ago and no real interchange of management personnel or ideas (except at the top corporate level) has taken place.

Since the acquisition, all bottle production has been absorbed by the perfume manufacturing plant. Each area is considered a separate profit center and evaluated as such. As the new corporate controller you are responsible for the definition of a proper transfer value to use in crediting the bottle production profit center and in debiting the packaging profit center.

At your request, the Bottle Division General Manager has asked certain other bottle manufacturers to quote a price for the quantity and sizes demanded by the perfume division. These competitive prices are:

Volume	Total Price	Price Per Case
2,000,000 eq. cases*	$ 4,000,000	$2.00
4,000,000	$ 7,000,000	$1.75
6,000,000	$10,000,000	$1.67

*An "equivalent case" represents six bottles each.

A cost analysis of the internal bottle plant indicates that they can produce bottles at these costs:

Volume	Total Price	Cost Per Case
2,000,000 eq. cases	$3,200,000	$1.60
4,000,000	$5,200,000	$1.30
6,000,000	$7,200,000	$1.20

(Your cost analysts point out that these costs represent fixed costs of $1,200,000 and variable costs of $1 per equivalent case.)

These figures have given rise to considerable corporate discussion as to the proper value to use in the transfer of bottles to the perfume division. This interest is heightened because a significant portion of a division manager's income is an incentive bonus based on profit-center results.

The perfume production division has the following costs in addition to the bottle costs:

Volume	Total Cost	Cost Per Case
2,000,000 cases	$16,400,000	$8.20
4,000,000	$32,400,000	$8.10
6,000,000	$48,400,000	$8.07

After considerable analysis, the marketing research department has furnished you with the following price-demand relationship for the finished product:

Sales Volume	Total Sales Revenue	Sales Price Per Case
2,000,000 cases	$25,000,000	$12.50
4,000,000	$45,600,000	$11.40
6,000,000	$63,900,000	$10.65

Required

1. The A. R. Oma Company has used market-price transfer prices in the past. Using the current market prices and costs, and assuming a volume of 6,000,000 cases, calculate the income for
   a. The bottle division.
   b. The perfume division.
   c. The corporation.

2. Is this production and sales level the most profitable volume for
   a. The bottle division?
   b. The perfume division?
   c. The corporation?

Explain your answer.

11-32. **Transfer-pricing principles.** A consulting firm, INO, is decentralized with 25 offices around the country. The headquarters is based in Orange County, Calif. Another operating division is located in Los Angeles, 50 miles away. A subsidiary printing operation, We Print, is located in the headquarters building. Top management has indicated the desirability of the Los Angeles office's utilizing We Print for printing reports. All charges are eventually billed to the client, but INO was concerned about keeping such charges competitive.

We Print charges Los Angeles the following:

Photographing page for offset printing (a setup cost)	$.30
Printing cost per page	$.015

At this rate, We Print sales have a 60 percent contribution margin to fixed overhead. Outside bids for 50 copies of a 135-page report needed immediately have been:

EZ Print	$145.00
Quick Service	$128.25
Fast Print	$132.00

These three printers are located within a five-mile radius of INO Los Angeles and can have the reports ready in two days. A messenger would have to be sent to drop off the original and pick up the copies. The messenger usually goes to headquarters, but, in the past, special trips have been required to deliver the original or pick up the copies. It takes three to four days to get the copies from We Print (because of the extra scheduling difficulties in delivery and pick-up).

Quality control of We Print is poor. Reports received in the past have had wrinkled pages and occasionally have been miscollated or had pages deleted. (In one circumstance an intracompany memorandum indicating INO's economic straits was inserted in a report. Fortunately, the Los Angeles office detected the error before the report was distributed to the clients.) The degree of quality control in the three outside print shops is unknown.

(Although the differences in costs may seem immaterial in this case, regard the numbers as significant for purposes of focusing on the key issues.)

Required

1. If you were the decision maker at INO Los Angeles, to which print shop would you give the business? Is this an optimal economic decision from the entire corporation's point of view?

2. What would be the ideal transfer price in this case, if based only on economic considerations?

3. Time is an important factor in maintaining the goodwill of the client. There is potential return business from this client. Given this perspective, what might be the optimal decision for the company?

4. Comment on the wisdom of top management in indicating that We Print should be utilized.

11-33. Transfer pricing in different situations. The Neumann Company, Ltd., adopted a philosophy of decentralization several years ago. All the company's autonomous manufacturing divisions are located in Great Britain, where the company manufactures a wide range of electronic controls and automated machine tools. Nominally, all divisions of the company are conducted as separate enterprises, which must negotiate all orders independently with prospective purchasers. Each division is then responsible for its own profitability and return on investment. However, all divisions are required to consider purchasing from other Neumann divisions whenever possible.

The Machine-Products Division (MPD), situated in London, manufactures small precision components that can be integrated with other Neumann components in a variety of automated systems. Both the components and the entire systems are generally quite profitable and in high demand by other Neumann divisions, as well as by independent purchasers. MPD is the only Neumann plant with the facilities to produce a very essential component, magnesium balance wheels. The market price for these items is £100, both in Great Britain and in the United States. However, an import duty of 10 percent (of the selling price without the duty) is charged on the import of this type of product into the United States. The MPD income statement for the last twelve months is as follows (in thousands of pounds):

Net sales		£1,100
Direct labor	£250	
Direct material	300	
Manufacturing overhead	250	800
Gross margin		300
Fixed selling expenses	100	
Fixed administrative expenses	80	180
Divisional profit		£ 120

The cost of a batch of balance wheels has been calculated in the following manner:

Direct labor	£25
Direct material	30
Manufacturing overhead*	25
Total cost	£80

* 100 percent of direct labor.

When the company was decentralized, several assembly and marketing divisions were opened in new areas to expand the size of the markets for existing manufacturing divisions. These divisions were expected to be less profitable than other Neumann divisions, especially where import duties might necessitate more burdensome costs. One of these new marketing and assembly divisions (Middle Continental) was headquartered in Chicago under Mr. Gorot. Gorot had previously worked in London under the divisional manager for MPD, Mr. Miller, a 35-year veteran of the company. Even though Gorot had been a highly successful department head while in London, Miller had surreptitiously instigated a transfer for Gorot because of a personality conflict. Needless to say, Miller was quite unhappy to hear of Gorot's recent successes as head of Middle Continental while he himself was struggling to eliminate unfavorable capacity variances in the MPD.

Miller has been reluctant in the past to sell MPD components to other divisions at less than the domestic price; he sees no reason why he should make less profit than if he sold them in Great Britain. Furthermore, he has stated categorically, "I will not hurt my own profits to help that upstart in Chicago!"

One of the most important systems sold by Middle Continental requires the use of magnesium balance wheels. In the past, Gorot has been under some pressure to purchase balance wheels from MPD at a base price of £100 plus £10 import duty. This practice has unduly affected his profit performance, and he is necessarily eager to obtain permission to purchase these components from local suppliers.

1. As the divisional controller at MPD, you are asked by Miller for advice in response to a memorandum from Gorot that he has obtained permission to purchase balance wheels in the United States unless MPD lowers its price. What would you advise Miller to do? Why? For this and the next part, assume that the manufacturing overhead is totally variable.

2. After you have given your advice to Miller, he receives a cablegram from Gorot indicating that several manufacturers in the United States have reduced their price on balance wheels to £85. How would you change your advice, if at all? Why?

3. Several days later, you determine that half the manufacturing overhead is fixed cost. Would this cause you to alter any of your previous decisions? In what way?

4. About a year later, MPD is operating at maximum capacity. Gorot sends MPD another order for balance wheels at the previously negotiated price in Requirement 1. Would you now recommend that this price be accepted? Why?

5. If the Neumann Company were to eliminate its divisions, what company guidelines should be established for transfers of goods between segments of the company?

6. Two years later, you are promoted to the controller's office of the entire Neumann Company. You are then asked to advise your new superior on whether some firm guidelines should be established for the determination of transfer prices between divisions as they were organized in Requirements 1 through 4. What would you recommend? Why?

SUGGESTED READINGS

ANTHONY, R. N., and J. DEARDEN, *Management Control Systems: Cases and Readings,* 3d ed. (Homewood, Ill.: Richard D. Irwin, Inc., 1976).

GOLDSCHMIDT, YAAQOV, *Information for Management Decisions* (Ithaca, N.Y., and London: Cornell University Press, 1970).

HORNGREN, CHARLES T., *Cost Accounting: A Managerial Emphasis,* 4th ed. (Englewood Cliffs, N.J.: Prentice-Hall, Inc. 1977), Chaps. 6, 22, 23.

MORRIS, WILLIAM T., *Decentralization in Management Systems* (Columbus, O.: Ohio State University Press, 1968).

SOLOMONS, DAVID, *Divisional Performance: Measurement and Control* (New York: Financial Executives Research Foundation, 1965). Reprinted in paperback form in 1968 by Richard D. Irwin, Inc.

PART THREE

Selected
Topics
for
Further Study

CHAPTER 12

Capital Budgeting

Should we replace the equipment? Should we add this product to our line? Managers must make these and similar decisions having long-range implications; they are called *capital-budgeting* decisions. Capital-budgeting decisions are faced by managers in all types of organizations, including religious, medical, and governmental subunits. Many different decision models are used for capital budgeting. In this chapter we deal mostly with the accountant's problem-solving function; we compare the uses and limitations of various capital-budgeting models, with particular emphasis on relevant-cost analysis.

FOCUS ON PROGRAMS OR PROJECTS

The planning and controlling of operations typically have a *time-period* focus. For example, the chief administrator of a university will be concerned with all activities for a given academic year. But he will also be concerned with longer-range matters that tend to have an individual *program* or *project* focus. Examples are new programs in educational administration or health-care education, joint law-management programs, new athletic facili-

351

ties, new trucks, or new parking lots. In fact, the ideas of *portfolio theory* in finance have sometimes been extended so that the operating management of many organizations is perceived as the ongoing overseeing of a collection of individual investments.

This chapter concentrates on the planning and controlling of those programs or projects that affect more than one year's financial results. Such decisions inevitably entail investments of resources that are often called **capital outlays.** Hence, the term **capital budgeting** has arisen to describe the long-term planning for making and financing such outlays.

Capital-budgeting problems affect almost all organizations. For example, decisions about hospital location, size, and equipment are usually crucial because of the magnitude of the financial stakes and the murkiness of future developments, particularly in technology. Because the unknowable factors are many, well-managed organizations tend to gather and quantify as many knowable factors as is feasible before a decision is made. In addition, because organizations have limited resources, they must choose *among* various investments. Thus, a basis of comparison must be established. In response to these concerns, many decision models have evolved, including discounted cash flow (DCF), payback, and accrual accounting models. The DCF model is becoming increasingly popular and has features that make it conceptually more attractive than the other two models.

DISCOUNTED-CASH-FLOW MODEL

Major Aspects of DCF

The old adage that a bird in the hand is worth two in the bush is applicable to the management of money. A dollar in the hand today is worth more than a dollar to be received (or spent) five years from today, because the use of money has a cost (interest), just as the use of a building or an automobile may have a cost (rent). **Because the discounted-cash-flow model explicitly and systematically weighs the time value of money, it is the best method to use for long-range decisions.**

Another major aspect of DCF is its focus on *cash* inflows and outflows rather than on *net income* as computed in the accrual accounting sense. As we shall see, the student without a strong accounting background has an advantage here. He does not have to unlearn the accrual concepts of accounting, which the accounting student often incorrectly tries to inject into discounted-cash-flow analysis.

There are two main variations of DCF: (a) net present value, and (b) internal rate of return. A brief summary of the tables and formulas used is included in Appendix B at the end of this book. Do not be frightened by the mathematics of compound interest. We shall confine our study to present-value tables, which may seem imposing but which are simple enough to be taught in many grade-school arithmetic courses. **Before reading on, be sure you understand Appendix B at the end of this book.**

Example. The following example will be used to illustrate the concepts. A buildings and grounds manager of a campus of the University of California is contemplating the purchase of some lawn maintenance equipment that will increase efficiency and produce cash operating savings of $2,000 per year. The useful life of this project is four years, after which the equipment will have a net disposal value of zero. Assume that the equipment will cost $6,074 now and that the minimum desired rate of return is 10 percent per year.

Required

1. Compute the project's net present value.
2. Compute the expected internal rate of return on the project.

Net Present Value

One type of discounted-cash-flow approach may be called the **net-present-value method.** It assumes some minimum desired rate of return. All expected future cash flows are discounted to the present, using this minimum desired rate. If the result is positive, the project is desirable, and vice versa. When choosing among several investments, the one with the largest net present value is most desirable.

EXHIBIT 12-1
Net-Present-Value Technique

Original investment, $6,074. Useful life, 4 years. Annual cash inflow from operations, $2,000. Minimum desired rate of return, 10 percent. Cash outflows are in parentheses; cash inflows are not.

	PRESENT VALUE OF $1, DISCOUNTED @ 10%	TOTAL PRESENT VALUE	SKETCH OF CASH FLOWS AT END OF YEAR				
			0	1	2	3	4
Approach 1: Discounting Each Year's Cash Inflow Separately*							
Cash flows:							
Annual savings	.909	$ 1,818		$2,000			
	.826	1,652			$2,000		
	.751	1,502				$2,000	
	.683	1,366					$2,000
Present value of future inflows		$ 6,338					
Initial outlay	1.000	(6,074)	$(6,074)				
Net present value		$ 264					
Approach 2: Using Annuity Table†							
Annual savings	3.170	$ 6,340		$2,000	$2,000	$2,000	$2,000
Initial outlay	1.000	(6,074)	$(6,074)				
Net present value		$ 264‡					

* Present values from Table 1, Appendix B, at the end of this book. (You may wish to put a paper clip on the page.)
† Present annuity values from Table 2. (Incidentally, hand-held calculators may give slightly-different answers than tables.)
‡ Rounded.

Requirement 1 of our example will be used to demonstrate the net-present-value approach. Exhibit 12-1 shows a net present value of $264, so the investment is desirable. The manager would be able to invest $264 more, or a total of $6,338 (i.e., $6,074 + $264), and still earn 10 percent on the project.

The higher the minimum desired rate of return, the less the manager would be willing to invest in this project. At a rate of 16 percent, the net present value would be $−478 (i.e., $2,000 × 2.798 = $5,596, which is $478 less than the required investment of $6,074). (Present-value factor, 2.798, is taken from Table 2 at the end of this book.) When the desired rate of return is 16 percent, rather than 10 percent, the project is undesirable at a price of $6,074.

Assumptions of DCF Model

Before proceeding, consider the assumptions of the DCF model. First, the model assumes a world of certainty: you are absolutely sure that the predicted cash flows will occur at the times specified. Second, the model assumes that the original amount of the investment can be looked upon as being either borrowed or loaned at some specified rate of return.

The assumptions of certainty and the interest effects apply to the net-present-value DCF model as follows. The net present value of $264 (as computed in Exhibit 12-1) implies that if you borrowed $6,074 from a bank at 10 percent per annum, invested in the project, and repaid the loan with the project cash flows, you would accumulate the same net amount of money as if you deposited $264 in a savings institution at 10 percent interest.

Exhibit 12-2 demonstrates these relationships. Suppose that at time zero a friend offered you $264 for the project that you had invested in thirty seconds before and that he would assume the obligation to pay the bank loan. You accept and invest the $264 in a savings account at a compound interest rate of 10 percent per annum. In our assumed world of certainty, you would be serenely indifferent as between the two alternatives. Pause a moment and study Exhibit 12-2.

Internal Rate of Return

Now consider Requirement 2. The internal rate of return has been defined as "the maximum rate of interest that could be paid for the capital employed over the life of an investment without loss on the project."[1] This rate corresponds to the effective rate of interest so widely computed for bonds, purchased or sold at discounts or premiums. Alternatively, the internal rate of return can be defined as the discount rate that makes the present value of

---

[1] *Return on Capital as a Guide to Managerial Decisions,* National Association of Accountants, Research Report No. 35 (New York), p. 57.

EXHIBIT 12-2

Rationale Underlying Net-Present-Value Model

Same data as in Exhibit 12-1.

Alternative One: Invest and hold the project.

YEAR	(1) LOAN BALANCE AT BEGINNING OF YEAR	(2) INTEREST AT 10% PER YEAR	(3) (1) + (2) ACCUMULATED AMOUNT AT END OF YEAR	(4) CASH FOR REPAYMENT OF LOAN	(5) (3) − (4) LOAN BALANCE AT END OF YEAR
1	$6,074	$607	$6,681	$2,000	$4,681
2	4,681	468	5,149	2,000	3,149
3	3,149	315	3,464	2,000	1,464
4	1,464	146	1,610	2,000	390*

*After repayment of the final $1,610 loan installment, the investor in the project would have $390 left over from the $2,000 cash provided by the project at the end of the fourth year. Therefore, he would be $390 wealthier at the end of the fourth year.

Alternative Two: Invest, sell the project for $264 an instant after
inception, and deposit the $264 in a savings institution paying
10 percent interest compounded annually.

YEAR	(1) INVESTMENT BALANCE AT BEGINNING OF YEAR	(2) INTEREST AT 10% PER YEAR	(3) (1) + (2) ACCUMULATED AMOUNT AT END OF YEAR
1	$264	$26	$290
2	290	29	319
3	319	32	351
4	351	35	386†

†The investor would have the same amount of wealth at the end of four years as in Alternative One. The $4 difference between the $386 and the $390 in Alternative One is because of the accumulation of a number of small differences from rounding off amounts. Note especially that stating the net present value at $264 at time zero is *equivalent* to stating the future amount at $386. The investor is indifferent (given equal riskiness of the two choices) as to whether he has $264 today or $386 four years hence.

the anticipated cash flows from a project equal to the cost of the project.

The mechanics of computing the internal rate of return are not too imposing when the annual cash inflows are uniform. In Exhibit 12-3, the following equation is used:

$6,074 = Present value of annuity of $2,000 at X percent for 4 years, or what factor F in Table 2 (end of the book) will satisfy the following equation:

$6,074 = $2,000F

$$F = \frac{\$6,074}{\$2,000} = 3.037$$

EXHIBIT 12-3
Two Proofs of Internal Rate of Return

	PRESENT VALUE OF $1, DISCOUNTED AT 12%	TOTAL PRESENT VALUE	SKETCH OF CASH FLOWS AT END OF YEAR				
Original investment, $6,074 / Useful life, 4 years / Annual cash inflow from operations, $2,000 / Rate of return (selected by trial-and-error methods), 12 percent			0	1	2	3	4
Approach 1: Discounting Each Year's Cash Inflow Separately*							
Cash flows:							
Annual savings	.893	$ 1,786		$2,000			
	.797	1,594			$2,000		
	.712	1,424				$2,000	
	.636	1,272					$2,000
Present value of future inflows		$ 6,074†					
Initial outlay	1.000	(6,074)	$(6,074)				
Net present value (the zero difference proves that the rate of return is 12 percent)		$ 0					
Approach 2: Using Annuity Table‡							
Annual savings	3,037	$ 6,074		$2,000	$2,000	$2,000	$2,000
Initial outlay	1.000	(6,074)	$(6,074)				
Net present value		$ 0					

* Present values from Table 1, Appendix B, at the end of this book.
† Sum is really $6,076, but is rounded.
‡ Present values of annuity from Table 2, Appendix B, at the end of this book.
Compare Table 2 with Table 1 in Appendix B. Note that Table 1 is the fundamental table, and Table 2 can only be used as a short-cut when a series of uniform cash flows occur; that is, Table 2 accomplishes in one computation what Table 1 accomplishes in four computations. Table 2 is really compiled by using the basic present value factors in Table 1; for example, 3.037 is equal to the sum (rounded) of .893 + .797 + .712 + .636.

On the Period 4 line of Table 2, find the column that is closest to 3.037. It happens to be exactly 12 percent.

But suppose that the cash inflow were $1,800 instead of $2,000:

$$\$6,074 = \$1,800F$$

$$F = \frac{\$6,074}{\$1,800} = 3.374$$

On the Period 4 line of Table 2, the column closest to 3.374 is 8 percent. This may be close enough for most purposes. To obtain a more accurate rate, interpolation is needed:

Present-Value Factors

6%	3.465	3.465
True rate		3.374
8%	3.312	
Difference	.153	.091

$$\text{True rate} = 6\% + \frac{.091}{.153}\,(2\%) = 7.2\%$$

These hand computations become more complex when the cash inflows and outflows are not uniform. Then trial-and-error methods are needed. See the Appendix to this chapter for examples. Of course, in practice, canned computer programs are commonly available for such computations.

Meaning of Internal Rate

Exhibit 12-3 shows that $6,074 is the present value, at a rate of return of 12 percent, of a four-year stream of inflows of $2,000 in cash. Twelve percent is the rate that equates the amount invested ($6,074) with the present value of the cash inflows ($2,000 per year for four years). In other words, if money were borrowed at an effective interest rate of 12 percent, as Exhibit 12-4 shows, the cash inflow produced by the project would exactly repay the hypothetical loan plus the interest over the four years.

Exhibit 12-4 can be interpreted from either the borrower's or lender's vantage point. Suppose you borrowed $6,074 from a bank at an interest rate of 12 percent per annum, invested in the project, and repaid the loan with the project cash flows of $2,000 per year. Each $2,000 payment would represent

EXHIBIT 12-4

Rationale of Internal Rate of Return

Note: Same data as in Exhibit 12-3: Original investment, $6,074; Useful life, 4 years; Annual cash inflow from operations $2,000; Rate of return, 12 percent. Unrecovered investment at the beginning of each year earns interest for the whole year. Annual cash inflows are received at the end of each year.

YEAR	(1) LOAN BALANCE AT BEGINNING OF YEAR	(2) INTEREST AT 12% PER YEAR	(3) (1) + (2) ACCUMULATED AMOUNT AT END OF YEAR	(4) CASH FOR REPAYMENT OF LOAN	(5) (3) − (4) LOAN BALANCE AT END OF YEAR
1	$6,074	$729	$6,803	$2,000	$4,803
2	4,803	576	5,379	2,000	3,379
3	3,379	405	3,784	2,000	1,784
4	1,784	216*	2,000	2,000	0

* Rounded

357

interest of 12 percent plus a reduction of the loan balance. At a rate of 12 percent, the borrower would end up with an accumulated wealth of zero. Obviously, if he could borrow at 12 percent, and the project could generate cash at more than the 12 percent rate (that is, in excess of $2,000 annually), the borrower would be able to keep some cash—and the internal rate of return, *by definition,* would exceed 12 percent. Again the internal rate of return is that which would provide a net present value of zero (no more, no less).

Depreciation and Discounted Cash Flow

Students are often mystified by the apparent exclusion of depreciation from discounted-cash-flow computations. A common homework error is to deduct depreciation. This is a misunderstanding of one of the basic ideas involved in the concept of the discounting. Because the discounted-cash-flow approach is fundamentally based on inflows and outflows of *cash* and not on the *accrual* concepts of revenues and expenses, no adjustments should be made to the cash flows for the periodic allocation of cost called depreciation expense (which is not a cash flow). In the discounted-cash-flow approach, the initial cost of an asset is usually regarded as a *lump-sum* outflow of cash at time zero. Therefore, it is wrong to deduct depreciation from operating cash inflows before consulting present-value tables. To deduct periodic depreciation would be a double counting of a cost that has already been considered as a lump-sum outflow.

Review of Decision Rules

Review the basic ideas of discounted cash flow. The decision maker cannot readily compare an outflow of $6,074 with a series of future inflows of $2,000 each because the outflows and inflows do not occur simultaneously. The net-present-value model expresses all amounts in equivalent terms (in today's dollars at time zero). An interest rate is used to measure the decision maker's time preference for money. At a rate of 12 percent, the comparison can be shown as follows:

Outflow in today's dollars	$(6,074)
Inflow equivalent in today's dollars @ 12%	6,074
Net present value	$ 0

Therefore, at a time preference for money of 12 percent, the decision maker is indifferent about having $6,074 now or a stream of four annual inflows of $2,000 each. If the interest rate were 16 percent, the decision maker would find the project unattractive because the net present value would be negative:

Outflow	$(6,074)
Inflow equivalent in today's dollars @ 16% =	
$2,000 × 2.798 (from Table 2) =	5,596
Net present value	$(478)

We can summarize the decision rules offered by these two models as follows:

Net Present Value	*Internal Rate of Return*
1. Calculate the net present value, using the minimum desired rate of return as the discount rate.	1. Using present-value tables, compute the internal rate of return by trial-and-error interpolation.
2. If the net present value is zero or positive, accept the project; if negative, reject the project.	2. If this rate equals or exceeds the minimum desired rate of return, accept the project; if not, reject the project.

Two Simplifying Assumptions

Two simplifying assumptions are being made here and throughout this book:

a. For simplicity in the use of tables, all operating cash inflows or outflows are assumed to take place at the *end* of the years in question. This is unrealistic because such cash flows ordinarily occur irregularly throughout the given year, rather than in lump sums at the end of the year. Compound-interest tables especially tailored for these more realistic conditions are available, but we shall not consider them here.[2]

b. We assume that the cost of capital is known, is given; it is the minimum desired rate of return, an opportunity investment rate on alternative uses of the funds to be invested. The cost of capital is discussed more fully in the next section.

Choosing the Minimum Desired Rate

Depending on risk (that is, the degree of variability in the likely rate of return) and available alternatives, investors usually have some notion of a minimum rate of return that would make various projects desirable investments. This minimum rate is often called the *cost of capital, hurdle rate, cutoff rate, target rate,* or *discount rate.* The problem of choosing the minimum acceptable rate of return is complex and is really more a problem of finance[3] than of accounting. In this book we shall assume that the minimum acceptable rate of return is given to the accountant by management, and that it repre-

[2] See J. Bracken and C. Christenson, *Tables for Use In Analyzing Business Decisions.* (Homewood, Ill.: Richard D. Irwin, Inc.)

[3] For an excellent discussion, see the chapter on cost of capital in James C. Van Horne, *Financial Management and Policy,* 4th ed. (Englewood Cliffs, N.J.: Prentice-Hall, Inc., 1977).

sents the rate that can be earned by the best alternative uses of investment capital.

Note too that we concentrate here on the *investing* decisions, as distinguished from the *financing* decisions. That is, the minimum desired rate is not affected by whether the *specific project* is financed by all debt, all ownership capital, or some of both. Thus, the cost of capital is not "interest expense" on borrowed money as the accountant ordinarily conceives it. For example, a mortgage-free house still has a cost of capital—the maximum amount that could be earned with the proceeds if the house were sold.[4]

CAPITAL BUDGETING AND NONPROFIT ORGANIZATIONS

Religious, educational, health-care, governmental, and other nonprofit organizations face a variety of capital-budgeting decisions. Examples include investments in buildings, equipment, weapons systems, and research programs. Thus, even when no revenue is involved, organizations try to choose projects with the least cost for any given set of objectives.

The unsettled question of the appropriate discount rate plagues all types of organizations, profit-seeking and not-for-profit. One thing is certain: As New York City has discovered, capital is not cost-free. A discussion of the appropriate hurdle rate is beyond the scope of this book. Nearly all U.S. departments use 10 percent. It represents a crude approximation of the opportunity cost to the economy of having investments made by public agencies instead of by private organizations.[5]

Progress in management practices and in the use of sophisticated techniques has generally tended to be faster in profit-seeking organizations. Although DCF is used by federal departments, it is almost unknown at state and local levels of government. Thus, there are many opportunities to introduce improved analytical techniques. In general, managers have more opportunities in nonprofit than in profit-seeking organizations to contribute to improved decision making by introducing newer management decision models such as DCF.

[4] Avoid a piecemeal approach. It is near-sighted to think that the appropriate hurdle rate is the interest expense on any financing associated with a specific project. Under this faulty approach, a project will be accepted as long as its expected internal rate of return exceeds the interest rate on funds that might be borrowed to finance the project. Thus, a project will be desirable if it has an expected internal rate of 11 percent and a borrowing rate of 9 percent. The trouble here is that a series of such decisions will lead to a staggering debt that will cause the borrowing rate to skyrocket or will result in an inability to borrow at all. Conceivably, during the next year, some other project might have an expected internal rate of 16 percent and will have to be rejected, even though it is the most profitable in the series, because the heavy debt permits no further borrowing.

[5] See H. Bierman and S. Smidt, *The Capital Budgeting Decision,* 4th ed. (New York: The Macmillan Company, 1976), Chap. 16; R. Anthony and R. Herzlinger, *Management Control in Nonprofit Organizations* (Homewood, Ill.: Richard D. Irwin, Inc., 1975), pp. 200–202.

UNCERTAINTY AND SENSITIVITY ANALYSIS

No Single Way

In this and other chapters, we almost always work with the expected values (single dollar amounts) of cash flows in order to emphasize and simplify various important points. These cash flows are subject to varying degrees of risk or uncertainty, defined here as the possibility that the actual cash flow will deviate from the expected cash flow. Nevertheless, as a minimum, a manager must predict the probable outcome of various alternative projects. These expected values really should be analyzed in conjunction with probability distributions, as we see in Chapter 16. However, to stress the fundamental differences among various decision models, in this chapter we deal only with the expected values.

General Electric Company requires planners to use more than just a single number, such as return on investment or assets, to justify programs. "In the last five years we have come to realize that a single-number criterion doesn't work. People can make that number come out whatever way they want." [6]

An alternative to developing probability distributions of anticipated cash flows is to use elaborate screening devices in the early stages of the decision. Consider the Monsanto Company:

> Projects are initiated with greater care than in the past. For instance, 47 planning units within Monsanto's six operating companies prepare two-page business-direction papers, which include financial data such as rates of return, information of market shares and competition, as well as an analysis of technology in the field. Top corporate management and operating executives then sift through proposed capital programs and assign priorities. A three-year list of projects is maintained. At present, about 200 are on the drawing boards for 1977–79; each involves a minimum investment of $2 million and must be cleared by the board of directors. [7]

Other ways to allow for uncertainty include the use of (a) high minimum desired rate of return, (b) short expected useful lives, (c) pessimistic predictions of annual cash flows, (d) simultaneous comparisons of optimistic, pessimistic, and best-guess predictions, and (e) sensitivity analysis. [8] Sensitivity analysis is a "what-if" technique that measures how the expected values in a decision model will be affected by changes in the data. In the context of capital budgeting, sensitivity analysis answers the question: "How

---

[6] "The Opposites: GE Grows While Westinghouse Shrinks," *Business Week,* January 31, 1977, p. 64.

[7] *Wall Street Journal,* December 30, 1976, pp. 1, 7.

[8] For a survey of how firms deal with uncertainty, see J. Fremgen, "Capital Budgeting Practices: A Survey," *Management Accounting* (May 1973), pp. 19-25.

will my internal rate of return or net present value be changed if my predictions of useful life or the cash flows are inaccurate?"

Applying Sensitivity Analysis

Although sensitivity analysis may be conducted at any time, it is usually conducted before a decision is made. Suppose in Exhibit 12-1 that the cash inflows were $1,500 annually instead of $2,000. What would be the net present value? The annuity factor of 3.170 would be multiplied by $1,500, producing a gross present value of $4,755 and a negative net present value of $4,755 − $6,074, or $ − 1,319. Alternatively, management may want to know how far cash inflows will have to fall to break even on the investment. In this context, "break even" means the point of indifference, the point where the net present value is zero. Let X = annual cash inflows and let net present value = 0; then

$$0 = 3.170(X) - 6,074$$

$$X = \frac{6,074}{3.170} = \$1,916$$

Thus, cash inflows can drop only $84 ($2,000 − $1,916) annually to reach the point of indifference regarding the investment.

Another critical factor is useful life. If useful life were only three years, the gross present value would be $2,000 multiplied by 2.487 (from the Period 3 row in Table 2, Appendix B) or $4,974, again producing a negative net present value, $4,974 − $6,074, or $ − 1,100.

These calculations can also be used in testing the sensitivity of rates of return. As we saw in the section on "Internal Rate of Return," a fall in the annual cash inflow from $2,000 to $1,800 reduces the rate of return from 12 percent to 7.2 percent.

Of course, sensitivity analysis works both ways. It can measure the potential increases in net present value or rate of return as well as the decreases. The major contribution of sensitivity analysis is that it provides an immediate financial measure of the consequences of possible errors in forecasting. Therefore, it can be very useful because it helps focus on decisions that may be very sensitive indeed, and it eases the manager's mind about decisions that are not so sensitive.

In addition, sensitivity analysis is applicable to the comparison of various capital-budgeting decision models. In other words, the results under the discounted-cash-flow model may be compared to the results, using the same basic data, generated under simpler models such as payback and accounting rate of return (discussed later in this chapter).

THE NET-PRESENT-VALUE COMPARISON
OF TWO PROJECTS

Incremental versus Total Project Approach

The mechanics of compound interest may appear formidable to those readers who are encountering them for the first time. However, a little practice with the interest tables should easily clarify the mechanical aspect. More important, we shall now combine some relevant cost analysis with the discounted-cash-flow approach. Consider the following example:

A company owns a packaging machine, which was purchased three years ago for $56,000. It has a remaining useful life of five years but will require a major overhaul at the end of two more years at a cost of $10,000. Its disposal value now is $20,000; in five years its disposal value is expected to be $8,000, assuming that the $10,000 major overhaul will be done on schedule. The cash operating costs of this machine are expected to be $40,000 annually.

A salesman has offered a substitute machine for $51,000, or for $31,000 plus the old machine. The new machine will reduce annual cash operating costs by $10,000, will not require any overhauls, will have a useful life of five years, and will have a disposal value of $3,000.

Required

Assume that the minimum desired rate of return is 14 percent. Using the net-present-value technique, show whether the new machine should be purchased, using: (1) a total project approach; (2) an incremental approach. Try to solve before examining the solution.

A difficult part of long-range decision making is the structuring of the data. We want to see the effects of each alternative on future cash flows. The focus here is on bona fide cash transactions, not on opportunity costs. Using an opportunity-cost approach may yield the same answers, but repeated classroom experimentation with various analytical methods has convinced the author that the following steps are likely to be the clearest:

Step 1. Arrange the relevant cash flows by project, so that a sharp distinction is made between total project flows and incremental flows. The incremental flows are merely algebraic differences between two alternatives. (There are always at least two alternatives. One is the status quo—i.e., doing nothing.) Exhibit 12-5 shows how the cash flows for each alternative are sketched.

Step 2. Discount the expected cash flows and choose the project with the least cost or the greatest benefit. Both the total project approach and the incremental approach are illustrated in Exhibit 12-5; which one you use is a matter of preference. However, to develop confidence in this area, you should work with both at the start. One approach can serve as proof of the accuracy of the other. In this example, the $8,425 net difference in favor of replacement is the ultimate result under either approach.

EXHIBIT 12-5

Total Project versus Incremental Approach to Net Present Value

	PRESENT-VALUE DISCOUNT FACTOR, @ 14%	TOTAL PRESENT VALUE	\multicolumn{6}{c}{SKETCH OF CASH FLOWS AT END OF YEAR}
			0	1	2	3	4	5
TOTAL PROJECT APPROACH								
A. Replace								
Recurring cash operating costs, using an annuity table*	3.433	$(102,990)		($30,000)	($30,000)	($30,000)	($30,000)	($30,000)
Disposal value, end of Year 5	.519	1,557						3,000
Initial required investment	1.000	(31,000)	($31,000)					
Present value of net cash outflows		$(132,433)						
B. Keep								
Recurring cash operating costs, using an annuity table*	3.433	$(137,320)		($40,000)	($40,000)	($40,000)	($40,000)	($40,000)
Overhaul, end of Year 2	.769	(7,690)			(10,000)			
Disposal value, end of Year 5	.519	4,152						8,000
Present value of net cash outflows		$(140,858)						
Difference in favor of replacement		$ 8,425						
INCREMENTAL APPROACH								
A – B Analysis Confined to Differences								
Recurring cash operating savings, using an annuity table*	3.433	$ 34,330		$10,000	$10,000	$10,000	$10,000	$10,000
Overhaul avoided, end of Year 2	.769	7,690			$10,000			
Difference in disposal values, end of Year 5	.519	(2,595)						(5,000)
Incremental initial investment	1.000	(31,000)	($31,000)					
Net present value of replacement		$ 8,425						

*Table 2 at end of book.

Analysis of Typical Items
under Discounted Cash Flow

1. Future disposal values. The disposal value at the date of termination of a project is an increase in the cash inflow in the year of disposal. Errors in forecasting terminal disposal values are usually not crucial because the present value is usually small.

2. Current disposal values and required investment. There are a number of correct ways to analyze this item, all having the same ultimate effect on the decision. Probably the simplest way was illustrated in Exhibit 12-5, where the $20,000 was offset against the $51,000 purchase price, and the actual cash outgo was shown. Generally, the required investment is most easily measured by offsetting the current disposal value of the old assets against the gross cost of the new assets.

3. Investments in receivables and inventories. Investments in receivables, inventories, and intangible assets are basically no different than investments in plant and equipment. In the discounted-cash-flow model, the initial outlays are entered in the sketch of cash flows at time zero. At the end of the useful life of the project, the original outlays for machines may not be recouped at all or may be partially recouped in the amount of the salvage values. In contrast, the entire original investments in receivables and inventories are usually recouped. Therefore, except that their expected "disposal" values are different, all investments are typically regarded as outflows at time zero, and their terminal disposal values are regarded as inflows at the end of the project's useful life.

Thus, the expansion of a retail store entails an additional investment in a building and fixtures *plus* inventories. Such investments would be shown in the format of Exhibit 12-5 as follows (numbers assumed):

SKETCH OF CASH FLOWS

End of Year	0	1	2	19	20
Investment in building and fixtures	(10)				1
Investment in working capital (inventories)	(6)				6

As the sketch shows, the residual value of the building and fixtures might be small. However, the entire investment in inventories would ordinarily be recouped when the venture was terminated.

4. Book value and depreciation. Depreciation is a phenomenon of accrual accounting that entails an allocation of cost, not a specific cash outlay. Depreciation and book value are ignored in discounted-cash-flow approaches for the reasons mentioned earlier in this chapter.

5. Income taxes. In practice, comparison between alternatives is best made after considering tax effects, because the tax impact may alter the picture. (The effects of income taxes are considered in Chapter 13 and may be studied now if desired.)

6. Overhead analysis. In relevant-cost analysis, only the overhead that will differ among alternatives is pertinent. There is need for careful study of the fixed overhead under the available alternatives. In practice, this is an extremely difficult phase of cost analysis, because it is hard to relate the individual costs to any single project.

7. Unequal lives. Where projects have unequal lives, comparisons may be made over the useful life either of the longer-lived project or of the shorter-lived one. For our purposes, we will estimate what the residual values will be at the end of the longer-lived project. We must also assume a reinvestment at the end of the shorter-lived project. This makes sense primarily because the decision maker should extend his time horizon as far as possible. If he is considering a longer-lived project, he should give serious consideration to what would be done in the time interval between the termination dates of the shorter-lived and longer-lived projects.

8. Mutually exclusive projects. When the projects are mutually exclusive, so that the acceptance of one automatically entails the rejection of the other (e.g., buying Dodge or Ford trucks), the project that maximizes wealth measured in net present value in dollars should be undertaken.

9. A word of caution. The foregoing material has been an *introduction* to the area of capital budgeting, which is, in practice, complicated by a variety of factors: unequal lives; major differences in the size of alternative investments; peculiarities in internal rate-of-return computations; various ways of allowing for uncertainty (see Chapter 16); changes, over time, in desired rates of return; the indivisibility of projects in relation to a fixed overall capital-budget appropriation; and more. These niceties are beyond the scope of this introduction to capital budgeting, but the Suggested Readings at the end of the chapter will help you pursue the subject in more depth.

CAPITAL BUDGETING AND INFLATION

As we have observed in our everyday living, inflation—the decline in the general purchasing power of the monetary unit—is pervasive and persistent. Investors typically cope with the risks of inflation by increasing their hurdle rate to incorporate their expected rate of inflation. For instance, if 8 percent inflation is expected, a hurdle rate of 10 percent without inflation becomes 18 percent with inflation.

DCF models should be adjusted for expected inflation in an internally consistent fashion. That is, if the discount rate of, say, 18 percent includes an element attributable to expected inflation, the predicted annual cash flows should also be adjusted for expected inflation. A common error is to adjust only one of the two factors. Both the *hurdle rate* and the *annual cash flows* should be adjusted.

The adjustment of the annual cash flow is made by either (a) using a general price-level index or (b) preferably using a specific index such as a wage index or a materials index. For example, suppose that a hospital is contemplating the purchase of some new dishwashing equipment that will save labor costs of $20,000 per year in terms of 19x0 dollars. If a 10 percent rise in labor rates is expected each year, the savings in 19x1 would be shown as $20,000 × 1.10 = $22,000; in 19x2 as $20,000 × (1.10)² = $24,200; and so forth.

The foregoing method expresses predictions in terms of the monetary units (the then-current dollars) that are supposed to appear at any given time. In this way, subsequent auditing of the capital budgeting is straight-forward.[9]

OTHER MODELS FOR ANALYZING LONG-RANGE DECISIONS

Although discounted-cash-flow models for business decisions are being increasingly used, they are still relatively new, having been developed and applied for the first time on any wide scale in the 1950s. There are other models with which the manager should be at least somewhat familiar, because they are entrenched in many businesses.[10]

[9] Another way of allowing for inflation is to think in terms of "real" monetary units (real dollars) exclusively. To be consistent, the DCF model would use an inflation-free hurdle rate plus inflation-free annual cash flows. Using the above numbers, the 18 percent hurdle rate would be lowered to exclude the expected inflation rate, the $20,000 labor savings in 19x0 dollars would be used in 19x1, 19x2, and so forth. Properly used, both ways lead to the same net present values. See Bierman and Smidt, *The Capital Budgeting Decision*, Chap. 13.

[10] Thomas Klammer, "Empirical Evidence of the Adoption of Sophisticated Capital Budgeting Techniques," *The Journal of Business*, Vol. VL, No. 3 (October 1972), surveyed 369 large firms and received 184 responses. Fifty-seven percent of the firms responding indicated that they use discounted-cash-flow techniques in 1970, as compared with only 19 percent in 1959:

	Percentage Using in:		
	1970	*1964*	*1959*
Discounting	57	38	19
Accounting rate of return	26	30	34
Payback	12	24	34
Urgency	5	8	13
	100	100	100

For a description of practices in the 1970s, see S. Hayes, "Capital Commitments and the High Cost of Money," *Harvard Business Review*, Vol. 55, No. 3 (May–June 1977), pp. 155–61.

These models, which we are about to explain, are conceptually inferior to discounted-cash-flow approaches. Then why do we bother studying them? First, because changes in business practice occur slowly. Second, because where older models such as payback are in use, they should be used properly, even if better models are available. The situation is similar to using a pocket knife instead of a scalpel for removing a person's appendix. If the pocket knife is used by a knowledgeable and skilled surgeon, the chances for success are much better than if it is used by a bumbling layman.

Of course, as always, the accountant and manager face a cost and value-of-information decision when they choose a decision model. Reluctance to use discounted-cash-flow models may be justified if the more familiar payback model or other models lead to the same investment decisions.

One existing technique may be called the **emergency-persuasion method.** No formal planning is used. Fixed assets are operated until they crumble, product lines are carried until they are obliterated by competition, and requests by a manager for authorization of capital outlays are judged on the basis of his past operating performance regardless of its relevance to the decision at hand. These approaches to capital budgeting are examples of the unscientific management that often leads to bankruptcy.

Payback Model

Payback, or **payout,** or **payoff,** is the measure of the time it will take to recoup, in the form of cash inflow from operations, the initial dollars of outlay. Assume that $12,000 is spent for a machine with an estimated useful life of eight years. Annual savings of $4,000 in cash outflow are expected from operations. Depreciation is ignored. The payback calculations follow:

$$P = \frac{I}{O} = \frac{\$12,000}{\$4,000} = 3 \text{ years} \tag{1}$$

where P is the payback time, I is the initial incremental amount of outlay, and O is the uniform annual incremental cash inflow from operations.

The payback model merely measures how quickly investment dollars may be recouped; it does *not* measure profitability. This is its major weakness, because a shorter payback time does not necessarily mean that one project is preferable to another.

For instance, assume that an alternative to the $12,000 machine is a $10,000 machine whose operation will also result in a reduction of $4,000 annually in cash outflow. Then

$$P_1 = \frac{\$12,000}{\$4,000} = 3.0 \text{ years}$$

$$P_2 = \frac{\$10,000}{\$4,000} = 2.5 \text{ years}$$

The payback criterion indicates that the $10,000 machine is more desirable. However, one fact about the $10,000 machine has been purposely withheld. Its useful life is only 2.5 years. Ignoring the impact of compound interest for the moment, the $10,000 machine results in zero benefit, while the $12,000 machine generates cash inflows for five years beyond its payback period.

The main objective in investing is profit, not the recapturing of the initial outlay. If a company wants to recover its outlay fast, it need not spend in the first place. Then no waiting time is necessary; the payback time is zero. When a wealthy investor was assured by the promotor of a risky oil venture that he would have his money back within two years, the investor replied, "I already have my money."

The payback approach may also be applied to the data in Exhibit 12-5. What is the payback time?

$$P = \frac{I}{O} = \frac{\$31,000}{\$10,000} = 3.1 \text{ years}$$

However, the formula may be used with assurance only when there are uniform cash inflows from operations. In this instance, $10,000 is saved by avoiding an overhaul at the end of the second year. When cash inflows are not uniform, the payback computation must take a cumulative form—that is, each year's net cash flows are accumulated until the initial investment is recouped:

Year	Initial Investment	Net Cash Inflows	
		Each Year	Accumulated
0	$31,000	—	—
1	—	$10,000	$10,000
2	—	20,000	30,000
2.1	—	1,000	31,000

The payback time is slightly beyond the second year. Straight-line interpolation within the third year reveals that the final $1,000 needed to recoup the investment would be forthcoming in 2.1 years.

Accounting Rate-of-Return Model

The label for this model or method is not uniform. It is also known as the *unadjusted rate-of-return model,* the *financial-statement model,* the *book-value model,* the *rate-of-return on assets model,* and the *approximate rate-of-return model.* Its computations supposedly dovetail most closely with conventional accounting models of calculating income and required investment. However, the dovetailing objective is not easily attained, because the purposes of the computations differ. The most troublesome aspects are depreciation and decisions concerning capitalization versus expense. For example, advertising and research are usually expensed, even though they often may be viewed as long-range investments.

The equations for the accounting rate of return are:

$$\text{Accounting rate of return} = \frac{\text{Increase in future average annual net income}}{\text{Initial increase in required investment}} \quad (2)$$

$$R = \frac{O - D}{I} \quad (3)$$

where R is the average annual rate of return on initial additional investment, O is the average annual incremental cash inflow from operations, D is the incremental average annual depreciation, and I is the initial incremental amount invested.

Assume the same facts as in our payback illustration: cost of machine, $12,000; useful life, eight years; estimated disposal value, zero; and expected annual savings in annual cash outflow from operations, $4,000. Annual depreciation would be $12,000 \div 8 = \$1,500$. Substitute these values in Equation (3):

$$R = \frac{\$4,000 - \$1,500}{\$12,000} = 20.8\%$$

Weighing Dollars Differently

The accounting model ignores the time value of money. Expected future dollars are unrealistically and erroneously regarded as equal to present dollars. The discounted-cash-flow model explicitly allows for the force of interest and the exact timing of cash flows. In contrast, the accounting model is based on *annual averages*. To illustrate, consider a petroleum company with three potential projects to choose from: an expansion of an existing gasoline station, an investment in an oil well, and the purchase of a new gasoline station. To simplify the calculations, assume a three-year life for each project. Exhibit 12-6 summarizes the comparisons. Note that the accounting rate of return would indicate that all three projects are equally desirable and that the internal rate of return properly discriminates in favor of earlier cash inflows.

Thus, the conflict of purposes is highlighted in Exhibit 12-6. The accounting model utilizes concepts of capital and income that were originally designed for the quite different purpose of accounting for periodic income and financial position. In the accounting model, the initial capital calculation is subject to questionable asset-versus-expense decisions (e.g., allocation of costs of research or of sales promotion outlays), while the effects of interest

EXHIBIT 12-6

Comparison of Accounting Rates of Return
and Internal Rates of Return

	EXPANSION OF EXISTING GASOLINE STATION	INVESTMENT IN AN OIL WELL	PURCHASE OF NEW GASOLINE STATION
Initial investment	$ 90,000	$ 90,000	$ 90,000
Cash inflows from operations:			
Year 1	$ 40,000	$ 80,000	$ 20,000
Year 2	40,000	30,000	40,000
Year 3	40,000	10,000	60,000
Totals	$120,000	$120,000	$120,000
Average annual cash inflow	$ 40,000	$ 40,000	$ 40,000
Less: Average annual depreciation			
($90,000 ÷ 3)	30,000	30,000	30,000
Increase in average annual net income	$ 10,000	$ 10,000	$ 10,000
Accounting rate of return on initial investment	11.1%	11.1%	11.1%
Internal rate of return, using discounted-cash-flow techniques	16.0%*	23.2%*	13.8%*

*Computed by trial-and-error approaches using Tables 1 and 2 at the end of the book. See the Appendix to this chapter for a detailed explanation.

on the timing of cash flows are ignored. The resulting accounting rate of return may be far from the real mark.[11]

However, the accounting model usually facilitates follow-up, because the same approach is used in the forecast as is used in the accounts. Yet exceptions to this ideal situation often occur, commonly arising from the inclusion in the forecast of some initial investment items that are not handled in the same manner in the subsequent accounting records. For example, the accounting for trade-ins and disposal values varies considerably. In practice, spot checks are frequently used on key items.

Conflict of Models

Many managers are reluctant to accept DCF models as the best way to make capital-budgeting decisions. Their reluctance stems from the wide usage of the accrual accounting model for evaluating performance. That is, managers become frustrated if they are instructed to use a DCF model for making

[11]For illustrations of the details, subtleties, and complexities of the unadjusted (accounting) rate of return see Charles T. Horngren, *Cost Accounting: A Managerial Emphasis,* 4th ed. (Englewood Cliffs, N.J.: Prentice-Hall, Inc., 1977), Chaps. 11 and 12.

decisions that are evaluated later by a non-DCF model, such as the typical accrual accounting rate-of-return model.

To illustrate, consider the potential conflict that might arise in the first example of this chapter. Recall that the expected rate of return was 12 percent, based on an outlay of $6,074 that would generate cash savings of $2,000 for each of four years and no terminal disposal value. Under accrual accounting, using straight-line depreciation, the first-year evaluation of performance would be:

Cash operating savings	$2,000
Straight-line depreciation,	
$6,074 ÷ 4 =	1,519
Effect on net income	$ 481
Accounting rate of return	
on initial book value,	
$481 ÷ $6,074 =	7.9%

Given the above facts, many managers of profit-seeking organizations (where performance is evaluated by accrual accounting models) would be inclined against replacing the equipment despite the internal rate of 12 percent. Such negative inclinations are especially likely where managers are transferred to new positions every year or two. As Chapter 5 indicated, the reluctance to replace is reinforced (see Problem 5-2) if a heavy book loss on old equipment would appear in Year 1's accrual income statement—even though such a loss would be irrelevant in a properly constructed decision model.

Reconciliation of Conflict

How can the foregoing conflict be reconciled? An obvious solution would be to use the same model for decisions and for evaluating performance. The accrual accounting model is often dominant for evaluating all sorts of performance; that is why many organizations use it for both purposes and do not use a DCF model at all. Critics claim that this nonuse of DCF may lead to many instances of poor capital-budgeting decisions.

Another obvious solution would be to use DCF for both capital-budgeting decisions and the performance evaluation audit. Several organizations use sampling procedures to perform such audits. A major reason for not auditing all capital-budgeting decisions routinely is that most accounting systems are designed to evaluate operating performances of products, departments, divisions, territories, and so on. In contrast, capital-budgeting decisions frequently deal with individual *projects,* not the collection of projects that are usually being managed simultaneously by divisional or department managers.

Some companies have solved the conflict by a dual approach. Managers use both the DCF model and the accrual accounting model at decision-making time. The decision is based on the DCF model, but the performance evaluation is tied back to the accrual accounting model.

The conflicts between the long-standing, pervasive accrual accounting model and various formal decision models represent one of the most serious unsolved problems in the design of management control systems. Top management cannot expect goal congruence if it favors the use of one collection of models for decisions and the use of other models for performance evaluation.[12]

SUMMARY

Product costing, income determination, and the planning and controlling of operations have a current-time-period orientation. Special decisions and long-range planning have primarily a project orientation. There is a danger in using ordinary accounting data for special purposes. Discounted-cash-flow techniques have been developed for the making of special decisions and for long-range planning because the time value of money becomes extremely important when projects extend beyond one or two years.

The field of capital budgeting is important because lump-sum expenditures on long-life projects have far-reaching effects on profit and on a business's flexibility. It is imperative that management develop its plans carefully and base them on reliable forecasting procedures. Capital budgeting is long-term planning for proposed capital outlays and their financing. Projects are accepted if their rate of return exceeds a minimum desired rate of return.

Because the discounted-cash-flow model explicitly and automatically weighs the time value of money, it is the best method to use for long-range decisions. The overriding goal is maximum long-run net cash inflows.

The discounted-cash-flow model has two variations: internal rate of return and net present value. Both models take into account the timing of cash flows and are thus superior to other methods.

The payback model is a popular approach to capital-spending decisions. It is simple and easily understood, but it neglects profitability.

The accounting rate-of-return model is also widely used in capital budgeting, although it is conceptually inferior to discounted-cash-flow models. It fails to recognize explicitly the time value of money. Instead, the accounting model depends on averaging techniques that may yield inaccurate answers, particularly when cash flows are not uniform through the life of a project.

A serious practical impediment to the adoption of discounted-cash-flow models is the widespread use of conventional accrual models for evaluating

---

[12]See Horngren, *Cost Accounting*, Chap. 23, for a fuller discussion.

performance. Frequently, the optimal decision under discounted cash flow will not produce a good showing in the early years, when performance is computed under conventional accounting methods. For example, heavy depreciation charges and the expensing rather than capitalizing of initial development costs will hurt reported income for the first year.

SUMMARY PROBLEM FOR YOUR REVIEW

Problem

Review the problem and solution shown in Exhibit 12-5. Conduct a sensitivity analysis as indicated below. Consider each requirement as independent of other requirements.

1. Compute the net present value if the minimum desired rate of return were 20 percent.

2. Compute the net present value if predicted cash operating costs were $35,000 instead of $30,000.

3. By how much may the cash operating savings fall before reaching the point of indifference, the point where the net present value of the project is zero, using the original discount rate of 14 percent?

Solution

1. Either the total project or the incremental approach could be used. The incremental approach would show:

	Total Present Value
Recurring cash operating savings, using an annuity table (Table 2): 2.991 × $10,000 =	$29,910
Overhaul avoided: .694 × $10,000 =	6,940
Difference in disposal values: .402 × $5,000 =	(2,010)
Incremental initial investment	(31,000)
Net present value of replacement	$ 3,840

2. Net present value in Exhibit 12-5 .... $ 8,425

Present value of original $10,000 annual cash operating savings, given in Exhibit 12-5	$34,330	
Present value of reduced savings of $5,000, which is 50 percent of above	17,165	
Decrease in net present value		17,165
New net present value		$(8,740)

3. Let x = annual cash operating savings and let net present value = 0. Then

$$0 = 3.433(x) + \$7,690 - \$2,595 - \$31,000$$
$$3.433x = \$25,905$$
$$x = \$ 7,546$$

(Note that the $7,690, $2,595, and $31,000 are at the bottom of Exhibit 12-5.)

If the annual savings fall from $10,000 to $7,546, a decrease of $2,454, the point of indifference will be reached.

An alternative way to obtain the same answer would be to divide the net present value of $8,425 (see bottom of Exhibit 12-5) by 3.433, obtaining $2,454, the amount of the annual difference in savings that will eliminate the $8,425 of net present value.

APPENDIX 12:
CALCULATIONS OF INTERNAL RATES
OF RETURN

Expansion of Existing Gasoline Station

(Data are from Exhibit 12-6.)

$90,000 = Present value of annuity of $40,000 at x percent for three years, or what factor F in the table of the present values of an annuity will satisfy the following equation:

$90,000 = $40,000F$

$F = $90,000 \div $40,000 = 2.250$

Now, on the Year 3 line of Table 2 at the end of the book, find the column that is closest to 2.250. You will find that 2.250 is extremely close to a rate of return of 16 percent—so close that straight-line interpolation is unnecessary between 14 percent and 16 percent. Therefore, the internal rate of return is 16 percent.

Investment in an Oil Well

Trial-and-error methods must be used to calculate the rate of return that will equate the future cash flows with the $90,000 initial investment. As a start, note that the 16 percent rate was applicable to a uniform annual cash inflow. But now use Table 1 (end of the book) because the flows are not uniform, and try a higher rate, 22 percent, because you know that the cash inflows are coming in more quickly than under the uniform inflow:

		Trial at 22 Percent		Trial at 24 Percent	
Year	Cash Inflows	Present-Value Factor	Total Present Value	Present-Value Factor	Total Present Value
1	$80,000	.820	$65,600	.806	$64,480
2	30,000	.672	20,160	.650	19,500
3	10,000	.551	5,510	.524	5,240
			$91,270		$89,220

The true rate lies somewhere between 22 and 24 percent and can be approximated by straight-line interpolation:

Interpolation	Total Present Values	
22%	$91,270	$91,270
True rate		90,000
24%	89,220	
Difference	$ 2,050	$ 1,270

Therefore

$$\text{True rate: } = 22\% + \frac{1,270}{2,050} \times 2\%$$

$$= 22\% + 1.2\% = 23.2\%$$

Purchase of a New Gasoline Station

In contrast to the oil-well project, this venture will have slowly increasing cash inflows. The trial rate should be much lower than the 16 percent rate applicable to the expansion project. Let us try 12 percent:

		Trial at 12 Percent		Trial at 14 Percent	
Year	Cash Inflows	Present-Value Factor	Total Present Value	Present-Value Factor	Total Present Value
1	$20,000	.893	$17,860	.877	$17,540
2	40,000	.797	31,880	.769	30,760
3	60,000	.712	42,720	.675	40,500
			$92,460		$88,800

Interpolation	Total Present Values	
12%	$92,460	$92,460
True rate		90,000
14%	88,800	
	$ 3,660	$ 2,460

$$\text{True rate } = 12\% + \frac{2,460}{3,660} \times 2\%$$

$$= 12\% + 1.3\% = 13.3\%$$

ASSIGNMENT MATERIAL

Special Note: **Ignore income taxes. The effects of income taxes are considered in Chapter 13.**

Fundamental Assignment Material

12-1. Terminology. Define: *capital budgeting; internal rate of return; net-present-value method; payback; payout; payoff; accounting rate of return; accounting method; book-value method; total project approach;* and *incremental approach.*

12-2. Exercises in compound interest: answers supplied.[13] Use the appropriate interest tables to compute the following:

a. It is your sixty-fifth birthday. You plan to work five more years before retiring. Then you want to take $5,000 for a round-the-world tour. What lump sum do you have to invest now in order to accumulate the $5,000? Assume that your minimum desired rate of return is:
   (1) 4 percent, compounded annually.
   (2) 10 percent, compounded annually.
   (3) 20 percent, compounded annually.
b. You want to spend $500 on a vacation at the end of each of the next five years. What lump sum do you have to invest now in order to take the five vacations? Assume that your minimum desired rate of return is:
   (1) 4 percent, compounded annually.
   (2) 10 percent, compounded annually.
   (3) 20 percent, compounded annually.
c. At age sixty, you find that your employer is moving to another location. You receive termination pay of $5,000. You have some savings and wonder whether to retire now.
   (1) If you invest the $5,000 now at 4 percent, compounded annually, how much money can you withdraw from your account each year so that at the end of five years there will be a zero balance?
   (2) If you invest it at 10 percent?
d. At 16 percent, compounded annually, which of the following plans is more desirable in terms of present values? Show computations to support your answer.

	Annual Cash Inflows	
Year	Mining	Farming
1	$10,000	$ 2,000
2	8,000	4,000
3	6,000	6,000
4	4,000	8,000
5	2,000	10,000
	$30,000	$30,000

[13]The answers appear at the end of the assignment material for this chapter.

12-3. Comparison of capital-budgeting techniques. The Putnam Company is considering the purchase of a new packaging machine at a cost of $20,000. It should save $4,000 in cash operating costs per year. Its estimated useful life is eight years, and it will have zero disposal value.

Required

1. What is the payback time?
2. Compute the net present value if the minimum rate of return desired is 10 percent. Should the company buy? Why?
3. Establish the internal rate of return.

12-4. Sensitivity analysis. The Midwest Railroad is considering the replacement of an old power jack tamper used in the maintenance of track with a new improved version that should save $5,000 per year in net cash operating costs. The old equipment has zero disposal value, but it could be used for the next twelve years. The estimated useful life of the new equipment is twelve years and it will cost $25,000.

Required

1. What is the payback time?
2. Compute the internal rate of return.
3. Management is unsure about the useful life. What would be the rate of return if the useful life were (a) six years instead of twelve and (b) twenty years instead of twelve?
4. Suppose the life will be twelve years but the savings will be $3,000 per year instead of $5,000. What would be the rate of return?
5. Suppose the annual savings will be $4,000 for eight years. What would be the rate of return?

Additional Assignment Material

12-5. "The higher the interest rate, the less I worry about errors in predicting terminal values." Do you agree? Explain.

12-6. "Double counting occurs if depreciation is separately considered in discounted-cash-flow analysis." Do you agree? Explain.

12-7. "Problem solving is project-oriented rather than time-period-oriented." Explain.

12-8. Why is capital budgeting likely to receive increasing attention?

12-9. Why is discounted cash flow a superior method for capital budgeting?

12-10. Why should depreciation be excluded from discounted-cash-flow computations?

12-11. Can net present value ever be negative? Why?

12-12. "The higher the minimum rate of return desired, the higher the price that a company will be willing to pay for cost-saving equipment." Do you agree? Explain.

12-13. Why should the incremental approach to alternatives always lead to the same decision as the total project approach?

12-14. "Current disposal values of equipment are always relevant to a replacement decision." Do you agree? Explain.

12-15. "Discounted-cash-flow approaches will not work if the competing projects have unequal lives." Do you agree? Explain.

12-16. Some perceptive observer in ancient times said, "A little knowledge is a dangerous thing." How might this apply in capital budgeting?

12-17. State a rule that can serve as a general guide to capital budgeting decisions.

12-18. "If discounted-cash-flow approaches are superior to the payback and the accounting methods, why should we bother to learn the others? All it does is confuse things." Answer this contention.

12-19. What is the basic flaw in the payback model?

12-20. How can the payback model be helpful in capital budgeting?

12-21. Compare the accounting rate-of-return approach and the discounted-cash-flow approach to the consideration of the time value of money.

12-22. **New equipment.** The Acme Company has offered to sell some new packaging equipment to the Zenith Company. The list price is $40,000, but Acme has agreed to accept some old equipment in trade. A trade-in allowance of $6,000 was agreed upon. The old equipment was carried at a book value of $7,700 and could be sold outright for $5,000 cash. Cash operating savings are expected to be $5,000 annually for the next twelve years. The minimum desired rate of return is 12 percent. The old equipment has a remaining useful life of twelve years. Both the old and new equipment will have zero disposal values twelve years from now.

Required

Should Zenith buy the new equipment? Show your computations, using the net-present-value method. Ignore income taxes.

12-23. **Illustration of trial-and-error method of computing rate of return.** Study Exhibit 12-3. Suppose the annual cash inflow will be $2,500 rather than $2,000.

Required

What is the internal rate of return?

12-24. **Assumptions of DCF Model.** (R. Jaffee.) A superintendent of a school district has asked you to explain the assumptions underlying the discounted-cash-flow model. He has just learned the *mechanics* of calculating net present value, but he is unclear on its *meaning* and its implications for financial analysis.

Prepare a memorandum of explanation for the superintendent, using an example of an initial investment of $1,000, a project life of three years, and an operating cash savings of $500 at the end of each of the three years. Assume that the minimum desired rate of return is 10 percent. Use Exhibit 12-2 as a guide for preparing your presentation. The superintendent admires clarity.

12-25. Replacement of equipment. Refer to Problem 5-2. Assume that the new equipment will cost $100,000 in cash, and that the old machine cost $81,000 and can be sold now for $16,000 cash.

Required

1. Compute the net present value of the proposed investment in new equipment, assuming that the minimum desired rate of return is 10 percent.
2. What will be the internal rate of return?
3. How long is the payback period on the incremental investment?

12-26. Discounted cash flow, uneven revenue stream, relevant costs. Mr. Divot, the owner of a nine-hole golf course on the outskirts of a large city, is considering the proposal that this course be illuminated and operated at night. Mr. Divot purchased the course early last year for $75,000. His receipts from operations during the 28-week season were $24,000. Total disbursements for the year, for all purposes, were $15,500.

The required investment in lighting this course is estimated at $20,000. The system will require 150 lamps of 1,000 watts each. Electricity costs 3.2¢ per kilowatt-hour. The expected average hours of operation per night is five. Because of occasional bad weather and the probable curtailment of night operation at the beginning and end of the season, it is estimated that there will be only 130 nights of operation per year. Labor for keeping the course open at night will cost $15 per night. Lamp renewals are estimated at $300 per year; other maintenance and repairs, per year, will amount to 4 percent of the initial cost of the lighting system. Property taxes on this equipment will be about 2 percent of its initial cost. It is estimated that the average revenue, per night of operation, will be $90 for the first two years.

Considering the probability of competition from the illumination of other golf courses, Mr. Divot decides that he will not make the investment unless he can make at least 10 percent per annum on his investment. Because of anticipated competition, revenue is expected to drop to $60 per night for Years 3 through 5. It is estimated that the lighting equipment will have a salvage value of $8,000 at the end of the five-year period.

Using discounted-cash-flow techniques, determine whether Mr. Divot should install the lighting system.

12-27. Replacing office equipment. The Gardner Co. is considering replacing its present manual bookkeeping machines (NCR) with faster machines purchased from IBM. The administration is very concerned about the rising costs of operations during the last decade.

In order to convert to IBM, two operators would have to be sent to school. Required remodeling would cost $6,000.

Gardner's three NCR machines were purchased for $10,000 each, five years ago. Their expected life was ten years. Their resale value now is $3,000 each, and will be zero in five more years. The total cost of the new IBM equipment will be $50,000; it will have zero disposal value in five years.

The three NCR operators are paid $8 an hour each. They usually work a 40-hour week. Machine breakdowns occur monthly on each machine, resulting in repair costs of $50 per month and overtime of four hours, at time-and-one-half, per machine per month, to complete the normal monthly workload. Paper, supplies, etc., cost $100 a month for each NCR.

The IBM system will require only two regular operators, on a reduced work week of 30 hours each, to do the same work. Rates are $10 an hour and no overtime is expected. Paper, supplies, etc., will cost $3,300 annually. Maintenance and repairs are fully serviced by IBM for $1,050 annually. (Assume a 52-week year.)

1. Using discounted-cash-flow techniques, compute the present value of all relevant cash flows, under both alternatives, for the five-year period discounted at 12 percent.
2. Should Gardner keep the NCR machines or replace them, if the decision is based solely on the given data?
3. What other considerations might affect the decision?

12-28. Replacement decision for railway equipment. The Milwaukee Railroad is considering replacement of a Kalamazoo Power Jack Tamper, used for maintenance of track, with a new automatic raising device that can be attached to a production tamper.

The present power jack tamper cost $18,000 five years ago and has an estimated life of twelve years. A year from now the machine will require a major overhaul estimated to cost $5,000. It can be disposed of now via an outright cash sale for $2,500. There will be no value at the end of twelve years.

The automatic raising attachment has a delivered selling price of $24,000 and an estimated life of twelve years. Because of anticipated future developments in combined maintenance machines, it is felt that the machine should be disposed of at the end of the seventh year to take advantage of newly developed machines. Estimated sale value at end of seven years is $5,000.

Tests have shown that the automatic raising machine will produce a more uniform surface on the track than the power jack tamper now in use. The new equipment will eliminate one laborer whose annual salary is $9,500.

Track maintenance work is seasonal, and the equipment normally works from May 1 to October 31 each year. Machine operators and laborers are transferred to other work after October 31, at the same rate of pay.

The salesman claims that the annual normal maintenance of the new machine will run about $1,000 per year. Because the automatic raising machine is more complicated than the manually operated machine, it is felt that it will require a thorough overhaul at the end of the fourth year at an estimated cost of $7,000.

Records show the annual normal maintenance of the Kalamazoo machine to be $1,200. Fuel consumption of the two machines is equal.

Should the Milwaukee keep or replace the Kalamazoo Power Jack Tamper? A 10 percent rate of return is desired.

The railroad is not currently paying any income tax.

12-29. Minimizing transportation costs. The Wegener Company produces industrial and residential lighting fixtures at its manufacturing facility located in Los Angeles. Shipment of company products to an eastern warehouse is presently handled by common carriers at a rate of 10¢ per pound of fixtures. The warehouse is located in Cleveland, 2,500 miles from Los Angeles.

The treasurer of Wegener Company is presently considering whether to purchase a truck for transporting products to the eastern warehouse. The following data on the truck are available:

Purchase price	$25,000
Useful life	5 years
Salvage value after five years	$5,000
Capacity of truck	10,000 lb
Cash costs of operating truck	$.40 per mile

The treasurer feels that an investment in this truck is particularly attractive because of his successful negotiation with X Company to back-haul X's products from Cleveland to Los Angeles on every return trip from the warehouse. X has agreed to pay Wegener $1,200 per load of X's products hauled from Cleveland to Los Angeles up to and including 100 loads per year.

Wegener's marketing manager has estimated that 500,000 lb of fixtures will have to be shipped to the eastern warehouse each year for the next five years. The truck will be fully loaded on each round trip.

Ignore income taxes. For income tax effects, see problem 13-25.

Required

1. Assume that Wegener requires a minimum rate of return of 20 percent. Should the truck be purchased? Show computations to support your answer.

2. What is the minimum number of trips that must be guaranteed by the X Company to make the deal acceptable to Wegener, based on the above numbers alone?

3. What qualitative factors might influence your decision? Be specific.

12-30. Uses of warehouse: review of Chapters 5 and 12.

a. The Miller Company is currently leasing one of its warehouses to another company for $3,000 per year, on a month-to-month basis.

b. The estimated sales value of the warehouse is $30,000. This price is likely to remain unchanged indefinitely—even if a contemplated public expressway results in the building's condemnation. The building originally cost $20,000 and is being depreciated at $500 annually. Its net book value is $9,000.

c. The Miller Company is seriously considering converting the warehouse into a retail outlet for selling furniture at ridiculously low discount prices. Such an endeavor would entail remodeling, at a cost of $15,000. The remodeling would be extremely modest because the major attraction will be flimsy furniture at rock-bottom prices. The remodeling can be accomplished over a single weekend.

d. The inventory, cash, and receivables needed to open and sustain the retail outlet would be $50,000. This total is fully recoverable whenever operations terminate.

e. The president, who paid an expressway engineer $1,000 to discover when and where the expressway will be built, is virtually certain that the warehouse will be available for no more than four years. He has asked you to give him an analysis of whether the company should continue to lease the warehouse or convert it to a retail outlet, assuming that the minimum annual rate of return desired is 14 percent over a four-year planning horizon. Estimated annual operating data, exclusive of depreciation, are:

f. Sales	$200,000
g. Operating expenses	177,000
h. Nonrecurring sales promotion costs at *beginning* of Year 1	20,000
i. Nonrecurring termination costs at *end* of Year 4	10,000

The president has definitely decided not to sell the warehouse until forced to by condemnation proceedings.

1. Show how you would handle the *individual* items on the company's analysis form, which is set up as follows:

		Net Present Value	Cash Flows in Year				
Item	*Description*	*Value*	*0*	*1*	*2*	*3*	*4*
a.							
b.							
.							
.							
.							
h.							
i.		_____					
		══════					

Use the following present-value factors: P.V. of $1 = $.60 and the P.V. of an annuity of $1 = $2.9. Ignore income taxes. If you think an item is irrelevant, leave the space blank.

2. After analyzing all the relevant data, compute the net present value. Indicate which course of action, based on the data alone, should be taken.

12-31. Investment in machine and working capital. The Brinow Company has an old machine with a net disposal value of $10,000 now and $4,000 five years from now. A new Speedee machine is offered for $60,000 cash or $50,000 with a trade-in. The new machine will result in annual operating cash outflow of $40,000 as compared with the old machine's annual outflow of $50,000. The disposal value of the new machine five years hence will be $4,000.

Because the new machine will produce output more rapidly, the average investment in inventories will be $160,000 by using the new machine instead of $200,000.

The minimum desired rate of return is 20 percent. The company uses discounted-cash-flow techniques to guide these decisions.

Should the Speedee machine be acquired? Show your calculations. Company procedures require the computing of the present value of each alternative. The most desirable alternative is the one with the least cost. Assume P. V. of $1 at 20 percent for five years, $40; P. V. of annuity of $1 at 20 percent for five years, $3.00.

12-32. Make or buy, discounted cash flow, and accounting rate of return. Refer to Problem 5-28, Requirement 1.

1. Using a net-present-value analysis, which alternative is most attractive? Assume that the minimum rate of return desired is 8 percent.
2. Using the accounting rate-of-return method, what is the rate of return on the initial investment?

12-33. Comparison of investment models. Tony's Pizza Company makes and sells frozen pizzas to local retail outlets. Tony just inherited $10,000 and has decided to invest it in the business. He is trying to decide between:

Alternative *a:* Buy a $10,000 contract, payable immediately, from a local reputable sales promotion agency. The agency would provide various advertising services, as specified in the contract, over the next ten years. Tony is convinced that the sales promotion would increase cash inflow from operations, through increased volume, by $2,000 a year for the first five years, and by $1,000 per year thereafter. There would be no effect after the ten years had elapsed.

Alternative *b:* Buy new mixing and packaging equipment, at a cost of $10,000, which would reduce operating cash outflows by $1,500 per year for the next ten years. The equipment would have zero salvage value at the end of the ten years. Ignore any tax effect.

1. Compute the rates of return on initial investment by the accounting model for both alternatives.
2. Compute the rates of return by the discounted-cash-flow model for both alternatives.
3. Are the rates of return different under the discounted-cash-flow model? Explain.

12-34. New equipment and analysis of operating costs: accounting rate of return. The processing department of Fay Company has incurred the following costs in producing 150,000 units, which is normal volume, during the past year:

Variable	$100,000
Fixed	50,000
	$150,000

The department has been offered some new processing equipment. The salesman says that the new equipment will reduce unit costs by 20¢. The department's old equipment has a remaining useful life of five years, has zero disposal value now, and is being depreciated on a straight-line basis at $5,000 annually. The new equipment's straight-line depreciation would be $30,000 annually. It would last five years and have no disposal value. The salesman pointed out that overall unit costs now are $1, whereas the new equipment is being used by one of Fay's competitors to produce an identical product at a unit cost of 80¢, computed as follows:

Variable costs	$ 80,000
Fixed costs*	80,000
Total costs	$160,000
Divide by units produced	200,000
Cost per unit	$.80

* Fixed costs include $30,000 depreciation on the new equipment. Fay's supervisory payroll is $10,000 less than this competitor's.

The salesman stated that a saving of 20¢ per unit would add $30,000 to Fay's annual net income.

Required

1. Show *specifically* how the salesman computed Fay's costs and prospective savings.

2. As adviser to the Fay Company, evaluate the salesman's contentions and prepare a quantitative summary to support your recommendations for Fay's best course of action. Include the accounting rate-of-return method and the net-present-value method in your evaluation. Assume that Fay's minimum desired rate of return is 10 percent.

12-35. Replacement decision. Amtrak, a passenger train company owned wholly by the United States Government, has included a dining car on the lone passenger train it operates from Buffalo to Albany, N.Y. Yearly operations of the dining car have shown a consistent loss, as follows:

Revenue (in cash)		$200,000
Expenses for food, supplies, etc. (in cash)	$100,000	
Salaries	110,000	210,000
Net loss (ignore depreciation on the dining car itself)		($ 10,000)

The Auto-vend Company has offered to sell automatic vending machines to Amtrak for $22,000, less a $3,000 trade-in allowance on old equipment (which is carried at $3,000 book value, and which can be sold outright for $3,000 cash) now used in the dining car operation. The useful life of the vending equipment is estimated at ten years, with zero scrap value. Experience elsewhere has led executives to predict that the equipment will serve 50 percent more food than the dining car, but prices will be 50 percent less, so the new gross receipts will probably be $150,000. The variety and mix of food sold are expected to be the same as for the dining car. A catering company will completely service and supply the machines, paying 10 percent of gross receipts to the Amtrak company and bearing all costs of food, repairs, etc. All dining car employees will be discharged immediately. Their termination pay will total $30,000. However, an attendant who has some general knowledge of vending machines will be needed for one shift per day. The annual cost to Amtrak for the attendant will be $14,000.

For political and other reasons, the railroad will definitely not abandon its food service. The old equipment will have zero scrap value at the end of ten years

Required Using the above data, carefully compute the following. Label computations. Ignore income taxes.

1. The incremental net present value, in dollars, of the proposed investment. Assume that Congress has specified that a minimum desired rate of return of 10 percent be used for these types of investments. For this problem, assume that the P.V. of $1 at 10% to be received at the end of ten years is $.4000 and that the P.V. of an annuity of $1 at 10% for ten years is $6.000.

2. What would be the minimum amount of annual *revenue* that Amtrak would have to receive from the catering company to justify making the investment? Show computations.

12-36. Sensitivity of capital budgeting and inflation. The president of the Haywood Company, a London manufacturer, is considering whether to invest £100,000 in some automatic equipment that will last five years, have zero scrap value, and produce cash savings in materials and labor usage as follows, using 19x0 prices and wage rates (in pounds sterling):

Year	19x1	19x2	19x3	19x4	19x5
	20,000	20,000	30,000	30,000	20,000

The minimum desired rate of return, which embodies an element attributable to inflation, is 12 percent per year. For purposes of this problem, assume that the present values of £1 at the end of each year are .89, .80, .71, .64, and .57, respectively. All analysis will be conducted on a before-tax basis.

Required
1. Compute the net present value of the project, using the above data.

2. Ms. Haywood is virtually certain that inflation will continue, although she is uncertain about its degree. She hopes that government control over prices and wages will dampen inflation, but she thinks that the existing rate of inflation, 6 percent annually, will prevail over the next five years. She wants to pinpoint price changes more precisely with respect to the materials and labor question, but she thinks 6 percent is probably as good an overall guess as any.

One pound invested at time zero will grow as follows, if the rates of interest are (rounded to the second decimal place):

End of Period	4%	6%	8%
1	1.04	1.06	1.08
2	1.08	1.12	1.17
3	1.12	1.19	1.26
4	1.17	1.26	1.36
5	1.22	1.34	1.47

Compute the net present value of the project, using the above data and an inflation rate of 6 percent throughout the five-year period. To make the decision model internally consistent, the cash savings should be adjusted upward in accordance with the 6 percent inflation rate. That is, there will be 6 percent inflation in year one.

3. Compare your results in Requirements 1 and 2. What generalizations seem warranted?

12-37. Effects of currency devaluation and qualitative factors. Phelan Glass Manufacturing Company is a large producer of high-quality crystal glassware in Dublin, Ireland. Its glassware is sold entirely on the export market, mostly in the United States and France. A small research group within the company has recently been investigating a new glass coating that, when applied to aluminum cooking ware, gives a finish that is cheap yet colorful, heat resistant, unbreakable, and nonstick. Patents on the process have been obtained by the company in many countries, including France and the U.S.

Mr. Phelan, the President, has ordered a market-research program to determine the approximate sales potential of the new product. At a conference called to discuss the product, he asked his marketing manager, "Why not kick off the meeting by telling us what the market-research fellows have come up with?"

John: "Basically, we can sell this new thing in the U.S. and France—tariffs and competition make other countries infeasible. In those two countries, the new line will tie in well with our present lines, since it will have the same high-quality image and be sold through the same distribution channels, over which we have strong influence in both countries. As accurately as we can predict, for the first five years, the net additional cash inflows by the new line will be $560,000 per year in the U.S. market, and 1,680,000 Francs in the French market. For the second five years, the average annual contribution will be only half of these figures, as the product line begins to decline. After ten years, other finishes and techniques will be taking over, so we plan on phasing the product out by the end of ten years. By the way, £1 equals $2.80, and £1 equals 14.0 francs."

The president then asked Jim Wood, the production manager, to describe what plant commitment would be involved.

Jim: "My predictions, based on the production levels that John is talking about, show that, apart from land, the total cost of buildings and normal equipment needed will be about £1.1 million. In addition to this, the glazing furnace and controls will have to be purchased in the U.S. for an estimated additional $2.1 million (dollars). I included installation of the furnace in the £1.1 million. The useful life should be ten years. The predicted value of the building at the end of ten years is £.8 million; of all equipment, zero."

The president then discussed the possible plant location. Adjoining the present factory was a five-acre site that would just be large enough for the proposed plant. It had been left over when the present factory had been built years ago. This site, landscaped into a recreation area and park, had won numerous awards for Phelan Glass in "best plant layout" competitions. Furthermore, it housed changing rooms and a football field for the factory's own football team, composed of amateur players among the company's 2,500 workers. Most large companies had such a football team, and Phelan Glass had among the best in the country—a fact in which most company workers took great pride.

Mr. Phelan was quite concerned that this area would have to go, because he felt that the image of the "well-groomed factory" was good employee and public relations. When the personnel manager had been informed of the proposal, he had flatly stated that the workers' high morale, for which the company was famous, "would disappear along with the football facilities." Investigation showed that another site, suitable for either a building or conversion to a football facility, was available five miles away at a cost of £90,000.

At this stage, the president turned to Patricia O'Shea, who had recently obtained a degree in management, and said, "Pat, you've been listening to us for the last few hours. We don't want to take on any project at present that does not give us a rate of return of 10 percent or more. Why don't you take our facts and predictions and give us your recommendations at our meeting tomorrow."

1. As Patricia, how accurate do you feel the predictions given in the cases are likely to be? What other information would you look for, if any?

2. Using the given data and predictions as the best available, would you recommend that the project be undertaken? Show computations in sterling. Assume that the value of the building sites will be unchanged over the next few years. Suppose that you favor proceeding. What would be your recommendation on the "site" problem?

3. Patricia finished her analysis late in the evening. Early next morning, she glanced at the newspaper and was startled to read the banner headline: *"POUND DEVALUED 14.3% LAST NIGHT."* The story stated that now £1 equalled $2.40, and £1 equalled 12 francs.

    Does this news affect your recommendations? If so, what recommendations will you make to the management group?

12-38. Capital-budgeting policies. Universal Engines Incorporated is a large manufacturer of small and medium-sized aircraft engines. The company has for many years enjoyed a reputation for building excellent quality piston engines and is now planning the introduction of a line of gas turbine engines.

Sales forecasts for the new family of gas turbine engines suggest 1,000 engines could be sold per year for a period of six years. Although a longer product life is possible, it is believed that rapidly changing technology will render the design obsolete at the end of the six-year period.

The Manufacturing Division is uncertain about what type of milling machine to purchase for machining the accessory gearbox casings for the new engines. A general-purpose milling machine could be purchased to do the job for $100,000. However, the machine tool manufacturer's salesman has recommended that the company purchase a custom-designed special-purpose milling machine, which would cost $140,000.

It has been estimated that the special-purpose machine will save two hours per gearbox produced. The company estimates cash operating costs for both types of machines to be $7.50 per hour. Both machines have an estimated life of about ten years, comfortably in excess of the estimated production period. However, whereas the special-purpose machine would be unsuitable for any other job at the end of the six-year production life of the new engines and would have zero salvage value, the general-purpose machine could be adapted to many other operations and would have a salvage value at the end of six years of $30,000.

The company attempts to maintain a minimum 10 percent accounting rate of return on gross assets used in each of its manufacturing programs. Because many of the manufacturing programs last only a few years, the manufacturing division has established the additional criterion of a minimum payback period of three years for machine tool purchases.

Manufacturing Division executives have made the following comments concerning the machine purchase decision.

"The $15,000 per year savings for $40,000 extra investment yields a return on investment of $37\frac{1}{2}$ percent and a payback period of 2.66 years. Both criteria are met; obviously we should buy the special-purpose machine.

"The additional investment for the special-purpose machine is really $70,000 if the salvage values are considered. Although the return on investment is still more than 21 percent, the payback period is 4.66 years. We should therefore buy the general-purpose machine."

"Our company should strive to maintain maximum flexibility in its manufacturing facilities. Special-purpose machines do not offer the kind of flexibility we want, and the payback period for them should be shorter, say one-half the length, than for general-purpose machines. We need the general-purpose machine."

The company eventually purchased the general-purpose machine. Comment upon the decision and upon the company's investment policies concerning machine tools. Show computations.

Solutions to Exercises
in Compound Interest, Problem 12-2

The general approach to these exercises centers about one fundamental question: Which of the two basic tables am I dealing with? No calculations should be made until after this question is answered with assurance. If you made any errors, it is possible that you used the wrong table.

a. From Table 1, at the end of the book:
  (1) $4,110
  (2) $3,105
  (3) $2,010

The $5,000 is an *amount* or *future worth*. You want the present value of that amount:

$$PV = \frac{S}{(1 + i)^n}$$

The conversion factor, $1/(1 + i)^n$, is on line 5 of Table 1. Substituting:

$$PV = \$5,000(.822) = \$4,110 \tag{1}$$
$$PV = \$5,000(.621) = \$3,105 \tag{2}$$
$$PV = \$5,000(.402) = \$2,010 \tag{3}$$

Note that the higher the interest rate, the lower the present value.

b. From Table 2, at the end of the book:
  (1) $2,226.00
  (2) $1,895.50
  (3) $1,495.50

The $500 withdrawal is a uniform annual amount, an annuity. You need to find the present value of an annuity for five years:

PV_A = Annual withdrawal (F), where F is the conversion factor.

Substituting:

$$PV_A = \$500(4.452) = \$2,226.00 \qquad (1)$$
$$PV_A = \$500(3.791) = \$1,895.50 \qquad (2)$$
$$PV_A = \$500(2.991) = \$1,495.50 \qquad (3)$$

c. From Table 2:
   (1) $1,123.09
   (2) $1,318.91

You have $5,000, the present value of your contemplated annuity. You must find the annuity that will just exhaust the invested principal in five years:

$$PV_A = \text{Annual withdrawal } (F) \qquad (1)$$

$$\$5,000 = \text{Annual withdrawal } (4.452)$$
$$\text{Annual withdrawal} = \$5,000 \div 4.452$$
$$= \$1,123.09$$
$$\$5,000 = \text{Annual withdrawal } (3.791) \qquad (2)$$
$$\text{Annual withdrawal} = \$5,000 \div 3.791$$
$$= \$1,318.91$$

d. From Table 1: Mining is preferable; its present value exceeds farming by $3,852.

Year	Present-Value Factors @ 16 Percent from Table 1	Present Value of Mining	Present Value of Farming
1	.862	$ 8,620	$ 1,724
2	.743	5,944	2,972
3	.641	3,846	3,846
4	.552	2,208	4,416
5	.476	952	4,760
		$21,570	$17,718

Note that the nearer dollars are more valuable than the distant dollars.

SUGGESTED READINGS

BIERMAN, H., and S. SMIDT, *The Capital Budgeting Decision,* 4th ed. (New York: The Macmillan Company, 1975).

BOWER, J., *Managing the Resource Allocation Process* (Boston: Harvard Business School, 1970).

MORRIS, WILLIAM T., *The Capacity Decision System* (Homewood, Ill.: Richard D. Irwin, Inc., 1967).

VAN HORNE, JAMES C., *Financial Management and Policy,* 4th ed. (Englewood Cliffs, N.J.: Prentice-Hall, Inc., 1977).

CHAPTER 13

Impact
of Income Taxes
on
Management Planning

Income taxes influence nearly all business decisions. In this chapter, we show how income taxes may be reckoned with in decision making. Our focus is on corporations, rather than on individuals or partnerships.

Managers have an obligation to avoid income taxes. Avoidance is not evasion. Avoidance is the use of legal means to minimize tax payments; evasion is the use of illegal means. Income tax problems are often exceedingly complex, so qualified counsel should be sought whenever the slightest doubt exists.

We are especially concerned with the effect of income taxes on the choice of depreciation methods and on capital-budgeting decisions. However, other topics will also be explored—the tax effects of last-in, first-out inventory valuations, of charitable contributions, and some miscellaneous matters. Obviously, in one chapter we can only scratch the surface of this vast and complicated subject.

INCOME TAXES AND CAPITAL BUDGETING

General Characteristics

Income taxes are cash disbursements. Income taxes can influence the *amount* and/or the *timing* of cash flows. Their basic role in capital budgeting is no different from that of any other cash disbursement. However, taxes tend to narrow the cash differences between projects. Cash savings in operations will cause an increase in net taxable income and, thus, an increase in tax outlays. A 60 percent income tax rate reduces the net attractiveness of $1,000,000 in cash operating savings to $400,000.

As of 1978, federal income tax rates on ordinary corporate taxable income were 20 percent of the first $25,000 per year, 22 percent of the second $25,000, and 48 percent of all income in excess of $50,000. These rates are sometimes subject to additional surcharges that may vary from year to year. State income tax rates vary considerably. In many instances, state plus federal income tax rates are more than 50 percent. We use a 60 percent rate in several examples to facilitate computations.

Effects of Depreciation Deductions

Exhibit 13-1 shows the interrelationship of income before taxes, income taxes, and depreciation. Please examine this exhibit carefully before reading on. Assume that the company has a single fixed asset, purchased for $100,000 cash, which has a four-year life and zero disposal value. The purchase cost, less the estimated disposal value, is tax-deductible in the form of yearly depreciation. Depreciation deductions (and similar deductions that are noncash expenses when deducted) have been called *tax shields* because they protect that amount of income from taxation. The term *tax shield* seems apt at first glance, but note that all deductions from gross income are really tax shields (including cost of goods sold, donations to charities, officer salaries, and so forth).

As Exhibit 13-2 shows, the asset represents a valuable future tax deduction of $100,000. The present value of this deduction depends directly on its specific yearly effects on future income tax payments. Therefore, the present value is influenced by the depreciation method selected, the tax rates, and the discount rate.

The Best Depreciation Method

The three most popular depreciation methods in the United States are straight-line depreciation, sum-of-the-years'-digits, and the double-declining balance. The effects of the first two are shown in Exhibit 13-2. Note that the present value of the income tax savings is greater if straight-line depreciation is *not* used. The general decision rule is to select accelerated methods because, as compared with the straight-line method, they maximize the

EXHIBIT 13-1

Basic Analysis of Income Statement,
Income Taxes, and Cash Flows

TRADITIONAL INCOME STATEMENT	
(S) Sales	$130,000
(E) Less: Expenses, excluding depreciation	$ 70,000
(D)　　　Depreciation (straight line)	25,000
Total expenses	$ 95,000
Income before taxes	$ 35,000
(T) Income taxes @ 60%	21,000
(I) Net income after taxes	$ 14,000

Net after-tax cash inflow from operations is

either S − E − T = $130,000 − $70,000 − $21,000 = $ 39,000

or I + D =　$14,000 + $25,000 = $39,000

ANALYSIS OF THE ABOVE FOR CAPITAL BUDGETING		
(S − E) Cash inflow from operations:	$130,000 − $70,000 =	$ 60,000
Income tax effects, @ 60%		36,000
After-tax effects of cash inflow from operations		$ 24,000
Effect of depreciation:		
(D) Straight-line depreciation: $100,000 ÷ 4 = $25,000		
Income tax savings @ 60%		15,000
Total cash effects		$ 39,000

present values of income tax savings. The cumulative *dollar* tax bills may not change when the years are taken together, but the early write-offs defer tax outlays to future periods. The measure of the latter advantage depends on the rate of return that can be gained from funds that otherwise would have been paid as income taxes. The mottoes in income tax planning are: When there is a legal choice, take the deduction sooner rather than later; and recognize taxable income later rather than sooner.

Comprehensive Illustration: Effects of Income Taxes on Cash Flow

The easiest way to visualize the effects of income taxes on cash flow is by a step-by-step analysis of a concrete situation. The following illustration is the same one used in the example in Chapter 12 (p. 363). However, an after-tax discount rate is now going to be used, and all income tax effects—including gains and losses on disposals—will now be considered.

A company owns a packaging machine, which was purchased three years ago for $56,000. It has a remaining useful life of five years, providing that it has a major overhaul, at the end of two more years of life, at a cost of $10,000, fully deductible in that year for income tax purposes. Its disposal value now is $20,000; in five years, its disposal value will be $8,000. The cash

EXHIBIT 13-2

After-Tax Effects of Depreciation

Assume: Original cost of equipment $100,000; four-year life; zero disposal value; annual cash inflow from operations, $60,000; income tax rate, 60 percent; minimum desired after-tax rate of return, 12 percent.

Straight-Line Depreciation

Annual depreciation: $100,000 ÷ 4 = $25,000
Savings in income tax disbursements,
@ 60% = .60 × $25,000 = $15,000

	12% DISCOUNT FACTOR, FROM APPROPRIATE TABLES	TOTAL PRESENT VALUE, @ 12%	SKETCH OF CASH FLOWS AT END OF YEAR				
			0	1	2	3	4
	3.037	$45,555	$—	$15,000	$15,000	$15,000	$15,000

Sum-of-the-Years'-Digits Depreciation

YEAR	MULTIPLIER*	DEDUCTION	INCOME TAX SAVINGS, @ 60%	12% DISCOUNT FACTOR, FROM APPROPRIATE TABLES	TOTAL PRESENT VALUE, @ 12%	0	1	2	3	4
1	4/10	$40,000	$24,000	.893	$21,432	—	$24,000			
2	3/10	30,000	18,000	.797	14,346			$18,000		
3	2/10	20,000	12,000	.712	8,544				$12,000	
4	1/10	10,000	6,000	.636	3,816					$ 6,000
Total present value					$48,138					

* The denominator for the sum-of-the-years'-digits method is:

$$1 + 2 + 3 + 4 = 10$$

or

$$S = \frac{n(n+1)}{2}$$

$$S = \frac{4(4+1)}{2} = 4 \times 2.5 = 10$$

where S = sum of the digits
n = years of estimated useful life

operating costs of this machine are expected to continue at $40,000 annually. The company has not used a residual value in allocating depreciation for tax purposes. Accumulated straight-line depreciation is $21,000.

A manufacturer has offered a substitute machine for $51,000 in cash. The new machine will reduce annual cash operating costs by $10,000, will not require any overhauls, will have a useful life of five years, and will have a disposal value of $3,000. The company would use sum-of-the-years'-digits depreciation for tax purposes, with no provision for residual value.

Assume that the minimum desired rate of return, after taxes, is 6 percent. Using the net-present-value technique, show whether the new machine should be purchased: (a) under a total project approach; (b) under an incremental approach. Assume that income tax rates are 60 percent on ordinary income. Assume that all taxes are paid in the same year in which the taxable income is earned. Also, assume that the zero residual values used in computing depreciation for tax purposes will not be challenged by the Internal Revenue Service.

Exhibits 13-3 and 13-4 show the complete solution. The following steps are recommended. The pertinent income tax aspects will be considered as each step is discussed.

Step 1. General Approach. Review the example in Chapter 12 (p. 363). The general approach to these decisions is unchanged by income tax considerations.

Step 2. Cash Operating Costs and Depreciation. Cash operating costs and their income tax effects are separated from the depreciation effects. **These can be combined, if preferred.** However, the approach illustrated facilitates comparisons of alternative depreciation effects and permits the use of annuity tables for the cash operating costs when they do not differ from year to year.

This illustration, in which we assume that any given cash flows and related tax flows occur in the same period, could be refined to account for any possible lags. For instance, the pretax operating cash inflows may occur in Year 1, and some related tax outflows may not occur until April in Year 2. **For simplicity, we are ignoring this possibility.**

Step 3. Disposals of Equipment. In general, gains and losses on disposals of equipment are taxed in the same way as ordinary gains and losses.[1]

[1] In this case, the old equipment was sold outright. Where there is a trade-in of old equipment for new equipment of like kind, special income tax rules result in the gain or loss being added to, or deducted from, the capitalized value of the new equipment. The gain or loss is not recognized in the year of disposal; instead, it is spread over the life of the new asset as an adjustment of the new depreciation charges.

Before 1962, gains from disposal of equipment were taxed at the existing capital gains rate. Since then, the general rule has been that gain on sale of equipment is not a capital gain except in special circumstances. This complicates the effect on taxes of gains arising on disposal, frequently resulting in part of the gain's being taxed at ordinary income tax rates and part at capital gain rates. For simplicity, this chapter does not introduce the latter complication.

EXHIBIT 13-3

After-tax Analysis of Equipment Replacement:
Total Project Approach

(A) Replace

		PRESENT-VALUE DISCOUNT FACTORS @ 6%	TOTAL PRESENT VALUE	SKETCH OF CASH FLOWS AT END OF YEAR					
				0	1	2	3	4	5
Recurring cash operating costs									
$30,000									
Income tax savings, @ 60%									
18,000									
After-tax cash operating costs									
$12,000		4.212	$(50,544)		($12,000)	($12,000)	($12,000)	($12,000)	($12,000)

Depreciation deductions (sum of digits
1 + 2 + 3 + 4 + 5 = 15):

YEAR	MULTIPLIED BY $51,000	DEDUCTION	INCOME TAX SAVINGS, @ 60%	PRESENT-VALUE DISCOUNT FACTORS @ 6%	TOTAL PRESENT VALUE	SKETCH OF CASH FLOWS AT END OF YEAR					
						0	1	2	3	4	5
1	5/15	$17,000	$10,200	.943	9,619		10,200				
2	4/15	13,600	8,160	.890	7,262			8,160			
3	3/15	10,200	6,120	.840	5,141				6,120		
4	2/15	6,800	4,080	.792	3,231					4,080	
5	1/15	3,400	2,040	.747	1,524						2,040

Residual value, all subject to tax
because book value will be zero $ 3,000
Less: 60% income tax   1,800

Net cash inflow	$ 1,200	.747	896						1,200

		PV factor	Total PV	Year 0	Year 1	Year 2	Year 3	Year 4
Initial required investment, actual cash outflow: $51,000	$51,000	1.000	(51,000)	($51,000)				
Disposal of old equipment:								
Book value now:								
$56,000 − $21,000 = $35,000								
Selling price	$20,000							
Net loss	$15,000							
Tax savings	× .60							
9,000								
Net immediate cash effects, including tax saving	$29,000	1.000	29,000	29,000				
Total present value of all cash flows			$(44,871)					
(B) Keep								
Recurring cash operating costs	$40,000							
Income tax savings, @ 60%	24,000							
After-tax cash operating costs	$16,000	4.212	$(67,392)		($16,000)	($16,000)	($16,000)	($16,000)
Savings in income tax disbursements because of depreciation, @ 60% = .60 × $7,000	4,200	4.212	17,690		4,200	4,200	4,200	4,200
Residual value, all subject to tax	$ 8,000							
Less: 60% income tax	4,800							
Net cash inflow	$ 3,200	.747	2,390					3,200
Overhaul, end of Year 2	$10,000							
Income tax savings, @ 60%	6,000							
Net effect on cash flow	$ 4,000	.890	(3,560)			(4,000)		
Total present value of all cash flows			$(50,872)					
Difference in favor of replacement			$ 6,001					

EXHIBIT 13-4

After-tax Analysis of Equipment Replacement
Incremental Approach

398

Analysis confined to differences between (A) and (B) in Exhibit 13-3:

		PRESENT-VALUE DISCOUNT FACTORS, @ 6%	TOTAL PRESENT VALUES
Recurring operating savings,			
$40,000 – $30,000	$10,000		
Income tax, @ 60%	6,000		
After-tax operating savings	$ 4,000	4.212	$ 16,848

Differences in depreciation:

YEAR	REPLACE	KEEP	DIFFERENCE	INCOME TAX EFFECT, @ 60%	PRESENT-VALUE DISCOUNT FACTORS, @ 6%	TOTAL PRESENT VALUES
1	$17,000	$7,000	$10,000	$6,000	.943	5,658
2	13,600	7,000	6,600	3,960	.890	3,524
3	10,200	7,000	3,200	1,920	.840	1,614
4	6,800	7,000	(200)	(120)	.792	(95)
5	3,400	7,000	(3,600)	(2,160)	.747	(1,614)

			PRESENT-VALUE DISCOUNT FACTORS, @ 6%	TOTAL PRESENT VALUES
Difference in disposal value, end of Year 5				
(see Exhibit 13-3 for details):				
$1,200 – $3,200 = $(2,000)			.747	(1,494)
Overhaul avoided, end of Year 2, net of tax effects			.890	3,560
Incremental initial investment				
(see Exhibit 13-3 for details): $51,000 – $29,000			1.000	(22,000)
Net present value of replacement				$ 6,001

SKETCH OF CASH FLOWS AT END OF YEAR

	0	1	2	3	4	5
After-tax operating savings		$4,000	$4,000	$4,000	$4,000	$4,000
Income tax effect		6,000	3,960	1,920	(120)	(2,160)
Overhaul avoided			4,000			
Difference in disposal value						(2,000)
Incremental initial investment	($22,000)					

Exhibit 13-3 is an analysis of the alternative dispositions of the asset. Disposal at the end of Year 5 entails the cash effect of the selling price, subject to a 60 percent tax. The tax is on the *gain,* the excess of the selling price over book value; the book value was zero in this case.

Immediate replacement entails the disposal of the old equipment at a loss. This loss is fully deductible from current income, so the cash-flow computations become a bit more subtle. The net loss must be computed to isolate its effect on current income tax, but the total **cash-inflow effect is the selling price plus the current income tax benefit.**

Step 4. Total Project or Incremental Approach? The relative merits of the total project and the incremental approaches were discussed in Chapter 12. Exhibits 13-3 and 13-4 demonstrate these approaches. Either yields the same net answer in favor of replacement. **Note, however, that the incremental approach rapidly becomes unwieldy when computations become intricate.** This becomes even more apparent when three or more alternatives are being considered.

Income Tax Complications

In the foregoing illustration, believe it or not, we deliberately avoided many possible income tax complications. As all taxpaying citizens know, income taxes are affected by many intricacies, including progressive tax rates, loss carrybacks and carryforwards, a variety of depreciation options, state income taxes, short- and long-term gains, distinctions between capital assets and other assets, offsets of losses against related gains, exchanges of property of like kind, exempt income, and so forth. Moreover, most depreciable asset purchases in the 1970s have qualified for an "investment tax credit," which is generally an immediate income tax credit of 10 percent of the initial cost. **This credit is a lump-sum reduction of the income tax cash outflow at time zero or in Year 1.** For example, an investment of $500,000 would generate an investment tax credit that would reduce current income tax outflows by .10 × $500,000, or $50,000. Furthermore, the full original cost, less the estimated disposal value, is deductible in the form of yearly depreciation.[2]

Keep in mind that miscellaneous changes in the tax law occur each year. For example, the investment tax credit has been suspended, reinstated, and changed in many respects through the years.

MISCELLANEOUS TAX PLANNING MATTERS

Form of Organization

The corporation is a distinct business entity subject to separate corporate income taxes. In contrast, individual proprietorships and partnerships are not

---

[2]For a book-length discussion of these and other complications, see W. L. Raby, *The Income Tax and Business Decisions,* 3rd ed. (Englewood Cliffs, N.J.: Prentice-Hall, Inc., 1975).

separate entities for income tax purposes. Instead, their income is attributed to the owners as individuals regardless of whether they make any cash withdrawals from the business. These distinctions are shown in Exhibit 13-5.

For a corporation, reasonable salaries paid to officers who are also stockholders are deductible for income tax purposes. For partnerships or proprietorships, no deductions are allowed for owners' salaries or for interest expense on invested ownership capital.

Corporate income is subject to double taxation. First, it is taxed to the separate entity. Second, any cash dividends are taxed to the individual at the recipient's income tax rate.

What form of business organization should be chosen? The answer depends on a myriad of legal and tax considerations, including the extent of personal liability of the owners for business debts, ease of transfer of ownership, and expected life of the business. But the personal income tax bracket of the owners is often paramount. For example, suppose an individual with a marginal income tax rate of 70 percent (because of other income) is considering how to organize his solely owned business.

Operating data may be analyzed as follows:

	Corporation		Proprietorship (or Partnership)	
Sales (all for cash)		$200,000		$200,000
Operating expenses:				
Owner's salary	$ 20,000[a]		$ 20,000[b]	
Other expenses	150,000[a]	170,000	150,000[a]	170,000
Income before income taxes		$ 30,000		$ 30,000
Corporate income tax				
20% on first $25,000	$ 5,000			
22% on excess of $5,000	1,100	6,100		—
Net income		$ 23,900		$ 30,000
Cash dividends		$ 23,900	Withdrawals	30,000[b]
Net income retained		$ —		$ —

[a] For simplicity, assume these are all cash expenses.

[b] Note that these amounts can be any number without affecting the personal income tax liability. "Salaries" and withdrawals are irrelevant as far as income tax liability is concerned. In this case, the proprietor will be subject to personal income taxes on the entity income of $30,000 plus the $20,000 owner's salary.

Incidentally, partnerships must file information returns disclosing the determination of net income and the share of each partner. However, under the income tax law, proprietorships and partnerships are regarded as a conduit through which taxable income flows to the owners. Thus, although salaries paid to proprietors and partners are deducted here in computing entity income, they must be reported as income by the recipients on their personal tax returns. In essence, then, the income tax laws would regard the entity income shown here ($30,000) and the owner's salary ($20,000) as arbitrary splits of a $50,000 income taxable to the owner. Therefore, if the owner wants to label the entity income as $40,000 and the salary as $10,000, it makes no difference regarding his taxable income, which will be $50,000 regardless. Furthermore, if the owner withdraws zero or $100,000, his taxable income will still be $50,000.

If the personal income tax brackets are low, the noncorporate forms may become more attractive. But high-bracket taxpayers will almost always find the corporate form more attractive if they do not need cash dividends.

EXHIBIT 13-5. Diagram of Tax Effects of Form of Business Organization

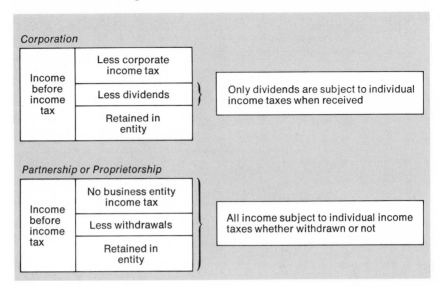

The tabulations in Exhibit 13-6 illustrate that (a) the need for high dividends will favor using the proprietorship form, and (b) little need for dividends will favor the corporate form of organization.[3]

Note that if heavy cash dividends are paid, the corporate form has no income tax advantage to the owner. If no cash dividends are paid, the corporate form is advantageous to an owner in a high tax bracket.

The remainder of this chapter will focus on planning for corporate taxes. However, unless specifically stated otherwise, most of the points are applicable to personal taxes and to any form of business organization.

Changes in Income Tax Rates

During World War II and the Korean War, the United States imposed an excess profits tax that considerably boosted effective income tax rates. At the time, the prospect of changes in income tax rates in a given year or series of years influenced management planning extensively. If income taxes were going to rise in the next year, the tendency would be to postpone certain expenses (e.g., repairs, advertising, legal services, purchases of supplies not usually inventoried) and to accelerate revenue recognition by boosting production to fill any existing orders before the higher tax rates took effect.

---

[3]Of course, there must be a legitimate business purpose, such as expansion of the corporation, for not paying dividends. Otherwise, penalty taxes are imposed on unjustified retentions of earnings.

EXHIBIT 13-6. Tax Effects on Form of Business Organization (Data from text)

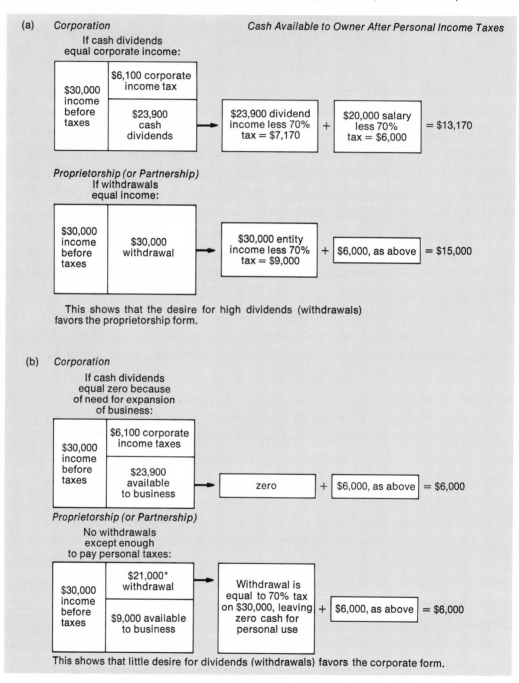

(a) Corporation — *Cash Available to Owner After Personal Income Taxes*

If cash dividends equal corporate income:

| $30,000 income before taxes | $6,100 corporate income tax |
| | $23,900 cash dividends |

$23,900 dividend income less 70% tax = $7,170 + $20,000 salary less 70% tax = $6,000 = $13,170

Proprietorship (or Partnership)
If withdrawals equal income:

| $30,000 income before taxes | $30,000 withdrawal |

$30,000 entity income less 70% tax = $9,000 + $6,000, as above = $15,000

This shows that the desire for high dividends (withdrawals) favors the proprietorship form.

(b) Corporation

If cash dividends equal zero because of need for expansion of business:

| $30,000 income before taxes | $6,100 corporate income taxes |
| | $23,900 available to business |

zero + $6,000, as above = $6,000

Proprietorship (or Partnership)
No withdrawals except enough to pay personal taxes:

| $30,000 income before taxes | $21,000* withdrawal |
| | $9,000 available to business |

Withdrawal is equal to 70% tax on $30,000, leaving zero cash for personal use + $6,000, as above = $6,000

This shows that little desire for dividends (withdrawals) favors the corporate form.

*The assumption is that proprietorship cash is withdrawn to pay all taxes on proprietorship income. Tax on proprietorship is based on total proprietorship income regardless of withdrawals.

Lifo or Fifo

The income tax planner does not have to be directly concerned with the relative conceptual merits of Lifo (last-in, first-out) or Fifo (first-in, first-out) inventory methods. The most desirable inventory method is that which postpones income tax payments, perhaps permanently. For instance, an expansion coupled with increasing price levels favors Lifo rather than Fifo; under Lifo, the highest (most recent) costs will be released to expense sooner rather than later.

The adoption of Lifo by one-third of the large American companies is directly attributable to the income tax benefits rather than to the conceptual justification of more "realistic" income measures so often cited. The only tax-planning reasons for not adopting Lifo would be: (1) the negligible prospect of income tax savings because of expected long-run declines in prices; (2) stability of prices; and (3) insignificance of inventories to particular organizations, such as service businesses.

If the prices of inventory are expected to rise, a company should adopt Lifo. The annual savings in cash flow will have compound effects and will result in a substantial financial advantage. Raby illustrates these effects as follows:

> Assume an effective income tax rate of 50 percent and after-tax rate of return of 7 percent. Inventory is $1,000,000 at time of adoption of Lifo. Prices increase in a straight line, so that inventory in Year 1 is $1,100,000 under Fifo but still $1,000,000 under Lifo; in Year 2 Fifo inventory is $1,200,000; in Year 3, $1,300,000; and so forth throughout 20 years. Meanwhile, Lifo inventory stays at $1,000,000, and income tax savings of $50,000 annually, invested at 7 percent compounded annually, will accumulate to $2,049,750 more assets under Lifo.[4]

Effect of Lifo on Purchase Decisions

When prices are rising, it may be advantageous—subject to prudent restraint as to maximum and minimum inventory levels—to buy unusually heavy amounts of inventory near year-end, particularly if income tax rates are likely to fall. For example, assume that a company has made the following transactions during 19x1, its first year in business:

Sales: 10 units, @ $5   Purchases: 8 units, @ $2
3 units, @ $3

Decision: Buy six more units, near year-end, @ $4? Current income tax rates, 50 percent, are expected to decline to 40 percent next year. Prices on inventory are not expected to decline next year.

[4] *Ibid.*, pp. 285–286.

		Do Not Buy	*Buy 6 More Units*
Sales: 10 units, @ $5		$50	$50
Cost of goods sold (Lifo basis):			
3 units, @ $3 =	$ 9		
7 units, @ $2 =	14	23	
or			
6 units, @ $4 =	$24		
3 units, @ $3 =	9		
1 unit, @ $2 =	2		35
Gross margin		$27	$15

Tax savings: 50 percent of ($27 − $15) = $6 this year. The effects on later years' taxes will depend on inventory levels, prices, and tax rates.

Tax savings can be generated because Lifo permits management to influence immediate net income by its purchasing decisions. In contrast, Fifo results would be unaffected by this decision:

		Do Not Buy	*Buy 6 More Units*
Sales		$50	$50
Cost of goods sold (Fifo basis):			
8 units, @ $2 =	$16		
2 units, @ $3 =	6	22	22
Gross margin		$28	$28

Contributions of Property Rather Than Cash

Donations to qualifying charitable, educational, and similar institutions are generally deductible, up to specified maximum limits, in computing income taxes. Giving property (such as marketable securities or land) rather than cash is more beneficial to both the donor and the donee. The reason is that any increase in the value of the property is not taxed, but the tax deduction is the fair market value of the contributed asset. For example:

Market price	$400,000
Cost of property	100,000
Capital gain	$300,000
Capital gain tax, @ 30%	$ 90,000*
Cash received by donor after tax, $400,000 − $90,000	$310,000

*For corporations, a capital gain on qualifying assets held more than one year is subject to a maximum tax at a rate of 30 percent, rather than at ordinary income tax rates. The tax law specifies which assets are subject to the capital gains rate (the most notable are land and marketable securities). Gains on sales of inventories and receivables are taxed at ordinary rates, while gains on sales of depreciable property are also taxed as ordinary income in many cases. However, the entire problem of computing taxes on long-term gains is too complex to be covered in this introductory chapter. Moreover, the contribution of appreciated property is subject to some complicated rules and limitations.

	Sell, and Donate Cash	*Donate Outright*
Income tax effects of contribution:		
Deduction	$310,000	$400,000
Assumed income tax rate of 50%	×.50	×.50
Income tax savings of donor	$155,000	$200,000
Charitable institution can receive:		
Cash = $400,000 in cash − $90,000 tax, or	$310,000	
Property, and then sell it for cash		$400,000

As the tabulation shows, compared to a cash donation, the direct donation of property can enable the donor to reap larger tax savings while the donee also receives a larger benefit. Therefore, charitable institutions have tried to attract donations by stressing the tax-saving features of giving property rather than cash.

Operating Losses

The net operating loss of a corporation may be used to offset net income by being carried back to each of the three preceding years and carried forward to each of the seven following years. This sequence must be followed strictly. No part of a given year's loss may be used to offset the second preceding year's income until all of the third preceding year's income has been absorbed. In short, a net operating loss enables the corporation to obtain tax refunds related to past years' operations or to reduce tax disbursements in future years.

The tax effects of a 19x4 net operating loss may be illustrated as follows (note that any loss carryforward unused after seven years becomes nondeductible):[5]

---

[5] A taxpayer may elect *not* to carry the loss back. The election is made annually and will not increase the carryover period. Such an election would generally be made only where carryback of the loss would cause tax credits utilized in the preceding years to expire unused.

	Net Income (Loss)	19x4 Carryback or Carryforward	Taxable Income
19x1	$ 5,000	$(5,000)	—
19x2	15,000	(15,000)	—
19x3	35,000	(35,000)	—
19x4	(100,000)	—	—
19x5	5,000	(5,000)	—
19x6	8,000	(8,000)	—
19x7	10,000	(10,000)	—
19x8	10,000	(10,000)	—
19x9	5,000	(5,000)	—
		(93,000)	
19x0	1,000	(1,000)	
19x1	2,000	(2,000)	
Used		(96,000)	
Unused and nondeductible		(4,000)	
Accounted for		(100,000)	

Strangely enough, a company may properly view a loss carryforward as an "asset," for planning purposes. It represents a valuable tax deduction as long as profitable operations are forthcoming. If the tax rate is 48 percent, a loss carryforward of $100,000 represents future tax savings of $48,000. In certain cases, this may prompt corporations to buy other profitable companies at higher-than-usual prices.

Suppose that Company A has a potential net operating cash inflow of $200,000 per year for the next five years. Suppose further that two companies, X and Y, are interested in buying Company A. Company X has a $1,000,000 net operating loss carryforward that can be offset against the next five years' net taxable income. Company Y has no such loss carryforward. Both companies are willing to buy all the capital stock of Company A at a price not to exceed the present value of the five years' after-tax cash inflows, discounted at 8 percent. What are the maximum prices that Company X and Company Y are willing to pay? Calculations follow:

Company Y

After-tax net cash inflow of Company A is $200,000 less .48(200,000)	=	$104,000
Present value of an annuity of $1, @ 8%, for 5 years	×	3.993
Maximum price		$415,272

Company X

After-tax net cash inflow of Company A would be the entire $200,000, because of the $1,000,000 loss carried forward over a five-year period		$200,000
Present value of an annuity of $1, @ 8%, for 5 years	×	3.993
Maximum price		$798,600

The relevance of the loss carryforward in the Company X analysis depends on the available alternatives. Perhaps the carryforward can be used to offset Company X's future taxable income—that is, there is danger of double-counting the carryforward. It cannot be used to offset both the Company A income and the Company X income.[6]

Tax-Free Interest

Interest on the bonds issued by a city, state, and certain nonprofit organizations is nontaxable to the investor. Because of this feature, such bonds have a lower pretax yield than industrial bonds. However, the high-bracket taxpayer and corporations will usually find tax-exempt bonds more attractive:

	Non-Tax-exempt Industrial Bond: Coupon Rate, 8%	*Tax-exempt Municipal Bond: Coupon Rate, 5%*
Investment in bonds	$100,000	$100,000
Interest income before taxes	$ 8,000	$ 5,000
Income taxes, @ 50%	4,000	—
Net income, after taxes	$ 4,000	$ 5,000

Capital Gains Alternative

Investments in stocks and bonds are usually cited as a common example of capital assets. The Internal Revenue Service defines capital assets negatively as being all assets except inventory, trade receivables, copyrights, depreciable property, and real property used in a trade or business. Unless a corporation has an operating loss, the gains from the sale of capital assets held more than one year are taxed at a maximum of 30 percent.

Depreciable property and real property used in a trade or business are not capital assets. Nevertheless, a special rule regarding these "Section 1231 assets" permits treating certain gains as long-term capital gains and certain losses as ordinary losses. If net gains exceed net losses, all the gains and losses are regarded as long-term capital gains and losses. If net losses exceed net gains, all the gains and losses are regarded as ordinary items in computing taxable income. Because the losses offset the gains dollar for dollar, the shrewd tax planner tries to time his transactions so that losses occur in one year and gains in another.

For example, assume that a company owns two parcels of land. One parcel can be sold at a capital gain of $500,000, the other at a capital loss of $500,000. If both were sold in the same year, the loss would offset the gain,

[6]A carryover may be disallowed if there has been a "substantial change" in ownership. These intricate rules severely limit the ability to "sell" a loss carryforward.

and there would be no impact on taxes. If they were sold in separate years, the tax bill would be 30 percent of $500,000 in one year, or $150,000, and lower (assuming an ordinary tax rate of 48 percent) by $240,000 in the next year. The second strategy would thus save the company $90,000 in income tax disbursements.

Other General Considerations

Purchases of assets. When a group of long-lived assets is acquired for a single overall price, care must be taken to see that as much of the total cost as permissible is allocated to those assets whose costs will be depreciated or amortized for income tax purposes. Otherwise, the excess of the total cost over those parts allocated is assigned to land and/or goodwill, which are not subject to amortization for income tax purposes. For example, suppose a purchaser paid $10 million for a group of assets having a book value of $6 million; individual assets such as inventories, buildings, and equipment would tend to be revalued upward.

Use of debt in the capital structure. Interest is deductible as an expense; dividends are not. Therefore, the relative after-tax cash drains on corporations favor using as much debt in the capital structure as seems prudent. Assume a 50 percent tax rate:

	Pretax Cost	*After-tax Cost*
8% Bonds payable	8%	4%
10% Preferred stock	10%	10%

Research and development. There is conceptual merit in capitalizing many research costs for internal purposes. These costs are then amortized over future periods. From a tax-planning standpoint, however, research costs should be deducted as quickly as possible.

Cash versus accrual accounting methods. The cash method of accounting allows more taxpayer control over the timing of revenue and expense than the accrual method. For example, a legal expense attributable to services rendered in December, 19x1, might be deductible in either 19x1 or 19x2, depending on whether the cash disbursement is made in December or delayed until January. However, where inventories exist, companies must use the accrual basis.

Deferral of income. Among the many ways of deferring income are installment sales methods, whereby income is geared to cash receipts rather than point of sale.

For example, a furniture store's taxable income for its first year in business could be computed as follows:

	Regular Basis	Installment Basis
Installment sales	$500,000	
Cost of goods sold	300,000	
Gross profit, @ 40%	$200,000	$160,000*
Expenses	150,000	150,000
Net taxable income	$ 50,000	$ 10,000

* Forty percent of current installment collections of $400,000.
Unrealized gross profit is 40 percent of ending receivables: 40
percent of $100,000, or $40,000.

If the owner chooses to report income on the installment basis, income tax on the uncollected gross profit—which is 40 percent of $100,000 (i.e., $500,000 − $400,000), or $40,000—is deferred until the years when the installments are collected.

Also available is the discretionary timing of shipments of merchandise to customers. At year-end, the choice between making a shipment at December 31 or January 1 can have a significant impact on income taxes, because the sale can thus be included in either of the two adjacent calendar years.

Dividends received. Corporations can generally exclude 85 percent of dividends received from taxable domestic corporations; in other words, only 15 percent of the dividend is taxable to the recipient. This provision enhances the attractiveness of investing excess cash in common stock rather than in federal or corporate bonds, whose interest is fully taxable.

Desirability of Losses

The often-heard expression, "What the heck, it's deductible," sometimes warps perspective. Even though losses bring income tax savings and gains bring additional income taxes, gains are still more desirable than losses. For example, business land (see earlier section, "Capital Gains Alternative") that cost $300,000 a few years ago and that is sold now, would have the following effect at two different selling prices:

	Gain		Loss	
Selling price	$1,000,000	$1,000,000	$ 100,000	$100,000
Cost	300,000		300,000	
Gain (loss)	$ 700,000		$(200,000)	
Tax, @ 30% of $700,000		−210,000		
Tax savings, @ 60% of $200,000				+120,000
Net cash effect		$ 790,000		$220,000

Income tax is a significant cost of conducting business. No accountant or manager should be indifferent to its impact. Income taxes may be necessary evils, but this does not mean that management should be resigned to tax burdens. Intelligent planning, assisted by expert advice, can minimize income taxes.

Income taxes are sometimes too influential in business decisions. Their effects may be overemphasized. The ogre of the income tax may reduce the emphasis on efficiency and may unduly hamper risk taking. Income tax is only one of a number of variables that bear on business administration.

SUMMARY PROBLEM FOR YOUR REVIEW

Problem

The Flan Company estimates that it can save $2,500 per year in annual cash operating costs for the next five years if it buys a special-purpose machine at a cost of $9,000. Residual value is expected to be $1,000, although no residual value is being provided for in using sum-of-the-years'-digits depreciation for tax purposes. The minimum desired rate of return, after taxes, is 10 percent. Income tax rates are 40 percent on ordinary income. Using discounted-cash-flow techniques, show whether the investment is desirable.

Solution

There is a net disadvantage in purchasing because the net present value is slightly negative, indicating an internal rate of return a shade below the minimum desired rate of 10 percent. However, such a slight quantitative disadvantage could be more than offset by positive factors not quantified here. The complete analysis is on the accompanying page.

Fundamental Assignment Material

13-1. Income taxes and disposal of assets. Assume that income tax rates are 60 percent.

1. The book value of an old machine is $20,000. It is to be sold for $8,000. What is the effect of this decision on cash flows, after taxes?

2. The book value of an old machine is $10,000. It is to be sold for $13,000. What is the effect on cash flows, after taxes, of this decision?

SOLUTION DATA FOR SUMMARY PROBLEM FOR YOUR REVIEW

	PRESENT-VALUE DISCOUNT FACTORS, @ 10%	TOTAL PRESENT VALUES
Recurring cash operating savings	$2,500	
Income taxes, @ 40%	1,000	
After-tax cash operating savings	$1,500	
	3.791	$5,686

Depreciation: Sum-of-the-years'-digits,
$1 + 2 + 3 + 4 + 5 = 15$

YEAR	MULTIPLIED BY $9,000	DEDUCTION	INCOME TAX SAVINGS, @ 40%	PRESENT-VALUE DISCOUNT FACTORS, @ 10%	TOTAL PRESENT VALUES
1	5/15	$3,000	$1,200	.909	1,091
2	4/15	2,400	960	.826	793
3	3/15	1,800	720	.751	541
4	2/15	1,200	480	.683	328
5	1/15	600	240	.621	149

Residual value, all subject to tax because book value will be zero	$1,000		
Less: 40% income tax on disposal gain*	400		
Net cash inflow	$ 600	.621	373
Initial required investment			(9,000)
Net present value of all cash flows			$(39)

SKETCH OF CASH FLOWS AT END OF YEAR

	0	1	2	3	4	5
		$1,500	$1,500	$1,500	$1,500	$1,500
		1,200	960	720	480	240
						600
	(9,000)					

* Assume that ordinary income tax rates, not capital gains rates, apply.

411

13-2. Equipment purchase. The Morax Company expects to save $6,000 in cash operating costs for each of the next four years if it buys a special machine at a cost of $20,000. Residual value is expected to be $1,000, although no residual value is being provided for in using the sum-of-the-years'-digits depreciation method for tax purposes. A major overhaul, costing $1,000, will occur at the end of the second year and is fully deductible, in that year, for income tax purposes. The minimum desired rate of return, after taxes, is 8 percent. Income tax rates are 60 percent.

Required

1. Using discounted-cash-flow techniques, show whether the investment is desirable.

2. Would your answer change if an investment tax credit of 10 percent were available on all assets having useful lives in excess of three years?

13-3. Tax shield and depreciation methods. A company has just paid $84,000 for some equipment that will have a six-year life and no residual value. The minimum rate of return desired, after taxes, is 10 percent.

The president has attended a management conference luncheon where an accounting professor adamantly stated: "Not using accelerated depreciation for tax purposes is outright financial stupidity." The president has a perpetual fear of rises in income tax rates and has favored straight-line depreciation "to have greater deductions against future income when taxes are higher."

He is having second thoughts now, and has asked you to prepare a financial analysis of the dollar benefits of using sum-of-the-years'-digits depreciation instead of straight-line depreciation under the following assumptions: (a) income tax rates of 60 percent throughout the coming six years, and (b) income tax rates of 60 percent for the first three years and 80 percent for the subsequent three years.

Additional Assignment Material

13-4. Distinguish between tax avoidance and tax evasion.

13-5. "Tax planning is unimportant because the total income tax bill will be the same in the long run, regardless of short-run maneuvering." Do you agree? Explain.

13-6. What are the major influences on the present value of a tax deduction?

13-7. Explain why accelerated depreciation methods are superior to straight-line methods for income tax purposes.

13-8. "Immediate disposal of equipment, rather than its continued use, results in a full tax deduction of the undepreciated cost now—rather than having such a deduction spread over future years in the form of annual depreciation." Do you agree? Explain, using the $35,000 cost of old equipment in Exhibit 13-3 as a basis for your discussion.

13-9. Name some income tax complications that were ignored in Exhibits 13-3 and 13-4.

13-10. What is an investment credit?

13-11. Why does Lifo save income taxes when prices are rising?

13-12. "If income tax rates are likely to rise, the tendency would be to increase year-end purchases of inventory under Lifo." Do you agree? Explain.

13-13. Why have charitable institutions tried to attract donations in the form of property rather than cash?

13-14. How was it possible that the drug companies' net income was increased in 1962 by their contribution to the ransom of Cuban prisoners?

13-15. "A loss carryforward has an economic value." Explain.

13-16. **Effects of Lifo on purchase decisions.** Solve Problem 20-32.

13-17. **Effects of Lifo and Fifo.** Solve Problem 20-33.

13-18. **Switch from Lifo to Fifo.** Effective January 1, 1970, Chrysler Corporation adopted the Fifo method for inventories previously valued by the Lifo method. The 1970 annual report stated: "This . . . makes the financial statements with respect to inventory valuation comparable with those of the other United States automobile manufacturers."

The Wall Street Journal reported:

The change improved Chrysler's 1970 financial results several ways. Besides narrowing the 1970 loss by $20 million it improved Chrysler's working capital. The change also made the comparison with 1969 earnings look somewhat more favorable because, upon restatement, Chrysler's 1969 profit was raised only $10.2 million from the original figures.

Finally, the change helped Chrysler's balance sheet by boosting inventories, and thus current assets, by $150 million at the end of 1970 over what they would have been under LIFO. As Chrysler's profit has collapsed over the last two years and its financial position tightened, auto analysts have eyed warily Chrysler's shrinking ratio of current assets to current liabilities.

Chrysler's current liabilities shrank last year because it was able to pay off sizable amounts of short-term debt with the help of a $200 million long-term financing last winter. Chrysler's short-term debt stood at $374 million at year-end, down from $477 million a year earlier but up slightly from $370 million on Sept. 30. Chrysler's cash and marketable securities shrank during the year to $156.4 million at year-end, down from $309.3 million a year earlier and $220 million on Sept. 30.

To get the improvements in its balance sheet and results, however, Chrysler paid a price. Roger Helder, vice president and comptroller, said Chrysler owed the government $53 million in tax savings it accumulated by using the LIFO method since it switched from FIFO in 1957. The major advantage of LIFO is that it holds down profit and thus tax liabilities. The other three major auto makers stayed on the FIFO method. Mr. Helder said Chrysler now has to pay back that $53 million to the government over 20 years, which will boost Chrysler's tax bills about $3 million a year.

Required

Given the content of this text chapter, do you think the Chrysler decision to switch from Lifo to Fifo was beneficial to its stockholders? Explain, being as specific and using as many data as you can.

13-19. Donations of property rather than cash. The Fantasy Company has 100 shares of Florence common stock that were acquired four years ago at $70 per share. Current market price is $120 per share. Income tax rates are 60 percent on ordinary income and 25 percent on capital gains. Compare the effects on Fantasy's income taxes of: (1) selling the stock and donating the net cash after taxes to a university, and (2) donating the stock outright. How much cash will the university net under each plan, assuming that all donations of property are immediately converted into cash?

13-20. Loss carryforward and purchase of a business. Company G's potential net operating cash inflow, before taxes, for the next five years is $500,000 annually. Two companies, P and Q, are interested in buying all of the capital stock of Company G. Company P has a $2,500,000 net operating loss, which it can carry forward to offset the next five years' net taxable income. Company Q has no such loss carryforward. Both companies are willing to buy all the capital stock of Company G at a price not to exceed the present value of the five years' cash inflow after taxes, discounted at 10 percent.

Required

What are the maximum prices that Company P and Company Q are willing to pay? Show your calculations. The ordinary income tax rate is 40 percent and the capital gains rate is 25 percent.

13-21. Timing of gains and losses. A company owns 10,000 shares each of the common stock of Company A and Company B. The Company A stock was acquired ten years ago for $100,000. It can now be sold for $400,000. The Company B stock was purchased five years ago for $900,000. It can now be sold for $600,000. It is now near the end of year 19x1. Capital gains tax rate is 30 percent, and ordinary income tax rate is 40 percent.

Required

1. If all the stock were sold in 19x1, what would be the effect on income taxes?
2. If the Company B stock were sold in 19x1, and the Company A stock were sold in 19x2, what would be the effect on income taxes? Assume that these are the only transactions affecting capital gains or losses. Which strategy will save the most income taxes? How much would be saved?

13-22. Form of organization. X and Y are attempting to decide whether to organize their new business as a corporation or as a partnership. Each will invest $100,000 and will receive annual compensation for services of $20,000 each. Sales will be $900,000 and cash expenses other than owners' salaries will be $760,000. All plant assets are rented, so there is no depreciation.

Each owner is in a 60 percent marginal income tax bracket. The corporate tax rate is 22 percent on the first $25,000 of income and 48 percent on the excess.

Required

1. Suppose that dividends or withdrawals are equal to net income. What is the income subject to tax for the corporation? The partnership? How much cash will be available to the business and to each owner after taxes?

2. Suppose that no dividends are paid. Suppose also that the withdrawals of the partners are equal to the salary equivalent of $20,000 each plus an additional withdrawal for payment of additional income taxes on the portion of partnership income that is not withdrawn. For the corporation and the partnership forms of organization, compute the cash available to each owner after taxes and the cash available to the business for expansion.

13-23. Football coaching contract. (H. Schaefer.) Bo Hays, a successful college football coach, has just signed a "million-dollar-plus" contract to coach a new professional team. The contract is a personal services contract for five years with the team's owner, I. M. Rich (if the team is disbanded Bo can still collect from Rich). Under the terms of the contract Bo will be paid $150,000 cash at the start of the contract plus $150,000 at the end of each of the five years. Rich also agrees to buy a $200,000 house that Bo can use rent-free for all five years.

Rich earns a substantial income from numerous business ventures. His marginal tax rate is about 60 percent. Bo's cash salary payments are tax deductible to Rich, as are the depreciation expenses on the house. Rich decides to depreciate the house over a 20-year life with zero salvage value using the straight-line method of depreciation. Rich is certain the house can be sold at the end of five years for a price equal to its remaining book value.

Required

1. Determine Rich's yearly after-tax cash flows under Bo's contract.

2. Given your answers to Requirement 1, calculate the net present value of the costs of Bo's contract to Rich, assuming Rich employs a 10 percent minimum desired rate of return. Show your calculations clearly and in an orderly fashion. You may round to the nearest thousand dollars.

13-24. Income taxes and replacement of equipment. Refer to Problem 5-2. Assume that income tax rates are 60 percent. The minimum desired rate of return, after taxes, is 6 percent. Using the net-present-value technique, show whether the proposed equipment should be purchased. Present your solution on both a total project approach and an incremental approach. For illustrative purposes, assume that old equipment would have been depreciated on a straight-line basis and the proposed equipment on a sum-of-the-years'-digits basis.

13-25. Minimizing transportation costs. Refer to Assignment 12-29, but ignore the requirements there and make the following assumptions:

a. Wegener requires a minimum 10 percent after-tax rate of return.
b. A 40 percent tax rate.
c. Sum-of-the-year's-digits depreciation with an allowance for the $5,000 salvage value of the truck.
d. No investment tax credit.

1. Should the truck be purchased? Show computations to support your answer.
2. What qualitative factors might influence your decision? Be specific.

13-26. Income taxes and make or buy. Refer to Problem 5-28, Requirement 1. Assume a tax rate of 40 percent. The minimum desired rate of return, after taxes, is 6 percent. Using the net-present-value technique, show whether the proposed purchase from the outside supplier is desirable. Use both a total project approach and an incremental approach. Assume straight-line depreciation.

13-27. Tax effects of equipment. (CMA, adapted.) R. Oliver and J. Rand have formed a corporation to franchise a quick food system for shopping malls. They have just completed experiments with the prototype machine, which will serve as the basis of the operation. Because the system is new and untried, they have decided to conduct a pilot operation in a nearby mall. When it proves successful, they will aggressively market the franchises.

The income statements in Exhibit 13-7 represent their best estimates of income from the mall operation for the next four years. At the end of the four-year period they intend to sell the operation and concentrate on the sale of and supervision of franchises. Based upon the income stream projected, they believe the operation can be sold for $190,000; the income tax liability from the sale will be $40,000.

1. Calculate the cash flow for the mall operation for the four-year period beginning January 1, 19x7, ignoring income tax implications.

EXHIBIT 13-7

Projected Income
for Years Ending December 31

	19x7	19x8	19x9	19x0
Sales	$120,000	$150,000	$200,000	$230,000
Less: Cost of goods sold	$ 60,000	$ 75,000	$100,000	$110,000
Wages	24,000	30,000	40,000	44,000
Supplies	2,000	2,300	2,400	3,200
Personal property taxes	1,000	1,200	1,600	1,800
Annual rental charge*	12,000	12,000	12,000	12,000
Depreciation†	11,000	11,000	11,000	11,000
Development costs‡	20,000	20,000	20,000	20,000
Total expenses	$130,000	$151,500	$187,000	$202,000
Net income before taxes	$ (10,000)	$ (1,500)	$ 13,000	$ 28,000
Income taxes @ 40%	— §	— §	600§	11,200
Net income after taxes	$ (10,000)	$ (1,500)	$ 12,400	$ 16,800

* The shopping mall requires tenants to sign a ten-year lease. Three years' rental is payable at the beginning of the lease period with annual payments at the end of each of the next seven years.

† Construction of an operational machine is estimated to be completed on December 31, 19x6. The $130,000 purchase price will be paid at that time. The salvage value at the end of its ten-year life is estimated at $20,000. Straight-line depreciation is to be used for statement purposes and sum-of-the-years'-digits for tax purposes.

‡ The prototype machine cost $200,000 to develop and build in 19x5. It is not suitable for commercial use. However, since it was the basis of the system, it is to be amortized at $20,000 per year. The same amount will be deducted for tax purposes.

§ The losses of the first two years are offset against the $13,000 income in 19x9 before income tax charges are calculated.

2. Adjust the cash flows for the tax consequences as appropriate.

3. Oliver and Rand plan to employ discounted-cash-flow techniques to judge whether the mall operation is a sound investment. Compute the net present value of the contemplated investment, using a minimum desired rate of return of 16 percent after taxes.

13-28. Acquiring equipment. (CMA, adapted.) Edwards Corporation is a manufacturing concern that produces and sells a wide range of products. The company not only mass-produces a number of products and equipment components but also is capable of producing special-purpose manufacturing equipment to customer specifications.

The firm is considering adding a new stapler to one of its product lines. More equipment will be required to produce the new stapler. There are two ways to acquire the needed equipment: (1) purchase general-purpose equipment, and (2) build special-purpose equipment. A third alternative, purchase of the special-purpose equipment, has been ruled out because it would be prohibitively expensive.

The general-purpose equipment can be purchased for $125,000. The equipment has an estimated salvage of $15,000 at the end of its useful life of ten years. At the end of five years the equipment can be used elsewhere in the plant or be sold for $40,000.

Special-purpose equipment can be constructed by the Contract Equipment Department of the Edwards Corporation. While the department is operating at a level that is normal for the time of year, it is below full capacity. The department could produce the equipment without interfering with its regular revenue-producing activities.

The estimated departmental costs for the construction of the special-purpose equipment are

Materials and parts	$ 75,000
Direct labor	60,000
Variable overhead (50% of DL$)	30,000
Fixed overhead (25% of DL$)	15,000
Total	$180,000

Corporation general and administrative costs average 20 percent of labor dollar content of factory production.

Engineering and management studies provide the following revenue and cost predictions (excluding depreciation) for producing the new stapler, depending upon the equipment used:

	General-Purpose Equipment	Self-Constructed Equipment
Unit selling price	$5.00	$5.00
Unit variable production costs:		
Materials	$1.80	$1.70
Conversion costs	1.65	1.40
Total unit variable production costs	$3.45	$3.10
Unit contribution margin	$1.55	$1.90
Estimated unit volume	40,000	40,000
Estimated total contribution margin	$62,000	$76,000

Other costs:		
Supervision	$16,000	$18,000
Taxes and insurance	3,000	5,000
Maintenance	3,000	2,000
Total	$22,000	$25,000

The company will depreciate the general-purpose machine over ten years on the sum-of-the-years-digits (S-Y-D) method. At the end of five years the accumulated depreciation will total $80,000. (The present value of this amount for the first five years is $62,100.) The special-purpose machine will be depreciated over five years on the S-Y-D method. Its salvage value at the end of that time is estimated to be $30,000.

The company uses an after-tax cost of capital of 10 percent. Its marginal tax rate is 40 percent.

Required

1. Calculate the net present value for each alternative. Round all discount factors to two decimal places.
2. Which alternative should be chosen? Explain.

13-29. **Comprehensive problem on equipment replacement.** A manufacturer who specializes in making aircraft parts developed a $68,000 special-purpose molding machine for automatically producing a special part. The machine will be useless after the total market potential, spread evenly over four years, is exhausted. The machine has been used for one year. The $68,000 original cost is being depreciated on a straight-line basis.

At the beginning of the second year, a machine salesman offers a new machine that is vastly more efficient. It will cost $45,000, will reduce annual cash operating costs from $45,000 to $26,500, and will have zero disposal value at the end of three years. Sum-of-the-years'-digits would be the depreciation method used for tax purposes for this machine.

The scrap value of the old machine is $30,000 now and will be $2,000 three years from now; however, no scrap value has been provided for in calculating straight-line depreciation for tax purposes.

Required

1. Assume that income tax rates are 60 percent. The minimum rate of return desired, after taxes, is 8 percent. Using the net-present-value technique, show whether the new machine should be purchased: (a) under a total project approach, and (b) under an incremental approach.
2. Recompute your answer in Requirement 1, assuming that a 10 percent investment tax credit is available on the new machine.

13-30. **Oil exploration.** (J. Patell.) During 19x6, Green and Trunk Oil Drilling expended $800,000 on oil exploration in Texarkana and succeeded in locating a small deposit. However, the nature of the oil-bearing formation (a salt dome) necessitates some long-range planning decisions now, before full-scale production begins.

Standard drilling and production equipment will require an immediate investment of $1,000,000. In addition, a sum of $100,000 must be deposited in advance with the Environmental Protection Agency as assurance that complete land reclamation will be provided by G&T when the well is finally closed down; the sum is returned in full plus 5 percent nontaxable annual interest if the required reclamation is performed. G&T estimates that the well will be productive for five years, and thus the investment will be depreciated on a straight-line basis over the five-year life. Owing to the size and shape of the formation, however, the oil production rate will not be constant over the five years. G&T's geologists predict that the well will yield approximately $500,000 worth of crude oil for each of the first three years, but the yield will drop to $400,000 in the fourth and fifth years *under normal production procedures*. Operating costs are estimated at $100,000 yearly for the entire life, and the land reclamation should require $50,000 at the end of the fifth year (fully tax deductible).

A secondary planning problem also must be solved now. Advanced forced-water pumping techniques have recently been perfected that would enable G&T to maintain the pressure in the well during Years 4 and 5 such that there would actually be *no decrease* in the flow rate. This technology would require an outlay of $50,000 at the end of Year 3 (to be depreciated over the last two years on a straight-line basis), but there would be no increase in annual operating expenses. Unfortunately, the initial production equipment would also have to be modified to accept the additional equipment later, raising the initial outlay from $1,000,000 to $1,100,000.

Green and Trunk pays a 40 percent corporate income tax and uses a 12 percent after-tax opportunity rate in evaluating investment proposals. For computational simplicity assume all operating cash flows and tax payments occur at the *end* of the year.

Assume that Green and Trunk will have enough taxable income from other sources to utilize all tax benefits from this project. The future amount of $1.00 at 5 percent is $1.00 $(1.05)^5 = \$1.2763$.

1. Assuming that G&T is going to develop the well, should the original equipment be constructed to accept the later addition of forced-water extraction gear? Support your answer with a net-present-value calculation.

2. Given your decision in Requirement 1, what is the net present value now to G&T of investing in production equipment and developing the well?

CHAPTER 14

Job
and Process Systems
and Overhead
Application

Thus far, we have paid little attention to the product costing-income determination purpose of an accounting system. The purpose of this and the next chapter is to show how data may be accumulated within an accounting system and how various alternative methods of applying costs to products affect inventories and income determination. These are essentially score-keeping tasks. Management makes policy decisions, at one time or another, regarding methods of product costing. Because such decisions affect the way net income will be determined, managers should know the various approaches to product costing. Moreover, as we have seen previously, a knowledge of product costing techniques will enhance a manager's understanding of his product costs, particularly when the latter are used for pricing and evaluating product lines.

Keep in mind that **product costing is separable from control.** That is, a good planning and control system may be coupled with any of a number of product costing practices. In short, how costs are held back in inventory and released to expense should have little bearing (except for income tax plan-

421

*Job and
Process
Systems and
Overhead
Application*

ning described in Chapter 14) on the planning and controlling decisions of intelligent managers.

This chapter is designed so that it may be studied immediately after Chapter 3 without loss of continuity. Therefore, to begin, please review the first two sections of Chapter 3 ("Classifications of Costs" and "Relationships of Income Statements and Balance Sheets") and the Chapter 3 Appendix ("Classification of Labor Costs"). It is not necessary to review the other parts of Chapter 3.

Our focus in this and the next chapter is on manufacturing costs, because accountants view selling, administrative, and other nonmanufacturing costs as being expenses immediately and therefore totally excludable from costs of *product.*

CONTROL
AND PRODUCT COSTING PURPOSES

Two Purposes and Two Cost Objectives

Recall that Chapter 3 defined a *cost objective* as any activity for which a separate measurement of costs is desired. Two principal cost objectives were illustrated: departments and products. Cost accounting systems have a twofold purpose fulfilled by their day-to-day operations: (1) allocate costs to departments for planning and control, hereafter for brevity's sake often called *control,* and (2) allocate costs to units of product for product costing.

Suppose a firm had direct-material usage of $10,000, direct-labor usage of $8,000, and manufacturing overhead incurred, $4,000, half of each of these in Department A and half in Department B. Three jobs (three special orders for batches of living room furniture) were started and completed, passing through both departments. Each received varying attention and effort, and therefore different costs were allocated to each job, as assumed in Exhibit 14-1.

If the jobs in Exhibit 14-1 are not completed at the end of the accounting period, their costs are the measure of the inventory of Work in Process. As the jobs are completed, their costs are transferred to another inventory, Finished Goods.

Direct material may be acquired and stored as Direct-Materials Inventory before it is requisitioned for use by departments. In schematic form, the flow of direct materials is shown in Exhibit 14-2. Pause and examine the exhibit before reading on.

Distinction between Job Costing and Process Costing

Two extremes of product costing are usually termed **job-order costing** and **process costing.** *Job-order* (or *job-cost* or *production-order*) accounting

EXHIBIT 14-1

Cost Allocation for Two Purposes

	TOTAL	DEPARTMENT A			DEPARTMENT B		
		DIRECT MATERIALS	DIRECT LABOR	FACTORY OVERHEAD	DIRECT MATERIALS	DIRECT LABOR	FACTORY OVERHEAD
1. Control purpose	$22,000	$5,000	$4,000	$2,000	$5,000	$4,000	$2,000
2. Product costing purpose:							
Job 1	$ 7,500	$1,000	$2,000	$1,000	$2,000	$1,000	$ 500
Job 2	7,550	2,000	1,500	750	1,800	1,000	500
Job 3	6,950	2,000	500	250	1,200	2,000	1,000
Costs accounted for	$22,000	$5,000	$4,000	$2,000	$5,000	$4,000	$2,000

In schematic form:

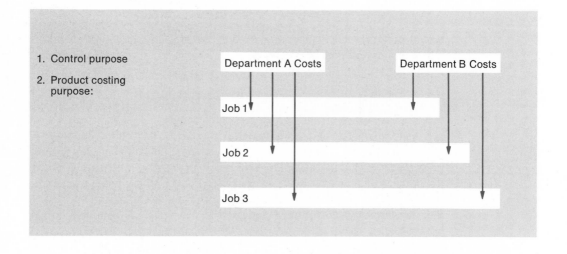

1. Control purpose

2. Product costing purpose:

methods were just illustrated. They are used by companies whose products are readily identified by individual units or batches, each of which receives varying degrees of attention and skill. Industries that commonly use job-order methods include construction, printing, aircraft, furniture, and machinery.

Process costing is most often found in such industries as chemicals, oil, textiles, plastics, paints, flour, canneries, rubber, lumber, food processors, glass, mining, cement, and meat packing. In these there is mass production of like units, which usually pass in continuous fashion through a series of uniform production steps called *operations* or *processes.* This is in contrast to

EXHIBIT 14-2. Flow of Direct Materials

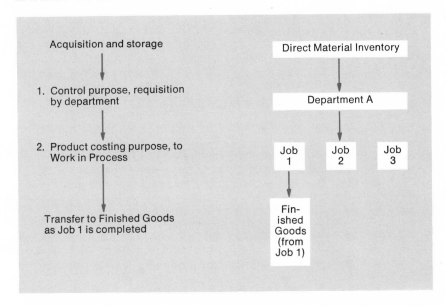

the production of tailor-made or unique goods, such as special-purpose machinery or printing.

Where manufacturing is conducted by continuous operations, costs are accumulated by departments (sometimes called *operations* or *processes*). The center of attention is the total department costs for a given time period in relation to the units processed. Accumulated department costs are divided by quantities produced during a given period in order to get broad, average unit costs. Then unit costs are multiplied by units transferred to obtain total costs applied to those units.

The distinction between the job-cost and the process-cost methods centers largely around how product costing is accomplished. Unlike process costing, which deals with broad averages and great masses of like units, the essential feature of the job-cost method is the attempt to apply costs to specific jobs, which may consist of either a single physical unit (such as a custom sofa) or a few like units (such as a dozen tables) in a distinct batch or job lot.

In job costing, the costs in Exhibit 14-1 might be applicable to, say, three different batches of furniture, each bearing a differing assortment of direct materials, direct labor, and manufacturing overhead. However, to indicate the essence of the process-costing system, assume the costs in Exhibit 14-1 ($10,000 + $8,000 + $4,000 = $22,000) are applicable to several manufacturing processes for the production of a *single product:* 22,000 gallons of chemicals at a unit cost of $1 per gallon of finished product:

423

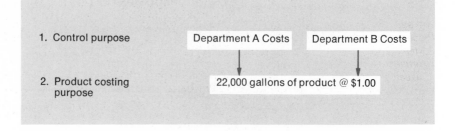

1. Control purpose	Department A Costs Department B Costs
2. Product costing purpose	22,000 gallons of product @ $1.00

The most important point is that product costing is an averaging process. The unit cost used for inventory purposes is the result of taking some accumulated cost that has been allocated to production departments and dividing it by some measure of production. **The basic distinction between job-order costing and process costing is the breadth of the denominator: in job-order costing, it is small** (for example, one painting, 100 advertising circulars, or one special packaging machine); **but in process costing, it is large** (for example, thousands of pounds, gallons, or board feet).

ILLUSTRATION OF JOB-ORDER COSTING

This section illustrates the principal aspects of the job-costing system. The first appendix to this chapter presents some technical details of job costing: source documents, journal entries, and ledgers. The second appendix explains some process-costing procedures.

Cost Application

Consider a new term, **cost application,** often called **cost absorption.** Until now the term **cost allocation** has been used indiscriminately to refer to the identifying or tracing of accumulated costs to *any* cost objective (whether a department or a product). Indeed, *cost allocation* is a general or generic term. However, when costs are allocated *to products,* the process of allocation is frequently called *application* or *absorption.* These latter terms will be used in this chapter. In any event, be alert to obtain the exact meanings of such terms when you encounter them in practice.

Predetermined Overhead Application Rates

To show how factory overhead is applied to jobs, consider the Singapore Electronics Company, which has a job-order cost system with the following inventories on December 31, 19x1:

424

425

*Job and
Process
Systems and
Overhead
Application*

Direct materials (12 types)	$110,000
Work in process	—
Finished goods (leftover	
units from two jobs)	12,000

The following manufacturing overhead budget has been prepared for the coming year, 19x2:

	Machining	Assembly
Indirect labor	$ 69,600	$ 28,800
Supplies	14,400	5,400
Utilities	20,000	9,000
Repairs	10,000	6,000
Factory rent	24,000	16,800
Supervision	18,600	20,400
Depreciation on equipment	114,000	14,400
Insurance, property taxes, etc.	7,200	2,400
	$277,800	$103,200

In order to cost units as they are worked on, a job-cost sheet is prepared for each job as it begins. Three classes of costs are applied to the units as they pass through the departments: material requisitions are used to apply costs of direct material; work tickets are used to apply costs of direct labor; and predetermined overhead rates are used to apply manufacturing overhead. The overhead rates are as follows:

	Year 19x2	
	Machining	Assembly
Budgeted manufacturing overhead	$277,800	$103,200
Budgeted machine-hours	69,450	
Budgeted direct-labor cost		$206,400
Predetermined overhead rate, per		
machine-hour: $277,800 ÷ 69,450 =	$4	
Predetermined overhead rate, per		
direct-labor dollar: $103,200 ÷ $206,400 =		50%

Overhead is a conglomeration of items which, unlike direct material or direct labor, cannot conveniently be applied on an individual basis. But the commonly accepted theory is that overhead is an integral part of a product's cost. Therefore, it is applied in an indirect manner, using a cost allocation base that is common to all jobs worked on and that is the best available index of the product's relative utilization of, or benefits from, the overhead items. In other words, there should be a strong correlation between the factory overhead incurred and the base chosen for its application, such as machine-hours or direct-labor cost.

Two or more machines in the machining department can often be operated simultaneously by a single direct laborer. Since utilization of machines is the major overhead cost in the machining department, machine-hours are the base for application of overhead costs. This necessitates keeping track of the machine-hours used for each job, and thus creates an added clerical cost. Both direct-labor costs and machine-hours must be accumulated for each job.

In contrast, the workers in the assembly department are paid uniform hourly rates, so the cost of direct labor is an accurate reflection of the relative attention and effort devoted to various jobs. No separate job records have to be kept of the labor *hours*. All that is needed is to apply the 50 percent overhead rate to the cost of direct labor already applied to the job. Of course, if the hourly labor rates differed greatly for individuals performing identical tasks, hours of labor, rather than dollars spent for labor, would have to be used as a base. Otherwise, a $4-per-hour worker would cause more overhead to be applied than a $3-per-hour worker, despite the probability that the same time would be taken and the same facilities utilized by each employee to do the same work.

These overhead rates will be used throughout the year to cost the various jobs as they are worked on by each department. All overhead will be applied to all jobs worked on during the year, in proportion to either the machine-hours or direct-labor costs of each job. If management predictions are accurate, the total overhead applied to the year's jobs on the basis of these predetermined rates should be equal to the total overhead costs actually incurred.

The Year's Events

In January, 19x2, several jobs were begun. For example, Job 404 was begun and completed. Exhibit 14-3 is the completed job cost sheet.

The bulk of the scorekeeping is a detailed recording and summarization of source documents such as requisitions, work tickets, invoices, and so on. The following is a summary of events for the year 19x2:

	Machining	*Assembly*	*Total*
1. Direct materials purchased	—	—	$1,900,000
2. Direct materials requisitioned	$1,000,000	$890,000	1,890,000
3. Direct-labor costs incurred	200,000	190,000	390,000
4a. Factory overhead *incurred*	290,000	102,000	392,000
4b. Factory overhead *applied*			
(50% of direct-labor costs,		95,000	95,000
70,000 machine-hours @ $4)	280,000		280,000
5. Cost of goods completed	—	—	2,500,000
6a. Sales	—	—	4,000,000
6b. Cost of goods sold	—	—	2,480,000

EXHIBIT 14-3
Completed Job Cost Sheet

				Job Order No.	404
MACHINING DEPARTMENT					
REFERENCE	DATE	QUANTITY	UNIT COST	AMOUNT	SUMMARY
Direct material:					
Type M—Various requisitions	Various	900	$2.00	$1,800	
Type N—Various requisitions	Various	900	5.00	4,500	$ 6,300
Direct labor:					
Various work tickets	Various	320 hrs	9.00	3,880	2,880
Factory overhead applied		424 mach. hrs	4.00	1,700	1,700
Total machining					$10,880
ASSEMBLY DEPARTMENT					
(Entries would be similar to above)					xxx
Total assembly (assumed)					$ 2,000
Total product cost					$12,880

The accounting for these events is displayed in Exhibit 14-4. The accumulated data would be allocated to departments and then to products. (If you wish a more detailed discussion, see the first appendix to this chapter.) These costs would appear in the financial statements for the year as shown in Exhibit 14-5, which warrants your close scrutiny. (Note how Exhibit 14-5 parallels the ideas in Chapter 3, Exhibit 3-2, page 58.)

PROBLEMS OF OVERHEAD APPLICATION

Most managements desire a close approximation of the costs of different products before the end of a fiscal period. Essentially, this need is for pricing, income determination, and inventory valuation. Moreover, there is a growing objection to the view that all costs incurred must be fully applied to the products. Some costs result from inefficiency, and these can hardly be viewed as being inventoriable as assets. Customers are rarely willing to pay for inefficiency.

Normalized Overhead Rates

Basically, Exhibit 14-4 demonstrates the normal costing approach. Overhead application rates are predetermined by dividing total *budgeted* overhead by

EXHIBIT 14-4

Control and Product Costing Illustration (in dollars)

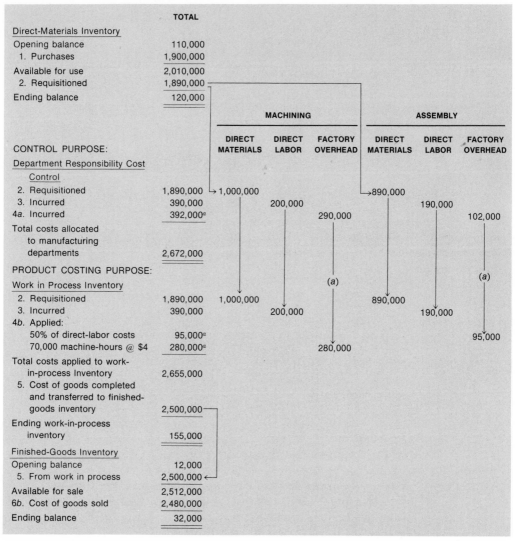

	TOTAL	MACHINING			ASSEMBLY		
		DIRECT MATERIALS	DIRECT LABOR	FACTORY OVERHEAD	DIRECT MATERIALS	DIRECT LABOR	FACTORY OVERHEAD
Direct-Materials Inventory							
Opening balance	110,000						
1. Purchases	1,900,000						
Available for use	2,010,000						
2. Requisitioned	1,890,000						
Ending balance	120,000						
CONTROL PURPOSE:							
Department Responsibility Cost Control							
2. Requisitioned	1,890,000	1,000,000			890,000		
3. Incurred	390,000		200,000			190,000	
4a. Incurred	392,000ᵃ			290,000			102,000
Total costs allocated to manufacturing departments	2,672,000						
PRODUCT COSTING PURPOSE:							
Work in Process Inventory							
2. Requisitioned	1,890,000	1,000,000			890,000		
3. Incurred	390,000		200,000			190,000	
4b. Applied:							
50% of direct-labor costs	95,000ᵃ						95,000
70,000 machine-hours @ $4	280,000ᵃ			280,000			
Total costs applied to work-in-process Inventory	2,655,000						
5. Cost of goods completed and transferred to finished-goods inventory	2,500,000						
Ending work-in-process inventory	155,000						
Finished-Goods Inventory							
Opening balance	12,000						
5. From work in process	2,500,000						
Available for sale	2,512,000						
6b. Cost of goods sold	2,480,000						
Ending balance	32,000						

ᵃ The $17,000 difference is underapplied overhead, $392,000 − ($95,000 + $280,000), which is explained later in the text.

an appropriate base such as machine-hours, direct-labor hours, or direct-labor dollars. The idea is to use an annual average overhead rate consistently throughout the year, for product costing, without altering it from day to day and from month to month. The resultant normal product costs include an average or normalized chunk of overhead.

As actual overhead costs are incurred by departments from month to month, they are charged, in detail, to the departments. These actual costs are

EXHIBIT 14-5

Relation of Costs to Financial Statements

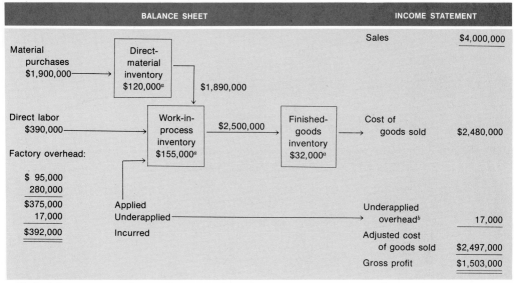

BALANCE SHEET	INCOME STATEMENT

Sales $4,000,000

Material purchases $1,900,000 → Direct-material inventory $120,000[a]

$1,890,000

Direct labor $390,000 →

Factory overhead:

Work-in-process inventory $155,000[a] $2,500,000 → Finished-goods inventory $32,000[a] → Cost of goods sold $2,480,000

$ 95,000
280,000
$375,000   Applied
17,000   Underapplied ————————————————→   Underapplied overhead[b]   17,000

$392,000   Incurred   Adjusted cost of goods sold $2,497,000

Gross profit $1,503,000

[a] Ending balance.
[b] Explained in the next section.

accumulated weekly or monthly and are then compared with budgeted costs to obtain budget variances for performance evaluation. This *control* process is completely divorced from the *product costing* process of applying overhead to specific jobs.

During the year and at year-end, it is unlikely that the amount incurred and applied will be equal. This variance between incurred and applied cost may be analyzed. The following are usually contributory causes: poor forecasting; inefficient use of overhead items; price changes in individual overhead items; erratic behavior of individual overhead items (e.g., repairs made only during slack time); calendar variations (i.e., 20 workdays in one month, 22 in the next); and, probably most important, operating at a different level of volume than the level used as a denominator in calculating the predetermined overhead rate (e.g., using 100,000 direct-labor hours as the denominator and then working 80,000 hours).

All these peculiarities of overhead are commingled in an annual overhead pool. Thus, an annual rate is predetermined and used regardless of the month-to-month peculiarities of specific overhead costs. Such an approach is more defensible than, say, applying the actual overhead for each month, because a *normal* product cost is more meaningful, and more representative for inventory costing purposes, than a so-called "actual" product cost that is distorted by month-to-month fluctuations in production volume and by the erratic behavior of many overhead costs. For example, the employees of a gypsum plant had the privilege of buying company-made

429

items "at cost." It was a joke common among employees to buy "at cost" during high-volume months. Unit costs were then lower under the actual overhead application system in use, whereby overhead rates would fall as volume soared, and vice versa:

	Actual Overhead			Direct-Labor Hours	Actual Overhead Application Rate* per Direct-Labor Hour
	Variable	Fixed	Total		
Peak-volume month	$60,000	$40,000	$100,000	100,000	$1.00
Low-volume month	30,000	40,000	70,000	50,000	1.40

* This overall rate can be separated into two rates, one for variable and one for fixed overhead. Note that the presence of fixed overhead causes the fluctuation in unit costs from $1.00 to $1.40. The variable rate is $.60 an hour in both months, but the fixed rate is $.40 in the peak-volume month ($40,000 ÷ 100,000) and $.80 in the low-volume month ($40,000 ÷ 50,000).

EXHIBIT 14-6. Disposition of Factory Overhead

Method One: Proration Among Inventories

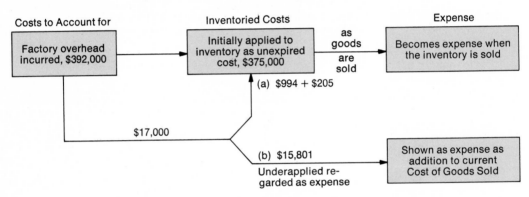

(a) $ 994 prorated to Work-in-Process Inventory
(a)   205 prorated to Finished Goods Inventory
(b) 15,801 regarded as expense
$17,000 underapplied overhead accounted for

Method Two: Immediate Writeoff

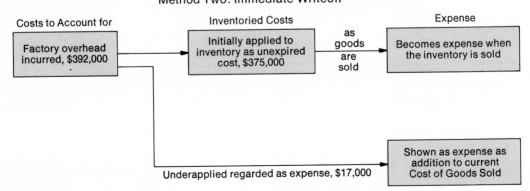

431

Job and
Process
Systems and
Overhead
Application

Another example of the difficulties of product costing was cited by James Lorie, who, after completing a consulting task for Chrysler Corporation in the middle 1950s, asked some top Chrysler executives if he could buy an Imperial automobile directly from the company "at cost." The response was, "We'll be happy to sell an Imperial to you at cost, which this year happens to be 120 percent of list price."

Disposition of Underapplied or Overapplied Overhead

When predetermined rates are used, the difference between incurred and applied overhead is typically allowed to accumulate during the year. When the amount applied to product exceeds the amount incurred by the departments, the difference is called *overapplied* or *overabsorbed* overhead; when the amount applied is less than incurred, the difference is called *underapplied* or *underabsorbed.* At year-end, the difference (which was $17,000 in Exhibit 14-4) is disposed of in one of two major ways, as shown in Exhibit 14-6:

1. *Proration.* This method prorates underapplied overhead among the accounts where the costs of the 19x2 jobs worked on are now lodged. Theoretically, if the objective is to obtain as accurate a cost allocation as possible, all of the overhead costs of the individual jobs worked on should be recomputed, using the actual rather than the original predetermined rates. This approach is rarely feasible, so the best practical attack is probably to prorate on the basis of the total manufacturing costs of the 19x2 jobs in each of three accounts (Work in Process, $155,000; Finished Goods, $32,000; and Cost of Goods Sold, $2,480,000), assuming that the beginning Finished-Goods Inventory was sold during 19x2:

	(1) *Unadjusted Balance,* *End of 19x2**	(2) *Deduct 19x1* *Jobs*	(3) (1) − (2) *Basis for* *Proration*
Work in Process	$ 155,000	$ —	$ 155,000
Finished Goods	32,000	—	32,000
Cost of Goods Sold	2,480,000	12,000	2,468,000
			$2,655,000

(4) *Proration of Underapplied* *Overhead*	(1) + (4) *Adjusted* *Balance* *End* *of 19x2*
155/2,655 × 17,000 = $ 994	$ 155,994
32/2,655 × 17,000 = 205	32,205
2,468/2,655 × 17,000 = 15,801	2,495,801
$17,000	

If overapplied subtract e from

*See Exhibits 14-4 and 14-5 for details.

The amounts prorated to inventories here are not significant. In practical situations, prorating is done only when inventory valuations would be significantly affected.

2. Immediate write-off. This is the most widely used approach; it was used in Exhibit 14-5. The $17,000 is regarded as a reduction in current income via adding the underapplied overhead to the cost of goods sold. (The same logic is followed for overapplied overhead, except that the result would be an addition to current income because cost of goods sold would be lessened.)

The theory underlying the direct write-off is that most of the goods worked on have been sold, and a more elaborate method of disposition is not worth the extra trouble. Another justification is that the extra overhead costs represented by underapplied overhead do not qualify as part of ending inventory costs because they do not represent assets. They should be written off because they largely represent inefficiency or the underutilization of available facilities.

In sum, overhead application will rarely coincide with overhead incurrence (e.g., entry 4*b* in Exhibit 14-4 will not exactly offset entry 4*a*). A difference will arise (i.e., entry 4*b*, compared with entry 4*a*, shows a $17,000 underapplication). This under- or overapplication is typically disposed of at year-end by a direct charge or credit to Income or to Cost of Goods Sold, even though it may also pertain to accounts other than Cost of Goods Sold. Conceptually, however, there is justification for prorating it.

The Use of Variable and Fixed Application Rates

As we have seen, overhead application is the most troublesome aspect of product costing. The presence of fixed costs is the biggest single reason for the costing difficulties. Most companies have made no distinction between variable- and fixed-cost behavior in the design of their accounting systems. For instance, reconsider the development of overhead rates in our illustration. The machining department developed the rate as follows:

$$\text{Overhead application rate} = \frac{\text{Expected total overhead}}{\text{Expected machine-hours}}$$

$$= \frac{\$277,800}{69,450} = \$4 \text{ per machine-hour}$$

Some companies distinguish between variable overhead and fixed overhead for product costing as well as for control purposes. This distinction could have been made in the machining department. Rent, supervision, depreciation, and insurance would have been considered the fixed portion of the total manufacturing overhead, and two rates could have been developed:

433

Job and
Process
Systems and
Overhead
Application

$$\text{Variable overhead application rate} = \frac{\text{Expected total variable overhead}}{\text{Expected machine-hours}}$$

$$= \frac{\$114,000}{69,450} = \$1.64 \text{ per machine-hour}$$

$$\text{Fixed overhead application rate} = \frac{\text{Expected total fixed overhead}}{\text{Expected machine-hours*}}$$

$$= \frac{\$163,800}{69,450} = \$2.36 \text{ per machine-hour}$$

*Alternatively, the denominator could be a measure of practical capacity, that is, a measure of the *maximum* feasible number of machine-hours.

As the next chapter explains, such rates can be used for product costing, and distinctions between variable and fixed overhead incurrence can also be made for control purposes.

Actual versus Normal Costing

The overall system we have just described is sometimes called an actual costing system, because every effort is made to trace the actual costs, as incurred, to the physical units benefited. However, it is only partly an actual system, because the overhead, by definition, cannot be definitely assigned to physical products. Instead, overhead is applied on an average or normalized basis, in order to get representative or normal inventory valuations. Hence, we shall label the system a normal system. The cost of the manufactured product is composed of *actual* direct material, *actual* direct labor, and *normal* applied overhead.

The two job-order costing approaches described in this chapter may be compared as follows:

	Actual Costing	*Normal Costing*
Direct materials	Actual	Actual
Direct labor	Actual	Actual
Manufacturing overhead:		
Variable	Actual	Predetermined rates*
Fixed	Actual	Predetermined rates*

*Actual inputs (such as direct-labor hours or direct-labor costs) multiplied by predetermined overhead rates (computed by dividing total budgeted manufacturing overhead by a budgeted application base such as direct-labor hours).

Reconsider the factory overhead cost in Exhibit 14-4. Actual factory overhead incurred, item 4a, would be the same under actual and normal costing: $290,000 + $102,000 = $392,000. However, applied factory overhead, item 4b, would differ. Under normal costing, it would be as shown in

Exhibit 14-4. That is, the total applications, which would occur as the jobs were worked on, would be: $280,000 + $95,000 = $375,000.

In contrast, under actual costing no overhead would be applied as jobs were worked on. Instead, overhead would be applied only after all overhead costs for the year were known. Then, using an "actual" average rate(s) instead of a predetermined rate(s), costs would be applied to all jobs that had been worked on throughout the year. In such a case, entry 4b for application under actual costing would be $392,000 instead of the $375,000 used under normal costing. All costs incurred would be exactly offset by costs applied to the Work-in-Process Inventory.

Normal costing has replaced actual costing in many organizations precisely because the latter approach fails to provide costs of products as they are worked on during the year. It is possible to use a normal costing system plus year-end adjustments to produce final results that closely approximate the results under actual costing. To do so in our illustration, the underapplied overhead is prorated among Work in Process, Finished Goods, and Cost of Goods Sold, as shown earlier in this chapter (Method 1 in Exhibit 14-6). Thus, because of the desire for yearly "actual" costing results, we often see normal costing used for inventory costing throughout the year supplemented by once-a-year prorations.

PRODUCT COSTING
IN NONPROFIT ORGANIZATIONS

This chapter has concentrated on how to apply costs to manufactured products. However, the job-costing approach is used in nonmanufacturing situations too. Examples include appliance repair, auto repair, dentistry, auditing, income tax preparation, and medical care.

In nonprofit organizations the "product" is usually not called a "job order." Instead, it may be called a program or a class of service. A "program" is an identifiable segment of activities that frequently produce outputs in the form of services rather than goods. Examples include a safety program, an education program, a family counseling program. Often many departments work simultaneously on many programs, so the "job-order" costing challenge is to "apply" the various department costs to the various programs. Then wiser management decisions may be made regarding the allocation of limited resources among competing programs.

The appraisal of nonprofit programs has special problems. The difficulties of *cost* measurement are similar to those in commercial enterprises. However, the *benefits* are tougher to evaluate, because there is seldom a marketplace. How do you measure the benefits from educating the mentally handicapped, placing children in foster homes, saving lives? Because market prices are rarely available, indirect measurements of value are used. (For further discussion, see Chapter 9.)

SUMMARY

Accounting systems should be designed to satisfy *control* and *product costing* purposes simultaneously. Costs are initially charged to department responsibility centers (cost centers); then they are applied to products in order to get inventory costs for balance sheets and income statements and in order to guide pricing and to evaluate product performance.

Product costing is an averaging process. Process costing deals with broad averages and great masses of like units. Job costing deals with narrow averages and a unique unit or a small batch of like units.

Indirect manufacturing costs (factory overhead) are often applied to products using predetermined overhead rates. The rates are computed by dividing total budgeted overhead by a measure of total activity such as expected labor-hours or machine-hours. These rates are usually annual averages. The resulting product costs are *normal costs*, consisting of actual direct material plus actual direct labor plus applied overhead using predetermined rates.

SUMMARY PROBLEM FOR YOUR REVIEW

Problem

The Cruze Co. began business on January 2, 19x1. It made a variety of products, each batch requiring varying attention and effort. Predetermined overhead rates were computed on January 2, 19x1, as follows:

$$\text{Variable overhead} = \frac{\text{Budgeted variable overhead}}{\text{Total expected activity}} = \frac{\$50,000}{100,000 \text{ hr}} = \$.50$$

$$\text{Fixed overhead} = \frac{\text{Budgeted fixed overhead}}{\text{Total expected activity}} = \frac{\$150,000}{100,000 \text{ hr}} = \$1.50$$

A summary of results follows:

Direct materials purchased	$110,000
Direct materials used	99,000
Direct labor incurred	
(85,000 hours @ $3.05)	259,250
Variable factory overhead incurred	42,000
Fixed factory overhead incurred	150,000

There was no ending work in process. A normal costing system is used. The cost of goods sold (before considering underapplied overhead) was $396,188.

Required

1. Prepare an exhibit like Exhibit 14-4, which provides an overview of how the costs would be accounted for to satisfy control and product costing purposes.

2. Suppose the following: sales, $600,000; selling and administrative expenses, $100,000. Prepare an income statement where the underapplied overhead is considered as a direct adjustment of cost of goods sold. Ignore income taxes.

Solution

1. See Exhibit 14-7.

EXHIBIT 14-7

Solution to Requirement (1)—in dollars

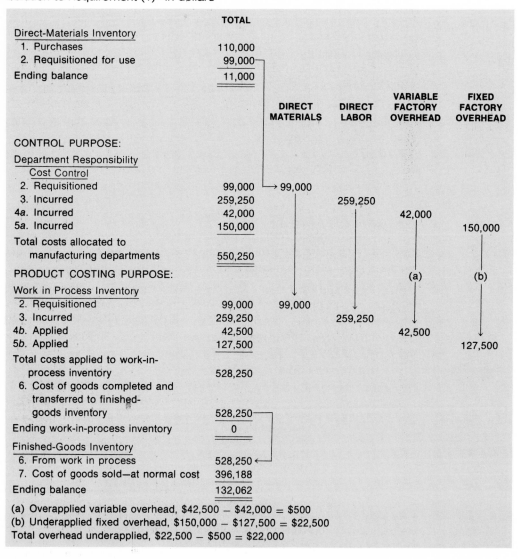

	TOTAL	DIRECT MATERIALS	DIRECT LABOR	VARIABLE FACTORY OVERHEAD	FIXED FACTORY OVERHEAD
Direct-Materials Inventory					
1. Purchases	110,000				
2. Requisitioned for use	99,000				
Ending balance	11,000				
CONTROL PURPOSE:					
Department Responsibility					
Cost Control					
2. Requisitioned	99,000	→ 99,000			
3. Incurred	259,250		259,250		
4a. Incurred	42,000			42,000	
5a. Incurred	150,000				150,000
Total costs allocated to manufacturing departments	550,250				
PRODUCT COSTING PURPOSE:				(a)	(b)
Work in Process Inventory					
2. Requisitioned	99,000	99,000			
3. Incurred	259,250		259,250		
4b. Applied	42,500			42,500	
5b. Applied	127,500				127,500
Total costs applied to work-in-process inventory	528,250				
6. Cost of goods completed and transferred to finished-goods inventory	528,250				
Ending work-in-process inventory	0				
Finished-Goods Inventory					
6. From work in process	528,250				
7. Cost of goods sold—at normal cost	396,188				
Ending balance	132,062				

(a) Overapplied variable overhead, $42,500 − $42,000 = $500
(b) Underapplied fixed overhead, $150,000 − $127,500 = $22,500
Total overhead underapplied, $22,500 − $500 = $22,000

437

*Job and
Process
Systems and
Overhead
Application*

2.

CRUZE CO.
Income Statement
for the Year Ended December 31, 19x1

Sales	$600,000
Cost of goods sold at normal cost	$396,188
Add underapplied overhead	22,000
Cost of goods sold, actual cost	$418,188
Gross profit	$181,812
Selling and administrative expenses	100,000
Net income	$ 81,812

APPENDIX 14A:
JOB-COSTING DETAILS:
JOURNAL ENTRIES AND LEDGERS

Exhibit 14-1 provides an overall perspective of the control and product costing purposes of accounting systems. This appendix uses the examples in the chapter as a basis for presenting the details of a job-order cost accounting system. **To understand this appendix, you must possess a familiarity with the fundamentals of double-entry bookkeeping.** In short, this appendix provides a grasp of how a cost bookkeeping system actually works. However, the overall conceptual framework described in the chapter is not expanded here.

General Systems Design

In principle, the general system design is straightforward and rests on a rigid distinction between control and product costing (see Exhibit 14-8). There is wide agreement among accountants, managers, and systems experts that control is best attained in *any* organization by initially charging the departments with the costs subject to their control. There is a wide divergence in theory and practice, however, as to the best way for *applying*[1] overhead costs to products.

Exhibit 14-8 illustrates the foregoing conceptual points and provides the focus for the journal entries in this appendix. However, company systems use a variety of approaches, including many shortcuts in the general ledger. For example, entries 1*a* and 1*b* are often condensed into a single entry:

Work-in-process inventory	10,000	
Direct-materials inventory		10,000

---

[1]The credit side of the Department Responsibility Cost Control account is often represented by a completely separate offsetting account, which could be termed "Department Responsibility Costs Applied." Such an *applied* account is roughly similar to Allowance for Depreciation and Allowance for Uncollectible Accounts, which are offsets to Plant and Equipment and Accounts Receivable.

EXHIBIT 14-8

General Systems Design:
Journal Entries for Cost Accumulation and Application

PURPOSE	JOURNAL ENTRIES		
	1. Direct-Material Usage, $10,000		
Control	(1a) Department A responsibility cost control	10,000	
	Direct materials inventory		10,000
Product costing	(1b) Work-in-process inventory	10,000	
	Department A responsibility cost control		10,000
	2. Direct-Labor Usage, $8,000		
Control	(2a) Department A responsibility cost control	8,000	
	Accrued payroll or cash		8,000
Product costing	(2b) Work-in-process inventory	8,000	
	Department A responsibility cost control		8,000
	3. Manufacturing Overhead Incurred, $4,000		
Control	(3a) Department A responsibility cost control	4,000	
	Accounts Payable, Allowance for Depreciation,		
	Accrued Payroll, and various other accounts		4,000
Product costing	(3b) Work-in-process inventory	4,000	
	Department A responsibility cost control		4,000

There is no harm in shortcuts, as long as the underlying concepts dominate the thinking about systems design. For example, departmental responsibility for *control* of direct-material usage is usually maintained by means other than general journals and ledgers. If so, the above journal entry illustrates the product costing purpose alone.

Again one must distinguish between costs for control and for product costing. Whether a process-cost or a job-cost approach is used, costs must be allocated to departments for control purposes. The typical job-order approach uses one account for tracing product cost and another account or accounts for accumulating department costs.

Basic Records

The basic record for the accumulation of job costs is the job order or job cost sheet. Exhibit 14-9 shows a job cost sheet and the related source documents. A file of current job cost sheets becomes the subsidiary ledger for the general ledger account, Work-in-process Inventory.

While job cost sheets are the primary scorekeeping device for *product costing*, department responsibility control sheets serve *control* purposes. For example, Exhibit 14-10 shows how the details of various costs charged to a particular department may be accumulated. The file of these sheets forms a subsidiary ledger for the general ledger account, Department Responsibility Cost Control or a similar account.

438

EXHIBIT 14-9

SOURCE DOCUMENTS

JOB COST SHEET

Job Order No._____

Description_____

Reference	Date	Amount	Summary
Direct material: (Requisition No. or Bill of Materials)	xx xx xx	xx xx xx	xx
Direct labor: (Work Ticket No.)	xx xx xx xx	xx xx xx xx	xx
Factory overhead applied: (Predetermined rate multiplied by actual machine hours or labor dollars or labor hours)	xx	xx	xx
Total product cost			xx

Direct Material Requisition

Job No._____ Date_____

Department_____ Account _Work in process_

Description	Quantity	Unit Cost	Amount
	xx	x	xx

Work Ticket

Job No._____ Date_____

Department _A_ Account _work in process_

Operation _Drill_

Units: Start _3:00 p.m._ Rate_____

Worked _10_ Stop _4:15 p.m._ Amount_____

Rejected _—_

Completed _10_

Estimated factory overhead for the year — $277,800

Estimated machine hours — 69,450

Predetermined overhead rate per labor hour* — $4

*Explained in the chapter

EXHIBIT 14-10.   Machining Department Responsibility Cost Control Sheet

MACHINING DEPARTMENT RESPONSIBILITY COST CONTROL SHEET

Month of_____

Date	Source Document	Direct Material	Direct Labor	Indirect Labor	Supplies	Utilities	Repairs	Rent	Supervision	Depreciation	Insurance
	Requisitions	xx			xx						
	Labor work tickets, analyses, or recapitulations		xx	xx					xx		
	Invoices					xx	xx	xx			
	Special memos on accruals, prepayments, etc.									xx	xx

440

441

*Job and
Process
Systems and
Overhead
Application*

Exhibit 14-11 shows how the general ledger accounts would be affected by the transactions originally analyzed in Exhibit 14-4. A careful study of this exhibit should yield insight into many relationships, particularly those between the subsidiary ledgers and the general ledger. A file of department cost sheets supports the charges to Department Responsibility Cost Control, while a file of job cost sheets supports Work in Process.

Relationships among Source Documents, Subsidiary Ledgers, and General Ledger

The source documents, such as material requisitions or work tickets, which were illustrated in Exhibit 14-9, are usually made in multiple copies, each being used for a specific task. For example, a materials requisition could be executed by a foreman in as many as six copies and disposed of as follows:

1. Kept by storekeeper who issues the materials.
2. Used by stores ledger clerk for posting to perpetual inventory cards for materials.
3. Used by job order cost clerk to post the Job Cost Sheet (Exhibit 14-9).
4. Used by cost control clerk to post the Direct Material Used column of Department Responsibility Cost Control Sheet (Exhibit 14-10).
5. Used by general ledger clerk as a basis for a summary monthly entry for all of the month's requisitions (Exhibit 14-11).
6. Retained by the foreman. He can use the requisition as a cross check against the performance reports which show his usage of material.

Of course, machine accounting and electronic computer systems can use a single punched card as a requisition. Sorting, re-sorting, classifications, reclassifications, summaries, and re-summaries can easily provide any desired information. Because these source documents are the foundation for data accumulation and reports, the importance of accurate initial recording cannot be overemphasized.

Copies of these source documents are used for direct postings to subsidiary ledgers. Sometimes the subsidiary ledgers will contain summarized postings of daily batches of source documents, rather than individual direct postings. Accounting data are most condensed in the general ledger and most detailed on the source documents, as the following listing shows.

Item	
Work in Process	General ledger (usually monthly totals only)
Job Cost Sheets	Subsidiary ledgers (perhaps daily summaries)
Material Requisitions	
or Work Tickets	Source documents (minute to minute, hour to hour)

EXHIBIT 14-11. Summary Effects of Job Costing: Normal Costing System

GENERAL JOURNAL

1.	Direct materials inventory	$1,900,000
	Accounts payable or cash	$1,900,000
	Purchases	
2a.	Department responsibility cost control	1,890,000
	Direct materials inventory	1,890,000
	Requisitions charged to departments for control purposes	
2b.	Work in process	1,890,000
	Department responsibility cost control	1,890,000
	Requisitions applied to jobs for product costing purposes	
3a.	Department responsibility cost control	390,000
	Accrued payroll or cash	390,000
	Work tickets charged to departments for control purposes	
3b.	Work in process	390,000
	Department responsibility cost control	390,000
	Work tickets applied to jobs for product costing purposes	
4a.	Department responsibility cost control	392,000
	Cash, accounts payable, and various accounts	392,000
	Overhead charged to departments as incurred for control purposes	
4b.	Work in process	375,000
	Department responsibility cost control	375,000
	Overhead applied to products, using predetermined application rates	
5.	Finished goods	2,500,000
	Work in process	2,500,000
	To transfer costs of goods completed	
6a.	Accounts receivable or cash	4,000,000
	Sales	4,000,000
6b.	Cost of goods sold	2,480,000
	Finished goods	2,480,000

GENERAL LEDGER (Selected accounts)

Department Responsibility Cost Control

Control Purpose:			Product Costing Purpose:	
2a. Direct material	$1,890,000		2b. Applied	$1,890,000
3a. Direct labor	390,000		3b. Applied	390,000
4a. Factory overhead	392,000		4b. Applied	375,000

Direct Materials

Bal.	$ 110,000	2a.	$1,890,000
1.	1,900,000		

Work in Process

2b.	$1,890,000	5.	$2,500,000
3b.	390,000		
4b.	375,000		

Finished Goods

Bal.	12,000	6b.	2,480,000
5.	2,500,000		

Cost of Goods Sold

6b.	2,480,000	

SUBSIDIARY LEDGER (Selected)

Department Cost Sheets

Assembly

Machining

Direct Material	Direct Labor	In-direct Labor	Supplies	Various

Job Cost Sheets

Direct material

Direct Labor

Applied Overhead

442

443

*Job and
Process
Systems and
Overhead
Application*

The daily scorekeeping duties are accomplished with source documents and subsidiary ledgers. Copies of the source documents are independently summarized, and are usually posted to the general ledger only once a month. See entry 2a, Exhibit 14-11, where, for convenience, a year was used, rather than a month.

In order to obtain a bird's-eye view of a system, we have been concentrating on general ledger relationships. However, keep in mind that the general ledger is a very small part of the accountant's daily work. Furthermore, current control is aided by hourly, daily, or weekly flash reports of material, labor, and machine usage. The general ledger itself is a summary device. Reliance on the general ledger for current control is ill-advised, because the resulting reports come too late and are often too stale for management control use.

Disposition of Factory Overhead

As incurred, factory overhead is allocated to departments and accumulates on the left side of the Department Responsibility Control account. The applied factory overhead accumulates on the right-hand side, and the difference between incurred and applied fluctuates from month to month. As Exhibit 14-6 demonstrates, there are two fundamental ways to eliminate the year-end difference. The journal entries are:

Either	1. Work in process	994	
	Finished goods	205	
	Cost of goods sold	15,801	
	Department responsibility cost control		17,000
	To prorate ending underapplied overhead among the accounts where the costs of the 19x2 jobs worked on are now lodged.		
or	2. Cost of goods sold (or a separate charge against revenue)	17,000	
	Department responsibility cost control		17,000
	To close ending underapplied overhead directly to Cost of Goods Sold.		

As is discussed near the end of the chapter, factory overhead is accounted for differently under actual costing and normal costing. Reconsider entry 4 in Exhibit 14-11 (in thousands of dollars):

	Actual Costing		*Normal Costing*	
4a. Department responsibility cost control	392		392	
Cash, accounts payable, etc.		392		392
4b. Work in process	—		375	
Department responsibility cost control		—		375
At end of year: Work in process	392		—	
Department responsibility cost control		392		—
Cost of goods sold	—		17	
Department responsibility cost control		—		17

ILLUSTRATION OF PROCESS COSTING

The major illustration in this chapter featured job-order costing. The same concepts pertain to process costing, but the application of costs to products is much easier.

Assume that the same company produced transistor radios in large quantities. Suppose it completed 1,000,000 units during the year. Then the unit cost of goods completed would be simply the total cost of $2,500,000 ÷ 1,000,000, or $2.50.

The major difficulty in process costing is applying costs to uncompleted products—goods still in process at the end of the accounting period. For example, suppose 100,000 radios were still in process at year-end; only 900,000 were started and completed. All the parts had been made or requisitioned, but only half of the assembly labor had been completed for each of the 100,000 radios.

What was the output for the year? An obvious answer would be 900,000 completed units plus 100,000 half-completed units. But we should hesitate to express the sum of the output as 1,000,000 units. After all, each of the partially completed units has received only half the assembly labor and overhead inputs applied to the fully completed output. Instead, we express output not as *physical* units, but as *equivalent* units.

Equivalent units is the expression of output in terms of *doses* or *amount* of work applied thereto. In process costing, a physical unit is looked upon as a collection of work applications (material and conversion costs).

Conversion costs are defined as direct labor plus manufacturing overhead. To illustrate the basic approach, we use the data in the assembly department only from Exhibit 14-4:

	Physical Flow	Equivalent Units	
		Direct Materials	Conversion Costs
Units started and completed	900,000	900,000	900,000
Work in process, end:	100,000		
Materials added: 100,000 × 1		100,000	
Conversion costs: 100,000 × ½			50,000
Units accounted for	1,000,000		
Total work done		1,000,000	950,000
Assembly costs:			
Direct materials added		$890,000	
Conversion costs ($190,000 + $102,000)			$292,000
Divide by equivalent units		1,000,000	950,000
Unit costs added in assembly		$.89	$.3073684

Note that costs are applied on the basis of costs per equivalent unit. The

445

*Job and
Process
Systems and
Overhead
Application*

ending work-in-process inventory (assembly department cost component only) would be:[2]

Direct materials, 100,000 × $.89	=	$ 89,000
Conversion costs, 50,000 × $.3073684	=	15,368
Assembly department component	=	$104,368

Processing industries (engaging in mass production of like units) tend to use standard product costing rather than the actual product costing or normal product costing described in this chapter.[3] Standard product costing is discussed in the next chapter.

ASSIGNMENT MATERIAL

Essential Assignment Material

14-1. **Terminology.** Define: *job-order costing; process costing; job order; normal cost system;* and *overapplied.*

14-2. **Balance sheets and income statements.** Consider the following (in millions of dollars):

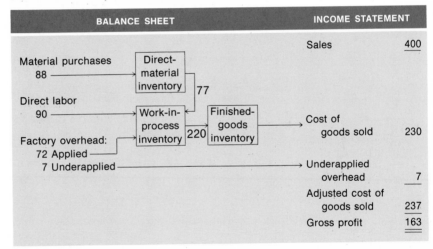

[2]The idea of equivalent units extends to all types of organizations, even though the terminology differs. For example, clinical laboratories often measure volume in terms of weight units. A *weight unit* is an arbitrary unit by which various lab procedures are ranked in terms of the relative combination of labor, supplies, and related costs devoted to each. For instance, a procedure with a weight of two is deemed to use twice the resources as a procedure with a weight of one. An average cost per weight unit is developed, which is then multiplied by the average number of weight units per laboratory procedure to obtain an average unit cost for each laboratory procedure. Radiology departments use a similar "process costing" system. For another example, the beer industry translates its productions into equivalent barrels, even though its output is in the form of various sizes of kegs, cans, and bottles.

[3]For an expanded discussion of process costing, see Charles T. Horngren, *Cost Accounting: A Managerial Emphasis,* 4th ed. (Englewood Cliffs, N.J.: Prentice-Hall, Inc., 1977), Chaps. 18 and 19.

The beginning inventory balances were (in millions): direct material, $19; work in process, $31; and finished goods, $90.

1. Compute the ending balances of the three inventories.
2. Compute the actual factory overhead incurred.

14-3. **Disposition of overhead.** Refer to the preceding problem. Assume that overhead was overapplied by $20 and that the ending inventories were $30, $30, and $70, respectively. Unadjusted cost of goods sold is still $230. Management has decided to prorate the $20 to the pertinent accounts (using their unadjusted ending balances) instead of writing it off solely as an adjustment of current cost of goods sold.

1. What accounts would be affected by the proration and by what amounts?
2. Your answer to Requirement 1 would affect current gross profit differently than if the $20 were all written off solely as an adjustment of current cost of goods sold. By how much? Would the current gross profit be higher or lower?

Additional Assignment Material

14-4. "Overhead application is overhead allocation." Do you agree? Explain.

14-5. Distinguish between job costing and process costing.

14-6. "The basic distinction between job-order costing and process costing is the breadth of the denominator." Explain.

14-7. What is the subsidiary ledger for work in process in a job-cost system?

14-8. Define *normal costing*.

14-9. "The special decision purpose of accounting is difficult to satisfy on a routine basis." Why?

14-10. "Cost application or absorption is terminology related to the product costing purpose." Why?

14-11. "I was looking at a trial balance the other day and was mystified by the account Department Responsibility Cost Applied. I just didn't know what it meant or where it fit." Briefly unravel the mystery.

14-12. What are some reasons for *incurred* and *applied* overhead differing?

14-13. Sometimes five copies of a stores requisition are needed. What are their uses?

447

*Job and
Process
Systems and
Overhead
Application*

14-14. "The general ledger is an incidental part of the accountant's daily work." Explain.

14-15. "Costs of inefficiency cannot be regarded as assets." Explain.

14-16. "Under actual overhead application, unit costs soar as volume increases, and vice versa." Do you agree? Explain.

14-17. What is the best theoretical method of allocating under- or overapplied overhead, assuming that the objective is to obtain as accurate a cost allocation as possible?

14-18. **Direct materials.** The MN Company has a beginning inventory of direct materials of $800,000. During the year it acquired $10 million in additional materials. Its ending inventory was $1 million. How much direct materials were used during the year?

14-19. **Normal costing system.** The following data summarize the factory operations of the Bensmeier Manufacturing Co. for the year 19x1, its first year in business:

1. Direct materials purchased for cash	$230,000
2. Direct materials issued and used	220,000
3. Labor used directly on production	100,000
4a. Indirect labor	80,000
4b. Depreciation of plant and equipment	40,000
4c. Miscellaneous factory overhead (ordinarily would be detailed))	30,000
5. Overhead: 180 percent of direct labor	?
6. Cost of production completed	450,000
7. Cost of goods sold	300,000

Required

Prepare an analysis similar to that in Exhibit 14-4. Show the ending balances in direct-materials inventory, work in process, and finished goods. For purposes of this analysis, combine the items in 4 as "overhead incurred." (For more detailed analyses of this problem, see Problems 14-30 and 14-31. Furthermore, Problem 14-23 is an alternate for this problem.)

14-20. **Accounting for overhead, predetermined rates.** Thomas Allan and Co. uses a predetermined overhead rate in applying overhead to individual job orders on a *machine-hour* basis for Department No. 1 and on a *direct-labor hour* basis for Department No. 2. At the beginning of 19x4, the company's management made the following budget predictions:

	Dept. No. 1	Dept. No. 2
Direct-labor cost	$1,200,000	$1,000,000
Factory overhead	1,200,000	800,000
Direct-labor hours	80,000	100,000
Machine-hours	240,000	15,000

Cost records of recent months show the following accumulations for Job Order No. 455:

	Dept. No. 1	Dept. No. 2
Material placed in production	$10,000	$30,000
Direct-labor cost	9,600	8,000
Direct-labor hours	800	1,000
Machine-hours	3,000	200

Required

1. What is the predetermined overhead *rate* that should be applied in Department No. 1? In Department No. 2?

2. What is the *total overhead* cost of Job Order No. 455?

3. If Job Order No. 455 consists of 100 units of product, what is the *unit cost* of this job?

4. At the *end* of 19x4, actual results for the year's operations were as follows:

	Dept. No. 1	Dept. No. 2
Actual overhead costs incurred	$1,000,000	$950,000
Actual direct-labor hours	800,000	100,000
Actual machine-hours	240,000	17,000

Find the under- or overapplied overhead for each department and for the factory as a whole.

14-21. **Disposition of overhead.** Refer to Problem 14-19.
1. Assume that under- or overapplied overhead is regarded as a reduction or addition to current income via adding or deducting the amount from the unadjusted cost of goods sold. What is the adjusted cost of goods sold?
2. Assume that the under- or overapplied overhead is prorated among the pertinent accounts in proportion to their ending unadjusted balances. What is adjusted cost of goods sold?
For a more detailed examination of the data, see Problem 14-29.

14-22. **Disposition of year-end underapplied overhead.** A company that uses a normal cost system has the following balances at the end of its first year's operations:

Work-in-process control	$200,000
Finished-goods control	300,000
Cost of goods sold	500,000
Actual factory overhead	360,000
Factory overhead applied	300,000

Show two different ways to dispose of the year-end overhead balances. By how much would net income differ?

14-23. **Straightforward job costing.** The Dunkel Custom Furniture Company has two departments. Data for 19x5 include the following.
Inventories, January 1, 19x5:

449

Job and
Process
Systems and
Overhead
Application

Direct materials (30 types)	$100,000
Work in process (in assembly)	60,000
Finished goods	20,000

Manufacturing overhead budget for 19x5:

	Machining	Assembly
Indirect labor	$200,000	$400,000
Supplies	40,000	50,000
Utilities	100,000	90,000
Repairs	150,000	100,000
Supervision	100,000	200,000
Factory rent	50,000	50,000
Depreciation on equipment	150,000	100,000
Insurance, property taxes, etc.	50,000	60,000
	$840,000	$1,050,000

Budgeted machine-hours were 84,000; budgeted direct-labor cost was $2,100,000. Manufacturing overhead was applied using predetermined rates on the basis of machine-hours in Machining and on the basis of direct-labor cost in Assembly.

The following is a summary of actual events for the year:

	Machining	Assembly	Total
1. Direct materials purchased			$ 1,700,000
2. Direct materials requisitioned	$1,000,000	$ 600,000	1,600,000
3. Direct-labor costs incurred	800,000	2,600,000	3,400,000
4a. Factory overhead incurred	1,000,000	1,000,000	2,000,000
4b. Factory overhead applied	800,000	?	?
5. Cost of goods completed	—	—	7,110,000
6a. Sales	—	—	12,000,000
6b. Cost of goods sold	—	—	7,100,000

The ending work in process (all in assembly) was $50,000.

Required

1. Compute the predetermined overhead rates.

2. Compute the amount of the machine-hours actually worked.

3. Compute the amount of factory overhead applied in the Assembly Department.

4. Prepare an exhibit similar to Exhibit 14-4, which shows how the costs are accounted for to satisfy control and product costing purposes. Show the ending inventory balances for direct materials, work in process, and finished goods.

5. Prepare a partial income statement similar to the one illustrated in Exhibit 14-5. "Overapplied or underapplied overhead is written off as an adjustment of current cost of goods sold."

This problem is pursued in more detail in Problem 14-32.

14-24. Nonprofit job costing. Job-order costing is usually identified with manufacturing companies. However, service industries and nonprofit organizations also use the method. Suppose that a social service agency has a cost accounting system that tracks cost by department (for example, family counseling, general welfare, and foster children) and by case. In this way, the manager of the agency is better able to determine how her limited resources (mostly professional social workers) should be allocated. Furthermore, her interchanges with her superiors and various politicians are more fruitful when she can cite the costs of various types of cases.

The condensed line-item budget for the general welfare department of the agency for 19x6 showed:

Professional salaries:

Level 12	6 @ $32,000 = $192,000	
Level 10	18 @ $24,000 =	432,000
Level 8	30 @ $16,000 =	480,000	$1,104,000
Other costs		441,600
Total costs		$1,545,600

For costing various cases, the manager favored using a single overhead application rate based on the ratio of total overhead to direct labor. The latter was defined as those professional salaries assigned to specific cases.

The professional workers filled out a weekly "case time" report, which approximated the hours spent for each case.

The instructions on the report were: "Indicate how much time (in hours) you spent on each case. Unassigned time should be listed separately." About 20 percent of available time was unassigned to specific cases. It was used for professional development (for example, continuing education programs). "Unassigned time" became a part of "overhead," as distinguished from the direct labor.

Required

1. Compute the "overhead rate" as a percentage of direct labor (that is, the assignable professional salaries).

2. Suppose last week a welfare case, Client No. 462, required two hours of Level 12 time, four hours of Level 10 time, and nine hours of Level 8 time. How much job cost should be allocated to Client No. 462 for the week? Assume that all professional employees work a 1,650-hour year.

14-25. **Job costing in a consulting firm.** AB Engineering Consultants is a firm of professional civil engineers. It mostly has surveying jobs for the heavy construction industry throughout California and Nevada. The firm obtains its jobs by giving fixed price quotations, so profitability is highly dependent on the ability to predict the time required for the various subtasks on the job. (This situation is similar to that in the auditing profession, where times are budgeted for such audit steps as reconciling cash, confirming accounts receivable, and so forth.)

A client may be served by various professional staff, who hold positions in the hierarchy from partners to managers to senior engineers to assistants. In addition, there are secretaries and other employees.

AB Engineering has the following budget for 19x4:

Compensation of professional staff	$2,000,000
Other costs	800,000
Total budgeted costs	$2,800,000

451

*Job and
Process
Systems and
Overhead
Application*

Each professional staff member must submit a weekly time report, which is used for charging hours to a client job-order sheet. The time report has seven columns, one for each day of the week. Its rows are as follows:

> Chargeable hours:
>> Client 234
>> Client 262
>> Etc.
>
> Nonchargeable hours:
>> Attending seminar on new equipment
>> Unassigned time
>> Etc.

In turn, these time reports are used for charging hours and costs to the client job-order sheets. The managing partner regards these job sheets as absolutely essential for measuring the profitability of various jobs and for providing an "experience base for improving predictions on future jobs."

Required

1. This firm applies overhead to jobs at a predetermined percentage of the professional compensation charged directly to the job ("direct labor"). For all categories of professional personnel, chargeable hours average 85 percent of available hours. The nonchargeable hours are regarded as additional overhead. What is the overhead rate as a percentage of the "direct labor," the chargeable professional compensation cost?

2. A senior engineer works 48 weeks per year, 40 hours per week. His compensation is $36,000. He has worked on two jobs during the past week, devoting 10 hours to Job 234 and 30 hours to Job 262. How much cost should be charged to Job 234 because of his work there?

14-26. Actual versus normal costing. B Company has the following costs:

Direct materials used	$200,000
Direct labor	300,000
Manufacturing overhead applied, 150%	
of direct labor	450,000
Actual manufacturing overhead incurred	500,000

There were no beginning inventories. At year-end, one-fourth of the production is unsold and is held as finished-goods inventory. The costs in finished-goods inventory are in the same proportion as the costs in cost of goods sold.

Required

1. Assume normal costing is used and that underapplied overhead is written off as an expense. Compute the finished-goods inventory.

2. Assume actual costing is used. Compute the finished-goods inventory.

3. What is the major difficulty with using actual costing? Do you favor proration of underapplied overhead when normal costing is used? Why?

14-27. Finding unknowns. The W Company has the following balances (in millions) as of December 31, 19x8:

Work-in-process inventory	7
Finished-goods inventory	150
Direct-materials inventory	70
Factory overhead incurred	150
Factory overhead applied at 150% of direct-labor cost	120
Cost of goods sold	300

The cost of direct materials purchased during 19x8 was $230. The cost of direct materials requisitioned for production during 19x8 was $200. The cost of goods completed was $404, all in millions.

Required

Before considering any year-end adjustments for over- or underapplied overhead, compute the beginning inventory balances of direct materials, work in process, and finished goods.

14-28. Appendix A problem

1. Prepare journal entries to record the information in the Summary Problem for Your Review at the end of the chapter. See Exhibit 14-11 for guidance.

2. Show the postings of the journal entries to T-accounts for Department Responsibility Cost Control, for Work in Process, and for Finished Goods.

14-29. Appendix A problem: overhead. Refer to Problem 14-21. For part 1, show the journal entry. Also show all the year's postings to the T-accounts for all inventories, and show their closing balances. For part 2, show the journal entry only.

14-30. Appendix A problem: journal entries. Refer to the data in Problem 14-19.

Required

1. Prepare general journal entries for a normal cost system. Number your entries.

2. Present the T-account for Department Responsibility Cost Control. Sketch how this account's subsidiary ledger would appear, assuming that there are four factory departments. You need not show any numbers in the subsidiary ledger.

This problem is probed in more detail in Problem 14-31.

14-31. Appendix A problem: source documents. Refer to Problems 14-19 and 14-30. For each journal entry, indicate: (a) the most likely name for the source documents that would authorize the entry, and (b) how the subsidiary ledgers, if any, would be affected.

14-32. Appendix A problem. Refer to Problem 14-23. Use those data to prepare an exhibit similar to Exhibit 14-11, which shows general journal entries and the major T-accounts. Work solely with the total amounts, not the details for Machining and Assembly. Explanations for the journal entries are not required, nor are subsidiary ledgers.

453

Job and
Process
Systems and
Overhead
Application

14-33. Process costing. Review the second appendix to the chapter. In the illustration there, suppose that 200,000 radios instead of 100,000 were in the ending work in process. The units started were 1,000,000. Prepare a statement that shows the total work done in equivalent units, the unit costs added in assembly, and the ending work in process (assembly department cost component only).

14-34. Nonprofit process costing. Read the second appendix to this chapter. The Internal Revenue Service must process millions of income tax returns yearly. When the taxpayer sends in his return, documents such as withholding statements and checks are matched against the data on page one. Then various other inspections of the data are conducted. Of course, some returns are more complicated than others, so the expected time allowed to process a return is geared to an "average" return.

Some work-measurement experts have been closely monitoring the processing at a particular branch. They are seeking ways to improve productivity.

Suppose 1,000,000 returns were received on April 15. On April 22, the work-measurement teams discovered that all supplies (punched cards, inspection check-sheets, and so on) had been affixed to the returns, but 40 percent of the returns still had to undergo a final inspection. The other returns were fully completed.

Required

1. Suppose that the final inspection represents 20 percent of the overall processing time in this process. Compute the total work done in terms of equivalent units.
2. The materials and supplies consumed were $150,000. For these calculations, materials and supplies are regarded just like direct materials. The conversion costs were $1,380,000. Compute the unit costs of materials and supplies and of conversion.
3. Compute the cost of the tax returns not yet completely processed.

14-35. Process costing. Read the second appendix to the chapter. Also reconsider the facts in the Summary Problem for Your Review in the body of the chapter. Suppose that, instead of being a job shop, the company manufactured and assembled basic hand-held calculators. Various materials were added at various stages of the process. The outer front shell and the carrying case, which represented 10 percent of the total material cost, were added at the final step of the assembly process. All other materials were considered to be "in process" by the time the calculator reached a 50 percent stage of completion.

Ninety thousand calculators were started in production during 19x1. At year-end, 5,000 calculators were in various stages of completion, but all of them were beyond the 50 percent stage and on the average they were regarded as being 80 percent completed.

Required

1. Prepare a schedule of physical flow, equivalent units, and unit costs.
2. Tabulate the cost of goods completed and the cost of ending work in process. Assume that the *actual* overhead is applied to production. In summary, the costs to account for were: materials, $99,000 and conversion costs, $451,250.

CHAPTER 15

Overhead Application: Direct and Absorption Costing

The preceding chapter concentrated on how an accounting system is used to *accumulate* costs by departments and to *apply* costs to the products (or services) that are produced by those departments. This chapter[1] concentrates on two major variations of product costing. We use a standard product costing system here for illustrative purposes. However, these variations can be used in nonstandard product costing systems too.

DIRECT VERSUS ABSORPTION COSTING

Accounting for Fixed Manufacturing Overhead

Two major methods of product costing will be compared in this chapter: direct costing (the contribution approach) and absorption costing (the func-

[1] Chapter 15 may be studied without having studied Chapter 14. However, Chapters 3 (particularly the first half, which is worth reviewing now) and 7 should be studied before undertaking Chapter 15. This book was written to permit the utmost flexibility. In particular, many instructors may prefer to follow Chapter 3 with Chapter 14 and then follow Chapter 7 with Chapter 15.

tional, full-costing, or traditional approach). These methods differ in only one conceptual respect: **Fixed manufacturing overhead is excluded from the cost of products under direct costing but included in the cost of products under absorption costing.** In other words, direct costing signifies that fixed factory overhead is not inventoried. In contrast, absorption costing signifies that fixed factory overhead is inventoried.

Absorption costing is much more widely used than direct costing, although the growing use of the contribution approach in performance measurement and cost analysis has led to increasing use of direct costing for internal-reporting purposes. Neither the public accounting profession nor the Internal Revenue Service approves of direct costing for external-reporting purposes.

Direct costing is more accurately called **variable** or **marginal costing,** because in substance it applies only the *variable* production costs to the product. As Exhibit 15-1 shows, **fixed manufacturing overhead is regarded as an expired cost to be immediately charged against sales rather than as an unexpired cost to be held back as inventory and charged against sales later as a part of cost of goods sold.**

The term "direct" costing is widely used, but "variable" costing is a more accurate description. Why? Because, as Exhibit 15-1 shows, the "direct" costing approach to the inventorying of costs is not confined to only "direct"

EXHIBIT 15-1. Comparison of Flow of Costs

Direct Costing

Costs to Account for	Inventoried Costs on Balance Sheet		Expense on Income Statement
Direct material* Direct labor* Variable manufacturing overhead*	Initially applied to inventory as unexpired costs	as goods are sold	Become expenses when the inventory is sold
Fixed manufacturing overhead	expires immediately		Becomes expense immediately

Absorption Costing

Costs to Account for	Inventoried Costs on Balance Sheet		Expense on Income Statement
Direct material* Direct labor* Variable manufacturing overhead* Fixed manufacturing overhead*	Initially applied to inventory as unexpired costs	as goods are sold	Become expenses when the inventory is sold

*As goods are manufactured, the costs are "applied" to inventory usually via the use of unit costs.

materials and labor; it also includes an "indirect" cost—the *variable* manufacturing overhead. Such terminological confusion is unfortunate but apparently unavoidable in a field such as management accounting, where new analytical ideas or approaches arise in isolated fashion. Newly coined terms, which may not be accurately descriptive, often become embedded too deeply to be supplanted later.

Take a moment to reflect on Exhibit 15-1. Also, reexamine Exhibit 3-2, which provides an overview of income statement and balance sheet relationships. (Exhibit 3-2 is on p. 58.)

Facts for Illustration

To make these ideas more concrete, consider the following example. The Tolman Company had the following operating characteristics in 19x4 and 19x5:

Basic Production Data at Standard Cost

Direct material	$1.30
Direct labor	1.50
Variable manufacturing overhead	.20
Standard variable costs per unit	$3.00

Fixed manufacturing overhead was $150,000. Expected production in each year was 150,000 units. Sales price, $5 per unit.

Selling and administrative expense is assumed for simplicity as being all fixed at $65,000 yearly, except for sales commissions at 5 percent of dollar sales.

	19x4	*19x5*
In units:		
Opening inventory	—	30,000
Production	170,000	140,000
Sales	140,000	160,000
Ending inventory	30,000	10,000

There were no variances from the standard variable manufacturing costs, and fixed manufacturing overhead incurred was exactly $150,000 per year.

Required

1. Prepare income statements for 19x4 and 19x5 under direct costing.

2. Prepare income statements for 19x4 and 19x5 under absorption costing.

3. Show a reconciliation of the difference in net income for 19x4, 19x5, and the two years as a whole.

The solution to this problem will be explained, step by step, in subsequent sections. The solution to Requirement 1 is in Exhibit 15-2, to Requirement 2 in Exhibit 15-3, and to Requirement 3 in Exhibit 15-5.

Direct-Costing Method

The solution to Requirement 1 is shown in Exhibit 15-2. It has a familiar contribution-approach format, the same format introduced in Chapter 3. The only new characteristic of Exhibit 15-2 is the presence of a detailed calculation of cost of goods sold, which is affected by changes in the beginning and ending inventories. (In contrast, the income statements in Chapters 3 through 7 assumed that there were no changes in the beginning and ending inventories.)

The costs of the product are accounted for by applying all variable manufacturing costs to the goods produced at a rate of $3 per unit; thus, inventories are valued at standard variable costs. In contrast, fixed manufacturing costs are not applied to any products but are regarded as expenses as actually incurred.

EXHIBIT 15-2

DIRECT COSTING

TOLMAN COMPANY

Comparative Income Statements (In thousands of dollars)
for the Years 19x4 and 19x5
(Data are in text)

		19x4	19x5
Sales	(1)	700	800
Opening inventory—at standard variable cost of $3		—	90
Add variable cost of goods manufactured at standard		510	420
Available for sale		510	510
Deduct ending inventory—at standard variable cost of $3		90	30
Variable manufacturing cost of goods sold		420	480
Variable selling expenses—at 5% of dollar sales		35	40
Total variable expenses	(2)	455	520
Contribution margin	(3) = (1) − (2)	245	280
Fixed factory overhead		150	150
Fixed selling and administrative expenses		65	65
Total fixed expenses	(4)	215	215
Net income	(3) − (4)	30	65

457

Again, before reading on, please trace the facts from the illustrative problem to the presentation in Exhibit 15-2, step by step.

Absorption-Costing Method

Exhibit 15-3 contains the following highlights of standard absorption costing.

1. The unit product cost is $4, not $3, because variable manufacturing costs ($3) plus fixed manufacturing overhead ($1) are applied to product.

2. The $1 predetermined application rate for fixed overhead was based on a denominator of 150,000 units ($150,000 ÷ 150,000 = $1). A **denominator variance**[2] appears whenever actual production (140,000 units in 19x5)

[2] The term *denominator variance* is relatively new, so it is not widely used in practice. The equivalent terms, *activity variance, capacity variance,* and especially *volume variance,* are widely used. The term *denominator variance* is favored here because it is a more precise description of the fundamental nature of the variance, which arises from the choice of some denominator and is measured by deviations from that denominator. In contrast, volume variance is a much looser term that may be applied to deviations in volume of all kinds for all kinds of costs and revenues.

EXHIBIT 15-3

Absorption Costing
TOLMAN COMPANY
Comparative Income Statements (In thousands of dollars)
for the Years 19x4 and 19x5
(Data are in text)

	19x4	19x5
Sales	700	800
Opening inventory—at standard absorption cost of $4*	—	120
Cost of goods manufactured at standard of $4	680	560
Available for sale	680	680
Deduct ending inventory at standard absorption cost of $4	120	40
Cost of goods sold—at standard	560	640
Gross profit at standard	140	160
Denominator variance†	20 F	10 U
Gross margin or gross profit—at "actual"	160	150
Selling and administrative expenses	100	105
Net income	60	45

* Variable cost $3
Fixed cost ($150,000 ÷ 150,000) 1
Standard absorption cost $4

† Computation of denominator variance based on denominator volume of 150,000 units:

19x4	$20,000 F	(170,000 − 150,000)× $1
19x5	10,000 U	(150,000 − 140,000) × $1
Two years together	$10,000 F	(310,000 − 300,000) × $1

U = Unfavorable; F = Favorable

459

*Overhead
Application:
Direct and
Absorption
Costing*

deviates from the level of activity selected as the denominator for computing the predetermined product costing rate. As the footnote in Exhibit 15-3
indicates, the measure of the variance is $1 multiplied by the difference
between the actual volume of output and the denominator volume.

3. Denominator variances (and other variances) are usually accounted for as
   expired costs, as expenses of the current period. They are often accounted
   for as adjustments that convert the gross profit at standard to gross profit at
   "actual," as shown in Exhibit 15-3.

The first of these three ideas was explained in the preceding chapter. The
denominator variance and the disposition of variances will be discussed in subsequent sections.

FIXED OVERHEAD AND
ABSORPTION COSTS OF PRODUCT

Variable and Fixed Unit Costs

A graphical presentation of how an absorption-costing system works for (1)
departmental budgeting and control purposes and (2) product costing purposes may help underscore the assumptions being made. Even though
absorption-costing systems rarely split their factory overhead into variable
and fixed components, we will do so here to stress the underlying assumptions. For *variable* costs, the graphs are:

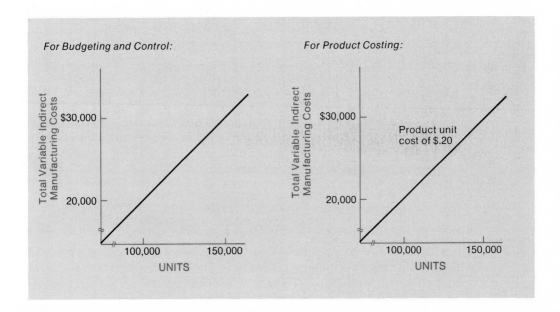

The two graphs are identical, so there is no conflict in the total results if the
second graph is used as a basis for predicting how total costs will behave.

Variable overhead will increase at a rate of $.20 per unit, as the slope of the graph shows.

Thinking in terms of *total costs* is the most popular way to budget (plan) and control operating activities. In contrast, thinking in terms of *unit costs* is the most popular way to allocate total costs for product costing purposes.

Under absorption costing, the accounting system for *fixed* manufacturing overhead is shown by the next graphs (which are not to the exact scale of the preceding graphs):

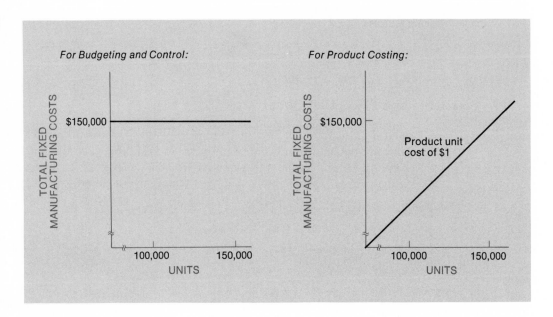

For product costing purposes, the accountant takes the total costs in the first graph and chooses a method for applying the costs to the product. He typically accomplishes this application via some unitization, using some predicted volume as a denominator:

$$\text{Unit product cost} = \frac{\text{Predicted total cost}}{\text{Denominator volume}} = \frac{\$150,000}{150,000} = \$1$$

For inventory purposes, as each unit is worked on, a $1 fixed indirect manufacturing cost will be applied to it. Thus, the first 100,000 units would bear a total *product cost* of $100,000, the next 100,000 units a total *product cost* of an additional $100,000, as the next graphs demonstrate.

The *total* fixed cost for budgetary planning and control will be unaffected by the specific predicted volume used as a denominator. For instance,

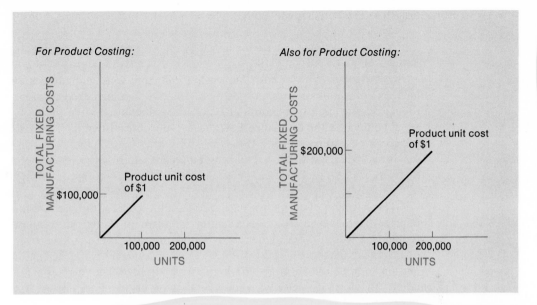

For Product Costing:

Also for Product Costing:

if the predicted volume were 100,000 instead of 150,000 units, the unit product cost would change:

$$\text{Unit product cost} = \frac{\text{Predicted total cost}}{\text{Denominator volume}} = \frac{\$150,000}{100,000} = \$1.50$$

But the first graph for fixed costs, the one that is of primary concern for planning and control, would not change:

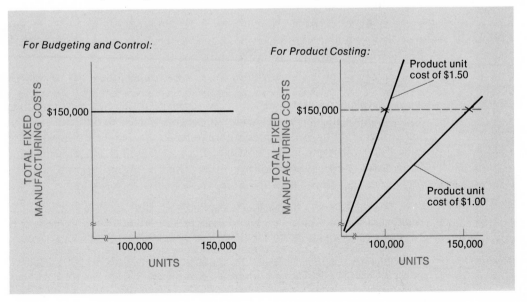

For Budgeting and Control:

For Product Costing:

Selecting the Denominator Level

As the preceding two graphs show, the unit cost depends on the activity level chosen as the denominator in the computation; the higher the level of activity, the lower the unit cost. The costing difficulty is magnified because management usually desires a single representative standard fixed cost for a product despite month-to-month changes in production volume.

The two graphs dramatize how the two purposes differ. The control-budget purpose regards fixed costs in a straightforward manner, viewing them in accordance with their actual cost behavior pattern. In contrast, as the graphs indicate, the absorption product costing approach views these fixed costs as though they had a variable cost behavior pattern.

The selection of an appropriate denominator level for the predetermination of fixed overhead rates is a matter of judgment. Thus, the standard product cost would differ, depending on how the rate is set for fixed overhead. Some managers favor using the expected actual activity for the year in question; others favor using some longer-run (three-to-five-year) approximation of "normal" activity; and others favor using maximum or full capacity (often called *practical capacity*) as the denominator.

Although fixed overhead rates are often important for product costing and long-run pricing, such rates *have limited significance for control purposes*. At the lower levels of supervision, almost no fixed costs are under direct control; even at higher levels of supervision, few fixed costs are controllable in the short run within wide ranges of anticipated activity.

Nature of Denominator Variance

A denominator variance arises whenever the actual outputs achieved deviate from the activity level selected as the denominator for computing the predetermined product costing rate.

The denominator variance is the conventional measure of the cost of departing from the level of activity originally used to set the overhead rate.[3] Most companies consider denominator variances to be beyond immediate control, although sometimes the top sales executive has to do some explaining or investigating. Sometimes failure to reach the denominator volume is caused by idleness due to poor production scheduling, unusual machine breakdowns, shortages of skilled workers, strikes, storms, and the like.

---

[3] Do not confuse the denominator variance described here with the marketing variance described in Chapter 7. The denominator variance arises because of the peculiarities of historical cost accounting for fixed overhead in an absorption-cost system. In contrast, the marketing variance in Chapter 7 is an entirely separate measure. It aims at estimating the effects on profit of deviating from an original master budget. It is the budgeted unit contribution margin multiplied by the difference between the master budgeted sales in units and the actual sales in units.

462

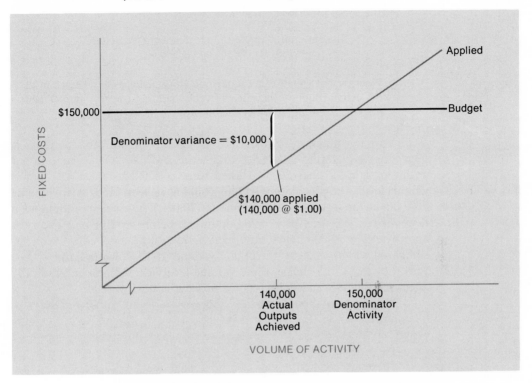

EXHIBIT 15-4. Denominator Variance for 19x5
(Data are from Exhibit 15-2)

There is no denominator variance for variable overhead. The concept of denominator variance arises for fixed overhead because of the conflict between accounting for control (by budgets) and accounting for product costing (by application rates). Note again that the fixed overhead budget serves the control purpose whereas the development of a product costing rate results in the treatment of fixed overhead *as if it were* a variable cost. In other words, the applied line in Exhibit 15-4 is artificial in the sense that, for product costing purposes, it seemingly transforms a fixed cost into a variable cost. This bit of magic forcefully illustrates the distinction between accounting for control and accounting for product costing.

To summarize, denominator variance arises because the actual production activity level achieved frequently does not coincide with the activity level used as a denominator for selecting a predetermined product-costing rate for fixed factory overhead.

1. When denominator production activity and actual production activity are identical, there is no denominator variance.

2. When actual activity is less than denominator activity, the denominator variance is unfavorable. It is measured in Exhibit 15-4 as follows:

(Denominator Activity − Actual Activity) × Predetermined Fixed-
Overhead Rate = Denominator Variance
(150,000 hours − 140,000 hours) × $1 = $10,000

or

Budget minus Applied = Denominator Variance
$150,000 − $140,000 = $10,000

3. Where actual activity exceeds denominator activity, as was the case in 19x4, the denominator variance is favorable because it is an index of better-than-expected utilization of facilities.

Note, too, that the dollar amount of the denominator variance depends on what activity level was selected to determine the application rate. In our example, suppose that 200,000 units were selected as the denominator volume level. The predetermined rate would have been $150,000 divided by 200,000, or 75¢. A subsequent volume of 170,000 hours would result in what denominator variance for 19x4? (Compute it before reading on.) The variance would be 30,000 hours multiplied by 75¢, or $22,500, unfavorable, as compared with the $20,000 favorable variance now shown in Exhibit 15-3. This shows how the choice of the volume-level denominator can radically affect the analysis and unit costs for product costing purposes.

Above all, we should recognize that fixed costs are simply not divisible like variable costs; they come in big chunks and they are related to the provision of big chunks of production or sales capability rather than to the production or sale of a single unit of product.

There are conflicting views on how fixed overhead variances are best analyzed. Obviously, the "best" way is the one that provides management with the most insight into its company's operations. Consequently, overhead analysis varies from company to company. In many companies denominator variances are most usefully expressed in physical terms only. For instance, a denominator variance could be expressed in machine-hours or kilowatt-hours.

RECONCILIATION OF DIRECT COSTING AND ABSORPTION COSTING

Exhibit 15-5 contains a reconciliation of the net incomes shown in Exhibits 15-2 and 15-3. The difference can be explained in a shortcut way by multiplying the fixed overhead product-costing rate by the *change* in the total units in the beginning and ending inventories. Consider 19x5: The change in units was 20,000, so the difference in net income would be 20,000 units multiplied by $1.00 = $20,000.

Exhibit 15-6 gives a more complete explanation of the difference in results. It traces the $30,000 of fixed costs held over from 19x4 under absorption costing, and shows how the 19x5 income statement must bear

EXHIBIT 15-5

Reconciliation of Net Income under Direct Costing
and Absorption Costing

	19x4	19x5	TOGETHER
Net income under:			
Absorption costing (see Exhibit 15-3)	$60,000	$ 45,000	$105,000
Direct costing (see Exhibit 15-2)	30,000	65,000	95,000
Difference to be explained	$30,000	$ – 20,000	$ 10,000
The difference can be reconciled by multiplying the fixed overhead rate by the *change* in the total inventory units:			
Fixed overhead rate	$1	$1	$1
Change in inventory units:			
Opening inventory	—	30,000	—
Ending inventory	30,000	10,000	10,000
Change	$30,000	$ – 20,000	$ 10,000
Difference in net income explained	$30,000	$ – 20,000	$ 10,000

these costs as well as the new costs of 19x5 (except for $10,000 lodged in the ending inventory of 19x5).

EFFECT OF OTHER VARIANCES

So far, our example has deliberately ignored the possibility of any variance except the denominator variance, which arises solely because of the desire for an application rate for fixed overhead in an absorption-costing situation (and the resultant likelihood that the chosen denominator level will differ from the actual production level achieved). Now we will introduce other variances that were explained in Chapter 7. Let us assume some additional facts for 19x5 (the second of the two years covered by our example):

Direct-material variances	None
Direct-labor variances	$ 34,000 *U*
Variable-manufacturing overhead variances	$ 3,000 *U*
Fixed-overhead budget-control variance	$ 7,000 *U*
Supporting data (which are analyzed in the appendix to this chapter):	
Standard direct-labor hours allowed for 140,000 units of output produced	35,000
Standard direct-labor rate per hour	$6.00
Actual direct-labor hours of input	40,000
Actual direct-labor rate per hour	$6.10
Variable manufacturing overhead actually incurred	$ 31,000
Fixed manufacturing overhead actually incurred	$157,000

465

EXHIBIT 15-6

Tracing of Fixed Manufacturing Costs During 19x5
(Data are from Exhibits 15-2 and 15-3)

COSTS TO ACCOUNT FOR	DIRECT COSTING— INVENTORIED COSTS	EXPENSE IN 19x5
No fixed overhead was unexpired in 19x4		
Fixed overhead of $150,000 actually incurred in 19x5 ────────────	expires immediately ────────────→	$150,000

COSTS TO ACCOUNT FOR	ABSORPTION COSTING— INVENTORIED COSTS	EXPENSE IN 19x5
Fixed overhead of $30,000 was held as unexpired cost at end of 19x4 ─────────→	Fixed overhead included in beginning inventory, 30,000 units × $1 = $ 30,000	
Fixed overhead of $150,000: Applied to product, $140,000 ──────────→	Additions to inventory 140,000 units × $1 = 140,000	
	Available for sale 170,000 units $170,000	
	160,000 units sold 160,000 ──── expires ────→ Part of cost of goods sold, at standard	$160,000
	Ending inventory 10,000 units $ 10,000	
Not applied to product, $10,000, expired as a denominator variance ────────────────	expires immediately ────────────→ Denominator variance	10,000
		$170,000

Note that net income must be $20,000 lower under absorption costing than under direct costing because $170,000 of fixed costs expire rather than $150,000.

466

467

Overhead
Application:
Direct and
Absorption
Costing

Exhibit 15-7 contains the income statement under absorption costing that incorporates these new facts. These new variances hurt income by $44,000 because, like the denominator variance, they are all charged against income in 19x5. When variances are favorable, they increase net income.

EXHIBIT 15-7

Absorption Costing
Modification of Exhibit 15-3 for 19x5
(Additional facts are in text)

Sales		$800
Opening inventory at standard	$120	
Cost of goods manufactured at standard	560	
Available for sale	$680	
Deduct ending inventory at standard	40	
Cost of goods sold at standard		640
Gross profit at standard		$160
Net variances for standard variable		
manufacturing costs ($34,000 + $3,000), unfavorable	$ 37	
Fixed-overhead budget-control variance, unfavorable	7	
Denominator variance (arises only because of fixed overhead),		
unfavorable	10	
Total variances		54
Gross profit at "actual"		$106
Selling and administrative expenses		105
Net income		$ 1

DISPOSITION OF STANDARD COST VARIANCES

The advocates of standard costing, particularly when the standards are viewed as being currently attainable, contend that variances are by and large subject to current control. Therefore, variances are not inventoriable and should be considered as adjustments to the income of the period instead of being prorated over inventories and cost of goods sold. In this way, inventory valuations will be more representative of desirable and attainable costs.

The countervailing view favors a proration of the variances[4] over inventories and cost of goods sold. In this way, inventory valuations will be more representative of the "actual" costs incurred to obtain the products. In

[4] For example, the Internal Revenue Service advocates proration. Why? Because most variances tend to be unfavorable. Therefore, proration of variances causes higher ending inventory values, higher immediate income, and higher income taxes than lack of proration. For instance, if, say, $6,000 of the $54,000 variances in Exhibit 15-7 were prorated to the ending inventory, the income would rise from $1,000 to $7,000.

practice, unless the variances are deemed significant in amount, they are usually not prorated because the managers who use standard cost systems favor the views in the preceding paragraph.

Therefore, in practice, variances are typically regarded as adjustments to current income. The form of the disposition is unimportant. Exhibit 15-7 shows the variances as a component of the computation of gross profit at "actual." The variances could also appear as a completely separate section elsewhere in the income statement. This helps to distinguish between product costing (that is, the cost of goods sold, at standard) and loss recognition (unfavorable variances are "lost" or "expired" costs because they represent waste and inefficiency that do not justify them as inventoriable costs. That is, waste is not an asset.)

SUMMARY

Standard cost accounting systems are usually designed to satisfy *control* and *product costing* purposes simultaneously. Many varieties of product costing are in use. For years, manufacturing companies regularly have used a version of absorption costing, which includes fixed factory overhead as a part of the cost of product based on some predetermined application rate (variances are not inventoried). In contrast, direct costing, which is more accurately called *variable costing*, charges fixed factory overhead to the period immediately—that is, fixed overhead is altogether excluded from inventories. Absorption costing continues to be much more widely used than direct costing, although the growing use of the contribution approach in performance measurement has led to increasing use of direct costing for internal purposes.

The denominator variance is linked with absorption costing, not direct costing. It arises from the conflict between the control-budget purpose and the product costing purpose of cost accounting. The denominator variance is measured by the predetermined fixed overhead rate multiplied by the difference between denominator production volume and actual production volume.

Standard costing uses fully predetermined product costs for direct material, direct labor, and factory overhead. If the standards are currently attainable, the variances are not inventoried. Instead, they are directly charged or credited to current operations.

Readers who study both this and the preceding chapter will readily see that various alternatives of *absorption product costing* are possible:[5]

---

[5] In addition, the same alternatives are available for *direct product costing*. The *only* change in the above tabulation would be to delete fixed factory overhead entirely because it is not a product cost under direct costing assumptions.

469

*Overhead
Application:
Direct and
Absorption
Costing*

		Actual Costing	Normal Costing	Standard Costing
Direct materials		Actual costs	Actual	Standard inputs allowed for actual output achieved × predetermined prices
Direct labor		Actual	Actual	
Variable factory overhead	{	Actual	{ Predetermined rates ×	
Fixed factory overhead	{	Actual	actual inputs }	

SUMMARY PROBLEMS FOR YOUR REVIEW

Problems

1. Reconsider Exhibits 15-2 and 15-3. Suppose in 19x5 that production was 145,000 units instead of 140,000 units, but sales were 160,000 units. Also assume that the net variances for all variable manufacturing costs were $37,000, unfavorable. Regard these variances as adjustments to standard cost of goods sold. Also assume that actual fixed costs were $157,000. Prepare income statements for 19x5 under direct costing and under absorption costing.

2. Explain why net income was different under direct costing and absorption costing. Show your calculations.

3. Without regard to Requirement 1, would direct costing or absorption costing give a manager more leeway in influencing his short-run net income through production-scheduling decisions? Why?

Solutions

1. See Exhibits 15-8 and 15-9. Note that the ending inventory will be 15,000 instead of 10,000 units.

2. Decline in inventory levels is 30,000 − 15,000, or 15,000 units. The fixed-overhead rate per unit in absorption costing is $1. Therefore, $15,000 more of fixed overhead was charged against operations under absorption costing than under direct costing. Generally, when inventories decline, absorption costing will show less income than direct costing; when inventories rise, absorption costing will show more income than direct costing.

3. Some version of absorption costing will give a manager more leeway in influencing his net income via production scheduling. Net income will fluctuate in harmony with changes in net sales under direct costing, but it is influenced by both production and sales under absorption costing. For example, compare the direct costing in Exhibits 15-2 and 15-8. As the

EXHIBIT 15-8

TOLMAN COMPANY

Income Statement (Direct Costing)
for the Year 19x5
(In thousands of dollars)

Sales			$800
Opening inventory—at variable standard cost			
of $3	$ 90		
Add variable cost of goods manufactured	435		
Available for sale	$525		
Deduct ending inventory—at variable standard			
cost of $3	45		
Variable cost of goods sold, at standard		$480	
Net variances for all variable costs, unfavorable		37	
Variable cost of goods sold, at actual		$517	
Variable selling expenses—at 5% of dollar sales		40	
Total variable costs charged against sales			557
Contribution margin			$243
Fixed factory overhead		$157*	
Fixed selling and administrative expenses		65	
Total fixed expenses			222
Net income			$ 21†

* This could be shown in two lines, $150,000 budget plus $7,000 variance.
† The difference between this and the $65,000 net income in Exhibit 15-2 occurs because of the $37,000 unfavorable variable cost variances and the $7,000 unfavorable fixed-cost control-budget variance.

second note to Exhibit 15-8 indicates, the net income may be affected by assorted variances (but not the denominator variance) under direct costing, but production scheduling *per se* will have no effect on net income. On the other hand, compare the net income of Exhibits 15-7 and 15-9. As the third note to Exhibit 15-9 explains, production scheduling as well as sales influence net income. Production was 145,000 rather than 140,000 units. So $5,000 of fixed overhead became a part of ending inventory (an asset) instead of part of the denominator variance (an expense)—that is, the denominator variance is $5,000 lower and the ending inventory contains $5,000 more fixed overhead in Exhibit 15-9 than in Exhibit 15-7.

APPENDIX 15:
COMPARISONS OF DENOMINATOR VARIANCES
WITH OTHER VARIANCES

Denominator Variance Is Unique

The only new variance introduced in this chapter is the denominator variance, which arises because fixed overhead accounting must serve two masters: the budget-control purpose and the product costing purpose. Let us

EXHIBIT 15-9

TOLMAN COMPANY

Income Statement (Absorption Costing)
for the Year 19x5
(In thousands of dollars)

Sales		$800
Opening inventory at standard cost of $4	$120	
Cost of goods manufactured at standard	580	
Available for sale	$700	
Deduct ending inventory at standard	60	
Cost of goods sold at standard	$640	
Net variances for all variable manufacturing costs, unfavorable	$37	
Fixed factory overhead budget-control variance, unfavorable	7	
Denominator variance, unfavorable	5*	
Total variances	49	
Cost of goods sold at actual		689†
Gross profit at "actual"		$111
Selling and administrative expenses		
Variable	$ 40	
Fixed	65	105
Net income		$ 6‡

*Denominator variance is $1 × (150,000 denominator volume − 145,000 actual production).

†This format differs slightly from Exhibit 15-7. The difference is deliberate; it illustrates that the formats of income statements are not rigid.

‡Compare this result with the $1,000 net income in Exhibit 15-7. The *only* difference is traceable to the *production* of 145,000 units instead of 140,000 units, resulting in an unfavorable denominator variance of $5,000 instead of $10,000.

examine these variances in perspective by using the approach originally demonstrated in Exhibit 7-6. The results of the approach are in Exhibit 15-10, which deserves your careful study, particularly the two notes. **Please ponder the exhibit before reading on.**

Exhibit 15-11 provides a graphical comparison of the variable and fixed overhead that were analyzed in Exhibit 15-10. Note how the control-budget line and the product costing line (the applied line) are superimposed in the graph for variable overhead but differ in the graph for fixed overhead.

Under- or overapplied overhead is always the difference between the actual overhead incurred and the overhead applied. An analysis may then be made:

$$\text{Underapplied overhead} = \text{Flexible budget-control variance} + \text{Denominator variance}$$

For variable overhead = $3,000 + 0 = $3,000

For fixed overhead = $7,000 + $10,000 = $17,000

EXHIBIT 15-10

Analysis of Variances
(Data are from text)

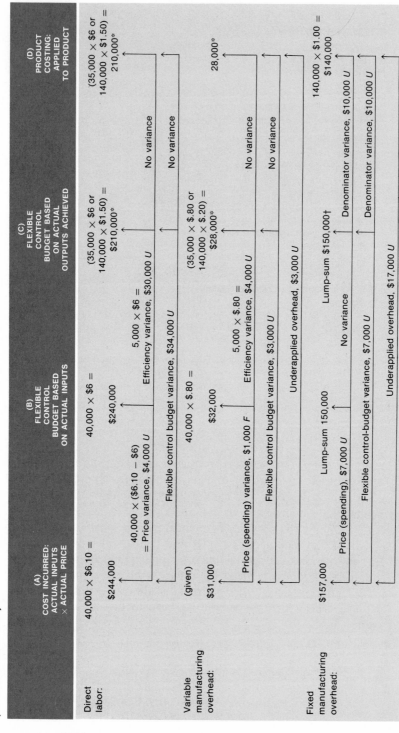

	(A) COST INCURRED: ACTUAL INPUTS × ACTUAL PRICE	(B) FLEXIBLE CONTROL BUDGET BASED ON ACTUAL INPUTS	(C) FLEXIBLE CONTROL BUDGET BASED ON ACTUAL OUTPUTS ACHIEVED	(D) PRODUCT COSTING: APPLIED TO PRODUCT
Direct labor:	40,000 × $6.10 = $244,000	40,000 × $6 = $240,000	(35,000 × $6 or 140,000 × $1.50) = $210,000*	(35,000 × $6 or 140,000 × $1.50) = 210,000*
	40,000 × ($6.10 − $6) = Price variance, $4,000 U	5,000 × $6 = Efficiency variance, $30,000 U	No variance	
	Flexible control budget variance, $34,000 U		No variance	
Variable manufacturing overhead:	(given) $31,000	40,000 × $.80 = $32,000	(35,000 × $.80 or 140,000 × $.20) = $28,000*	28,000*
	Price (spending) variance, $1,000 F	5,000 × $.80 = Efficiency variance, $4,000 U	No variance	
	Flexible control budget variance, $3,000 U		No variance	
		Underapplied overhead, $3,000 U		
Fixed manufacturing overhead:	$157,000	Lump-sum 150,000	Lump-sum $150,000†	140,000 × $1.00 = $140,000
	Price (spending), $7,000 U	No variance	Denominator variance, $10,000 U	
	Flexible control-budget variance, $7,000 U		Denominator variance, $10,000 U	
		Underapplied overhead, $17,000 U		

U = Unfavorable F = Favorable

*Note especially that the control budget for variable costs rises and falls in direct proportion to production. Note also that the control-budget purpose and the product costing purpose harmonize completely; the total costs in the flexible budget will always agree with the standard variable costs applied to product because they are based on standard costs per unit multiplied by units produced.

†In contrast with variable costs, the control budget total will always be the same regardless of the units produced. However, the control-budget purpose and the product costing purpose conflict; whenever actual production differs from denominator production, the standard costs applied to product will differ from the control budget. This difference is the denominator variance. In this case, the denominator variance may be computed by multiplying the $1 rate times the difference between the 150,000 denominator volume and the 140,000 units of output achieved.

472

EXHIBIT 15-11. Comparison of Control and Product Costing Purposes,
Variable Overhead and Fixed Overhead (Not to scale)

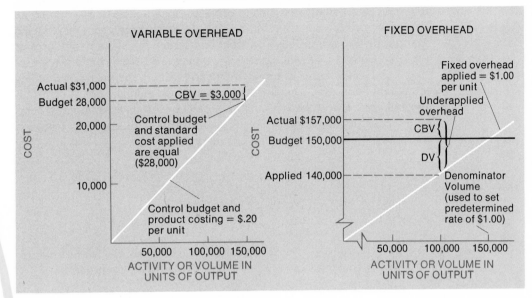

Lost-Contribution Margins

Finally, what is the economic significance of unit fixed costs? Unlike variable costs, total fixed costs do not change in the short run as production or sales fluctuate. **Management would obtain a better measure of the cost of underutilization of physical facilities by trying to approximate the related lost-contribution margins instead of the related historical fixed costs.**[6] Fixed-cost incurrence often involves lump-sum outlays based on a pattern of expected recoupment. But ineffective utilization of existing facilities has no bearing on the amount of fixed costs currently incurred. The economic effects of the inability to reach target volume levels are often directly measured by lost-contribution margins, even if these have to be approximated. The historical-cost approach fails to emphasize the distinction between *fixed-cost incurrence,* on the one hand, and the objective of *maximizing the total contribution margin,* on the other hand. These are separable management problems, and the utilization of existing capacity is more closely related to the latter.

For instance, the denominator variance in our example was computed at $10,000 by multiplying a unit fixed cost of $1 by the 10,000-unit difference between the 150,000 units of denominator activity and 140,000 units produced. This $10,000 figure may be helpful in the sense that management is

[6] For an expanded discussion, see C. Horngren, "A Contribution Margin Approach to the Analysis of Capacity Utilization," *The Accounting Review,* Vol. XLII, No. 2, pp. 254–64.

alerted in some crude way to the probable costs of failure to produce 150,000 units. But the more relevant information is the lost-contribution margins that pertain to the 10,000 units. This information may not be so easy to obtain. The lost-contribution margins may be zero in those cases where there are no opportunities to obtain any contribution margin from alternative uses of available capacity; in other cases, however, the lost-contribution margins may be substantial. For example, if demand is high, the breakdown of key equipment may cost a company many thousands of dollars in lost-contribution margins. Unfortunately, in these cases, existing accounting systems would show denominator variances based on the unitized fixed costs and entirely ignore any lost-contribution margins.

ASSIGNMENT MATERIAL

Fundamental Assignment Material

15-1. Terminology. Define: *absorption costing; direct costing; variable costing; marginal costing; standard absorption costing; and standard direct costing.*

15-2. Comparison of direct costing and absorption costing. From the following information pertaining to a year's operation, answer the questions below:

Units produced	2,400
Units sold	2,000
Selling and administrative expenses (all fixed)	$ 800
Fixed manufacturing overhead	2,400
Variable manufacturing overhead	1,100
Direct labor	3,400
Direct material used	2,700
All beginning inventories	-0-
Gross margin (gross profit)	2,000
Direct-materials inventory, end	300
Work-in-process inventory, end	-0-

Required

1. What is the ending finished-goods inventory cost under traditional costing procedures (absorption costing)?

2. What is the ending finished-goods inventory cost under variable-costing procedures (direct costing)?

3. Would net income be higher or lower under direct costing? By how much? Why? (Answer: $400 lower.)

15-3. Extension of chapter illustration. Reconsider Exhibits 15-2 and 15-3. Suppose that in 19x5 production was 156,000 units instead of 140,000 units, and sales were 150,000 units. Also assume that the net variances for all variable manufacturing costs were $24,000, unfavorable. Also assume that actual fixed manufacturing costs were $157,000.

1. Prepare income statements for 19x5 under direct costing and under absorption costing. Use a format similar to Exhibits 15-8 and 15-9.

2. Explain why net income was different under direct costing and absorption costing. Show your calculations.

15-4. Extension of appendix illustration. Study the analysis of variances in Exhibit 15-10. Suppose that production is 156,000 units. Also assume:

Standard direct-labor hours allowed per unit produced	.25
Standard direct-labor rate per hour	$6.00
Actual direct-labor hours of input	42,000
Actual direct-labor rate per hour	$6.10
Variable manufacturing overhead actually incurred	$33,000
Fixed manufacturing overhead actually incurred	$157,000

Prepare an analysis of variances similar to that shown in Exhibit 15-10.

Additional Assignment Material

15-5. "Direct costing means that only direct material and direct labor are inventoried." Do you agree? Why?

15-6. Why do advocates of currently attainable standard costs as a method for product costing claim that it is conceptually superior to actual costing?

15-7. "Absorption costing regards more categories of costs as product costs." Explain. Be specific.

15-8. "Direct costing is used in several corporate annual reports." Do you agree? Explain.

15-9. How is fixed overhead applied to product?

15-10. Define the *denominator variance* as conventionally measured.

15-11. "The dollar amount of the denominator variance depends on what activity level was chosen to determine the application rate." Explain.

15-12. Why is it artificial to unitize fixed costs?

15-13. "The fixed cost per unit is directly affected by the denominator selected." Do you agree? Explain.

15-14. Simple comparison of direct and absorption costing. B Company began business on January 1, 19x1, with assets of $100,000 cash and equities of $100,000 capital stock. In 19x1 it manufactured some inventory at a cost of $50,000, including $10,000 for factory rent and other fixed factory overhead. In 19x2 it manufactured nothing and sold half of its inventory for $32,000 cash. In 19x3 it manufactured nothing and sold the remaining half for another $32,000 cash. It had no fixed expenses in 19x2 or 19x3.

There are no other transactions of any kind. Ignore income taxes.

Required

Prepare an ending balance sheet plus an income statement for 19x1, 19x2, and 19x3 under (1) absorption costing and (2) variable (direct) costing.

15-15. Comparison of direct costing and absorption costing. From the following information pertaining to a year's operations, answer the questions below:

Units sold	1,000
Units produced	1,100
Fixed manufacturing overhead	$2,200
Variable manufacturing overhead	500
Selling and administrative expenses (all fixed)	900
Direct labor	4,000
Direct material used	2,100
Beginning inventories	-0-
Contribution margin	4,000
Direct-material inventory, end	1,000

There are no work-in-process inventories.

Required

1. What is the ending finished-goods inventory cost under traditional costing procedures (absorption costing)?

2. What is the ending finished-goods inventory cost under variable-costing procedures (direct costing)?

15-16. Comparisons over four years. The E corporation began business on January 1, 19x7, to produce and sell a single product. Reported net income figures (before tax) under both absorption and direct (variable) costing for the first four years of operation are:

Year	Direct Costing	Absorption Costing
19x7	40,000	40,000
19x8	20,000	50,000
19x9	60,000	40,000
19x0	60,000	50,000

Standard production costs per unit, sales prices, application (absorption) rates, and denominator volume levels were the same in each year. There were no under- or overapplied overhead costs, and no variances in any year. All nonmanufacturing expenses were fixed, and there were no nonmanufacturing cost variances in any year.

Required

1. In what year(s) did "units produced" equal "units sold"?

2. In what year(s) did "units produced" exceed "units sold"?

3. What is the dollar amount of the December 31, 19x0, finished-goods inventory? (Give absorption-costing value.)

4. What is the difference between "units produced" and "units sold" in 19x8, if you know that the absorption-costing fixed-manufacturing-overhead application rate is $2 per unit? (Give answer in units.)

477

Overhead
Application:
Direct and
Absorption
Costing

15-17. All-fixed costs. (Suggested by Raymond P. Marple.) The Marple Company has built a massive water-desalting factory next to an ocean. The factory is completely automated. It has its own source of power, light, heat, etc. The salt water costs nothing. All producing and other operating costs are fixed; they do not vary with output because the volume is governed by adjusting a few dials on a control panel. The employees have flat annual salaries.

The desalted water is not sold to household consumers. It has a special taste that appeals to local breweries, distilleries, and soft-drink manufacturers. The price, 10¢ per gallon, is expected to remain unchanged for quite some time.

The following are data regarding the first two years of operations:

	In Gallons		Costs (All fixed)	
	Sales	Production	Manufacturing	Other
19x1	5,000,000	10,000,000	$450,000	$100,000
19x2	5,000,000	0	450,000	100,000

Orders can be processed in four hours, so management decided, in early 19x2, to gear production strictly to sales.

Required

1. Prepare three-column income statements for 19x1, for 19x2, and for the two years together using (a) direct costing and (b) absorption costing.
2. What is the break-even point under (a) direct costing and (b) absorption costing?
3. What inventory costs would be carried on the balance sheets on December 31, 19x1 and 19x2, under each method?
4. Comment on your answers in Requirements 1 and 2. Which costing method appears more useful?

15-18. Semifixed costs. The McFarland Company differs from the Marple Company (described in Problem 15-17) in only one respect: it has both variable and fixed manufacturing costs. Its variable costs are $.025 per gallon and its fixed manufacturing costs are $225,000 per year.

Required

1. Using the same data as in the previous problem, except for the change in production-cost behavior, prepare three-column income statements for 19x1, for 19x2, and for the two years together using (a) direct costing and (b) absorption costing.
2. Why did McFarland earn a profit for the two-year period while Marple suffered a loss?
3. What inventory costs would be carried on the balance sheets on December 31, 19x1 and 19x2, under each method?

15-19. Fundamentals of overhead variances. The Green Company is installing an absorption standard cost system and a flexible overhead budget. Standard costs have been recently developed for its only product and are as follows:

Direct material, 2 pounds @ $15	$30
Direct labor, 6 hours @ $6	36
Variable overhead, 6 hours @ $1	6
Fixed overhead	?
Standard cost per unit of finished product	$?

Denominator activity (expected activity) is expressed as 12,000 standard direct-labor hours per month. Fixed overhead is expected to be $18,000 per month. The predetermined fixed overhead rate for product costing is not changed from month to month.

Required

1. Calculate the proper fixed overhead rate per standard direct-labor hour and per unit.

2. Graph the following for activity from zero to 15,000 hours:
   a. Budgeted variable overhead.
   b. Variable overhead applied to product.

3. Graph the following for activity from zero to 15,000 hours:
   a. Budgeted fixed overhead.
   b. Fixed overhead applied to product.

4. Assume that 10,000 standard direct-labor hours are allowed for the output achieved during a given month. Actual variable overhead of $10,200 was incurred; actual fixed overhead amounted to $18,500. Calculate the:
   a. Fixed-overhead control-budget variance.
   b. Fixed-overhead denominator variance.
   c. Variable-overhead control-budget variance.

5. Assume that 12,500 standard direct-labor hours are allowed for the output achieved during a given month. Actual overhead incurred amounted to $29,900, $18,900 of which was fixed. Calculate the:
   a. Variable-overhead control-budget variance.
   b. Fixed-overhead denominator variance.
   c. Fixed-overhead control-budget variance.

15-20. Analysis of fixed overhead; various activity levels. The fixed overhead items of the lathe department of Costanzo Company include for the month of January, 19x4:

Item	Actual	Budget
Supervision	$ 900	$ 800
Depreciation—Plant	750	750
Depreciation—Equipment	1,750	1,750
Property taxes	350	400
Insurance—Factory	400	300
	$4,150	$4,000

Expected activity for the lathe department is 1,000 standard hours per month. Practical capacity is 1,600 standard hours per month. Standard hours allowed for work done (good units actually produced) were 1,250.

Required

1. Prepare a summary analysis of fixed overhead variances using expected activity as the activity base.
2. Prepare a summary analysis of fixed overhead variances using practical capacity as the activity base.

3. Explain why the control-budget variances in Requirements 1 and 2 are identical whereas the denominator variances are different.

15-21. Direct and absorption costing. (H. Schaefer.) Data for 19x2:

Sales: 10,000 units at $12 each	
Actual production	12,000 units
Denominator activity	15,000 units
Manufacturing costs *incurred:*	
Variable	$60,000
Fixed	30,000
Nonmanufacturing costs *incurred:*	
Variable	$15,000
Fixed	14,000

1. Determine net income for 19x2, assuming the firm uses the direct-costing approach to product costing. (Do not prepare a statement.)

2. Assume that (a) there is *no* January 1, 19x2, inventory, (b) *no* variances are allocated to inventory, and (c) the firm uses a "full absorption" approach to product costing. Compute: (a) the cost assigned to December 31, 1972, inventory; and (b) net income for the year ended December 31, 19x2. (Do not prepare a statement.)

15-22. **Analysis of operating results.** (CMA, adapted.) Sun Company, a wholly owned subsidiary of Guardian, Inc., produces and sells three main product lines. The company employs a standard cost accounting system for record-keeping purposes.

At the beginning of 19x4, the president of Sun Company presented the budget to the parent company and accepted a commitment to contribute $15,800 to Guardian's consolidated profit in 19x4. The president has been confident that the year's profit would exceed budget target, since the monthly sales reports that he has been receiving have shown that sales for the year will exceed budget by 10 percent. The president is both disturbed and confused when the controller presents an adjusted forecast as of November 30, 19x4, indicating that profit will be 11 percent under budget. The two forecasts are presented below:

SUN COMPANY
Forecasts of Operating Results

	Forecasts as of	
	1/1/x4	11/30/x4
Sales	$268,000	$294,800
Cost of sales at standard	212,000*	233,200
Gross margin at standard	$ 56,000	$ 61,600
Over- (Under-) absorbed fixed manufacturing overhead		⟨6,000⟩
Actual gross margin	$ 56,000	$ 55,600
Selling expenses	$ 13,400	$ 14,740
Administrative expenses	26,800	26,800
Total operating expenses	$ 40,200	$ 41,540
Earnings before tax	$ 15,800	$ 14,060

*Includes fixed manufacturing overhead of $30,000.

There have been no sales price changes or product-mix shifts since the 1/1/x4 forecast. The only cost variance on the income statement is the underabsorbed manufacturing overhead. This arose because the company produced only 16,000 standard machine-hours (budgeted machine-hours were 20,000) during 19x4 as a result of a shortage of raw materials while its principal supplier was closed by a strike. Fortunately, Sun Company's finished goods inventory was large enough to fill all sales orders received.

Required

1. Analyze and explain why the profit has declined in spite of increased sales and good control over costs. Show computations.

2. What plan, if any, could Sun Company adopt during December to improve their reported profit at year-end? Explain your answer.

3. Illustrate and explain how Sun Company could adopt an alternative internal cost reporting procedure that would avoid the confusing effect of the present procedure. Show the revised forecasts under your alternative.

4. Would the alternative procedure described in Requirement 3 be acceptable to Guardian, Inc., for financial reporting purposes? Explain.

15-23 **Standard absorption and standard direct costing.** Coleman Company has the following results for a certain year. All variances are written off as additions to (or deductions from) the standard cost of goods sold. Find the unknowns, designated by letters.

Sales: 200,000 units, @ $22	$4,400,000
Net variance for standard variable manufacturing costs	$ 36,000, unfavorable
Variable standard cost of goods manufactured	$ 10 per unit
Variable selling and administrative expenses	$ 2 per unit
Fixed selling and administrative expenses	$1,000,000
Fixed manufacturing overhead	$ 240,000
Maximum capacity per year	240,000 units
Denominator volume for year	200,000 units
Beginning inventory of finished goods	30,000 units
Ending inventory of finished goods	10,000 units
Beginning inventory: direct-costing basis	a
Contribution margin	b
Net income: direct-costing basis	c
Beginning inventory: absorption-costing basis	d
Gross margin	e
Net income: absorption-costing basis	f

15-24. **Fill in the blanks.** Read the appendix.

	Factory Overhead	
	Fixed	Variable
Actual incurred	$5,500	$10,800
Budget for standard hours allowed for output achieved	5,000	9,000
Applied	4,800	9,000
Budget for actual hours of input	5,000	9,800

481

*Overhead
Application:
Direct and
Absorption
Costing*

From the above information fill in the blanks below:

The control budget variance is $_____   Fixed $_____
                                             Variable $_____
The denominator variance is $_____   Fixed $_____
                                             Variable $_____
The price variance is $_____   Fixed $_____
                                             Variable $_____
The efficiency variance is $_____   Fixed $_____
                                             Variable $_____

Mark your variances *F* for favorable and *U* for unfavorable.

15-25. **Straightforward appendix problem on standard cost system.** Read the appendix. The Mellor Company uses a standard cost system. The month's data regarding its single product follow:

> Fixed overhead costs incurred, $6,150
> Variable overhead applied at $.90 per hour
> Standard direct-labor cost, $4 per hour
> Denominator production per month, 2,500 units
> Standard direct-labor hours per finished unit, 5
> Direct-labor costs incurred, 11,000 hours, $41,800
> Variable overhead costs incurred, $9,500
> Fixed-overhead budget variance, $100, favorable
> Finished units produced, 2,000

Required | Prepare an analysis of all variances (similar to Exhibit 15-10).

15-26. **Analysis of variances.** (CPA, adapted.) Read the appendix. The Groomer Company manufactures two products, florimene and glyoxide, used in the Singapore plastics industry. The company uses a flexible budget in its standard cost system to develop variances. Selected data follow:

	Florimene	*Glyoxide*
Data on standard costs:		
Raw material per unit.........	3 pounds at $1.00 per pound	4 pounds at $1.10 per pound
Direct labor per unit	5 hours at $2.00 per hour	6 hours at $2.50 per hour
Variable factory overhead per unit	$3.20 per direct-labor hour	$3.50 per direct-labor hour
Fixed factory overhead per month	$20,700	$26,520
Denominator activity per month	5,750 direct-labor hours	7,800 direct-labor hours
Units produced in September	1,000	1,200

Costs incurred for September:

Raw material..................	3,100 pounds at $.90 per pound	4,700 pounds at $1.15 per pound
Direct labor....................	4,900 hours at $1.95 per hour	7,400 hours at $2.55 per hour
Variable factory overhead.....	$16,170	$25,234
Fixed factory overhead........	$20,930	$26,400

Required

Select the best answer for each of the following items. Show computations to support your answer.

1. The total variances (that is, the difference between total costs incurred and total standard costs applied to product) to be explained for both products for September are
   a. Florimene, $255, favorable; Glyoxide, $909, unfavorable.
   b. Florimene, $7,050, favorable; Glyoxide, $6,080, favorable.
   c. Florimene, $4,605, favorable; Glyoxide, $3,431, favorable.
   d. Florimene, $2,445, unfavorable; Glyoxide, $2,949, unfavorable.
   e. None of the above.

2. The labor-efficiency variances for both products for September are
   a. Florimene, $195, favorable; Glyoxide, $510, unfavorable.
   b. Florimene, $1,700, favorable; Glyoxide, $1,000, favorable.
   c. Florimene, $200, favorable; Glyoxide, $500, unfavorable.
   d. Florimene, $195, favorable; Glyoxide, $510 favorable.
   e. None of the above.

3. The labor-price (rate) variances for both products for September are
   a. Florimene, $245, favorable; Glyoxide, $370, unfavorable.
   b. Florimene, $200, favorable; Glyoxide, $500, unfavorable.
   c. Florimene, $1,945, favorable; Glyoxide, $630 favorable.
   d. Florimene, $245, unfavorable; Glyoxide, $370, favorable.
   e. None of the above.

4. The "price" variances for variable overhead for both products for September are
   a. Florimene, $490, unfavorable; Glyoxide, $666, favorable.
   b. Florimene, $167, unfavorable; Glyoxide, $35, unfavorable.
   c. Florimene, $170, unfavorable; Glyoxide, $34, unfavorable.
   d. Florimene, $1,900, favorable; Glyoxide, $1,960, favorable.
   e. None of the above.

15-27. Three-Year Comparison. (SMA.) The management of X Ltd. is concerned about recent profit trends. The following condensed income statements were viewed with some alarm by the executive committee. The president is particularly disturbed. "Why," he asks, "has the profit from increased sales failed to materialize?"

483

*Overhead
Application:
Direct and
Absorption
Costing*

X LTD
Condensed Income Statements

	19x0	19x1	*Profit Increase/Decrease*
Sales: units	80,000	120,000	
revenue	$2,000,000	$3,000,000	$ 1,000,000
Manufacturing cost	1,000,000	2,050,000	(1,050,000)
	1,000,000	950,000	(50,000)
General expense	480,000	620,000	(140,000)
Net income	$ 520,000	$ 330,000	$ (190,000)

Investigation provides the following facts:

1. The company operates an absorption-cost accounting system. Unabsorbed manufacturing overhead is charged to manufacturing cost.
2. Manufacturing-cost estimates, prepared at a denominator volume of 100,000 units, are as follows:

Material	$ 3
Labor	1
Overhead:	
Variable	1
Fixed	10
	$15

There is no reason to suspect any significant departure from the budgeted cost behavior in either year.

3. General expenses were incurred at a variable rate of $1 per unit sold in both years. Fixed expenses totalled $400,000 in 19x0 and $500,000 in 19x1. The increase reflected a sales promotion program initiated to raise sales volume to 125,000 units. Actual sales were only 5,000 units short of this target.
4. Production levels in 19x0 were 120,000 units. As in preceding years, sales fell short of anticipation and year-end inventories rose 40,000 units. Management decided to cut inventory levels to 150,000 units in 19x1 and reduced production levels to 75,000 units in that year. By December 31, 19x1, inventory was at the 150,000-unit level. It is expected that in 19x2 sales will equal production at 125,000 units.

Required

1. Reconstruct the income statements for 19x0 and 19x1 on a variable (direct) costing basis.
2. a. Submit a short note explaining to the president the reasons for the strange profit performance exhibited by his original statement.
   b. If expectations are realized in 19x2 and assuming no cost or price changes from 19x1, what profit will the *company system report?* By how much will it differ from a variable-cost based income report?

15-28. Inventory measures, production scheduling, and evaluating divisional performance. The Mark Company stresses competition between the heads of its various divisions and rewards stellar performance with year-end bonuses that vary between 5 and 10 percent of division net operating income (before considering the bonus or income taxes). The divisional managers have great discretion in setting production schedules.

Division Y produces and sells a product for which there is a longstanding demand but which can have marked seasonal and year-to-year fluctuations. On November 30, 19x2, George Craft, the Division Y manager, is preparing a production schedule for December. The following data are available for January 1 through November 30:

Beginning inventory, January 1, in units	10,000
Sales price, per unit	$ 500
Total fixed costs incurred for manufacturing	$11,000,000
Total fixed costs: other (not inventoriable)	$11,000,000
Total variable costs for manufacturing	$22,000,000
Total other variable costs (fluctuate with units sold)	$ 5,000,000
Units produced	110,000
Units sold	100,000
Variances	None

Production in October and November was 10,000 units each month. Practical capacity is 12,000 units per month. Maximum available storage space for inventory is 25,000 units. The sales outlook, for December through February, is 6,000 units monthly. In order to retain a core of key employees, monthly production cannot be scheduled at less than 4,000 units without special permission from the president. Inventory is never to be less than 10,000 units.

The denominator used for applying fixed factory overhead is regarded as 120,000 units annually. The company uses a standard absorption-costing system. All variances are disposed of at year-end as an adjustment to standard cost of goods sold.

Required

1. Given the restrictions as stated, and assuming that the manager wants to maximize the company's net income for 19x2:
   a. How many units should be scheduled for production in December?
   b. What net operating income will be reported for 19x2 as a whole, assuming that the implied cost behavior patterns will continue in December as they did throughout the year, to date? Show your computations.
   c. If December production is scheduled at 4,000 units, what would reported net income be?

2. Assume that standard direct costing is used rather than standard absorption costing.
   a. What would net income for 19x2 be, assuming that the December production schedule is the one in Requirement 1, part (a)?
   b. Assuming that December production was 4,000 units?
   c. Reconcile the net incomes in this requirement with those in Requirement 1.

3. From the viewpoint of the long-run interests of the company as a whole, what production schedule should the division manager set? Explain fully. Include in your explanation a comparison of the motivating influence of absorption and direct costing in this situation.

485

*Overhead
Application:
Direct and
Absorption
Costing*

4. Assume standard absorption costing. The manager wants to maximize his after-income-tax performance over the long run. Given the data at the beginning of the problem, assume that income tax rates will be halved in 19x3. Assume also that year-end write-offs of variances are acceptable for income tax purposes.

How many units should be scheduled for production in December? Why?

15-29. Dispute about variance allocation. G Manufacturing Company has been buying $\frac{1}{4}$-horsepower motors from L Manufacturing Company for several years. L Manufacturing Company has supplied such motors to several large customers. Each customer pays a predetermined price per motor, which is changed annually. The procedure follows (data simplified to ease calculations):

	Customer			
	F	*G*	*H*	*Total*
Three customers predict their annual volume	100	100	100	300
Standard costs:				
Direct material	$10	$10	$10	
Direct labor	10	10	10	
Variable overhead	5	5	5	
Fixed overhead $3,000 ÷ 300	10	10	10	
Absorption cost per unit	$35	$35	$35	
Add a margin	7	7	7	
Predetermined price	$42	$42	$42	

Each year L Manufacturing also allocates any year-end "unabsorbed overhead denominator variance" as an additional charge or rebate to its customers.

1. Suppose that Customers F, G, and H each bought 75 motors for the year. Compute the additional charge to each customer.

2. Suppose that Customers F and G each bought 75 motors, but H bought 150. Compute the additional charge to each customer.

3. Refer to Requirement 2. In 19x8 L Company changed its method of computing the denominator variance after its top executive commented: "We're not playing fair with our customers by computing the denominator variance in such an aggregate way. Instead, we should compute individual denominator variances." Compute the charges or rebates under this new allocation method. As an impartial observer, do you favor using the aggregated method or the disaggregated method? Why?

CHAPTER 16

Influences of Quantitative Techniques on Management Accounting

Because the branches of knowledge overlap, it is always an oversimplification to specify where the field of accounting starts and where it ends. Some accountants take the view that accounting should restrict itself to scorekeeping, the compilation of financial history. Others feel that if accountants do not move quickly to assimilate a working knowledge of computer technology and assorted mathematical techniques, their attention-directing and problem-solving functions will be seized by the expanding field of management science.

We need not be concerned with the controversy over what accounting is and what it is not. Regardless of its label, the subject matter of this chapter has a bearing on management planning and control and is therefore important to accountants and to managers. One of the marks of an educated person is his ability to recognize and accept changes that promise better ways of accomplishing objectives. The accountant is still the top quantitative

487

*Influences of
Quantitative
Techniques on
Management
Accounting*

expert in nearly all organizations, and few companies employ full-time mathematics specialists. To retain and improve his status, the accountant should be aware of how mathematical models may improve planning and control. The alert manager would naturally expect his accountants to keep abreast of the newer quantitative techniques.

This chapter is a survey. Technical competence in any of the areas mentioned can be achieved only by thorough specialized study. We shall explore decision theory and uncertainty, linear-programming models, and inventory-control models.

The accountant often provides many of the data that are included in these decision models. His understanding of the nature of decision models should have a direct effect on how he designs a formal information system.

DECISION THEORY AND UNCERTAINTY

Formal Decision Models

A **model** is a depiction of the interrelationships among the recognized factors in a real situation. Most models spotlight the key interrelationships and deemphasize the unimportant factors. Models take many forms. Museums contain model rockets and model ships. Automobile companies distribute miniature model cars. Accountants continually work with accounting systems and financial reports, which are models. Operations researchers principally use mathematical equations as models.

Decision models are often expressed in mathematical form. The careful use of mathematical models supplements hunches and implicit rules of thumb with explicit assumptions and criteria. Mathematical models have been criticized because they may oversimplify and ignore important underlying factors. Still, many examples of successful applications can be cited. For example, inventory-control and linear-programming models are widely used. The test of success is not whether mathematical models lead to perfect decisions, but whether such models lead to better decisions than via alternative techniques. How is this test applied? Sometimes it is difficult, but conceptually the test is to compare the net financial impact (after deducting the cost of accumulating the information used in the decision) of the decision generated by the mathematical model versus the net financial impact of the decision generated by other techniques. In other words, the relative attractiveness of using mathematical decision models is again subject to the cost-benefit test.

Decision theory is a complex, somewhat ill-defined body of knowledge developed by statisticians, mathematicians, economists, and psychologists that tries to prescribe how decisions should be made and to describe systematically which variables affect choices. The basic approach of decision theory has the following characteristics:

1. An organizational objective that can be quantified. This objective can take many forms. Most often, it is expressed as a maximization (or minimization) of some form of profit (or cost). This quantification is often called a *choice criterion* or an *objective function.* This objective function is used to evaluate the courses of action and to provide a basis for choosing the best alternative.

2. A set of the alternative courses of action under explicit consideration. This set of *actions* should be collectively exhaustive and mutually exclusive.

3. A set of all relevant *events* (sometimes called *states*) that can occur. This set should also be collectively exhaustive and mutually exclusive. Therefore, only one of the states will actually occur.

4. A set of *probabilities* that describes the likelihood of occurrence for each event.

5. A set of *outcomes* (often called *payoffs*) that measure the consequences of the various possible actions in terms of the objective function. Each outcome is conditionally dependent on a specific course of action and a specific event.

Payoff Tables and Decision Tables

An example may clarify the essential ingredients of a formal model. Suppose a decision maker has two mutually exclusive and exhaustive alternative courses of action regarding the quality-control aspects of his project: accept or reject. He also predicts that two mutually exclusive and exhaustive events will affect his outcomes: either the product conforms to the quality standards, or it does not. The combination of actions, events, and outcomes can be presented in a *payoff table:*

Alternative Actions	Alternative Events and Outcomes	
	Conform	*Nonconform*
Accept	$12[1]	$2[2]
Reject	$ 7[3]	$7[4]

Note: The number references in this table relate to the corresponding numbers in the list that follows.

The outcomes in this example are the dollar contributions to profit; they are assumed to take the pattern shown here because:

1. Acceptance and conformance should produce the normal contribution to profit.

489

*Influences of
Quantitative
Techniques on
Management
Accounting*

2. Acceptance and nonconformance eventually results in expensive rework after the product is processed through later stages, so the contribution is lower.

3. Rejection and conformance results in immediate unnecessary rework that reduces the normal contribution.

4. Rejection and nonconformance results in the same immediate necessary rework described in item 3.

The payoff table includes three of the five ingredients of the formal model: actions, events, and outcomes. The other two ingredients are the probabilities and the choice criterion. Assume that the probability of conform is 0.6 and that of nonconform is 0.4. Assume also that the choice criterion is to maximize the expected value of the outcome, the contribution to profit. The payoff table can now be expanded to a *decision table:*

	Events		
	Conform	*Nonconform*	
Probability of event:	*0.6*	*0.4*	*Expected Value*
	Contribution	*Contribution*	*of Contribution*
Actions:			
Accept	$12	$2	$8
Reject	$ 7	$7	$7

Given this model, the decision maker would always accept the product, because the expected value of the outcome is larger for Accept than for Reject. Let $\bar{A}$ = the "average" or expected value;[1] then:

If Accept, $\bar{A} = \$12(0.6) + \$2(0.4) = \$7.20 + \$.80 = \$8$

If Reject, $\bar{A} = \$7(0.6) + \$7(0.4) = \$4.20 + \$2.80 = \$7$

As you can see, an expected value is simply a weighted average using the probability of each event to weight the outcomes for each action.

Decisions under Certainty

Decisions are frequently classified as those made under certainty and those made under uncertainty. Certainty exists when there is absolutely no doubt

---

[1] An expected value is an arithmetic mean, a weighted average using the probabilities as weights. The formula is

$$\bar{A} = \sum_{x=1}^{n} A_x P_x$$

where A_x is the outcome or payoff or cost or cash flow for the xth possible event or state of nature, P_x is the probability of occurrence of that outcome, and $\bar{A}$ is the expected value of the outcome.

about which event will occur and when there is a single outcome for each possible action. The payoff table would appear as follows (data assumed):

Action	Outcome
Buy *A*	$1,000
Buy *B*	1,400
Buy *C*	1,900
Buy *D*	800

Note that there is only one column in the payoff table because there is only one possible event. The decision obviously consists of choosing the action that will produce the best outcome. However, decisions under certainty are not *always* obvious. There are often countless alternative actions, each of which may offer certain outcomes. The problem then is finding the best one. For example, the problem of allocating 20 different job orders to 20 different machines, any one of which could do the job, can involve literally *billions* of different combinations. Each way of assigning these jobs is another possible action. The payoff table would have only one *column,* because the costs of production using the various machines are assumed as known; however, it would have 2½ quintillion *rows.* This demonstrates that decision making under certainty can be more than just a trivial problem.[2]

When an outcome is certain, the prediction is a single point with no dispersion on either side. There is a 100 percent chance of occurrence if the action is taken; in other words, the probability is 1.0. For example, the expected cash inflow on a federal Treasury note might be, say, $4,000 for next year. This might be graphed as follows:

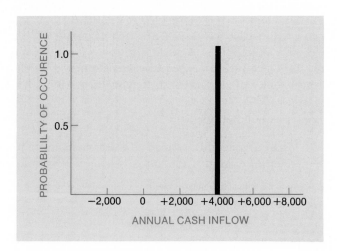

[2] See D. W. Miller and M. K. Starr, *Executive Decisions and Operations Research,* 2nd ed. (Englewood Cliffs, N.J.: Prentice-Hall, Inc., 1969), pp. 104–5. Their distinctions among certainty, risk, and uncertainty are used here.

Of course, the decision maker must frequently contend with uncertainty rather than certainty; he faces a number of possible events, given a particular course of action. The distinction among various degrees of uncertainty centers on the degree of objectivity by which probabilities are assigned. The probabilities may be assigned with a high degree of objectivity.[3] That is, if the decision maker knows the probability of occurrence of each of a number of events, his assignment of probabilities is "objective," because of mathematical proofs or the compilation of historical evidence. For example, the probability of obtaining a head in the toss of a symmetrical coin is 0.5; that of drawing a particular playing card from a well-shuffled deck, $\frac{1}{52}$. In a business, the probability of having a specified percentage of spoiled units may be assigned with great confidence, which is based on production experience with thousands of units.

If the decision maker has no basis in past experience or in mathematical proofs for assigning the probabilities of occurrence of the various events, he must resort to the *subjective* assignment of probabilities. For example, the probability of the success or failure of a new product may have to be assessed without the help of any related experience. This assignment is subjective, because no two individuals assessing a situation will necessarily assign the same probabilities. Executives may be virtually certain about the *range* of possible events or possible outcomes, but they may differ about the likelihoods of various possibilities within that range.

The concept of uncertainty can be illustrated by considering two investment proposals on new projects.[4] The manager has carefully considered the risks. He has subjectively determined the following discrete probability distribution of expected cash flows for the next year (assume that the useful life of the project is one year):

Proposal A		Proposal B	
Probability	*Cash Inflow*	*Probability*	*Cash Inflow*
0.10	$3,000	0.10	$2,000
0.20	3,500	0.25	3,000
0.40	4,000	0.30	4,000
0.20	4,500	0.25	5,000
0.10	5,000	0.10	6,000

[3] This is sometimes called decision making under risk, as distinguished from decision making under certainty. See Miller and Starr, *op cit.*, p. 105. The distinction between risk and uncertainty in the current literature and in practice is so blurred that the terms are used interchangeably here.

[4] James C. Van Horne, *Financial Management and Policy*, 4th ed. (Englewood Cliffs, N.J.: Prentice-Hall., Inc., 1977), Chap. 2.

Expected Value and Standard Deviation

Exhibit 16-1 shows a graphical comparison of the probability distributions. The usual approach to this problem is to compute an expected value for each probability distribution.

The expected value of the cash inflow in Proposal A is

$\bar{A}$ = 0.1(3,000) + 0.2(3,500) + 0.4(4,000) + 0.2(4,500) + 0.1(5,000)
= $4,000

The expected value for the cash inflow in Proposal B is also $4,000:

$\bar{A}$ = 0.1(2,000) + 0.25(3,000) + 0.3(4,000) + 0.25(5,000) + 0.1(6,000)
= $4,000

Incidentally, the expected value of the cash inflow in the federal Treasury note is also $4,000:

$$\bar{A} = 1.0(4,000) = \$4,000$$

Note that mere comparison of these $4,000 expected values is an oversimplification. These three single figures are not strictly comparable; one represents certainty, whereas the other two represent the expected values over a range of possible outcomes. The decision maker must explicitly or implicitly (by "feel" or hunch) recognize that he is comparing figures that are really representations of probability distributions; otherwise the reporting of the expected value alone may mislead him.[5]

To give the decision maker more information, the accountant could provide the complete probability distribution for each proposal. However, often that course means flooding the manager with too much data for his comprehension. Therefore, a middle ground is often used. A summary measure of the underlying dispersion is supplied. The conventional measure of the dispersion of a probability distribution for a single variable is the standard deviation—the square root of the mean of the squared deviations from the expected value:

$$\sigma = \sqrt{\sum_{x=1}^{n}(A_x - \bar{A})^2 P_x}$$

The standard deviation for Proposal A is smaller than that for Proposal B:

[5] For example, how would you feel about choosing between the following two investments? First, invest $10 today with a probability of 1.0 of obtaining $11 in two days. Second, invest $10 today with a probability of 0.5 of obtaining $22 in two days and 0.5 of obtaining $0. The expected value is $11 in both cases.

EXHIBIT 16-1.   Comparison of Probability Distributions

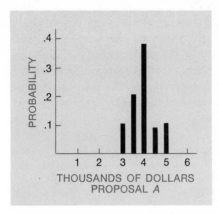

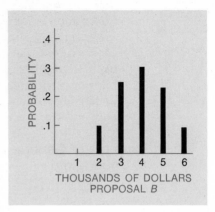

For A: $\sigma = [0.1(3,000 - 4,000)^2 + 0.2(3,500 - 4,000)^2$
$$+ 0.4(4,000 - 4,000)^2 + 0.2(4,500 - 4,000)^2$$
$$+ 0.1(5,000 - 4,000)^2]^{1/2}$$
$$= [300,000]^{1/2} = \$548$$

For B: $\sigma = [0.1(2,000 - 4,000)^2 + 0.25(3,000 - 4,000)^2$
$$+ 0.3(4,000 - 4,000)^2 + 0.25(5,000 - 4,000)^2$$
$$+ 0.1(6,000 - 4,000)^2]^{1/2}$$
$$= [1,300,000]^{1/2} = \$1,140$$

For the Treasury note: $\sigma = \sqrt{1.0(4,000 - 4,000)^2} = 0$

A measure of relative dispersion is the coefficient of variation, which is the standard deviation divided by expected value. The coefficient for Proposal B is $1,140 \div 4,000 = 0.29$; for A it is $548 \div 4,000 = 0.14$; and for the Treasury note it is $0 \div 4,000 = 0$. Therefore, because the coefficient is a relative measure of risk or uncertainty, B is said to have a greater degree of risk than A, which, in turn, has a greater degree of risk than the Treasury note.

The Accountant and Uncertainty

Many accounting practitioners and businessmen shudder at the notion of using subjective probabilities to quantify things that are supposedly "intangible" or "unmeasurable" or "qualitative" or "unquantifiable." However, their position is weak, simply because decisions *do* have to be made. The attempts by statisticians, mathematicians, and modern accountants to measure the unmeasurable is an old and natural chore that scientists have performed for centuries. The use of subjective probabilities merely formalizes the intuitive judgments and hunches that businessmen so often use. It forces the decision maker to expose and evaluate what he may have done unconsciously for years.

Many statisticians and accountants favor presenting the entire probability distribution directly to the decision maker. Others first divide the information into a threefold classification of optimistic, middle, and pessimistic categories. Still others provide summary measures of dispersion, such as the standard deviation or the coefficient of variation. In any event, we are likely to see the accountant's formal recognition of uncertainty and probability distributions in his reporting. In this way, the information will portray underlying phenomena in a more realistic fashion instead of as if there were only a world of certainty.

Example of General Approach to Uncertainty

An example of the general approach to dealing with uncertainty may clarify some of the preceding ideas.

Problem

Once a day, a retailer stocks bunches of fresh-cut flowers, each of which costs 40¢ and sells for $1. The retailer never cuts his price; leftovers are given to a nearby church. He estimates characteristics as follows:

Demand	Probability
0	0.05
1	0.20
2	0.40
3	0.25
4	0.10
5 or more	0.00
	1.00

Required

He wants to know how many units he should stock in order to maximize profits. Try to solve before consulting the solution that follows.

Solution

The profit, per unit sold, is 60¢; the loss, per unit unsold, is 40¢. All the alternatives may be assessed in the following *decision table.*

Events: Demand of	0	1	2	3	4	Expected
Probability of Event:	0.05	0.20	0.40	0.25	0.10	Value
Actions, Units Purchased:						
0	$ 0	$ 0	$ 0	$ 0	$ 0	$ 0
1	− .40	.60	.60	.60	.60	.55
2	− .80	.20	1.20	1.20	1.20	.90
3	− 1.20	− .20	.80	1.80	1.80	.85
4	− 1.60	− .60	.40*	1.40	2.40	.55

*Example of computation: (2 × $1.00) − (4 × $.40) = $.40

495

*Influences of
Quantitative
Techniques on
Management
Accounting*

As shown in an earlier section, the computation of expected value ($\bar{A}$) for each action is affected by the probability weights and the conditional payoff associated with each combination of actions and events:

$$\bar{A} \text{ (Stock 1)} = 0.05(-.40) + 0.20(.60) + 0.40(.60) + 0.25(.60) + 0.10(.60)$$
$$= \$.55$$

$$\bar{A} \text{ (Stock 2)} = 0.05(-.80) + 0.20(.20) + 0.40(1.20) + 0.25(1.20) + 0.10(1.20)$$
$$= \$.90$$

and so on.

To maximize expected payoff, the retailer should stock two units ($\bar{A} = \$.90$).

Obtaining Additional Information

Sometimes the executive is hesitant about making a decision. He would like to obtain more information before making a final choice. Some additional information is nearly always obtainable—at a price. Schlaifer[6] describes a technique for computing the maximum amount that should be paid for such additional information. The general idea is to compute the expected value under ideal circumstances—that is, circumstances that would permit the retailer to predict, with absolute certainty, the number of units to be sold on any given day. A decision table *with perfect information* would appear as follows:

Event: Demand of	0	1	2	3	4	Expected
Probability of Event:	0.05	0.20	0.40	0.25	0.10	Value
Actions, Units Purchased:						
0	$0					$ 0
1		$.60				.12
2			$1.20			.48
3				$1.80		.45
4					$2.40	.24
Total expected value						$1.29

The total expected value with perfect information is computed as follows:

$$\bar{A} \text{ (Perfect Information)} = 0.05(0) + 0.20(.60) + 0.40(1.20) + 0.25(1.80)$$
$$+ 0.10(2.40) = \$1.29$$

In this table, it is assumed that the retailer will never err in his forecasts and that demand will fluctuate from zero to four exactly as indicated by the

---

[6] Robert Schlaifer, *Analysis of Decisions Under Uncertainty* (New York: McGraw-Hill Book Company, 1969), pp. 585–88.

probabilities. The maximum day-in, day-out profit is $1.29. Consequently, the most he should be willing to pay for perfect advance information would be the difference between the expected value with perfect information and the expected value with existing information—$1.29 minus the $.90 expected value computed in the previous example, or 39¢. Schlaifer calls the latter the expected value of perfect information, the top price the retailer should pay for additional knowledge.

In the real world, of course, the retailer would not pay 39¢, because no amount of additional information is likely to provide perfect knowledge. But businesses often obtain additional knowledge through sampling, and sampling costs money. The executive needs a method, such as the one described at length by Schlaifer, (a) of assessing the probable benefits, in relation to its cost, of additional information from sampling; and (b) of determining the best sample size. In the present example, no sampling technique would be attractive if its cost allocated to each day's operations equaled or exceeded the 39¢ ceiling price.

LINEAR-PROGRAMMING MODELS

Characteristics

Linear programming is a potent mathematical approach to a group of business problems that contain many interacting variables and that basically involve the utilization of limited resources in such a way as to increase profit or decrease cost. There are nearly always limiting factors or scarce resources that are restrictions, restraints, or constraints on available alternatives. Linear programming has been applied to a vast number of business decisions, such as machine scheduling, product mix, raw-material mix, scheduling flight crews, production routing, shipping schedules, transportation routes, blending gasoline, blending sausage ingredients, and designing transformers. In general, linear programming is the best available technique for combining materials, labor, and facilities to best advantage, when all the relationships are approximately linear and many combinations are possible.

Note that linear programming is a decision model under conditions of *certainty*, where constraints affect the allocation of resources among competing uses. That is, the model analyzes a total list of actions whose outcomes are known with certainty and chooses the combination of actions that will maximize profit or minimize cost.

The Techniques, the Accountant, and the Manager

All of us are familiar with linear equations (e.g., $X + 3 = 9$). We also know that simultaneous linear equations with two or three unknowns become

497

*Influences of
Quantitative
Techniques on
Management
Accounting*

progressively more difficult to solve with pencil and paper. Linear programming essentially involves: (1) constructing a set of simultaneous linear equations, which represent the model of the problem and which include many variables; and (2) solving the equations with the help of the digital computer.

The formulation of the equations—that is, the building of the model—is far more challenging than the mechanics of the solution. The model aims at being a valid and accurate portrayal of the problem. Computer programmers can then take the equations and process the solution.

As a minimum, accountants and executives should be able to recognize the types of problems in their organizations that are most susceptible to analysis by linear programming. They should be able to help in the construction of the model—i.e., in specifying the objectives, the constraints, and the variables. Ideally, they should understand the mathematics and should be able to talk comfortably with the operations researchers who are attempting to express their problem mathematically. However, the position taken here is that the accountant and the manager should concentrate on formulating the model and *analyzing* the solution and not worry too much about the technical intricacies of *obtaining* the solution. The latter may be delegated to the mathematicians; the feasibility and advisability of delegating the former is highly doubtful.

Illustration of Product Mix

Consider the following illustration: Machine 1 is available for 24 hours, and Machine 2 is available for 20 hours, for the processing of two products. Product X has a contribution margin of $2 per unit; Product Y, $1 per unit. These products must be sold in such combination that the quantity of X must be equal to or less than the quantity of Y. X requires 6 hours of time on Machine 1 and 10 hours of time on Machine 2. Product Y requires 4 hours of time on Machine 1 only. What daily production combination will produce the maximum profit?

The linear-programming approach may be divided into four steps, although variations and shortcuts are available in unique situations:

1. Formulate the objectives. The objective is usually to maximize profit or minimize cost.
2. Determine the basic relationships, particularly the constraints.
3. Determine the feasible alternatives.
4. Compute the optimum solution.

Techniques may differ. In the uncomplicated situation in our example, the graphic approach is easiest to understand. In practice, the *simplex method* is used—a step-by-step process that is extremely efficient. Basically, the simplex method begins with one feasible solution and tests it algebraically, by substitution, to see if it can be improved. These substitutions continue until further improvement is impossible, given the constraints. The optimum solution is therefore achieved.

These four steps may be applied to the example.

Step 1. **Formulate the objectives.** In our case, find the product combination that results in the maximum total contribution margin. Maximize:

$$\text{Total contribution margin} = \$2X + \$1Y \tag{1}$$

This is called the objective function. X represents the number of X product units and Y represents the number of Y units.

Step 2. **Determine the basic relationships.** The relationships may be depicted by the following inequalities:

For Machine 1:	$6X + 4Y \leq 24$
For Machine 2:	$10X \quad\quad \leq 20$
Sales of X and Y:	$X - Y \leq 0$
Because negative production is impossible:	$X \quad\quad \geq 0 \text{ and } Y \geq 0$

The three solid lines in Exhibit 16-2 will help you to visualize the machine constraints and the product-mix constraint. (To plot a constraint line, assume for Machine 1 that $X = 0$; then $Y = 6$. If $Y = 0$, then $X = 4$. Connect points $(0, 6)$ and $(4, 0)$ with a straight line.)

Step 3. **Determine the feasible alternatives.** Alternatives are feasible if they are technically possible. We do not want to bother with computations for impossible solutions. The shaded area in Exhibit 16-2 shows the boundaries of the feasible product combinations—that is, combinations of X and Y that satisfy all constraining factors.

Step 4. **Compute the optimum solution.** Steps 2 and 3 focused on physical relationships alone. We now return to the economic relationships expressed as the objective in Step 1. We test various feasible product combinations to see which one results in a maximum total contribution margin. It so happens that the best solution must lie on one of the corners of the Area of Feasible Product Combinations in Exhibit 16-2. The corners represent the limits of at least two constraints, so those constraints (resources) are being fully utilized. Intuitively, full utilization suggests optimality. The total contribution margin is calculated for each corner. The steps, which are similar to the simplex method, which uses digital computers, are:

a. Start with one possible combination.
b. Compute the profit.
c. Move to another possible combination to see if it will improve the result in step b. Keep moving from corner to corner until no further improvement is possible. (The simplex method is more efficient because it does not necessitate testing all possible combinations before finding the best solution.)

These steps are summarized below. They show that the optimum combination is two units of X and three units of Y:

EXHIBIT 16-2. Linear Programming: Graphic Solution

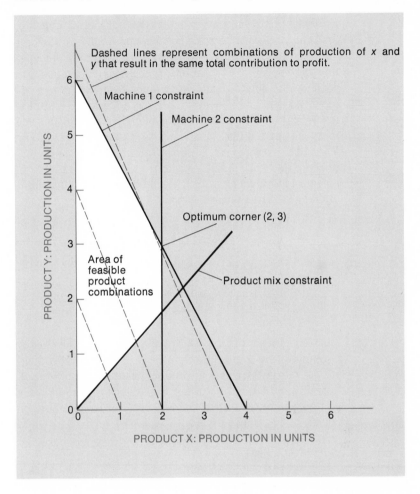

Trial	Corner	Combination		$2X + $1Y =$ Total Contribution Margin
		Product X	Product Y	
1	0,0	0	0	$2(0) + $1(0) = $0
2	0,6	0	6	2(0) + 1(6) = 6
3	2,3	2	3	2(2) + 1(3) = 7
4	2,2	2	2	2(2) + 1(2) = 6

Why must the best solution lie on a corner? Consider all possible combinations that will produce a total contribution margin of $1 ($2X + 1Y = \$1$). This is a straight line through $(0, 2)$ and $(1, 0)$. Other total contribution margins are represented by the dashed lines parallel to this one. Their associated total contribution margins increase the further the lines get

499

from the origin. The optimum line is the one furthest from the origin that has a feasible point on it; intuitively, we know that this happens at a corner (2, 3). Furthermore, if you put a ruler on the graph and move it parallel with the $1 line, the optimum corner becomes apparent.

As these trials show, the central problem of linear programming is to find the specific combination of variables that satisfies all constraints and achieves the objective sought. Moving from corner to corner (which is really moving from one possible solution to another) implies that the scarce resource, productive capacity, is being transferred between products. Each four-hour period that Machine 1 is productively used to produce one unit of Y may be sacrificed (i.e., given or traded) for one six-hour period required to produce one unit of X. Consider the exchange of twelve hours of time. This means that three units of Y will be traded for two units of X. Will this exchange add to profits? Yes:

Total contribution margin at corner (0, 6)		$6
Additional contribution margin from Product X:		
2 units, @ $2	$4	
Lost contribution margin, Product Y:		
3 units, @ $1	3	
Net additional contribution margin		1
Total contribution margin at corner (2, 3)		$7

It is not simply a matter of comparing margins per unit of *product* and jumping to the conclusion that the production of Product X, which has the greater margin per unit of product, should be maximized.[7] These substitutions are a matter of trading a given contribution margin per unit of a limiting factor (i.e., a critical resource) for some other contribution margin per unit of a limiting factor.

INVENTORY PLANNING AND CONTROL MODELS

Characteristics

Comprehensive inventory-planning and control systems have been successfully installed in many companies. The major objective of inventory management is to discover and maintain the optimum level of investment in the inventory. Inventories may be too high or too low. If too high, there are unnecessary carrying costs and risks of obsolescence. If too low, production may be disrupted or sales permanently lost. The optimum inventory level is that which minimizes the total costs associated with inventory.

[7] This point is also discussed in Chapter 4 in the section, "Contribution to Profit Per Unit of Limiting Factor."

EXHIBIT 16-3

Some Relevant Costs of Inventories

COSTS OF ORDERING
1. Preparing purchase or production orders.
2. Receiving (unloading, unpacking, inspecting).
3. Processing all related documents.
4. Extra purchasing or transportation costs for frequent orders.
5. Extra costs of numerous small production runs, overtime, set-ups, and training.

plus

COSTS OF CARRYING
1. Desired rate of return on investment.*
2. Risk of obsolescence and deterioration.
3. Storage-space costs.
4. Personal property taxes.
5. Insurance.

* Cost that ordinarily does not explicitly appear on formal accounting records.

The costs of buying or manufacturing the inventory (that is, the acquisition costs) would usually be irrelevant to the inventory-control decisions considered here, because we assume that the total annual quantity required would be the same for the various alternatives. Exhibit 16-3 shows the main relevant costs that must be considered, the costs of ordering plus the costs of carrying.

The two significant cost items tend to offset one another. The total relevant costs of carrying, including interest, rise as orders decrease in frequency and grow in size, but the total costs of ordering, delivery, etc., decrease; and vice versa.

How Much to Order?

The two main questions in inventory control are how much to order at a time and when to order. A key factor in inventory policy is computing the optimum size of either a normal purchase order for raw materials or a shop order for a production run. This optimum size is called the *economic order quantity*, the size that will result in minimum total annual costs of the item in question. Consider this example:

Problem

A refrigerator manufacturer buys certain steel shelving in sets from outside suppliers at $4 per set. Total annual needs are 5,000 sets at a rate of twenty sets per working day. The following cost data are available:

Desired annual return on inventory investment,	
10% × $4	$.40
Rent, insurance, taxes, per unit per year	.10
Carrying costs per unit per year	$ .50
Costs per purchase order:	
Clerical costs, stationery, postage, telephone, etc.	$10.00

What is the economic order quantity?

Solution

Exhibit 16-4 shows a tabulation of total relevant costs under various alternatives. The column with the least cost will indicate the economic order quantity.

Exhibit 16-4 shows minimum costs at two levels, 400 and 500 units. The next step would be to see if costs are lower somewhere between 400 and 500 units—say, at 450 units:

Average inventory, 225 × $.50	= $113	Carrying costs
Number of orders (5,000/450), 11.1 × $10 =	111	Purchase-order costs
	$224	Total relevant costs

EXHIBIT 16-4

Annualized Relevant Costs of Various Standard Orders
(250 working days)

SYMBOLS										
E	Order size	50	100	200	400	500	600	800	1,000	5,000
E/2	Average inventory in units*	25	50	100	200	250	300	400	500	2,500
A/E	Number of purchase orders†	100	50	25	12.5	10	8.3	6.3	5	1
S(E/2)	Annual carrying cost @ $.50	$ 13	$ 25	$ 50	$100	$125	$150	$200	$ 250	$1,250
P(A/E)	Annual purchase-order cost @ $10	1,000	500	250	125	100	83	63	50	10
C	Total annual relevant costs	$1,013	$525	$300	$225	$225	$233	$263	$ 300	$1,260

Least cost

E = Order size
A = Annual quantity used in units
S = Annual cost of carrying one unit in stock one year
P = Cost of placing a purchase order
C = Total annual relevant costs

* Assume that stock is zero when each order arrives. (Even if a certain minimum inventory were assumed, it has no bearing on the choice here as long as the minimum is the same for each alternative.) Therefore, the average inventory relevant to the problem will be one-half the order quantity. For example, if 600 units are purchased, the inventory on arrival will contain 600. It will gradually diminish until no units are on hand. The average inventory would be 300; the carrying cost, $.50 × 300 or $150.
  † Number to meet the total annual need for 5,000 sets.

EXHIBIT 16-5. Graphic Solution of Economic Lot Size

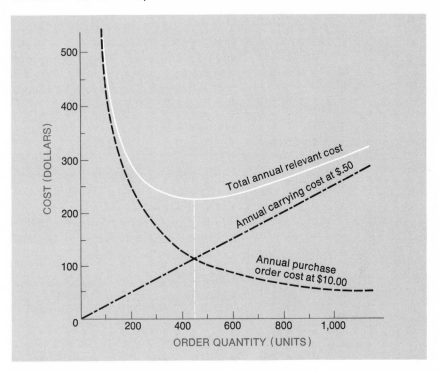

The dollar differences here are extremely small, but the approach is important. The same approach may be shown in graphic form. See Exhibit 16-5. Note that in this case, total cost is at a minimum where total purchase-order cost and total carrying cost are equal.

Order-Size Formula

The graphic approach has been expressed as a formula (derived via calculus):

$$E = \sqrt{\frac{2AP}{S}}$$

where E = order size; A = annual quantity used in units; P = cost of placing an order; and S = annual cost of carrying one unit in stock for one year.

Substituting:

$$E = \sqrt{\frac{2(5,000)(\$10)}{\$.50}} = \sqrt{\frac{\$100,000}{\$.50}} = \sqrt{200,000}$$

$E = 448$, the economic order quantity (often referred to as EOQ)

As we may expect, the order size gets larger as A or P gets bigger or as S gets smaller.

Note in Exhibit 16-5 that the approach to economic lot-size centers on locating a minimum-cost *range* rather than a minimum-cost *point. The total-cost curve tends to flatten between 400 and 800 units.* In practice, there is a definite tendency to (a) find the range, and (b) select a lot size at the lower end of the range. In our example, there would be a tendency to select a lot size of 400 or slightly more.

When to Order?

Although we have seen how to compute economic order quantity, we have not yet considered another key decision: When to order? This question is easy to answer only if we know the *lead time,* the time interval between placing an order and receiving delivery, know the EOQ, and are *certain* of demand during lead time. The graph in Exhibit 16-6 will clarify the relationships among the following facts:

Economic order quantity	448 sets of steel shelving
Lead time	2 weeks
Average usage	100 sets per week

Exhibit 16-6, Part A, shows that the *reorder point*—the quantity level that automatically triggers a new order—is dependent on expected usage during lead time; that is, if shelving is being used at a rate of 100 sets per week and the lead time is two weeks, a new order will be placed when the inventory level reaches 200 sets.

Minimum Inventory: Safety Allowance

Our previous example assumed that 100 sets would be used per week—a demand pattern that was known with certainty. Businesses are seldom blessed with such accurate forecasting; instead, demand may fluctuate from day to day, from week to week, or from month to month. Thus, the company will run out of stock if there are sudden spurts in usage beyond 100 per week, delays in processing orders, or delivery delays. Obviously, then, nearly all companies must provide for some safety stock—some minimum or buffer inventory as a cushion against reasonable expected maximum usage. Part B of Exhibit 16-6 is based on the same facts as Part A, except that reasonable expected maximum usage is 140 sets per week. The safety stock might be, say, 80 sets (excess usage of 40 sets per week multiplied by two weeks). The reorder point is commonly computed as safety stock plus the average usage during the lead time.

The foregoing discussion of inventory control revolved around the so-called two-bin or constant-order-quantity system: When inventory levels

EXHIBIT 16-6. Demand in Relation to Inventory Levels

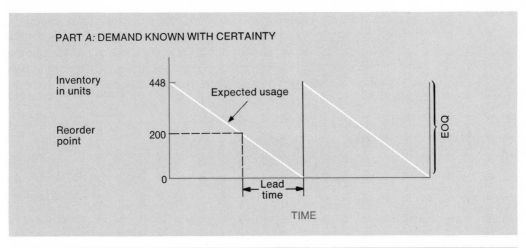

PART *A:* DEMAND KNOWN WITH CERTAINTY

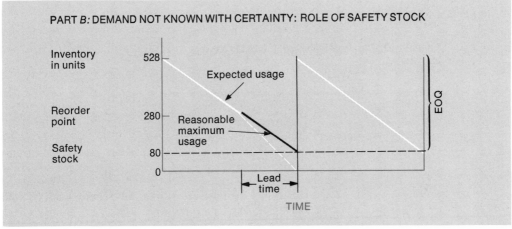

PART *B:* DEMAND NOT KNOWN WITH CERTAINTY: ROLE OF SAFETY STOCK

recede to *X*, then order *Y*. Another widely used model is the constant-order-cycle system. For example, every month, review the inventory level on hand and order enough to bring the quantity on hand and on order up to some predetermined level of units. The reorder date is fixed, and the quantity ordered depends on the usage since the previous order and the outlook during the lead time. Demand forecasts and seasonal patterns also should be considered in specifying the size of orders during the year.

SUMMARY

Mathematical decision models are used increasingly, because they replace or supplement hunches with explicit assumptions and criteria. As these decision

505

models become more widely utilized, accounting reports for decision making will tend to give more formal, explicit recognition of uncertainty. For example, the reporting of some measure of probability distributions is more likely.

Accountants often provide inputs to assorted decision models, such as linear-programming models and inventory-control models. Therefore, both accountants and managers need to understand the uses and limitations of the models.

SUMMARY PROBLEM FOR YOUR REVIEW

Problem

Review this chapter's examples on statistical probability theory, linear programming, and inventory control by trying to solve them before studying their solutions.

ASSIGNMENT MATERIAL

Fundamental Assignment Material

16-1. Terminology. Define: *model; conditional value; expected value; payoff table; linear programming; economic standard order quantity; safety stock;* and *lead time.*

16-2. Influence of uncertainty in forecasts. The figures used in many examples and problems in the previous chapters were subject to uncertainty. For simplicity, the expected future amounts of sales, direct material, direct labor, and other operating costs were presented as if they were errorless predictions. For instance, this textbook and others tend to state that a facilities rearrangement "should result in cash operating savings of $2,000 per year."

The industrial engineers who studied the situation had really prepared three estimates:

Event	Percentage Chance of Occurrence	Savings
Pessimistic	.1	$1,200
Most likely	.6	1,800
Optimistic	.3	2,500

Required | Using an expected-value table, show how the estimate of $2,000 was probably computed.

16-3. Inventory levels and sales forecasting. Each day, an owner of a sidewalk stand stocks bunches of fresh flowers, which cost 30¢ and sell for 50¢ each. Leftovers are given to a nearby hospital. Demand characteristics are:

507

*Influences of
Quantitative
Techniques on
Management
Accounting*

Demand	Probability
Less than 20	0.00
20	0.10
21	0.40
22	0.30
23	0.20
24 or more	0.00

Required

How many units should be stocked to maximize expected net income? Show your computations.

16-4. Costs and benefits of perfect information. If the owner of the stand in Assignment 16-3 were clairvoyant, so that he could perfectly forecast the demand each day and stock the exact number of flowers needed, what would be his expected profit per day? What is the maximum price that he should be willing to pay for perfect information?

16-5. Fundamental approach of linear programming. A company has two departments, machining and finishing. The company's two products require processing in each of two departments. Data follow:

Product	Contribution Margin per Unit	Daily Capacity in Units Department 1: Machining	Daily Capacity in Units Department 2: Finishing
A	$2.00	200	120
B	2.50	100	200

Severe shortages of material for Product B will limit its production to a maximum of 90 per day.

Required

How many units of each product should be produced to obtain the maximum net income? Show the basic relationships as inequalities. Solve by using graphical analysis.

Additional Assignment Material

16-6. "The management accountant must be technically competent in computer technology and modern mathematics." Do you agree? Explain.

16-7. What are the distinguishing features of operations research?

16-8. What is a payoff table?

16-9. "OR is mainly a planning tool rather than a controlling tool." Why?

16-10. "Models must conform to reality in two major respects." Explain.

16-11. "Simulation is game playing in the world of make-believe. It has no practical value." Do you agree? Explain.

16-12. "I'm not certain what uncertainty is." Explain uncertainty briefly.

16-13. What is the difference between a conditional value and an expected value?

16-14. Consider the following probability distribution:

Daily Sales Event in Units	Probability
1,000	0.1
1,500	0.5
2,000	0.2
2,500	0.1
3,000	0.1
	1.0

A student commented: "If a manager has perfect information, he will always sell 3,000 units." Do you agree? Explain.

16-15. Which of the following are linear equations?

$$x + y + 4z + 6a = 8c + 4m$$
$$x^2 = y$$
$$x^2 - y = 4$$
$$4c = 27$$

16-16. What is the minimum competence in linear programming that managers should have?

16-17. What is an infeasible alternative?

16-18. What are the four basic steps in linear programming?

16-19. "The major objective of inventory management is to minimize cash outlays for inventories." Do you agree? Explain.

16-20. What are the principal costs of having too much inventory? Too little inventory?

16-21. "The safety stock is the average amount of inventory used during lead time." Do you agree? Explain.

16-22. "If demand and lead time were known with certainty, no safety stock would be needed." Do you agree? Explain.

16-23. Production scheduling and linear programming. A factory can produce either Product A or Product B. Machine 1 can produce 15 units of B or 20 units of

509

*Influences of
Quantitative
Techniques on
Management
Accounting*

A per hour. Machine 2 can produce 20 units of B or 12 units of A per hour. Machine 1 has a maximum capacity of 10,000 hours and Machine 2 a maximum capacity of 8,000 hours.

Product A has a unit contribution margin of 20¢; B, 16¢. There is an unlimited demand for either product; however, both products must be produced together through each machine in a combination such that the quantity of B is at least 20 percent of the quantity of A.

Which combination of products should be produced? Solve by graphic analysis. Express all relationships as inequalities.

16-24. **Linear programming.** (CPA.) The Golden Hawk Manufacturing Company wants to maximize the profits on products A, B, and C. The contribution margin for each product follows:

Product	Contribution Margin
A	$2
B	$5
C	$4

The production requirements and departmental capacities, by departments, are as follows:

Department	Production Requirements by Product (Hours)		
	A	B	C
Assembling	2	3	2
Painting	1	2	2
Finishing	2	3	1

Department	Departmental Capacity (Total hours)
Assembling	30,000
Painting	38,000
Finishing	28,000

1. What is the profit-maximization formula for the Golden Hawk Company?
   a. $\$2A + \$5B + \$4C = X$ (where X = profit).
   b. $5A + 8B + 5C \leqslant 96,000$.
   c. $\$2A + \$5B + \$4C \leqslant X$ (where X = profit).
   d. $\$2A + \$5B + \$4C = 96,000$.

2. What is the constraint for the Painting Department of the Golden Hawk Company?
   a. $1A + 2B + 2C \geqslant 38,000$.
   b. $\$2A + \$5B + \$4C \geqslant 38,000$.
   c. $1A + 2B + 2C \leqslant 38,000$.
   d. $2A + 3B + 2C \leqslant 30,000$.

16-25. Linear programming and minimum cost. The local agricultural center has advised George Junker to spread at least 4,800 pounds of a special nitrogen fertilizer ingredient and at least 5,000 pounds of a special phosphate fertilizer ingredient in order to increase his crops. Neither ingredient is available in pure form.

A dealer has offered 100-pound bags of VIM @ $1 each. VIM contains the equivalent of 20 pounds of nitrogen and 80 pounds of phosphate. VOOM is available in 100-pound bags @ $3 each; it contains the equivalent of 75 pounds of nitrogen and 25 pounds of phosphate.

Required

Express the relationships as inequalities. How many bags of VIM and VOOM should Junker buy in order to obtain the required fertilizer at minimum cost? Solve graphically.

16-26. Change in LP constraints. (CMA, adapted.) The Frey Company manufactures and sells two products—a toddler bike and a toy high chair. Linear programming is employed to determine the best production and sales mix of bikes and chairs. This approach also allows Frey to speculate on economic changes. For example, management is often interested in knowing how variations in selling prices, resource costs, resource availabilities, and marketing strategies would affect the company's performance.

The demand for bikes and chairs is relatively constant throughout the year. The following economic data pertain to the two products:

	Bike (B)	Chair (C)
Selling price for unit	$12	$10
Variable cost per unit	8	7
Contribution margin per unit	$ 4	$ 3
Raw materials required:		
Wood	1 board foot	2 board feet
Plastic	2 pounds	1 pound
Direct labor required	2 hours	2 hours

Estimates of the resource quantities available in a nonvacation month during the year are:

Wood	10,000 board feet
Plastic	10,000 pounds
Direct labor	12,000 hours

The algebraic formulation of the linear-programming model that Frey Company has developed for the nonvacation months is as follows:

Objective function: $\text{Max } Z = 4B + 3C$

Constraints:

$$B + 2C \leq 10,000 \text{ board feet}$$
$$2B + C \leq 10,000 \text{ pounds}$$
$$2B + 2C \leq 12,000 \text{ direct-labor hours}$$
$$B, C \geq 0$$

The results from the linear-programming model indicate that Frey Company can maximize its contribution margin (and thus profits) for a nonvacation month by producing and selling 4,000 toddler bikes and 2,000 toy high chairs. This sales mix will yield a total contribution margin of $22,000 in a month.

Required

1. Prepare a graph of the constraints, placing the bikes on the vertical axis.

2. During the months of June, July, and August the total direct-labor hours available are reduced from 12,000 to 10,000 hours per month due to vacations.

   a. What would be the best product mix and maximum total contribution margin when only 10,000 direct-labor hours are available during a month?

   b. The "shadow price" of a resource is defined as the marginal contribution of a resource or the rate at which profit would increase (decrease) if the amount of resource were increased (decreased). Based upon your solution for Requirement 2a, what is the shadow price on direct-labor hours in the original model for a nonvacation month?

3. Competition in the toy market is very strong. Consequently, the prices of the two products tend to fluctuate. Can analysis of data from the linear-programming model provide information to management that will indicate when price changes made to meet market conditions will alter the optimum product mix? Explain your answer.

16-27. Change in LP constraints. (CMA, adapted.) Girth, Inc., makes two kinds of men's suede leather belts. Belt A is a high-quality belt, while Belt B is of somewhat lower quality. The company earns $7 for each unit of Belt A that is sold, and $2 for each unit sold of Belt B. Each unit (belt) of type A requires twice as much manufacturing time as a unit of type B. Further, if only Belt B is made, Girth has the capacity to manufacture 1,000 units per day. A long-term contract makes available to Girth enough suede leather to make 800 belts per day (A and B combined). Belt A requires a fancy buckle, of which only 400 per day are available. Belt B requires a plain buckle, of which 700 per day are available. The demand for the suede leather belts (A or B) is such that Girth can sell all that it produces.

Required

1. Prepare a graph of the constraint functions, placing Belt B on the vertical axis.

2. Using the graph, determine how many units of Belt A and Belt B should be produced to maximize daily profits.

3. Assume the same facts as above except that the sole supplier of buckles for Belt A informs Girth, Inc., that it will be unable to supply more than 100 fancy buckles per day. How many units of each of the two belts should be produced each day to maximize profits?

4. Assume the same facts as in Requirement 2 except that Texas Buckles, Inc., could supply Girth, Inc., with the additional fancy buckles it needs. The price would be $3.50 more than Girth is paying for such buckles. How many, if any, fancy buckles should Girth buy from Texas Buckles? Explain how you determined your answer.

16-28. Probabilities: automatic or semiautomatic equipment. The Click Company is going to produce a new product. Two types of production equipment are being considered. The more costly equipment will result in lower labor and related variable costs:

Equipment	Total Original Cost	Salvage Value	Variable Costs, per Unit of Product
Semiautomatic	$40,000	—	$4
Automatic	95,000	—	3

Marketing executives believe that this unique product will be salable only over the next year. The unit selling price is $5. Their best estimate of potential sales follows:

Total Units	Probability
30,000	0.2
50,000	0.4
60,000	0.2
70,000	0.2

Required | Prepare an analysis to indicate the best course of action.

16-29. Money on the table. The search for oil is a chancy and costly undertaking. For example, in December, 1972, the United States government sold a parcel of Louisiana offshore oil leases covering 536,000 acres for $1.6 billion. The previous record was $900 million in the Alaska North Slope in 1969.

The leases are sold on blocks of acreage. Sealed bids are received on various blocks from joint ventures of several oil companies or from a single company. A news item concerning the bidding stated:

The left-on-the-table aggregate this time came to a stunning $660 million or 40% of the winning total. By far, the most open-handed bidder was the group headed by Shell which grabbed fourteen tracts with bids totaling $230 million or more than twice the $93 million sum of the runner-up bids.

Required | Describe what you think is meant by money-on-the-table. Why does it occur? Who collects it?

16-30. Probability assessment and new product. A new manager, Emil Frang, has just been hired by the Nattelle Company. He is considering the market potential for a new toy, Marvo, which, like many toys, may have great fad appeal.

Frang is experienced in the fad market and is well qualified to assess Marvo's chances for success. He is certain that sales will not be less than 25,000 units. Plant capacity limits total sales to a maximum of 80,000 units during Marvo's brief life. Frang thinks that there are two chances in five for a sales volume of 50,000 units. The probability that sales will exceed 50,000 units is four times the probability that they will be less than 50,000.

513

*Influences of
Quantitative
Techniques on
Management
Accounting*

If sales are less than 50,000, he feels quite certain that they will be 25,000 units. If sales exceed 50,000, unit volumes of 60,000 and 80,000 are equally likely. A 70,000-unit volume is four times as likely as either.

Variable production costs are $3 per unit, selling price is $5, and the special manufacturing equipment (which has no salvage value or alternate use) costs $125,000. Assume, for simplicity, that the above-mentioned are the only possible sales volumes.

Required

Should Marvo be produced? Show detailed computations to support your answer.

16-31. Net present values, probabilities, and capital budgeting. At the recent stockholders meeting of a large utility company, a stockholder raised the question of the profitability of the satellite communications project undertaken by the company. The project was undertaken two years ago. The president stated that $10 million had been invested in the project in each of the previous years and that an equal amount must be invested in each of the next three years. There would be no income from the project until the total investment was completed. At that time the probability of receiving $4 million cash inflow from operations would be 0.8; the probability of receiving $8 million in the second year after completion would be 0.7; the probability of receiving $15 million in the third year after completion would be 0.6; the probability of receiving $30 million for the following seven years would be 0.5.

This company expects a minimum rate of return of 10 percent on investments.

Required

As a stockholder, would you have approved of this project when it was first undertaken? Support your answer with figures, using the net-present-value approach.

16-32. Long-distance phone calls. A memorandum from the president of Stanford University contained the following:

As of October 20, 1972, the placement of person-to-person telephone calls from the University extensions will cease; rather, you are asked to place station-to-station calls instead. . . . We anticipate that this change in policy will save over $30,000 per year in toll charges.

You will be interested to know that for the same cost approximately two station-to-station calls can be made for each person-to-person call. Further, a sampling of Stanford users indicates that there is the probability of 66⅔% that a station-to-station call will be successfully completed the first time.

Required

Using the data given, compute the annual Stanford long-distance phone bill for person-to-person calls before the new policy took effect. In all cases, assume that two station-to-station calls will obtain the desired person.

16-33. Evaluation of degree of risk: standard deviation and coefficient of variation. Suppose that you are the manager of a bottling company. You are trying to choose between two types of equipment, F and G. The proposals had the following discrete probability distributions of cash flows in each of the next four years:

Proposal F			Proposal G	
Probability	*Net Cash Inflow*		*Probability*	*Net Cash Inflow*
0.10	$3,000		0.10	$1,000
0.25	4,000		0.25	2,000
0.30	5,000		0.30	3,000
0.25	6,000		0.25	4,000
0.10	7,000		0.10	5,000

Required

1. For each proposal, compute (a) the expected value of the cash inflows in each of the next three years, (b) the standard deviation, and (c) the coefficient of variation.

2. Which proposal has the greater degree of risk? Why?

16-34. Expected value, standard deviation, and risk. Suppose that the Van Horne Company is planning to invest in a common stock for one year. An investigation of the expected dividends and expected market price has been conducted. The probability distribution of expected returns for the year, as a percent, is:

Probability of Occurrence	Possible Return
0.05	.284
0.10	.224
0.20	.160
0.30	.100
0.20	.040
0.10	−.024
0.05	−.084

Required

1. Compute the expected value of possible returns, the standard deviation of the probability distribution, and the coefficient of variation.

2. Van Horne could also earn 6 percent for certain on federal bonds. What are the standard deviation and the coefficient of variation of such an investment?

3. Relate the computations in Requirement 1 with those in Requirement 2. That is, what role does the coefficient of variation play in determining the relative attractiveness of various investments?

16-35. Break-even in executive education. (SMA.) Management Development Ltd. is deciding which one of two new executive courses to offer. The costs associated with course development would be $5,000 for either course. Administrative facilities are available within the firm for one additional course without additional costs. The course would have a one-year life. Enrollment in either course would be $100 and the variable costs associated with offering the course would be $60 per executive.

To decide which course to offer, the management of M.D.L. has estimated the demand for the courses and utilized subjective probabilities to estimate the likelihood of varying levels of course enrollment. The information derived from this process is as follows:

515

*Influences of
Quantitative
Techniques on
Management
Accounting*

Course Enrollments	Probability Course A	Probability Course B
50	0.1	0.1
100	0.1	0.2
200	0.2	0.4
300	0.4	0.2
400	0.2	0.1
	1.0	1.0

Required

1. Calculate the number of course enrollments required to break even for each course.

2. Which course should M.D.L. select? Explain why and show all computations.

3. Suppose instead that M.D.L. were absolutely certain that the enrollment in Course A would be 205. Which course should be offered? Discuss the key factor that would lead to a decision in this situation.

16-36. Cost-volume-profit analysis under uncertainty. (CMA, adapted.) Aplet Inc. purchased Avcont Company in 19x0 during Aplet's expansion period. The subsidiary has been quite profitable until recently. Beginning in 19x3 the market share dropped; costs increased, owing primarily to increased prices of inputs; and the profits turned into losses. The income statements for 19x3 and 19x4 are presented along with an estimate of the 19x5 income made in October 19x5.

AVCONT COMPANY
Income Statement for Years Ending December 31
(000 omitted)

	19x3	19x4	19x5 (Est.)
Industry unit sales	1,300	1,200	1,200
Avcont unit sales	120	110	110
Sales	$1,200	$1,100	$1,100
Less: Variable expenses	660	649	680
Contribution Margin	540	451	420
Fixed expenses	460	495	520
Net income (loss)	$ 80	$ (44)	$ (100)

The subsidiary management is optimistic about the volume of sales for 19x6. Recent sales promotion efforts seem to be beneficial, and Avcont expects to increase unit sales 10 percent during 19x6 even though industry volume is expected to decline to 1,100,000 units. However, Avcont management also knows its variable cost rates will increase 10 percent in 19x6 over 19x5 levels.

Avcont management wants to take action to reverse the unsatisfactory results the company has been experiencing. One proposal under consideration is to increase the price of Avcont's product. Some members of management believe that the market might accept an 8 percent increase in prices at this time without affecting the expected 10 percent increase in unit sales volume because no price increases have taken place in this market since 19x2. Several other companies are also considering price increases for 19x6.

Other members of Aplet management question the feasibility of a price increase because Avcont is operating in an industry that is experiencing declining sales. In addition, the marketing department believes a price increase will have an impact on the expected increase in unit sales volume during 19x6. Its estimate of the possible outcomes on unit sales and the related probabilities for the 8 percent price increase are as follows:

Increase (Decrease) in 19x6 Unit Sales Volume	Probability
10%	0.4
5	0.3
0	0.2
(5)	0.1
	1.0

Required

1. Calculate Avcont Co.'s profits for 19x6 if the 8 percent price increase takes place and unit sales volume increases 10 percent.

2. What are Avcont Co.'s expected profits for 19x6 if the probabilistic sales data assembled by the marketing department are used?

3. A member of the analysis team made the following observation to support his recommendation for a price increase: "Inflationary pressures make it reasonable for a company to forecast increased costs, increased product prices, and increased or at least constant volume because consumers can be expected to accept the product price increases." Comment on the validity of this statement for planning purposes.

16-37. Cost and value of information. An oil-well driller, Mr. George, is thinking of investing $50,000 in an oil-well lease. He estimates the probability of finding a producing well as 0.4. Such a discovery would result in a net gain of $100,000 ($150,000 revenue—$50,000 cost). There is a 0.6 probability of not getting any oil, resulting in the complete loss of the $50,000.

Required

1. What is the net expected value of investing?

2. Mr. George desires more information because of the vast uncertainty and the large costs of making a wrong decision. There will be an unrecoverable $50,000 outlay if no oil is found; there will be a $100,000 opportunity cost if he does not invest and the oil is really there. What is the most he should be willing to pay for perfect information regarding the presence or absence of oil? Explain.

16-38. Payoff tables and perfect information. (CMA, adapted.) Vendo, Inc., has been operating the concession stands at a university's football stadium. The university has had successful football teams for many years; as a result the stadium is always full. The university is located in an area that suffers no rain during the football season. From time to time, Vendo has found itself very short of hot dogs and at other times it has had many left. A review of the records of sales of the past nine seasons revealed the following frequency of hot dogs sold:

10,000 hot dogs	5
20,000 hot dogs	10
30,000 hot dogs	20
40,000 hot dogs	15
	50

Hot dogs sell for 50¢ each and cost Vendo 30¢ each. Unsold hot dogs are given to a local orphanage without charge.

Required

1. Assuming that only the four quantities listed were ever sold and that the occurrences were random events, prepare a payoff table (ignore income taxes) to represent the four possible strategies of ordering 10,000, 20,000, 30,000, or 40,000 hot dogs.

2. Using the expected value decision rule, determine the best strategy.

3. What is the dollar value of perfect information?

16-39. Inventory control and television tubes. The Nemmers Company assembles private-brand television sets for a retail chain, under a contract requiring delivery of 100 sets per day for each of 250 business days per year. Each set requires a picture tube, which Nemmers buys outside for $20 each. The tubes are loaded on trucks at the supplier's factory door and are then delivered by a trucking service at a charge of $100 per trip, regardless of the size of the shipment. The cost of storing the tubes (including the desired rate of return on investment) is $2 per tube per year. Because production is stable throughout the year, the average inventory is one-half the size of the truck lot. Tabulate the relevant annual cost of various truck-lot sizes at 5, 10, 15, 25, 50, and 250 trips per year. Show your results graphically. (Note that the $20 unit cost of tubes is common to all alternatives and hence may be ignored.)

16-40. Reorder point. A utility company uses 5,000 tons of coal per year to generate power at one of its plants. The company orders 500 tons at a time. Lead time for the orders is five days, and the safety stock is a three-day supply. Usage is assumed to be constant over a 360-day year. Calculate the reorder point.

16-41. Inventory policy. (CMA.) Breakon, Inc., manufactures and distributes machine tools. The tools are assembled from approximately 2,000 components manufactured by the company. For several years the production schedule called for one production run of each component each month. This schedule has resulted in a high inventory turnover rate of 4.0 times but requires 12 set-ups for each component every year. In a normal year $3,500 of cost is incurred for each component to produce the number of units sold. The company has been successful in not letting the year-end inventory drop below $100 for each component.

The production manager recommends that the company gradually switch to a schedule of producing the annual needs of each component in one yearly production run. He believes this would reduce costs, because only one set-up cost would be incurred each year for every component rather than 12. At the present time the costs for each set-up are $36. Estimated annual costs associated with carrying inventory, per $1 of inventory value, are: property tax, 4 percent; insurance, 2 percent; and storage cost, 20 percent. The firm estimates its cost of capital to be 10 percent after taxes and pays income taxes at 40 percent of taxable income.

Required

1. If Breakon converts to the "once-a-year" production schedule for its components, calculate the total investment released or additional investment required once the changeover is completed.

2. If Breakon converts to the "once-a-year" production schedule, calculate the after-tax savings or added expenses once the changeover is completed.

3. What factors other than those referred to in Requirements 1 and 2 should be considered in reaching a decision to change the production policy?

4. Do your calculations support a change to the proposed policy? Explain your answer.

16-42. **EOQ and relevant costs.** (CMA, adapted.) Evans, Inc., is a large wholesale distributor dealing exclusively in baby shoes. Owing to the substantial costs related to ordering and storing the shoes, the company has decided to employ the economic order quantity method (EOQ) to help determine the optimum quantities of shoes to order from the different manufacturers.

Before Evans, Inc., can employ the EOQ model, they need to develop values for two of the cost parameters, which they call ordering costs (C_o) and storage costs (C_s). As a starting point, management has decided to develop the values for the two cost parameters by using cost data from the most recent fiscal year, 19x5.

The company placed 4,000 purchase orders during 19x5. The largest number of orders placed during any one month was 400 in June and the smallest number was 250 in December. Selected cost data for these two months and the year for the purchasing, accounts payable, and warehousing operations appear below.

	Costs for High-Activity Month (June; 400 orders)	Costs for Low-Activity Month (December; 250 orders)	Annual Costs
Purchasing Department			
Purchasing manager	$ 1,750	$ 1,750	$ 21,000
Buyers	2,500	1,900	28,500
Clerks	2,000	1,100	20,600
Supplies	275	150	2,500
Accounts Payable Department			
Clerks	2,000	1,500	21,500
Supplies	125	75	1,100
Data processing	2,600	2,300	30,000
Warehouse			
Foreman	1,250	1,250	15,000
Receiving clerks	2,300	1,800	23,300
Receiving supplies	50	25	500
Shipping clerks	3,800	3,500	44,000
Shipping supplies	1,350	1,200	15,200
Freight out	1,600	1,300	16,800
	$21,600	$17,850	$240,000

519

*Influences of
Quantitative
Techniques on
Management
Accounting*

The purchasing department is responsible for placing all orders. The costs listed for the accounts payable department relate only to the processing of purchase orders for payment. The warehouse costs reflect two operations—receiving and shipping. The receiving clerks inspect all incoming shipments and place the orders in storage. The shipping clerks are responsible for processing all sales orders to retailers.

The company leases space in a public warehouse. The rental fee is priced according to the square feet occupied during a month. The annual charges during 19x5 totaled $34,500. Annual insurance and property taxes on the shoes stored in the warehouse amounted to $5,700 and $7,300, respectively. Investments are expected to produce a rate of return of 20 percent before taxes.

The inventory balances tend to fluctuate during the year, depending upon the demand for baby shoes. Selected data on inventory balances are shown below.

Inventory, January 1, 19x5	$160,000
Inventory, December 31, 19x5	120,000
Highest inventory balance (June)	220,000
Lowest inventory balance (December)	120,000
Average monthly inventory	190,000

The boxes in which the baby shoes are stored are all approximately the same size. Consequently, the shoes all occupy about the same amount of storage space in the warehouse.

Required

1. Using the 19x5 data, determine estimated values appropriate for
   a. C_o—cost of placing an order.
   b. C_s—the annual cost of storage per dollar of investment in inventory.

2. Should Evans, Inc., use the cost parameters developed solely from the historical data in the employment of the EOQ model? Explain your answer.

SUGGESTED READINGS

BIERMAN, HAROLD, and THOMAS R. DYCKMAN, *Managerial Cost Accounting,* 2nd ed. (New York: The Macmillan Company, 1976).

DEMSKI, JOEL S., *Information Analysis* (Reading, Mass.: Addison-Wesley Publishing Co., Inc., 1972.

FELTHAM, GERALD A., *Information Evaluation* (Sarasota, Fla.: American Accounting Association, 1972).

HORNGREN C., *Cost Accounting: A Managerial Emphasis,* 4th ed. (Englewood Cliffs, N.J.: Prentice-Hall, Inc., 1977), Chaps. 14, 24–27.

LIVINGSTONE, JOHN LESLIE, ed., *Management Planning and Control: Mathematical Models* (New York: McGraw-Hill Book Company, 1970).

MILLER, D. W., and M. K. STARR, *Executive Decisions and Operations Research,* 2nd ed. (Englewood Cliffs, N.J.: Prentice-Hall, Inc., 1969).

STOCKTON, R. STANSBURY, *Introduction to Linear Programming* (Homewood, Ill.: Richard D. Irwin, Inc., 1971).

WAGNER, HARVEY M., *Principles of Operations Research with Applications to Managerial Decisions,* 2nd ed. (Englewood Cliffs, N.J.: Prentice-Hall, Inc., 1975).

PART FOUR

Basic
Financial Accounting
for Managers

CHAPTER 17

Basic Accounting: Concepts, Techniques, and Conventions

This chapter provides an overview of the accounting process for individuals with little or no background in accounting and for those who want to review some fundamental ideas. We shall become acquainted with some terminology and with what financial statements say and do not say. Knowing what financial statements do *not* communicate is just as important as knowing what they do communicate. We shall be mainly concerned with how to measure the managers' custodial or stewardship responsibilities for the assets entrusted to them. This is basically a scorekeeping task.

This chapter covers the fundamentals without employing some of the bookkeeping techniques (for example, ledger accounts) and language (for example, debit and credit) that are commonplace in accounting. The chapter appendix probes the ideas of the chapter in greater depth, using a more technical approach.

We consider the essence of profit-making activities and how the accountant portrays them. As we examine what the accountant does, we shall introduce the concepts and conventions that he uses.

The Accounting Process

Managers, investors, and other interested groups usually want the answers to two important questions about an organization: How well did the organization perform for a given period of time? Where does the organization stand at a given point in time? The accountant answers these questions with two major financial statements—an income statement and a balance sheet. To obtain these statements, he continually records the history of an organization or entity. Through the financial accounting process, he accumulates, analyzes, quantifies, classifies, summarizes, and reports the seemingly countless events and their effects on the entity.

Economic Activity

Most organizations exist to serve a desire for some type of goods or services. Whether they are profit seeking or not, they typically follow a similar, somewhat rhythmic, cycle of economic activity. Consider the following example. A retail business usually engages in some version of the following "operating cycle" in order to earn profits:

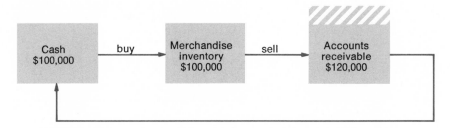

The box for Accounts Receivable (amounts owed to the business by customers) is bigger than the other two boxes because the objective is to sell goods at a price higher than acquisition cost. Retailers and nearly all other businesses buy goods and services and perform acts (such as placing them in a convenient location or changing their form) that merit selling prices that hopefully will yield a profit. The total amount of profit earned during a particular period heavily depends on the excess of the selling prices over the costs of the goods and services (*the markup*) and on the speed of the operating cycle (*turnover*).

For example, Retailer No. 1, as illustrated above, may earn an operating income of $20,000 in, say, one month. His competitor, Retailer No. 2, may have lower prices, realizing in each cycle only $110,000 in sales instead of $120,000. But his lower prices attract three times as many customers in the same span of a month. He will earn $30,000 (sales of $330,000 minus the cost of merchandise sold, $300,000) because his lower prices have resulted in a

524

turnover of merchandise three times faster than that of Retailer No. 1. This is the fundamental approach of the owner of the discount store. He trades off lower prices for quicker turnover with the hope that he will earn larger profits than the conventional retailer.

Financial Statements

The accountant records these acts and other events and measures their financial effects on the organization. Financial statements, which are summarized reports of these financial activities, can be produced at any instant and can apply to any span of time. Suppose that Retailer No. 1 began business as a corporation on March 1. An opening balance sheet (more accurately called **statement of financial position or statement of financial condition**) follows:

RETAILER No. 1
Balance Sheet (Statement of Financial Position)
As of March 1, 19x1

Assets		*Equities*	
Cash	$100,000	Capital stock (issued as evidence of ownership)	$100,000

The balance sheet is a photograph of financial status at an instant of time. It has two counterbalancing sections—assets and equities. Assets are economic resources that are expected to benefit future activities. Equities are the claims against, or interests in, the assets.

The accountant conceives of the balance sheet as an equation:

$$\text{Assets} = \text{Equities}$$

The equities side of this fundamental equation is often divided as follows:

$$\text{Assets} = \text{Liabilities} + \text{Owners' Equity}$$

The **liabilities** are the economic obligations of the entity. The **owners' equity** is the excess of the assets over the liabilities. For a corporation, the owners' equity is called **stockholders' equity.** In turn, the stockholders' equity is composed of the ownership claim against, or interest in, the total assets arising from any paid-in investment **(capital stock),** plus the ownership claim arising as a result of profitable operations **(retained income or retained earnings).**

The following is a summary of the **transactions** that occurred in March. A transaction is any event that affects the financial position of the organization, and that requires recording:[1]

1. Initial investment by owners, $100,000 cash.

2. Acquisition of inventory for $75,000 cash.

3. Acquisition of inventory for $35,000 on open account. A purchase (or a sale) on open account is an agreement whereby the buyer pays cash sometime after the date of sale, often in thirty days. Amounts owed on open accounts are usually called **accounts payable**.

4. Merchandise carried in inventory at a cost of $100,000 were sold on open account for $120,000. These open customer accounts are called **accounts receivable**.

5. Collections of accounts receivable, $30,000.

6. Payments of accounts payable, $10,000.

7. On March 1, $3,000 cash was disbursed for store rent for March, April, and May. Rent is $1,000 per month, payable quarterly in advance, beginning March 1.

Note that these are indeed *summarized* transactions. For example, all the sales will not take place at once, nor will purchases of inventory, collections from customers, or disbursements to suppliers. A vast number of repetitive transactions occur in practice, and specialized data collection techniques are used to measure their effects on the entity.

The above transactions can be analyzed using the balance sheet equation, as shown in Exhibit 17-1.

Transaction 1 has been explained previously. Note, in this illustration, that capital stock represents the claim arising from the owners' total initial investment in the corporation.[2]

Transactions 2 and 3, the purchases of inventory, are steps toward the ultimate goal—the earning of a profit. But stockholders' equity is not affected. That is, no profit is realized until a sale is made.

Transaction 4 is the sale of $100,000 of inventory for $120,000. Two things happen simultaneously: A new asset, Accounts Receivable, is acquired (4*a*) in exchange for the giving up of Inventory (4*b*).

Transaction 5, the collection, is an example of an event that has no impact on stockholders' equity. It is merely the transformation of one asset (Accounts Receivable) into another (Cash).

[1]The meaning of "transaction" is explored more fully in a later section, "Formal Adjustments."

[2]Stock certificates usually bear some nominal "par or stated value" that is far below the actual cash invested. For example, the par or stated value of the certificates might be only $10,000; if so, the ownership claim arising from the investment might be split between two ownership equity claims, one for $10,000 "capital stock, at par" and another for $90,000 "paid-in capital in excess of par value of capital stock."

EXHIBIT 17-1
RETAILER NO. 1

Analysis of Transactions (in dollars)
For March, 19x1

Transactions	ASSETS				=	LIABILITIES	+	EQUITIES STOCKHOLDERS' EQUITY	
	CASH	ACCOUNTS RECEIVABLE	INVENTORY	PREPAID RENT		ACCOUNTS PAYABLE		CAPITAL STOCK	RETAINED INCOME
1. Initial investment	+100,000				=		+	+100,000	
2. Acquire inventory for cash	−75,000		+75,000		=				
3. Acquire inventory on credit			+35,000		=	+35,000			
4a. Sales on credit		+120,000			=				+120,000 (revenue)
4b. Cost of inventory sold			−100,000		=				−100,000 (expense)
5. Collect from customers	+30,000	−30,000			=				
6. Pay accounts of suppliers	−10,000				=	−10,000			
7a. Pay rent in advance	−3,000			+3,000	=				
7b. Recognize expiration of rental services				−1,000	=				−1,000 (expense)
Balance, 3/31/x1	+42,000	+90,000	+10,000	+2,000	=	+25,000	+	+100,000	+19,000

527

Transaction 6, the payment, also has no effect on stockholders' equity—it affects assets and liabilities only. In general, **collections from customers and payments to suppliers of the** *principal* **amounts of debt have no direct impact on stockholders' equity. Of course, as will be seen in a subsequent section,** *interest* **on debt does affect stockholders' equity as an item of expense.**

Transaction 7, the rent disbursement, is made to acquire the right to use store facilities for the next three months. At March 1, the $3,000 measures the future benefit from these services, so the asset *Prepaid Rent* is created (7*a*). At the end of March, one-third of these rental services have expired, so the asset is reduced and stockholders' equity is also reduced by $1,000 as rent expense (7*b*).

For simplicity, we have assumed no expenses other than cost of goods sold and rent. The accountant would ordinarily prepare at least two financial statements:

RETAILER NO. 1

Income Statement

For the Month Ending March 31, 19x1

Sales (revenue)		$120,000
Expenses:		
Cost of goods sold	$100,000	
Rent	1,000	
Total expenses		101,000
Net income		$ 19,000

RETAILER NO. 1

Balance Sheet

As of March 31, 19x1

Cash	$ 42,000	Liabilities: Accounts payable		$ 25,000
Accounts receivable	90,000	Stockholders' equity:		
Inventory	10,000	Capital stock	$100,000	
Prepaid rent	2,000	Retained income	19,000	119,000
Total assets	$144,000	Total equities		$144,000

Relationship of Balance Sheet and Income Statement

The income statement has measured the operating performance of the corporation by matching its accomplishments (revenue from customers, which usually is called *sales*) and its efforts (cost of goods sold and other expenses). **The balance sheet shows the financial position at an instant of time, but the income statement measures performance for a span of time,** whether it be a month, a quarter, or longer. The income statement is the major link between balance sheets:

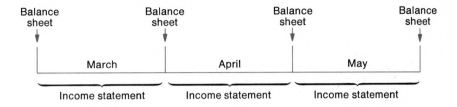

Examine the changes in stockholders' equity in Exhibit 17-1. The accountant records revenue and expense so that they represent increases (revenues) and decreases (expenses) in the owners' claims. At the end of a given period, these items are summarized in the form of an income statement.

Each item in a financial statement is frequently called an *account*, so that term will be used occasionally throughout this book. In the above example, the outflows of assets are represented by decreases in the Inventory and Prepaid Rent accounts and corresponding decreases in stockholders' equity in the form of Cost of Goods Sold and Rent Expense. Expense accounts are basically negative elements of stockholders' equity. Similarly, the Sales (revenue) account is a positive element of stockholders' equity.

The Analytical Power of the Balance Sheet Equation

As you study Exhibit 17-1, the following points should become clearer about how accountants use the fundamental balance sheet equation as their framework for analyzing and reporting the effects of transactions:

$$\text{Assets } (A) = \text{Liabilities } (L) + \text{Stockholders' equity } (SE) \qquad (1)$$

SE equals original ownership claim plus the increase in ownership claim due to profitable operations. That is, *SE* equals the claim arising from paid-in capital plus the claim arising from retained income. Therefore,

$$A = L + \text{Capital stock} + \text{Retained income} \qquad (2)$$

But, ignoring dividends for the moment, Retained income equals Revenue minus Expenses. Therefore,

$$A = L + \text{Capital stock} + \text{Revenue} - \text{Expenses} \qquad (3)$$

Revenue and *expense accounts* are nothing more than subdivisions of stockholders' equity—temporary stockholders' equity accounts, as it were. Their

529

purpose is to summarize the volume of sales and the various expenses, so that management is kept informed of the reasons for the constant increases and decreases in stockholders' equity in the course of ordinary operations. In this way comparisons can be made, standards or goals can be set, and control can be better exercised.

The entire accounting system is based on the simple balance sheet equation. As you know, equations in general possess enormous analytical potential because of the dual algebraic manipulations that they permit. The equation is always kept in balance because of the duality feature.

Exhibit 17-1 illustrates the dual nature of the accountant's analysis. For each transaction, the equation is always kept in balance. If the items affected are confined to one side of the equation, you will find the total amount added equal to the total amount subtracted on that side. If the items affected are on both sides, then equal amounts are simultaneously added or subtracted on each side.

The striking feature of the balance sheet equation is its universal applicability. No transaction has ever been conceived, no matter how simple or complex, that cannot be analyzed via the equation. The top technical partners in the world's largest professional accounting firms, when confronted with the most intricate transactions of multinational companies, will inevitably discuss and think about their analyses in terms of the balance sheet equation and its major components: assets, liabilities, and owners' equity (including the explanations of changes in owners' equity that most often take the form of revenues and expenses).

Accrual Basis and Cash Basis

The process of determining income and financial position is anchored to the **accrual basis** of accounting, as distinguished from the **cash basis.** In accrual accounting, the impact of events on assets and equities is recognized in the time periods when services are rendered or utilized instead of when cash is paid or received. That is, **revenue is recognized as it is** *earned,* **and expenses are recognized as they are** *incurred*—**not when cash changes hands.** For example, Transaction 4*a* in Exhibit 17-1 recognizes revenue when sales are made on credit. Similarly, Transactions 4*b* and 7*b* show that expenses are recognized as efforts are expended or services utilized to obtain the revenue (regardless of when cash is disbursed). Therefore, income is affected by measurements of noncash resources and obligations. The accrual basis is the principal conceptual framework for matching accomplishments (revenue) with efforts (expenses).

If the **cash basis** of accounting were used instead of the accrual basis, **revenue and expense would depend on the timing of various cash receipts and disbursements.** In our Retailer No. 1 example, the March income statement would contain the following:

Revenue (cash collected from customers)		$ 30,000
Expenses:		
Cash disbursed for merchandise ($75,000		
in Transaction 2 plus $10,000 in		
Transaction 6)	$85,000	
Cash disbursement for rent	3,000	
Total expenses		88,000
Net loss		−$58,000

The March 31 balance sheet would have:

Cash	$42,000	Capital stock	$ 100,000
		Retained income	− 58,000
		Stockholders' equity	$ 42,000

The major deficiencies of the cash basis of accounting are apparent from this example: it ignores the impact on net income and financial position of the liability for accounts payable and the impact of such very real assets as accounts receivable, inventory, and prepaid rent.

Despite the incompleteness of the cash basis of accounting, it is used widely by individuals when they measure their income for personal income tax purposes. For this limited purpose, the cash basis often gives a good approximation of what might also be reported on the accrual basis. Long ago, however, accountants and managers found cash basis financial statements such as those above to be unsatisfactory as a measure of both performance and position. Now more than 95 percent of all business is conducted on a credit basis; cash receipts and disbursements are not the critical transactions as far as the recognition of revenue and expense is concerned. Thus, the accrual basis evolved in response to a desire for a more complete, and therefore more accurate, report of the financial impact of various events.

Formal Adjustments

To measure income under the accrual basis, certain formal adjustments must be made for some of the transactions already recorded. An example of such an adjustment is Transaction 7b in Exhibit 17-1. Earlier, we mentioned that a "transaction" is any economic event that should be recorded by the accountant. Note that this definition is not limited to market transactions, which are explicit exchanges between the entity and another party. Transactions also include internal conversions (such as raw materials into finished goods), losses of assets from fire or theft, and any other changes in assets and equities that occur because of the passage of time or some other event. The latter changes, such as the expiration of Prepaid Rent, are generally recognized formally in the accounting records at periodic intervals—when the financial statements are about to be prepared—through the use of these adjustments.

The principal adjustments concern prepayments, accruals, deferrals, and depreciation (the regular periodic write-off of the original costs of long-lived physical assets such as equipment). All have an important common characteristic. They reflect implicit transactions, in contrast to the explicit transactions that trigger nearly all of the day-to-day routine entries.

To illustrate: Entries for sales, purchases, cash receipts, and cash disbursements are supported by explicit evidence. This evidence is usually in the form of source documents (for example, sales slips, purchase invoices, employee time records, cash receipts, or cash payments). On the other hand, adjustments for accrued interest, accrued wages, prepaid insurance, subscriptions collected in advance, depreciation, and the like are prepared from special schedules or memoranda that recognize events (such as the passage of time) that are ignored in day-to-day recording procedures.

These adjustments refine the accountant's accuracy and provide a more complete and meaningful measure of efforts, accomplishments, and financial position. They are an essential part of accrual accounting.

The Measurement of Expenses: Assets Expire

Transactions 4*b* and 7*b* demonstrate how assets may be viewed as bundles of economic services awaiting future use or expiration. It is helpful to think of assets, other than cash and receivables, as prepaid or stored costs (for example, inventories or plant assets) that are carried forward to future periods rather than immediately charged against revenue:

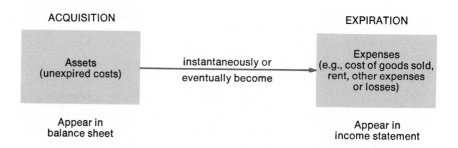

Expenses are used-up assets. Thus assets are unexpired costs held back from the expense stream and carried in the balance sheet to await expiration in future periods.

The analysis of the inventory and rent transactions in Exhibit 17-1 maintains this distinction of acquisition and expiration. The unexpired costs of inventory and prepaid rent are assets until they are used up and become expenses.

Sometimes services are acquired and utilized almost instantaneously. Examples are advertising services, interest services (the cost of money, which is a service), miscellaneous supplies, and sales salaries and commissions. **Conceptually, these costs should, at least momentarily, be viewed as assets upon acquisition before being written off as expenses.** For example, suppose there was an eighth transaction in Exhibit 17-1, whereby newspaper advertising was acquired for $1,000 cash. To abide by the acquisition-expiration sequence, the transaction would be analyzed in two phases:

Trans-action		Assets		=	Liabilities	+	Stockholders' Equity	
	Cash	+ Other assets	+ Unexpired advertising =				Capital stock	+ Retained income
8a.	− 1,000		+ 1,000 =					
8b.			− 1,000 =					− 1,000 (expense)

Frequently, services are acquired and used up so quickly that accountants do not bother recording an asset such as Unexpired Advertising or Prepaid Rent for them. Instead, a shortcut is taken:

Transaction	Cash + Other assets = Liabilities + Capital stock + Retained income
8	− 1,000 = − 1,000 (expense)

Making the entry in two steps instead of one may seem cumbersome, and it is—from a practical bookkeeping viewpoint. **But our purpose is not to learn how to be efficient bookkeepers. We want an orderly way of thinking about what the manager does. He acquires goods and services, not expenses** *per se.* **These goods and services become expenses as they are utilized in obtaining revenue.**

Some of the most difficult issues in accounting center on when an unexpired cost expires to become an expense. For example, some accountants believe that research and development costs should be accounted for as unexpired costs (often found on balance sheets as "Deferred Research and Development Costs") and written off (amortized) in some systematic manner over a period of years. But the regulators of financial accounting in the United States have ruled that such costs have vague future benefits that are difficult to measure and thus have required writing them off as expenses immediately; in cases such as this, research costs would never be found on balance sheets.

Pause for Reflection

If you have never studied accounting before, or if you studied it long ago, you should not proceed further with your study of this chapter until you have solved the following problem. There are no shortcuts. Pushing a pencil is an absolute necessity for becoming comfortable with accounting concepts. The cost-benefit test will easily be met; your gain in knowledge will exceed your investment of time.

Another suggestion is to do the work on your own. In particular, do not ask for help from any professional accountant if he or she introduces any new terms beyond those already covered. For example, the technical terms of debits, credits, and ledger accounts will only confuse, not clarify, at this stage. Instead, scrutinize Exhibit 17-1. Note how the balance sheet equation is affected by each transaction. Then do the review problem that follows.

SUMMARY PROBLEM FOR YOUR REVIEW

Problem One

The Retailer No. 1 transactions for March were analyzed early in this chapter. The balance sheet showed the following balances as of March 31, 19x1:

Cash	$ 42,000	
Accounts receivable	90,000	
Inventory	10,000	
Prepaid rent	2,000	
Accounts payable		$ 25,000
Capital stock		100,000
Retained income		19,000
	$144,000	$144,000

The following is a summary of the transactions that occurred during April:
1. Collections of accounts receivable, $88,000.

2. Payments of accounts payable, $24,000.

3. Acquisitions of inventory on open account, $80,000.

4. Merchandise carried in inventory at a cost of $70,000 were sold on open account for $85,000.

5. Adjustment for recognition of rent expense for April.

6. Wages (which were ignored for simplicity in March) *incurred* in April were $8,000. The acquisition of these employee services was recognized by the asset Unexpired Wages Services and the liability Accrued Wages Payable.

7. Wages *paid* on four Fridays in April totaled $6,000. The payment of these wages was recognized by decreasing Accrued Wages Payable and by decreasing Cash.

8. All the Unexpired Wages Services acquired in Transaction 6 were deemed to have no benefit beyond April, so the asset is written off and Wages Expense is recognized.

9. Some customers paid $3,000 in advance for merchandise they ordered but that is not expected in inventory until mid-May. (What asset must rise? Does this transaction increase liabilities or stockholders' equity?)

10. Cash dividends declared and disbursed to stockholders on April 29 equaled $18,000. (What account besides Cash is affected?)

1. Using the accrual basis of accounting, prepare an analysis of transactions, employing the equation approach demonstrated in Exhibit 17-1. To have plenty of room for new accounts, put your analysis sideways.

2. Prepare a balance sheet as of April 30, 19x1, and an income statement for the month of April. Also prepare a new report, the Statement of Retained Income, which should show the beginning balance, followed by a description of any major changes, and end with the balance as of April 30, 19x1.

3. Using the cash basis of accounting, prepare an income statement for April. Compare the net income with that computed in Requirement 2. Which net income figure do you prefer as a measure of the economic performance for April? Why?

Solution to Problem One

Part 1. The answer is in Exhibit 17-2. The first five transactions are straightforward extensions or repetitions of the March transactions. But the rest of the transactions are new. They are discussed in the sections that follow the solutions to the second and third parts of this problem.

Part 2. See Exhibits 17-3, 17-4, and 17-5. The first two of these exhibits show financial statements already described in this chapter: the balance sheet and the income statement. Exhibit 17-5 presents a new statement, the *Statement of Retained Income,* which is merely a formal reconciliation of the Retained Income. It consists of the beginning balance, adds net income for the period in question, and deducts cash dividends to arrive at the ending balance. Frequently, this statement is tacked on to the bottom of an income statement. If so, the result is a *combined* statement of income and statement of reconciliation of retained income.

Part 3. See Exhibit 17-6. The net income is $61,000 on the cash basis, but only $6,000 on the accrual basis. Accountants prefer the accrual basis because it provides a more complete and precise measurement of economic performance, a better matching of accomplishments with efforts. For example, the timing of disbursements to reduce accounts payable obviously is not as closely related to sales in April as the cost of inventory that was sold.

ACCOUNTING FOR WAGES

The analysis of wages is the most difficult to understand, but it is covered here because it provides an excellent illustration of what is meant by accrual accounting.

Most companies pay their employees at predetermined times, for example, each Friday. However, strictly speaking, an employee should be paid each hour or each day. That is, an entity "accrues" a debt or liability to its employees as the clock ticks. For measurement purposes under the accrual basis of accounting, **the critical event is when the wages are incurred (that is, earned by the employees),** *not* **when the wages are paid in cash.** Therefore, the logical accounting steps are:

EXHIBIT 17-2
RETAILER NO. 1

Analysis of Transactions (In dollars)
For April, 19x1

| | ASSETS | | | | | = | EQUITIES | | | | |
| | | | | | | | LIABILITIES | | | STOCKHOLDERS' EQUITY | |
Transaction	CASH	ACCOUNTS RECEIVABLE	INVENTORY	PREPAID RENT	UNEXPIRED WAGES SERVICES	=	ACCOUNTS PAYABLE	ACCRUED WAGES PAYABLE	DEFERRED SALES REVENUE*	CAPITAL STOCK	RETAINED INCOME
Bal. 3/31/x1	+42,000	+90,000	+10,000	+2,000		=	+25,000			+100,000	+19,000
1.	+88,000	−88,000				=					
2.	−24,000					=	−24,000				
3.			+80,000			=	+80,000				
4a.		+85,000				=					+85,000 (revenue)
4b.			−70,000			=					−70,000 (expense)
5.				−1,000		=					−1,000 (expense)
6.					+8,000	=		+8,000			
7.	−6,000					=		−6,000			
8.					−8,000	=					−8,000 (expense)
9.	+3,000					=			+3,000*		
10.	−18,000					=					−18,000 (dividend)
Bal. 4/30/x1	+85,000	+87,000	+20,000	+1,000	0	=	+81,000	+2,000	+3,000	+100,000	+7,000

*Some managers and accountants would call this account "Customer Deposits" or "Advances from Customers."

EXHIBIT 17-3
RETAILER NO. 1

Balance Sheet
As of April 30, 19x1

ASSETS		EQUITIES		
Cash	$ 85,000	Liabilities:		
Accounts receivable	87,000	Accounts payable	$ 81,000	
Inventory	20,000	Accrued wages		
Prepaid rent	1,000	payable	2,000	
		Deferred sales		
		revenue	3,000	$ 86,000
		Stockholders' equity:		
		Capital stock	$100,000	
		Retained income	7,000	107,000
Total assets	$193,000	Total equities		$193,000

EXHIBIT 17-4
RETAILER NO. 1

Income Statement (Multiple-Step)*
for the Month Ending April 30, 19x1

Sales		$85,000
Cost of goods sold		70,000
Gross profit		$15,000
Operating expenses:		
Rent	$1,000	
Wages	8,000	9,000
Net income		$ 6,000

> * A "single-step" statement would not draw the gross profit figure,
> but would merely list all the expenses—including cost of goods
> sold—and deduct the total from sales. *Gross profit* is defined as the
> excess of sales over the cost of the inventory that was sold. It is
> sometimes called *gross margin*.

EXHIBIT 17-5
RETAILER NO. 1

Statement of Retained Income
for the Month Ending April 30, 19x1

Balance, March 31, 19x1	$19,000
Net income for April	6,000
Total	$25,000
Cash dividends	18,000
Balance, April 30, 19x1	$ 7,000

EXHIBIT 17-6
RETAILER NO. 1

Income Statement (Cash Basis)
for the Month Ending April 30, 19x1

Sales (collections from customers, including advance payments)		$91,000
Expenses:		
Disbursements for merchandise	$24,000	
Wages	6,000	30,000
Net income		$61,000

	Assets		*Equities*
First, acquire wages services.	+ Unexpired Wages Services	=	+ Accrued Wages Payable
Second, pay for wages services.	− Cash	=	− Accrued Wages Payable
Third, recognize wage expense.	− Unexpired Wages Services	=	− Retained Income (as Wages Expense)

Many systems designers follow this three-step logic when payroll accounting systems are installed. First, as entry 6 in Exhibit 17-2 summarizes, all labor costs result in an increase in a liability account, Accrued Wages Payable (or Accrued Payroll), and an increase in an asset account, Unexpired Wages Services (at least temporarily). Consider an April calendar:

			APRIL			
S	M	T	W	T	F	S
			1	2	3	4
5	6	7	8	9	10	11
12	13	14	15	16	17	18
19	20	21	22	23	24	25
26	27	28	29	30		

The wages *incurred* (earned by employees) during April could be recorded daily, weekly, or only on April 30 if no financial statements were prepared before the end of the month.

Second, as wages are paid each payday (say each Friday for work done on Monday through Friday), the liability is diminished by decreasing Accrued Wages Payable and decreasing Cash, as entry 7 summarizes. This automatically provides a month-end balance of Accrued Wages Payable that represents the wages incurred but unpaid (for Monday through Thursday, April 27–30). Those wages will not be *paid* until the first Friday in May, but the accrual method demands that they be recognized in April, when they were *incurred*.

Third, as entry 8 summarizes, the Unexpired Wages Services acquired during April are judged as having no future benefit, so they are written off as expenses.

Many alert readers will think the foregoing three steps are too cumbersome, particularly the third step. After all, labor services always have temporary benefit, so why not take a shortcut and skip the Unexpired Wages Services account altogether by recognizing Wages Expenses immediately? Obviously, such a practice may be adopted, but here we are concerned with *concepts,* not bookkeeping shortcuts.

Moreover—and this is important—you can readily visualize where the wages shown in Unexpired Wages Services are *not* always written off as expenses immediately. As Chapter 14 explains, in manufacturing companies the wages of factory labor that works directly on goods being produced (often called *direct labor*) finds its way into an account such as Unexpired Wages Services (or Direct Labor) and then is transferred to another *asset* account, Finished Goods Inventory. Why? Because the labor is looked upon as an asset that should not be written off to expense until the inventory to which it relates is sold. Thus, such "direct labor" becomes expense as a part of Cost of Goods Sold and not necessarily in the same month that the payroll is paid.

ACCOUNTING FOR DEFERRED REVENUE

Entry 9 is an example of **deferred revenue,** sometimes called **unearned revenue,** which is a liability because the retailer is obligated to deliver the goods ordered or to refund the money if the goods are not delivered. Some managers might prefer to call this account *advances from customers,* or *customer deposits,* instead of *deferred sales revenue,* but it is a deferred revenue account no matter what its label. That is, it is revenue collected in advance that has not been earned as yet. Advance collections of rent and magazine subscriptions are other examples.

Sometimes it is easier to see how accountants analyze transactions by vizualizing the financial positions of both parties to a contract. For instance, for the rent transaction of March 1 compare the financial impact on Retailer No. 1 with the impact on the landlord who received the rental payment:

	Landlord				Retailer No. 1		
	A	=	L	+	SE	A	= L + SE
	Cash		Deferred Rent Revenue	Rent Revenue		Cash	Prepaid Rent	Rent Expense
1. Prepayment	+3,000	=	+3,000			−3,000	+3,000 =	
2. March expiration		=	−1,000	+1,000			−1,000 =	−1,000
3. April expiration		=	−1,000	+1,000			−1,000 =	−1,000

A similar analysis could be conducted for magazine publishers, who receive payments in advance, and who must recognize Deferred Subscription Revenue.

Deferred revenue is often called *deferred income,* but *revenue* is a more accurate description than *income* because the latter is, strictly speaking, a difference or "what's left over" after deducting appropriate expenses from revenue. This kind of revenue will generate income later only if it exceeds the cost of goods or services delivered to customers.

DIVIDENDS AND RETAINED INCOME

As entry 10 shows, **cash dividends are *not* expenses like rent and wages.** They are not directly related to the generation of sales or the conduct of operations. Cash dividends are distributions of assets to owners that reduce their ownership claim (which is represented as retained income). Moreover, although the amount of a dividend often is some fraction of net income, dividends are not necessarily tied to current net income, as this illustration shows.

Retained income, retained earnings, undistributed earnings, or reinvested earnings is the accumulated increase in stockholders' equity arising from profitable operations. As a company grows, this account can soar enormously if dividends are not paid. Retained income can easily be the largest stockholders' equity account.

Retained income is *not* a pot of cash that is awaiting distribution to stockholders. Consider the following illustration:

Step 1. Assume an opening balance sheet of:

Cash	$100	Capital stock	$100

Step 2. Purchase inventory for $50 cash. The balance sheet now reads:

Cash	$ 50	Capital stock	$100
Inventory	50		
	$100		

Step 3. Now sell the inventory for $80:

Cash	$130	Capital stock	$100
		Retained income	30
			$130

At this stage, the retained income might be reflected by a $30 increase in cash. **But the $30 in retained income connotes only a *general* claim against *total* assets.** This may be clarified by the transaction that follows.

Step 4. Purchase equipment and inventory, in the amounts of $40 and $50, respectively. Now:

Cash	$ 40	Capital stock	$100
Inventory	50	Retained income	30
Equipment	40		$130
	$130		

Where is the $30 in retained income reflected? Is it reflected in Cash, in Inventory, or in Equipment? The answer is indeterminate. This example helps to explain the nature of the Retained Income account. It is a *claim,* not a pot of gold. Retained income is increased by profitable operations, but the cash inflow from sales is an increment in assets (see Step 3). When the cash inflow takes place, management will use the cash, most often to buy more inventory or equipment (Step 4). **Retained income is a *general* claim against, or undivided interest in, *total* assets, *not* a preferred claim against cash or against any other particular asset.**

A term that is virtually archaic, **earned surplus,** is sometimes still found in stockholders' equity sections. Fortunately, its use is fading fast. Earned surplus is an interchangeable term for retained income. The trouble with the term is that *surplus* is misleading. It connotes something superfluous or unessential or left over; therefore, consequent misunderstandings of the term might be expected. As the above example shows, earned surplus (retained income) is not an asset, nor does it represent an unnecessary ownership interest.

As stated above, **dividends** are distributions of assets that reduce ownership claims. The cash assets that are distributed typically arose from profitable operations. Thus, dividends or withdrawals are often spoken of as "distributions of profits" or "distributions of retained income." Dividends are often erroneously described as being "paid *out of* retained income." **In reality, cash dividends are distributions of assets and liquidate a portion of the ownership claim. The distribution is made possible by profitable operations.**

The amount of cash dividends declared by the board of directors of a company depends on many factors, the least important of which is the balance in Retained Income. Although profitable operations are generally essential, dividend policy is also influenced by the company's cash position and future needs for cash to pay debts or to purchase additional assets. It is also influenced by whether the company is committed to a stable dividend policy or to a policy that normally ties dividends to fluctuations in net income. Under a stable policy, dividends may be paid consistently even if a company encounters a few years of little or no net income.

PROPRIETORSHIPS AND PARTNERSHIPS

The owners' equity section of the balance sheet can be affected by four basic types of transactions, (1) investments, (2) withdrawals, (3) revenues, and (4) expenses:

$$\text{Assets} = \text{Liabilities} + \overline{\qquad\qquad\qquad\text{Owners' Equity}\qquad\qquad\qquad}$$

$-$Owners' withdrawals (e.g., corporate cash dividends)	$+$Owners' investments
$-$Expenses	$+$Revenues

The basic accounting concepts that underlie the owners' equity are unchanged regardless of whether ownership takes the form of a corporation, sole proprietorship, or partnership. However, in proprietorships and partnerships, distinctions between contributed capital (that is, the investments by owners) and retained income are rarely made. Compare the possibilities for Retailer No. 1 as of April 30:

Owners' Equity for a Corporation

Stockholders' equity:		
Capital stock	$100,000	
Retained income	7,000	
Total stockholders' equity		$107,000

Owners' Equity for a Sole Proprietorship

Alice Walsh, Capital	$107,000

Owners' Equity for a Partnership

Susan Zingler, Capital	$ 53,500
John Martin, Capital	53,500
Total partners' equity	$107,000

In contrast to corporations, sole proprietorships and partnerships are not legally required to account separately for contributed capital (that is, proceeds from issuances of capital stock) and for retained income. Instead, they typically accumulate a single amount for each owner's original investments, subsequent investments, share of net income, and withdrawals. In the case of a sole proprietorship, then, the owner's equity will consist of a lone capital account.

Other terms for owners' equity are *equity capital* and *net worth*. The latter term is fading (the faster, the better). Net worth is a poor term because it implies that the owners' equity is a measure of the "current value" of the business. The total owners' equity is a measure of the ownership claim against the total assets, but it does not necessarily yield an accurate approximation of what some outsider is willing to pay for such an ownership interest. The selling price of a business is the subject of independent bargaining that seldom has a direct relationship to the accounting records of the assets or equities of the entity.

NONPROFIT ORGANIZATIONS

The examples in this chapter have focused on profit-seeking organizations, but balance sheets and income statements are also used by not-for-profit organizations. For example, hospitals and universities have income statements, although they will be called *statements of revenue and expense.* The "bottom line" is frequently called "excess of revenue over expense" rather than "net income."

The basic concepts of assets, liabilities, revenue, and expense are applicable to all organizations, whether they be utilities, symphony orchestras, private, public, American, Asian, and so forth. However, some nonprofit organizations have been slow to adopt some ideas that are widespread in progressive companies. For example, in many governmental organizations the accrual basis of accounting has not supplanted the cash basis. This has hampered the evaluation of the performance of such organizations.

GENERALLY ACCEPTED ACCOUNTING PRINCIPLES

"Principles" Is a Misnomer

The balance sheet and income statement[3] of publicly held corporations and many other corporations are subject to an independent audit that forms the basis for a professional accounting firm's opinion, typically including the following key phrasing:

> In our opinion, the accompanying financial statements present fairly the financial position of the ABC Company at December 31, 19x1, and the results of its operations for the year then ended, in conformity with generally accepted accounting principles applied on a basis consistent with that of the preceding year.

The auditor's opinion, usually appearing at the end of annual reports prepared for stockholders and other external users, is often mistakenly relied on as an infallible guarantee of financial truth. Somehow accounting is thought to be an exact science, perhaps because of the aura of precision that financial statements possess. But accounting is more art than science. The financial reports may appear accurate because of their neatly integrated numbers, but they are the results of a complex measurement process that rests on a huge bundle of assumptions and conventions called accounting principles.

What are these generally accepted accounting principles? This technical

---

[3]Another key financial statement, the statement of changes in financial position, is discussed in Chapter 18.

term covers much territory. It includes both broad concepts or guidelines and detailed practices. It includes all conventions, rules, and procedures that together make up accepted accounting practice at any given time.

Accounting principles become "generally accepted" by agreement. Such agreement is not influenced solely by formal logical analysis. Experience, custom, usage, and practical necessity contribute to the set of principles. Accordingly, it might be better to call them conventions, because *principles* connotes that they are the product of airtight logic.

During the 1960s and 1970s, American generally accepted accounting principles have been most heavily influenced by the Accounting Principles Board (APB) and its successor body, the Financial Accounting Standards Board (FASB). These Boards have been financially supported by various professional accounting associations. In addition, these Boards have had the general backing of the Securities and Exchange Commission, which has had legal authority over most financial reporting to investors. In other words, the public body (the SEC) has informally delegated much rule-making power regarding accounting theory to the private bodies (the APB and FASB). These Boards have rendered a series of pronouncements on various accounting issues. Independent auditing firms, which issue opinions concerning the fairness of corporate financial statements prepared for external use, are required to see that corporate statements do not depart from these pronouncements.

Three broad measurement or valuation conventions (principles) establish the basis for implementing accrual accounting: *realization* (when to recognize revenue), *matching* (when to recognize expense), and the *stable dollar* (what unit of measure to use).

Realization

The realization concept usually pertains to the recording of revenue from sales of products and services to customers. When is revenue realized by a seller—when the inventory is acquired, when sales orders are received, when materials are put into process, when they are finished, when the finished products are delivered to customers, or when the sales proceeds are finally collected in cash? Generally, the accountant has maintained that revenue is realized when the goods or services are *delivered* to customers, even though delivery is only one of a series of events related to the sale. He defends this entrenched practice by pointing out that, for most businesses, delivery is the occasion that validates a legal claim against the customer for goods or services rendered. He maintains that although the importance of purchasing, production, and distribution may differ from business to business, revenue is generally regarded as an indivisible totality. In this sense, revenue cannot be allocated in bits and pieces to individual business functions such as purchasing inventory, obtaining orders, manufacturing products, delivering goods, and collecting cash.

In sum, to be realized, revenue must meet the following two tests: First, the earning process must be virtually complete in that the goods or services must be fully rendered. Second, an exchange of resources evidenced by a market transaction must occur.

There are two major exceptions to the notion that an exchange (delivery, in most cases) is needed to justify the realization of revenue. First, long-run construction contracts often necessitate a *percentage-of-completion method.* For example, the builder of an ocean liner or a huge office building may portray his performance better by spreading prospective revenues, related costs, and resulting net income over the life of the contract in proportion to the work accomplished. Otherwise, all of the net income would appear in one chunk upon completion of the project, as if it were earned on a single day. Second, in exceptionally rare cases (such as in the retail sales of undeveloped lots), where receivables are collectible over an extended period of time and there is no reliable basis for estimating the degree of collectibility, revenue is regarded as being realized under such long-run installment contracts in proportion to the cash collections. In the first instance, revenue is realized earlier than under the general realization test; in the second instance, revenue is realized later.

Matching

The matching process has already been described. Many accountants claim that the principal concern of accounting is the periodic matching of accomplishments (as measured by the selling prices of goods and services rendered) with efforts (as measured by the cost of the goods and services rendered). Much of the accountant's work deals with the difficult measurement problems to be overcome in the evaluation of an organization's performance—the relationship between efforts and accomplishments—during a given period.

Stable Dollar

The monetary unit (the dollar in the United States and Canada) is the principal means for measuring assets and equities. It is the common denominator for quantifying the effects of a wide variety of transactions. Accountants record, classify, summarize, and report in terms of the dollar.

Such measurement assumes that the principal counter—the dollar—is an unchanging yardstick. Yet we all know that a 1980 dollar does not have the same purchasing power as a 1970 or 1960 dollar. Therefore, accounting statements that include different dollars must be interpreted and compared with full consciousness of the limitations of the basic measurement unit. (For an expanded discussion, see Chapter 20.)

Accountants have been extensively criticized for not making explicit and formal adjustments to remedy the defects of their measuring unit. In the face of this, they maintain that price-level adjustments would lessen objectivity and would add to general confusion. They claim that the price-level problem has been exaggerated, and that the adjustments would not significantly affect the vast bulk of corporate statements because most accounts are in current or nearly current dollars.

On the other hand, inflation has been steady and its effects are sometimes surprisingly pervasive. We can expect to see increasing experimentation with reporting that measures the effects of changes in the general economywide price level and in the prices of specific assets. The most troublesome aspect, however, is how to interpret the results after they are measured. Investors and managers are accustomed to the conventional statements. The intelligent interpretation of statements adjusted for changes in the price level will require extensive changes in the habits of users.

Additional Conventions

The foregoing conventions of measurement are only three of many conventions that heavily influence generally accepted accounting principles. We shall now consider **entity, going concern, consistency, objectivity, conservatism, disclosure, materiality, and cost benefit.**

The Entity

The accounting process focuses upon events as they affect an *entity,* which is a specific area of accountability. This entity may be a single corporation, a partnership, a tax district, a department, a paper-making machine, or a consolidated group of many interrelated corporations. The concept of an entity helps the accountant relate events to a sharply defined unit of activity. He separates *business* transactions from *personal* transactions. A purchase of groceries for inventory is an accounting transaction for a grocery store (the entity), but the owner's payment for a diamond necklace by personal check is not.

Going Concern

Many accountants would regard *going concern* as a fact of life rather than as a convention or assumption. **To view an entity as a going concern is to assume that it will continue indefinitely or at least that it will not be liquidated in the near future.** This notion implies that existing *resources,* such as plant assets, *will be used* to fulfill the general purposes of a continuing concern, *rather than sold* in tomorrow's real estate or equipment markets. It also implies that existing liabilities will be paid at maturity in an orderly manner.

The opposite view to this going-concern or continuity convention is an immediate-liquidation assumption, whereby all items on a balance sheet are valued at the amounts appropriate if the entity were to be liquidated in piecemeal fashion within a few days or months. This liquidation approach to valuation is usually used only when the entity is in severe, near-bankrupt straits.

Consistency

In reporting information, accountants are often free to select any one of a variety of procedures, all of which conform to "generally accepted accounting principles." There are, for example, various inventory cost-flow assumptions and various methods of allocating depreciation. Unless they are informed otherwise, users of financial statements assume that the particular procedures adopted by a given organization are consistent from year to year. If consistency could not be assumed, chaos would result. An organization could, for example, switch at whim from one method of accounting for inventory to another and back again.

Although consistency is desirable, it does not in itself constitute virtue. An accounting procedure can be consistently wrong. A company could, for example, consistently write off all acquisitions of plant assets as expenses in the year of purchase. What is desired is described as "generally accepted accounting principles applied on a basis consistent with that of the preceding year." Where such consistency is not maintained, adequate disclosure and explanation should be mandatory.

Objectivity or Verifiability

Users want assurance that the numbers in the financial statements are not fabricated by management or by accountants in order to mislead or to falsify the financial position and performance. Consequently, accountants seek and prize objectivity as one of their principal strengths and regard it as an essential characteristic of measurement. Objectivity results in accuracy that is supported by convincing evidence that can be verified by independent accountants. **It is a relative rather than an absolute concept.** Some measurements can be extremely objective (such as cash in a cash register) in the sense that the same measurement would be produced by each of a dozen CPAs. But there are gradations of objectivity. A dozen CPAs are less likely to arrive at the same balances for receivables, inventories, plant and equipment, and intangible assets. Yet they strive for measurement rules that will produce results that are subject to independent check. That is why accountants are generally satisfied with existing tests of realization; requiring an exchange to occur before revenue is realized helps assure verifiability.

Many critics of existing accounting practices want to trade objectivity (accuracy) for what they conceive as more relevant or valid information. For example, the accounting literature is peppered with suggestions that accounting should attempt to measure "economic income," even though objectivity may be lessened. This particular suggestion often involves introducing asset valuations at replacement costs, when these are higher than historical costs. The accounting profession has generally rejected these suggestions, even when reliable replacement price quotations are available, because no evidence short of a bona fide sale is regarded as sufficient to justify income recognition. However, inflation during the 1970s has led to experimentation with the use of replacement costs and other versions of current values for external purposes. (See Chapter 20 for a fuller discussion.)

Conservatism

In a technical sense, **conservatism** means selecting the method of measurement that yields the gloomiest immediate results. This attitude is reflected in such working rules as: "Anticipate no gains, but provide for all possible losses," and "If in doubt, write it off."

Accountants have traditionally regarded the historical costs of acquiring an asset as the ceiling for its valuation. Assets may be written up only upon an exchange, but they may be written down without an exchange. For example, consider *lower-of-cost-or-market* procedures. Inventories are written down when replacement costs decline, but they are never written up when replacement costs increase.

Conservatism has been criticized as being inherently inconsistent. If replacement market prices are sufficiently objective and verifiable to justify write-downs, why aren't they just as valid for write-ups? Furthermore, the critics maintain, conservatism is not a fundamental concept. Accounting reports should try to present the most accurate picture feasible—neither too high nor too low. Accountants defend their attitude by saying that erring in the direction of conservatism usually would have less severe economic consequences than erring in the direction of overstating assets and net income.

Disclosure

Accountants are obliged to transmit all significant financial data, preferably in the body of the financial reports but also in explanatory footnotes. Especially since they may disagree about which particular inventory or depreciation method is best, accountants should disclose all the major facts so that the user can make his own adjustments and comparisons. The need for ample disclosure is paramount. There is no rule against providing supplementary information on price-level adjustments, depreciation methods, or market values. A working rule should be: "When in doubt, disclose." **Disclosure is perhaps one of the most important of the underlying conventions.**

Materiality

Because accounting is a practical art, the practitioner often tempers accounting reports by applying the convention of materiality. Many outlays that theoretically should be recorded as assets are immediately written off as expenses because of their lack of significance. For example, many corporations have a rule that requires the immediate write-off to expense of all outlays under a specified minimum of, say, $100, regardless of the useful life of the asset acquired. In such a case, coat hangers may be acquired that may last indefinitely but that may never appear in the balance sheet as assets. The resulting $100 understatement of assets and stockholders' equity would be too trivial to worry about.

When is an item material? There probably will never be a universal clear-cut answer. What is trivial to General Motors may be material to Joe's Tavern. **An item is material if its omission or misstatement would tend to mislead the user of the financial statements under consideration.** A working rule is that an item is material if its proper accounting would probably affect the decision of a knowledgeable user. The continued emphasis in the stock market on earnings per share has lowered this threshold to 3 percent or lower in some cases. For example, if reported earnings per share would drop from $1.00 to $.97, the item in question is material. In sum, materiality is an important convention. But it is difficult to use anything other than prudent judgment to tell whether an item is material.

Cost-Benefit

Accounting systems vary in complexity from the minimum crude records kept to satisfy governmental authorities to the sophisticated budgeting and feedback schemes that are at the heart of management planning and controlling. As a system is changed, its potential benefits usually must exceed its additional costs. Often the benefits are difficult to measure, but this cost-benefit criterion at least implicitly underlies the decisions about the design of accounting systems. **The reluctance to adopt suggestions for new ways of measuring financial position and performance is frequently because of inertia, but it is often because the apparent benefits do not exceed the obvious costs of gathering and interpreting the information.**

SUMMARY

An underlying structure of concepts, techniques, and conventions provides a basis for accounting practice. The major ideas that guide accountants in their recording, classifying, and reporting are *realization, matching, stable dollar, entity, going concern, consistency, objectivity, conservatism, disclosure,*

549

materiality, and last but not least, the *cost-benefit approach* to designing accounting systems.

Accountants have precise meanings for their terms. Among the more important terms are *revenue, assets, expired costs, expense, income, accrual basis,* and *retained income.*

The word *value,* used alone, is vague; it should be used cautiously and always with a descriptive modifier, such as in the term *replacement value.* Accountants traditionally have measured assets in terms of their historical cost. Therefore, it is more precise to refer to the *costs* of plant, equipment, and inventories rather than to their *values.*

Finally, readers who have had no or little exposure to accounting should solve the Summary Problems for Your Review before proceeding to the next chapter. To read about basic accounting concepts is not enough. Work some problems too—the more, the better.

SUMMARY PROBLEM FOR YOUR REVIEW

The first problem appeared earlier in the chapter.

Problem Two

The following interpretations and remarks are sometimes encountered with regard to financial statements. Do you agree or disagree? Explain fully.

1. "If I purchase 100 shares of the outstanding common stock of General Motors Corporation (or Retailer No. 1), I invest my money directly in that corporation. General Motors must record that transaction."
2. "Sales shows the cash coming in from customers and the various expenses show the cash going out for goods and services. The difference is net income."
3. "Why can't that big steel company pay higher wages and dividends too? It can use its hundreds of millions of dollars of retained income to do so."
4. "The total stockholders' equity measures the amount that the shareholders would get today if the corporation were liquidated."
5. "Conservatism is desirable because investors will be misled if the financial report is too rosy."

Solution to Problem Two

1. Money is invested directly in a corporation only upon original issuance of the stock by the corporation. For example, 100,000 shares of stock may be issued at $80 per share, bringing in $8,000,000 to the corporation. This is a transaction between the corporation and the stockholders. It affects the corporate financial position:

Cash	$8,000,000	Stockholders' equity	$8,000,000

In turn, 100 shares of that stock may be sold by an original stock-holder (A) to another individual (B) for $130 per share. This is a private transaction; no funds come to the corporation. Of course, the corporation records the fact that 100 shares originally owned by A are now owned by B, but the corporate financial position is unchanged. Accounting focuses on the business entity; the private dealings of the owners have no direct effect on the financial position of the entity and hence are unrecorded except for detailed records of the owners' identities.

In sum, B invests his money in the shares of the corporation when he buys them from A. However, individual dealings in shares already issued and held by stockholders have no direct effect on the financial position of the corporation.

2. Cash receipts and disbursements are not the fundamental basis for the accounting recognition of revenues and expenses. Credit, not cash, lubri-cates the economy. Therefore, if services or goods have been rendered to a customer, a legal claim to cash in the form of a receivable is deemed sufficient justification for recognizing revenue; similarly, if services or goods have been used up, a legal obligation in the form of a payable is justifica-tion for recognizing expense.

This approach to the measurement of net income is known as the accrual method. Revenue is recognized as it is earned by (a) goods or services rendered and (b) an exchange in a market transaction. Expenses or losses are recognized when goods or services are used up in the obtaining of revenue (or when such goods or services cannot be justifiably carried forward as an asset because they have no potential future benefit). The expenses and losses are deducted from the revenue, and the result of this matching process is net income, the net increase in stockholders' equity from the conduct of operations.

Depreciation is probably the best example of an expense that does not entail a cash outlay at its time of recognition.

3. As the chapter indicated, retained income is not cash. It is a stockholders' equity account that represents the accumulated increase in ownership claims due to profitable operations. This claim or interest may be partially liquidated by the payment of cash dividends, but a growing company will reinvest cash in sustaining the added investments in receivables, inventories, plant, equipment, and other assets so necessary for expansion. As a result, the ownership claims become "permanent" in the sense that, as a practical matter, they will never be liquidated as long as the company remains a going concern.

This linking of retained income and cash is only one example of fallacious interpretation. As a general rule, there is no direct relationship between the individual items on the two sides of the balance sheet.

4. Stockholders' equity is a difference, the excess of assets over liabilities. If the assets were carried in the accounting records at their liquidating value today, and the liabilities were carried at the exact amounts needed for their extinguishment, the remark would be true. But such valuations would be

coincidental, because assets are customarily carried at historical cost expressed in an unchanging monetary unit. Intervening changes in markets and general price levels in inflationary times may mean that the assets are woefully understated. Investors may make a critical error if they think that balance sheets indicate current values.

5. Conservatism is an entrenched practice among accountants, and it is also favored by many managers and investors. However, it has some ramifications that should be remembered. Conservatism will result in fast write-offs of assets with consequent lower balance sheet values and lower net incomes. But later years may show higher net incomes because of the heavier write-offs in early years.

So being conservative has some long-run countereffects because, for any asset, early fast write-offs will lighten expenses in later years. This countervailing effect is especially noteworthy when a company is having trouble making any net income. In such cases, the tendency is to wipe the slate clean by massive write-offs that result in an enormous net loss for a particular year. Without such assets to burden future years, the prospects brighten for reporting future net profits rather than net losses.

Conservatism has another boomerang effect. The understatement of assets and net income may prompt anxious stockholders to sell their shares when they should hold them. A dreary picture may be every bit as misleading as a rosy one.

APPENDIX 17: USING LEDGER ACCOUNTS

This chapter offered some insight into the overall approach of the accountant to the measuring of economic activity. This appendix focuses on some of the main techniques that the accountant would use to analyze the illustration in the chapter.

The Account

Reconsider Exhibit 17-1. You can readily see that changes in the balance sheet equation happen several times daily. In large businesses, such as in a department store, hundreds of repetitive transactions occur hourly. *Ledger accounts* may be used to keep track of how these transactions affect each particular asset, liability, revenue, expense, and so forth. The accounts used here are simplified versions of those used in practice. They are called T-accounts because they take the form of the letter T. To begin, consider only the first three transactions in Exhibit 17-1:

(1) Initial investment, $100,000 cash
(2) Acquire inventory for cash, $75,000
(3) Acquire inventory on credit, $35,000

Each account summarizes the changes in a particular asset or equity. Each transaction is keyed in some way, such as by the numbering used in this illustration or by date or both. This keying facilitates the rechecking (auditing) process by facilitating the tracing of transactions to orginal sources. A

Cash				Accounts Payable			
Increases		Decreases		Decreases		Increases	
(1)	100,000	(2)	75,000			(3)	35,000
Bal.	25,000						

Inventory				Capital Stock			
Increases		Decreases		Decreases		Increases	
(2)	75,000					(1)	100,000
(3)	35,000						
Bal.	110,000						

balance is computed by deducting the smaller amount from the larger and placing the remainder on the side with the larger amount. These accounts can be kept in various forms, from fancy account paper with pen and ink to magnetic computer tape. Whatever their form, their objective is to keep an up-to-date summary of the changes in a specific asset or equity account.

A balance sheet may be prepared at any instant if desired. The necessary information is tabulated in the accounts. For example, the balance sheet after the first three transactions would contain:

Assets		Equities	
Cash	$ 25,000	Liabilities:	
Inventory	110,000	Accounts payable	$ 35,000
Total assets	$135,000	Stockholders' equity:	
		Capital stock	100,000
		Total equities	$135,000

General Ledger

Exhibit 17-7 is the *general ledger* of Retailer No. 1. The **general ledger** is defined as the group of accounts that supports the amounts shown in the major financial statements.[4] Exhibit 17-7 is merely a recasting of the facts that were analyzed in Exhibit 17-1. Study Exhibit 17-7 by comparing

---

[4] The general ledger is usually supported by various *subsidiary ledgers,* which provide details for several accounts in the general ledger. For instance, an accounts receivable subsidiary ledger would contain a separate account for each credit customer. The accounts receivable balance that appears in the Sears balance sheet is in a single account in the Sears general ledger. However, that lone balance is buttressed by detailed individual accounts receivable with millions of credit customers. You can readily visualize how some accounts in general ledgers might have subsidiary ledgers supported by subsubsidiary ledgers, and so on. Thus, a subsidiary accounts receivable ledger might be subdivided alphabetically into Customers A–D, E–H, and so forth.

EXHIBIT 17-7

General Ledger of RETAILER NO. 1

1. Initial investment
2. Acquire inventory for cash
3. Acquire inventory on credit

4a. Sales on credit
4b. Cost of inventory sold
5. Collect from customers

6. Pay accounts of suppliers
7a. Pay rent in advance
7b. Recognize expiration of rental services

ASSETS (INCREASES ON LEFT, DECREASES ON RIGHT)

EQUITIES (DECREASES ON LEFT, INCREASES ON RIGHT)

Cash

(1)	100,000	(2)	75,000
(5)	30,000	(6)	10,000
		(7a)	3,000
3/31 Bal.	42,000		

Accounts Receivable

(4a)	120,000	(5)	30,000

Inventory

(2)	75,000	(4b)	100,000
(3)	35,000		
3/31 Bal.	10,000		

Prepaid Rent

(7a)	3,000	(7b)	1,000

Accounts Payable

(6)	10,000	(3)	35,000

Capital Stock

	(1)	100,000

Retained Income

	3/31 Bal.	19,000 *

EXPENSE AND REVENUE ACCOUNTS

Cost of Goods Sold

(4b)	100,000

Sales

	(4a)	120,000

Rent Expense

(7b)	1,000

*The details of the revenue and expense accounts appear in the income statement. Their net effect is then transferred to a single account, Retained Income, in the balance sheet.
Note: An ending balance should be drawn for each account, but all balances are not shown here because some can be computed easily by inspection.

its analysis of each transaction against its corresponding analysis in Exhibit 17-1.

Debits and Credits

The balance sheet equation has often been mentioned in this chapter. Recall:

$$A = L + \text{Capital stock} \tag{1}$$

$$A = L + \text{Capital stock} + \text{Retained income} \tag{2}$$

$$A = L + \text{Capital stock} + \text{Revenue} - \text{Expense} \tag{3}$$

The accountant often talks about his entries in a technical way:

Transposing, $A + \text{Expenses} = L + \text{Capital stock} + \text{Revenue}$ (4)

Finally, $\text{Left} = \text{Right}$ (5)

$$\text{Debit} = \text{Credit}$$

Debit means one thing and one thing only—"left" (not "bad," "something coming," etc.). *Credit* means one thing and one thing only—"right" (not "good," "something owed," etc.). The word *charge* is often used instead of *debit*, but no single word is used as a synonym for *credit*.

For example, if you asked an accountant what entry to make for Transaction 4*b*, his answer would be: "I would debit (or charge) Cost of Goods Sold for $100,000; and I would credit Inventory for $100,000." Note that the total dollar amount of the debits (entries on the left side of the account(s) affected) will *always* equal the total dollar amount of the credits (entries on the right side of the account(s) affected) because the whole accounting system is based on an equation. The symmetry and power of this analytical debit-credit technique is indeed impressive.

Assets are traditionally carried as left-hand balances. Why do assets and expenses both carry debit balances? They carry left-hand balances for different reasons. *Expenses* are temporary stockholders' equity accounts. Decreases in stockholders' equity are entered on the left side of the accounts because they offset the normal (i.e., right-hand) stockholders' equity balances. Because expenses decrease stockholders' equity, they are carried as left-hand balances.

ASSIGNMENT MATERIAL

Fundamental Assignment Material

17-1. **Analysis of transactions and preparation of financial statements.** The Retailer No. 1 transactions for April were analyzed in Problem One of the Summary

Problems for Your Review. The balance sheet as of April 30 is shown in Exhibit 17-3. The following is a summary of transactions that occurred during May:

1. Collections of accounts receivable, $80,000.

2. Acquisitions of inventory on open account, $90,000.

3. Payments of accounts payable, $84,000.

4. Merchandise carried in inventory at a cost of $78,000 was sold on open account for $97,000.

5. In addition to the Transaction 4, Retailer No. 1 delivered inventory that cost $2,000 to customers who had paid $3,000 in advance. This represented the complete fulfillment of these customer orders.

6. Adjustment for rent expense for May.

7. Paid $4,000 cash on May 31 for a fire and burglary insurance policy covering the next twelve months.

Before analyzing Transactions 8 through 10, review entries 6 through 8 in Exhibit 17-2, page 536.

8. Wages *incurred* in May were $10,000. The acquisition of these employee services was recognized through the asset Unexpired Wages Services and the liability Accrued Wages Payable.

9. Wages *paid* on four Fridays in May totaled $9,000. The payments of these wages was recognized by decreasing Accrued Wages Payable and by decreasing Cash.

10. All Unexpired Wages Services acquired in Transaction 8 were deemed to have no benefit beyond May, so the asset is written off and Wages Expense is recognized.

11. On May 31, Retailer No. 1 received $2,000 in advance as a year's rental payment from a costume jewelry vendor who will occupy some space within the store.

12. On May 31, cash dividends of $4,000 were declared and disbursed to stockholders.

Required

1. Using the accrual basis of accounting, prepare an analysis of May transactions, employing the equation approach demonstrated in Exhibit 17-2. Place your analysis sideways. To save space, make all entries in thousands of dollars. Allow room for new accounts.

2. Prepare a balance sheet as of May 31, 19x1, and an income statement and a statement of retained income for May.

3. Using the cash basis of accounting, prepare an income statement for May. Compare the net income with that computed in Requirement 2. Which net income figure do you prefer as a measure of the economic performance for May? Why?

4. Examine the balance sheet. Based on the limited information available what advice would you, as a consultant, be inclined to give the manager? What additional information would you seek before giving your advice with more assurance?

17-2. Describe the usual "operating cycle" of a business.

17-3. Give five examples of accounting entities.

17-4. Define *going concern.*

17-5. What is the major criticism of the dollar as the principal accounting measure?

17-6. Define *consistency.*

17-7. What is a major exception to the idea that an exchange is needed to justify the realization of revenue?

17-8. What does the accountant mean by *objectivity?*

17-9. Define *conservatism.*

17-10. How important is disclosure in relation to other fundamental accounting concepts?

17-11. Criticize: "Assets are things of value owned by the entity."

17-12. Criticize: "Net income is the difference in the ownership capital account balances at two points in time."

17-13. Distinguish between the accrual basis and the cash basis.

17-14. How do adjusting entries differ from routine entries?

17-15. Why is it better to refer to the *costs,* rather than *values,* of assets such as plant or inventories?

17-16. Give at least two synonymous terms for each of the following: *balance sheet; income statement; assets.*

17-17. Give at least three other terms for *retained earnings.*

17-18. Criticize: "As a stockholder, I have a right to more dividends. You have millions stashed away in retained earnings. It's about time that you let the true owners get their hands on that pot of gold."

17-19. Criticize: "Dividends are distributions of profits."

17-20. Explain why advertising should be viewed as an asset upon acquisition.

17-21. What is the role of economic feasibility in the development of accounting principles?

17-22. If gross profit is 60 percent, express the relationship of cost of goods sold to gross profit in percentage terms.

17-23. Balance sheet effects. The Wells Fargo Bank showed the following items (among others) on its balance sheet at December 31, 19x1:

Cash	$ 947,000,000
Total deposits	$6,383,000,000

Required

1. Suppose that you made a deposit of $1,000 in the Wells Fargo Bank. How would the bank's assets and equities be affected? How would your personal assets and equities be affected? Be specific.

2. Suppose that the bank makes a $1,000 loan to a local merchant. What would be the effects on the bank's assets and equities immediately after the loan is made? Be specific.

3. Suppose that you borrowed $10,000 from the Wells Fargo Bank on a personal loan. How would such a transaction affect your personal assets and equities?

17-24. Accrual basis for banks and physicians. Prepare balance sheets on the accrual basis for the following:

1. A bank has $10,000,000 in deposits, $2,000,000 in cash, $11,000,000 in loans and other investments, $5,000,000 in other assets, and miscellaneous liabilities of $3,000,000.

2. A physician has business cash of $10,000, personal artwork of $2000, miscellaneous payables of $1,000, uncollected amounts from patients of $20,000, equipment and furniture at a net depreciated cost of $40,000. During the final two days of December, she received advance payments of $2,000 from a few patients who owed her nothing but did anticipate receiving future services. The physician also had $1,000 in a personal checking account, a home that cost $100,000 and had a current market value of $125,000, and marketable securities that cost $80,000 and had a current market value of $90,000. There was a home mortgage of $70,000.

17-25. Find unknowns. The following data pertain to the Bunce Corporation. Total assets at January 1, 19x1, were $100,000; at December 31, 19x1, $120,000. During 19x1, sales were $200,000, cash dividends were $4,000, and operating expenses (exclusive of cost of goods sold) were $50,000. Total liabilities at December 31, 19x1, were $55,000; at January 1, 19x1, $40,000.

Required

(These need not be computed in any particular order.)

1. Net income for 19x1
2. Cost of goods sold for 19x1
3. Stockholders' equity, January 1, 19x1.

17-26. Conservatism and consistency. The new president and the controller of a chain of fast-food restaurants are having a dispute regarding the first-year operating losses of new restaurants. The president favors amortization of such losses over a three-year period, but the controller does not favor regarding such losses as an asset. The president maintains that amortization is industry practice and that such accounting would be conservative and consistent with industry practice. Evaluate the president's use of the words *conservative* and *consistent* from the standpoint of accounting terminology. What accounting treatment do you recommend? Why?

17-27. Revenue realization. Calhoun Company contracted to build a huge shopping center for the Zenith Realty Company. The contract price was $80 million. The top management estimated that the total cost of the project to Calhoun would be $72 million. The contract provided that Calhoun be paid on a percentage-of-completion basis. An independent architect determined when four equal payments would be made in proportion to an appropriate percentage of completion—except that the final payment would be made 90 days after occupancy.

The construction was completed in approximately two years. Payments were authorized and paid as indicated:

November 20, 19x0	Construction begins
May 12, 19x1	25% payment made
November 29, 19x1	25% payment made
June 4, 19x2	25% payment made
November 14, 19x2	Construction completed. Occupancy begins
February 14, 19x3	Final 25% payment made

Calhoun Company is on a calendar-year reporting basis:

Required

1. In general, accountants recognize revenue when a sale is made; that is, when goods or services are delivered to a customer. When would the $80 million in revenue be realized under this rule? Suppose that the actual costs were $74 million. When would net income be realized? Explain.

2. When should revenue be realized under a percentage-of-completion basis? Net income? Explain. Comment on the results as compared with those in Requirement 1.

3. A small minority of accountants feel that no revenue or net income should be realized until all cash is collected. How would this affect reported net income in the four calendar years?

17-28. Effects of error. The bookkeeper of a certain firm, the Dark Co., included the cost of a new motor truck, purchased on December 30 for $5,000 to be paid in January, as an operating expense instead of as an addition to the proper asset account. What was the effect of this error ("no effect," "overstated," or "understated"—use symbols *n*, *o*, or *u*, respectively) on:

1. Operating expenses for the year ended December 31.   _____

2. Net profit from operations for the year.   _____

3. Retained earnings as of the close of business on December 31.   _____

4. Total liabilities as of December 31.   _____

5. Total assets as of December 31.   _____

17-29. Conversion from accrual to cash basis. From the following data, calculate the cash collected for subscriptions for the month of December. The Subscription Revenue Earned balance that was reported in the income statement for the month of December was $200,000. These data pertain to a magazine company's operations:

	Dec. 1	Dec. 31
Deferred subscription revenue	$100,000	$170,000
Accrued subscriptions receivable	9,000	7,000

17-30. Balance sheet equation; solving for unknowns. Compute the unknowns (X, Y, and Z) in each of the individual cases, Columns a through g.

Given	a	b	c	d	e	f	g
Assets at beginning of period		$10,000				Z	$ 8,200
Assets at end of period		11,000					9,600
Liabilities at beginning of period		6,000				$12,000	4,000
Liabilities at end of period		Y					6,000
Stockholders' equity at beginning of period	$5,000						X
Stockholders' equity at end of period	X	5,000				10,000	
Sales			$15,000		X	14,000	20,000
Inventory at beginning of period			6,000	$ 8,000		Y	
Inventory at end of period			7,000	6,000		7,000	
Purchases			10,000	10,000		6,000	
Gross profit			Y		2,000	6,000	
Cost of goods sold			X	X	4,500	X	Z
Other expenses			4,000			4,000	5,000
Net profit	3,000	X	Z				Y
Dividends	1,000					1,500	400
Additional investments						5,000	

17-31. Measuring income for tax and other purposes. The following are the summarized transactions of Dr. Cristina Faragher, a dentist, for 19x7, her first year in practice:

1. Acquired equipment and furniture for $50,000. Its expected useful life is five years. Straight-line depreciation will be used.

2. Fees collected, $80,000. These fees included $2,000 paid in advance by some patients on December 31, 19x7.

3. Rent is paid at the rate of $500 monthly, payable on the twenty-fifth of each month for the following month. Total disbursements during 19x7 for rent were $6,500.

4. Fees billed but uncollected, December 31, 19x7, $15,000.

5. Utilities expense paid in cash, $600. Additional utility bills unpaid at December 31, 19x7, $100.

6. Salaries expense of dental assistant and secretary, $16,000 paid in cash. In addition, $1,000 was earned but unpaid on December 31, 19x7.

Dr. Faragher may elect either the cash basis or accrual basis of measuring income for income tax purposes, provided that she uses it consistently in subsequent years. Under either alternative, the original cost of the equipment and furniture must be written off over its five-year useful life rather than being regarded as a lump-sum expense in the first year.

Required

1. Prepare a comparative income statement on both the cash and accrual bases, using one column for each basis.

2. Which basis do you prefer as a measure of Dr. Faragher's performance? Why? What is the justification for the government allowing the use of the cash basis?

17-32. Transactions and financial statements. Sincere Company was formed on March 1, 19x1, to sell used cars. Its initial capital was cash of $20,000. During March, the corporation had a total of only three transactions: (1) the initial investment was $20,000; (2) three cars were acquired as inventory for $2,000 cash; and (3) seven more cars were acquired for $8,000 ($3,000 in cash plus $5,000 on open account to be paid in 30 days).

Required

A. Prepare an analysis of March transactions. Use the accrual basis of accounting and the equation approach demonstrated in Exhibit 17-2. Place your analysis sideways. To save space, use abbreviated headings. Allow room for new accounts; this analysis will be continued in April.

B. Prepare a balance sheet as of March 31.

C. The following is a summary of transactions for April. Continue the analysis that you began in Requirement A.

    1, 2, and 3. See the transactions in Requirement A.

    4. The Sincere Company sold six cars during April for $9,000 including $5,000 on open accounts receivable. These cars were carried in inventory at a cost of $6,000. The two phases of this summary transaction are 4a, the inflow of assets, which increased stockholders' equity by $9,000 (revenue); and 4b, the outflow of assets, which decreased stockholders' equity by $6,000 (expense). The latter method of accounting for inventory is called the **perpetual method,**

whereby the inventory account is immediately reduced as sales are made.

5a. Effective April 1, the company rented a building on a quarter-to-quarter basis. Rent for April and May, totaling $2,000, was paid in cash on April 1. The payment is to acquire rental services. At April 1, the $2,000 measures the future benefit from those services and the asset Prepaid Rent is created.

5b. This benefit expires as time elapses. Therefore, at April 30, the accountant should recognize that the services of the asset have been utilized to the extent of $1,000, one month's rent. Entry 5b should show how the asset expires with a corresponding negative effect on stockholders' equity (rent expense).

6a. The company bought some furniture and fixtures on April 1 for $2,600 cash plus a three-month promissory note payable of $1,000 with interest payable at an annual rate of 6 percent. Note that the total of the cash and the note is the measure of the asset, not just the cash payment at the date of acquisition.

6b-1. The furniture and fixtures are expected to be useful for ten years. Part of the original cost should be allocated to each month's operations as depreciation expense. Because no scrap value is expected, the entire $3,600 cost is spread over ten years, or 120 months, at a rate of $3,600 ÷ 120, or $30 monthly.

6b-2. The company has had the service benefit of a $1,000 loan for one month. The creditor is now owed $\frac{1}{12}$ × .06 × $1,000, or $5, for these interest services. The amount is insignificant, but the idea is important. The acquisition of these services is recorded as an asset, Unexpired Interest, or Unexpired Interest Services, with a corresponding increase in a liability Accrued Interest Payable.

6b-3. The interest services have expired because the company has had the benefit of a $1,000 loan for one month. Therefore, the asset is immediately written off and Interest Expense is recognized.

7a. Advertising services of $300 for the month are paid in cash. The acquisition is recognized by the asset Unexpired Advertising, or Unexpired Advertising Services.

7b. The benefits from the advertising have expired by the end of the month, so the asset is written off and Advertising Expense is recognized.

8a. Salaries and commissions services of $1,100 were *incurred* in April. The acquisition of these employee services is recognized by the asset Unexpired Salaries and Commissions Services and the liability Accrued Salaries and Commissions Payable.

8b. Salaries and commissions *paid* on four Thursdays in April totaled $900. The payments are recognized by decreasing Accrued Salaries and Commissions Payable and decreasing Cash.

8c. All Unexpired Salaries and Commissions Services acquired in 8a were deemed to have no benefit beyond April, so the asset is written off and Salaries and Commission Expense is recognized.

9a. On April 15, the company subleased two of its offices for two months at $100 per month. The first month's rent was received in cash. Note that this is a payment in advance of services rendered. It is often called **deferred income**; a more accurate description is **unearned revenue** or **deferred revenue**. It is a liability, a claim by an outside party, until the service is rendered.

9b. As the service is rendered, revenue is recognized by decreasing the liability, Deferred Rent Revenue, and recognizing Rent Revenue (often called **Rent Income**) in the amount of $50, half of the rent received on April 15.

D. Prepare an income statement for April and a balance sheet as of April 30.

17-33. Fundamental transaction analysis and preparation of statements. Three women who were college classmates have decided to pool a variety of work experiences by opening a women's clothing store. The business has been incorporated as Sartorial Choice, Inc. The following transactions occurred during April:

1. On April 1, 19x1, each woman invested $9,000 in cash in exchange for 1,000 shares of stock each.

2. The corporation quickly acquired $50,000 in inventory, half of which had to be paid for in cash. The other half was acquired on open accounts which were payable after thirty days.

3. A store was rented for $500 monthly. A lease was signed for one year on April 1. The first two months' rents were paid in advance. Other payments were to be made on the second of each month.

4. Advertising during April was purchased on open account for $3,000 from a newspaper owned by one of the stockholders. Additional advertising of $6,000 was acquired for cash.

5. Sales were $65,000. The average markup above the cost of the merchandise was two-thirds of cost. Eighty percent of the sales were on open account.

6. Wages and salaries incurred in April amounted to $11,000, of which $5,000 was paid.

7. Miscellaneous services paid for in cash were $1,410.

8. On April 1, fixtures and equipment were purchased for $6,000 with a down payment of $1,000 plus a $5,000 note payable in one year. The annual interest rate was 9.6 percent, payable when the note matures; recognize the interest effects for April. The estimated useful life of the fixed assets was ten years. Depreciation is taken on a straight-line basis.

9. Cash dividends of $300 were declared and disbursed to stockholders on April 29.

1. Using the accrual basis of accounting, prepare an analysis of transactions, employing the equation approach demonstrated in Exhibit 17-2. Place your analysis sideways; to save space, use abbreviated headings.

2. Prepare a balance sheet and income statement. Also prepare a statement of retained income.

3. What advice would you give the owners based on the information compiled in the financial statements?

17-34. **Accrual basis of accounting.** Christiane Jose runs a small consulting-engineering firm that specializes in designing and overseeing the installation of environmental-control systems. However, even though she is the president, she has had no formal training in management. She has been in business one year and has prepared the following income statement for her fiscal year ended June 30, 19x4:

JOSE CONSULTING ENGINEERS, INC.
Income Statement
for the Year Ended June 30, 19x4

Fees collected in cash		$500,000
Expenses paid in cash except for depreciation:		
Rent	$ 12,500	
Utilities	10,000	
Wages	200,000	
President's salary	46,000	
Office supplies	14,000	
Travel	30,000	
Miscellaneous	80,000	
Depreciation	10,000	402,500
Operating income		$ 97,500

Jose realized that the entire $50,000 cost of the equipment acquired on July 1, 19x3, should not be an expense of one year. She predicted a useful life of five years and deducted $10,000 as depreciation for the first year.

Jose is thinking about future needs for her expanding business. For example, although she now uses rented space in an office building, she is considering buying a small building. She showed her income statement to a local banker, who reacted: "Christiane, this statement may suffice for filing income tax forms, but the bank will not consider any long-term financing until it receives a balance sheet and income statement prepared on the accrual basis of accounting. Moreover, the statements must be subjected to an audit by an independent certified public accountant."

As a CPA, you are asked to audit her records and fulfill the bank's request. The following data are gathered:

1. On July 1, 19x3, Jose invested $25,000 cash, and two friends each invested $2,000 cash in the firm in return for capital stock.

2. Jose acquired $50,000 of equipment on July 1, 19x3. A down payment of $20,000 cash was made. A $30,000 two-year note bearing an annual interest rate of 15 percent was signed. Principal plus interest were both payable at maturity.

3. On June 30, 19x4, clients owed Jose $95,000 on open accounts.

4. Salaries are paid on the fifteenth of every month. As business expanded throughout the fiscal year, additional employees were added. The total payroll paid on June 15, 19x4, including the president's monthly salary of $4,000, was $40,000.

5. Rent was paid in advance on the fifteenth of every month. An initial payment of $1,500 covered July 1, 19x3–August 15, 19x4. Payments of $1,000 monthly were paid beginning August 15, 19x3.

6. Office supplies on hand on June 30, 19x4, were $5,000.

7. On April 1, 19x4, a local oil refinery gave Jose a retainer fee of $60,000 cash in exchange for twelve months of consulting services beginning at that date.

Required

1. Using the accrual basis of accounting, prepare an income statement for the fiscal year. Submit supporting computations properly labeled.

2. Prepare a balance sheet, dated June 30, 19x4. Assume that the cash balance is $116,500.

17-35. **Reconstruct the cash account in Assignment 17-34.** Show a summary analysis of the cash flow in 17-34 that proves that the ending cash balance is indeed $116,500. Label your analysis fully.

17-36. **The case of the president's wealth.** From the *Chicago Tribune*, August 20, 1964:

Accountants acting on President Johnson's orders today reported his family wealth totaled $3,484,098.

The statement of capital, arrived at through conservative procedures of evaluation, contrasted with a recent estimate published by *Life* magazine, which put the total at 14 million dollars.

The family fortune, which is held in trust while the Johnsons are in the White House, was set forth in terms of book values. The figures represent original cost rather than current market values on what the holdings would be worth if sold now.

Announced by the White House press office, but turned over to reporters by a national accounting firm at their Washington branch office, the financial statement apparently was intended to still a flow of quasi-official and unofficial estimates of the Johnson fortune. . . .

Assets

Cash	$ 132,547
Bonds	398,540
Interest in Texas Broadcasting Corp.	2,543,838
Ranch properties and other real estate	525,791
Other assets, including insurance policies	82,054
Total assets	$3,682,770

Liabilities

Note payable on real estate holding, 5 percent due 1971	$ 150,000
Accounts payable, accrued interest, and income taxes	48,672
Total liabilities	$ 198,672
Capital	$3,484,098

The report apportions the capital among the family, with $378,081 credited to the President; $2,126,298 to his wife Claudia T., who uses the name Lady Bird; $490,141 to their daughter Lynda Bird; and $489,578 to their daughter Luci Baines.

The statement said the family holdings—under the names of the President, his wife, and his two daughters, Lynda Bird and Luci Baines—had increased from $737,730 on January 1, 1954, a year after Johnson became Democratic leader of the Senate, to $3,484,098 on July 31 this year, a gain of $2,746,368. . . .

A covering letter addressed to Johnson said the statement was made "in conformity with generally accepted accounting principles applied on a consistent basis."

By far the largest part of the fortune was listed as the Johnsons' interest in the Texas Broadcasting Corporation, carried on the books as worth $2,543,838.

The accountants stated that this valuation was arrived at on the basis of the cost of the stock when the Johnsons bought control of the debt-ridden radio station between 1943 and 1947, plus accumulated earnings ploughed back as equity, less 25 percent capital gains tax.

Editorial, *Chicago Tribune,* August 22, 1964:

> An accounting firm acting on Mr. Johnson's instructions and employing what it termed "generally accepted auditing standards" has released a statement putting the current worth of the Lyndon Johnson family at a little less than $3\frac{1}{2}$ million dollars. . . .
>
> Dean Burch, chairman of the Republican National Committee, has remarked that the method used to list the Johnson assets was comparable to placing the value of Manhattan Island at $24, the price at which it was purchased from the Indians. The Johnson accounting firm conceded that its report was "not intended to indicate the values that might be realized if the investment were sold."
>
> In fact, it would be interesting to observe the response of the Johnson family if a syndicate of investors were to offer to take Texas Broadcasting off the family's hands at double the publicly reported worth of the operation. . . .

Evaluate the criticisms, making special reference to fundamental accounting concepts or "principles."

ASSIGNMENT MATERIAL FOR APPENDIX

Fundamental Assignment Material

17-37. Using T-accounts. Refer to Assignment 17-1. Make entries for May in T-accounts. Key your entries and check to see that the ending balances agree with the financial statements.

17-38. Debits and credits. Determine for the following transactions whether the account *named in parentheses* is to be debited or credited.

1. Sold merchandise (Merchandise Inventory), $1,000.
2. Paid Johnson Associates $3,000 owed them (Accounts Payable).
3. Bought merchandise on account (Merchandise Inventory), $2,000.
4. Received cash from customers on accounts due (Accounts Receivable), $1,000.
5. Bought merchandise on open account (Accounts Payable), $5,000.
6. Borrowed money from a bank (Notes Payable), $10,000.

17-39. True or false. Use *T* or *F* to indicate whether each of the following statements is true or false.

1. Debit entries must always be recorded on the left.
2. Decreases in accounts must be shown on the debit side.
3. The bank balance is the best evidence of stockholders' equity.
4. Both increases in liabilities and decreases in assets should be entered on the right.
5. From a single balance sheet you can find stockholders' equity for a period of time but not for a specific day.
6. Money borrowed from the bank should be credited to Cash and debited to Notes Payable.
7. Purchase of inventory on account should be credited to Inventory and debited to Accounts Payable.
8. It is not possible to determine change in the condition of a business from a single balance sheet.
9. Decreases in liability accounts should be recorded on the right.
10. Increases in asset accounts must always be entered on the left.
11. Increases in stockholders' equity always should be entered as credits.
12. Equipment purchases for cash should be debited to Equipment and credited to Cash.
13. Asset credits should be on the right and liability credits on the left.
14. Payments on mortgages should be debited to Cash and credited to Mortgages Payable.
15. Retained Earnings should be accounted for as a current asset item.
16. Cash should be classified as a stockholders' equity item.
17. Machinery used in the business should be recorded as a fixed asset item.

17-40. Using T-accounts. Refer to Problem One of the Summary Problems for Your Review. The transactions are analyzed in Exhibit 17-2. Make entries in

T-accounts and check to see that the ending balances agree with the financial statements in Exhibits 17-3, 17-4, and 17-5.

17-41. T-accounts. Refer to Assignment 17-32. Use T-accounts to present an analysis of April transactions. Key your entries and check to see that the ending balances agree with the financial statements.

17-42. T-accounts. Refer to Assignment 17-33. Use T-accounts to present an analysis of April transactions. Key your entries and check to see that the ending balances agree with the financial statements.

CHAPTER 18

Understanding Corporate Annual Reports— Part One

Accounting has often been called the language of business. But it is a language with a special vocabulary aimed at conveying the financial story of organizations. To understand corporate annual reports, a reader must learn at least the fundamentals of the language. This chapter presents the basic meanings of the terms and relationships used in the financial statements found in annual reports.

Accounting is commonly misunderstood as being a precise discipline that produces exact measurements of a company's financial position and performance. As a result, many individuals regard accountants as little more than mechanical tabulators who grind out financial reports after processing an imposing amount of detail in accordance with stringent predetermined rules. Although accountants take methodical steps with masses of data, their rules of measurement allow much room for judgment. Managers and accountants who exercise this judgment have more influence on financial reporting than is commonly believed.

This chapter extends the discussion of the financial statements in the preceding chapter. It also introduces the Statement of Changes in Financial Position. Additional coverage (including investments in subsidiaries, consolidated statements, deferred income taxes, and accounting for inflation) will be found in the final two chapters of this book.

CLASSIFIED BALANCE SHEET

Current Assets

Assets are usually grouped in the manner shown in Exhibit 18-1. The *current assets* **are cash plus assets that are reasonably expected to be converted to cash or sold or consumed during the normal operating cycle.** They are the assets directly involved in the operating cycle, including cash; temporary investments in marketable securities; receivables of nearly all kinds, including installment accounts and notes receivable if they conform to normal industry practice and terms; inventories; and prepaid expenses.

Several operating cycles may occur during one year. But some businesses need more than one year to complete a single cycle. The distillery, tobacco, and lumber industries are examples. Inventories in such industries are nevertheless regarded as current assets. Similarly, installment accounts and notes receivable are typically classified as current assets even though they will not be fully collected within one year.

Some comments on specific kinds of current assets follow:

Cash consists of bank deposits in checking accounts plus money on hand. Incidentally, visualize how a deposit would be accounted for by a bank. Its cash will increase and its liabilities increase in the form of "Deposits," which are really "Deposits Payable."

Marketable securities is a misnomer, although the expression is encountered frequently. Strictly speaking, marketable securities may be held for either a short-term or a long-term purpose. A better expression would be temporary or short-term investments (as distinguished from long-term investments in capital stock or bonds of other companies, which are not current assets). They represent an investment of excess cash not needed immediately. The idea is to get earnings on otherwise idle cash. The money is typically invested in securities that are highly liquid (easily convertible into cash) and that have relatively stable prices, such as short-term notes or government bonds. These securities are usually shown at cost or market price, whichever is lower. The market price is disclosed parenthetically if it is above cost.

Accounts receivable is the total amount owed to the company by its customers. Because some accounts will ultimately be uncollectible, the total is reduced by an allowance or provision for doubtful accounts (that is, possible "bad debts" arising from credit extended to customers who do not pay). The difference represents the net amount that probably will be collected.

Inventories consist of merchandise, finished products of manufacturers, goods in the process of being manufactured, and raw materials. These are frequently carried at cost or market (defined as replacement cost), whichever is lower. Cost of manufactured products normally is composed of raw

570

EXHIBIT 18-1

THE GREEN CO.

Balance Sheet
(In thousands of dollars)

ASSETS	DECEMBER 31 19x1	DECEMBER 31 19x0
Current assets:		
Cash	$ 2,600	$ 2,200
Temporary investments in marketable securities	600	600
Receivables, net of allowance for doubtful accounts	5,300	5,100
Inventories at cost	14,600	14,400
Prepaid expenses	600	600
Total current assets	$23,700	$22,900
Plant assets:		
Land	$ 300	$ 300
Buildings and equipment, net of accumulated depreciation	7,000	5,800
Total plant assets	$ 7,300	$ 6,100
Total assets	$31,000	$29,000

EQUITIES		
Current liabilities:		
Notes payable	$ 3,900	$ 2,800
Accounts payable	3,200	2,400
Accrued expenses payable	1,600	1,700
Accrued income taxes payable	500	400
Total current liabilities	$ 9,200	$ 7,300
5% Mortgage bonds payable	$16,000	$16,000
Total liabilities	$25,200	$23,300
Stockholders' equity:		
Preferred stock, 6%, $100 par value, $100 liquidating value	$ 1,600	$ 1,600
Common stock, $10 par value	2,000	2,000
Additional paid-in capital	1,000	1,000
Retained earnings	1,200	1,100
Total stockholders' equity	$ 5,800	$ 5,700
Total equities	$31,000	$29,000

material plus the costs of its conversion (direct labor and manufacturing overhead) into a finished product.

Once the total cost of goods purchased or produced by a company is measured, how should it be allocated between the goods sold (an expense) and goods still on hand (an asset)? This is easy to do if the products are readily identifiable, like the cars of an automobile dealer or the expensive merchandise of a jewelry store. But it is infeasible to have an elaborate identification system for goods that are purchased and sold in vast numbers and variety. Therefore, some version of average cost is often used.[1]

Prepaid expenses are usually unimportant in relation to other assets. They are short-term prepayments or advance payments to suppliers. Examples are short-term prepaid expenses such as rent, operating supplies, and insurance that will be used up within the current operating cycle. They belong in current assets, because if they were not present more cash would be needed to conduct current operations.[2]

Plant Assets

Plant assets are sometimes called **fixed assets** or **property, plant, and equipment.** Because they are physical items that can be seen and touched, they are often called **tangible assets.**

Land is typically accounted for as a separate item and is carried indefinitely at its original cost.

Plant and equipment are initially recorded at cost: the invoice amount, plus freight and installation, less cash discounts. The major difficulties of measurement center about the choice of a pattern of depreciation—that is, the allocation of the original cost to the particular periods or products that benefit from the utilization of the assets.

Accountants often stress that depreciation is a process of *allocation of the original cost* of acquisition; it is not a process of valuation in the ordinary sense of the term. The usual balance sheet presentation does **not** show replacement cost, resale value, or the price changes since acquisition.

The amount of original cost to be allocated over the total useful life of the asset as depreciation is the difference between the total acquisition cost and the estimated terminal disposal value. The depreciation allocation to each year may be made on the basis of time or service. The estimate of useful life, which is an important factor in determining the yearly allocation of depreciation, is influenced by estimates of physical wear and tear, technological change, and economic obsolescence.

For example, suppose that equipment with an estimated useful life of four years is acquired for $41,000. Its estimated scrap value is $1,000. Exhibit 18-2 shows how the asset would be displayed in the balance sheet if a

---

[1] First-in, first-out and last-in, first-out methods are discussed in Chapter 20. Accounting for manufacturing costs is discussed in Chapters 14 and 15. Incidentally, recent progress in data-processing capabilities at lower and lower costs has made specific identification more and more economical.

[2] Sometimes prepaid expenses are lumped with *deferred charges* as a single amount, *prepaid expenses and deferred charges,* that appears at the bottom of the current asset classification or at the bottom of all the assets as an "other asset." Deferred charges are like prepaid expenses, but they have longer-term benefits. For example, the costs of relocating a mass of employees to a different geographical area or the costs of rearranging an assembly line may be carried forward as deferred charges and written off as expense over a three- to five-year period.

EXHIBIT 18-2
Straight-Line Depreciation*

	BALANCES AT END OF YEAR			
	1	2	3	4
Plant and equipment (at original acquisition cost)	$41,000	$41,000	$41,000	$41,000
Less: Accumulated depreciation (the portion of original cost that has already been charged to operations as expense)	10,000	20,000	30,000	40,000
Net book value (the portion of original cost that will be charged to future operations as expense)	$31,000	$21,000	$11,000	$ 1,000

*Other patterns of depreciation are discussed later in this chapter.

straight-line method of depreciation were used. The annual depreciation expense that would appear on the income statement would be:

$$\frac{\text{Original cost} - \text{Estimated disposal value}}{\text{Years of useful life}}$$

or

$$\frac{\$41,000 - \$1,000}{4} = \$10,000 \text{ per year}$$

An understanding of how the accountant reports plant assets and depreciation will highlight the limitations of financial statements. Professor William A. Paton, a leading scholar in accounting for more than fifty years, once compared accounting for fixed assets with a boy's acquisition of a jelly-filled doughnut (the original cost, $41,000). The boy is so eager to taste the jelly that he licks it and creates a hole in the center of the doughnut (the accumulated depreciation of $10,000 at the end of Year 1). He continues his attack on the doughnut, and the hole enlarges. The hole is the accumulated depreciation. The net book value or carrying amount of the asset diminishes as the hole gradually becomes larger throughout the useful life of the doughnut. At the end of the useful life, the book value consists of the original doughnut ($41,000) less its gaping hole ($40,000), leaving a crumbly $1,000.

If you remember that accumulated depreciation is like a hole in a doughnut, you will be less likely to fall into the trap of those who think that accumulated depreciation is a sum of cash being accumulated for the replacement of plant assets. Accumulated depreciation is not cash; if specific cash is being accumulated for the replacement of assets, such cash will be an asset specifically labeled as a cash fund for replacement and expansion or a fund of marketable securities for replacement and expansion. Such funds are rare, because most companies can earn better returns by investing any available cash in ordinary operations rather than in special funds. Companies will use or acquire cash for the replacement and expansion of plant assets as specific needs arise.

Leasehold improvements are not illustrated in the Exhibit 18-1 balance sheet, but they are often grouped with plant assets. Such improvements may be made by a lessee (tenant) who invests in painting, decorating, fixtures, and air conditioning equipment that cannot be removed from the premises when a lease expires. The costs of leasehold improvements are written off in the same manner as depreciation; however, their periodic write-off is called amortization.

Natural resources such as mineral deposits are not illustrated here, but they are typically grouped with plant assets. Their original cost is written off in the form of depletion as the resources are used. For example, a coal mine may cost $10,000,000 and originally contain an estimated 5,000,000 tons. The depletion rate would be $2 per ton. If 500,000 tons were mined during the first year, depletion would be $1,000,000 for that year; if 300,000 tons were mined the second year, depletion would be $600,000; and so forth.

Intangible Assets

Intangible assets are a fuzzy class of long-lived assets that are not physical in nature. They are not illustrated in the Exhibit 18-1 balance sheet, but examples are goodwill, franchises, patents, trademarks, and copyrights. Goodwill, which is discussed in more detail in Chapter 19, is defined as the excess of the cost of an acquired company over the sum of the market value of its identifiable net assets. For example, suppose Company A acquires Company B at a cost to A of $10,000,000 and can assign only $9,000,000 to various identifiable assets such as receivables, plant, and patents; the remainder, $1,000,000, is goodwill. Identifiable intangible assets, such as franchises and patents, may be acquired singly but goodwill cannot be acquired separately from a related business.

Intangible assets are accounted for like plant and equipment—that is, the acquisition costs are "capitalized" as assets and then written off over their estimated useful lives, which, because of obsolescence, are often much shorter than their legal lives. For instance, a patent might be written off over five or ten years rather than its seventeen-year legal life. This periodic write-off, called amortization, is similar to depreciation of plant and equipment.

Although many managers and accountants maintain that some franchises, trademarks, and goodwill have perpetual lives, the Accounting Principles Board (APB) concluded otherwise. The Board ruled that the value of intangible assets eventually disappears. Therefore, the costs of all intangible assets must be amortized in a straight-line manner over the periods benefited. In no case should such "useful lives" exceed forty years.

575

*Understanding
Corporate
Annual
Reports—
Part One*

Accountants tend to be extremely conservative about intangible assets (and the deferred charges discussed earlier), and most intangibles are swiftly amortized. The contrast between the accounting for tangible and intangible long-lived assets raises some provocative and knotty theoretical issues. Accountants are sometimes overly concerned with physical objects or contractual rights, tending to overlook the underlying reality of future economic benefits.

This preoccupation with physical evidence often results in the expensing of outlays that should be treated as assets. Thus, expenditures for research, advertising, employee training, and the like are expensed, although it seems clear that in an economic sense such expenditures represent expected future benefit. The difficulty of measuring future benefits is the reason usually advanced for expensing these items. The Financial Accounting Standards Board (FASB) requires that all internal research and development costs be written off to expense as incurred.

In summary, accounting practice for intangible assets is not consistent, as this excerpt from the 1976 Annual Report of Omark Industries exemplifies: "Costs incurred for internally developed patents, trademarks and formulae are charged to current operations. The costs of purchased patents, trademarks and formulae are amortized over their respective legal or economic lives. The excess of purchase price over value ascribed to assets of businesses purchased is amortized over periods presently ranging up to 20 years."

Liabilities

Current liabilities are those that fall due within the coming year or within the normal operating cycle if longer than a year. Accounts payable are amounts owed to suppliers who extended credit for purchases on open account. These open account purchases from trade creditors are ordinarily supported by signatures on purchase orders or similar business documents. Notes payable are backed by formal promissory notes held by a bank or business creditors.

Accrued expenses payable are recognized for wages, salaries, interest, and similar items. The accountant tries to recognize expenses as they occur in relation to the operations of a given time period regardless of when they are paid for in cash. Accrued income taxes payable is a special accrued expense of enough magnitude to warrant a separate classification.

Long-term liabilities are those that fall due beyond one year. Bonds payable are formal certificates of indebtedness that are accompanied by a promise to pay interest at a specified annual rate.

Mortgage bonds are supposed to provide some additional safety for the bondholders in case the company is unable to meet its regular obligations on the bonds. If such an undesirable event occurs, the bondholders will have a prior lien on a specific asset(s). This means that such an asset may be sold and the proceeds used to liquidate the obligations to the bondholders. If no such lien exists, the bondholders have no special claims against the assets beyond the general claim against the *total* assets enjoyed by the general creditors such as trade creditors.

Subordinated debentures (not illustrated in Exhibit 18-1) are like any long-term debt except that *subordinated* means such bondholders are junior to the other general creditors in exercising claims against assets, and *debenture* means a general claim against all unencumbered assets rather than a specific claim against particular assets.

The following example should clarify these ideas. Suppose a company is liquidated. **Liquidation** means converting assets to cash and terminating outside claims. The company had miscellaneous assets, including a building, that were converted into $110,000 cash.

	Proceeds		*Owed*
Cash	$110,000	Accounts payable	$ 30,000
		First mortgage bonds	
		payable	90,000
		Subordinated debentures	
		payable	40,000
		Stockholders' equity	(50,000)
			$110,000

The mortgage bonds would be paid in full, the trade creditors would get paid two-thirds on the dollar ($20,000 for a $30,000 claim), and the other claimants would get nothing. If the debentures were **unsubordinated**, the $20,000 of cash remaining after paying $90,000 to the mortgage holders would be used to settle the $70,000 claims of the unsecured creditors as follows:

To trade creditors	$\frac{3}{7} \times \$20,000 =$	$ 8,571
To debenture holders	$\frac{4}{7} \times \$20,000 =$	11,429
Total cash distributed		$20,000

Deferred income taxes, which arise because the timing of income tax payments is delayed beyond the current operating cycle, are not shown in Exhibit 18-2, but are commonly found in the annual reports of American companies. These deferrals are discussed in Chapter 20.

Stockholders' Equity

Stockholders' equity (also called **owners' equity** or **capital** or **net worth**) as an overall class is the total residual interest in the business. It is a balance sheet difference, the excess of total assets over total liabilities. There may be many subclasses. It arises from two main sources: (1) contributed or paid-in capital and (2) retained income.

577

*Understanding
Corporate
Annual
Reports—
Part One*

Paid-in capital typically comes from owners who invest in the business in exchange for stock certificates, which are issued as evidence of shareholder rights. It is often composed of a number of classes of capital stock with a variety of different attributes. Preferred stock typically has some priority over other shares regarding dividends or the distribution of assets upon liquidation. A cumulative preferred stock means that if a specified annual dividend of, say, $5 per share is not paid, this preferred claim accumulates and must be paid in full before any dividends are paid to any other classes of stock. Preferred shareholders do not ordinarily have voting privileges regarding the management of the corporation.

Stock frequently has a designated par or legal or stated value that is printed on the face of the certificate. For preferred stock (and bonds), par is a basis for designating the amount of dividends or interest. Many preferred stocks have $100 par values; therefore, a 9 percent, $100-par preferred stock would carry a $9 annual dividend. Similarly, an 8 percent bond usually means that the investor is entitled to annual interest of $80 because most bonds have par values of $1,000. Par value of common stock has no practical importance. Historically, it was used for establishing the maximum legal liability of the stockholder in case the corporation could not pay its debts. Currently, it is set at a nominal amount (for example, $5) in relation to the market value of the stock upon issuance (for example, $70). It is generally illegal for a corporation to sell an original issue of its common stock below par. Common shareholders typically have limited liability, which means that creditors cannot resort to them as individuals if the corporation itself cannot pay its debts.

Common stock has no predetermined rate of dividends and is the last to obtain a share in the assets when the corporation is dissolved. Common shares usually have voting power in the management of the corporation. Common stock is usually the riskiest investment in a corporation, being unattractive in dire times but attractive in prosperous times because, unlike other stocks, there is no limit to the stockholder's potential participation in earnings.

Paid-in capital in excess of par (formerly called capital surplus or paid-in surplus) is the excess received over the par or stated or legal value of the shares issued. Common shares are often issued at a price substantially greater than par. The balance sheet effects of selling 100,000 shares of $5 par common at $80 per share would be:

Cash	$8,000,000	Common stock	$ 500,000
		Paid-in capital in excess of par	7,500,000
		Stockholders' equity	$8,000,000

Retained income, also called retained earnings or reinvested earnings, is the increase in stockholders' equity due to profitable operations. It was explained more fully in Chapter 17. Retained income is the dominant item of stockholders' equity for most companies. For instance, as of January 27,

1977, J. C. Penney Company had a stockholders' equity of $1,538 million, of which $1,264 million was retained income.

Treasury stock is a corporation's issued stock that has subsequently been repurchased by the company. Such repurchase is a liquidation of an ownership claim. It should therefore appear on a balance sheet as a deduction from total stockholders' equity. The stock is not retired; it is only held temporarily "in the treasury" to be distributed later as a part of an employee stock purchase plan or as an executive bonus or for use in an acquisition of another company. Cash dividends are not paid on shares held in the treasury; cash dividends are distributed only to the shares outstanding (in the hands of stockholders), and treasury stock is not outstanding stock. Treasury stock is usually of minor significance in the financial picture of a corporation.

Meaning of Stockholders' Equity Section: Stock Splits and Stock Dividends

Distinguishing among the par or stated value, capital surplus, and retained income has little practical importance. It is simpler to think of stockholders' equity as a single amount.

Many companies occasionally split their stock. A stock split or split-up refers to the issuance of additional shares for no payments by stockholders and under conditions indicating that the objective is to increase the number of outstanding shares for the purpose of reducing their unit market price, in order to bring the stock price down into a more popular range. This, supposedly, encourages wider distribution and a higher total market value for the same ownership interest. Corporate management naturally wants the stock to be as attractive as possible, easing the task of raising additional investment capital when needed. For a given ownership interest, the higher the total market value, the more capital can be raised for each additional share issued.

Stock split-ups can be achieved by issuing new shares for old shares or simply by issuing additional shares to conform to the size of the split. Suppose that Company A has the following stockholders' equity section:

	Before 2-for-1 Split	Changes	After 2-for-1 Split
Common stock, 100,000 shares @ $10 par	$1,000,000	200,000 shares @ $5 par	$1,000,000
Paid-in capital in excess of par	4,000,000		4,000,000
Retained income	6,000,000		6,000,000
Stockholders' equity	$11,000,000		$11,000,000
Overall market value of stock @ assumed $150	$15,000,000	@ assumed $80	$16,000,000

579

*Understanding
Corporate
Annual
Reports—
Part One*

There is no effect on the reported amount of the total stockholders' equity. A person who previously owned 1,000 shares (a 1 percent interest) now owns 2,000 shares (still a 1 percent interest). Professor Willard Graham explained a stock split as being akin to taking a gallon of whiskey and pouring it into five individual bottles. The resulting packaging will attract a price for each fifth that will produce a higher total value than if the gallon were not split (less the amount spilled when pouring into the five bottles—that's the legal, printing, and clerical costs). Therefore, Company A splits its stock with the hope that the market value of the total ownership interest will increase from $15,000,000 to $16,000,000 because one share that previously sold for $150 will now be in the form of two shares that might sell for $80, or a total of $160.

Stock dividends is a misnomer because such dividends are totally different from cash dividends. A stock dividend is a distribution of additional certificates of any class of the distributing company's stock. The most frequently encountered type of stock dividend is the distribution of additional common stock to existing holders of common stock already outstanding; usually anywhere from 1 to 10 percent of the number of common shares already outstanding are distributed.

In substance, stock dividends are not dividends at all, as the term is usually understood. The shareholders' proportionate interest in the corporation is unchanged, and the unit market price of each share tends to decline in response to the additional shares outstanding without any corresponding infusion of new capital. Again, an example may clarify. Suppose the market price of common stock is $80:

	Before 5% Stock Dividend		*Changes*	*After 5% Stock Dividend*
Common stock, 200,000 shares @ $5 par	$ 1,000,000	+	(10,000 shares @ $5 par)	$ 1,050,000
Paid-in capital in excess of par	4,000,000	+	[10,000 shares @ ($80 − $5)]	4,750,000
Retained income	6,000,000	−	(10,000 @ $80)	5,200,000
Stockholders' equity	$11,000,000			$11,000,000
Fractional ownership interest of a stockholder	2,000 shares 1%		100 shares	2,100 shares Still 1%

First, note that the individual shareholder receives no assets from the corporation. Moreover, his fractional interest is unchanged; if he sells his dividend shares, his proportionate ownership interest in the company will decrease.

Second, the company records the transaction by transferring the market value of the additional shares from retained income to common stock and "paid-in capital in excess of par." This entry is often referred to as being a "capitalization of retained income." It is basically a signal to the shareholder that $800,000 of retained income cannot be reduced by future cash dividends.

Stock dividends are prime examples of have-your-cake-and-eat-it-too manipulations that in substance are meaningless but that seemingly leave all interested parties happy. The company pays a "dividend" but gives up no assets. The stockholder thinks he's getting a dividend even though to realize it in cash he must sell some of his fractional interest in the company.

The stock dividend device is particularly effective where a low percentage, such as 1 or 2 percent, of additional shares are issued that may have an imperceptible effect on the market price. The recipient, who is not particularly concerned about his fractional ownership interest anyway, may hold 100 shares @ $80 before the dividend and 101 shares @ $80 after the dividend. His reaction is likely to be favorable because he is $80 richer because of the dividend. Why? Because the peculiarities of the stock market somehow avoided the logical lowering of the market price per share, and not because the corporation gave him anything directly.

A stock split is often achieved via the use of the stock dividend device by issuing an enormous stock "dividend" of 50 or 100 percent or more. The use of such high-percentage stock dividends is merely another way of obtaining a stock split. Such a transaction should not really be called a stock dividend; it would be better to call it a "split-up effected in the form of a stock dividend." This requires a decrease in Retained Income and an increase in Common Stock in the amount of the par value (rather than the market value) of the additional shares. For example, if the two-for-one split described earlier were achieved through a 100 percent stock dividend, the total stockholders' equity would be unaffected. However, its composition would change:

Common stock, 200,000 shares @ $10 par	$ 2,000,000
Paid-in capital in excess of par	4,000,000
Retained income	5,000,000
Stockholders' equity	$11,000,000

Reserves and Funds

Accountants frequently use the term reserve in their reports. To a layman, reserve normally means setting aside a specific amount of cash or securities for a special purpose such as vacations, illness, Christmas gifts, and so on. The accountant *never* uses the word reserve to describe such an amount; instead he calls such assets a *fund.* For example, a pension fund is cash or other highly liquid assets segregated for meeting the pension obligations. Similarly, a sinking fund is usually cash or securities segregated for meeting obligations on bonded debt.

The word *reserve* is on the wane, but it is used frequently enough to warrant an acquaintance with its three broad meanings in accounting:

581

*Understanding
Corporate
Annual
Reports—
Part One*

1. **Retained income reserve.** A restriction of dividend-paying power denoted by a specific subdivision of retained income. The term appropriated or restricted is better terminology than reserve. Examples are reserves for contingencies (which can refer to any possible future losses from such miscellany as foreign devaluations of currency, lawsuits, natural disasters, and so on) and reserves for self-insurance (which refer to possible future losses from fires or other casualty losses). This reserve is *not* a reduction of total retained income; it is merely an earmarking or subdividing of part of retained income.

2. **Asset valuation.** An offset to an asset. Examples: reserves for depreciation, depletion, uncollectible accounts, or reduction of inventory or investments to market value. "Allowance for . . ." is much better terminology.

3. **Liability.** An estimate of a definite liability of indefinite or uncertain amount. Examples: reserves for income taxes, warranties, pensions, and vacation pay. "Estimated liability for . . ." is much better terminology.

Note that asset valuation reserves and liability reserves are created by charges to expense (and, hence, reductions of stockholders' equity).

Alternate Form of Balance Sheet

The balance sheet in Exhibit 18-1 is sometimes presented in a different format. The most popular alternative is to deduct current liabilities from current assets. The difference is called net working capital, which measures the ownership equity (or net investment) in the current assets. The main change in Exhibit 18-1 would be that the current liabilities would appear on the left side as negative assets:

December 31, 19x1

Current assets (detailed)	$23,700
Less current liabilities (detailed)	9,200
Net working capital	$14,500
Plant assets	7,300
Total assets, less current liabilities	$21,800

Thus, the right side of the balance sheet would be reduced to the same $21,800 total, consisting of only two elements:

Long-term liability (5% mortgage bonds payable)	$16,000
Stockholders' equity	5,800
Total	$21,800

INCOME STATEMENT

Use of Subtotals

Most investors are vitally concerned about the company's ability to produce long-run earnings and dividends. In this regard, income statements are much more important than balance sheets. The income statement is straightforward and, for the most part, is stated in terms of current dollars. Revenue is shown first; this represents the total sales value of products delivered and services rendered to customers. Expenses are then listed and deducted. The statement can take two major forms: single-step and multiple-step. The single-step statement merely lists all expenses without drawing subtotals, whereas the multiple-step statement contains one or more subtotals, as illustrated in Exhibit 18-3.

Subtotals often highlight significant relationships. As explained in the preceding chapter, sometimes cost of goods sold is deducted from sales to show gross profit or gross margin. This indicates the size of the margin above merchandise costs—an important statistic for many managers and analysts.

Depreciation expense, various selling expenses, and various administrative expenses are often grouped as "operating expenses" and deducted from the gross profit to obtain operating income which is also called operating profit. (Of course, cost of goods sold can actually be viewed as an operating expense, because it is also deducted from sales revenue to obtain "operating income.")

EXHIBIT 18-3
THE GREEN CO.

Statement of Income
For the Year Ending December 31, 19x1
(In thousands of dollars)

Sales		$55,000
Cost of goods sold		40,000
Gross profit on sales		$15,000
Operating expenses:		
Selling expenses	$8,900	
Administrative expenses	2,000	
Depreciation expense	1,000	11,900
Operating income		$ 3,100
Interest expense		800
Income before income taxes		$ 2,300
Income taxes		1,150
Net income		$ 1,150
Earnings per share of common stock		$5.27*

*Computation of earnings per share:

Net income	$1,150,000
Deduct preferred dividends	96,000
Net income for holders of common stock	$1,054,000
Divide by common shares	200,000
Earnings per share of common stock	$5.27

Operating and Financial Management

Operating income is a popular subtotal because of the oft-made distinction between operating management and financial management. *Operating management* is mainly concerned with the major day-to-day activities that generate sales revenue (that is, utilizing a given set of resources). In contrast, *financial management* is mainly concerned with where to get cash and how to use cash for the benefit of the entity (that is, obtaining and investing the needed capital). Examples of questions of financial management include: how much cash should be held in checking accounts? should we pay a dividend? should we borrow or issue common stock? The best managements perform both operating management and financial management superbly. However, many managers are superior operating managers and inferior financial managers, or vice versa.

Because interest expense is usually a result of financial rather than operating decisions, it appears as a separate item after operating income. In this way, comparisons of operating income between years and between companies are facilitated. Some companies make heavy use of debt, which causes high interest expenses, whereas other companies incur little debt and interest expenses.

Income, Earnings, Profits

Although this book does tend to use *income* most often, the terms income, earnings, and profits are often used as synonyms. The income statement is also called the statement of earnings, the statement of profit and loss, and the P & L statement. For some strange reason, many companies, as illustrated in Exhibits 18-3 and 18-4, will use net *income* on their income statements but will refer to retained income as retained *earnings*.

The term net income is the residual after deducting income taxes. The term "net" is seldom used for any subtotals that precede the calculation of net income; instead, the subtotals are called "income." Thus, the appropriate term is "operating income" or "income from operations," not "net operating income."

Income taxes are often a prominent expense and are not merely listed with operating expenses. Instead, income taxes are often deducted as a separate item immediately before net income.

RECONCILIATION OF RETAINED EARNINGS

The analysis of the changes in retained earnings is frequently placed in a separate statement, the statement of reconciliation of retained earnings, also called statement of reconciliation of retained income. As Exhibit 18-4 demonstrates, the major reasons for changes in retained income are dividends

EXHIBIT 18-4

THE GREEN COMPANY

Reconciliation of Retained Earnings
For the Year Ended December 31, 19x1
(In thousands of dollars)

Retained earnings, December 31, 19x0		$ 900
Net income (Exhibit 18-3)		1,150
Total		$2,050
Deduct dividends:		
On preferred stock	$ 96	
On common stock	954	1,050
Retained earnings, December 31, 19x1		$1,000

and net income. **Note especially that dividends are *not* expenses. They are not deductions in computing net income,** as Chapter 17 explained in more detail.

STATEMENT OF CHANGES IN FINANCIAL POSITION

Concept and Format of Funds Statement

In 1971, in *Opinion No. 19,* the Accounting Principles Board added an additional financial report to its requirements. A statement of changes in financial position must be presented as a basic financial statement in corporate annual reports. Before 1971, the statement was most widely known as a statement of sources and applications of funds. For brevity in the ensuing discussion, the statement will frequently be called a **funds statement.** The term is convenient, but not descriptive.

The funds statement summarizes the financing and investing activities of the enterprise. The statement shows directly information that can otherwise be obtained only by makeshift analysis and interpretation of balance sheets and statements of income and retained earnings.

Balance sheets are statements of financial position, whereas funds statements are statements of *changes* in financial position. **Balance sheets show the status at a day in time. In contrast, funds statements, income statements, and retained earnings statements cover periods of time; they**

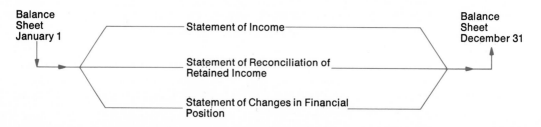

584

585

*Understanding
Corporate
Annual
Reports—
Part One*

provide the explanations of why the balance sheet items have changed. This linkage may be depicted as shown in the diagram at the bottom of the preceding page.

The statement of changes in financial position is still in its infancy as a required major financial report. It is undergoing experimentation as more experience is gained with it. There has been long-standing disagreement on the concept and format of the funds statement. The most popular approach has been to view it as an explanation of why net working capital (the excess of current assets over current liabilities) has changed for a given period. Thus, in this approach, "funds" are defined as net working capital. Therefore, most funds statements have displayed the sources and applications of net working capital, as follows:

Sources of funds:

Operations (excess of revenue over charges against revenue requiring funds)
Sale of noncurrent assets (plant, equipment, long-term stocks and bonds)
Issuance of long-term debt
Issuance of capital stock

Applications of funds:

Declaration of cash dividends
Purchase of noncurrent assets (plant, equipment, long-term stocks and bonds)
Redemption of long-term debt
Repurchase of outstanding capital stock

Financial analysts have cited the following information as being revealed by a funds statement: the major sources from which funds have been obtained (that is, profitable operations, borrowing, sale of capital stock); clues as to the financial management habits of the executives (that is, management attitudes toward spending and financing); the proportion of funds applied to plant, dividends, debt retirement, etc.; indications of the impact of fund flows upon future dividend-paying probabilities; and an indication of the company's trend toward general financial strength or weakness.

Example of Funds Statement

The preparation of a funds statement can become complex, but the basic ideas are straightforward. Generally, as the example will show, a funds statement can be prepared from visual inspection of the changes in balance-sheet items, the availability of a few additional facts, and a familiarity with the typical components of the funds statement.

Consider the example of the B Company, which had net income of $43,000 in 19x2. Sales were $200,000, expenses requiring working capital, $140,000, and depreciation, $17,000. The B Company had the following balance sheets (in thousands of dollars):

	December 31			December 31	
	19x2	*19x1*		*19x2*	*19x1*
Current assets:			Current		
Cash	$ 5	$ 25	liabilities	$100	$ 10
Net receivables	45	25	Long-term debt	105	5
Inventories	100	60	Stockholders'		
Total current assets	$150	$110	equity	425	315
Plant assets, net of			Total equities	$630	$330
accumulated					
depreciation	480	220			
Total assets	$630	$330			

In 19x2, the company issued long-term debt and capital stock for cash of $100,000 and $87,000, respectively. Cash dividends were $20,000. New plant and equipment was acquired for $277,000 cash.

Because the funds statement explains the *causes* for the change in net working capital, the first step is to compute such a change (which represents the effects):

	December 31	
	19x2	*19x1*
Current assets	$150	$110
Current liabilities	100	10
Net working capital	$ 50	$100
Net decrease		$50

Exhibit 18-5 illustrates how this computation can be shown in detail in the lower part of the funds statement as the schedule of changes in net working capital.

When business expansion occurs, as in this case where there is a strong net-working-capital position at the outset, net working capital will probably decline because maximum use of current trade credit limits and slower payments to creditors are likely. Cash balances will also fall to a bare minimum because the cash is needed for investment in miscellaneous business assets.

The statement in Exhibit 18-5 gives a direct picture of where the funds came from and where they went. In this instance, the excess of applications over sources reduced net working capital by $50,000. Without the statement of funds, the reader would have to conduct his own analysis of the balance sheets, income statement, and statement of retained income to get a grasp of the financial management decisions.

Role of Depreciation

The most crucial aspect of a funds statement is how depreciation and other expenses that do not require cash outflows relate to the flow of funds (net

EXHIBIT 18-5
B COMPANY

Statement of Changes in Financial Position
(Explaining Changes in Net Working Capital)
for the Year Ending December 31, 19x2

Sources of net working capital:		
Net income	$ 43,000	
Add charges against income not requiring net working capital:		
depreciation	17,000	
Funds provided by operations		$ 60,000
Issuance of long-term debt		
($105,000 − $5,000)		100,000
Issuance of additional capital stock*		87,000
Total sources		$247,000
Applications of net working capital:		
Acquisition of plant and equipment†	$277,000	
Payment of cash dividends	20,000	
Total applications		297,000
Decrease in net working capital (see schedule)		$(50,000)

Schedule of Changes in Net Working Capital

	December 31	
	19x2	19x1
Current assets:		
Cash	$ 5	$ 25
Net receivables	45	25
Inventories	100	60
Total current assets	$150	$110
Current liabilities (detailed)	100	10
Net working capital	$ 50	$100
Decrease in net working capital		$50

* In this example, the amounts of inflows and outflows were given. In cases where the exact amounts of inflows or outflows are not explicitly given, they can usually be computed by analyzing the changes in the beginning and ending balances of the accounts in question.
Let X = amount of additional capital stock issued.

$315,000 beginning balance + $43,000 net income
− $20,000 dividends + X = $425,000 ending balance
$338,000 + X = $425,000
X = $ 87,000

† There were two changes in the plant asset accounts, an increase from new acquisitions and a decrease from depreciation.
Let X = amount spent for new acquisitions.

$220,000 beginning balance − $17,000 depreciation + X = $480,000 ending balance
X = $277,000

working capital). There is widespread misunderstanding of the role of depreciation in financial reporting, so let us examine this point in detail.

Accountants view depreciation as an allocation of historical cost to expense. Therefore, depreciation expense does not entail an outflow of current resources in the form of cash, which is the prime form of working capital. Exhibit 18-6 shows the typical relationship of current operations to the production of net working capital. Net income is a residual; by itself, it provides no funds. Sales to customers is almost always *the* major source of funds. The excess of sales over the expenses that require outflows of funds is called **net funds provided by operations,** which is labeled as a major source of funds. This figure can be computed and shown in a funds statement in two ways. Exhibit 18-6 is used as a basis for illustration. The most straightforward way is to begin with the total sales figure and then deduct all the operating expenses that drained working capital ($A - B = \$60,000$ in Exhibit 18-6). Because a detailed listing of such operating expenses is a cumbersome way of arriving at funds provided by operations, accountants and financial analysts use a shortcut. Instead of beginning with the Sales total and working down, accountants usually start with Net Income and work up ($E + D = \$60,000$ in Exhibit 18-6) by adding back all charges not requiring working capital. The funds statement usually presents this shortcut computation as follows:

Sources:		
Net income		$43,000
Add charges not requiring working capital:		
Depreciation	$17,000	
Other (amortization of patents, etc.)	—	17,000
Total funds provided by operations		$60,000
Other sources		xx

Unfortunately, the use of this shortcut method creates an erroneous impression that depreciation is, by itself, a source of funds. If that were really true, a corporation could merely double or triple its depreciation charges when funds were badly needed. What would happen? Funds provided by operations

EXHIBIT 18-6

Analysis of Income Statement to Show Effects of Operations on Net Working Capital

Sales	$200,000 (A)
Less: All expenses requiring working capital (detailed)	140,000 (B)
Net funds provided by operations	$ 60,000 (C)
Less: Depreciation	17,000 (D)
Net income	$ 43,000 (E)

Note: Figures are from the preceding example. In this example, depreciation is the only expense not requiring net working capital.

589

*Understanding
Corporate
Annual
Reports—
Part One*

would be unaffected. Suppose that depreciation in Exhibit 18-6 is doubled:

Sales	$200,000
Less: All expenses requiring working capital (detailed)	140,000
Net funds provided by operations	$ 60,000
Less: Depreciation	34,000
Net income	$ 26,000

The doubling affects depreciation *and* net income, but it has no direct influence on funds provided by operations, which, of course, still amounts to $60,000.

Effects of Different Patterns of Depreciation

Federal income tax laws permit faster write-offs for depreciation than were previously allowed. Exhibit 18-7 is a comparison of the annual depreciation produced by three methods. **Note how income taxes paid can be affected substantially by the depreciation method chosen.**

Depreciation, Income Taxes, and Cash Flow

One of the reasons for the liberalizing of these deductions for depreciation has been "to provide more funds for industrial expansion." The business press and financial analysts' reports are replete with such phrasing as "cash

EXHIBIT 18-7

Annual Depreciation Expense: Three Methods
Assume equipment costs $85,000, no scrap value,
five-year life.

YEAR	STRAIGHT-LINE*	DECLINING BALANCE AT TWICE THE STRAIGHT-LINE RATE†	SUM-OF-YEARS DIGITS‡
1	$17,000	$34,000	$28,333
2	17,000	20,400	22,667
3	17,000	12,240	17,000
4	17,000	7,344	11,333
5	17,000	4,406	5,667
Total	$85,000	$78,390	$85,000

* 20% of $85,000 each year.
† 40% of $85,000; 40% of ($85,000 − $34,000); etc. This method will never fully depreciate the existing balance. Therefore, in the later years of an asset's life, companies typically switch to a straight-line method.
‡ Sum of digits is 1 + 2 + 3 + 4 + 5 = 15. Then 5/15 × $85,000: 4/15 × $85,000; etc.

provided by depreciation" or "funds generated by depreciation." Accountants quarrel with such phrasing because depreciation in itself is not a direct source of funds, as we saw in the previous section.

The use of faster depreciation permits larger deductions in the computation of income taxes and thus reduces the outflow of funds for current income taxes. So faster depreciation conserves funds by reducing current income tax disbursements:

	Straight-Line Depreciation	Double-Declining-Balance Depreciation
(C) Income before depreciation	$60,000	$60,000
Depreciation deduction on income tax return	17,000	34,000
Income before income taxes	$43,000	$26,000
(T) Income taxes @ 40%	17,200	10,400
Net income	$25,800	$15,600
Net after-tax inflow from operations:		
$\quad$ C − T = $60,000 − $17,200 =	$42,800	
$\qquad$ = $60,000 − $10,400 =		$49,600

As the tabulation shows, the effect of more depreciation on fund flows is indirect; it reduces income taxes by 40 percent of the extra depreciation deduction of $17,000, or $6,800, and **therefore keeps more funds in the business for a longer period of time because of the postponement of income taxes.**

Alternative Concepts and Formats

Income statements and retained income statements have a sharp focus regarding their purposes, but funds statements have a less-clear focus that differs from entity to entity. Some organizations focus on a change in cash; others, on a change in net liquid assets (that is, cash plus receivables, less current liabilities); others, on all the balance sheet items (called the "all-financial-resources" approach); and others on the net-working-capital approach already described.

The net-working-capital focus of the funds statement provides only a relatively crude look at a company's debt-paying capability. For example, net working capital can soar if inventories are piling up; sales might be slowing, and soaring inventories might foretell severe impending cash shortages. In short, the critics of the net-working-capital concept maintain that inventories hardly justify being included in any sensible definition of funds. The defenders of the net-working-capital concept of funds claim that

591

*Understanding
Corporate
Annual
Reports—
Part One*

the funds statement does not pretend to be a substitute for a statement of cash receipts and disbursements. Moreover, they state that the detailed comparison of current assets and current liabilities is satisfactorily supplied by the comparative balance sheet or by a supplementary schedule of changes in net working capital at the bottom of the funds statement, as Exhibit 18-5 illustrates.

Critics of the net-working-capital approach have stressed that it excludes the disclosure of some important financing and investing activities that do not entail the direct use of net working capital but that belong in any statement of changes in financial position. Consequently, *APB Opinion No. 19* requires disclosure of all the important aspects of financing and investing activities "regardless of whether cash or other elements of working capital are directly affected." For example, acquisitions of property by issuance of securities or in exchange for other property should be appropriately reflected on the statement. In our B Company example (Exhibit 18-5), suppose that some plant and equipment were acquired in exchange for the issuance of capital stock having a market value of $87,000. Strictly interpreted, the net-working-capital concept of funds would exclude that transaction from the statement in Exhibit 18-5 because there was no impact on net working capital. However, *Opinion No. 19* would include the issuance as a source and the acquisition as an application.

Although *Opinion No. 19* has required a statement of changes in financial position, it allows flexibility (some commentators might say fuzziness) in form, content, and terminology. Thus "net change in financial position" may be expressed in terms of any of the alternative concepts enumerated above (cash, net working capital, and so on).

Cash Flow

Sometimes a statement of sources and applications of cash is found in an annual report. For practical purposes, **cash** in many of these instances is **loosely** defined so that it is equivalent to net working capital. Therefore, in such cases, statements of sources and applications of cash may be essentially another type of funds statement.

Some companies like to stress a cash-flow-per-share figure as well as an earnings-per-share figure. Cash flow per share and funds provided by operations per share are usually equivalent. Net income is an attempt to summarize management performance. **Cash flow or funds provided by operations gives an incomplete picture of that performance because it ignores noncash expenses that are just as important as cash expenses for judging overall company performance. Because they give an incomplete picture, cash-flow-per-share figures can be downright misleading.** They should be interpreted cautiously.

SUMMARY

This chapter explained the meaning of the account titles most often found in the major financial statements. Accountants have narrow meanings for many of their terms, including *funds, reserves, net working capital, depreciation, cash flow* and others. In particular, the term *depreciation* is misunderstood. Unless these terms are clear, the user is likely to misinterpret financial reports.

Statements of changes in financial position, also (less accurately) called *funds statements,* are increasing in importance because they yield direct insights into the financial management policies of a company. They also directly explain why a company with high net income may nevertheless be unable to pay dividends because of the weight of other financial commitments to plant expansion or retirement of debt.

SUMMARY PROBLEMS FOR YOUR REVIEW

Problem One

"The net book value of plant assets is the amount that would be spent today for their replacement." Do you agree? Explain.

Problem Two

On December 31, 19x1, a magazine publishing company receives $300,000 in cash for three-year subscriptions. This is regarded as deferred revenue. Show the balances in that account at December 31, 19x2, 19x3, and 19x4. How much revenue would be earned in each of those three years?

Problem Three

B Company splits its $10 par common stock 5 for 1. How will its balance sheet be affected? Its earnings per share?

Problem Four

C Company distributes a 2 percent stock dividend on its 1,000,000 outstanding $5 par common shares. Its stockholders' equity section before the dividend was:

Common stock, 1,000,000 shares @ $5 par	$ 5,000,000
Paid-in capital in excess of par	20,000,000
Retained income	75,000,000
	$100,000,000

The common was selling on the open market for $150 per share when the dividend was distributed.

592

How will the stockholders' equity section be affected? If net income were $10,200,000 next year, what would earnings per share be before considering the effects of the stock dividend? After considering the effects of the stock dividend?

Problem Five

"A reserve for depreciation provides cash for the replacement of fixed assets." Do you agree? Explain.

Problem Six

"A reserve for taxes is cash set aside in a special bank account so that the cash is readily available when taxes are due." Do you agree? Explain.

Problem Seven

"A reserve for contingencies is cash earmarked for use in case of losses on lawsuits or fires." Do you agree? Explain.

Problem Eight

1. Using Exhibits 18-1, 18-3, and 18-4, prepare a statement of changes in financial position for the Green Company.
2. In your own words, explain why net working capital declined. What other sources of funds are likely to be available?

Solution to Problem One

Net book value of the plant assets is the result of deducting accumulated depreciation from original cost. This process does not attempt to capture all the technological and economic events that may affect replacement value. Consequently, there is little likelihood that net book value will approximate replacement cost.

Solution to Problem Two

The balance in Deferred Revenue would decline at the rate of $100,000 yearly; $100,000 would be recognized as earned revenue in each of three years.

Solution to Problem Three

Total stockholders' equity would be unaffected, but there would be five times more outstanding shares than previously at $2 par rather than $10 par. Earnings per share would be one-fifth of that previously reported, assuming no change in total net income applicable to the common stock.

Solution to Problem Four

Stockholders' equity:

	Before 2% Stock Dividend	*Changes*	*After 2% Stock Dividend*
Common stock 1,000,000 shares @ $5 par	$ 5,000,00	+ (20,000 @ $5)	$ 5,100,000
Paid-in surplus	20,000,000	+ [20,000 @ ($150 − $5)]	22,900,000
Retained income	75,000,000	− (20,000 @ $150)	72,000,000
	$100,000,000		$100,000,000

Earnings per share before considering the effects of the stock dividend would be $10,200,000 ÷ 1,000,000, or $10.20. After the dividend: $10,200,000 ÷ 1,020,000 or $10.

Note that the dividend has no effect on net income, the numerator of the earnings-per-share computation. But it does affect the denominator and causes a mild dilution which, in theory, should be reflected by a slight decline in the market price of the stock.

Solution to Problem Five

Reserve for depreciation is a synonym for accumulated depreciation. It is a negative asset, an offset to or deduction from original cost. It is a "hole in a doughnut" and in no way represents a direct stockpile of cash for replacement.

Solution to Problem Six

Reserve for taxes is a liability reserve, not a fund gathered for a particular purpose. It is a misleading label because it means "estimated income taxes payable." This does not preclude the establishment of a special *fund* if one is desired, although this is seldom done in practice.

Solution to Problem Seven

Reserve for contingencies is a retained income reserve, a formal restriction of dividend-paying power often made voluntarily by a board of directors. Its purpose is to warn stockholders that future dividend-paying possibilities are constrained by future possible events that might bear sad economic consequences.

Often restrictions on dividend-paying power are the result of legal agreements with bondholders or other creditors who do not want resources paid to shareholders in the form of dividends until creditor claims are met.

Solution to Problem Eight

1.

GREEN CO.
Statement of Changes in Financial Position
for the Year Ending December 31, 19x1

Sources:		
Net income	$1,150,000	
Add charges against income not requiring net		
working capital: depreciation	1,000,000	
Funds provided by operations		$ 2,150,000
Other sources		—
Total sources		$ 2,150,000
Applications:		
Purchases of plant and equipment	$2,200,000*	
Cash dividends:		
On preferred stock	96,000	
On common stock	954,000	
Total applications		3,250,000
Decrease in net working capital (see schedule)		$(1,100,000)

Schedule of Changes in Net Working Capital

	19x1	19x0
Current assets:		
Cash	$ 2,600,000	$ 2,200,000
Temporary investments in marketable		
securities	600,000	600,000
Receivables, net	5,300,000	5,100,000
Inventories	14,600,000	14,400,000
Prepaid expenses	600,000	600,000
Total current assets	$23,700,000	$22,900,000
Current liabilities:		
Notes payable	$ 3,900,000	$ 2,800,000
Accounts payable	3,200,000	2,400,000
Accrued expenses payable	1,600,000	1,700,000
Accrued income taxes payable	500,000	400,000
Total current liabilities	$ 9,200,000	$ 7,300,000
Net working capital	$14,500,000	$15,600,000
Decrease in net working capital (explained		
above)	($1,100,000)	

*($7,000,000 − $5,800,00) + depreciation of $1,000,000 = $2,200,000

2. The decline in net working capital came from the inability to generate enough funds from operations to cover expenditures for plant and equipment and dividends. In view of the pressure on working capital, one may question the wisdom of paying a $954,000 cash dividend to common shareholders. Other sources of funds might be sales of long-term investments, if any; sales of plant and equipment; issuance of long-term debt; or sale of capital stock.

595

ASSIGNMENT MATERIAL

Fundamental Assignment Material

18-1. **Net book value of land and building.** Y Company purchased an office building twenty years ago for $1 million, $200,000 of which was attributable to land. The mortgage has been fully paid. The current balance sheet follows:

Cash		$400,000	Stockholders'	
Land		200,000	equity	$750,000
Building at cost	$800,000			
Accumulated				
depreciation	650,000			
Net book value		150,000		
Total assets		$750,000		

The company is about to borrow $1,800,000 on a first mortgage to modernize and expand the building. This amounts to 60 percent of the combined appraised value of the land and building before the modernization and expansion.

Required

Prepare a balance sheet after the loan is made and the building is expanded and modernized. Comment on its significance.

18-2. **Funds statement.** The D Company has the following balance sheets (in millions of dollars):

	As of December 31			As of December 31	
	19x4	19x3		19x4	19x3
Current assets (detailed)	$ 90	$ 80	Current liabilities (detailed)	$ 50	$ 45
Fixed assets (net of depreciation)	60	40	Long-term debt	5	—
Goodwill	5	10	Stockholders' equity	100	85
	$155	$130		$155	$130

Net income was $25 million. Cash dividends paid were $10 million. Depreciation was $7 million. Half the goodwill was amortized. Fixed assets of $27 million were purchased.

Required

Prepare a statement of changes in financial position (sources and applications of net working capital).

18-3. **Funds statement and analysis of growth.** The Denny Company has the following balance sheets (in millions):

| | December 31 | | | December 31 | |
	19x7	19x6		19x7	19x6
Current assets:			Current liabilities		
Cash	$ 2	$ 10	(detailed)	$105	$ 30
Receivables, net	60	30	Long-term debt	150	—
Inventories	100	50	Stockholders'		
Total current			equity	207	160
assets	$162	$ 90	Total equities	$462	$190
Plant assets (net of					
accumulated					
depreciation)	300	100			
Total assets	$462	$190			

Net income was $54 million. Cash dividends paid were $7 million. Depreciation was $20 million. Fixed assets were purchased for $220 million, $150 million of which was financed via the issuance of long-term debt outright for cash.

Denny Alain, the president and majority stockholder, was a superb operating executive. He was an imaginative, aggressive marketing man and an ingenious, creative production man. But he had little patience with financial matters. After examining the most recent balance sheet and income statement he muttered, "We've enjoyed ten years of steady growth; 19x7 was our most profitable ever. Despite such profitability, we're in the worst cash position in our history. Just look at those current liabilities in relation to our available cash! This whole picture of the more you make, the poorer you get just does not make sense. These statements must be cockeyed."

Required

1. Prepare a statement of changes in financial position (sources and applications of net working capital).

2. Using the funds statement and other information, write a short memorandum to Mr. Alain, explaining why there is such a squeeze on cash.

18-4. **Depreciation, income taxes, and cash flow.** Mr. Hawtrey, president of the Vaunt Transportation Company, had read a newspaper story which stated: "The Zenith Steel Company had a cash flow last year of $1,500,000, consisting of $1,000,000 of net income plus $500,000 of depreciation. New plant facilities helped the cash flow, because depreciation was 25 percent higher than in the preceding year."

Hawtrey was encouraged by the quotation because the Vaunt Company had just acquired a vast amount of new transportation equipment. These acquisitions had placed a severe financial strain on the company. Hawtrey was heartened because he thought that the added cash flow provided by the depreciation on the new equipment should ease the financial pressures on the company.

The income before income taxes of the Vaunt Company last year (19x2) was $200,000. Depreciation was $200,000; it will also be $200,000 on the old equipment in 19x3.

In 19x3, the new equipment is expected to help increase revenue by $1,000,000. However, operating expenses other than depreciation will increase by $800,000.

1. Suppose that depreciation on the new equipment for financial reporting purposes is $100,000. What would be the "cash flow" from operations (funds provided by operations) for 19x3? Show computations. Ignore income taxes.

2. Repeat Requirement 1, assuming that the depreciation on the new equipment is $50,000. Ignore income taxes.

3. Assume an income tax rate of 40 percent. (a) Repeat Requirement 1; (b) repeat Requirement 2. Assume that the same amount of depreciation is shown for tax purposes and for financial-reporting purposes.

4. In your own words, state as accurately as possible the effects on "cash flow" of depreciation. Comment on Requirements 1, 2, and 3 above in order to bring out your points. This is a more important requirement than Requirements 1, 2, and 3.

Additional Assignment Material

18-5. "Asset valuation reserves are created by charges to stockholders' equity." Do you agree? Explain.

18-6. Define *current assets*.

18-7. Why is the term *marketable securities* a misnomer?

18-8. Define *depreciation*.

18-9. "Accumulated depreciation is a hole in a doughnut." Explain.

18-10. "Accumulated depreciation is a sum of cash being accumulated for the replacement of fixed assets." Do you agree? Explain.

18-11. "Goodwill may have nothing to do with the personality of the manager or employees." Do you agree? Explain.

18-12. Why should short-term prepaid expenses be classified as current assets?

18-13. Why are intangible assets and deferred charges usually swiftly amortized?

18-14. Define *current liabilities*.

18-15. What is a subordinated debenture?

18-16. "Mortgage bonds are always safer investments than debentures." Do you agree? Explain.

18-17. What is the role of a par value of stock or bonds?

599

Understanding
Corporate
Annual
Reports—
Part One

18-18. "Common shareholders have limited liability." Explain.

18-19. "Treasury stock is negative stockholders' equity." Do you agree? Explain.

18-20. What is a stock split?

18-21. What is a stock dividend?

18-22. What are the major sources of funds? Applications?

18-23. What type of insights are provided by a funds statement?

18-24. Define *a funds statement.*

18-25. What is net working capital?

18-26. What are some examples of expenses and losses not affecting working capital?

18-27. What are the two major ways of computing funds provided by operations?

18-28. "The ordinary purchase of inventory has no effect on working capital." Why?

18-29. "Net losses mean drains on working capital." Do you agree? Explain.

18-30. "Depreciation is usually a big source of funds." Do you agree? Explain.

18-31. What are some weaknesses of the idea that funds are net working capital?

18-32. Give other definitions of funds.

18-33. What is the major difference between a funds statement and a cash flow statement?

18-34. Criticize the following presentation of part of a funds statement:

Sources:	
Sales	$100,000
Less expenses requiring working capital	70,000
Funds provided by operations	$ 30,000

18-35. The gain on the sale of a fixed asset represents part of the funds received by the X Company. How should this item be presented on a funds statement? Why?

18-36. What are the effects on funds flows of the following transaction: The purchase of fixed assets at a cost of $100,000, of inventories at a cost of $200,000, and of receivables at a cost of $50,000, paid for by the assumption of a $70,000 mortgage on the fixed assets and the giving of a ninety-day promissory note for $280,000.

18-37. The net income of the Lear Company was $1,500,000. Included on the income statement are the following:

Uninsured loss of inventory, by flood	$100,000
Gain on the sale of equipment	200,000
Dividend income	10,000
Interest income, including $5,000 not	
yet received	20,000
Amortization of patents	50,000
Depreciation	400,000

Compute the funds provided by operations, assuming that interest and dividend income are a part of operating income.

18-38. How can a stock split be achieved via the use of a stock dividend?

18-39. What are convertible securities?

18-40. What is a reconciliation of retained income?

18-41. What are the three major types of reserves?

18-42. Enumerate the items most commonly classified as current assets.

18-43. "Sometimes 100 shares of stock should be classified as current assets and sometimes not." Explain.

18-44. What is the proper measure for an asset newly acquired through an exchange (e.g., an exchange of land for securities)? Explain.

18-45. Criticize: "Depreciation is the loss in value of a fixed asset over a given span of time."

18-46. What factors influence the estimate of useful life in depreciation accounting?

18-47. "Accountants sometimes are too concerned with physical objects or contractual rights." Explain.

18-48. How may the distinction between contributed and accumulated capital be blurred by traditional accounting?

18-49. Traveler's checks. The American Express Company had $1 billion of traveler's checks outstanding on December 31, 1977. Each May, the First National

City Bank of New York conducts a special sale of its traveler's checks whereby up to $5,000 of its checks can be purchased for a flat fee of $2.

Required
When a company issues $1,000 of its traveler's checks, how are its assets and equities affected? Describe how profits might be made in the traveler's checks business.

18-50. Advances and deposits. Airlines typically have accounts such as Customer Deposits and Advance Ticket Sales on their balance sheets. Customer deposits often are required from large customers who have not yet established a credit rating. This money is ordinarily fully refunded at a later date. (In the bottling business, customer deposits typically are refundable when the containers are returned.) Advance ticket sales means that cash has been received from customers who have not yet used their tickets.

Required
In what section of the balance sheet would such accounts appear? Why? Explain in detail how the balances are usually extinguished, including their effects on the income statement.

18-51. Franchises and trademarks. The 19x9 annual report of the ABC Corporation contained the following account at the bottom of the asset side of the consolidated balance sheet:

Franchises and trademarks $2,347,900

Explain how this account probably arose. Will it be carried indefinitely on the balance sheet? Why?

18-52. Stock dividends. The St. Regis Paper Company had 13,700,000 shares of $5 par value common stock issued and outstanding in 19x8 when a 2 percent stock dividend was issued. The market value of the stock at the time was $36 per share.

Required
Indicate what accounts would be affected by the issuance of the dividend and by how much.

18-53. Effects on stockholders' equity. Indicate the effect ($+$, $-$, or 0) on *total* stockholders' equity of General Motors Corporation of each of the following:

1. Declaration of a cash dividend.
2. Payment of item 1.
3. Declaration of a stock dividend (common on common).
4. Issuance of a stock dividend (common on common).
5. Failing to declare a regular dividend on cumulative preferred stock.
6. Sale of 100 shares of General Motors by David Rockefeller to Tom Jones.
7. Operating loss for the period.
8. Purchase of ten shares of treasury stock for $1,000 cash.

601

9. Sale of treasury stock, purchased in item 8, for $1,200.

10. Sale of treasury stock, purchased in item 8, for $900.

11. Creation of a reserve for contingencies.

12. Creation of a construction fund.

13. Creation of a reserve for current income taxes.

14. Creation of a reserve for depreciation.

18-54. Creation and disposition of reserves. Show how the items listed below are created and disposed of, using the following letters:

For Creation	*For Disposition*
A. By increase in an asset	*A.* Usually written off against the related asset
E. By increase in an expense	*I.* Carried indefinitely
R. By decrease in retained earnings	*L.* Written off when the liability is liquidated
	R. Restored to retained earnings when its purpose is fulfilled
	O. Added as other income to current net income

Each item below will have two answers, one for creation and one for disposition.

1. Reserve for holiday pay.

2. Reserve for contingencies.

3. Reserve for possible future price declines in inventory.

4. Reserve for redemption of S & H green merchandise savings stamps.

5, Reserve for bad debts.

6. Reserve for plant expansion.

7. Reserve for bond-sinking fund.

8. Reserve for depletion.

9. Reserve for income taxes.

10. Reserve to reduce inventories from acquisition cost to current market price.

18-55. Balance sheet classification of reserves and funds. Designate whether each of the following is essentially an asset account (*A*); asset valuation account (*AV*); liability account (*L*); or retained earnings account (*R*).

1. Reserve for sinking fund.

2. Reserve for vacation pay.

3. Reserve for possible future losses in foreign operations.

4. Sinking fund for retirement of bonds.

5. Reserve for employees' bonuses.

6. Reserve for purchases of other companies.

7. Construction fund.

8. Reserve for impending economic recession.

9. Reserve for replacement of facilities at higher price levels.

10. Reserve to reduce investments from cost to market value.

18-56. Stock split. The 19x7 annual report of Essex International Corporation included the following in the statement of consolidated retained earnings:

Charge relating to stock split in May, 19x7 $4,392,800

The comparative balance sheets showed:

	December 31	
	19x7	*19x6*
Common stock $1 par value	$8,785,600	$4,392,800

Required

Define *a stock split.* What did Essex International do to achieve its stock split? Does it conflict with your definition? Explain fully.

18-57. Meaning of stock dividends. A *Wall Street Journal* story stated:

The Securities and Exchange Commission moved to bolster its control over companies that use stock dividends to misrepresent their operating results.

The agency proposed a rule generally prohibiting a company from distributing stock to its shareholders unless it has enough "earned surplus" to cover the "fair value" of the distributed shares and has transferred that amount from its earned surplus to its capital accounts.

The SEC said the proposed rule wouldn't affect traditional stock splits involving the distribution of at least an additional share for each share outstanding. It applies to distributions made "on a pro-rata basis and without consideration."

The Commission said a number of companies use stock dividends to create the impression "that a distribution is being made out of the earned surplus . . . without the drain on current assets that would result from the distribution of a cash dividend."

It added that some instances have occurred "recently" where "such distributions were utilized by companies having little or no earned surplus, thus creating a misleading impression concerning the results of operations of the company."

Required

Suppose that A Company owned 10,000 common shares of B Company, which declared a 3 percent dividend in common stock. The market price of the shares before the dividend was $50. B Company had the following stockholders' equity before declaring the stock dividend:

Capital stock, 100,000 shares issued and
      outstanding, par value $10 per share $1,000,000
Paid-in capital in excess of par value   2,000,000
Retained income   3,000,000
                                               $6,000,000

1. How would the stockholders' equity of B Company be changed upon issuance of the dividend? Assuming that 3,000 additional shares of $10 par value would be issued? Give dollar amounts.

2. How would the accounts of A Company be affected? Give dollar amounts.

3. What are the overall dollar effects on the total assets and total stockholders' equity of A Company? B Company?

18-58. Format of funds statement. Criticize the following excerpts from actual annual reports:

FMC Corporation:

Source of funds:
  Net income $ 60,822,770
  Provision for depreciation and amortization   49,296,594
  Cash flow from operations $110,119,364

Trans World Airlines:

Source of funds (amounts in millions):
  Operations:
    Net income for the year $ 21.5
  Add noncash expense:
    Depreciation and amortization   83.3
  Total from operations $104.8

Tenneco, Inc.:

Source of funds:
  Net income $166,931,748
  Depreciation, depletion and amortization   156,901,757
  Preferred stock sold   30,000,000
  Disposal of properties   50,506,439
  Etc.   Etc.

St. Regis Paper Company:

Source:
  Operations:
    Net earnings $ 34,022,000
    Expenses that did not require outlay of cash:
      Depreciation   36,365,000
      Deferred items   6,101,000
      Other   1,569,000
  Total $ 78,057,000

18-59. Valuation of intangible assets of football team. New owners acquired the Los Angeles Rams football team in 1962 for $7.2 million. They valued the

605

*Understanding
Corporate
Annual
Reports—
Part-One*

contracts of their 40 players at a total of $3.5 million. For income tax purposes, the Rams amortized the $3.5 million over five years; therefore, they took a tax deduction of $700,000 annually.

The Internal Revenue Service challenged the deductions. It maintained that only $300,000 of the $7.2 million purchase price was attributable to the player contracts and that the bulk of the purchase price was attributable to the league franchise rights. Such franchise rights are regarded by the Internal Revenue Service as a valuable asset with an indefinite future life; therefore, no amortization is permitted for tax-reporting purposes.

Required

Reports to stockholders by American companies do not have to adhere to the same basis used for income tax purposes. Assume that the operating income reported to stockholders (before considering any possible amortization of the $3.5 million cost) was $1,000,000 each year. There may have been additional amortization deducted in arriving at the $1,000,000 figure, but ignore such amortization for purposes of this problem. That is, concentrate solely on the effects of accounting for the $3.5 million in dispute. Also assume that $300,000 is identified with the player contracts and $3.2 million with the franchise rights. Under generally accepted accounting principles as now existing rather than those that existed in the 1960s, by how much would the annual operating income reported to stockholders be changed for each of the five years in question? Comment on your answer; that is, do you think that your answer is an appropriate measure of operating income? Why? By how much would taxable income increase if the IRS position were upheld?

18-60. Depreciation, income taxes, and cash flow. The Howell Company has purchased special-purpose automated machinery for the production of electronic gear. The useful life of this machinery is four years because rapid technological and market changes make the products obsolete by that time. The scrap value will be negligible. The original cost is $100,000.

The company expects annual sales of $2.0 million and annual operating expenses other than depreciation of $1.8 million.

Required

1. Show a tabulation of net income and funds provided by operations for each of the four years using (a) straight-line depreciation and (b) sum-of-the-years'-digits depreciation. Ignore income taxes.

2. Assume an income tax rate of 40 percent. Show a tabulation of net income before income taxes, income taxes, net income after taxes, and net after-tax funds provided by operations for (a) straight-line depreciation and (b) sum-of-the-years'-digits depreciation.

3. In your own words, express as precisely as possible the effects on fund flows of using the sum-of-the-years'-digits method rather than the straight-line method.

Note: Additional assignment material on the statement of changes in financial position (the funds statement) is given at the end of the next chapter. See Assignments 19-39 and 19-40.

CHAPTER 19

Understanding Corporate Annual Reports— Part Two

This chapter continues the discussion of corporate annual reporting begun in the preceding chapter. It examines accounting for intercorporate investments, consolidated statements, goodwill, and the analysis of financial statements.

ACCOUNTING FOR INTERCORPORATE INVESTMENTS

Investments in the equity securities of one company by another company are accounted for in different ways, depending on the type of the relationship between the "investor" and "investee." For example, the ordinary stockholder is a passive investor who follows the **cost method,** whereby the initial investment is recorded at cost and dividends are recorded as income as received.

Beginning in 1970 (*APB Opinion No. 18*) U.S. companies were required to use the *equity method* instead of the cost method if the investor exerts a "significant influence" over the operating and financial policies of an investee

607

*Understanding
Corporate
Annual
Reports—
Part Two*

even though the investor holds 50 percent or less of the outstanding voting stock. The **equity method** is defined as the cost at date of acquisition adjusted for the investor's share of the earnings or losses of the investee subsequent to the date of investment. Dividends received from the investee reduce the carrying amount of the investment. The equity method is generally used for a 20 through 50 percent interest, because such a level of ownership is regarded as a presumption that the owner has the ability to exert significant influence, whereas the cost method is generally used to account for interests of less than 20 percent.

The equity method is relatively new. Long-term investments in equity securities were carried at acquisition cost for many years by U.S. companies and are still carried at cost by parent companies in many countries.

Compare the cost and equity methods. Suppose Company A acquires 40 percent of the voting stock of Company B for $80 million. In year one, B has a net income of $30 million and pays cash dividends of $10 million. A's 40 percent share would be $12 and $4 million, respectively.

The balance sheet equation of A would be affected as follows:

	Equity Method					*Cost Method*		
	Assets		=	*Equities*		*Assets*		= *Equities*
	Cash	*Investments*		*Liab. Stk. Eq.*		*Cash*	*Investments*	*Liab. Stk. Equity*
1. Acquisition	−80	+80	=			−80	+80	=
2. Net income of B		+12	=	+12		No entry and no effect		
3. Dividends from B	+4	−4	=			+4		= +4
Effects for year	−76	+88	=	+12		−76	+80	+4

<table>
<tr><td>The investment account will have a net increase of $8 million for the year. The dividend will increase the cash account by $4 million.</td><td>The investment account will be unaffected. The dividend will increase the cash account by $4 million.</td></tr>
</table>

Under the equity method, income is recognized by A as it is earned by B rather than when dividends are received. Cash dividends do not affect net income; they increase Cash and decrease the Investment balance. In a sense, the dividend is a partial liquidation of the investor's "claim" against the investee. The receipt of a dividend is similar to the collection of an account receivable. The revenue from a sale of merchandise on account is recognized when the receivable is created; to include the collection also as revenue would be double-counting. **Similarly, it would be double-counting to include the $4 million of dividends as income after the $12 million of income is already recognized as it is earned.**

The major justification for requiring the use of the equity method is that it is more appropriate than the cost method for recognizing increases or decreases in the economic resources underlying the investments. The most striking difference between the two methods is that the cost method allows management to influence reported net income. Under the cost method, the net income of the investor could be directly affected by the dividend policies of the investee, over whom the investor might have significant influence. Under the equity method, the reported net income could not be influenced by the manipulation of dividend policies.

CONSOLIDATED FINANCIAL STATEMENTS

United States companies having substantial ownership of other companies must issue **consolidated financial statements,** which are explained in this section. **An American cannot hope to understand a corporate annual report without understanding the assumptions underlying consolidations. Furthermore, the early 1970s have been marked by a worldwide movement toward requiring consolidated financial statements instead of parent-company-only statements.**[1]

A publicly-held business is typically composed of two or more separate legal entities that constitute a single overall economic unit. This is almost always a parent-subsidiary relationship where one corporation (the parent) owns more than 50 percent of the outstanding voting shares of another corporation (the subsidiary).

Why have subsidiaries? Why not have the corporation take the form of a single legal entity? The reasons include limiting the liabilities in a risky venture, saving income taxes, conforming with government regulations with respect to a part of the business, doing business in a foreign country, and expanding in an orderly way. For example, there are often tax advantages in acquiring the capital stock of a going concern rather than its individual assets.

Consolidated statements combine the financial positions and earnings reports of the parent company with those of various subsidiaries into an overall report as if they were a single entity. The aim is to give the reader better perspective than could be obtained by his examining a large number of separate reports of individual companies.

The Acquisition

When parent and subsidiary financial statements are consolidated, double-counting of assets and equities must be avoided via "intercompany eliminations." Suppose Company P acquired a 100 percent voting interest in S for $213 million cash at the beginning of the year. Their balance sheet accounts immediately after the acquisition are (in millions):

	P	S	Intercompany Eliminations	Consolidated
Investment in S	$213	$ —	$213	$ —
Other assets	437	400		837
Total assets	$650	$400		$837
Accounts payable, etc.	$200	$187		$387
Stockholders' equity	450	213	(213)	450
Total equities	$650	$400		$837

---

[1] For example, in 1977 Japanese companies were required to use consolidated statements. See "Japan's Accounting Shake-up," *Business Week,* April 25, 1977, pp. 112–114.

609

*Understanding
Corporate
Annual
Reports—
Part Two*

Each legal entity has its individual set of books, but the consolidated entity is the summation of the individual assets and liabilities after the elimination of any duplications. If the $213 million elimination of the reciprocal accounts did not occur, there would be a double-counting in the consolidated statement.

After Acquisition

As we saw in the preceding section, long-term investments in equity securities, such as this Investment in S, are carried by the equity method in the investor's balance sheet. Suppose S has a net income of $50 million for the year. If the parent company were reporting alone, it would have to account for the net income of its subsidiary by increasing its investment in S account and its stockholders' equity account (in the form of Retained Income) by 100 percent of $50 million.

The income statements for the year would contain (in millions):

	P	S	Consolidated
Sales	$900	$300	$1,200
Expenses	800	250	1,050
Operating income	$100	$ 50	$ 150
Pro-rata share (100%) of unconsolidated			
subsidiary net income	50	—	
Net income	$150	$ 50	

P's parent-company-only income statement would show its own sales and expenses plus its pro-rata share of S's net income (as the equity method requires). Reflect on the changes in P's balance sheet equation (in millions):

	Assets			=	Liabilities + Stockholders' Equity		
	Investment in S	+	Other Assets	=	Accounts Payable	+	Stockholders' Equity
Beginning of year	$213	+	$437	=	$200	+	$450
Operating income		+	100	=		+	100 in retained income
Share of S income	+50					+	50 in retained income
End of year	$263	+	$537	=	$200	+	$600

S's balance sheet accounts would have increased by $50 million. A consolidated balance sheet at the end of the year would be prepared as follows (in millions):

	P	S	Intercompany Eliminations	Consolidated
Investment in S	$263[a]	$ —	$263	—
Other assets	537[b]	450[d]		$987
Total assets	$800	$450		$987
Accounts payable, etc.	$200	$187		$387
Stockholders' equity	600[c]	263[e]	(263)	600
Total equities	$800	$450		$987

[a] $213 + $50
[b] $437 + 100
[c] $450 + $100 + $50
[d] $400 + $50
[e] $213 + $50

Review at this point to see that consolidated statements are the summation of the individual accounts of two or more separate legal entities. They are prepared periodically via worksheets. **The consolidated entity does not have a separate continuous set of books like the legal entities.** Moreover, a consolidated income statement is merely the summation of the revenue and expenses of the separate legal entities being consolidated after eliminating double-counting.

Minority Interests

A consolidated balance sheet usually includes an account on the equities side called **Outside Stockholders' Interest in Subsidiaries,** often also termed simply **Minority Interests.** It arises because the consolidated balance sheet is a combination of all the assets and liabilities of a subsidiary. If the parent owns, for example, 90 percent of the subsidiary stock, then outsiders to the consolidated group own the other 10 percent. The account Outside Stockholders' Interest in Subsidiaries is a measure of this minority interest. The diagram that follows shows the area encompassed by the consolidated statements; it includes all the subsidiary assets, item by item. The creation of an account for minority interests, in effect, corrects this overstatement:

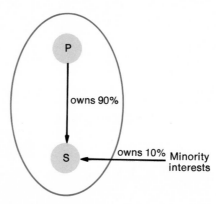

611

*Understanding
Corporate
Annual
Reports—
Part Two*

The next table, using the basic figures of the previous example, shows the overall approach to a consolidated balance sheet immediately after the acquisition. P owns 90 percent of the stock of S for a cost of .90 × $213, or $192 million. The minority interest is 10 percent, or $21 million.

	P	*S*	*Intercompany Elimination*	*Consolidated*
Investment in S	$192	$ —	$192	$ —
Other assets	458	400		858
Total assets	$650	$400		$858
Accounts payable, etc.	$200	$187		$387
Minority interest	—	—	21	21
Stockholders' equity	450	213	(213)	450
Total equities	$650	$400		$858

Again, suppose S has a net income of $50 million for the year. The same basic procedures are followed by P and by S regardless of whether S is 100 percent owned or 90 percent owned. However, the presence of a minority interest changes the *consolidated* statements slightly. The income statements would include:

	P	*S*	*Consolidated*
Sales	$900	$300	$1,200
Expenses	800	250	1,050
Operating income	$100	$ 50	$ 150
Pro-rata share (90%) of unconsolidated subsidiary net income	45	—	
Net income	$145	$ 50	
Outside interest (10%) in consolidated subsidiaries' net income (minority interest in income)			5
Net income to consolidated entity			$ 145

Consolidated balance sheets at the end of the year would be prepared as follows (changes from beginning balances are footnoted):

	P	*S*	*Intercompany Eliminations*	*Consolidated*
Investment in S	$237[a]	$ —	$237	$ —
Other assets	558[b]	450[d]		1,008
Total assets	$795	$450		$1,008
Accounts payable, etc.	$200	$187		$ 387
Minority interest	—	—	26[e]	26
Stockholders' equity	595[c]	263	(263)	595
Total equities	$795	$450		$1,008

[a] $192 + .90 ($50) = $192 + $45 = $237
[b] $458 + $100 = $558
[c] $450 + $100 + $45 = $595
[d] $400 + $50 = $450
[e] $21 + .10 ($50) = $21 + $5 = $26

EXHIBIT 19-1
GOLIATH CORPORATION

Consolidated Balance Sheets
As of December 31
(In millions of dollars)

ASSETS	19x3	19x2	CHANGE
Current assets:			
Cash	$ 90	$ 56	
Marketable securities at cost (which approximates market value)	—	28	
Accounts receivable (less allowance for doubtful accounts of $2,000,000 and $2,100,000 at their respective dates)	91	95	
Inventories at average cost	120	130	
Total current assets	301	309	(8)
Investments in unconsolidated subsidiaries	63	55	8
Property, plant, and equipment:			
Land at original cost	60	48	12
Plant and equipment	19x3	19x2	
Original cost	$192	$135	57
Accumulated depreciation	126	112	(14)
Net plant and equipment	66	23	
Total property, plant, and equipment	126	71	
Other assets:			
Franchises and trademarks	15	16	
Deferred charges and prepayments	3	4	
Total other assets	18	20	(2)
Total assets	$508	$455	53

EQUITIES	19x3	19x2	CHANGE
Current liabilities:			
Accounts payable	$100	$ 84	
Notes payable	10	—	
Accrued expenses payable	32	22	
Accrued income taxes payable	34	38	
Total current liabilities	176	144	32
Long-term liabilities:			
First mortgage bonds, 5% interest, due Dec. 31, 19x6	25	25	
Subordinated debentures, 6% interest, due Dec. 31, 19x9	30	20	
Total long-term liabilities	55	45	10
Deferred income*	12	9.3	2.7
Outside stockholders' interest in subsidiaries (minority interests)	6	5.7	0.3
Total liabilities	249	204	
Stockholders' equity:			
Preferred stock, 100,000 shares $30 par†	3	3	
Common stock, 1,000,000 shares, $1 par	1	1	
Paid-in capital in excess of par	55	55	
Retained income	200	192	8
Total stockholders' equity	259	251	
Total equities	$508	$455	53

* Advances from customers on long-term contracts. Other examples are collections for rent and subscriptions, which often are classified as current liabilities.

† Divided rate is $5 per share; each share is convertible into two shares of common stock. The shares were originally issued for $100. The excess over par is included in "paid-in capital in excess of par." Liquidating value is $100 per share.

613

*Understanding
Corporate
Annual
Reports—
Part Two*

Exhibits 19-1 through 19-3 are included to provide an overall perspective on how financial statements appear in corporate annual reports. On balance sheets the minority interest typically appears just above the stockholders' equity section, as Exhibit 19-1 shows. However, some accountants place it as a subpart of the stockholders' equity section. On income statements, the minority interest in net income is deducted as if it were an expense of the consolidated entity, as Exhibit 19-2 demonstrates.

EXHIBIT 19-2

GOLIATH CORPORATION

Consolidated Income Statements
for the Year Ending December 31
(000's omitted)

	19x3	19x2
Net sales and other operating revenue	$500,000	$600,000
Cost of goods sold and operating expenses, exclusive of depreciation	468,750	554,550
Depreciation	14,000	11,000
Total operating expenses	482,750	565,550
Operating income before share of unconsolidated net income	17,250	34,450
Pro-rata share of unconsolidated subsidiary net income	8,000	10,000
Total income before interest expense and income taxes	25,250	44,450
Interest expense	2,450	2,450
Income before income taxes	22,800	42,000
Income taxes	12,000	21,900
Income before minority interests	10,800	20,100
Outside stockholders' interest (minority interests) in consolidated subsidiaries' net income	300	600
Net consolidated income to Goliath Corporation*	10,500	19,500
Preferred dividends	500	500
Net income to Goliath Corporation common stock	$ 10,000	$ 19,000
Earnings per share of common stock: On shares outstanding (1,000,000 shares)†	$10.00	$19.00
Assuming full dilution, reflecting conversion of all convertible securities (1,200,000 shares)‡	$ 8.75	$16.25

* This is the total figure in dollars that the accountant traditionally labels net income. It is reported accordingly in the financial press.
† This is the figure most widely quoted by the investment community.
‡ Computed, respectively: 10,500,000 ÷ 1,200,000 = $8.75; $19,500,000 ÷ 1,200,000 = $16.25.

EXHIBIT 19-3

GOLIATH CORPORATION

Consolidated Statement of Retained Income
for the Year Ending December 31
(000's omitted)

	19x3	19x2
Balance beginning of year	$192,000	$176,000
Add: Net income to Goliath Corporation	10,500	19,500
Total	202,500	195,500
Deduct:		
Cash dividends on preferred stock (also shown in Exhibit 19-2)	500	500
Cash dividends on common stock	2,000	3,000
Total dividends	2,500	3,500
Balance, end of year	$200,000	$192,000

Unconsolidated Subsidiaries

We have already seen how the equity method is used on a parent company's books to account for its investment in subsidiaries. Most often, such investment accounts are eliminated as consolidated statements are prepared, as was just illustrated. Sometimes there is justification for not consolidating one or two subsidiaries whose business is totally different from the parent and other subsidiaries. Examples are a merchandiser's subsidiary finance companies and insurance companies. For instance, a consolidated statement of Sears Roebuck and Allstate Insurance Company would produce a meaningless hodgepodge, so the Allstate statements are shown as an Investment on the Sears consolidated balance sheet. A separate set of Allstate statements is included in the Sears annual report.

Investments in domestic unconsolidated subsidiaries are carried via the equity method. The use of the equity method necessitates recognition of the parent's share of unconsolidated subsidiary net income. Exhibit 19-2 is an example of how this income usually appears as a separate item in the consolidated income statement. Note also that the beginning balance of the Investment account in Exhibit 19-1 was $55 million. It has risen by $8 million for the year because of the consolidated enterprise's share in the unconsolidated subsidiary net income.

Exhibits 19-1 and 19-2 indicate that the unconsolidated subsidiary did not declare dividends during 19x3. But suppose that the parent received $6 million in dividends. The equity method would have the following effects:

Equity Method:

Original investment	$55	
Share of subsidiary net income	8	→ Same as now appears in the
Balance	$63	income statement in
Dividends received	6	Exhibit 19-2
Balance, December 31, 19x3	$57	

614

615

*Understanding
Corporate
Annual
Reports—
Part Two*

The $6 million dividend does not appear in the income statement because it would represent a double-counting. Instead, it is regarded as a partial liquidation of the $63 million ownership "claim" as measured in the Investment account. Thus, net income of the subsidiary increases this claim and dividends reduce this claim.

Investments in foreign subsidiaries are often carried at cost because of a long-standing reluctance to recognize gains prior to the receipt of a corresponding amount of funds from the foreign subsidiaries. This conservative approach is an outgrowth of many unhappy experiences with wars, expropriations of assets, devaluations of currencies, and currency restrictions.

RECAPITULATION OF ACCOUNTING FOR INVESTMENTS

As we have seen, the accounting for investments in voting stock depends on the nature of the investment:

1. Except for those subsidiaries in insurance and finance activities, nearly all investments that represent more than a 50 percent ownership interest are usually consolidated. A subsidiary is a corporation controlled by another corporation. The usual condition for control is ownership of a majority (more than 50 percent) of the outstanding voting stock.

2. (a) If the subsidiary is not consolidated, it is carried by the parent under the equity method, which is cost at date of acquisition adjusted for the investor's share of the earnings or losses of the investee subsequent to the date of investment. Dividends received from the investee reduce the carrying amount of the investment.

   (b) The equity method is also generally used for a 20 through 50 percent interest because such a level of ownership is regarded as a presumption that the owner has the ability to exert significant influence.

   (c) Investments in corporate joint ventures should also be accounted for under the equity method. "Corporate joint ventures" are corporations owned and operated by a small group of businesses (the "joint venturers") as a separate business or project for the mutual benefit of the members of the group. Joint ventures are common in the petroleum and construction industries.

3. All other investments are generally carried by the cost method, or more accurately at the lower of cost or market value.[2]

---

[2] *FASB Statement No. 12,* "Accounting for Certain Marketable Securities," requires that a portfolio of securities (rather than each security as an individual investment) should be stated at the lower of cost or market. If the investment is classified as a current asset, any write-downs to market should affect current net income. If the investment is a noncurrent asset, the write-down shall be recorded directly in the stockholders' equity section of the balance sheet as a separate valuation account and not as a component of the determination of net income.

ACCOUNTING FOR GOODWILL

Purchased Goodwill

The major example on intercorporate investments assumed that the acquisition cost of Company S by Company P was equal to the *book values* of Company S. However, the total purchase price paid by P often exceeds the book values of the assets acquired. In fact, the purchase price also often exceeds the sum of the fair market values (current values) of the identifiable individual assets less the liabilities. Such excess of purchase price over fair market value is called "goodwill" or "purchased goodwill" or more accurately "excess of cost over fair value of net identifiable assets of businesses acquired."

To see the impact on the consolidated statements, refer to our initial example on consolidations, where there was an acquisition of a 100 percent interest in S by P for $213 million. Suppose that the price were $40 million higher, or a total of $253 million. For simplicity, assume that all other assets and liabilities in P and S were unaffected by paying $253 million. Also assume that the fair values of the individual assets of S are equal to their book values. The balance sheets immediately after the acquisition are:

	P	S	Intercompany Eliminations	Consolidated
Investment in S	$253	$ —	$213	$ 40[a]
Other assets	437	400		837
Total assets	$690	$400		$877
Accounts payable, etc.	$200	$187		$387
Stockholders' equity	490	213	(213)	490
Total equities	$690	$400		$877

[a] The $40 million "goodwill" would appear in the consolidated balance sheet as a separate intangible asset account. It often is shown as the final item in a listing of assets. It is usually amortized in a straight-line manner as an expense in the consolidated income statement over a span of no greater than 40 years.

If the book values of the S individual assets are not equal to their fair values, the usual procedures are:

1. S continues as a going concern and keeps its accounts on the same basis as before.
2. P records its investment at its acquisition cost (the agreed purchase price).
3. For consolidated reporting purposes, the excess of the acquisition cost over the book values of S is identified with the individual assets, item by item. (In effect, they are revalued at the current market prices prevailing when P acquired S.) Any *remaining excess* that cannot be identified is labeled as purchased goodwill.

Suppose in our example that the fair value of the other assets (e.g., equipment) of S exceeded its book value by $30 million. The balance sheets immediately after acquisition would be:

617

*Understanding
Corporate
Annual
Reports—
Part Two*

	P	*S*	Intercompany *Eliminations*	*Consolidated*
Investment in S	$253	$ —	$213	$30ᵃ / 10ᵇ
Other assets	437	400		837
Total assets	$690	$400		$877
Accounts payable, etc.	$200	$187		$387
Stockholders' equity	490	213	(213)	490
Total equities	$690	$400		$877

ᵃ The $30 million would appear in the consolidated balance sheet as an integral part of the "other assets." That is, the S equipment would be shown at $30 million higher in the consolidated balance sheet than the carrying amount on the S books. Similarly, the depreciation expense on the consolidated income statement would be higher. For instance, if the equipment had five years of useful life remaining, the straight-line depreciation would be $30 ÷ 5, or $6 million higher per year.
ᵇ As in the preceding tabulation, the $10 million "goodwill" would appear in the consolidated balance sheet as a separate intangible asset account.

Nature of Goodwill

Goodwill is frequently misunderstood. The layman often thinks of goodwill as the friendly attitude of the neighborhood store manager. Goodwill may have nothing to do with the personality of the managers or employees. A company may be willing to pay more than the current values of the individual assets received because the acquired company is able to generate abnormally high earnings. This excess earning power may be traceable to:

1. Saving in time and costs by purchasing a corporation having a share of the market in a type of business or in a geographical area where the acquiring corporation planned expansion;

2. Excellent general management skills or a unique product line;

3. Potential efficiency by combination, rearrangement, or elimination of duplicate facilities and administration.

Of course, "goodwill" is originally generated internally. For example, a happy combination of advertising, research, management talent, and timing may give a particular company a dominant market position for which another company is willing to pay dearly. This ability to command a premium price for the total business is goodwill. Nevertheless, such goodwill is never recorded by the selling company. **Therefore, the *only* goodwill generally recognized as an asset is that identified when one company is purchased by another. The consolidated company then must show in its financial statements the purchased goodwill.**

Goodwill must be amortized by systematic charges in the income statement over the period estimated to be benefited. The maximum amortization period should not exceed forty years. (Before 1970, amortization was not required.) Managers, investors, and accountants tend to be uncomfortable about the presence of goodwill on the balance sheet. Somehow, it is regarded as an inferior asset even though management decided that it was valuable enough to warrant a total outlay in excess of the total current value of the individual assets. As a practical matter, many accountants feel that the income-producing factors of goodwill are unlikely to have a value in perpetuity even though expenditures may be made to maintain their value.

As already mentioned, the allocation of a total purchase price among individual assets is often a difficult task. Before 1970, some managers were inclined to take advantage of the fuzziness in this area by insisting that goodwill be loaded with a heavy share of the total purchase price. In this way, future earnings would bear lighter charges because the individual assets would have lower assigned acquisition costs and the goodwill would not be amortized. The requirement for mandatory amortization of goodwill should reduce this questionable practice.

ANALYSIS OF FINANCIAL STATEMENTS

Financial statements should facilitate comparison and prediction, the two major analytical tasks of both internal and external users. In this section, we consider some techniques and ratios commonly used in financial analysis and interpretation. Although internal and external users share an interest in these techniques, our present emphasis is on external uses, particularly because internal uses—evaluation of management performance—are discussed at length in other chapters. The techniques discussed in this chapter will be helpful both to managers and to investors.

Do Ratios Provide Answers?

Some analysts maintain that financial ratios merely provide clues that necessitate deeper probing to discover underlying causes. However, a growing body of evidence shows that ratios can be directly helpful as a basis for making predictions. The most commonly used ratios, numbered 1 through 17, are presented on the following pages.

There are two major purposes of financial-statement analysis: (1) solvency determination and (2) profitability evaluation. Solvency determination is the assessment of the likelihood of a firm's ability to meet its financial obligations as they mature. Profitability evaluation is the assessment of the likelihood of a particular future rate of return on a given security. Empirical studies have shown that ratios related to income (the ratios in Equations 1 through 13) possess the highest predictive power for both purposes.[3] In

[3] For a summary of these studies, see William H. Beaver, "Financial Statement Analysis," in Sidney Davidson and Roman Weil, eds., *Handbook of Modern Accounting,* 2nd ed. (New York: McGraw-Hill Book Company, 1977).

Research in finance and accounting during the 1970s has reinforced the idea that ratios provide preliminary inputs to formal models of the explorations and predictions of such economic phenomena as earnings growth or financial failure. Moreover, many ratios are used simultaneously rather than one at a time for such predictions. Further, accounting reports are only one source of information. See Baruch Lev, *Financial Statement Analysis: A New Approach* (Englewood Cliffs, N.J.: Prentice-Hall, Inc., 1974), and George Foster, *Financial Statement Analysis* (Englewood Cliffs, N.J.: Prentice-Hall, Inc., 1978).

619

*Understanding
Corporate
Annual
Reports—
Part Two*

contrast, the liquidity and turnover ratios (in Equations 14 through 17) are poor bases for prediction.

Our illustrative analysis will focus on one company and one or two years. This is sufficient as a start, but other firms in the industry and a series of years should be examined to get the best overall perspective. That is why annual reports typically contain a table of comparative statistics for five or ten years.

Operating Performance

An important measure of overall accomplishment is the rate of return on invested capital:

$$\text{Rate of return on investment} = \frac{\text{Income}}{\text{Invested capital}} \quad (1)$$

On the surface, this measure is straightforward, but its ingredients may differ according to the purpose it is to serve. What is Invested Capital, the denominator of the ratio? What income figure is appropriate?

The measurement of operating performance (i.e., how profitably assets are employed) should not be influenced by the management's financial decisions (i.e., how assets are obtained). Operating performance is best measured by operating rate of return on average total assets:

$$\begin{array}{c}\text{Pretax operating rate}\\\text{of return on total assets}\end{array} = \frac{\begin{array}{c}\text{Income before}\\\text{interest expense and income taxes}\end{array}}{\text{Average total assets available}} \quad (2)$$

The right-hand side of Equation 2 consists, in turn, of two important ratios:

$$\frac{\begin{array}{c}\text{Income before}\\\text{interest expense and income taxes}\end{array}}{\text{Average total assets available}}$$

$$= \frac{\begin{array}{c}\text{Income before}\\\text{interest expense and income taxes}\end{array}}{\text{Sales}} \times \frac{\text{Sales}}{\begin{array}{c}\text{Average total}\\\text{assets available}\end{array}} \quad (3)$$

Using Exhibits 18-1 and 18-3 from the preceding chapter, we may compute the following 19x1 results for Green Company:

$$\frac{\$3,100,000}{\frac{1}{2}(\$31,000,000 + \$29,000,000)} = \frac{\$3,100,000}{\$55,000,000} \times \frac{\$55,000,000}{\$30,000,000}$$

The right-hand terms in Equation 3 are often called the **margin percentage on sales** and the **total asset turnover**, respectively. Equation 3 may be re-expressed:

Pretax operating rate of return on total assets
$$= \text{Margin percentage on sales} \times \text{Total asset turnover}$$
$$10.33\% = 5.64\% \times 1.833 \text{ times} \tag{4}$$

If ratios are used to evaluate operating performance, they should exclude extraordinary items because they are regarded as nonrecurring items that do not reflect normal performance.

A scrutiny of Equation 4 shows that there are two basic factors in profit making: operating margin percentages and turnover. An improvement in either will, by itself, increase the rate of return on total assets. This phase of performance measurement is discussed fully in Chapter 11.

The ratios used can also be computed on the basis of figures after taxes. However, the peculiarities of the income tax laws may sometimes distort results—for example, the tax rate may change, or losses carried back or forward might eliminate the tax in certain years.

Trading on the Equity

Another measure of invested capital is stockholders' equity:

After-tax rate of return on stockholders' equity
$$= \frac{\text{Net income after taxes}}{\text{Average total stockholders' equity}}$$
$$= \frac{\$1,150,000}{\frac{1}{2}(\$5,800,000 + \$5,700,000)} = 20.0\% \tag{5}$$

This ratio focuses on the ultimate rate of return being earned by the preferred and common stockholders.

Equation 5 can be refined to compute the rate of return on common equity:

Rate of return on common equity
$$= \frac{\text{Net income after taxes} - \text{Preferred dividends}}{\text{Average total stockholders' equity} - \text{Liquidating value of preferred equity}}$$
$$= \frac{\$1,150,000 - \$96,000}{\$5,750,000 - \$1,600,000} = 25.4\% \tag{6}$$

This rate of return is higher than the 20 percent rate in Equation 5

621

*Understanding
Corporate
Annual
Reports—
Part Two*

because the holders of preferred shares are entitled to a limited return based on the 6 percent preferred dividend rate.

Note that the capitalization structure provides limited returns to bondholders and preferred shareholders. This means that common shareholders enjoy the benefits from all income in excess of interest and preferred dividends. When the overall rate of return on total assets exceeds the 5 and 6 percent rates needed to pay interest and preferred dividends, the rate of return to the common shareholders will be magnified. This is an example of *trading on the equity.*

Trading on the equity, which is also referred to as **using financial leverage,** generally means using borrowed money at fixed interest rates and/or paying preferred dividends in the hope of enhancing the rate of return on common stockholders' equity.

Exhibit 19-4, regarding hypothetical companies, shows that results differ, depending on whether the version of invested capital used is total assets or stockholders' equity. Borrowing is a two-edged sword. In Year 1, Company A paid 5 percent for the use of $30,000,000, which in turn earned 15 percent. This method of financing benefited the stockholders handsomely, resulting in an ultimate return on equity of 21 percent, compared with the 15 percent earned by debt-free Company B.

In Year 3, the picture is reversed. When a company is unable to earn at least the interest rate on the funds it borrows, the return on equity will be lower than for the debt-free company.

Real estate promoters are classical examples of traders on the equity. They use layers of mortgage debt, a minimum amount of ownership capital, and enjoy very high returns on investment as long as revenues are ample.

EXHIBIT 19-4

Trading on the Equity: Effects of Debt
on Rates of Return
(In thousands of dollars)

		EQUITIES					RETURN ON INVESTED CAPITAL	
	ASSETS	BONDS PAYABLE	STOCKHOLDERS' EQUITY	INCOME BEFORE INTEREST	5% INTEREST	NET INCOME	ASSETS	EQUITY
Year 1								
Co. A	$80,000	$30,000	$50,000	$12,000	$1,500	$10,500	15.0%	21.0%
Co. B	80,000	—	80,000	12,000	—	12,000	15.0	15.0
Year 2								
Co. A	80,000	30,000	50,000	4,000	1,500	2,500	5.0	5.0
Co. B	80,000	—	80,000	4,000	—	4,000	5.0	5.0
Year 3								
Co. A	80,000	30,000	50,000	2,000	1,500	500	2.5	1.0
Co. B	80,000	—	80,000	2,000	—	2,000	2.5	2.5

Obviously, the more stable the business, the less dangerous it is to trade on the equity. Moreover, the *prudent* use of debt is part of intelligent financial management. Managers who brag about having no long-term debt may not be obtaining the maximum return on equity. On the other hand, too much debt can cause financial disaster when operations become unprofitable.

Common Stock Statistics

Because stock market prices are quoted on a per-share basis, many of the popular ratios are expressed per share (and after taxes). Some of the more important of these ratios follow:

Earnings per share of common stock

$$= \frac{\text{Net income} - \text{Preferred dividends}}{\text{Number of shares outstanding}}$$

$$= \frac{\$1,150,000 - \$96,000}{200,000} = \$5.27 \tag{7}$$

Price/earnings ratio

$$= \frac{\text{Average market price per share of common stock}}{\text{Earnings per share of common stock}}$$

$$= \frac{\$63.25 \text{ (assumed)}}{\$5.27} = 12 \text{ times} \tag{8}$$

Dividend-payout ratio

$$= \frac{\text{Common dividends per share}}{\text{Common earnings per share}}$$

$$= \frac{\$4.77}{\$5.27} = 90.5\% \tag{9}$$

Dividend-yield ratio

$$= \frac{\text{Common dividends per share}}{\text{Average market price per share of common stock}}$$

$$= \frac{\$4.77}{\$63.25} = 7.5\% \tag{10}$$

The above ratios focus on net income and dividends per share—by far, the two factors that most influence investors. When earnings are materially affected by an extraordinary charge, they are reported both before and after the extraordinary charge. Equation 8, the price/earnings ratio (sometimes called an **earnings multiple**), generally measures how much the investing

623

*Understanding
Corporate
Annual
Reports—
Part Two*

public is willing to pay for the company's prospects for earnings. Note especially that the price/earnings ratio is a consensus of the marketplace. This earnings multiplier may differ considerably for two companies within the same industry. It may also change for the same company through the years. Glamour stocks often have astronomical ratios. In general, a high price/earnings ratio indicates that investors are optimistic about the prospective stability and growth of the company's net income. The dividend ratios may be of particular importance to investors in common stock who seek regular cash returns on their investments. For example, an investor who favors high current returns would not buy stock in growth companies. Growth companies have conservative dividend policies because they are using their resources to help finance expansion.

Another oft-quoted statistic is **book value:**

Book value per share of common stock

$$= \frac{\text{Stockholders' equity} - \text{Liquidating value of preferred stock}}{\text{Number of common shares outstanding}}$$

$$= \frac{\$5,800,000 - \$1,600,000}{200,000} = \$21.00 \tag{11}$$

Note the low book value as compared with market value. The shareholders are paying for earning power rather than for assets *per se*. The usefulness of this computation is highly questionable, except in the cases of investment companies. Supposedly, if a stock's market price is below its book value, the stock is attractively priced. The trouble is that market prices are geared to forecasted earnings and dividends—not to book values, which are based on balance sheet values. Consequently, some companies may perpetually have market prices in excess of book values, and vice versa. Book value may, however, be pertinent when companies have heavy investments in liquid assets and are contemplating liquidation. In these cases, book values probably approximate the market values of the assets.

Senior Securities and Safety

Long-term bonds and preferred stocks are sometimes called **senior securities.** Investors who buy senior securities want assurance that future operations will easily provide funds sufficient to pay bond interest, make repayments of principal on bonds, and pay dividends on preferred stock. Senior securities often have protective provisions, such as mortgage liens on real estate or restrictions on dividend payments to holders of common stock, but these are of minor importance compared with prospective earnings. Bondholders don't care for the trouble and inconvenience of foreclosure; they would rather receive a steady stream of interest and repayments of principal. The guiding rule regarding investments in senior securities is to look to **earnings coverage** (also called **interest coverage**), not to liens or legal restrictions on common stock dividends, for protection. The presence of restrictive clauses in bond or preferred stock agreements is secondary; sole reliance on them as justification for investment is foolhardy.

The most informative way to calculate earnings coverage is:

Times bond interest earned

$$= \frac{\text{Net income before bond interest and extraordinary items}}{\text{Bond interest expense}}$$

$$= \frac{\$3,100,000}{\$800,000} = 3.88 \text{ times} \tag{12}$$

Times interest and preferred dividends earned

$$= \frac{\text{Net income before interest, extraordinary items, and taxes}}{\text{Bond interest} + (\text{Preferred dividends} \div 1 \text{ minus tax rate})}$$

$$= \frac{\$3,100,000}{\$800,000 + (\$96,000 \div .5)}$$

$$= \frac{\$3,100,000}{\$800,000 + \$192,000} = 3.13 \text{ times} \tag{13}$$

Equation 12 is self-explanatory. One rule of thumb for adequate safety of an industrial bond is that the interest charges should be earned at least five times in the poorest year in a span of seven to ten years that might be under review. The numerator does not deduct income taxes because interest expense is deductible for income tax purposes. In effect, income taxes have a lower priority than interest. For example, if the numerator were only $800,000, interest would be paid, leaving a net taxable income of zero. This tax deductibility feature is a major reason why bonds are used so much more widely than preferred stock.

Equation 13 highlights the difference between bonds and preferred stock. Because interest payments precede both taxes and preferred dividends, the coverage of preferred dividends is affected by both interest and taxes. The denominator must include an adjustment of preferred dividends for the income tax rate to determine the amount of pretax income needed to cover the taxes and the preferred dividends. The minimum amount of income needed is $992,000, which can be proven as follows:

Income before interest and taxes	$992,000
Interest	800,000
Income before taxes	$192,000
Income taxes	96,000
Net income	$ 96,000
Preferred dividends	96,000
Net income to common stock	0

Short-Term Credit Analysis

Although all investors are interested in any clues that may yield insights into the operating and financial outlook for a company, the short-term lender is naturally more concerned with immediate prospects than with whether bonds due in 2010 will be paid. The direct way for him to obtain his answers is from a **budgeted statement of cash receipts and disbursements** covering the period of the loan (discussed in Chapter 6). The indirect way is to rely on the following ratios that attempt to measure liquidity in a less precise manner:

$$\text{Current ratio} = \frac{\text{Current assets}}{\text{Current liabilities}}$$

$$= \frac{\$23,700,000}{\$9,200,000} = 2.58 \text{ to } 1 \tag{14}$$

Acid-test ratio or Quick ratio

$$= \frac{\text{Cash} + \text{Receivables} + \text{Short-term investments}}{\text{Current liabilities}}$$

$$= \frac{\$8,500,000}{\$9,200,000} = .92 \text{ to } 1 \tag{15}$$

Inventory turnover

$$= \frac{\text{Cost of goods sold}}{\text{Average inventory}}$$

$$= \frac{\$40,000,000}{\frac{1}{2}(\$14,600,000 + \$14,400,000)} = 2.76 \text{ times} \tag{16}$$

Average collection period

$$= \frac{\text{Average accounts receivable}}{\text{Sales on account}} \times 365 \text{ (or 360) days}$$

$$= \frac{\frac{1}{2}(\$5,300,000 + \$5,100,000)}{\$55,000,000^*} \times 365 = 34.5 \text{ days} \tag{17}$$

*Assumed all on account.

The current ratio (Equation 14), although it is probably as widely used as any ratio, is subject to many criticisms. For example, a high current ratio may be due to increases in inventories that have not been selling well. A low current ratio may be traceable to a high current liability for income taxes because of a prosperous year. An increase in the current ratio does not necessarily mean that the business is currently doing well, or vice versa. In other words, changes in current ratios are difficult to interpret. (The current ratio is often called the **working-capital ratio.**)

The acid-test ratio (Equation 15), or quick ratio, attempts to show the ability of the company to pay its current liabilities without having to liquidate its inventory. The time-honored rules of thumb are that a company is below standard if (1) its quick ratio is not at least 1 to 1 and (2) its current ratio is not at least 2 to 1.

These rules of thumb are, of course, subject to countless exceptions, depending on a specific industry's or company's financial picture.

Inventory turnover (Equation 16, the number of times a given amount of stock is sold in a year), computed for classes of inventory, is a useful technique for discovering slow-moving items, for comparing present with past performance, and for spotting possible pricing problems. All these factors are related to the gross profit associated with each turnover.

Turnover standards also differ from industry to industry. Turnovers are faster in grocery stores than in jewelry stores, for example, and turnover traditionally receives more attention in retail than in manufacturing companies.

The average collection period (Equation 17) is a crude indicator of how well the credit terms are being enforced. The shorter the collection period, the better the quality of the receivables. On the other hand, too-stringent credit terms may result in the loss of credit sales and thus may adversely affect profits. Again, variations from rule-of-thumb ratios may mean only that a company performs differently, not less effectively.

SUMMARY

Nearly all corporate annual reports contain consolidated financial statements, as well as "investment" accounts of various sorts. Therefore, acquiring a basic understanding of accounting for intercorporate investments seems essential.

There are many aids to the intelligent analysis of statements. Financial ratios are widely used as a basis for prediction. Above all, financial analysts want to assess future earnings and dividend-paying prospects. If analysts are investigating senior securities, they are concerned with the adequacy with which earnings cover interest payments and related yearly cash requirements. Short-term creditors are less interested in long-run earning power. They want to know the immediate outlook for smooth payment.

Earnings per share seems to be the single number that gets the widest attention as a measure of company performance. Its surface appeal is probably attributable to its deceptive simplicity. However, the difficulties of measuring net income plus the complexities of modern capitalization structures mean that both the numerator and denominator are far from being simple computations.

SUMMARY PROBLEM FOR YOUR REVIEW

Problem

1. Review the section on minority interests. Suppose that P owns 60 percent of the stock of S for a cost of .60 × $213, or $128 million. The total assets of P consist of this $128 million plus $522 million of other assets, a total of $650 million. The S assets and equities are unchanged from the amount given in the example. Prepare an analysis showing what amounts would appear in a consolidated balance sheet immediately after the acquisition.

2. Suppose S has a net income of $50 million for the year, and P has an operating income of $100 million. Other details are described in the example. Prepare an analysis showing what amounts would appear in a consolidated income statement and year-end balance sheet.

Solution

1.

	P	S	Intercompany Eliminations	Consolidated
Investment in S	$128		$128	$ —
Other assets	522	$400		922
Total assets	$650	$400		$922
Accounts payable, etc.	$200	$187		$387
Minority interest	—	—	85	85
Stockholders' equity	450	213	(213)	450
Total equities	$650	$400		$922

2.

	P	S	Consolidated
Sales	$900	$300	$1,200
Expenses	800	250	1,050
Operating income	$100	$ 50	$ 150
Pro-rata share (60%) of unconsolidated subsidiary net income	30	—	
Net income	$130	$ 50	
Outside interest (40%) in consolidated subsidiary net income (minority interest in income)			20
Net income to consolidated entity			$ 130

	P	*S*	Intercompany Eliminations	Consolidated
Investments in S	$158[a]	$ —	$158	$ —
Other assets	622[b]	450[d]		1,072
Total assets	$780	$450		$1,072
Accounts payable, etc.	$200	$187		$ 387
Minority interest	—	—	105[e]	105
Stockholders' equity	580[c]	263	(263)	580
Total equities	$780	$450		$1,072

[a] $128 + .60($50) = $128 + $30 = $158
[b] $522 + $100 = $622
[c] $450 + $100 + $30 = $580
[d] $400 + $50 = $450
[e] $85 + .40($50) = $105

ASSIGNMENT MATERIAL

Fundamental Assignment Material

19-1. Equity method. Company A acquired 30 percent of the voting stock of Company B for $90 million cash. In year one, B had a net income of $50 million and paid cash dividends of $30 million.

Required

Prepare a tabulation that compares the equity method and the cost method of accounting for A's investment in B. Show the effects on the balance sheet equation under each method. What is the year-end balance in the Investment in B account under the equity method? Under the cost method?

19-2. Consolidated financial statements. Suppose Company P acquired a 100 percent voting interest in Company S for $200 million cash at the beginning of the year. Their balance sheet accounts immediately after the acquisition were (in millions):

	P	*S*
Investment in S	$200	$ —
Other assets	600	450
Total assets	$800	$450
Accounts payable, etc.	$300	$250
Stockholders' equity	500	200
Total equities	$800	$450

Required

1. Prepare a consolidated balance sheet upon acquisition.

2. Suppose S had sales of $400 million and expenses of $360 million for the year. P had sales of $950 and expenses of $825. Prepare income statements and balance sheets for P, for S, and for the consolidated company.

3. Prepare a year-end balance sheet for P, S, and the consolidated entity.

4. Suppose S paid a cash dividend of $40 million. What accounts in Requirement 3 would be affected and by how much?

629

*Understanding
Corporate
Annual
Reports—
Part Two*

19-3. Minority interests. This is an extension of the preceding problem. However, it may be solved independently, because all facts are self-contained below. Suppose Company P acquired an 80 percent voting interest in S for $160 million cash at the beginning of the year. Their balance sheet accounts immediately after the acquisition were (in millions):

	P	S
Investment in S	$160	$ —
Other assets	640	450
Total assets	$800	$450
Accounts payable, etc.	$300	$250
Stockholders' equity	500	200
Total equities	$800	$450

Required

1. Prepare a consolidated balance sheet upon acquisition.

2. Suppose S had sales of $400 million and expenses of $360 million for the year. P had sales of $950 and expenses of $825. Prepare income statements and balance sheets for P, for S, and for the consolidated entity.

3. Prepare a year-end balance sheet for P, S, and the consolidated entity.

4. Suppose S paid a cash dividend of $30 million. What accounts in Requirement 3 would be affected and by how much? Prepare a year-end balance sheet for P, S, and the consolidated entity.

19-4. Goodwill. This is an elaboration of Problem 19-2. However, it may be solved independently, because all facts are self-contained below. Suppose Company P acquired a 100 percent voting interest in Company S for $230 million cash at the beginning of the year. The balance sheet accounts immediately after the acquisition were (in millions):

	P	S
Investment in S	$230	$ —
Other assets	570	450
Total assets	$800	$450
Accounts payable, etc.	$300	$250
Stockholders' equity	500	200
Total equities	$800	$450

Required

1. Prepare a consolidated balance sheet upon acquisition, assuming that the book values of the S individual assets are equal to their fair market values. "Goodwill" is going to be amortized as an expense on a straight-line basis over forty years. How much was amortized in the first year?

2. Assume that the book values of the S individual assets are equal to their fair market values, except for equipment. The book value of the S equipment is $100 million, but its fair market value is $120 million. The equipment has a remaining useful life of ten years. Straight-line depreciation is used.
   a. Prepare a consolidated balance sheet upon acquisition.
   b. By how much will consolidated income differ in comparison to the consolidated income in Requirement 1?

19-5. What criterion is used to determine whether a parent-subsidiary relationship exists?

19-6. Why have subsidiaries? Why not have the corporation take the form of a single legal entity?

19-7. What is a minority interest?

19-8. When is there justification for not consolidating subsidiaries in accounting reports?

19-9. What is the equity method?

19-10. Contrast the cost method and the equity method.

19-11. What are the major analytical tasks of internal and external users of financial statements?

19-12. How does the analyst approach depreciation?

19-13. "Ratios are mechanical and incomplete." Explain.

19-14. "Trading on the equity means exchanging bonds for stock." Do you agree? Explain.

19-15. "Borrowing is a two-edged sword." Do you agree? Explain.

19-16. "Senior securities are all those issued before 1940." Do you agree? Explain.

19-17. What is the guiding rule for investing in senior securities?

19-18. "Sale and leasing back entails invisible debt." Explain.

19-19. "The objective of credit management is to avoid credit losses." Do you agree? Explain.

19-20. What is the argument for departing from the use of historical cost as a basis of recording depreciation of fixed assets?

19-21. "Depreciation may be viewed in at least two different ways." Explain.

19-22. Classification on balance sheet. The following accounts appeared in the annual report of the Jewel Companies, Inc.:

1. Accumulated earnings—reserved for self-insured losses and general contingencies.

631

*Understanding
Corporate
Annual
Reports—
Part Two*

2. Long-term indebtedness, due within one year

3. Investments: minority interest in foreign affiliates (at cost)

4. Prepaid expenses and supplies

5. Dividends payable

6. Treasury stock at cost

Required

Indicate in detail in what section of the balance sheet each account should appear.

19-23. Meaning of account descriptions. The following account descriptions were found in various annual reports:

Montgomery Ward: Net earnings of subsidiaries not consolidated
Tenneco: Equity in undistributed earnings of 50% owned companies
St. Regis Paper: Equity in net earnings of subsidiaries not consolidated and associated companies

In your own words, explain what this account represents.

19-24. Consolidations in Japan. *Business Week* (April 25, 1977, p. 112) reported that Japan's finance ministry issued a directive requiring the 600 largest Japanese companies to produce consolidated financial statements after April 1, 1977. The story said: "Financial observers hope that the move will help end the tradition-honored Japanese practice of 'window dressing' the parent company financial results by shoving losses onto hapless subsidiaries, whose red ink was seldom revealed. . . . When companies needed to show a bigger profit, they would sell their product to subsidiaries at an inflated price. . . . Or the parent company charged a higher rent to a subsidiary company using its building."

Required

Could a parent company follow the quoted practices and achieve window dressing in its parent-only financial statements if it used the equity method of accounting for its intercorporate investments? The cost method? Explain.

19-25. Investments in equity securities. Clark Equipment Company is a multinational corporation with subsidiaries and affiliations throughout the world. Its annual report for 1976 showed total assets of $900.1 million. Investments in companies in which Clark owned 20 percent or more minority interest was $25.0 million. The remaining investments in companies in which Clark owned less than 20 percent amounted to $4.3 million.

Required

How did Clark report the investments in which it owned more than 50 percent interest? Indicate briefly how the following three classes of investments should be accounted for: (a) greater than 50 percent interest; (b) 20 percent through 50 percent interest; and (c) less than 20 percent interest.

19-26. Earnings per share. The Koss Corporation reported earnings per share of $5 for 19x4. The company had outstanding 4,000,000 common shares and 200,000 shares of 4% convertible preferred stock, $100 par, each share convertible into four common shares.

1. Net income for 19x4.

2. Earnings per share on a fully diluted basis.

19-27. Equity method of accounting for unconsolidated subsidiaries. Trans World Airlines owns 100 percent of Hilton International Company. The airline and hotel operations are now being reported on a consolidated basis. However, in past years the hotel operations have not been consolidated with the airline operations for financial reporting purposes. The following data are extracted from the TWA 1972 annual report (in millions):

From statement of consolidated income:	*12-31-72*	*12-31-71*
Income from airline operations	(5.3)	
Income from hotel operations	8.8	
Net income for the year	$ 3.5	
From consolidated balance sheet:		
Investments: equity in Hilton International	$47.0	$38.2

If Hilton International had paid cash dividends of $4.1 million in 1972, how would the payment have affected TWA net income for the year? How would it have affected the investment balance at December 31, 1972?

19-28. Consolidated statements. Consider the following for D Company as of December 31, 19x4:

	Parent	*Subsidiary**
Assets	$700,000	$200,000
Liabilities to creditors	$200,000	$ 80,000
Stockholders' equity	500,000	120,000
Total equities	$700,000	$200,000

*80 percent owned by parent

The $700,000 of assets of the parent include a $96,000 investment in the subsidiary. The $96,000 includes the parent's pro-rata share of the subsidiary's net income for 19x4. The parent's sales were $990,000 and operating expenses were $922,000. These figures exclude any pro-rata share of the subsidiary's net income. The subsidiary's sales were $700,000 and operating expenses were $660,000. Prepare a consolidated income statement and a consolidated balance sheet.

19-29. Consolidated financial statements. Fresno Company (the parent) owns 100 percent of the common stock of Grand Company (the subsidiary). Their financial statements follow:

Income Statements for the year Ended December 31, 19x3

	Parent	*Subsidiary*
Revenue and "other income"	$40,000,000	$10,000,000
Expenses	38,000,000	9,000,000
Net income	$ 2,000,000	$ 1,000,000

Assets	$10,000,000	$ 4,000,000
Liabilities to creditors	$ 4,500,000	$ 1,000,000
Stockholders' equity	5,500,000	3,000,000
Total equities	$10,000,000	$ 4,000,000

Required

1. The subsidiary had enjoyed a fantastically profitable year in 19x3. The parent's income statement had been prepared by showing the parent's claim to the subsidiary's income as a part of the parent's "other income." On the other hand, the parent's balance sheet is really not completed. The $10,000,000 of assets of the parent company include a $2,000,000 investment in the subsidiary and do *not* include the parent's claim to subsidiary's 19x3 net income.

   Prepare a consolidated income statement and a consolidated balance sheet.

2. Suppose that Fresno Company owned 60 percent of the Grand Company. Liabilities to creditors are unchanged. The assets of the parent company include a $1,200,000 investment in the subsidiary instead of $2,000,000. Therefore, the total assets are $9.2 million, not $10.0 million. The balance sheet is really not completed because the investment account does not reflect the claim to the subsidiary's 19x3 net income. Similarly, the parent's revenue and other income is $39,600,000, not $40,000,000.

   Prepare a consolidated income statement and a consolidated balance sheet.

19-30. Determination of goodwill. Refer to Assignment 19-29, Requirement 1. Suppose that the investment in the subsidiary in Requirement 1 was $2,800,000 instead of the $2,000,000 as stated. This would mean that the "other assets" would be $7,200,000 instead of $8,000,000. Would the consolidated income differ? How? Be as specific as possible. Would the consolidated balance sheet differ? How? Be as specific as possible.

19-31. Purchased goodwill. Consider the following balance sheets (in millions of dollars):

	COMPANY X	COMPANY Y
Cash	150	20
Inventories	60	30
Plant assets, net	60	30
Total assets	270	80
Common stock and paid-in capital	70	30
Retained income	200	50
Total equities	270	80

X paid $120 million to Y stockholders for all of their stock. The "fair value" of the plant assets is $70 million. The fair value of cash and inventories is equal to their carrying amounts. X and Y continued to keep separate books as individual entities.

Required
1. Prepare a tabulation showing the balance sheets of X, of Y, Intercompany Eliminations, and Consolidated immediately after the acquisition.

2. Suppose that only $60 million rather than $70 million of the total purchase price of $120 million could be logically assigned to the plant assets. How would the consolidated accounts be affected?

3. Refer to the facts in Requirement 1. Suppose X had paid $144 million rather than $120 million. State how your tabulation in Requirement 1 would change.

19-32. Amortization and depreciation. Refer to Assignment 19-31, Requirement 3. Suppose a year passes, and X and Y generate individual net incomes of $20 million and $13 million, respectively. The latter is after a deduction of $6 million of straight-line depreciation. Compute the consolidated net income if goodwill is amortized (1) over forty years and (2) over ten years.

19-33. Purchases and goodwill. The B Company and the Y Company have the following accounts at December 31, 19x1:

	B	Y
Net assets	$99,000,000	$27,000,000
Stockholders' equity	$99,000,000	$27,000,000
Net income	$10,000,000	$10,000,000

B combined with Y by issuing stock with a market value of $67,000,000 in exchange for the shares of Y. Assume that the book value and the current value of the individual assets of Y were equal.

Required
1. Show the balance sheet accounts and immediate net income for the combined companies as they would appear if the combination were accounted for as a $67,000,000 purchase with recognition of purchased goodwill. Assume that goodwill is not amortized.

2. How would net income in Requirement 1 above be affected if goodwill were amortized on a straight-line basis over five years? Comment on the results.

19-34. Allocating total purchase price to assets. Two entities had the following balance sheet accounts as of December 31, 19x1 (in millions):

	Grey-mont	Para-delt		Grey-mont	Para-delt
Cash and receivables	$ 30	$ 22	Current liabilities	$ 50	$ 20
Inventories	120	3	Common stock	100	10
Plant assets, net	150	95	Retained income	150	90
Total assets	$300	$120	Total equities	$300	$120
Net income for 19x1	$ 19	$ 4			

634

635

*Understanding
Corporate
Annual
Reports—
Part Two*

On January 4, 19x2, these entities combined. Greymont issued $180 million of its shares (at market value) in exchange for all of the shares of Paradelt, a motion picture division of a large company. The inventory of films acquired through the combination had been fully amortized on Paradelt's books.

During 19x2, Greymont entered into many television distribution contracts that called for $21 million in film rentals over a prolonged span of years. These rentals were to be collected over this period of time, but the contracts were used as support for immediate recognition of revenue (and consequent net income).

Greymont earned $20 million on its other operations during 19x2. Paradelt broke even on its other operations during 19x2.

Required

1. Prepare a consolidated balance sheet for the combined company immediately after the combination on a purchase basis. Assume that on a purchase basis $80 million would be assigned to the inventory of films.

2. Prepare a comparison of net income between 19x1 and 19x2 where 25 percent of the cost of the film inventories would be properly matched against the revenue from the television contracts. What would be the net income for 19x2 if the $80 million were assigned to goodwill rather than to the library of films, and goodwill were amortized over forty years?

19-35. Analysis of ratios. (CMA.) Thorpe Company is a wholesale distributor of professional equipment and supplies. The company's sales have averaged about $900,000 annually for the three-year period 19x3–19x5. The firm's total assets at the end of 19x5 amounted to $850,000.

The president of Thorpe Company has asked the controller to prepare a report summarizing the financial aspects of the company's operations for the past three years. This report will be presented to the Board of Directors at their next meeting.

In addition to comparative financial statements, the controller has decided to present a number of relevant financial ratios that can assist in the identification and interpretation of trends. At the request of the controller, the accounting staff has calculated the following ratios for the three-year period 19x3–19x5:

	19x3	19x4	19x5
Current ratio	2.00	2.13	2.18
Acid-test (quick) ratio	1.20	1.10	0.97
Accounts receivable turnover	9.72	8.57	7.13
Inventory turnover	5.25	4.80	3.80
Percent of total debt to total assets	44%	41%	38%
Percent of long-term debt to total assets	25%	22%	19%
Sales to fixed assets (fixed-asset turnover)	1.75	1.88	1.99
Sales as a percent of 1973 sales	1.00%	1.03%	1.06%
Gross margin percentage	40.0%	38.6%	38.5%
Net income to sales	7.8%	7.8%	8.0%
Return on total assets	8.5%	8.6%	8.7%
Return on stockholders' equity	15.1%	14.6%	14.1%

In the preparation of his report, the controller has decided first to examine the financial ratios independently of any other data to determine if the ratios themselves reveal any significant trends over the three-year period.

Required Answer the following questions. Indicate in each case which ratio(s) you used in arriving at your conclusion.

1. The current ratio is increasing while the acid-test (quick) ratio is decreasing. Using the ratios provided, identify and explain the contributing factor(s) for this apparently divergent trend.

2. In terms of the ratios provided, what conclusion(s) can be drawn regarding the company's use of financial leverage during the 19x3–19x5 period?

3. Using the ratios provided, what conclusion(s) can be drawn regarding the company's net investment in plant and equipment?

19-36. Effects of transactions on financial statements. For each of the following numbered items, select the lettered transaction that indicates its effect on the corporation's financial statements. If a transaction has more than one effect, list all applicable letters. Assume that the total current assets exceed the total current liabilities both before and after every transaction described.

Numbered Transactions

1. The appropriation of retained earnings as a reserve for contingencies.
2. Issue of new shares in a three-for-one split of common stock.
3. Issuance of additional common shares as a stock dividend.
4. Sale and leaseback of factory building at a selling price that substantially exceeds the book value.
5. The destruction of a building by fire. Insurance proceeds, collected immediately, slightly exceed book value.
6. Payment of trade account payable.
7. Purchase of inventory on open account.
8. Collection of account receivable.
9. Sale on account (ignore related cost of goods sold).

Lettered Effects

a. Increases current ratio.
b. Decreases current ratio.
c. Increases net working capital.
d. Decreases net working capital.
e. Increases total stockholders' equity.
f. Decreases total stockholders' equity.
g. Increases the book value per share of common stock.
h. Decreases the book value per share of common stock.

i. Increases total retained earnings.

j. Decreases total retained earnings.

19-37. Computation of financial ratios. You are given the financial statements of the Maxim Co.

Required

Compute the following for the 19x2 financial statements:

1. Pretax operating rate of return on total assets.

2. Divide your answer in Requirement 1 into two components: margin percentage on sales and total asset turnover.

3. After-tax rate of return on total stockholders' equity.

4. Rate of return on common equity. Did the common stockholders benefit from the existence of preferred stock? Explain fully.

5. Earnings per share.

6. Suppose the preferred stock were convertible into common on a basis of ten shares of common for each share of preferred. What would be the "fully diluted" earnings per share?

7. The average market price of the stock was $9\frac{3}{8}$. What was the price/earnings ratio?

8. Dividend yield ratio. Explain why cash dividends might be so high.

9. Book value per share of common stock.

THE MAXIM CO.
Balance Sheet
(In thousands of dollars)

	December 31	
Assets	*19x2*	*19x1*
Current assets:		
Cash	$ 1,000	$ 1,000
Marketable securities		1,000
Receivables, net	5,000	4,000
Inventories at cost	12,000	9,000
Prepayments	1,000	1,000
Total current assets	$19,000	$16,000
Plant and equipment, net	22,000	23,000
Total assets	$41,000	$39,000
Equities		
Current liabilities:		
Accounts payable	$10,000	$ 6,000
Accrued expenses payable	500	500
Income taxes payable	1,500	1,500
Total current liabilities	$12,000	$ 8,000
4% bonds payable	$10,000	$10,000

	December 31	
	19x2	19x1
Stockholders' equity:		
Preferred stock, 6%, par value and liquidating value are $100 per share	$ 5,000	$ 5,000
Common stock, $10 par value	8,000	8,000
Premium on common stock	4,000	4,000
Retained earnings	1,000	3,000
Reserve for plant expansion	1,000	1,000
Total stockholders' equity	$19,000	$21,000
Total equities	$41,000	$39,000

THE MAXIM CO.
Statement of Income and Reconciliation of Retained Earnings
for the Year Ended December 31, 19x2
(In thousands of dollars)

Sales (all on credit)		$40,000
Cost of goods sold		30,100
Gross profit on sales		$ 9,900
Other operating expenses:		
Selling expenses	$ 5,000	
Administrative expenses	2,000	
Depreciation	1,000	8,000
Net operating income		$ 1,900
Interest expense		400
Net income before income taxes		$ 1,500
Income taxes		700
Net income after income taxes		$ 800
Dividends on preferred stock		300
Net income for common stockholders		$ 500
Dividends on common stock		2,500
Net income retained		$(2,000)
Retained earnings, December 31, 19x1		3,000
Retained earnings, December 31, 19x2		$ 1,000

19-38. Short-term ratios. Refer to Problem 19-37. Compute (1) current ratio (2) acid-test or quick ratio, (3) inventory turnover, and (4) average collection period of receivables outstanding.

19-39. Prepare funds statement. Refer to Problem 19-37. Prepare a statement of changes in financial position using the net working capital concept of "funds."

19-40. Funds statement. (This is more difficult than the other problems on the funds statement.) Using Exhibits 19-1, 19-2, and 19-3, prepare a consolidated statement of changes in financial position using the net working capital concept of "funds" for the Goliath Corporation.

19-41. Prepare classified financial statements. The Crown Company has the following balances in accounts and miscellaneous data (in millions of dollars) that pertain to operations for 19x2 or to December 31, 19x2:

639

*Understanding
Corporate
Annual
Reports—
Part Two*

Minority interests	$ 10
Cash	10
Capital surplus	30
Revenue received in advance	5
Franchise at amortized cost	9
Reserve for contingencies	5
Plant and equipment—at original cost	100
Outside stockholders' interest in consolidated subsidiaries' net income	1
Depreciation expense	10
Land—at current realizable value	70
Preferred stock, not convertible	20
Unappropriated reinvested earnings	35
Accounts payable	20
Prepaid rent	1
Net sales and other operating revenue	200
Inventories at average cost	50
Income taxes	23
Preferred dividends	1
Prepaid insurance	1
Accounts receivable	39
Accumulated depreciation	30
Cost of goods sold and operating expenses, exclusive of depreciation	144
Temporary investments in marketable securities—at cost	14
Notes payable	10
Treasury common stock—at cost	3
Accrued wages payable	4
Interest expense	2
Land—at original cost	9
Pro-rata share of unconsolidated subsidiary net income	2
Trademarks—at amortized cost	10
Accrued income taxes payable	5
Common stock	40
Deferred charges (e.g., plant rearrangement costs)	2
Plant and equipment—current replacement cost	110
Long-term debt	45
Investments in unconsolidated subsidiaries	12
Franchise—at current realizable value	13
Accrued interest payable	1

The company had issued 10,150,000 shares of common stock, of which 150,000 have been repurchased and held in the treasury. Note that all the above data need not necessarily appear in the financial statements as prepared under generally accepted accounting principles.

Required Prepare a formal consolidated balance sheet and income statement. Include appropriate classifications of the various accounts.

CHAPTER 20

Difficulties in Measuring Net Income

The income statement summarizes the performance of a company. This chapter examines the effects on the determination of net income of a selected few of the major accounting practices. Unless these effects are understood, the user of an income statement will be unable to interpret it intelligently.

This discussion attempts to focus on the major issues without getting bogged down in techniques. First, various *theoretical* concepts of income are explored. Then various *generally accepted alternative accounting methods* are inspected to highlight their divergent effects on income. The aim is to alert the reader to the imprecision of a reported net income figure and to the need for awareness of the assumptions and limitations of generally accepted accounting measurements. The issues discussed include inflation, inventory methods, the investment tax credit, and deferral of income taxes. There are, of course, many other controversial issues in accounting, including, for example, accounting for long-term leases, pensions, intangible exploratory drilling costs, foreign currency revaluation, and whether companies should publish financial forecasts. However, space limitations preclude our discussion of these accounting controversies.

640

INFLATION AND INCOME MEASUREMENT

The middle 1970s were marked by unprecedented levels of inflation in nearly all countries. As a result, influential persons attacked the traditional financial statements as "unrealistic," "misleading," "useless," and so on. Suggestions for change led to regulatory actions that departed from the historical cost measures that had almost exclusively dominated financial reporting throughout the century. These departures will now be described. **In essence, the controversies center around how income should be defined.** One concept of income will lead to one set of measurement rules, another concept to a different set.

Although various approaches to income measurement are subject to dispute, the crudest approach, that of matching cash disbursements against cash receipts in a given period, has been generally rejected in favor of the accrual basis that was discussed in Chapter 17. To illustrate, nearly all "cash-basis" income measurement systems have at least been modified to provide for depreciation. After all, depreciation is central to an accrual basis. All variations in the concepts of income discussed below have the accrual basis as an anchor.

The following facts are used to compare various concepts of income:

At December 31, 19x2, two identical parcels of land are acquired for $50,000 each. One parcel is sold on December 31, 19x3, for $80,000. The second parcel is sold on December 31, 19x4, for $90,000. The general price-level index was 100 on December 31, 19x2, 110 on December 31, 19x3 (a first rise of 10 percent), and 132 on December 31, 19x4 (a subsequent rise of 20 percent).

Historical Cost and Current Value

Four basic concepts of income are presented, two using nominal dollars and two using constant dollars. **Nominal dollars** are those that are not restated for fluctuations in the general purchasing power of the monetary unit, whereas **constant dollars** are restated.

Exhibit 20-1, which illustrates these four concepts of income, should be studied closely now and as you read the explanations that follow in the next several pages. As the first column of Exhibit 20-1 shows, income (= gain) is the excess of realized revenue ($80,000 in 19x3) over the "not restated" historical costs of assets used in obtaining that revenue. As Chapter 17 points out, an exchange transaction is ordinarily necessary before revenues or gains are measured. No income appears until the asset is sold; intervening price fluctuations are ignored.

Exhibit 20-1 (second column) illustrates a version of the *current-value* approach. Net income is the increase in wealth as achieved by operations plus changes in the current value of assets held. This current-value approach

641

EXHIBIT 20-1

Four Ways to Measure Income

	NOMINAL DOLLARS: NOT RESTATED FOR GENERAL INDEX		CONSTANT DOLLARS: RESTATED FOR GENERAL INDEX	
	HISTORICAL COST (1)	CURRENT VALUE (2)	HISTORICAL COST (3)	CURRENT VALUE (4)
19x3				
Selling price	$80,000	$80,000	$80,000	$80,000
Current value at Dec. 31, 19x2;		50,000		
adjusted for general price-level change				
($50,000 × 1.10)				55,000
Historical cost	50,000		55,000	
Gain on parcel sold	$30,000	$30,000	$25,000	$25,000
Land not sold:				
Current value of land held at Dec. 31, 19x3		$80,000		$80,000
Current value at Dec. 31, 19x2		50,000		55,000
Gain on land not sold	—	$30,000	—	$25,000
Total gain recognized	$30,000	$60,000	$25,000	$50,000
19x4				
Selling price	$90,000	$90,000	$90,000	$90,000
Current value at Dec. 31, 19x3;		80,000		
adjusted for general price-level change				
($80,000 × 1.20)				96,000
Historical cost ($50,000) and ($55,000 × 1.20)	50,000		66,000	
Gain (loss) on parcel sold	$40,000	$10,000	$24,000	$ (6,000)
Cumulative gain:				
Two years together	$70,000[a]	$70,000[a]	$54,000[b]	$54,000[b]

[a] Note that the total gain for the two years is the same.
[b] In order to compare current with past net income figures, the past must be restated in terms of current dollars.

Two-year summary of income:
19x3 restated in terms of 19x4 general purchasing power;

$25,000 × 1.20 and $50,000 × 1.20	$30,000	$60,000
19x4 gain	24,000	(6,000)
Two years together	$54,000	$54,000

The cumulative sums are not the same as those in columns (1) and (2) because no income can emerge under the general index approach until the general purchasing power of the original capital has been maintained.

abandons the well-entrenched concept of realization; it includes "unrealized" gains in net income.[1]

The second column shows how rising current values would be reported as income even if the land were unsold. The essential difference between the historical-cost basis and the current-value basis is one of timing. The bottom line shows that the cumulative gain for the two years is the same.

[1] For an elaboration, see the section, "Measurement Alternatives," in Chapter 11.

Current value is a term widely used to describe the fundamental basis for valuation in column (2). However, it is a general term that embraces several variations. Be on guard as to its meaning in a particular situation.

Sometimes current value represents *replacement cost,* today's cost of obtaining a similar asset *that would produce the same expected cash flow* as the existing asset. Other times, the term current value represents *net realizable value,* the estimated selling price in the ordinary course of business, less reasonably predictable costs of completion and disposal.

For some assets (for example, marketable securities), replacement cost and net realizable value should be approximately equal. However, for assets whose markets are inactive or fragmented (for example, highly specialized equipment), replacement cost and net realizable value may differ significantly, because net realizable value may approximate scrap value whereas replacement cost may be large.

During the late 1970s accountants in the English-speaking countries struggled with the problem of measuring the current values of assets. For example, in 1976 the U.S. Securities and Exchange Commission issued a new requirement for footnote disclosure of the replacement value of inventories and plant and equipment of companies having total assets in excess of $100 million.

Regulatory authorities in the United Kingdom have proposed a form of current-value accounting, effective in 1978. However, their version of profit differs from that in column (2) in one major respect. No "profit" would be recognized if a going concern were planning to replace the land in question. Instead, the "gains" in Exhibit 20-1 would be excluded from profit and shown separately in a summary of total gains and losses immediately after the income statement. This approach is illustrated in the appendix to this chapter.

Restated Historical Cost

Column (3) of Exhibit 20-1 shows the results of applying general index numbers to historical costs. Essentially, the income measurements in each year are restated in terms of *constant dollars* (possessing the same general purchasing power of the current year) instead of the *nominal dollars* (possessing different general purchasing power of various years).

The fundamental reasoning underlying the column (3) approach goes to the heart of measurement theory itself. Additions or subtractions must use a *common measuring unit,* be it dollars, francs, meters, ounces, or any chosen measure.

Consider the objections to column (1). Deducting 50,000 19x2 dollars from 80,000 19x3 dollars to obtain $30,000 is akin to deducting 50 centimeters from 80 meters and calling the result 30. **Grade-school tests are marked wrong when such nonsensical arithmetic is discovered, but accountants have been paid well for years for performing similar arithmetic.**

Column (3) shows how general indexes may be used to restate column (1) and thereby remedy the foregoing objections. An example of such an index is the Gross National Product Implicit Price Deflator. Anyone who has lived long enough to be able to read this book is aware that the purchasing power of the dollar is unstable. Index numbers are used to gauge the relationship between current conditions and some norm or base condition (which is assigned the index number of 100). For our purposes, a general price index compares the average price of a group of goods and services at one date with the average price of a similar group at another date. **A price index is an average; it does not measure the behavior of the individual component prices.** Some individual prices may move in one direction and some in another. The general consumer price level may soar while the prices of eggs and chickens decline.

Maintaining Invested Capital

The column (3) approach is *not* a fundamental departure from historical costs. Instead, it maintains that all historical costs to be matched against revenue should be restated on some constant-dollar basis so that all revenue and all expenses can be expressed in dollars of the same (usually current) purchasing power. The restated figures *are historical costs* expressed in constant dollars via the use of a general price index.

The current dollar is typically employed because users of financial statements tend to think in such terms instead of in terms of old dollars with significantly different purchasing power. The second parcel of land would be updated on each year's balance sheet along with its effect on stockholders' equity as follows:

December 31, 19x3

	Not Restated Cost	*Multiplier*	*Restated Cost*
Land	$50,000	110/100	$55,000
Stockholders' equity	50,000	110/100	55,000

December 31, 19x4

	Restated Cost $12/31/x3$	*Multiplier*	*Restated Cost* $12/31/x4$
Land	$55,000	132/110	$66,000[a]
Stockholders' equity	55,000	132/110	66,000[a]

[a] The same result could be tied to the year of acquisition:

Land	$50,000 × 132/100 = $66,000
Stockholders' equity	$50,000 × 132/100 = $66,000

The restated amount is just that—a restatement of original *cost* in terms of current dollars—not a gain in any sense. Therefore, this approach should *not* be labeled as an adoption of "current value" accounting. Thus, under this approach, **if the specific appraisal value of the land goes up or down, the restated cost is unaffected.**

The restated-historical-cost approach harmonizes with the concept of maintaining the general purchasing power of the invested capital in total rather than maintaining "specific invested capital," item by item. More will be said about this distinction after we examine column (4).

Restated Current Value

Column (4) of Exhibit 20-1 shows the results of applying general index numbers to current values. As footnote *b* of the exhibit explains in more detail, the *nominal* gains reported in column (2) are adjusted so that only gains in *constant dollars* are reported. For example, suppose you buy land on December 31, 19x2, for $50,000 cash. If the current appraisal value of your land at December 31, 19x3, is $80,000, but the general price index has risen from 100 to 110, your nominal gain is $30,000 but your "real" gain in constant dollars on that parcel in 19x3 is only $25,000: the $80,000 current value minus the restated historical cost of $55,000.

Note too that holding the parcel throughout 19x4 would provide a $10,000 nominal gain but a $6,000 real loss after the maintenance of the general purchasing power of your invested capital is considered [column (2) versus column (4)].

Many theorists disagree on the relative merits of historical-cost approaches versus miscellaneous versions of current-value approaches to income measurement. But there is general agreement among the theorists that restatements in constant dollars would be an improvement (ignoring practical barriers), because otherwise income includes illusory gains caused by using an unstable measuring unit.

Misinterpretations of Current-Value Accounting

Restatements in constant dollars can be applied to *both* the historical-cost and the current-value basis of income measurement, as columns (3) and (4) illustrate. **Avoid the misconception that the choices are among the first three columns only.** In fact, many advocates of the column (4) approach insist it is the best approximation of net income. Their definition of net income is the *total* change in *wealth* (overall command over goods and services) measured in constant dollars—units of general purchasing power including realized and unrealized components.

When inflation accounting is discussed, accountants and managers frequently confuse and blur the various concepts of income just covered. Highlights of Exhibit 20-1 include:

1. Column (3), constant-dollar accounting applied to historical cost statements, is *not* concerned with current-value concepts of income, whatever their strengths and weaknesses.

2. **Write-ups of nonmonetary assets under column (3) do *not* result in the recognition of gains. They are restatements of *costs* in dollars of equivalent purchasing power.**

3. The difference between current-value and historical-cost concepts of income is primarily the *timing* of the recognition of income. Historical cost only looks at realized gains, whereas current value also encompasses unrealized gains. The cumulative effects of both concepts of income are identical under the nominal-dollar approach. The cumulative effects are also identical under the constant-dollar approach, as the bottom computation in Exhibit 20-1 shows.

4. The choice among accounting measures is often expressed as either historical-cost accounting or general-price-level accounting or current-value (specific-price-level) accounting. **But this is an inaccurate statement of choices. A correct statement would be that there are four basic choices.** General-price-level (constant-dollar) accounting may be combined with either historical-cost accounting [column (3)] or current-value accounting [column (4)].

UNIFORMITY VS. FLEXIBILITY

Despite the weaknesses of historical cost, generally accepted accounting principles in the United States and Canada continue to view it as the primary basis for determining net income. Even within the historical-cost framework, there are many ways of computing net income. Given the same set of facts, two companies within the same industry may have accounting policies that show quite different results. The use of different patterns of depreciation is one example.

The user of financial statements wants to make comparisons over time and among companies. He is obviously hampered by the lack of uniformity in accounting. Uniformity does not mean rigid adherence to a detailed encyclopedia of stringent rules. It does mean that variations should be eliminated that cannot be justified by differences in circumstances. The trouble is that managers and accountants interpret "differences in circumstances" in a variety of ways.

Almost everybody is for narrowing the differences in accounting as long as flexibility is not inhibited. Such a position is self-contradictory because flexibility must be reduced to obtain more uniformity, and vice versa. It is hard to assail the idea that differences in circumstances may justify differences in accounting. The key need is to define what "differences in circumstances" means. So far, the authoritative professional bodies have not directly discussed that issue. Nevertheless, some progress is being made. *APB Opinion No. 11,* on deferred income taxes, which is discussed later in this chapter, narrowed the differences, even though many accountants felt strongly that the method supported was not defensible accounting theory.

The remainder of this chapter examines the possible effects of alternative accounting methods on financial statements with particular stress on net income computed on the historical-cost basis.

INVENTORY METHODS

Fifo and Lifo

Accountants argue vigorously about the theoretical merits of two widely used inventory-costing methods that entail totally opposite cost-flow assumptions:

1. **First-in, first-out (Fifo).** The stock acquired earliest is assumed to be used first; the stock acquired latest is assumed to be still on hand.

2. **Last-in, first-out (Lifo).** The stock acquired earliest is assumed to be still on hand; the stock acquired latest is assumed to have been used first. In the Lifo method, the most recent, or last, inventory costs are considered to be the cost of goods used or sold. The attempt is to match the current cost of materials against current sales. As compared to Fifo, the Lifo technique of valuing inventory usually results in the reporting of less income when prices are rising and more income when prices are falling.

If unit prices did not fluctuate, all inventory methods would show identical results. But prices change, and these changes appear on the financial records in different ways, depending on the specific inventory methods used. Under Lifo, current purchase prices immediately affect current operating results; under Fifo, recognition of price effects is delayed. If prices are volatile, year-to-year incomes may differ dramatically under the two approaches to inventory valuation.

Balance sheet presentations are also affected by the choice of Lifo or Fifo. Under the Lifo method, older and older, and hence less useful inventory prices are shown, especially if stocks grow through the years. Under the Fifo method, the balance sheet tends to reflect current prices.

When prices are rising, Lifo shows less income than Fifo, thus minimizing current taxes. Also, Lifo permits the immediate influencing of net income by the timing of purchases, a feature that has not received the attention it deserves. For example, if prices are rising and a company desires, for income tax or other reasons, to show less income in a given year, all it need do is to buy a large amount of inventory near the end of the year—thus releasing, as expenses, higher costs than would ordinarily be released.

Note that neither the Fifo nor the Lifo approach isolates and measures the effects of price fluctuations as special managerial problems. In Exhibit 20-2, consider the $50 rise in price pertaining to the beginning inventory

EXHIBIT 20-2

Comparison of Lifo, Fifo, and Replacement Cost

	LIFO			FIFO			REPLACEMENT COST		
	UNITS	UNIT PRICE	TOTAL	UNITS	UNIT PRICE	TOTAL	UNITS	UNIT PRICE	TOTAL
Sales	5,000	$.22	$1,100	same		$1,100	same		$1,100
Beginning inventory	1,000	.10	$ 100	same		$ 100			
Purchases	5,000	.15	750	same		750			
Available for sale	6,000		$ 850	same		$ 850			
Ending inventory	1,000	.10	100	1,000	.15	150			
Cost of goods sold	5,000	.15	$ 750	$\left\{\begin{matrix}1{,}000\\4{,}000\end{matrix}\right.$ $\begin{matrix}.10\\.15\end{matrix}$		$ 700	5,000	.15	$ 750*
Gross profit			$ 350			$ 400			$ 350
Other expenses			100			100			100
Net income			$ 250			$ 300			
Operating income									$ 250
Holding gain: 1,000 units @ $.05									50
Net income									$ 300

*Under the replacement-cost method, cost of goods sold is computed by multiplying the number of units sold times the unit replacement cost.

(1,000 units $\times$ $.05 = $50). Fifo buries the $50 in income as part of the gross profit of $300. Lifo excludes the $50 from income by showing a gross profit of $250 and ignoring the $50. In contrast, the replacement-cost method pinpoints the price effects by showing the $50 as a holding gain and including it in income. Keep in mind that the replacement-cost method is not allowed under generally accepted accounting principles as practiced in the United States.

The continued inflation in the United States since 1940 has generally encouraged the adoption of Lifo. Almost one-third of the 600 companies whose practices are tabulated in the annual volume *Accounting Trends and Techniques*[2] use Lifo. The major theoretical justification hinges on the matching of current costs with current revenues. By so doing, the resulting net income is a better reflection of the increase in "distributable" assets. Thus, Lifo achieves this goal better than Fifo. For instance, Exhibit 20-2 shows that if $300 were paid out in dividends instead of $250, a company using Fifo would not have enough funds to replenish its stocks to sustain sales of 5,000 units again during the next period. In contrast, Lifo would be more likely to conserve sufficient funds:

[2]Published by American Institute of CPAs, New York.

	Lifo	Fifo
Revenue	$1,000	$1,000
Dividends equal to net income	250	300
Funds left for replenishment of stock to maintain sales of 5,000 units next period	$ 750	$ 700
Funds needed, 5,000 units @ $15	$ 750	$ 750
Shortage of funds		$ − 50

This argument has some appeal, but it is not really the reason why companies have adopted Lifo. Dividend payouts are not made before considering many of their financial ramifications. The fundamental reason is that Lifo became acceptable for income tax purposes. If prices rise and if inventory quantities are maintained, current taxable income will be less under Lifo than Fifo and income taxes will be postponed; intelligent financial management would therefore be very tempted to adopt Lifo.

Lower of Cost or Market

When the concept of the market price is superimposed upon a cost method, the combined method is often called the lower-of-cost-or-market method. That is, the current market price is compared to cost (derived by Fifo, average, or other method), and the lower of the two is selected as the basis for the valuation of goods at a specific inventory date. **Market** generally means the current replacement cost or its equivalent. It does not mean the ultimate selling price to customers.

Assume that an ending inventory is valued at $10,000 at cost and $7,000 at market. If the lower market price is indicative of lower ultimate sales prices, an inventory write-down of $3,000 is in order. Of the cost, $3,000 is considered to have expired during the current period because it cannot be justifiably carried forward to the future. Furthermore, the decision to purchase was probably made during the current period, but unfortunate fluctuations occurred in the replacement market during the same period. These downward price fluctuations caused the inventory to lose some utility, some revenue-producing power. (On the other hand, if **selling prices** are not also likely to fall, the revenue-producing power of the inventory will be maintained and no write-down would be justified.)

If a writedown occurs, the new $7,000 valuation is what is left of the original cost of the inventory. In other words, the new market price becomes, for accounting purposes, the new cost of the inventory.

Compared to a strict cost method (see Exhibit 20-3), the lower-of-cost-or-market method reports less net income in the current period and more net income in the future period. Assuming that there are no sales in the

EXHIBIT 20-3

Effects of Lower-of-Cost-or-Market Method

	COST		LOWER OF COST OR MARKET	
	PERIOD 1	PERIOD 2	PERIOD 1	PERIOD 2
Net sales	$100,000	$11,000	$100,000	$11,000
Cost of goods available	$ 80,000	$10,000	$ 80,000	$ 7,000
Ending inventory after write-down	10,000	—	7,000	—
Cost of goods sold*	$ 70,000	$10,000	$ 73,000	$ 7,000
Gross profit	$ 30,000	$ 1,000	$ 27,000	$ 4,000

* Cost of goods sold is increased by the $3,000 inventory write-down in this example. Many accountants favor isolating the write-down and deducting it separately after the ordinary gross profit.

second period shown in Exhibit 20-3, except for the disposal of the inventory in question, total income for both periods will be the same (ignoring income tax). Note that the total gross profit for the two periods is $31,000, under both methods. The lower-of-cost-or-market method has been termed a conservative valuation method. However, it results in a favorable impact upon the net income of the next period.

THE INVESTMENT TAX CREDIT

Although Congress may suspend or alter its provisions from time to time, the investment tax credit is highly likely to continue to affect financial reporting for many years. The United States Internal Revenue Code has allowed **investment tax credits** (hereafter called *investment credits,* for brevity) that are equal to various percentages of the original costs of the depreciable assets acquired (usually 10 percent if the useful life is eight years or more). Tax credits are used as direct reductions of income taxes. For example, suppose that a company spends $100,000 for an asset with an estimated useful life of ten years. If the expenditure qualifies for a 10 percent tax credit, the company is permitted to deduct $10,000 from its liability for income taxes and is also permitted to deduct the full $100,000 as depreciation expense through the years of useful life, provided, of course, that there is no predicted scrap value at the end of the useful life. Many observers maintain that these credits are equivalent to discounts on the purchase of assets.

How should this credit be measured for corporate annual reporting purposes? Should the beneficial effects on net income of the $10,000 credit be recognized in full for the year of purchase (the **flow-through** method)? Or should the effects be reflected in net income over the productive life of the asset (the **deferral method**)? What do you think? There is no uniform agreement on this issue. In many industries (such as airlines and others that have heavy capital expenditures), the method chosen will have a material effect on reported net income. Exhibit 20-4 compares the two methods.

The proponents of the flow-through method claim that the investment credit is a selective tax reduction in the year in which taxes otherwise payable are reduced by the credit. It is not a determinant of cost of acquisition or use of the related assets. The majority of companies use this method. Note that if a company is expanding, its current reported net income will benefit greatly from the flow-through method in comparison with the deferral method.

Supporters of the deferral method are particularly critical of the idea that net income can be directly affected by the amount spent for depreciable assets in a given year; within constraints, the more the company *buys,* the more it earns. Such an implication conflicts with the generally accepted concept that net income is earned only via *using* assets in the production of revenue from customers. The deferral method prevents current net income from being so significantly affected by unrelated management actions in buying depreciable assets.

The advocates of deferral maintain that the amount of the investment credit is associated primarily with the use of the property qualifying for the credit. In addition, the property must be held for a minimum period of time. Deferral of the credit and its subsequent amortization associates the credit with the useful life of the related property. This matching is consistent with the objectives of income measurement because it spreads a purchase discount over the useful life of the asset purchased.

The investment credit is an excellent example of the existence of alternative accounting methods not justified by changes in underlying circumstances. This provision of the Internal Revenue Code affects all

EXHIBIT 20-4

Effects of Investment Tax Credit on Net Income

    Assumptions: Net income before considering investment credit of $10,000 is $50,000 annually. The asset acquired for $100,000 will be used ten years and have no scrap value.

| | | FLOW-THROUGH EFFECTS | | DEFERRAL EFFECTS | |
| | (1) | (2) | (3) (1) + (2) | (4) | (5) (1) + (4) |
YEAR	NET INCOME BEFORE INVESTMENT CREDIT EFFECT	RECOGNIZED IMMEDIATELY	NET INCOME	RECOGNIZED GRADUALLY	NET INCOME
1	$50,000	$10,000	$60,000	$1,000	$51,000
2	50,000	—	50,000	1,000	51,000
3	50,000	—	50,000	1,000	51,000
4	50,000	—	50,000	1,000	51,000
5	50,000	—	50,000	1,000	51,000
	Etc. through Year 10				

companies alike, and there seems little reason for permitting two such diametrically different accounting methods.

DEFERRED FEDERAL INCOME TAXES

In recent years, American companies have had increasing opportunities to postpone disbursements for income taxes. For example, the Internal Revenue Service permits companies to use accelerated methods of depreciation when computing taxable income even though straight-line methods of depreciation are used in annual reports to stockholders. Therefore, as the top of Exhibit 20-5 shows, income tax payments are lower in the early years of the useful life of the asset and higher in the later years than they would be if straight-line depreciation were used for both tax and stockholder reporting purposes.

These differences in the timing of cash payments for income tax purposes have spurred great controversy regarding how income should be measured for stockholder-reporting purposes. An example should clarify the issues. Suppose that B Company purchases an asset for $15 million with an estimated useful life of five years and an estimated scrap value of zero. The sum-of-the-years'-digits-depreciation (SYD) method is used for tax purposes. The straight-line method is used for financial reporting purposes. Prospective annual net income before depreciation and income taxes is $10 million. The income tax rate is 60 percent. Exhibit 20-5 shows the effect on net income after tax if (1) no income tax allocation is used and (2) allocation is used.

As Method 1 in Exhibit 20-5 shows, some accountants believe that the income tax expense on the income statement should be the actual amount paid to the government for the year in question—no more, no less. Again

EXHIBIT 20-5

Comparison of Alternative Reporting Practices
for Depreciation and Income Taxes
    Facts: Purchase asset for $15 million; five-year life; 60 percent tax rate. Company takes SYD for tax purposes, but uses straight-line depreciation for financial reporting purposes.

YEAR	INCOME BEFORE DEPRECIATION AND TAXES	REPORTING FOR TAX PURPOSES SYD DEPRECIATION	INCOME BEFORE TAX	INCOME TAX PAID	NET INCOME AFTER TAX
1	$10	$\frac{5}{15} \times \$15 = \$ 5$	$ 5	$ 3.0	$ 2.0
2	10	$\frac{4}{15} \times \$15 = 4$	6	3.6	2.4
3	10	$\frac{3}{15} \times \$15 = 3$	7	4.2	2.8
4	10	$\frac{2}{15} \times \$15 = 2$	8	4.8	3.2
5	10	$\frac{1}{15} \times \$15 = 1$	9	5.4	3.6
Cumulative	$50		$15	$35	$21.0	$14.0

EXHIBIT 20-5 (cont.)

REPORTING TO STOCKHOLDERS

1. Straight-Line Depreciation and No Tax Allocation

YEAR	INCOME BEFORE DEPRECIATION AND TAXES	STRAIGHT-LINE DEPRECIATION	INCOME BEFORE TAX	INCOME TAX EXPENSE	NET INCOME AFTER TAX	BALANCE SHEET EFFECT: DEFERRED INCOME TAXES
1	$10	$ 3	$ 7	$ 3.0	$ 4.0	—
2	10	3	7	3.6	3.4	—
3	10	3	7	4.2	2.8	—
4	10	3	7	4.8	2.2	—
5	10	3	7	5.4	1.6	—
Cumulative	$50	$15	$35	$21.0	$14.0	

2. Straight-Line Depreciation and Tax Allocation

YEAR	INCOME BEFORE DEPRECIATION AND TAXES	STRAIGHT-LINE DEPRECIATION	INCOME BEFORE TAX	INCOME TAX EXPENSE TAX PAID	INCOME TAX EXPENSE TAX ALLOCATED	INCOME TAX EXPENSE TOTAL TAX EXPENSE	NET INCOME AFTER TAX	BALANCE SHEET EFFECT: DEFERRED INCOME TAXES*
1	$10	$3	$ 7	$ 3.0	$ 1.2	$ 4.2	$ 2.8	$1.2
2	10	3	7	3.6	0.6	4.2	2.8	1.8
3	10	3	7	4.2	0	4.2	2.8	1.8
4	10	3	7	4.8	−0.6	4.2	2.8	1.2
5	10	3	7	5.4	−1.2	4.2	2.8	0
Cumulative	$50		$35	$21.0	$ 0	$21.0	$14.0	—

* This would ordinarily appear in the liability section of the balance sheet as a separate item just above the stockholders' equity section.

note that the favorable effect of lower taxes on net income in earlier years is offset by higher taxes in later years. This method has been outlawed in favor of Method 2 as a basis for reporting to stockholders.

As Method 2 in Exhibit 20-5 shows, the Accounting Principles Board (after heated debate) concluded in favor of interperiod allocation of income taxes, "both in the manner in which tax effects are initially recognized and in the manner in which deferred taxes are amortized in future periods." Method 2 demonstrates that the effect for a particular asset would be to regard any reported income as if it were subject to the full current tax rate even though a more advantageous depreciation method were used for tax purposes. As Exhibit 20-5 shows, this results in a smoothing effect on income in these particular circumstances when the year-by-year effects are viewed over the five-year span.

The deferred income tax payable is a deferred credit in the sense that it is intended to offset the income tax expense in future years. Years 4 and 5 show how the credit is utilized to bring the reported tax expense down to a lower amount. More fundamentally, the deferred tax payable is a liability (rather than a part of stockholders' equity) that should be recognized under the accrual basis of accounting. Proponents of allocation maintain that failure to allocate is tantamount to retrogressing to a cash basis of accounting. Therefore, deferred income taxes should be recognized as a legitimate claim on the assets of the enterprise; it is an obligation to the government that arises because the firm elects to postpone some income tax payments from the present to some future date.

For growing companies, these deferred income tax accounts are likely to accumulate to enormous amounts that will never diminish unless the company starts reducing the level of its operations. For example, in Exhibit 20-5, if the company spent $15 million each year for more plant assets, the additional deferrals in each of these years would more than offset the decline in deferrals in Years 4 and 5 associated with the original $15 million outlay. Exhibit 20-6 summarizes this point.

The objectors to the deferral method point out that tax-allocation procedures should not apply to the recurring differences between taxable income and pretax accounting income in Exhibit 20-6 if there is a relatively stable or growing investment in depreciable assets. This results in an indefinite postponement of the additional tax, a mounting deferred taxes payable that may never be reduced, and a consequent understatement of net income. Note from Year 6 in Exhibit 20-6 that the income taxes payable will never decline unless the company fails to maintain its $15 million annual expenditure each year. Furthermore, if the company continued to grow at the rate of $15 million per year, the expenditure in Year 6 would be $30 million and the deferred income tax account would soar even more.

The proponents of deferral reject the growing-firm argument as fallacious. The ever-increasing aggregate amount of deferred income taxes is an example of a phenomenon that affects many other accounts in a growing firm. For example, accounts payable and liabilities for product warranties may also grow, but that is not justification for assuming that liabilities for these obligations are unnecessary.

Whatever your reactions to these conflicting arguments, the Board's action on deferred income taxes has reduced the number of available accounting alternatives and increased comparability. The Board supports the view that the amount of taxes payable for a given period does not necessarily measure the appropriate income tax expense related to transactions for that period as measured and reported to stockholders. Income tax expense includes any accrual, deferral, or estimation necessary to adjust the amount of income taxes payable for the period to measure the tax effects of all revenue and expenses included in the pretax income reported to stockholders. As *Opinion No. 11,* paragraph 29, states:

> Those supporting comprehensive allocation believe that the tax effects of initial timing differences should be recognized and that the tax effects should

EXHIBIT 20-6

Analysis of Growing Firm and Deferred Income Taxes

Facts: Same as in Exhibit 20-5, except that $15 million is spent each year for additional assets and income increases $10 million each year until leveling off in Year 6. In Year 6, the $15 million represents a replacement of the asset originally purchased in Year 1.

REPORTING FOR TAX PURPOSES

YEAR	INCOME BEFORE DEPRECIATION AND TAXES	SYD DEPRECIATION	NET INCOME BEFORE TAX	INCOME TAX PAID	NET INCOME AFTER TAX
1	$10	$5	$ 5	$ 3.0	$ 2.0
2	20	4 + 5 = 9	11	6.6	4.4
3	30	3 + 4 + 5 = 12	18	10.8	7.2
4	40	2 + 3 + 4 + 5 = 14	26	15.6	10.4
5	50	1 + 2 + 3 + 4 + 5 = 15	35	21.0	14.0
6	50	1 + 2 + 3 + 4 + 5 = 15	35	21.0	14.0

REPORTING TO STOCKHOLDERS
Straight-Line Depreciation and Tax Allocation

YEAR	INCOME BEFORE DEPRECIATION AND TAXES	STRAIGHT-LINE DEPRECIATION	NET INCOME BEFORE TAX	INCOME TAX EXPENSE			NET INCOME AFTER TAX	BALANCE SHEET EFFECT DEFERRED INCOME TAXES PAYABLE
				TAX PAID	TAX ALLOCATED	TOTAL TAX EXPENSE		
1	$10	$ 3	$ 7	$ 3.0	$1.2	$ 4.2	$ 2.8	$1.2
2	20	6	14	6.6	1.8	8.4	5.6	3.0
3	30	9	21	10.8	1.8	12.6	8.4	4.8
4	40	12	28	15.6	1.2	16.8	11.2	6.0
5	50	15	35	21.0	—	21.0	14.0	6.0
6	50	15	35	21.0	—	21.0	14.0	6.0

be matched with or allocated to those periods in which the initial differences reverse [Years 4 and 5 in Exhibit 20-5]. The fact that when the initial differences reverse other initial differences may offset any effect on the amount of taxable income [Years 4, 5, and 6 in Exhibit 20-6] does not . . . nullify the fact of the reversal. . . . These initial differences do reverse, and the tax effects thereof can be identified as readily as can those of other timing differences. While new differences may have an offsetting effect, this does not alter the fact of the reversal; without the reversal there would be different tax consequences. Accounting principles cannot be predicated on reliance that offsets will continue.

SUMMARY

The matching of historical costs with revenue is the generally accepted means of measuring net income. But basing such computations on some version of current values has been proposed as a better gauge of the corresponding net increase in net wealth.

General price indexes are used to adjust historical costs so that all expenses are measured in current dollars of the same purchasing power. Such adjustments do not represent a departure from historical cost. In contrast, specific price indexes are often used to implement the current-value approach to measuring net income.

Within the historical-cost framework, an immense diversity of accounting alternatives have quite different impacts on net income. Examples include Fifo and Lifo inventory methods and accounting for the investment tax credit on a flow-through or deferral basis.

There is a need for more uniformity in accounting where underlying circumstances are the same.

SUMMARY PROBLEMS FOR YOUR REVIEW

Problem One

In 1930, a parcel of land was purchased for $1,200. An identical parcel was purchased today for $3,600. The general price-level index has risen from 100 in 1930 to 300 now. Fill in the blanks:

Parcel	*(1)* *Historical Cost* *Measured in 1930* *Purchasing Power*	*(2)* *Historical Cost* *Measured in Current* *Purchasing Power*	*(3)* *Historical Cost* *As Originally* *Measured*
1			
2			
Total			

1. Compare the figures in the three columns. Which total presents a nonsense result. Why?

2. Does the write-up of parcel 1 in column 2 result in a gain? Why? Assume that these parcels are the only assets of the business. There are no liabilities. Prepare a complete balance sheet for each of the three columns.

Problem Two

Suppose that a parcel of land is acquired for $1,000 on December 31, 19x1, when the general index is 100. The general price level rises 20 percent during 19x2 and 10 percent during 19x3. The land is sold on December 31, 19x3, for $3,000; it could have been sold on December 31, 19x2, for $1,800.

1. Using four columns, show the balance sheet amount for land plus net income for 19x2 and 19x3 under (1) historical cost—not restated, (2) his-

torical cost—restated, (3) current value—not restated, and (4) current value restated for general-price-level effects.

2. At the bottom of your presentation in Requirement 1 show comparative income statistics for the two years and the cumulative gain for the two years.

3. What major points can be learned from the tabulations in Requirements 1 and 2?

Problem Three

"When prices are rising, Fifo results in fool's profits because more resources are needed to maintain operations than previously." Do you agree? Explain.

Problem Four

"The lower-of-cost-or-market method is inherently inconsistent." Do you agree? Explain.

Problem Five

Examine Exhibit 20-4. The flow-through method would reduce income taxes by $10,000 in Year 1. How would the relevant balance-sheet and income-statement accounts be affected by the deferral method? Show accounts and amounts for each of the first three years. Assume that income taxes before considering the investment tax credit were $52,000.

Problem Six

Examine Exhibit 20-6. In Year 7 suppose that $30 million was spent on depreciable assets with five-year lives and that income before depreciation and taxes reached $60 million. For Year 7, fill in all the columns in Exhibit 20-6.

Solution to Problem One

1.

Parcel	(1) Historical Cost Measured in 1930 Purchasing Power	(2) Historical Cost Measured in Current Purchasing Power	(3) Historical Cost as Originally Measured
1	$1,200	$3,600	$1,200
2	1,200	3,600	3,600
Total	$2,400	$7,200	$4,800

The addition in column 3 produces a nonsense result. In contrast, the other sums are the results of applying a standard unit of measure. The computations in columns 1 and 2 are illustrations of a restatement of historical cost in terms of a common dollar, a standard unit of measure. Such computations have been frequently termed as adjustments for changes in the general price level. Whether the restatement is made using the 1930 dollar or the current dollar is a matter of personal preference; columns 1 and 2 yield equivalent results. The preponderance of opinion seems to favor restatement in terms of the current dollar (column 2) because the current dollar has more meaning to the reader of the financial statements.

The mere restatement of identical assets in terms of different but equivalent measuring units cannot be regarded as a gain. Expressing parcel 1 as $1,200 in column 1 and $3,600 in column 2 is like expressing parcel 1 in terms of, say, either 1,200 square yards or 10,800 square feet. Surely, the "write-up" from 1,200 square yards to 10,800 square feet is not a gain; it is merely another way of measuring the same asset. The 1,200 square yards and the 10,800 square feet are equivalent; they are different ways of describing the same asset. That is basically what general-price-level accounting is all about. It says you cannot measure one plot of land in square yards and another in square feet and add them together before converting to some common measure. Unfortunately, column 3 fails to perform such a conversion before adding the two parcels together; hence, the total is internally inconsistent.

2. Note especially that write-ups under general-price-level accounting do not result in the recognition of gains. They are restatements of costs in dollars of equivalent purchasing power. The balance sheets would be:

	(1)	(2)	(3)
Land	$2,400	$7,200	$4,800
Stockholders' equity	$2,400	$7,200	$4,800

Solution to Problem Two

1.

	(1)	(2)	(3)	(4)
	Historical Cost		Current Value	
	Not Restated	Restated	Not Restated	Restated
Balance sheet amount of land:				
Dec. 31, 19x1	$1,000	$1,000	$1,000	$1,000
Dec. 31, 19x2	1,000	1,200	1,800	1,800
Dec. 31, 19x3, before sale	1,000	1,320	3,000	3,000
Income-statement gains reported:				
19x2:				
Current value	$ —	$ —	$1,800	$1,800
Historical cost				
Not restated			1,000	
Restated, 120% of 1,000				1,200
Gain	—	—	$ 800	$ 600

	(1)	(2)	(3)	(4)
	Historical Cost		Current Value	
	Not Restated	Restated	Not Restated	Restated
19x3:				
Selling price	$3,000	$3,000	$3,000	$3,000
Historical cost				
Not restated	1,000			
Restated		1,320		
Current value				
Not restated			1,800	
Restated, 110% of				
$1,800				1,980
Gain	$2,000	$1,680	$1,200	$1,020
2. Two-year comparative summary:				
19x2	$ —	$ —	$ 800	$ 660*
19x3	2,000	1,680	1,200	1,020
Cumulative	$2,000	$1,680	$2,000	$1,680

*When statements are recast for the general price level, to compare current with past net income figures, the past net income must be restated in terms of current dollars: $600 × 1.10 = $660.

3. (a) Column 1 depicts the concept of income as usually applied in practice. General-price-level accounting as recommended (but not required) by the Accounting Principles Board is concerned with the income concept demonstrated in column 2; it is *not* concerned with current value concepts of income.

(b) The choices among accounting measures are often expressed as either historical-cost accounting or general-price-level accounting or specific-price-level (current-value) accounting. *But this is an inaccurate and confusing statement of choices.* A correct statement would be that general-price-level accounting may be combined with either historical-cost accounting (Column 2) or current-value accounting (Column 4).

(c) The difference between current-value and historical-cost concepts of income is primarily the *timing* of the recognition of income. The cumulative effects of both concepts on income are identical.

Solution to Problem Three

The merit of this position is directly dependent on the concept of income favored. As Exhibit 20-2 shows, Lifo does give a better measure of "distributable" income than Fifo. Fifo increases profits by the $50 difference in ending inventory valuation (1,000 units @ 5¢). The $50 in a sense is "tied up" in maintaining the same inventory level as previously; therefore, it cannot be distributed as a cash dividend without reducing the current level of operations.

Solution to Problem Four

The inconsistency is the willingness of accountants to have replacement costs used as a basis for *write-downs* below historical costs, even though a market exchange has not occurred, but the unwillingness to have replacement costs used as a basis for *write-ups* above historical costs. Historical cost is an upper limit for valuation under generally accepted accounting principles.

Solution to Problem Five

The deferral method would appear as follows in each of the three years:

Income before taxes ($50,000 + $52,000)		$102,000
Income tax expense:		
Taxes before investment credit	$52,000	
Less allocation of credit (10% × $10,000)	1,000	51,000
Net income		$51,000

The balance sheet at the end of the first year would show a deferred credit of $10,000 − $1,000, or $9,000. This balance would decline by $1,000 annually as the beneficial effects of the investment credit were spread out over the useful life of the asset in the form of an annual reduction of income taxes. At the end of Year 3, the balance in deferred income taxes would be $10,000 − 3($1,000), or $7,000.

Solution to Problem Six

For tax purposes:

Income Before Depreciation and Taxes	SYD Depreciation	Net Income Before Tax	Income Tax Paid	Net Income After Tax
$60	$1 + 2 + 3 + 4 + 10* = $20	$40	$24	$16

*5/15 × 30 = 10.

For stockholders:

Income Before Depreciation and Taxes	Straight-line Depreciation	Net Income Before Tax	Income Tax Expenses Paid	Income Tax Expenses Allocated	Income Tax Expenses Total	Net Income After Tax	Balance Sheet Effect: Deferred Income Taxes Payable
$60	$18	$42	$24	$1.2	$25.2	$16.8	$7.2

APPENDIX 20:
DISPUTES ABOUT INCOME MEASUREMENT

This appendix expands the discussion of the first section of this chapter. Two major topics are covered: (1) effects of current value and (2) general purchasing-power gains and losses.

EFFECTS OF CURRENT VALUE

What Is Income?

This section explores the current-value, nominal-dollar approach shown in column 2 of Exhibit 20-1, which takes a clear-cut approach to a definition of income. *All* value increases, whether or not they have been "realized" in the form of a sale, are income of the period when the prices rose. Many accountants want to *recognize* the gain on the unsold land, but want to exclude it from the reported net income of 19x3. Instead, this "unrealized gain" would be placed in a separate "revaluation equity" account as a part of stockholders' equity.

Essentially all gains are recognized as they occur (in the economic sense), but they are divided between realized gains and unrealized gains. A summary is in Exhibit 20-7, which uses data from Exhibit 20-1. Assume that original capital was $100,000, all in cash, which was then used to purchase the two $50,000 parcels of land.

The issue is whether the $30,000 increase in current value of the unsold land in 19x3 should be recognized as a gain of 19x3, as it is in Exhibit 20-1, column (2). Some accountants favor creating a realized-unrealized distinction whereby the gain is held "in suspense" in a special account that would increase a new stockholders' equity account, called Revaluation Equity in Exhibit 20-7. This approach is really a half-way house between columns (1) and (2) in Exhibit 20-1. Why? Because the reported net income in each year would be the same $30,000 and $40,000 shown in column (1); at the same time the $30,000 value increase would appear as an unrealized gain of 19x3.

Does the $30,000 special account in Exhibit 20-7 appear in the income statement? No, because it is not realized income. The $30,000 gain in unsold land is a direct increase to Revaluation Equity; of course, it would appear in a statement of changes in stockholders' equity or of changes in Revaluation Equity. When the land is sold, the $30,000 is transferred to current income [item (b) in the exhibit] and thus becomes "realized" in the income statement of 19x4 and then a part of Retained Income.

Replacement-Cost Basis

The regulatory authorities in the United Kingdom and Australia have proposed rules based on a "current-cost" approach, which is largely tied to replacement costs via either specific appraisals or specific material or construction indexes.

A popular version of the replacement-cost basis contains a separation of **operating income,** which is defined as the excess of revenue over the replacement costs of the assets consumed in obtaining that revenue, and

EXHIBIT 20-7

Realized and Unrealized Gains
(Data are in thousands of dollars)

BALANCE SHEET ACCOUNTS	DECEMBER 31 19x3	19x4
Assets		
Cash (100 − 100 + 80) and (100 − 100 + 80 + 90), respectively	80	170
Land—at acquisition cost	50	—
Add: Unrealized appreciation	30	—
Land— at current value	80	—
Total assets	160	170
Stockholders' Equity		
Original capital	100	100
Retained income [confined to realized net income, from (c) below]	30	70
Revaluation equity [confined to unrealized income, from (d) below minus transfer to (b)]	30	—
Total stockholders' equity	160	170

INCOME ACCOUNTS	FOR YEAR 19x3	19x4
(a) Gain (loss) recognized and realized during current year on land actually sold	30	10
(b) Gain (loss) recognized in prior years and realized during current year	—	30
(c) Total effects on current net income	30	40

SPECIAL ACCOUNT	FOR YEAR 19x3	19x4
(d) Gain recognized but unrealized during current year, which is shown separately as an increase in Revaluation Equity	30	—

holding gains (or **losses**), which are increases (or decreases) in the replacement costs of the assets held during the current period.

Consider the following example. Company A bought 12,000 units of Product Y for $10 each, a total cost of $120,000. It sold 10,000 of the units for $15 each, a total revenue of $150,000. Other expenses were $12,000. The replacement cost of these items soared to $13 each almost immediately after they were acquired. The price is still $13. The two approaches would show the following:

662

	Historical Cost		Replacement Cost
Revenue	$150,000	Revenue	$150,000
Cost of goods		Cost of goods	
sold @ $10	$100,000	sold @ $13	$130,000
Other expenses	12,000	Other expenses	12,000
Total expenses	$112,000	Total expenses	$142,000
Net income	$ 38,000	Operating income	$ 8,000
		Holding gain*	$ 36,000

* Consisting of $30,000 on goods sold (10,000 × $3) plus $6,000 (2,000 × $3) on goods held in inventory.

As shown in the above tabulation, the United Kingdom and Australian approaches would not add together the $8,000 operating income and the $36,000 holding gain. Instead, the $8,000 is the only defensible approximation of "distributable" income. That is, the company in our example could pay dividends in an amount of $8,000, leaving enough resources to allow for replenishment of the inventory that has just been sold. The $38,000 figure is misleading as a measure of income because it does not reflect the net increment in distributable assets. If a $38,000 dividend were paid, the company would be less able to continue operations at the same level as before.

Income Tax Effects
of Current Value

If the current-value basis is adopted (probably in the form of some "current-cost" or "replacement-cost" approach), most business managers will favor not including unrealized holding gains as part of current income subject to income taxes. That is, the managers would favor the item (c) version of income in Exhibit 20-7, not the version that would add item (d) to item (c) when computing taxable income. So income taxes would be postponed and not levied until the land was sold for cash and not replaced.

The managers in capital-goods industries especially favor the replacement-cost approach for income tax purposes because of the prominence of their depreciation expenses. If historical depreciation is restated to a replacement-cost basis, expenses are increased, income subject to tax is decreased, and income tax outflows are decreased. Consider an example (figures assumed):

663

	Historical-Cost Basis	Replacement-Cost Basis
Income before depreciation	$100	$100
Depreciation	30	80
Income before income taxes	$ 70	$ 20
Income taxes @ 50%	35	10[3]
Net income	$ 35	$ 10

GENERAL PURCHASING-POWER GAINS AND LOSSES

Now we return to constant-dollar, historical-cost accounting, the comparison of columns (1) and (3) in Exhibit 20-1 that was introduced in the body of this chapter.

Monetary Items

A **monetary item** is a claim receivable or payable in a specified number of dollars; the claim remains fixed regardless of changes in either specific or general price levels. Examples are cash, accounts receivable, accounts payable, and bonds payable. In contrast, **nonmonetary items** have prices that can vary. Examples are inventory, land, equipment, and liabilities for product warranties.

The distinction between monetary and nonmonetary assets is the key to understanding the impact of general-price-level accounting on income measurement and stockholders' equity. Reconsider the facts depicted in column 1 of Exhibit 20-1, which omitted any consideration of the proceeds related to the $80,000 selling price of December 31, 19x3. Suppose that $80,000 cash was received and held throughout 19x4 in a noninterest-bearing checking account. Let us consider a comparative balance sheet as it would be conventionally prepared as of December 30, 19x4 (one day before the disposal of the second parcel of land):

---

[3]If taxes were levied as shown in the example, the capital-goods industries would have relatively lower incomes subject to tax than other industries. However, keep in mind that a country usually has the same target *total* income taxes to be generated by the corporate sector. If the taxable income of all corporations declined, all income tax *rates* would undoubtedly be raised so as to produce the same *total* tax collections as before. Thus, a replacement-cost basis may redistribute the tax burden among companies so that capital-goods industries pay less total tax. But the chances are high that the 50 percent rate in the example would increase, so that the tax savings would not be as large as indicated.

	December 31, 19x3	December 30, 19x4
Cash	$ 80,000	$ 80,000
Land	50,000	50,000
Total assets	$130,000	$130,000
Original capital	$100,000	$100,000
Retained income	30,000	30,000
Total stockholders' equity	$130,000	$130,000

Before reading on, reflect on the intuitive meaning of holding cash during a time of inflation. The holder of cash or claims to cash gets burned by inflation. In contrast, the debtor benefits from inflation because he can pay his creditors with a fixed amount of dollars that have less current purchasing power than when the debt was originally contracted.

How do we measure the economic effects of holding cash during inflation? Using the basic approach of column 3 in Exhibit 20-1, let us restate in constant dollars, using 19x4 dollars. Because the general price-level index rose from 110 to 132, the restatements would be:

Cash: 132/110 × 80,000 19x3 dollars	$ 96,000	$ 80,000
Land: 132/100 × 50,000 19x2 dollars	66,000	66,000
Total assets	$162,000	$146,000
Original capital:		
132/100 × 100,000 19x2 dollars	$132,000	$132,000
Retained income	30,000	14,000
Total stockholders' equity	$162,000	$146,000

The cash balance is not restated in 19x4 because it is already measured in 19x4 dollars. A formal income statement does not accompany this balance sheet. Why? Because, assuming no transactions, the constant-dollar income statement would consist of a lone item: purchasing-power loss on monetary item, $16,000. The purchasing-power loss on monetary item (cash) is $96,000 − $80,000 = $16,000. In turn, this loss would reduce retained income as shown: $30,000 − $16,000 = $14,000.

Nonmonetary Items

Before reading on, reflect on the intuitive meaning of holding a nonmonetary asset during a time of inflation. Assets in the form of physical things have prices that can fluctuate and thus, unlike cash, offer more protection against the risks of inflation.

As of the end of 19x3, the $80,000 cash balance represented the **equivalent of $96,000 in terms of 19x4 purchasing power,** but at the end of 19x4 it is only worth $80,000. In contrast, the $50,000 historical investment in land, which does not represent a fixed monetary claim, represented $66,000 in terms of *19x4 purchasing power;* its purchasing power has not been eroded. The land (and original capital) is *restated* to an amount of $66,000. But the $66,000 investment in land is unaffected by changes in the general price-level index during 19x4.

Two difficulties and subtleties of constant-dollar accounting deserve emphasis here. First, all past balance sheets are *restated* in today's dollars. Second, the balance sheet changes are computed among the *monetary* items to produce purchasing-power gains or losses. No such gains or losses will ever appear for nonmonetary items. For example, suppose the $80,000 cash had been immediately reinvested in a similar parcel of land. How would the constant-dollar statements be affected? No purchasing-power loss or gain would have occurred in 19x4:

	December 31, 19x3	December 31, 19x4
Land (instead of cash)		
132/110 × $80,000	$ 96,000	$ 96,000
Land (as before)	66,000	66,000
Total assets	$162,000	$162,000
Original capital	$132,000	$132,000
Retained income	30,000	30,000
Total stockholders' equity	$162,000	$162,000

Many accountants and managers confuse these restatements of *historical-cost* statements with current-value notions of income. However, these constant-dollar statements adhere to historical cost. The aim is to see whether the *general* purchasing power of the original invested capital has been maintained. Hence, whether *specific* land prices have gone up, down, or sideways is of no concern.

In sum, general-purchasing-power accounting will modify historical-cost statements in two major ways. First, historical costs are restated in constant dollars. Second, purchasing-power gains and losses arising from having monetary assets and monetary liabilities will be recognized and will affect net income.[4]

Finally, constant-dollar accounting may be linked with *either* historical-cost statements or current-value statements. Thus, the $16,000 purchasing-power loss computed above would also appear under the column (4) approach as well as the column (3) approach of Exhibit 20-1.

ASSIGNMENT MATERIAL

Note: These problems are generally grouped sequentially in accordance with the topical coverage of the chapter.

[4] Note that "unrealized" holding gains on monetary items are linked with constant-dollar accounting. They do not exist under nominal-dollar accounting. "Unrealized" holding gains on nonmonetary items are associated exclusively with "current-value" accounting and are not an integral part of "historical-cost" accounting.

20-1. What are the two polar approaches to income measurement?

20-2. Explain how net income is measured under the market-value approach.

20-3. What is *distributable income?*

20-4. Explain what a general price index represents.

20-5. Distinguish between general indexes and specific indexes.

20-6. Enumerate four ways to measure income.

20-7. What does uniformity mean in accounting?

20-8. Briefly distinguish the difference between Fifo and Lifo.

20-9. Does Fifo or Lifo isolate and measure the effects of price fluctuations as special management problems?

20-10. What is meant by the term *market* in inventory accounting?

20-11. What are the relative effects on net income of a strict-cost method and the lower-of-cost-or-market method?

20-12. Why has Lifo been so widely adopted?

20-13. "Lifo reflects current prices in the financial statements." Do you agree? Explain.

20-14. How does goodwill usually arise in accounting?

20-15. "Lifo consistently results in less net income than Fifo." Do you agree? Explain.

20-16. What is an investment tax credit?

20-17. What are the two most widely used methods for accounting for the investment tax credit?

20-18. Which of the two methods of accounting for the investment credit will benefit current income the most?

20-19. Why do deferred federal income taxes arise?

20-20. In brief, why did the Accounting Principles Board favor deferral of income taxes?

20-21. "General-price-level accounting is a loose way of achieving replacement-cost income accounting." Do you agree? Explain.

20-22. Meaning of general index applications and choice of base year. Mays Company acquired land in mid-1958 for $2,000,000. In mid-1978 it acquired a substantially identical parcel of land for $4,000,000. The gross national product implicit price deflator annual averages were:

$$1978—160.0 \qquad 1968—100.0 \qquad 1958—66.7$$

Required

1. In four columns, show the computations of the total cost of the two parcels of land expressed in (a) costs as traditionally recorded, (b) dollars of 1978 purchasing power, (c) 1968 purchasing power, and (d) 1958 purchasing power. For ease of computation, round all adjusted figures to the nearest hundred thousand dollars.

2. Explain the meaning of the figures that you computed in Requirement 1.

20-23. Concepts of income. Suppose that on December 31, 19x2, a parcel of land has a historical cost of $100,000 and a current value (measured via use of a specific price index) of $300,000; the general price level had doubled since the land was acquired. Suppose also that the land is sold on December 31, 19x3, for $360,000. The general price level rose by 5 percent during 19x3.

Required

1. Compute net income for 19x3 on the historical-cost basis, the current-value basis, the historical-cost basis adjusted for changes in the general price level, and the current-value basis also so adjusted.

2. In your own words, explain the meaning of each net income figure.

20-24. Four ways to compute income. Suppose that a parcel of land is acquired at the end of 19x3 for $100,000 when the general price index is 100. Its current value at the end of 19x4 is $140,000; the general price index is 115. There are at least four ways to portray these events:

(*1*) Historical cost—not restated for general-price-level effects.
(*2*) Historical cost—restated for general-price-level effects.
(*3*) Current value (specific price level)—not restated for general-price-level effects.
(*4*) Current value (specific price level)—restated for general-price-level effects.

Required

1. Using the above four ways as column headings, tabulate the amounts to be shown at the end of 19x4 for land, original capital, retained earnings, and "gain" on the income statement.

2. Suppose that one more year transpires with absolutely no change in either the general price level or in the specific price of the land. Suppose that the land is sold for $140,000 cash. Repeat Requirement 1 for 19x5.

3. Explain the composition of the gain that you show in Requirements 1 and 2. What other major points flow from the tabulations in Requirements 1 and 2?

20-25. Four ways to compute a gain. Land was purchased in Year 1 for $20,000. Market price did not change in Year 1. It was held during Year 2, and its market price increased to $26,000. It was sold for $33,000 at the end of Year 3. The

GNP deflator indexes were 100, 110, and 120 for the successive years. There are at least four ways to measure these events:

(*1*) Historical cost—not restated for general-price-level effects.
(*2*) Historical cost—restated for general-price-level effects.
(*3*) Current value—not restated for general-price-level effects.
(*4*) Current value—restated for general-price-level effects.

Required

1. Using the above four ways as column headings, tabulate the amounts to be shown for land on the balance sheet at the end of Year 1, Year 2, and before the sale at the end of Year 3. Also show the gains to be reported in the income statement for each year.

2. Explain the composition of the gains shown in Requirement 1. What other major points flow from the tabulations?

20-26. Depreciation and price-level adjustments. The Klaman Company purchased a computer for $260,000. It has an expected life of four years and an expected residual value of zero. Straight-line depreciation is used. The general price index is 100 at the date of acquisition; it increases 20 points annually during the next three years. The results follow:

Year	Price-Level Index	Unadjusted Depreciation	Multiplier	Adjusted Depreciation As Recorded
1	100	$ 65,000	$\frac{100}{100}$	$ 65,000
2	120	65,000	$\frac{120}{100}$	78,000
3	140	65,000	$\frac{140}{100}$	91,000
4	160	65,000	$\frac{160}{100}$	104,000
		$260,000		

Required

1. Convert the figures in the last column so that they are expressed in terms of fourth-year dollars.

2. Suppose in Requirement 1 that revenue easily exceeds expenses for each year and that cash equal to the annual depreciation charge was invested in a noninterest-bearing cash account. If amounts equal to the unadjusted depreciation charge were invested each year, would sufficient cash have accumulated to equal the general purchasing power of $260,000 invested in the asset four years ago? If not, what is the extent of the total financial deficiency measured in terms of fourth-year dollars?

3. Suppose in Requirement 2 that amounts equal to the adjusted depreciation for each year were used. What is the extent of the total financial deficiency?

4. Suppose in Requirement 3 that the amounts were invested each year in assets that increased in value at the same rate as the increase in the general price level. What is the extent of the total financial deficiency?

20-27. Lifo and Fifo. The inventory of the Kiner Coal Company on June 30 shows 1,000 tons at $6 per ton. A physical inventory on July 31 shows a total of 1,200 tons on hand. Revenue from sales of coal for July totals $30,000. The following purchases were made during July:

July 5	2,000 tons @ $7 per ton	
July 15	500 tons @ $8 per ton	
July 25	600 tons @ $9 per ton	

Required

Compute the inventory value, as of July 31, using (a) Lifo: last-in, first-out, (b) Fifo: first-in, first-out.

20-28. Lower of cost or market. The company uses cost or market, whichever is lower. There were no sales or purchases during the periods indicated, and there has been no change in the salability of the merchandise. At what amount would you value merchandise on the dates listed below?

	Invoice cost	Replacement cost
December 31, 19x1	$100,000	$ 80,000
April 30, 19x2	100,000	90,000
August 31, 19x2	100,000	105,000
December 31, 19x2	100,000	65,000

20-29. Multiple choice: comparison of inventory methods. The Byron Corporation began business on January 1, 19x4. Information about its inventories under different valuation methods is shown below. Using this information, you are to choose the phrase which best answers each of the following questions. For each question, insert on an answer sheet *the number that identifies the answer* you select.

		Inventory		
	Lifo Cost	Fifo Cost	Market	Lower of Specifically Identified Cost or Market
December 31, 19x4	$10,200	$10,000	$ 9,600	$ 8,900
December 31, 19x5	9,100	9,000	8,800	8,500
December 31, 19x6	10,300	11,000	12,000	10,900

1. The inventory basis that would show the *highest net income for 19x4* is: (a) Lifo cost; (b) Fifo cost; (c) market; (d) lower of cost or market.

2. The inventory basis that would show the *highest net income for 19x5* is: (a) Lifo cost; (b) Fifo cost; (c) market; (d) lower of cost or market.

3. The inventory basis that would show the *lowest net income for the three years combined* is: (a) Lifo cost; (b) Fifo cost; (c) market; (d) lower of cost or market.

4. For the year 19x5, how much higher or lower would profits be on the *Fifo-cost basis* than on the *lower-of-cost-or-market basis?* (a) $400 higher; (b) $400 lower; (c) $600 higher; (d) $600 lower; (e) $1,000 higher; (f) $1,000 lower; (g) $1,400 higher; (h) $1,400 lower.

5. On the basis of the information given, it appears that *the movement of prices* for the items in the inventory was: (a) up in 19x4 and down in 19x6; (b) up in both 19x4 and 19x6; (c) down in 19x4 and up in 19x6; (d) down in both 19x4 and 19x6.

20-30. Fifo and Lifo. Two companies, the Lifo Company and the Fifo Company, are in the scrap metal warehousing business as arch-competitors. They are about the same size and in 19x1 coincidentally encountered seemingly identical operating situations.

Their beginning inventory was 10,000 tons; it cost $50 per ton. During the year, each company purchased 50,000 tons at the following prices:

$$20,000 @ \$70$$
$$30,000 @ \$90$$

Each company sold 45,000 tons at average prices of $100 per ton. Other expenses in addition to cost of goods sold but excluding income taxes were $700,000. The income tax rate is 60 percent.

Required

1. Compute net income for the year for both companies. Show your calculations.

2. As a manager, which method would you prefer? Why? Explain fully. Include your estimate of the overall effect of these events on the cash balances of each company, assuming that all transactions during 19x1 were direct receipts or disbursements of cash.

20-31. Lifo effects. (CMA.) The management of Stark Products Company has asked its accounting department to describe the effect upon the company's financial position and its financial statements of accounting for inventories on the LIFO rather than FIFO basis during 19x4 and 19x5. The accounting department is to assume that the change to LIFO would have been effective on January 1, 19x4, and that the initial LIFO base would have been the inventory value on December 31, 19x3. Presented below are the company's financial statements and other data for the years 19x4 and 19x5 when the FIFO method was in fact employed.

Financial Condition as of	12/31/x3	12/31/x4	12/31/x5
Cash	$ 67,700	$121,300	$176,050
Accounts receivable	40,000	54,000	61,750
Inventory	69,000	75,000	84,000
Other assets	114,000	114,000	114,000
Total assets	$290,700	$364,300	$435,800
Accounts payable	$ 23,000	$ 30,000	$ 36,400
Other liabilities	40,000	40,000	40,000
Common stock	140,000	140,000	140,000
Retained earnings	87,700	154,300	219,400
Total equities	$290,700	$364,300	$435,800

Income for Years Ended		12/31/x4	12/31/x5
Sales		$540,000	$617,500
Less: Cost of goods sold		$294,000	$355,000
Other expenses		135,000	154,000
Sub-total		$429,000	$509,000
Net income before income taxes		$111,000	$108,500
Income taxes (40%)		44,400	43,400
Net income		$ 66,600	$ 65,100

Other data:

1. Inventory on hand at 12/31/x3 consisted of 30,000 units costing $2.30 each

2. Sales (all units sold at the same price in a given year):
   19x4—120,000 units @ $4.50 each
   19x5—130,000 units @ $4.75 each

3. Purchases (all units purchased at the same price in a given year):
   19x4—120,000 units @ $2.50 each
   19x5—130,000 units @ $2.80 each

4. Income taxes at the effective rate of 40 percent are paid on December 31 each year.

Required

Name the account(s) presented in the financial statements that would have different amounts for 19x5 if LIFO rather than FIFO had been used and state the new amount for each account that is named.

20-32. Effects of Lifo on purchase decisions. The Bjork Corporation is nearing the end of its first year in business. The following purchases of its single product have been made:

	Units	Unit Price	Total Cost
January	1,000	$10	$10,000
March	1,000	10	10,000
May	1,000	11	11,000
July	1,000	13	13,000
September	1,000	14	14,000
November	1,000	15	15,000
	6,000		$73,000

Sales for the year will be 5,000 units for $120,000. Expenses other than cost of goods sold will be $20,000.

The president is undecided about whether to adopt Fifo or Lifo for income tax purposes. The company has ample storage space for up to 7,000 units of inventory. Inventory prices are expected to stay at $15 per unit for the next few months.

Required

1. If the president decided to purchase 4,000 units @ $15 in December, what would be the net income before taxes, the income taxes, and the net income after taxes for the year under: (a) Fifo; and (b) Lifo? Income tax rates are 30 percent on the first $25,000 of net taxable income and 50 percent on the excess.

2. If the company sells its year-end inventory in Year 2 @ $24 per unit and goes out of business, what would be the net income before taxes, the income taxes, and the net income after taxes under: (a) Fifo; and (b) Lifo? Assume that other expenses in Year 2 are $20,000.

3. Repeat Requirements 1 and 2, assuming that 4,000 units, @ $15, were not purchased until January of the second year. Generalize on the effect on net income of the timing of purchases under Fifo and Lifo.

20-33. Effects of Lifo and Fifo. (Adapted from a problem originated by George H. Sorter.) The Cado Company is starting in business on December 31, 19x0. In each *half year,* from 19x1 through 19x4, they expect to purchase 1,000 units and sell 500 units for the amounts listed below. In 19x5, they expect to purchase no units and sell 4,000 units for the amount indicated below.

	19x1	19x2	19x3	19x4	19x5
Purchases:					
First 6 months	$ 2,000	$ 4,000	$ 6,000	$ 6,000	0
Second 6 months	4,000	9,000	6,000	8,000	0
Total	$ 6,000	$13,000	$12,000	$14,000	0
Sales (at selling price)	$10,000	$10,000	$10,000	$10,000	$40,000

Assume that there are no costs or expenses other than those shown above. The tax rate is 60 percent, and taxes for each year are payable on December 31 of each year. Cado Company is trying to decide whether to use periodic Fifo or Lifo throughout the five-year period.

1. What was net income after taxes under Fifo for each of the five years? Under Lifo? Show calculations.
2. Explain briefly which method, Lifo or Fifo, seems more advantageous, and why.

20-34. Investment credit. The Scott Company purchased machinery for $300,000. Its estimated useful life is eight years; its expected scrap value is zero. Net income (after taxes but before considering a 10 percent investment tax credit) is $160,000 annually. Income taxes before considering the investment credit were $100,000.

1. Net income for Year One under the flow-through method.
2. Net income for Years 1, 2, and 3 under the deferral method. Show how the income statement and balance-sheet accounts will be affected by the deferral method for each of the first three years.

20-35. Investment credit and airlines. Suppose that United Airlines purchases ten new airplanes for $7,000,000 each. Their estimated useful life is fourteen years. Ignore scrap value. Net earnings before considering the investment credit are averaging $50 million annually. Twenty million common shares are outstanding.

1. This problem will probe the effects of a differing investment tax credit rate, which has been varied by Congress through the years. First assume that the rate is 7 percent. For the first four years, show how net income and earnings per share would differ between flow-through and deferral of the investment credit.
2. Repeat Requirement 1, but assume that $70 million is spent in each of the four years to replace ten worn-out airplanes that were originally not subject to the investment credit.

3. Suppose there is a severe economic recession. To encourage investment, Congress increases the investment tax credit from 7 percent to 40 percent for a duration of one year. Repeat Requirement 1. Which of the two computations of net income "presents fairly" the results of operations? Why?

4. Examine the results in Requirements 1 and 2. If United Airlines steadily expands, how will net income be affected under the two methods? Compute the difference for Years 1 and 2 if United spent $105 million on new equipment in Year 2.

20-36. **Deferred income taxes.** Examine Exhibit 20-6. Suppose in Year 7 that $45 million were spent on fixed assets with five-year lives and that income before depreciation and taxes reached $70 million. For Year 7, fill in all the columns in Exhibit 20-6.

20-37. **Fundamentals of income tax allocation.** Suppose that the Norfolk & Western Railroad purchases a group of highly specialized freight cars for $2.1 million dollars. They will have a six-year life and no residual value. The company uses sum-of-the-years'-digits depreciation for tax purposes and straight-line depreciation for financial reporting purposes.

The income of this division before depreciation and taxes is $1.0 million. The applicable income tax rate is 40 percent.

1. For the six years, tabulate the details of how these facts would influence the Norfolk & Western reporting for tax purposes and for reporting to stockholders. Ignore the investment tax credit.

2. How will the Deferred Income Taxes account be affected if capital expenditures are the same each year? Grow each year?

20-38. **Installment sales and deferred income taxes.** On January 2, 19x1, Retail Appliance Company sold a refrigerator for $540 on an installment sale basis. The sales contract required no down payment and thirty-six payments of $15 per month plus interest on the unpaid balance. The gross margin was 20 percent of the sales price. For purposes of this problem, ignore interest and any carrying charges.

1. For financial reporting purposes, what is the pretax gross profit on the sale? The Internal Revenue Code gives the retailer the option of using either the accrual or the installment method, whereby 20 percent of each installment payment would be taxable in the period received. Under this method, what would be the pretax gross profit for each of the three years?

2. Assume a 50 percent tax rate. Prepare a table for three years showing the effects of income tax deferral. Use the following columns: pretax gross profit, tax paid, tax allocated, total tax expense, net income after tax, and balance-sheet effect: deferred income taxes.

3. Repeat Requirement 2, assuming that a refrigerator is sold for the same price and terms on January 2, 19x2, and also on January 2, of 19x3, 19x4, and 19x5. Extend the analysis through Year 5.

4. Repeat Requirement 3, assuming that two units are sold on January 2, 19x2, three in 19x3, four in 19x4, and five in 19x5.

5. Study the results in the above parts. What conclusions can you draw about the long-run effects of income tax allocation on financial statements?

20-39. Investment credit and deferred taxes. The Wonder Steel Company had used accelerated depreciation for both financial reporting and tax purposes. It had also amortized the investment credit for financial reporting purposes. After enjoying steady growth in earnings for several years, the company encountered severe competition from foreign sources. This had a leveling effect on reported earnings per share.

In 19x8, the company invested $50 million in a mammoth plant construction program. Some of the $50 million was not eligible for the investment tax credit; in any event, the net result was an investment credit of $3.5 million for 19x8. Management is seriously considering changing its method of reporting from Requirements 2a to 2d below. Other data:

Useful life of $50 million investment, 20 years with no scrap value

Double-declining-balance depreciation rate of 10 percent used for tax purposes

Net income before depreciation on new assets and income taxes and investment credit effects, $20 million

Depreciation on new assets for 19x8:

Straight-line	$2.5 million
Double-declining-balance	$5 million
Income tax rate, 60 percent	

1. Compute net taxable income and the total income taxes for 19x8.

2. Suppose that the Wonder Steel Company has 10,000,000 common shares outstanding and no preferred shares outstanding. For financial-reporting purposes, compute net income and earnings per share where:
   a. The company uses accelerated depreciation and defers the investment credit.
   b. The company uses accelerated depreciation and "flows through" the investment credit.
   c. The company uses straight-line depreciation and defers the investment credit.
   d. The company uses straight-line depreciation and "flows through" the investment credit.

20-40. Effects of various accounting methods on net income. You are the manager of Drivo Company, a profitable new company that has high potential growth. It is nearing the end of your first year in business and you must make some decisions regarding accounting policies for financial reporting to stockholders. Your controller and your certified public accountant have gathered the following information (in thousands):

Revenue	$30,000
Beginning inventory	-0-
Purchases	14,000
Ending inventory—Lifo	4,000
Ending inventory—Fifo	5,000
Depreciation—straight-line	1,000
Depreciation—double-declining-balance	2,000
Product promotion costs	2,000
Product promotion costs (amortized amount)	400
Other expenses	4,000
Common shares outstanding (in thousands)	1,000
Income tax rate	50%
Investment credit—total received on tax returns this year	500
Investment credit—amortized amount per year	50

Double-declining-balance depreciation and flow-through of the investment credit will be used for tax purposes regardless of the method chosen for reporting to stockholders. For all other items, assume that the same method is used for tax purposes and for financial reporting purposes.

1. Prepare a columnar income statement. In column (1) show the results using Lifo, double-declining-balance depreciation, direct write-off of product promotion costs and amortization of the investment credit. Show earnings per share as well as net income. In successive columns, show the separate effects on net income and earnings per share of: (2) Fifo inventory, (3) straight-line depreciation, (4) amortization of product promotion costs, (5) flow-through of investment credit. In column (6), show all the effects of choosing (2) through (5). Note that in columns (2) through (5) only single changes in column (1) should be shown; that is, column (3) does not show the effects of (2) and (3) together, nor does column (4) show the effects of (2), (3), and (4) together.

2. As the manager, which accounting policies would you adopt? Why?

20-41. Monetary items. Read the appendix. Refer to Assignment 20-24. Suppose the same company also had $100,000 of cash, which it had acquired at the end of 19x3. It held the cash in a safety deposit box through the end of 19x4.

1. Fill in the blanks for the cash held in the safety box:

	(1) Measured in 19x3 Purchasing Power	(2) Measured in 19x4 Purchasing Power	(3) As Conventionally Measured
Cash balance, December 31, 19x3			
Cash balance, December 31, 19x4			
Purchasing-power loss from holding monetary item			

2. Prepare a similar tabulation for the land balance, except that the final line would refer to a "nonmonetary" rather than a "monetary" item.

20-42. Monetary versus nonmonetary assets. Read the appendix. Sloan Company owns land acquired for $100,000 one year ago, when the general price index was 100. It also owns $100,000 of government bonds acquired at the same time. The index today is 110. Operating expenses and operating revenue, including interest income, resulted in net income (and an increase of cash) of $4,000 measured in historical-dollar terms. Assume that all income and expense transactions occurred yesterday. The Sloan Company has no other assets and no liabilities. Its cash balance one year ago was zero.

1. Prepare comparative balance sheets for the two instants of time plus an income statement summary based on historical costs. Then prepare such statements on a basis restated for changes in the general price level.

2. This is a more important requirement. In your own words, explain the meaning of the price-level-adjusted statement. Why should the holding of a monetary asset generate a monetary loss while the holding of land causes neither a loss nor a gain?

20-43. Price-level accounting concepts questionnaire. (J. Shank.)

1. In preparing general-price-level adjusted financial statements, "monetary" items consist of:
   a. Only cash.
   b. Cash, other assets expected to be converted into cash, and current liabilities.
   c. Assets and liabilities whose amounts are fixed by contract or otherwise in terms of dollars, regardless of price-level changes.
   d. Assets and liabilities that are classified as current on the balance sheet.
   e. None of the above.

2. An unacceptable practice in presenting general-price-level adjusted financial statements is:
   a. The inclusion of general-price-level gains and losses on monetary items in the general-price-level adjusted income statement.
   b. The inclusion of extraordinary gains and losses in the general-price-level adjusted income statement.
   c. The use of charts, ratios, and narrative information.
   d. The use of specific price indices to restate inventories, plant and equipment.
   e. None of the above.

3. General-price-level adjusted financial statements do not incorporate:
   a. The "lower of cost or market" rule in the valuation of inventories.
   b. Replacement cost in the valuation of plant assets.
   c. The historical-cost basis in reporting income tax expense.
   d. The actual amounts payable in reporting liabilities on the balance sheet.
   e. Any of the above.

4. During a period of rising price levels, if a firm's combined holdings of cash, short-term marketable securities, and accounts receivable exceed its total liabilities, the general-price-level adjusted financial statements will exhibit:

a. Purchasing-power gains increasing net income.
b. Purchasing-power losses decreasing net income.
c. Purchasing-power gains with no effect on net income.
d. Purchasing-power losses with no effect on net income.
e. None of the above.

5. With regard to a firm's holdings of plant and equipment, when price levels are rising, its general-price-level adjusted financial statements will show:
   a. Holding gains that increase net income.
   b. Holding gains credited directly to capital with no effect on net income.
   c. Holding losses that reduce net income.
   d. Holding losses charged directly against capital with no effect on net income.
   e. None of the above.

The following information is applicable to items 6 and 7: Equipment was purchased for $120,000 on January 1, Year 1, when the general price index was 100. It was sold on December 31, Year 3, at a price of $85,000. The equipment originally was expected to last six years with no salvage value and was depreciated on a straight-line basis. The general price index at the end of Year 1 was 125, at the end of Year 2 was 150, and at the end of Year 3 was 175.

6. In comparative general-price-level adjusted balance sheets prepared at the end of Year 2, the end-of-Year 1 balance sheet would show equipment (net of accumulated depreciation) at:
   a. $150,000.
   b. $125,000.
   c. $100,000.
   d. $80,000.
   e. None of the above.

7. The general-price-level adjusted income statement prepared at the end of Year 2 should include depreciation expense of:
   a. $35,000.
   b. $30,000.
   c. $24,000.
   d. $20,000.
   e. None of the above.

20-44. Comprehensive review of appendix. A company has the following comparative balance sheets at December 31 (based on historical costs in nominal dollars):

	19x1	19x2
Cash	$2,000	$3,400
Inventory, 20 units and 10 units, respectively	2,000	1,000
Total assets	$4,000	$4,400
Original capital	$4,000	$4,000
Retained income	—	400
Stockholders' equity	$4,000	$4,400
General price-level index	160	176

The company had acquired all the inventory at $100 per unit on December 31, 19x1, and had held the inventory throughout 19x2; ten units were sold for cash on December 31, 19x2. The replacement cost of the inventory at that date was $125.

Required

Prepare a four-column tabulation of income statements: (1) historical cost—nominal dollars; (2) current value—nominal dollars; (3) historical cost—constant dollars, and (4) current value—constant dollars. Also show beginning and ending balance sheet accounts for each of the four columns. For example, the above accounts accompany column (1).

20-45. Extension of appendix problem. Suppose in the preceding problem that sales equipment had been purchased on December 31, 19x1 for $1,000 cash provided by an extra $1,000 of capital. The equipment was being fully depreciated over a ten-year life on a straight-line basis. The replacement cost of the equipment (new) at the end of 19x2 was $1,500.

Prepare a four-column summary of how your tabulations in the preceding problem would be affected by this additional information. Include the following items: Equipment, Accumulated Depreciation, Retained Income, Depreciation Expense, Holding Gain—Equipment. For Retained Income, present the new balances plus footnotes showing how the new balances were obtained. Thus, the footnotes would show the old balances of the preceding problem plus or minus the changes arising from obtaining and using equipment.

20-46. Replacement costs. (P. Griffin.) Accompanying this problem are excerpts from the 1974 Annual Report of Barber-Ellis Limited of Canada. Note 1 to the financial report includes the following passage:

The current replacement costs of inventories and of property, plant and equipment are shown on the balance sheet and earnings are determined by matching current costs with current revenues. Adjustments of the historical cost of physical assets to their current replacement cost are considered as restatements of shareholders' equity and are shown on the balance sheet under "Revaluation Surplus."

Since 1974 is the first year that the company has prepared current replacement cost financial statements, comparatve figures are not available.

Required

From information in the Balance Sheet, Statement of Earnings and Retained Earnings, and Statement of Revaluation Surplus determine, as of December 31, 1974:

1. Current replacement cost "Inventories."
2. Current replacement cost "Property, Plant and Equipment."
3. Current replacement cost "Accumulated Depreciation."
4. Current replacement cost "Total Assets."
5. Current replacement cost "Retained Earnings."

Also, for the year ended December 31, 1974, determine:

6. Current replacement cost "Cost of Products Sold."

7. Current replacement cost "Net Earnings."

Finally, explain in words the nature of:

8. The difference between the current replacement cost "Net Earnings" and the historical cost "Net Earnings" for the year ended December 31, 1974.

BARBER-ELLIS OF CANADA, LIMITED

Current Replacement Cost Balance Sheet
As at December 31, 1974

	CURRENT REPLACEMENT COST (NOTE 1)	HISTORICAL COST (NOTE 3)		CURRENT REPLACEMENT COST (NOTE 1)	HISTORICAL COST (NOTE 3)
ASSETS			**LIABILITIES**		
Current:			Current:		
Cash	$ 29,783	$ 29,783	Bank indebtedness	$ 7,573,983	$ 7,573,983
Accounts receivable	12,074,945	12,074,945	Accounts payable and accrued liabilities	4,109,189	4,109,189
Inventories	(1)	10,117,804	Income taxes	1,296,693	1,296,693
Prepaid expenses	249,545	249,545	Dividends—preference shares	700	700
Current assets	$22,721,077	$22,472,077	Current portion of long-term debt	486,650	486,650
			Current liabilities	$13,467,215	$13,467,215
Property, plant and equipment	(2)	11,261,927	Deferred income taxes	278,362	278,362
Accumulated depreciation	(3)	(5,817,772)	Long-term debt (Note 1)	4,133,650	4,133,650
Unamortized excess of purchase price of subsidiaries over fair value of net assets acquired	—	816,067	Total liabilities	$17,879,227	$17,879,227
			SHAREHOLDERS' EQUITY		
			Capital Stock	$ 565,705	$ 565,705
			Contributed surplus	45,000	45,000
			Retained earnings	(5)	10,242,367
			Revaluation surplus	4,319,204	—
Total assets	$ (4)	$28,732,299	Total equities	$ (4)	$28,732,299

Current Replacement Cost Statement
of Earnings and Retained Earnings
for the year ended December 31, 1974

	CURRENT REPLACEMENT COST (NOTE 2)	HISTORICAL COST (NOTE 3)
Net sales	$69,058,300	$69,058,300
Cost of products sold	$ (6)	$50,389,580
Selling, general and administration	10,705,281	10,705,281
Depreciation and amortization	1,095,567	786,969
Interest—long-term debt	381,884	381,884
Interest—current	590,284	590,284
Cost and expenses	$	$62,853,998
Earnings before income taxes	$	$ 6,204,302
Provision for income taxes	2,927,442	2,927,442
Net Earnings	$ (7)	$ 3,276,860
Retained earnings, beginning of year	7,939,344	7,939,344
Sub-total	$	$11,216,204
Adjustment of prior years' depreciation on current replacement cost of plant and equipment	$ 1,948,116	—
Dividends	973,837	$ 973,837
Retained Earnings, End of Year	$	$10,242,367
Earnings Per Share		
Basic	$ 4.30	$ 7.09
Fully diluted	4.22	6.96

Statement of Revaluation Surplus
for the year ended December 31, 1974

Revaluation of physical assets to reflect current replacement cost as at December 31, 1974	
Inventories	$ 249,000
Property, plant and equipment	3,902,271
Excess of purchase price over fair value of assets acquired	(816,067)
Revaluation of cost of products sold during the year ended December 31, 1974	
Portion of 1974 earnings determined on historical cost basis which are required to replace inventory sold at the current cost in effect at the date of sale	984,000
Revaluation surplus December 31, 1974	$4,319,204

Report on Supplementary Financial Statements

To the Shareholders,
Barber-Ellis of Canada, Limited

In conjunction with our examination of and report on the financial statements of Barber-Ellis of Canada, Limited for 1974 we have also examined the accompanying supplementary financial statements which have been prepared on a current replacement cost basis.

Uniform criteria for the preparation and presentation of such supplementary financial information have not yet been established and accordingly, acceptable alternatives are available as to their nature and content. In our opinion, however, the accounting basis described in the notes to the supplementary financial statements has been applied as stated and is appropriate in these circumstances.

Touche Ross & Co.
Chartered Accountants

Toronto, Ontario
February 21, 1975

PART FIVE

Appendixes

Recommended
Readings

The following readings are suggested as an aid to those readers who want to pursue some topics in more depth than is possible in this book. Of course, many of the chapters have footnotes or suggested readings on a particular topic. Therefore, the specific chapters should be consulted for direct references.

There is a hazard in compiling a group of recommended readings. Inevitably, some worthwhile books or periodicals are overlooked. Moreover, such a list cannot include books published subsequent to the compilation here.

Professional journals are typically available in university libraries. *Management Accounting* and *The Financial Executive* tend to stress articles on management accounting. The *Journal of Accountancy* emphasizes financial accounting and is directed at the practicing CPA. The *Harvard Business Review* and *Fortune,* which are aimed at general managers, contain many articles on planning and control.

The Accounting Review and the *Journal of Accounting Research* cover all phases of accounting at a more theoretical level than the preceding publications.

The *Opinions* of the Accounting Principles Board are available from the American Institute of CPAs, 1211 Avenue of the Americas, New York, N.Y. 10036. The Institute also has a series of research studies on a variety of topics. The pronouncements of the Financial Accounting Standards Board are available from the Board's officers, High Ridge Park, Stamford, Conn. 06905.

The Financial Executives Institute, 50 West 44th Street, New York, N.Y. and the National Association of Accountants, 919 Third Avenue, New York, N.Y. have long lists of accounting research publications.

There are many books on elementary management accounting. Also, many books entitled *Cost Accounting* stress a management approach, including those published since 1977 by Charles Horngren (Prentice-Hall), and Gordon Shillinglaw (Richard D. Irwin).

The following books on planning and control should be helpful:

ANTHONY, R. N., and JOHN DEARDEN, *Management Control Systems,* 3rd ed., Homewood, Ill.: Richard D. Irwin, 1976.

BEYER, ROBERT, and DONALD TRAWICKI, *Profitability Accounting for Planning and Control,* 2nd ed., New York: Ronald Press, 1972.

SOLOMONS, DAVID, *Divisional Performance: Measurement and Control.* Homewood, Ill.: Richard D. Irwin, 1968. This book has an extensive bibliography. It is especially strong on transfer pricing.

Books of readings on management accounting topics published since 1970 include:

ANTON, HECTOR R., and PETER A. FIRMIN (eds.), *Contemporary Issues in Cost Accounting,* 2nd ed. Boston: Houghton Mifflin Company, 1972.

BENSTON, GEORGE J., *Contemporary Cost Accounting and Control.* Belmont, Cal.: Dickenson Publishing Company, Inc., 1970.

DeCOSTER, D., K. RAMANTHAN, and G. SUNDEM (eds.), *Accounting for Managerial Decision Making.* Los Angeles: Melville Publishing Company, 1974.

LIVINGSTONE, JOHN LESLIE (ed.), *Management Planning and Control: Mathematical Models.* New York: McGraw-Hill Book Company, 1970.

RAPPAPORT, ALFRED (ed.), *Information for Decision Making: Quantitative and Behavioral Dimensions,* 2nd ed. Englewood Cliffs, N.J.: Prentice-Hall, Inc., 1974.

ROSEN, L. S. (ed.), *Topics in Managerial Accounting,* 2nd ed. Toronto: McGraw-Hill Ryerson, Ltd., 1974.

SCHIFF, MICHAEL, and ARIE Y. LEWIN (eds.), *Behavioral Aspects of Accounting.* Englewood Cliffs, N.J.: Prentice-Hall, Inc., 1974.

THOMAS, W., (ed.), *Readings in Cost Accounting, Budgeting and Control,* 4th ed. Cincinnati: South-Western Publishing Co., 1973.

For a book-length study of management accounting in not-for-profit organizations, see:

ANTHONY, R. N., and R. HERZLINGER, *Management Control in Nonprofit Organizations.* Homewood, Ill.: Richard D. Irwin, Inc., 1975.

Fundamentals of Compound Interest and the Use of Present-Value Tables

NATURE OF INTEREST

Interest is the cost of using money. It is the rental charge for cash, just as rental charges are often made for the use of automobiles or boats.

Interest does not always entail an outlay of cash. The concept of interest applies to ownership funds as well as to borrowed funds. The reason why interest must be considered on *all* funds in use, regardless of their source, is that the selection of one alternative necessarily commits funds that otherwise could be invested in some other opportunity. The measure of the interest in such cases is the return foregone by rejecting the alternative use. For instance, a wholly owned home or business asset is not cost-free. The funds so invested could alternatively be invested in government bonds or in some other venture. The measure of this opportunity cost depends on what alternative incomes are available.

Interest cost is often unimportant when short-term projects are under consideration, but it becomes extremely important when long-run plans are being considered. The longer the time span, the higher the interest or rental

687

charge. If you place $10,000 in a savings account at 4 percent interest, compounded annually, you accumulate "interest on interest," which is what "compounding" means. The original $10,000 will grow to $10,400 at the end of Year 1 ($10,000 × 1.04); to $10,816 at the end of Year 2 ($10,400 × 1.04); to $11,249 at the end of Year 3 ($10,816 × 1.04); and to $21,911 at the end of Year 20 ($10,000 × 1.04²⁰). If the rate of interest were 10 percent compounded annually, the original $10,000 would grow to $13,310 at the end of Year 3, ($10,000 × 1.10³); and to $67,276 at the end of Year 20 ($10,000 × 1.10²⁰).

TABLE 1: PRESENT VALUE OF $1

Two basic tables are used in capital budgeting. The first table (Table 1, p. 692, the Present Value of $1, deals with a single lump-sum cash inflow or outflow at a given instant of time, the *end* of the period in question. An example should clarify the reasoning underlying the construction and use of the table.

Illustration: assume that a prominent corporation is issuing a three-year noninterest-bearing note payable that promises to pay a lump sum of $1,000 exactly three years from now. You desire a rate of return of exactly 6 percent, compounded annually. How much would you be willing to pay now for the three-year note? The situation is sketched as follows:

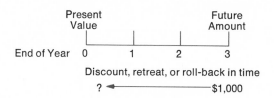

Let us examine the chart, period by period. First, let us assume that you are to purchase the $1,000 note at the end of Year 2 instead of at time zero. How much would you be willing to pay? If you wish to earn 6¢ annually on every $1 invested, you would want to receive $1.06 after one year for every $1 you invest today. Therefore, at the end of Year 2 you would be willing to pay $\frac{\$1.00}{\$1.06}$ × $1,000 for the right to receive $1,000 at the end of Year 3, or $.943 × $1,000 = $943. Let us enter this in a tabular calculation:

End of Year	Interest per Year	Cumulative Discount, Called Compound Discount	Present Value at the End of Year
3	$57	$ 57	$1,000
2	53	110	943
1	50	160	890
0	—	—	840

689

*Fundamentals
of Compound
Interest and
the Use of
Present-Value
Tables*

Note that what is really being done in the tabulation is a series of computations that could be formulated as follows:

$$PV_2 = \$1,000 \left[\frac{1.00}{1.06} \right] = \$943$$

$$PV_1 = \$1,000 \left[\frac{1.00}{(1.06)^2} \right] = \$890$$

$$PV_0 = \$1,000 \left[\frac{1.00}{(1.06)^3} \right] = \$840$$

This can be written as a formula for the present value of $1:

$$PV = \frac{S}{(1 + i)^n}$$

where PV = Present value at time zero; S = Future amount; i = Interest rate; and n = Number of periods.

Check the answers in the tabulation by using Table 1 (p. 692). For example, the Period 3 row and the 6 percent column show a factor of .840. Multiply this factor by the future cash flow, $1,000, to obtain its present value, $840.

Use Table 1 to obtain the present values of:

1. $1,600, @ 20 percent, at the end of 20 years.
2. $8,300, @ 10 percent, at the end of 12 years.
3. $8,000, @ 4 percent, at the end of 4 years.

Answers:

1. $1,600 (.026) = $41.60.
2. $8,300 (.319) = $2,648.
3. $8,000 (.855) = $6,840.

TABLE 2: PRESENT VALUE
OF AN ORDINARY ANNUITY OF $1

An ordinary annuity is a series of equal cash flows to take place at the *end* of successive periods of equal length. Assume that you buy a noninterest-bearing serial note from a corporation that promises to pay $1,000 at the end of each of three years. How much should you be willing to pay, if you desire a rate of return of 6 percent, compounded annually?

The tabulation on p. 690 shows how the formula for PV_A, *the present value of an ordinary annuity,* is developed.

END OF YEAR		0	1	2	3
1st payment:	$\dfrac{1{,}000}{1.06}$	$ 943	$1,000		
2nd payment:	$\dfrac{1{,}000}{(1.06)^2}$	$ 890		$1,000	
3rd payment:	$\dfrac{1{,}000}{(1.06)^3}$	$ 840			$1,000
		$2,673			

$$PV_A = \text{Sum of present values of each item} \qquad (1)$$

For the general case, the present value of an ordinary annuity of $1 may be expressed as follows:

$$PV_A = \frac{1}{1+i} + \frac{1}{(1+i)^2} + \frac{1}{(1+i)^3} \qquad (2)$$

Substituting values from our illustration:

$$PV_A = \frac{1}{1.06} + \frac{1}{(1.06)^2} + \frac{1}{(1.06)^3} \qquad (3)$$

Multiply by $\dfrac{1}{1.06}$:

$$PV_A\left(\frac{1}{1.06}\right) = \frac{1}{(1.06)^2} + \frac{1}{(1.06)^3} + \frac{1}{(1.06)^4} \qquad (4)$$

Subtract Equation 4 from Equation 3:

$$PV_A - PV_A\left(\frac{1}{1.06}\right) = \frac{1}{1.06} - \frac{1}{(1.06)^4} \qquad (5)$$

Factor:
$$PV_A\left(1 - \frac{1}{1.06}\right) = \frac{1}{1.06}\left[1 - \frac{1}{(1.06)^3}\right] \qquad (6)$$

or
$$PV_A\left(\frac{.06}{1.06}\right) = \frac{1}{1.06}\left[1 - \frac{1}{(1.06)^3}\right] \qquad (7)$$

Multiply by $\dfrac{1.06}{.06}$:
$$PV_A = \frac{1}{.06}\left[1 - \frac{1}{(1.06)^3}\right] \qquad (8)$$

691

*Fundamentals
of Compound
Interest and
the Use of
Present-Value
Tables*

The general formula for the present worth of an annuity of $1 is:

$$PV_A = \frac{1}{i}\left[1 - \frac{1}{(1+i)^n}\right] \tag{9}$$

Solving:

$$PV_A = \frac{1}{.06}(1 - .840) = \frac{.160}{.06} = 2.67 \tag{10}$$

This formula is the basis for Table 2 (p. 693). Check the answer in the table. Minor differences are due to rounding.

Finally, note that Table 2 is convenient, but it is really a compilation of the basic data in Table 1. For example, the present value of each of the three payments could be computed individually, using Table 1:

$$
\begin{array}{rcl}
 & P.V. & \\
 & Factor & \\
.943 \times \$1,000 & = & \$\ \ 943 \\
.890 \times \$1,000 & = & 890 \\
.840 \times \$1,000 & = & \underline{\ \ \ 840} \\
 & & \overline{\$2,673} \\
\end{array}
$$

Alternatively, a shortcut computation would use the present-value factor from Table 2, which is merely the sum of the three individual factors = .943 + .890 + .840 = 2.673. Therefore, the shortcut computation would be 2.673 × $1,000 = $2,673. If you were marooned on a deserted island with one table, Table 1 would be preferable to Table 2.[1]

Use Table 2 to obtain the present values of the following ordinary annuities.

1. $1,600 at 20 percent for 20 years.
2. $8,300 at 10 percent for 12 years.
3. $8,000 at 4 percent for 4 years.

Answers:

1. $1,600 (4.870) = $7,792.
2. $8,300 (6.814) = $56,556.
3. $8,000 (3.630) = $29,040.

---

[1] For additional tables, see D. Thorndike, *The Thorndike Encyclopedia of Banking and Financial Tables* (Boston: Warren, Gorham & Lamont, Inc., 1977).

TABLE 1:

Present Value of $1

$$PV = \frac{S}{(1 + i)^n}$$

PERIODS	4%	6%	8%	10%	12%	14%	16%	18%	20%	22%	24%	26%	28%	30%	40%
1	0.962	0.943	0.926	0.909	0.893	0.877	0.862	0.847	0.833	0.820	0.806	0.794	0.781	0.769	0.714
2	0.925	0.890	0.857	0.826	0.797	0.769	0.743	0.718	0.694	0.672	0.650	0.630	0.610	0.592	0.510
3	0.889	0.840	0.794	0.751	0.712	0.675	0.641	0.609	0.579	0.551	0.524	0.500	0.477	0.455	0.364
4	0.855	0.792	0.735	0.683	0.636	0.592	0.552	0.516	0.482	0.451	0.423	0.397	0.373	0.350	0.260
5	0.822	0.747	0.681	0.621	0.567	0.519	0.476	0.437	0.402	0.370	0.341	0.315	0.291	0.269	0.186
6	0.790	0.705	0.630	0.564	0.507	0.456	0.410	0.370	0.335	0.303	0.275	0.250	0.227	0.207	0.133
7	0.760	0.665	0.583	0.513	0.452	0.400	0.354	0.314	0.279	0.249	0.222	0.198	0.178	0.159	0.095
8	0.731	0.627	0.540	0.467	0.404	0.351	0.305	0.266	0.233	0.204	0.179	0.157	0.139	0.123	0.068
9	0.703	0.592	0.500	0.424	0.361	0.308	0.263	0.225	0.194	0.167	0.144	0.125	0.108	0.094	0.048
10	0.676	0.558	0.463	0.386	0.322	0.270	0.227	0.191	0.162	0.137	0.116	0.099	0.085	0.073	0.035
11	0.650	0.527	0.429	0.350	0.287	0.237	0.195	0.162	0.135	0.112	0.094	0.079	0.066	0.056	0.025
12	0.625	0.497	0.397	0.319	0.257	0.208	0.168	0.137	0.112	0.092	0.076	0.062	0.052	0.043	0.018
13	0.601	0.469	0.368	0.290	0.229	0.182	0.145	0.116	0.093	0.075	0.061	0.050	0.040	0.033	0.013
14	0.577	0.442	0.340	0.263	0.205	0.160	0.125	0.099	0.078	0.062	0.049	0.039	0.032	0.025	0.009
15	0.555	0.417	0.315	0.239	0.183	0.140	0.108	0.084	0.065	0.051	0.040	0.031	0.025	0.020	0.006
16	0.534	0.394	0.292	0.218	0.163	0.123	0.093	0.071	0.054	0.042	0.032	0.025	0.019	0.015	0.005
17	0.513	0.371	0.270	0.198	0.146	0.108	0.080	0.060	0.045	0.034	0.026	0.020	0.015	0.012	0.003
18	0.494	0.350	0.250	0.180	0.130	0.095	0.069	0.051	0.038	0.028	0.021	0.016	0.012	0.009	0.002
19	0.475	0.331	0.232	0.164	0.116	0.083	0.060	0.043	0.031	0.023	0.017	0.012	0.009	0.007	0.002
20	0.456	0.312	0.215	0.149	0.104	0.073	0.051	0.037	0.026	0.019	0.014	0.010	0.007	0.005	0.001
21	0.439	0.294	0.199	0.135	0.093	0.064	0.044	0.031	0.022	0.015	0.011	0.008	0.006	0.004	0.001
22	0.422	0.278	0.184	0.123	0.083	0.056	0.038	0.026	0.018	0.013	0.009	0.006	0.004	0.003	0.001
23	0.406	0.262	0.170	0.112	0.074	0.049	0.033	0.022	0.015	0.010	0.007	0.005	0.003	0.002	
24	0.390	0.247	0.158	0.102	0.066	0.043	0.028	0.019	0.013	0.008	0.006	0.004	0.003	0.002	
25	0.375	0.233	0.146	0.092	0.059	0.038	0.024	0.016	0.010	0.007	0.005	0.003	0.002	0.001	
26	0.361	0.220	0.135	0.084	0.053	0.033	0.021	0.014	0.009	0.006	0.004	0.002	0.002	0.001	
27	0.347	0.207	0.125	0.076	0.047	0.029	0.018	0.011	0.007	0.005	0.003	0.002	0.001	0.001	
28	0.333	0.196	0.116	0.069	0.042	0.026	0.016	0.010	0.006	0.004	0.002	0.002	0.001	0.001	
29	0.321	0.185	0.107	0.063	0.037	0.022	0.014	0.008	0.005	0.003	0.002	0.001	0.001	0.001	
30	0.308	0.174	0.099	0.057	0.033	0.020	0.012	0.007	0.004	0.003	0.002	0.001	0.001	0.001	
40	0.208	0.097	0.046	0.022	0.011	0.005	0.003	0.001	0.001						

TABLE 2:

Present Value of Ordinary Annuity of $1

$$PV_A = \frac{1}{i}\left[1 - \frac{1}{(1+i)^n}\right]$$

PERIODS	4%	6%	8%	10%	12%	14%	16%	18%	20%	22%	24%	25%	26%	28%	30%	40%
1	0.962	0.943	0.926	0.909	0.893	0.877	0.862	0.847	0.833	0.820	0.806	0.800	0.794	0.781	0.769	0.714
2	1.886	1.833	1.783	1.736	1.690	1.647	1.605	1.566	1.528	1.492	1.457	1.440	1.424	1.392	1.361	1.224
3	2.775	2.673	2.577	2.487	2.402	2.322	2.246	2.174	2.106	2.042	1.981	1.952	1.923	1.868	1.816	1.589
4	3.630	3.465	3.312	3.170	3.037	2.914	2.798	2.690	2.589	2.494	2.404	2.362	2.320	2.241	2.166	1.849
5	4.452	4.212	3.993	3.791	3.605	3.433	3.274	3.127	2.991	2.864	2.745	2.689	2.635	2.532	2.436	2.035
6	5.242	4.917	4.623	4.355	4.111	3.889	3.685	3.498	3.326	3.167	3.020	2.951	2.885	2.759	2.643	2.168
7	6.002	5.582	5.206	4.868	4.564	4.288	4.039	3.812	3.605	3.416	3.242	3.161	3.083	2.937	2.802	2.263
8	6.733	6.210	5.747	5.335	4.968	4.639	4.344	4.078	3.837	3.619	3.421	3.329	3.241	3.076	2.925	2.331
9	7.435	6.802	6.247	5.759	5.328	4.946	4.607	4.303	4.031	3.786	3.566	3.463	3.366	3.184	3.019	2.379
10	8.111	7.360	6.710	6.145	5.650	5.216	4.833	4.494	4.192	3.923	3.682	3.571	3.465	3.269	3.092	2.414
11	8.760	7.887	7.139	6.495	5.938	5.453	5.029	4.656	4.327	4.035	3.776	3.656	3.544	3.335	3.147	2.438
12	9.385	8.384	7.536	6.814	6.194	5.660	5.197	4.793	4.439	4.127	3.851	3.725	3.606	3.387	3.190	2.456
13	9.986	8.853	7.904	7.103	6.424	5.842	5.342	4.910	4.533	4.203	3.912	3.780	3.656	3.427	3.223	2.468
14	10.563	9.295	8.244	7.367	6.628	6.002	5.468	5.008	4.611	4.265	3.962	3.824	3.695	3.459	3.249	2.477
15	11.118	9.712	8.559	7.606	6.811	6.142	5.575	5.092	4.675	4.315	4.001	3.859	3.726	3.483	3.268	2.484
16	11.652	10.106	8.851	7.824	6.974	6.265	5.669	5.162	4.730	4.357	4.033	3.887	3.751	3.503	3.283	2.489
17	12.166	10.477	9.122	8.022	7.120	6.373	5.749	5.222	4.775	4.391	4.059	3.910	3.771	3.518	3.295	2.492
18	12.659	10.828	9.372	8.201	7.250	6.467	5.818	5.273	4.812	4.419	4.080	3.928	3.786	3.529	3.304	2.494
19	13.134	11.158	9.604	8.365	7.366	6.550	5.877	5.316	4.844	4.442	4.097	3.942	3.799	3.539	3.311	2.496
20	13.590	11.470	9.818	8.514	7.469	6.623	5.929	5.353	4.870	4.460	4.110	3.954	3.808	3.546	3.316	2.497
21	14.029	11.764	10.017	8.649	7.562	6.687	5.973	5.384	4.891	4.476	4.121	3.963	3.816	3.551	3.320	2.498
22	14.451	12.042	10.201	8.772	7.645	6.743	6.001	5.410	4.909	4.488	4.130	3.970	3.822	3.556	3.323	2.498
23	14.857	12.303	10.371	8.883	7.718	6.792	6.044	5.432	4.925	4.499	4.137	3.976	3.827	3.559	3.325	2.499
24	15.247	12.550	10.529	8.985	7.784	6.835	6.073	5.451	4.937	4.507	4.143	3.981	3.831	3.562	3.327	2.499
25	15.622	12.783	10.675	9.077	7.843	6.873	6.097	5.467	4.948	4.514	4.147	3.985	3.834	3.564	3.329	2.499
26	15.983	13.003	10.810	9.161	7.896	6.906	6.118	5.480	4.956	4.520	4.151	3.988	3.837	3.566	3.330	2.500
27	16.330	13.211	10.935	9.237	7.943	6.935	6.136	5.492	4.964	4.524	4.154	3.990	3.839	3.567	3.331	2.500
28	16.663	13.406	11.051	9.307	7.984	6.961	6.152	5.502	4.970	4.528	4.157	3.992	3.840	3.568	3.331	2.500
29	16.984	13.591	11.158	9.370	8.022	6.983	6.166	5.510	4.975	4.531	4.159	3.994	3.841	3.569	3.332	2.500
30	17.292	13.765	11.258	9.427	8.055	7.003	6.177	5.517	4.979	4.534	4.160	3.995	3.842	3.569	3.332	2.500
40	19.793	15.046	11.925	9.779	8.244	7.105	6.234	5.548	4.997	4.544	4.166	3.999	3.846	3.571	3.333	2.500

APPENDIX C

Glossary

For a more elaborate description of each term, consult the chapter indicated in parentheses.

Absorption costing. That type of product costing which assigns fixed manufacturing overhead to the units produced as a product cost. Contrast with *direct costing*. (Chap. 15)

Account. Summary of the changes in a particular asset or equity. (Chap. 17)

Accounting method. See *Unadjusted rate of return*. (Chap. 12)

Accounting rate of return. An expression of the utility of a given project as the ratio of the increase in future average annual net income to the initial increase in required investment. Also called *book value rate* and *unadjusted rate*. (Chap. 12)

Accrual basis. A matching process whereby revenue is recognized as services are rendered and expenses are recognized as efforts are expended or services utilized to obtain the revenue. (Chap. 17)

Activity accounting. See *Responsibility accounting*. (Chap. 9)

Allocation. Assigning one or more items of cost or revenue to one or more segments of an organization according to benefits received, responsibilities, or other logical measure of use. (Chap. 10)

Appropriation. An authorization to spend up to a specified dollar ceiling. (Chap. 8)

Assets. Economic resources that are expected to benefit future activities. (Chap. 17)

695

Asset turnover. The ratio of sales to total assets available. (Chap. 11)

Attention directing. That function of the accountant's information-supplying task which focuses on problems in the operation of the firm or which points out imperfections or inefficiencies in certain areas of the firm's operation. (Chap. 1)

Balance sheet. A statement of financial status at an instant of time. (Chap. 17)

Bill of materials. A specification of the quantities of direct material allowed for manufacturing a given quantity of output. (Chap. 7)

Book value. See *Net book value.* (Chap. 18)

Book value method. See *Unadjusted rate of return.* (Chap. 12)

Budget. A plan of action expressed in figures. (Chaps. 1, 6)

Capacity costs. An alternate term for fixed costs, emphasizing the fact that fixed costs are needed in order to provide operating facilities and an organization ready to produce and sell at a planned volume of activity. (Chap. 8)

Capital budgeting. Long-term planning for proposed capital outlays and their financing. (Chap. 12)

Capital surplus. The excess received over the par or stated or legal value of the shares issued. (Chap. 18)

Capital turnover. Revenue divided by invested capital. (Chap. 11)

Cash budget. A schedule of expected cash receipts and disbursements. (Chap. 6)

Cash flow. A general term that must be interpreted carefully. Most strictly, cash flow means inflows or outflows of cash. Frequently, the term is used loosely to represent funds provided by operations. (Chaps. 12, 18)

Committed costs. Those fixed costs arising from the possession of plant and equipment and a basic organization and thus affected primarily by long-run decisions as to the desired level of capacity. (Chap. 8)

Common cost. A cost which is common to all the segments in question and which is not clearly or practically allocable except by some questionable allocation base. (Chaps. 4, 5)

Comptroller. See *Controller.* (Chap. 1)

Conditional value. The value which will ensue if a particular event occurs. (Chap. 16)

Conservatism. Selecting that method of measurement which yields the gloomiest immediate results. (Chap. 18)

Consolidated financial statements. The combination of the financial positions and earnings reports of the parent company with those of various subsidiaries into an overall report as if they were a single entity. (Chap. 19)

Continuous budget. A budget which perpetually adds a month in the future as the month just ended is dropped. (Chap. 6)

Contribution approach. A method of preparing income statements which separates variable costs from fixed costs in order to emphasize the importance of cost behavior patterns for purposes of planning and control. (Chap. 3)

Contribution margin. Excess of sales price over variable expenses. Also called marginal income. May be expressed as a total, as a ratio, or on a per unit basis. (Chap. 2)

Controllable cost. A cost which may be directly regulated at a given level of managerial authority, either in the short run or in the long run. (Chap. 9)

Controller. The chief management accounting executive. Also spelled *comptroller.* (Chap. 1)

Controlling. Obtaining conformity to plans through action and evaluation. (Chap. 1)

Cost application. Also called *cost absorption.* The allocation to products rather than to departments. (Chap. 10)

Cost-benefit philosophy. Accounting systems are economic goods whose additional benefits must exceed their incremental costs. (Chap. 1)

Cost center. An area of responsibility for costs. (Chap. 9)

Cost objective. Any activity for which a separate measurement of costs is desired. Examples include departments, products, territories, etc. (Chap. 3)

Cost of goods sold. Cost of the merchandise that is acquired and resold. (Chap. 3)

Cost pool. A group of costs that is allocated to cost objectives in some plausible way. (Chap. 10)

Credit. An entry on the right side of an account. (Chap. 17)

Current assets. Cash plus those assets which are reasonably expected to be converted to cash or sold or consumed during the normal operating cycle. (Chap. 18)

Current liabilities. Liabilities that fall due within the coming year or within the normal operating cycle if longer than a year. (Chap. 18)

Currently attainable standards. Standards expressing a level of economic efficiency which can be reached with skilled, diligent, superior effort. (Chap. 7)

Debenture. A security with a general claim against all unencumbered assets rather than a specific claim against particular assets. (Chap. 18)

Debit. An entry on the left side of an account. (Chap. 17)

Decentralization. The relative freedom to make decisions. The lower the level in the organization that decisions are made, the greater the decentralization. (Chap. 11)

Decision model. A formal method for making a choice that often involves quantitative analysis. (Chap. 4)

Decision table. A convenient technique for showing the total expected value of each of a number of contemplated acts in the light of the varying probabilities of the events which may take place and the varying values of each act under each of the events. (Chap. 16)

Deferral method. Reflection in net income of an investment tax credit over the productive life of the asset acquired. Contrast with *Flow-through method*. (Chap. 20)

Deferred federal income taxes. A deferred credit in the balance sheet that represents the additional federal income taxes that would have been due if a company had not been allowed to deduct greater amounts for expenses (such as depreciation) for income tax reporting purposes than are recorded for financial reporting purposes. (Chap. 20)

Denominator variance. Difference between *budgeted* fixed overhead and the fixed overhead *applied* to product. (Chap. 15)

Depreciation. The allocation of the original cost of plant, property, and equipment to the particular periods or products that benefit from the utilization of the assets. (Chap. 18)

Differential cost. See *Incremental cost*. (Chap. 5)

Direct costing. That type of product costing which charges fixed manufacturing overhead immediately against the revenue of the period in which it was incurred, without assigning it to specific units produced. Also called *variable costing* or *marginal costing*. (Chap. 15)

Direct labor. All labor which is obviously related and specifically and conveniently traceable to specific products. (Chap. 3)

Direct material. All raw material which is an integral part of the finished good and which can be conveniently assigned to specific physical units. (Chap. 3)

Discretionary costs. Those fixed costs that arise from periodic, usually yearly, appropriation decisions that directly reflect top management policies. Also called *programmed costs* and *managed costs*. (Chap. 8)

Earned surplus. See *Retained income*. (Chap. 17)

Earnings per share. Net income divided by the number of common shares outstanding. However, where preferred stock exists, the preferred dividends must be deducted in order to compute the net income applicable to common stock. (Chap. 18)

Economic standard order quantity. The amount of inventory which should be ordered at one time in order to minimize the associated annual costs of the inventory. (Chap. 16)

Efficiency variance. The standard price for a given resource, multiplied by the difference between the actual quantity of inputs used and the total standard quantity of inputs allowed for the number of good outputs achieved. (Chap. 7)

Entity. A specific area of attention and effort that is the focus of the accounting process. It may be a single corporation, a tax district, a department, a papermaking machine, or a consolidated group of many interrelated corporations. (Chap. 17)

Equities. The interests in the assets. (Chap. 17)

Equity method. A basis for carrying long-term investments at cost plus a prorata share of accumulated retained income since acquisition. (Chap. 19)

Equivalent units. The expression of output in terms of doses or amount of work applied thereto. (Chap. 14)

Excess material requisitions. A form to be filled out by the production staff to secure any materials needed in excess of the standard amount allotted for output. (Chap. 7)

Expected value. A weighted average of all the conditional values of an act. Each conditional value is weighted by its probability. (Chap. 16)

Expenses. Expired costs that are deducted from revenue for a given period. (Chap. 17)

Factory burden. See *Factory overhead.* (Chap. 3)

Factory overhead. All factory costs other than direct labor and direct material. Also called *factory burden, indirect manufacturing costs, manufacturing overhead,* and *manufacturing expense.* (Chap. 3)

First in, first out. The stock which is acquired earliest is assumed to be used first; the stock acquired latest is assumed to be still on hand. (Chap. 20)

Fixed cost. A cost which, for a given period of time and range of activity called the *relevant range, does not change in total* but becomes progressively smaller on a *per unit* basis as volume increases. (Chap. 2)

Flexible budget. A budget, often referring to overhead costs only, which is prepared for a range, rather than for a single level, of activity—one which can be automatically geared to changes in the level of volume. Also called *variable budget.* Direct material and direct labor are sometimes included in the flexible budget. (Chap. 7)

Flow-through method. Recognition in full in one year of the income benefits of an investment tax credit. Contrast with *Deferral method.* (Chap. 20)

Functional costing. Classifying costs by allocating them to the various functions performed, such as manufacturing, warehousing, delivery, billing, and so forth. (Chap. 2)

Fund. A specific amount of cash or securities earmarked for a special purpose. (Chap. 18)

Funds provided by operations. The excess of revenue over all expenses requiring net working capital. (Chap. 18)

Funds statement. A statement of sources and applications of net working capital. (Chap. 18)

Goal congruence. Sharing of the same goals by top managers and their subordinates. (Chap. 9)

Going concern. The assumption that an entity will continue indefinitely or at least that it will not be liquidated in the near future. (Chap. 17)

Goodwill. The total purchase price of assets acquired in a lump-sum purchase that exceeds the total of the amounts that can be justifiably assigned to the individual assets. (Chap. 20)

Gross margin. Also called *gross profit.* Excess of sales over the *cost of goods sold* that is, over the cost of the merchandise inventory that is acquired and resold. (Chap. 2)

Gross profit. See *Gross margin.* (Chap. 2)

Historical cost. See *Sunk cost.* (Chap. 5)

Ideal capacity. The absolute maximum number of units that could be produced in a given operating situation, with no allowance for work stoppages or repairs. Also called *theoretical capacity.* (Chap. 8)

Idle time. A classification of *indirect labor* which constitutes wages paid for unproductive time due to circumstances beyond the worker's control. (Chap. 3)

Income statement. A statement that evaluates the operating performance of the corporation by matching its accomplishments (revenue from customers, which usually is called *sales*) and efforts (cost of goods sold and other expenses). (Chap. 17)

Incremental approach. A method of determining which of two alternative courses of action is preferable by calculating the present value of the difference in net cash inflow between one alternative and the other. (Chap. 12)

Incremental cost. The difference in total cost between two alternatives. Also called *differential cost.* (Chap. 5)

Indirect manufacturing costs. See *Factory overhead.* (Chap. 3)

Internal rate of return. The rate of interest at which the present value of expected cash inflows from a particular project equals the present value of expected cash outflow of the same project. Also called *Time-adjusted rate.* (Chap. 12)

Investment center. An area of responsibility for costs, revenues, and related investment. (Chap. 9)

Investment tax credit. Direct reductions of income taxes arising from the acquisition of depreciable assets. (Chap. 20)

Job order costing. The method of allocating costs to products that receive varying attention and effort. (Chap. 14)

Joint product costs. Costs of two or more manufactured goods, of significant sales values, that are produced by a single process and that are not identifiable as individual products up to a certain stage of production, known as the splitoff point. (Chap. 5)

Last in, first out. A cost-flow assumption that the stock acquired earliest is still on hand; the stock acquired latest is used first. (Chap. 20)

Lead time. The time interval between placing an order and receiving delivery. (Chap. 16)

Liability. The economic obligation of the entity to creditors. (Chap. 17)

Limiting factor. The item that restricts or constrains the production or sale of a product or service. (Chap. 4)

Linear programming. A mathematical approach to a group of business problems which contain many interacting variables and which basically involve combining limited resources to maximize profits or minimize costs. (Chap. 16)

Line authority. Authority which is exerted downward over subordinates. (Chap. 1)

Managed costs. See *Discretionary costs.* (Chap. 8)

Management by exception. The practice by the executive of focusing his attention mainly on significant deviations from expected results. It might also be called *management by variance.* (Chap. 1)

Management science. The formulation of mathematical and statistical models applied to decision making and the practical application of these models through the use of digital computers. (Chap. 16)

Manufacturing expenses. See *Factory overhead.* (Chap. 3)

Manufacturing overhead. See *Factory overhead.* (Chap. 3)

Marginal costing. See *Direct costing.* (Chap. 15)

Marginal income. See *Contribution margin.* (Chap. 2)

Marketing variance. The budgeted unit contribution margin multiplied by the difference between the master-budgeted sales in units and the actual sales in units. (Chap. 7)

Master budget. The budget which consolidates the organization's overall plans. (Chap. 6)

Master budgeted sales. The expected sales employed in formulating the master budget for the period. (Chap. 6)

Matching. Establishing a relationship between efforts (expenses) and accomplishments (revenues). (Chap. 17)

Minority interest. The total shareholder interest (other than the parent's) in a subsidiary corporation. (Chap. 19)

Mixed cost. A cost that has both fixed and variable elements. (Chap. 8)

Negotiated market price. A transfer price negotiated by the buying and selling segments when there is no market mechanism to fix a price clearly relevant to the situation. (Chap. 11)

Net book value. The asset amount (usually unexpired cost) carried on the financial records of the organization. (Chap. 17)

Net present value method. A method of calculating the expected utility of a given project by discounting all expected future cash flows to the present, using some predetermined minimum desired rate of return. (Chap. 12)

Net working capital. The excess of current assets over current liabilities. (Chap. 18)

Normal activity. The rate of activity needed to meet average sales demand over a period long enough to encompass seasonal and cyclical fluctuations. (Chap. 15)

Normal costing. The method of allocating costs to products using *actual* direct materials, *actual* direct labor, and *predetermined* overhead rates. (Chap. 14)

Object of costing. See *Cost objective.* (Chap. 3)

Objectivity. Accuracy supported by convincing evidence that can be verified by independent accountants. (Chap. 17)

Operations research. A diffused collection of mathematical and statistical models applied to decision making. (Chap. 16)

Opportunity cost. The maximum alternative earning that might have been obtained if the productive good, service, or capacity had been applied to some alternative use. (Chap. 5)

Order-filling cost. A marketing cost incurred in the storing, packing, shipping, billing, credit and collection, and in other similar aspects of selling merchandise. (Chap. 8)

Order-getting cost. A marketing cost incurred in the effort to attain a desired sales volume and mix. (Chap. 8)

Overabsorbed overhead. See *Overapplied overhead.* (Chap. 14)

Overapplied overhead. The excess of amount of overhead cost applied to product over the amount of overhead cost incurred. Also called *overabsorbed overhead.* (Chap. 14)

Overtime premium. A classification of *indirect labor costs,* consisting of the wages paid to *all* factory workers in excess of their straight-time wage rates. (Chap. 3)

Paid-in surplus. See *Capital surplus.* (Chap. 18)

Par value. The value printed on the face of the security certificate. (Chap. 18)

Parameter. A constant, such as *a,* or a coefficient, such as *b,* in a model or system of equations, such as $y = a + bx$. (Chap. 8)

Payback. The measure of the time needed to recoup, in the form of cash inflow from operations, the initial dollars invested. Also called *payout* and *payoff.* (Chap. 12)

Payoff. See *Payback.* (Chap. 12)

Payoff table. See *Decision table.* (Chap. 16)

Payout. See *Payback.* (Chap. 12)

Performance report. The comparison of actual results with the budget. (Chap. 1)

Period costs. Those costs being deducted as expenses during the current period without having been previously classified as product costs. (Chap. 3)

Planning. Selecting objectives and the means for their attainment. (Chap. 1)

Practical capacity. The maximum level at which the plant or department can realistically operate most efficiently, i.e., ideal capacity less allowances for unavoidable operating interruptions. Also called *practical attainable capacity.* (Chap. 15)

Preferred stock. Stock that has some priority over other shares regarding dividends or the distribution of assets upon liquidation. (Chap. 18)

Price variance. The difference between the actual price and the standard price, multiplied by the total number of items acquired. The term "price variance" is usually linked with direct material; the term "rate variance," which is conceptually similar to the price variance, is usually linked with direct labor. (Chap. 7)

Problem solving. That function of the accountant's information supplying task which expresses in concise, quantified terms the relative advantages and disadvantages to the firm of pursuing a possible future course of action, or the relative advantages of any one of several alternative methods of operation. (Chap. 1)

Process. A series of actions or operations leading to a definite end. (Chap. 1)

Process costing. The method of allocating costs to the products resulting from the mass production of like units. (Chap. 14)

Product costs. Costs that are identified with goods produced or purchased for resale. (Chap. 3)

Profitability accounting. See *Responsibility accounting.* (Chap. 9)

Profit center. A segment of a business that is responsible for both revenue and expense. (Chaps. 9, 11)

Pro-forma statements. Forecasted financial statements. (Chap. 6)

Programmed costs. See *Discretionary costs.* (Chap. 8)

P/V chart. A graph showing volume on the horizontal axis and net income on the vertical axis. (Chap. 2)

Qualitative factor. A factor which is of consequence but which cannot be measured precisely and easily in dollars. (Chap. 4)

Quantity variance. *Efficiency variance,* applied to materials. (Chap. 7)

Quote sheet. An analysis of costs used as a basis for determining selling prices. (Chap. 4)

Rate variance. The difference between actual wages paid and the standard wage rate, multiplied by the total actual hours of direct labor used. See *Price variance.* (Chap. 7)

Realization. The recognition of revenue. Generally, two tests must be met. First, the earning process must be virtually complete in that the goods or services must be fully rendered. Second, an exchange of resources evidenced by a market transaction must occur. (Chap. 17)

Reallocation. Allocation of the costs of operating the service departments to the various production departments in proportion to the relative benefits or services received by each production department. (Chap. 10)

Reapportionment. See *Reallocation.* (Chap. 10)

Relevant data for decision making. Expected future data which will differ among alternatives. (Chap. 4)

Relevant range. The band of activity in which budgeted sales and expense relationships will be valid. (Chap. 2)

Reserve. Should not be confused with *fund. Reserve* has one of three meanings: (1) A restriction of dividend-paying power denoted by a specific subdivision of retained income. (2) An offset to an asset. (3) An estimate of a definite liability of indefinite or uncertain amount. (Chap. 18)

Residual income. The net income of a profit center or investment center, less the "imputed" interest on the net assets used by the center. (Chap. 11)

Responsibility accounting. A system of accounting which recognizes various responsibility centers throughout the organization and which reflects the plans and actions of each of these centers by allocating particular revenues and costs to those having the pertinent responsibilities. Also called *profitability accounting* and *activity accounting.* (Chap. 9)

Retained earnings. See *Retained income.* (Chap. 17)

Retained income. The accumulated increase in stockholders' equity arising from profitable operations. (Chap. 17)

Safety stock. A minimum inventory that provides a cushion against reasonably expected maximum demand and against variations in lead time. (Chap. 16)

Sales mix. The relative combination of the quantities of a variety of company products that compose total sales. (Chap. 2)

Scorekeeping. That data accumulation function of the accountant's information supplying task which enables both internal and external parties to evaluate the financial performance of the firm. (Chap. 1)

Segment. Any line of activity or part of an organization for which separate determination of costs and/or sales is wanted. (Chaps. 9, 10)

Segment margin. The contribution margin for each segment less all separable fixed costs, both discretionary and committed. A measure of long-run profitability. (Chap. 10)

Sensitivity analysis. Measuring how the basic predicted results will be affected by variations in the critical data inputs that will influence those results. (Chap. 12)

Separable cost. A cost directly identifiable with a particular segment. (Chap. 5)

Service departments. Those departments that exist solely to aid the production departments by rendering specialized assistance with certain phases of the work. (Chap. 10)

Short-run performance margin. The contribution margin for each segment, less separable discretionary costs. (Chap. 10)

Source document. The original record of any transaction, internal or external, which occurs in the firm's operation. (Chaps. 1, 9)

Spending variance. Basically, a price variance applied to variable overhead. However, other factors besides price may influence the amount of the variance. (Chap. 7)

Staff authority. The authority to *advise* but not to command; it may be exerted laterally or upward. (Chap. 1)

Standard absorption costing. That type of product costing in which the cost of the finished unit is calculated as the sum of the costs of the standard allowances for

factors of production, *including* fixed factory overhead, without reference to the costs actually incurred. (Chap. 15)

Standard cost. A carefully predetermined cost that should be attained, usually expressed per unit. (Chap. 7)

Standard direct costing. That type of product costing in which the cost of the finished unit is calculated as the sum of the costs of the *standard allowances* for the factors of production, *excluding* fixed factory overhead, which is treated as a period cost, and without reference to the costs actually incurred. (Chap. 15)

Statement of sources and applications of funds. See *Funds statement.* (Chap. 18)

Static budget. A budget prepared for only one level of activity and, consequently, one which does not adjust automatically to changes in the level of volume. (Chap. 7)

Step-down method. Allocation of service department costs to other service departments as well as production departments. Once a department's costs are allocated to other departments, no subsequent service department costs are allocated back to it. (Chap. 10)

Step-variable costs. Those variable costs which change abruptly at intervals of activity because their acquisition comes in indivisible chunks. (Chap. 8)

Stockholders' equity. The excess of assets over liabilities. (Chap. 17)

Stock split. The issuance of additional shares for no consideration and under conditions indicating that the objective is to increase the number of outstanding shares for the purpose of reducing their unit market price. (Chap. 18)

Subordinated. A creditor claim that is junior to other creditor claims. (Chap. 18)

Subordinated debenture. See *Subordinated* and *Debenture.* (Chap. 18)

Sunk cost. A cost which has already been incurred and which, therefore, is irrelevant to the decision-making process. Also called *historical cost.* (Chap. 5)

System. A formal means of gathering data

to aid and coordinate the process of making decisions. (Chap. 1)

Tax shield. Noncash items (e.g., depreciation) charged against income, thus protecting that amount from tax. (Chap. 13)

Time-adjusted rate of return. See *Internal rate of return.* (Chap. 12)

Total project approach. A method of comparing two or more alternative courses of action by computing the total expected inflows and outflows of each alternative and then converting these flows to their present value by applying some predetermined minimum rate of return. (Chap. 12)

Trading on the equity. Using borrowed money at a fixed interest rate and/or using funds provided by preferred stockholders with the aim of enhancing the rate of return on common stockholders' equity. (Chap. 19)

Transaction. Any event that affects the financial position or results of the organization; it is the happening that requires recording. (Chap. 17)

Transfer price. The price charged by one segment of an organization for a product or service which it supplies to another segment of the same organization. (Chap. 11)

Treasury stock. Outstanding stock that has subsequently been repurchased and not cancelled by the company. (Chap. 18)

Unadjusted rate of return. See *Accounting rate of return.* (Chap. 12)

Usage variance. Efficiency variance applied to materials. (Chap. 7)

Variable budget. See *Flexible budget.* (Chap. 7)

Variable cost. A cost which is uniform *per unit,* but which fluctuates in total in direct proportion to changes in the related total activity or volume. (Chap. 2)

Variable costing. See *Direct costing.* (Chap. 15)

Variance. The deviation of actual results from the expected or budgeted result. (Chaps. 1 and 7)

Volume variance. See *Denominator variance.* (Chap. 15)

Zero-based budgeting. Budgeting from the ground up as though the budget were being initiated for the first time. (Chap. 9)

Index

Note: Also see the glossary, pages 695-703.

Absorption costing, 64-65
  compared to direct costing,
    455-59
Account Analysis, 218
Accountant's role:
  role in an organization, 3, 4,
    12
  role in special decisions, 82
Accounting:
  external, 16
  for deferred revenue, 539-40
  for wages, 535
  internal, 16
  manufacturing compared to
    merchandising, 61
  rate of return model, 369-70
  readings on, 685-86
  types of information supplied
    by, 9, 10
  weakness, 370-71

Accounting method, income tax
    effect of cash vs. accrual,
    408
Accounting principles, 543
  effect on determination of net
    income, 640
  uniformity vs. flexibility, 646-
    47
Accounting Principles Board,
    544, 685
  require statement of changes
    in financial position, 584
Accounting process, 524
Accounting system, 8
  purposes, 4
Accounts payable, example, 526
Accounts receivable, 526, 570
  average collection period, 625
Accrual basis accounting:
  distinguished from cash basis,
    530

Accrual basis accounting (*cont.*)
  formal adjustments, 531
  three measurement principles,
    544
Accrued expenses payable, 575
Accrued income taxes payable,
    575
Accumulated depreciation, 573
Accuracy, compared to rele-
    vancy, 82
Acid-test ratio, 625
Acquisitions, of subsidiary
    companies, accounting
    for, 608-10, 614-15
Activity:
  accounting, 240
  level, 462
  variance, 458n
Actual costing system, com-
    pared to normal, 433-34
Advances from customer, 539

Allocation of costs (see also Cost allocation)
Alternatives, examining long run alternatives, 123
Amortization:
    of intangible assets, 575
    of leasehold improvements, 574
Annuity, ordinary:
    present value of, examination of formula for, 689-91
    table, 693
APB, 544
    Opinion No. 11, 654-55
Approximate rate-of-return model, 369-70
Asset turnover, total, 620
Asset valuation:
    as a measurement alternative, 327-28
    income tax effect, 408
Assets:
    current, 570-72
    intangible, 574-75
    plant, 570-72
Attention directing, 9, 10
Auditor's opinion, 543
Autonomy, decentralization, 317
Average collection period, 625
Avoidability criteria, divisional allocation of invested capital, 327

Balance sheet:
    alternate forms of, 581
    budgeted, 157-58
    classified, 570-81
    equation, 529-30
    illustration, 525
    manufacturing:
        compared to retailer, 59
        inventory accounts, 57
        relationship to income statement, 528-29
Bonds:
    long-term, 623-24
    mortgage, 575
Book value:
    DCF analysis, 365
    defined, 121
    definition of, 623
    relevant costs, 121
    sunk value, 121
Book Value Model, 369-70
Break-even analysis (see Cost-volume-profit analysis), 28

Break-even point, 28
    computational techniques,
        contribution margin, 30
        equation, 29
        graphical, 31
Budget:
    advantages, 148
    and the cost-benefit approach, 324-25
    balance sheet, 157-58
    cash budget explanation, 156
    classifications, 151
    definition, 148
    flexible, 315
    formalized planning, 148-49
    framework for judging performance, 149
    illustration of master budget preparation, 151-55
    importance of human relations, 150
    long range capital, 150
    master, 147-60
    middle management's attitude, 150
    preparation of master budget, basic steps, 155
    purchases budget, 155
    role in coordination and communication, 149
    role in operations and finance, 147
    role of expected future data, 147
    sales forecast, 155
    short range:
        continuous, 150-51
        static, 315
        time span, 150-51
        types, 150-51
Budget period, fixed costs, 26
Budgeted:
    allocation bases, 292-93
    balance sheet, role in master budget, 157-58
    cost, 179
    performance, 179
    statement of cash receipts and disbursements, 625
Budgeting:
    mixed costs, 220
    program, 262
    responsibility in nonprofit organizations, 259-63
    zero-based, 260
Budgets:
    capital, 207
    departmental overhead, 179
    flexible, 171-78
    problem of padding, 257

Budgets (cont.)
    static, 315
    limitations of, 171-75
    variable, 173
Buffer inventory, 504
Business plan (see Master budget)

Capacity variance, 458n
Capital (see also Stockholders' equity), 576
Capital budgeting, 350-73
    and inflation, 366-67
    discounted-cash-flow (see Discounted-cash-flow)
    effect of income taxes, 393-99
    focus on programs or projects, 351-52
    internal rate of return, 352-57
    net present value, 352-54
    nonprofit organizations, 360
    uncertainty and sensitivity analysis, 361-62
    use of present value tables, 688-91
Capital budgets, 207, 150
Capital gains, income tax effect, 407-8
Capital outlays, 352
Capital structure, tax effect of debt, 408
Capital surplus, 577
Carrying amount, 573
Cash, 570, 591
Cash basis accounting, example, 530-31
Cash budget, explanation, 156-57
Cash disbursements, role in cash budget, 156
Cash flows, 591-92
    annual inflation adjustment in DCF, 367
    effects of depreciation, 589
    focus of DCF, 352
    impact of income taxes, 392, 393-99
    per-share, 591
Cash forecasting, role of accounts receivable, 156
Cash receipts and disbursements, budgeted statement of, 625
Central costs, allocation of, 292
Certainty:
    decisions under, 489-90
    definition of term, 489-90

Certified Management Accountant, 17
Choice criterion, 488
Classified balance sheet, 570-81
Coefficient of dispersion, as measure of uncertainty, 493
Collection period, average, 625
Committed costs, 206-7
Common cost, 119
Common measuring unit, 643
Common stock, 577-80
    statistics and ratios, 622-23
Communication, role of budget, 149
Compound interest, fundamentals of, 687-91
Consistency, 547
Conservatism, 548
Consolidated financial statements, 608-15
    acquisitions, accounting for, 608-10
    minority interests, accounting for, 610-13
    unconsolidated subsidiaries, 614-15
Constant dollars, defined, 641
Constant-order-cycle system, 505
Constant-order-quantity system, 504-5
Continuous budgets
Contribution approach:
    income statement, 65-66
    limited capacity decisions, 96
    relevant costing, 81-97
    to cost allocation, 283-87
    to segment performance, 286
    vs. full-costing, 455-59
Contribution margin:
    and linear programming, 500
    compared to gross margin, 36
    use in cost allocation, 283-85
Contribution margin technique, break-even analysis, 30
Contributions, income tax effect, 405
Control process, overhead application, 429
Control systems, 213-14
    behavioral problems, 256-58
    development of, 178
    in nonprofit organizations, 259-63
Control-factor units, 210
Controllability, 324
Controllable contribution, 285-86

Controllable costs, 251
    versus uncontrollable, 254-56
Controller:
    distinctions between controller and treasurer, 15
    functions, 15
    role analyzed, 12-15
Conversion cost, 56
Coordination, role of budget, 149
Corporate joint ventures, accounting for, 615
Cost: (see also Costs)
    accumulation, 55
    full, 88
    objective, 55
    absorption, 424
    allocation to, 55
    of capital, 359
    of control, 421
    of goods sold, 37
    opportunity, 687
Cost accounting:
    bookkeeping system, 437-43
    purpose, 421
Cost allocation (see also Allocation of costs), 424
    and management incentive, 291
    and responsibility accounting, 280-98
    bases, 282, 288
    budgeted, 292-93
    compared to transfer pricing, 318
    contribution approach, 283-87
    cost of inefficiency, 291
    cost pools, 289-91
    direct method, 296
    dual method of, 288
    for planning and control, 288-93
    of central costs, 292
    of intangible assets, 575
    of plant assets, 572-74
    of service department costs, 294-96
    purposes of, 281, 296
    step-down method, 296
    to outputs, 293-96
    trouble with using lump sums, 291-92
Cost application, 424, 420-34
Cost behavior patterns, 214-19
Cost-benefit, 549
    of accounting systems tests, 315
Cost centers, 247
Cost comparison, equipment replacement, 123, 124

Cost estimation, 214
Cost functions:
    criteria for choosing, 215-16
    definition, 214
    determination of, 214-19
    methods of approximation, 218-19
    examples, 219-25
Cost method of accounting, for intercorporate investments, 606
Cost of goods sold, as product costs, 57
Cost-profit-volume:
    analysis, P/V chart or profit-volume graph, 39-40
    break-even analysis:
        effects of sales mix, 40-41
        impact of income taxes, 41-42
Costing:
    absorption, 90
    absorption (see also Absorption costing), 455
    absorption and variable, 87-88
    comparison of job-order to process, 67
    contribution approach, advantages over absorption costing, 91, 94
    direct (see also Direct costing), 455
    job and process, 66-68
    marginal, 455
    product (see Product costing)
    variable, 455
    variable and absorption, 87-88
Costs: (see also Cost)
    accuracy and relevancy, 82
    activity base, 28
    behavior patterns, determination of, 214-19
    budgeted, 179
    capacity, 206
    causes of, 288
    classification of, 205, 255
    control of, comparison of systems, 213-14
    controllable, 251
        versus uncontrollable, 254-56
    direct labor graphical analysis, 184
    discretionary fixed, 207-8, 212
    discretionary variable, 208-9
    engineered:
        and work measurement, 210-11
        definition of, 208-9

Costs (*cont.*)
  engineered (*cont.*)
    versus discretionary, 208-14
  fixed, 25
    assumptions:
      budget period of time, 26
      relevant range of activity, 26
      relevant range, graphic illustration, 27
    budgeted, 26
    committed, 206-7
    comparison to variable, 26
    discretionary and work measurement, 212
    effect of changes on break-even point, 32
    fixed unit, 459-61
    relation to capacity, 206
    relation to total volume, 26
    spreading, 89
  irrelevance of past costs, 120-23
  managed, 207
  manufacturing:
    absorption costing, 64-65
    balance sheet, compared to retailer, 59
    classification of, 54-56
    cost of goods sold, 57
    difference between costs and expenses, 60
    direct costing, 66
    direct and indirect, 63
    direct labor, 56
    direct materials, 56
    elements of, 56
      conversion cost, 56
      prime cost, 56
    factory overhead, 56
      fixed, 56
      variable, 56
    fixed indirect, 88
    full costing, 64-65
    income statements, 59-60
      compared to retailer, 60
      primary classification of costs, 65
      two types, 63-66
    income statement and balance sheet, relationships, 57-63
    inventory:
      direct material, 57-58
      finished goods, 59
      work in process, 57-59
    job-order-costing, 66-68
    joint product (see also Joint product costs)

Costs (*cont.*)
  manufacturing (*cont.*)
    labor costs, 69-71
      indirect and direct, 70
      indirect idle time, 70-71
      indirect overtime premium, 70
      payroll fringe costs, 71
    marginal costing, 66
    period costs, 57
    process costing, 66-68
    product costing, relation to balance sheet equation, 61, 62
    use of unit costs, 59
    product costs, 57
    product costs and period costs, distinction between, 57
    traditional costing, 64-65
    variable costing, 66
  mixed, 217, 219-25
  nonlinear, 27
  opportunity (see also Opportunity costs), 116-17
  outlay, 116
  pooled, 282
  pricing role, 90-94
  programmed, 207
  relevant, 81-97
    relevant definition, 83
    relevant examples, 83-84
    relevant pricing role (see also Pricing)
    relevant qualitative and quantitative factors, 82
    relevant range, 214, 222
    relevant role of predictions, 84
    relevant special sales order (see also Sales order, special)
  semivariable (see also Costs, mixed), 217
  standard, 178-79
  step-function, 217
  unit-total distinction, 88-89
  variable, 25
    comparison to fixed, 26
    cost ratio, 36, 37
    discretionary, 208-9
    proportionately, 216
    relation to total volume, 25
    unit, 459-61
Costs and expenses, difference between, 60
Cost-volume-profit:
  analysis, 24
    break-even point, 28-34
    illustration, 28

Cost-volume-profit (*cont.*)
  analysis (*cont.*)
    limiting assumptions, 35-36
    optimum combination of factory
    relevant range, 35
    summary, 37-38
    uses and limitations, 35-37
  break-even analysis:
    changes in contribution margin per unit, 32
    changes in fixed expenses, 32
    multiple changes in the key factors, 34
    target net profit and an incremental approach, 33-34
Credit, short term, analysis of, 625-26
Credits and debits, defined, 555
Critical success factors, 244
Critical variables, 244
Cumulative preferred stock, 577
Current assets, 570-72
Current liabilities, 575
Current ratio, 625
Current value:
  compared to historical cost approach, 641-43
  effects, 660-66
  income tax effects, 663
  replacement cost or net realizable value, 643
  restated, 645
Current value accounting, misinterpretations, 645-46
Current value reporting, use in asset valuation, 328
Currently attainable standards, 180
Cutoff rate, 359

DCF (see also Discounted-cash-flow)
Debentures, subordinated vs. unsubordinated, 576
Debits and credits, defined, 555
Debt capital, income tax effect, 408
Decentralization, 315-17
  autonomy problem, 317
  costs and benefits, 315-16
  middle ground, 316-17
Decision:
  make or buy, 113-15
  model, 84
  utilization of facilities, 115

Decision making (see also Decision theory), use of quantitative models, 486-506
Decision models:
and uncertainty, 127-28
definition of term, 487 (see also Decision theory)
mathematical evaluation of usefulness, 487
role in financial planning, 160
Decision process, and role of information, 85
Decision relevance:
past decision performance, 124-25
to book value of old equipment, 122
to cost of new equipment, 122
to disposal value of old equipment, 122
to gain or loss on disposal, 122
Decision table:
compared to payoff table, 489
example of, 489
Decision theory:
description of basic approach, 488
under certainty, 489-90
use of linear programming, 496-500
under risk, 491-96
under uncertainty, 491-96
value of perfect information, 496
Decisions:
capital budgeting (see also Capital budgeting)
special, 81-97
accountant's role, 82
and opportunity costs, 116
Deferral method, of investment tax credit, 650, 652
Deferral of income, tax effect, 408
Deferred charges (see also Prepaid expenses), 572n
Deferred federal income taxes, 652-55
Deferred income taxes, 576
Deferred revenue accounting, 539-40
Denominator level, 462
Denominator variance, 458, 462-64
Departmental overhead budgets, 179
Depletion, of natural resources, 574

Depreciation:
accounting for, 573-74
and discounted cash flow, 358
DCF analysis, 365
effects of different patterns of depreciation, 589
effects on income taxes and cash flow, 589
role of, in statement of changes in financial position, 586-89
Depreciation methods:
financial reporting purposes, 652-53
income tax effect, 392-99
tax purposes, 652-53
Direct costing, 66
and inventory valuation, 455, 464-65
compared to absorption costing, 455-59
Direct material inventory, 57-58
Disclosure, 548
Discount rate, 359
Discounted-cash-flows, 352-60
analysis of typical items, 365-66
and depreciation, 358
assumptions, 359
decision rules, 358-59
disposal values, 365
investing vs. financing decision, 360
minimum desired rate of return, 359-60
model assumptions, 354
unequal lives, 366
Discretionary fixed costs, 207-8, 212
Discretionary variable costs, 208-9
Disposal gain or loss, 122
Disposal of equipment, tax analysis, 395-98
Disposal value of old equipment, 122
Disposal values, DCF analysis, 365
Dividend-payout ratio, 622
Dividend-yield ratio, 622
Dividends:
and retained income, 540-41
common stock tax effect, 409
defined, 541
not an expense, 584
Double-entry bookkeeping, in cost accounting system, 437

Earned surplus, 541

Earnings (see also Income), 583
Earnings coverage, 623
multiple, 622
per share ratio, 622
Economic activity cycle, 524-25
Economic lot size, 501-4
Economic order quantity, 501-4
Effectiveness variance, 175n
Efficiency defined, 181-82
Efficiency variances, 175
Engineered costs (see also Costs engineered), 208-9
Entity, defined, 546
Equation technique, break-even analysis, 29
Equipment replacement, tax analysis, 395-98
Equity capital, 542
Equity method of accounting for intercorporate investments, 606-7
unconsolidated subsidiaries, 614-15
Equity, stockholders', 576-80
Equity, trading on the, 620-22
Equivalent units, 444-45
Expected value, definition of, 489n
Expected value, use of in decision theory, 489, 492-93
Expenses:
considered as assets acquired, 533
measurement, 532
prepaid, 570

Factory burden (see also Costs; Manufacturing; Factory overhead)
Factory overhead:
bookkeeping for disposition, 443
disposition methods, 430-31
Federal income taxes, deferred, 652-55
Feedback reports, format of, 248
FIFO:
defined, 647
income tax effects, 403
Financial accounting:
basic concepts, techniques, and conventions, 522-55
compared to management accounting, 16
emphasis of, 4
Financial Accounting Standards Board (FASB), 544, 685

Financial Accounting Standards (*cont.*)
    opinion regarding Research and Development costs, 575
Financial analysis (see also Financial statements, analysis of), 618-26
Financial leverage, 621
Financial management, 583
Financial planning, role of decision models, 159-60
Financial statement model, 369-70
Financial statements, 525-28
    analysis of, 618-26
        common stock statistics, 622-23
        operating performance, 619-20
        ratios, use of, 618-19
        short-term credit analysis, 625-26
        trading on the equity, 620-22
    distinctions between balance sheets and funds statements, income statements and retained earnings statements, 584-85
Financing, role of short-term, self-liquidating in cash budgets, 156-57
Financing requirements, and cash budgeting, 156
Finished goods inventory, 59
Fixed assets (see also Plant Assets), 572-74
Fixed budget variance defined, 184
Fixed cost pool, 289-90
Fixed costs (see also Costs, fixed)
    allocation of, 289-90
Fixed factory overhead, 56
Fixed manufacturing overhead, accounting for (see also Overhead), 455-56
Fixed overhead application rate, 432-33
Fixed unit costs, 459-61
Flexible budgets, 171-78, 315
Flow of direct materials, 423
Flow-through method, of investment tax credit, 650-52
Full costing, 64-65
Functional approach, income statement, 64-65
Funds, 580-81

Funds statement (see also Statement of changes in financial position), 584
Future expected data, role in budgets, 147

General ledgers, 441-43
    defined, 553-55
General purchasing-power gains and losses, 664-66
Generally Accepted Accounting Principles (G.A.A.P.), 543-44
Goal congruence, 242
Goals:
    multiple use of, 245
    obtaining acceptance, 256
    specification of, 244
Going concern, 546
Goodwill:
    accounting for, 616-18
    amortization of, 617
    nature of, 617-18
    purchased, 616-17
Graphic technique, break-even analysis, 31
Graphs, analysis of, 221
Gross book value method, instead of net, 328-29
Gross margin, compared to contribution margin, 36-37

High-low method, 218, 223-24
Historical cost:
    compared to current value approach, 641-43
    restated, 643-44
    use in asset valuation, 327-28
Holding gains and losses; separated from operating income, 661-62
Human relations, aspect of budgeting, 150
Hurdle rate, 359
    DCF inflation adjustment, 367

Ideal standards, 180
Idle time, 70-71
Incentive, 243
    and cost allocation systems, 291
    use in transfer pricing, 320-21
Income:
    and invested capital defined, 325-27

Income (*cont.*)
    definitions compared, 661
    effect of inflation on measurement, 640-46
    net, 583
    operating, 582
    theoretical concepts, 640-46
Income deferral, tax effect, 408
Income statement, 581-83
    contribution and functional form, 86
    contribution approach, 65-66, 87
    functional and contribution form, 86
    functional approach, 64-65
    manufacturing, two types, contribution approach, 65-66, 87
    functional approach, 64-65
Income statement, relationship to balance sheet, 528-29
Income taxes:
    accrued, 575
    allocation, 652-55
    complications, 399
    DCF analysis, 366
    deferred, 576
    depreciation effect, 392-93
    effect on form of business organization, 401-2
    effect on inventory method, 403
    effect of depreciation on, 589
    effects of current value, 664
    federal rates, 392
    impact on cost-volume-profit analysis, 41, 42
    impact on planning, 391-409
    total project vs. incremental approach, 395-99
Incremental approach, income tax analysis, 395-99
Incremental costs; and joint product costs, 118-20
Indirect manufacturing costs (see also Costs; Manufacturing; Factory overhead)
Inefficiency, costs of, 291
Inflation, and capital budgeting, 366-67
Information (see also Perfect information), 495
    value of in decision-making, 496
Institute of Management Accounting, 17
Intangible assets, 574-75
Intercompany eliminations, 608

Intercorporate investments, ac- counting for (see also Investments, intercorporate), 606-7, 615
Interest:
 coverage, 624
 nature of, 687-88
 tax-free, 407
Internal rate of return:
 calculations, 375-77
 meaning, 357-58
Interperiod allocation of income taxes, 652-55
Inventories, accounting for, 570-72
 turnover ratio, 625
 valuation of direct vs. absorption costing, 464-65
Inventory:
 constant-order-cycle system, 505
 constant-order-quantity system, 504-5
 cost of, 570
 direct-materials, 421-23
 economic order quantity, 501-4
 finished goods, 421-23
 lead time, 504
 manufacturing classes:
  direct material, 57-58
  finished goods, 59
  work-in-process, 57-59
 methods, 647-50
  income tax effects, 403
 obsolete, 121
 planning and control models, 500-5
 relevant costs, 501
 reorder point, 504
 safety, or buffer, stock, 504
 two-bin system, 504-5
 work-in-process, 421, 423
Invested capital:
 allocated to divisions, 326-27
 as performance measure of division managery, 325-26
 definitions, 325-27
 maintenance of, 644-45
Investment centers, 247
Investment tax credit, 650-52
Investments:
 in receivables and inventories, 365
 intercorporate:
  accounting for consolidated statements, 608-15
  accounting for cost vs. equity method, 606-7

Investments (cont.)
 intercorporate (cont.)
  accounting for summary of methods, 615
  marketable securities, 615, 615n
  short vs. long-term, 570

Japan, consolidated statements required, 608n
Job and process systems, 420-34
Job-costing, 423
 compared with process costing, 421-24
 sheets, 427, 438-40
Job-order costing, 424-27
 actual compared to normal, 433-34
 cost application, 424
 over-head application, 424-26
Job-order sheet, as a basic record, 438-40
Joint product costs:
 and incremental costs, 118-20
 common cost
 defined, 118
 incremental and total analysis, 120
 incremental or differential costs, 120
 separable costs, 119
 split-off point, 118
Joint ventures, corporate, accounting for, 615
Journal entries and ledgers, job-costing accounting system, 437-43

Key-result areas, 244
Key variables, 244

Labor costs:
 classification of, 69-71
 indirect, 70
  idle time, 70-71
  overtime premium, 70
  payroll fringe costs, 71
Lead time, inventory, 504
Leasehold improvements, 574
Least squares method, 228
Ledger accounts, use of, 552
Legal value, of common stock, 577
Leverage, financial, 621
Liabilities, 575-76
 defined, 525

LIFO:
 defined, 647
 income tax effect, 403
Limited liability, 577
Limiting factors, 96-97
Line and staff authority, 12-14
Line departments, 12
Linear programming, 496-500
Liquidation, 576
Long-range decisions, other models, 367
Long-term investments, 570
Long-term liabilities, 575
Long-term planning, to describe capital budgeting, 352
Loss, motivational influence, 124
Loss carryforward, income tax effect, 405-7
Lower-of-cost-or-market, 548, 649-50

McNamara, Robert, 89
Managed costs, 207
Management:
 by exception, 248
 operating versus financial, 583
 process, 4, 8
Management accounting, 4
 behavioral impact, 17
 compared to financial accounting, 16
 recommended readings on, 686
Management objectives and accounting systems, 242
Managers, distinction between managers and investments, 324
Manufacturing accounting, compared to merchandise accounting, 61
Manufacturing costs, 54-68
Manufacturing expenses (see also Costs; Manufacturing; Factory overhead)
Manufacturing overhead (see also Costs; Manufacturing; Factory overhead)
Margin percentage on sales, 620
Marginal costing, 66, 455
Market pricing, application to transfer pricing, 318
Marketable securities, 570
 accounting for, 615, 615n
Marketing variance, 175-76
Master budget, 147-60, 150
 basic preparation steps, 155

Master budget (*cont.*)
 budgeted balance sheet, 157-58
 preparation illustrated, 151-55
Master budgets, 150
Matching principle, 545
Materiality, 549
Measures of profitability (see also Profitability measures)
Minimum rate, 359
Minority interests, accounting for, 610-13
Mixed costs, 217, 219-25
Models:
 conflict and motivation, 124-25
 conflict between DCF and accrual accounting, 371-72
 conflict reconciliation, 125-26
 decision, 84
 definition of term, 487
 discounted-cash-flow (see also Discounted-cash-flow)
 financial planning, 159-60
 long-range decision, 367-73
 quantitative, use of in decision-making, 486-506
Monetary items, 664-65
Mortgage bonds, 575
Motivation, 244
 and conflict of models, 124-25
Multiple goals, use of, 245
Mutual price and efficiency effects, 191-92
Mutually exclusive projects, DCF analysis, 366

National Association of Accountants, 17
Natural resources, 574
Net book value, 573
Net funds provided by operations, 588
Net income, 583
Net marketing variance, 176
Net-present-value, comparison of two projects, 363-66
Net working capital, 581
Net worth (see also Stockholders' equity), 542, 576
Nominal dollars, defined, 641
Nonmonetary items, 664-66
Nonprofit organization, 11
 capital budgeting, 360
 financial statements, 543
 profit costing, 434

Nonprofit organization (*cont.*)
 responsibility budgeting in, 259-63
Normal costing, overhead application, 427-31
Normal costing system, compared to actual, 433-34
Normal product cost, purpose, 429
Notes payable, 575
Not-for-profit organization, 11
 management accounting in, 11
 recommended readings, 686

Objective function, 488
Objectivity or verifiability, 547-48
Operating cycle, 524
Operating expense budget, role in master budget, 156
Operating income, 582
 separated from holding gains or losses, 661-62
Operating losses, income tax effect, 405
Operating management, 583
Operating profit, 582
Opportunity costs, 116-17, 687
 accounting treatment, 117
 outlay costs compared to, 116
Ordinary annuity, present value of, formula for, 689-91
Organization chart of controllers department, 13, 14
Organization form, income tax effect, 400
Outlay cost, 116
Outputs, costing of, 293-96
Outside stockholders' interest in subsidiaries, accounting for, 610-13
Overhead (see also Budgets):
 accounting for, budgeting and control vs. product costing, 459-64
 application problems, 427-34
 application rates, 424-26
 control process application, 429
 fixed and absorption costs of product, 459-63
 fixed manufacturing, 455-56
 fixed selection of denominator level, 462
 immediate write-off of overapplied overhead, 432
 normal costing approach, 427-31

Overhead (*cont.*)
 underapplied or overapplied, 431
 underapplied proration, 431
 use of variable and fixed application rates, 432-33
 variable, 459
Overhead analysis, DCF analysis, 366
Overhead application, 420-34
Overhead costs, application of, 454-68
 direct and absorption costing compared, 469
Overtime premium, 70
Owners' equity (see also Stockholders' equity), 576-80
 defined, 525

Paid-in capital in excess of par, 577
Paid-in surplus, 577
Par value, of common stock, 577
Partnerships and proprietorships, 541-42
 accounting distinction, 542
Past costs, irrelevance of, 120-23
Payback model, 368-69
Payoff model, 368-69
Payoff table:
 compared to decision table, 489
 example of, 488
Payroll fringe costs, 71
Pension fund, 580
Percentage-of-completion method, 545
Perfect information:
 definition of term, 495
 determining value of, 496
Perfection standards, 180
Performance:
 budgeted, 179
 evaluation, 243
  and controllable contribution concept, 285-87
  feedback reports, 248-50
  measures of (see also Financial statements, analysis of), 606-26
 report, 173
 role of budgets in evaluation of, 149
 standard, 179
Period costs, 57
Planning, impact of income taxes, 391-409

Planning and controlling, 4
  accounting framework, 5
  and cost allocation, 288-93
  budgets, 5, 6
  inventory models, 500-5
  management by exception, 5
  performance reports, 5, 6
  recommended readings on, 686
  time-period vs. program or project focus, 351
  use of quantitative techniques in, 486-506
  variances, 5, 7
Plant assets, 572-74
  allocation of cost of, 572-74
  depreciation of, 573
Pooled costs, 282
Portfolio theory, operating management viewpoint, 351
Predictions, role in relevant costs, 84
Preferred stock, 577
Prepaid expenses, 572, 623-24
Present value tables, 692-93
  use of, 687-89
Price/earnings ratio, 622
Price index, 644
Price variances, 175
Pricing:
  effect on sales forecasts, 159
  role in costs, 90-94
  target, 91
  transfer (see also Transfer pricing)
Prime Cost, 56
Probabilities (see also Subjective Probability) use of in decision theory, 491, 493-94
Problem solving, 9, 10
Process costing, illustrated, 444-45
Process systems, 420-34
Product costing, 57, 87, 293-96, 420, 423-24
  absorption costing method, 458-64
  direct costing method, 457
  distinction between job costing and process costing, 421-24
  in nonprofit organizations, 434
  job-cost method, 423
  job-order costing, 66-68, 424-27
  pricing, 87-90
  process-cost method, 423-24
  process costing, 66-68

Product costing (cont.)
  reconciliation of absorption and direct costing, 87-90, 464-65
  use of unit costs, 59
Products, allocation of costs to, 293-96
Professional journals in accounting field, 685
Profit, operating, 582
Profit, when realized, 526
Profit and loss statement (see also Income statement), 583
Profit centers, 247, 314-31
  compared to cost center, 317
  meaning, 317
  reason for, 330-31
  timing alternatives, 330
Profit-volume graph, 39-40
Profitability accounting, 246
Profitability evaluation, 618
Profitability measures, 322
Profits (see also Income), 583
Pro-forma statements, budgets, 151
Program budgeting, 262
Programmed costs, 207
Property contributions, income tax effect, 404
Property, plant, and equipment (see also Plant Assets), 572-74
Proportionately variable costs, 216
Proprietorships and partnerships, 541-42
Purchase decisions, inventory method tax effect, 403
Purchased goodwill (see also Goodwill)
Purchases budget, role in master budget, 155
P/V chart, 39-40

Qualitative and quantitative factors, 82
Quantitative techniques, use of in decision-making, 486-506
Quantity variance, 181 (notes)
Quick ratio, 625

Rate-of-return on assets, model, 369-70
Rate-of-return on investment, 314
Rate variance, 181 (notes)

Ratios:
  common stock statistics, 622-23
  operating performances, measures of, 619-20
  short-term credit analysis, 625-26
  trading on the equity, 620-22
  use of in financial analysis, 618-19
  variable expense ratio, 36-37
Realization, concept, 544-45
Record-keeping, importance of accuracy of, 258
Regression methods, use of, 218-19, 221
Reinvested earnings (see also Retained income), 577
Relevance:
  definition, 83
  examples, 83-84
Relevant costs, 81-97
  fixed vs. variable, 126
  future costs, 126
  long-run alternatives examined, 123
  make or buy decision, 113-15
  obsolete inventory, 121
Relevant range, 214, 222
  cost-volume-profit analysis, 35
  fixed costs, 26
  graphic illustration, 27
Relevancy, compared to accuracy, 82
Reorder point, 504
Replacement cost, use in asset valuation, 320-27
Replacement-cost basis, 661-63
Research and development:
  accounting for costs of, 575
  income tax treatment, 408
Reserves, meanings of term in accounting, 580-81
Residual income, 323-24
Responsibility accounting, 314
  and cost allocation, 280-98
  definition of, 246
  feedback reports, 248-50
Responsibility budgeting in non-profit organizations, 259-63
Retained earnings (see also Retained income), 577
  statement of reconciliation of, 583-84
Retained income, 577
  in consolidated statements, 609
  or earnings, defined, 540-41

Retained income (*cont.*)
reserve, 581
Return on investment (see also
ROI), 314, 322-23 ·
choice of rate of return, 329
compared to RI, 323-24
ratio, 619
Return on total assets ratio, 619
Revenue center, 247n
Revenue, zero-based, 261
Risk (see also Uncertainty)
Role, accountant's organization,
12

Safety stock, 504
Sales forecast:
difficulties, 158-59
factors, 159
quantitative techniques, 159
role in master budget, 155
Sales-mix analysis, 40
Sales order:
special, 86-90
correct analysis, 87
example, 86
fixed cost analysis
incorrect analysis, 88
total costs and unit costs,
90
variable and absorption
costing, 87-88
Sampling, value of in decision
theory, 496
Scorekeeping, 9, 10
Securities and Exchange Commission (SEC), 544
Securities, marketable, accounting for, 615, 615n
Semivariable costs (see also
Costs, mixed), 217
Senior securities (see also
Bonds, long-term; pre-
ferred stock), 623-24
Sensitivity analysis, and uncertainty in capital budget-
ing, 361-62
Separate costs, 119
Service departments, allocation
of costs of, 294-96
Service organizations:
characteristics, 11
management accounting and.
10, 11
Short-term credit, analysis of,
625-26
Short-term investments, 570
Simplex method, 497-98
Sinking fund, 580

Solvency determination, 618
Source documents, 441-43
Sources and applications of
funds, 585
Special decisions:
costs avoidable and unavoidable, 94
deletion or addition of product lines or departments,
94-96
limited capacity, 96-97
Specification analysis, 215n
Split-off point, 118
Stable dollar principle, 545-46
Staff departments, 12
Standard bill of materials, 187
Standard cost, 178-79
variances, disposition of, 467-
68
Standard deviation:
as measure of uncertainty,
492
formula for, 492
Standard formula, 187
Standard performance, 179
Standards:
compared to budgets, 178-79
currently attainable, 180
ideal, 180
nature of, 178
perfection, 180
role of past experience, 179
Stated value, of common stock,
577
Statement of changes in finan-
cial position, 584-92
alternative concepts and
formats, 590
example, 585-86
role of depreciation, 586-89
Statement of earnings (see also
Income statement), 583
Statement of profit and loss (see
also Income Statement),
583
Statement of reconciliation of
retained earnings, 583-84
Statement of reconciliation of
retained income, 583-84
Static budget, 315
Step-function costs, 217
Stock dividends, 578-80
Stockholders' equity (see also
Capital), 576-80
Stock splits, 578-80
Subjective probabilities:
definition of term, 491
reasons for using, 491, 493-94
Subordinated debentures, 576

Subsidiaries:
accounting for:
consolidated basis, 608-13
foreign, 615
unconsolidated basis, 614-
15
reasons for having, 608
Subsidiary ledgers, 441-43

T-accounts, 552
Target net profit, incremental
approach to break-even
analysis, 33-34
Target pricing, 91
Target rate, 359
Tax-free interest, 407
Tax planning, 399-409
Tax shields, 392
Temporary investments, 570
Time analysis, 210
Time value of money, weighed
by DCF, 352
Top-management objectives,
242
Total asset turnover, 620
Total project, income tax analysis, 395-99
Trading on the equity, 620-22
Traditional costing, 64-65
Transactions:
analysis, 527-28
defined, 526
effect on stockholder's equity,
528
Transfer pricing, 314-31, 317-
21
based on variable costs, 319
causing dysfunctional be-
havior, 320
compared to cost allocation,
318
nature of, 317-18
need for many transfer prices,
321
use of budgeted or standard
costs, 318
use of incentives, 320-21
use of market pricing, 318
Treasurer:
distinctions between con-
troller and treasurer, 15
functions, 15
Treasury stock, 577
Turnover, 524-25
Turnover ratio, 625
Two-bin system, 504-5

Unadjusted rate-of-return,
model, 369-70

713

Uncertainty:
  and sensitivity analysis in
      capital budgeting, 361-62
  decision models, 127-28
  decisions under, 491-96
  description of term, 491
  distinction between risk and
      uncertainty, 491n
  measures of, 491-93
  value of perfect information,
      496
Unconsolidated subsidiaries, ac-
    counting for, 614-15
Unearned revenue, 539
Unit costs, relevance, 126-27
Unsubordinated debenture, 576
Usage variance, 181n
Using financial leverage, 621
Utilization of facilities, 115

Variable budget, 173
Variable cost, use in transfer
    pricing, 318-19
Variable cost pool, 289
Variable costs, allocation of,
    289
Variable costing (see also Di-
    rect costing), 66, 455
Variable factory overhead, 56

Variable overhead application
    rate, 432-33
Variable unit costs, 459-61
Variance:
  activity, 458n
  between incurred and ap-
      plied cost, 429
  capacity, 458n
  causes, 429
  denominator, 458, 462-64
  effectiveness, 175n
  flexible budget, 184
  marketing, 175-76
  quantity, 181n
  rate, 181n
  spending, 185
  usage, 181n
Variances:
  analysis of, 174-84
      variable costs graphical ap-
          proach, 182-84
  controllability, 186
  efficiency, 175, 181
      causes of, 187
      limitations, 185-86
  expected, 180 (notes)
  labor responsibility for, 186-
      87
  material responsibility for,
      186

Variances (cont.)
  need to isolate, 174
  price, 175, 181
      limitations of, 185-86
  standard cost disposition of,
      467-68
  trade-offs among, 187
  when to investigate, 187-88
Visual-fit method, 218

Wages, accounts for, 535
Weighted average, definition of,
    489n
Work capital, net, 581
Work-in-process inventory, 57-
    59
Work measurement, 209-10
  discretionary fixed cost ap-
      proach, 212
  engineered cost approach,
      210-11
Work sampling, 210
Working-capital ratio, 625
Worksheets, use of in preparing
    consolidated statements,
    610

Zero-based budgeting, 260
Zero-based revenue, 261